Plant User Handbook

A Guide to Effective Specifying

Edited by

James Hitchmough
Reader in Landscape, Department of Landscape,
University of Sheffield

and

Ken Fieldhouse
former editor of *Landscape Design Journal*

Blackwell
Science

Editorial offices:
Blackwell Science Ltd, 9600 Garsington Road, Oxford OX4 2DQ, UK
  Tel: +44 (0) 1865 776868
Blackwell Publishing Inc., 350 Main Street, Malden, MA 02148-5020, USA
  Tel: +1 781 388 8250
Blackwell Science Asia Pty Ltd, 550 Swanston Street, Carlton, Victoria 3053, Australia
  Tel: +61 (0)3 8359 1011

First published 2004

Library of Congress Cataloging-in-Publication Data
Plant user handbook : a guide to effective specifying / edited by Ken
Fieldhouse and James Hitchmough.
      p.   cm.
Includes bibliographical references and index.
  ISBN 0-632-05843-9 (pbk. : alk. paper)
  1. Landscape plants—Handbooks, manuals, etc.   2. Planting
design—Handbooks, manuals, etc.   I. Fieldhouse, Ken.   II. Hitchmough,
James.

SB435.P59 2003
715—dc21

                                        2003011786

ISBN 0-632-05843-9

A catalogue record for this title is available from the British Library

Set in 9.5/12 pt Sabon
by SNP Best-set Typesetter Ltd., Hong Kong
Printed and bound in India using acid-free paper
by Replika Press Pvt. Ltd., Kundli 131 028

For further information on Blackwell Publishing, visit our website:
www.blackwellpublishing.com

This book is dedicated to Ken Fieldhouse who worked unstintingly to disseminate knowledge and understanding of landscape so that genius and creativity could flourish.

Contents

Foreword

There is a wide constituency of potential users for this long awaited book; we offer a landscape architect's perspective on it. The information contained within its chapters forms an essential and scientific reference for more appropriate and imaginative plant use. It formulates positions on 'appropriateness' that could be the basis for endless and interesting discussions (within practices and across disciplines) making reference to plant tolerances rather than ideal growing conditions.

It also supports the principle that plant selection and use could and should be imaginative: constantly experimenting with plant palettes; analysing the suitability of plants for the site microclimate; considering existing soil conditions; being receptive to the dynamic seasonal patterns and changes; being mindful of long term mangement issues and implications; and ultimately by acknowledging the requirements of the perceived users, and reflecting on the changing ways in which people use parks and other urban landsapes.

While these principles provide a scientific framework and a series of guiding tools for the landscape architect, the framework has to be part of an overall design vision. This implies a creative interpretation, sensitivity and instinctiveness in response to the objective conditions of the place.

Planting is only one element and material in the creation of space. It has the unique potential to impart particular character to space (of beauty, mutability, dynamism, unpredictability, grace, mysteriousness, impermanence).

The inseparable nature of this relationship between art and science means that on a fundamental level one must inform the other. Landscape architecture becomes fragile when it is not underpinned by solid knowledge.

The sharing of knowledge, in terms of the research and practical experience of other professionals, represents an invaluable resource. The information contained within this book, and the discussions that it will inspire, can only lead to a better understanding of the living materials and processes that form the basis of our profession. We look forward to seeing landscape architects and horticulturalists apply these ideas and principles to future project: leading, we hope, to richer, more diverse and sustainable landscapes. And inevitably, to further editions of the book.

Frances Christie
Sibylla Hartel
Gustafson Porter
July 2003

Preface

Tom La Dell

Landscape practice has long been in need of a book that not only gives a guide to plant specification but also shows how they are developed through an understanding of plants and their cultivation. This book is primarily aimed at professional designers, scientists, horticulturists and managers, who whilst needing to produce precise specifications on plant use also need to maintain a big view of plants, people and their environment.

The design and management of landscape planting are relatively recent concepts. Planting associated with public spaces and new development has evolved slowly over the last two hundred years. Planting and management for nature conservation is even more recent and has made its first steps in the last fifty years. Both have to be based on an appropriate knowledge of plants and the environment in which they grow. Designers need to know the relevant facts about the materials they design with if they are to use them effectively. The function and performance of any materials are as important as their aesthetic impact and how their form and character are expressed in the design.

This book aims to make sense of plants and their cultivation for the designers and managers of landscape planting. It provides the factual and scientific background for practical planting design and its implementation through specification writing and contracts. Each chapter covers a well-defined topic about the plants themselves, their establishment or their management. They all focus on a creative approach to problem solving by design and practical implementation.

Cultivation and the environment – from crops to design

It is useful to place the relatively recent concept of landscape planting in the long history of plants and their cultivation for food and pleasure; it shows a sense of continuity in what we do.

Plants are fundamental to our survival: all life on the planet depends on them. They trap energy from the sun to form the organic molecules that fuel their growth. All other forms of life (including humans) depend on this energy to grow, survive and reproduce. Early humans selectively gathered and prepared wild plants as their staple diet. They survived in the landscape in small numbers but in a very wide variety of habitats. As they spread out across the globe they learnt how to use plants in each of the varied environments they occupied. The big change in their relationship to their environment, and to each other, came when people realised they could cultivate plants rather than just collect them in the wild. They could get a higher yield of energy for a given area and support a larger population. This could be done in less time than it took to harvest wild plants and with less effort.

A new type of society evolved, organised around production and sharing and creating time for leisure. Villages and then towns grew up around productive farmland. As cultivation spread, wild and cultivated plants became more distinct and plants began to be grown for their beauty and not just for food or medicine. At the same time wild plants came to be regarded as an expendable resource first for exploitation and soon for over-exploitation to extinction. Whole eco-systems, whether forest or grassland, have been and are still being destroyed on a huge scale, without a thought for their long-term value. It is only relatively recently that wild habitats have been seen again as being important to our survival.

Most food plants are cultivated in monocultures, with areas devoted to a single plant. This is true of agriculture and the more intensive systems used in horticulture. Areas of plants can all be given the same treatment from sowing to cropping. Agriculture and horticulture have been mechanised, followed by the use of chemical fertilisers and then chemicals to control the pests, diseases and weeds.

Control of soil conditions has always been part of cultivation. For example, the irrigation of desert soils has been practised from very early times. Techniques have developed, to the extent that some topsoils are relegated from being complex growing media to become lifeless templates to which water and nutrients are added as required. This loss of complexity leads to vulnerability to dramatic environmental changes. Land may become unproductive, for example, due to erosion of topsoil, acidification or salt accumulation.

Landscape planting has learnt from these rationalised cropping systems and most designs use mass planting – if for no other reason than they are cheap to maintain. With a better knowledge of plants, designs can be more complex, interesting and responsive to their site and location.

From gardens to landscape

The cultivation of ornamental plants in gardens developed alongside the cultivation of crops in fields. The hanging gardens of Babylon were surrounded by the first agricultural areas in Mesopotamia. As garden designs and concepts developed in different cultures and environments, horticulture evolved with them to create new garden styles. Landscape horticulture developed later from garden practice at a time when designed public spaces became part of the fabric of industrial towns and cities.

When the first public parks were created in Britain fashionable designs and horticultural techniques were being developed for the rich. They were creating ornamental parks, full of the latest plant introductions from around the world, displayed in shrubberies, flower gardens and arboreta. The first formally commissioned public park, the Derby Arboretum, was intended to educate but this was soon eclipsed by the more flexible, 'ornamental' parks from Birkenhead onwards. The designers of both (Loudon and Paxton) had been apprenticed in large private gardens. They brought garden horticulture into the public arena. A new horticulture developed as tropical plants were introduced, carpet bedding became the main attraction and horticulture became an entertainment. The management of public parks was handed to this new breed of horticulturist.

Meanwhile, in the late nineteenth century, the idea of the garden city was being developed by Howard in 'Garden Cities of Tomorrow'. This envisaged a complete landscape structure for new cities. The green public realm would be everywhere, not just in parks or 'green lungs'. The original concepts have been expanded for new conditions and contexts. We now include the regeneration of the old areas of the cities – and even quite recent ones where the areas were unliveable or the industry has moved on.

Landscape horticulture has grown from both traditions: the public park and the green city. It has evolved from these and from garden horticulture into a new branch of the science, using plants in new ways and developing techniques for plant establishment in new site conditions to make new landscapes. But as these skills have developed, the rationalised management of the labour to implement and maintain the schemes has led to a de-skilled workforce. This trend will only be reversed if planting is well detailed and specified.

It is not only towns and cities that need regeneration. The ecology and wildlife of rural landscapes have lost their diversity from the 1950s onwards, as farming became mechanised and dependent on chemical controls. Habitat creation and restoration are becoming more common, to redress the balance in favour of wildlife and create rich environments for people. Some of the techniques in the book are relevant to this evolving discipline and more are being developed.

There is no separate science for ornamental or ecological planting. It follows the same understanding of biology and ecology that has allowed us to develop the crop plants and cultivation systems that feed huge populations. The book shows how the science they have in common can be understood, interpreted and used by the majority of landscape professionals without a scientific education. The examples are all in the temperate landscape but the approach can be used in any climate.

Landscape planting principles

This science enables us to design the public landscape, and revitalise natural ecosystems, responsibly and effectively, using techniques that create sustainable solutions. Landscape professionals work with a great variety of initially unfamiliar conditions, trying to select and establish appropriate plants (unlike gardeners who develop a long-term relationship with their site).

The principles of sustainable development can be applied to landscape planting. A simple overview of sustainable landscape techniques is to see the process as inputs and outputs.

In modern agricultural systems the output is high when the crop is taken off for food or fuel or grazed by animals. The input is also high, in the energy used in cultivation of the crop and the fertilisers and pesticides applied to it. This is a high-input/high-output system. The crop may be taken off annually, or even more frequently in the tropics. In forestry it may be cropped decades after planting. Gardens and ornamental horticulture tend to be high-input/low-output as they are primarily decorative.

Landscape design should follow the principles of sustainable development and aim for a low-input/low-output energy system. The implementation and use of resources should be as effective and economical as possible while the establishing landscape should require lowest possible energy inputs. There is no crop to be taken off so the outputs are low. There should though be a high aesthetic output and cultural value as these are simply down to the skills of the designer, by making best use of the available physical resources.

Low-input systems like these can and should be designed to respond to the environmental conditions of the site and the plants available to make them diverse and complex. These systems are described as being well 'buffered'. The impact of change in one part of the plant/environment relationship will be absorbed by the rest of it, with a much reduced risk of catastrophic failure. This is built in to the design by creating the right soil conditions for good long-term growth and by selecting plants that will survive in these conditions and have predictable maintenance inputs.

We return to the fact that designers need to understand the materials they design with. Good design is an expression of many things but the materials are the basis of that expression. Managers have the same need to understand what they are managing; they are the custodians of both the aesthetic and practical qualities of designed and 'natural' landscapes.

Landscape aesthetics is about the beauty of using materials but it is also about wildlife and the expression of the human spirit in our instinctive relationship to the environment. Science and rationalism gives us the facts to work with. Expression through design and management can then be whatever we wish to make it for pleasure and enlightenment.

Acknowledgements

Many people have given their time freely both in writing the original Specification Guides in *Plant User* and updating and expanding them for this book. Some chapters have been written specially to ensure that we have a comprehensive coverage of plants in landscape design and management. Every chapter has a fresh approach to its subject to ensure that it is relevant to landscape and horticulture professionals. It makes each subject clear and accessible to those with no scientific background.

We are fortunate that so many both within and outside the landscape professions have given their time and expertise to help us be more competent in the work we do. It should also be a long-term foundation for better landscape planting and more adventurous design.

A lot of people, from many professions, helped to launch the professional Plant Users Group in 1987. We all agreed that we needed a stronger voice in the industry. Many plants being used were quite unsuitable – largely because we accepted that we had to provide the growing conditions for whatever nurserymen produced. Every discussion about how we could change this came up against the lack of knowledge in the profession about plants and how they should be cultivated in landscape schemes at any scale. There was little literature and selective teaching of this on landscape and related courses.

When we agreed that a magazine would be a good start, I approached the late Ken Fieldhouse at the Landscape Design Trust and he straightaway said 'Come and see me'. We wanted a weighty core to each issue of *Plant User*, as it became. The Specification Guides were the way to get a specialist to explain the background to each topic and get the benefits of a sound approach to readers. The editorial board met to plan each issue and these have always been lively affairs, pushing forward the ideas of the skills needed for successful landscape planting.

When we suggested a book, Ken took this forward and James Hitchmough agreed to edit it with him. He has carried this through since Ken's tragically early death, with editorial assistance from Janet Prescott.

Thank you to everyone involved who have made the Specification Guides, and now the book, possible and to Professor Tony Bradshaw, Peter Thoday and Derek Patch as a botanist, horticulturalist and arboriculturalist respectively, who have long shown the need for a scientific basis for this aspect of landscape practice. The test is the difference this book will make to the quality of landscape planting.

Contributors

Neil Bayfield is a Principal Scientific Officer at the Centre for Ecology and Hydrology, Banchory, Scotland AB31 4BW.

Richard Bisgrove is Senior Lecturer and Course Director for Landscape Management, at the Centre for Horticulture and Landscape, University of Reading, PO Box 221, Reading RG6 6AS.

Andy Boorman is Senior Lecturer in Horticulture at Writtle College, Chelmsford, Essex CM1 3RR.

Mike Browell is Principal Landscape Architect at Weddle Landscape Design, Landscape Research Office, 27 Wilkinson Street, Sheffield S10 2GB.

Jed Bultitude was a Country Manager for the British Trust for Conservation Volunteers at the time of writing.

Nick Coslett is an independent landscape consultant at 5 Gun Back Lane, Horsemonden, Tonbridge, Kent TN12 8NL.

Nigel Dunnett is Senior Lecturer in the Department of Landscape, University of Sheffield, Sheffield S10 2TN.

Rory Dusoir worked at Great Dixter gardens after his Classics degree and is now at the Royal Botanical Gardens at Kew.

Tony Edwards is Director of EDCO Design Ltd, 16 West Barnes Lane, London SW20 0BU.

Ken Fieldhouse was an experienced landscape architect and town planner, and Editor of the *Landscape Design Journal* until his death in 2002.

Bob Froud-Williams is Senior Lecturer in Weed Science at the Department of Agricultural Botany, University of Reading, Reading RG6 6AU.

Tim Gale is a Director of Whitelaw Turkington Landscape Architects, 354 Kennington Road, London SE11 4LD.

Fergus Garrett is Head Gardener at Great Dixter gardens, Northiam, Rye, East Sussex TN31 6PH.

John Hacker is Director of Professional Sportsturf Design (NW) Ltd, 42 Garstang Road, Preston PR1 1NA.

Terence Henry is Lecturer in Biology and Environmental Science at Greenmount College of Agriculture and Horticulture, Antrim, Northern Ireland, BT41 4PU.

James Hitchmough is Associate Professor in the Department of Landscape, University of Sheffield, Sheffield S10 2TN.

Nerys Jones is Chief Executive of the National Urban Forestry Unit, The Science Park, Stafford Road, Wolverhampton WV10 9RT.

Tony Kendle is Mission Director at the Eden Project, St Austell, Cornwall and a lecturer in the

Department of Horticulture and Landscape, University of Reading, Reading RG6 6AS.

Tom La Dell is a chartered landscape architect at Stocks Studio, Grafty Green, Maidstone, Kent ME17 2AP and a founder member of the *Plant User* Editorial Board.

John Parker was Head of Property Services at Kent County Council until his retirement.

Kevin Patrick is Associate Director of Hankinson Duckett Associates, Landscape Studio, Reading Road, Lower Basildon, Reading RG8 9NE.

Glynn Percival is a plant physiologist and technical support specialist at R.A. Bartlett Tree Research Laboratory (Europe) Ltd, 2 Earley Gate, Whiteknights, University of Reading RG6 6AU.

Richard Scott is Senior Project Manager of Landlife, The National Wildflower Centre, Court Hey Park, Liverpool L16 3NA.

Steve Scrivens is Senior Consultant at Technical Landscapes, Fawkham Green, Longfield, Kent DA3 8NL.

Bob Sherman is Head of Horticulture at HDRA, Ryton Organic Gardens, Coventry CV8 3LG.

Mike Smith is a partner in Macgregor Smith, The Malthouse, Sydney Buildings, Bath BA12 6BZ.

Gordon Spoor is former Professor of Applied Soil Physics at Silsoe College, Cranfield University and Director of Gordon Spoor Associates, Model Farm, Maulden, Bedford MK45 2BQ.

Caroline Swann is Marketing Manager at Hillier Nurseries Ltd, Ampfield, Romsey, Hants SO51 9PA.

Peter Thoday is Principal of Thoday Associates, Landscape Consultants, Faircross House, Box Hill, Corsham, Wilts SN13 8MA, and a founder member of the *Plant User* Editorial Board.

James Wilson was principal author and editor of the National Plant Specification, a horticulturist and landscape architect and a founder member of the *Plant User* Editorial Board.

Tom Wright is a consultant on landscape design and management, and formerly Senior Lecturer at Wye College, University of London.

I Preliminaries to Plant Use and the Landscape

1 Introduction to Plant Use in the Landscape

James Hitchmough and Peter Thoday

The majority of books on plants and plant use are concerned with the cultivation of plants in gardens. For the private gardener, plants are a recreation and an adventure. It is good to succeed, but if a plant fails, there is always another chance next year.

This book is aimed at practitioners who are professionally engaged in the use of plants in public, commercial and institutional landscapes. The vast majority of these plantings are undertaken on the basis of a binding contract, generally between the client who owns or leases the landscape and the implementer (a landscape contractor), with the designer as specifier and contract administrator.

Landscape practitioners working on such sites require very different information from the private gardener, and this book represents the compilation of the knowledge and understanding of some of the leading practitioners and academics involved in the use of plants in the British landscape.

1.1 Planting and the designed landscape

In the contractual relationship in which landscape practitioners work it is common to implement schemes quickly and to a rigid timetable. At times this procedure generates its own problems: plants chosen may be unavailable and less appropriate ones substituted; designs may be planted under inappropriate conditions and/or by poorly trained staff. In such circumstances even species and cultivars that are otherwise regarded as tough and reliable can fail. This leads to a tendency to standardise design, producing dull landscapes and solutions that do not respond to environmental conditions.

Beyond the twelve months immediately following the planting of the design, there is a considerable risk that plants which fail will not be replaced, and that maintenance will be unreliable and in some cases non-existent (Fig. 1.1). The need for intelligent long-term maintenance is largely underplayed by the entire industry, and in many cases designers and managers fail to convince clients to pay for such work, even when the funds are available. Unskilled maintenance can result in plantings that fall considerably short of the designer's aspirations. In short, the world of professional plant users, and particularly those involved in contractual procedures, is often frustrating.

It is easy to see what needs to be done to improve matters but landscape professionals often find it extremely difficult to get this to happen. Relationships between designers, contractors and clients are discussed in more detail in Chapter 3, but it is clear that those responsible for designing, implementing and managing plantings need to have access to information that recognises the realities of the situation, and provides advice that is informed and based upon best practice. The aim of this text is to provide such information.

Many of the chapters and sub-sections in this book were originally written as part of the Plant User series of Specification Guides, and distributed via the Landscape Design Trust publications and other professional journals, latterly, *Garden Design* and *The Horticulturist*. The *Plant User* magazine was the brainchild of Tom La Dell, Peter

Fig. 1.1   Planting adds a great deal of richness and complexity to urban environments for little cost. This is particularly evident when planting is absent. (Photo: James Hitchmough)

Thoday and others who set up the Professional Plant Users Group (PPUG) in 1987. The key aim of PPUG was to elevate the standard of plant use in the landscape by improving the information available to users of plant material.

Responsibility for the selection of plants in public landscapes has shifted away from horticulturally-trained staff to landscape architects. In Britain this process has occurred over the last 50 years, and has brought many benefits: not least the use of plants as living elements contributing to the overall design. Nevertheless it has also created problems, the most obvious of which is that the selection and initial cultivation of the plants is now primarily controlled by members of a broad-ranging discipline with varying specialisations.

There are landscape architects for whom plants and plantings are a great passion, but on the whole such people appear to be in a minority. This situation causes considerable concern, but it is difficult to see how things will improve significantly in the short term, unless this is addressed in the university education of landscape architects and through continuing professional development courses.

The successful use of plants in the landscape often relies on the participants involved having a good understanding of at least the following factors.

The biological and visual characteristics of the plants selected

There is a huge range of literature on the cultivation and use of decorative plants, largely aimed at the amateur gardener, and of substantially variable quality. A great deal of valuable information can be drawn from it, especially on plant morphology (appearance) and phenology (times of flowering, fruiting, leaf fall etc.). However professional users of this literature have to learn to interpret its often highly garden-focused pronouncements.

For example, the recommendations on cultivation are nearly always expressed in terms of requirements rather than tolerances. Readers are informed that nearly all plants need to grow in a moist, well-structured loam. This is hardly surprising. Such topsoils represent the ideal: biological optima in terms of the supply of moisture and oxygen to roots, and ease of root penetrability. Good quality soils with these characteristics are often not available to professional plant users (see Chapter 4) so it is more useful to know what conditions plants will tolerate outside such biological optima and still perform satisfactorily. This information is rarely presented or even discussed in garden-orientated literature; the goal is generally to grow excellent specimens rather than a satisfactory mass planting.

Professional plant users who are familiar with the conditions in which a plant grows in its natural habitat will appreciate, for example, that a considerable number of plants recommended by garden writers for well-drained soil may in nature occupy very wet soils. Apart from texts describing the native flora of a region, there are few books available that discuss the ecological regimes under which plants exist in nature; yet it is precisely these conditions that shape a plant's range of tolerance when brought into cultivation. Some authors writing in the late nineteenth and early twentieth century were aware of this, – for example the great plantsmen William Robinson (1874) and W.J. Bean (1914, edited by Clarke 1976–) – but with the conspicuous exception of garden writers such as Beth Chatto (e.g. Chatto, 1982) British gardening literature is relatively silent on this, providing instead a cover-all recipe for optimal cultivation.

This ecological approach to understanding plants is best developed in the garden and landscape literature of Germany, for example in the very useful if rather prescriptive *Perennials and their Garden Habitats* (Hansen and Stahl, 1993). Much of this understanding can also be gained by observing the performance of cultivated plants in a range of landscape and garden sites across the north-south and east-west climatic gradients of Britain. With a better understanding of plant tolerances, based on a combination of reading and observation of plants in their habitats, future plantings are likely to be more successful.

The physical and biological context of the planting site

Most landscape development is directly or indirectly associated with some form of construction works. Inevitably, some of this work takes place during wet weather and entails the use of heavy machinery that compacts soil and destroys its structure. It is possible to establish vegetation in the resulting conditions, which are often a long way from any kind of biological optimum for the species concerned, but it requires a fundamental understanding of how soils work with regard to the movement of water, air and root penetration. These issues are discussed in Chapters 4 and 5.

It is equally important to understand how climate influences plant success. Britain is a small island which experiences marked differences in the warmth of the growing season across a north-south and altitudinal gradient; this has a significant impact on the successful growth of species requiring either cool or warm conditions. There is also a marked rainfall gradient from east to west with, for example, less than 500 mm rain per year on the Essex coast and in excess of 1500 mm on the west coast of Wales. These contrasting conditions can provide a challenge for plant users drawing on a small, standardised palette; but they also offer an opportunity to use other taxa whose requirements are in harmony with these regional conditions. Such selections can create plantings

that form distinctive relationships with the local physical, ecological and even cultural contexts.

The cultural context in which planting takes place

For some landscape architects, sensitivity to place or context is a key idea governing their work; for many, however, design style is an end in itself. The most common form of approach to contextual recognition involves historical period, or geographical notions of place. An understanding of the cultural context of plantings is often rather less well developed.

One of the most important ways in which this cultural context expresses itself is in understanding the history of plant use in gardens and landscapes. Britain probably has the most developed gardening culture of any nation state on earth. This plant culture has a long history and is rich and complex, varying not only across time, in relation to social class and political change (see Crouch and Ward, 1988; Brown, 1999) but also in relation to geographic location within Britain. It extends from the world of the window box, patio and hanging basket to the naturalistic woodland and meadow gardens exemplified by Robinson and Jekyll in the early part of the twentieth century.

The diversity of styles in the way that plants are used can easily be observed by those who visit gardens, and understood by reading the garden literature. Unfortunately we rarely see evidence of such cultural sensitivity being applied by those who create and maintain frequently uninspiring public and institutional landscapes. In this context planting based either around nature conservation or historical restoration are increasingly seen as the only alternatives.

Landscape professionals have their own approach to the use of plants, which they first learn at university, and then reinforce and develop through practice. At times this appears to be at odds with the plant use cultures of the public as a whole.

In landscape architecture low diversity planting is popular for both philosophical (design) reasons and pragmatic ones (you can get away with very limited plant knowledge and it is easier to detail). Native as opposed to non-native planting has become popular over a wide range of sites for similar reasons, when it should be used creatively and respond to the huge variety of forms and habitats in the landscape that depend upon native species.

By contrast, popular garden culture is about high plant diversity, seasonal change and colour. There is a growing acceptance of native plants, but more often as a complement or framework to more exotic offerings than as an alternative. The sites addressed in this book are not gardens, and are subject to very different public pressures. Nonetheless their designers should understand and reflect on how plants and plantings appeal to the public at large.

Fashion is an extremely important cultural factor in shaping the views of plant users. It is important to appreciate these changes, to know that the archetypal herbaceous border is an early twentieth century invention that has evolved little in the past hundred years, and that flowering cherries were planted in parks from their introduction in the 1930s until replaced by the genus *Sorbus* from 1970 onwards (Plate 1). It is more important though to recognise that these fashions merely represent a new paradigm, rather than a truth that will last forever.

Vegetation that is now in vogue will be superseded by plantings derived from future paradigms. Many landscape professionals currently favour native wildflower meadows in urban parks; these are sometimes viewed differently by residents, who remember the same site resplendent with past plantings of annual bedding or exotic herbaceous borders. Similarly, landscape professionals decry avenues of flowering cherries as an aberration belonging to the past, as they formulate plans to replace them with some other tree species more in line with their own personal approach. Greater clarity by designers in the aesthetic and practical choice of plants would produce longer-lasting designs.

1.2   Conclusion

Plants and planting are key components of landscape works. In functional terms they can ameliorate atmospheric conditions, and provide habitats for a wide range of living creatures. They also allow physical as well as intellectual connections to be established or re-established between old and new landscapes. Through colour, scent, touch, and their physical changes in response to the seasons, plants add richness to the experience of landscape. To obtain all these dividends in practice, plant users need to be prepared to adopt a thoughtful approach to selecting, designing and managing plants. In particular their decision making must take into account the ecological characteristics of plants and planting sites, plus the cultural context in which planting and long-term management takes place.

References

Brown, J. (1999) *The Pursuit of Paradise: A Social History of Gardens and Gardening.* HarperCollins, London.

Chatto, B. (1982) *The Damp Garden.* Dent, London.

Clarke, D. (1976–) *Bean's Trees and Shrubs Hardy in the British Isles*, 8th edn, John Murray, London.

Crouch, D. & Ward, C. (1988) *The Allotment, Its Landscape and Culture.* Faber and Faber, London.

Hansen, R. & Stahl, F. (1993) *Perennials and their Garden Habitats.* Cambridge University Press, Cambridge.

Robinson, W. (1874) *The Wild Garden.* (Reprinted by Century, London, 1983)

Acknowledgement

The original Specification Guides as published in *Plant User* have been revised and updated in the preparation of this book. Wherever possible, the original authors have contributed to this process and their support and considerable experience have formed a vital element in ensuring accuracy and relevance in the topics discussed.

2 Selecting Plant Species, Cultivars and Nursery Products

James Hitchmough

Much of this chapter is devoted to trying to shed some light on the confusion that currently reigns when specifying the origin of native species used in landscape projects. It is difficult to reduce the arguments that underpin this debate down to clear black and white courses of action. This is because many of the supposed facts in this debate are as heavily influenced by the personal values and attitudes of people as by objective science. Making essentially objective decisions is possible; however this does require practitioners to develop understanding of some of the genetic concepts underpinning plant conservation.

2.1 Setting clear objectives for plant selection

Recently graduated (and some less-recently graduated) landscape professionals are often ill-at-ease when confronted with the enormous wealth of plant material on offer in Britain. Estimates vary widely but in total there are in excess of 60 000 cultivated taxa available through British nurseries, plus many more available via the international nursery industry and seed trade. Within mainstream wholesale nurseries a much smaller range of plants is available, but even here the number is probably still in excess of 3000 taxa.

Given this abundance of plants, users need to adopt a process to identify the most appropriate taxa for use on a given project or site. Some landscape offices and local authorities have put together an office 'list' of species that have proved to be reliable in past works. These lists are helpful in one sense, as they may in some cases incorpo-

rate valuable lessons learnt through prior research and by trial and error. However on another level they are potentially undesirable, perpetuating the excessive use of particular species and cultivars and essentially freezing the development of plant use at a point in time that may restrict the adoption of superior species and new cultivars.

In terms of biological diversity and of the richness of public experience of the landscape, it seems undesirable that so many schemes use the same plants. Most planting schemes in Britain draw on a pool of approximately 100 plants, with some practitioners using only a fraction of this number. Some would argue that taxonomic diversity is counter-productive to good, strong design, and this may often be true. However, this is a separate argument, and does not deal with the stagnation of plant use.

Even if a landscape practitioner only ever uses a maximum of ten taxa or less on each landscape project, it is not always necessary to use the same ten. A cynic would say that this minimalist approach is mobilised by some to provide a professionally acceptable cover for underdeveloped appreciation of the role of plant materials within landscape architecture.

If plant use is to be responsive to both the site and its users, plant selection for landscape sites should begin with the development of a clear planting or vegetation strategy for each project. Key elements to consider in developing this are shown in Box 2.1. A planting strategy provides a clear and reasoned framework for how plant use can contribute to the overall goals for the landscape in question, and avoid the (all too common)

> **Box 2.1   Important factors in developing a planting strategy for a site.**
>
> 1. Aspirations of the client(s):
>   How do the client perceive themselves?
> 2. External policy constraints:
>   Assessment of the environment planting must take cognisance of these.
>
> 3. Practicalities:
>   What are the limitations/opportunities posed by the site, i.e. what is reasonably possible, what can be afforded, what time scales are involved and skills available for management?
> 4. Social-cultural considerations:
>   What design style-genre, how will this relate to and be perceived by site users? Who are these people and what are their cultural norms? Is it legible or meaningful, could it enrich understanding of a place or idea?
> 5. Ecological considerations:
>   Is the scheme sustainable, does it contribute to enhanced biodiversity? Is there a local ecological character to connect to? Do the plants (whether native or exotic) fit the likely environment of the site?
> 6. Place-time context:
>   Is there a well-defined context set by social and cultural history, location, visual characteristics, geology, past and present land use, or visual references? Should one respond to this slavishly, or at the other extreme conscientiously ignore it?

situation of plants being used as wallpaper to fill spaces. In the same way that clients have a right to expect that a designer can explain why a certain spatial arrangement was adopted within the overall site masterplan, it should always be possible to perceive and indeed to debate the intellectual decisions that underpin planting.

Most of the factors inherent in developing a planting strategy can be pigeon-holed under the headings of aesthetic, biological and functional requirements. These headings act as aide memoire, after the planting strategy is completed and plants selected to meet the objectives of the planting strategy. This process of sieving through the pool of plants that are commercially available is illustrated in Fig. 2.1.

Clearly the process is far less mechanical in practice than is suggested by this simplistic figure, but it reinforces the notion of plant selection as a process rather than a series of whimsical or uninformed decisions. Plant selection is one of the most powerful tools available to plant users to contribute to the development of landscapes that are

manageable both technically and economically, as sustainable as possible and yet rich and meaningful to site users.

To make the best possible plant selection decisions, plant users need to access information on plant characteristics. As yet there is very little information on plants that has been published with the needs on professional plant users in mind. It is nearly always necessary to re-interpret plant literature from the perspective of conditions prevailing on landscape sites. Key sources of information on plant materials and inherent strengths and weaknesses are shown in Box 2.2.

2.2   Genetic and plant origin issues in plant selection

With rising awareness of bio-diversity and sustainability, understanding of the importance of genetic variation within plants has become an increasingly important issue for plant specifiers. It has always been a significant factor in successful usage even though some landscape practitioners

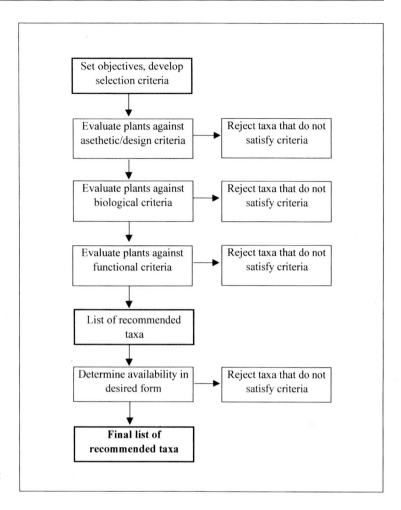

Fig. 2.1 An idealised plant selection process.

have significantly under-appreciated this, and the nursery industry has generally failed to exploit the potential of genetic variation to the extent that is possible. These characteristics of plants can be considered at a series of levels.

Native versus exotic

This concept doesn't quite fit in this categorisation but is an important idea and is included here for convenience. Over the past 20 years there has been a considerable increase in the use of native species in landscape planting. Nearly all planting in rural locations is now typically native, as is an increasing percentage of naturalistic and/or structural woodland and woodland edge planting in urban areas. This can only be seen as a positive trend, as native species do in many cases visually link new plantings with the surrounding landscape character.

Native species also bring habitat benefits, providing opportunities for native fauna (and particularly invertebrates) that have evolved specific relationships with a native plant species during the past 10 000 years. The use of non-native species (exotics) has generally been constricted to urban sites that strongly represent the cultural landscape.

This landscape is itself the product of the multi-cultural and ethnic society of modern Britain. In this diverse range of environments exotic species

---

Box 2.2   Information sources on plant materials.

Literature on plants aimed at amateur gardeners

Enormously variable in quality of information; users need to be selective. The best is very useful. The Phillips and Rix garden plants series are excellent, not least because they show many plants in their habitats from which useful ecological information can be gleaned. Also good are most Batsford Press monographs on particular genera, and those by Timber Press. Jellito and Schacht (1990) is a good source for herbaceous spp. None of these texts provide information on plant tolerance of the hostile conditions found on many landscape sites.

Nursery catalogues

Can be useful, but again tend to make pronouncements based on performance under garden conditions. Generally an inexpensive information source.

Literature on plants aimed at professional users

Good when available, but there are very few examples of this type of literature in Britain. The USA is better supplied, for example *Dirr's Hardy Trees and Shrubs* (Dirr 1997). Hansen and Stahl (1993) is an excellent text on herbaceous plants.

Experimental and other studies on plants in the peer-reviewed literature

Again, useful when you can find it but requires access to the abstracting service databases, which is expensive. Suffers from poor coverage of species you are likely to be interested in, but information contained is less anecdotal than in the above. Interpretation for actual landscape site conditions is often required.

Commercially available computer databases on plants

The chief merit of these is speed and ease of use. Information content varies in quality and applicability depending on geographical origin. Some packages merely re-package the typical pronouncements of the amateur gardening literature.

Your own experiences and observations

When cross-referenced with the above sources, this is probably the most useful. There are abundant plant collections in Britain to observe (Fig. 2.2), as well as plant performance in everyday practice. Beware of basing attitudes to plants on the behaviour of one or only a few plants. It is easy to misinterpret relationships between cause and effect when only a few plants or incidents are involved.

---

are valuable in that they are a part of the highly developed garden culture of Britain, and as such are familiar and valued by the public. As a result of our separation from mainland Europe following the rise in sea level at the end of the last glaciation, Britain has a relatively depauperate native flora of approximately 1500 species. This is much lower than that of our continental European neighbours. However by contrast, our horticultural flora offers a wider range of plant forms, flowering seasons etc. Observation of private gardens suggests that this flora is clearly valued by most people in Britain.

It is unfortunate that the use of native and exotic plant species in Britain has become a rather polarised debate in the past decade, as it is perfectly feasible to value both native and non-native species and use them as appropriate. In simplistic terms, exotics have become seen as a direct or indirect threat to the native flora, and of little or no value as habitat to native fauna. These perspectives are increasingly accepted at face value by landscape practitioners. Approximately 4000 non-native species are naturalised in Britain (Clement and Foster 1994), however in contrast to some other countries, for example the USA, relatively few are sufficiently abundant to have a significant ecological impact.

Ecological studies conducted over the past century (Rich and Woodruff 1996) show that

Fig. 2.2 A *Potentilla fruticosa* trial at RHS Wisley. While this is useful for generating morphological information, assessments made in good quality soil tell you little about how such plants will perform in the often hostile soil conditions of many urban landscapes. (Photo: James Hitchmough)

while some naturalised species increase their range and become significant problems, others decline, or colonise specific ecological niches that are not fully exploited by native species (for example the riparian draw-down zones most favoured by *Impatiens glandulifera*). The plants with the most profound adverse impacts on the native flora are in many cases ubiquitous, highly productive native species such as the grass *Arrhenatherum elatius*, which invade species-rich grasslands, leading to the loss of many less robust species. The losses these species cause are rarely discussed because they are native.

The claim that exotic plants support little if any native fauna is frequently made. Observant gardeners will be aware that this is clearly not the case. Owen (1991) has exhaustively documented the extensive invertebrate fauna associated with plantings of non-native species, and research is currently in train at the University of Sheffield to extend understanding of these relationships. This

importance of plants as support systems for life (and in particular invertebrate life) entered the consciousness of landscape professionals after the work of Southwood (1964), and Kennedy and Southwood (1984) into how many species of insects and mites were associated with common native and exotic trees and shrubs. Much-quoted data by these authors clearly shows how native trees such as *Quercus robur* support the most diverse range of invertebrates but also that some native trees (for example *Taxus*) support far fewer.

Clearly it would be highly undesirable to increase the number and range of aggressive exotic species in Britain, but the risks of this happening through using non-aggressive exotics need to be assessed in a rational context. The notion that exotic equals invasive is just as nonsensical as the notion that native equals non-invasive. Exotic invasive species are invasive because they have certain ecological, physiological and morphological traits, such as high seed production, effective seed distribution, high capacity for vegetative spread and large size at maturity. Native species with these characteristics are also aggressive and 'weedy' (Thompson 1995).

Most of the exotic plants that can be grown outdoors in Britain have now been in cultivation for at least a hundred years and in many cases much longer. Many herbaceous exotic species that are recorded as naturalised are a result of fly-tipping of garden waste on roadsides (Hitchmough, 1999), rather than the overtly aggressive behaviour of the species themselves. The risks of future naturalisations need to be set against the real cultural and environment benefits of the use of these plants in urban areas (Fig. 2.3).

A significant number of plant species now accepted as natives (and in some cases seen as worthy of specific conservation action) are themselves long-naturalised aliens, for example the corn marigold, *Chrysanthemum segetum*. The invasive species *Rhododendron ponticum* was a native species during a past interglacial period, only to be eliminated eventually by a more recent ice-age, then re-introduced in the nineteenth century by human agency. At what point in history does one finalise the list of native species, and say

Fig. 2.3 Exotic species can look perfectly comfortable with native species if selected with care, even in naturalistic planting arrangements. Here a spring-flowering *Spiraea* is used in a woodland edge planting mix in a new town to give additional spring colour. (Photo: James Hitchmough)

'this is it, there can be no more'? Some botanists have proposed that plants that arrived prior to the sixteenth century can be natives, but new plants establishing after this must be forever considered as aliens. From a philosophical perspective this is clearly ludicrous! Even without obvious human agency new species will arrive.

One of the reasons why exotic plants are increasingly vilified appears to have little to do with assessment of an actual biological threat, but rather to a philosophical, aesthetic perception that these plants are out of place and somehow demean the native landscape. Alien plants simply don't fit in this 'nature' paradigm. This in itself is simultaneously interesting and paradoxical, because it is based on the rather old-fashioned view that human beings and their activities lie outside of nature, even though in Britain it is being applied to a landscape that is demonstrably and significantly the creation of humans.

In a philosophical sense this particular nature paradigm denies the reality of our species' relationship throughout history with native and non-native plant species. The complexities and paradoxes of the native-exotic conundrum are dealt with in much greater detail in Kendle and Rose (2000). Outside of the 'countryside' the native-exotic debate is a very grey, rather than black and white issue.

Sub-specific variation and plant selection

Dealing with species

In practice many plant users tend to see species as indivisible, almost immutable commodities. The North American tree *Liquidambar styraciflua* is perceived as much the same whether purchased from Notcutts, Coblands or any other nursery. Plant species do of course often occur naturally over a wide geographical, altitudinal and ecological range. Over evolutionary time natural selection works on individuals across a species range to produce individuals that are better fitted to the conditions prevailing across this range. *Liquidambar styraciflua* is, for example, naturally distributed across eastern North America from New York to the Gulf of Mexico. It is likely that the populations growing at the most northern, and elevated parts of the range will have evolved to cope with much cooler summers than the most southerly populations. It is reasonable to assume that these northern populations would be better fitted to cultivation in the cool summers of Britain, (where *Liquidambar* is demonstrably ill-fitted) than southern populations.

These principles have been extensively researched and utilised in forestry to arrive at plant provenances (plants derived from a particular geographical location) which grow faster and more reliably when planted in a part of Britain or elsewhere in the world. With forestry, the scale of operation and the impossibility of intensive management of trees post-planting makes such research economically worthwhile. Outside of forestry there have been very few scientifically rigorous attempts by nurseries or botanic-horticultural institutions to identify better-fitted forms of important but relatively poorly-fitted species (Fig. 2.4). The key exceptions to this statement largely lie within *Eucalyptus*, and latterly *Rhododendron*, where nurserymen such as Cox and Son have attempted to re-collect from different provenances in the search for greater cold hardiness and other traits.

With *Liquidambar* and most other North American trees that require higher summer temperatures for reliable, vigorous growth than many locations in the UK offer, you cannot buy selections made from the cooler parts of the range. They simply are not on offer, because there is no funded research into such problems, and little appreciation of these issues within either the nursery stock industry, or professional plant users. If you ask a nurseryman where does the stock of a particular (non-cultivar) tree originate from (in terms of habitat-geographical location), in most cases they will have no idea. The precise provenance origins of most populations of cultivated plants are lost in the mists of time, because the biological traits these origins may have influenced are largely invisible to nursery growers and plant users.

Nurserymen have selected *Liquidambar* cultivars with reliable dark purple autumn colour, with variegated leaves, and so on; unfortunately there are no cultivars selected for cool summers, or for extra wet or extra dry soils. Appearance is the main (often the only) issue in cultivar selection. In a time of growing awareness of the value of biological diversity, the lack of research and rational thought in this area is rather tragic.

Cultivars

Many of these selections of a species are maintained by vegetative propagation, which ensures that each subsequent individual is identical to the original selection. In practice, ongoing mutations within the DNA of cultivars do lead to genetic change or 'drift' across time. This is often demonstrated in the variation in different nurseries' stocks of a given cultivar in trials organised by the Royal Horticultural Society and other agencies. Another type of cultivar is raised from seed. A significant number of herbaceous perennials sold in wholesale nurseries as cultivars are in actual fact grown from seed produced under conditions of controlled pollination, to greatly limit variation in the resultant plants. Such plants are similar to one another but never identical as with a vegetatively produce clone. However this is often perfectly satisfactory for general use (Fig. 2.5).

Fig. 2.4 Screening tree species for tolerance of low soil oxygen (a frequent problem for street trees) using a water bath immersion experiment. (Photo: James Hitchmough)

Fig. 2.5 Seedlings of a species are often very different, and this can be both desirable and undesirable. Here it is manifested in radically different growth form in two randomly-planted seedlings. (Photo: James Hitchmough)

Cultivars are useful in situations where a desired set of plant properties is required. Most cultivars have been selected because they possess certain desirable aesthetic characteristics: flowers of a given colour, size or shape, length of flowering season, leaf or branch texture, autumn colour, etc. Cultivars also differ in growth rates in some cases and probably also in tolerance of urban stresses such as deoxygenation, salt spray, etc. Where such traits occur they are just part of the lucky dip of past cultivar selection, rather than an organised search for more profound biological tolerances. Very little is known about the characteristics of cultivars other than those associated with phenology or morphology.

Cultivars and bio-diversity

Because of growing awareness of the concept of bio-diversity, some plant users have come to regard cultivars as less desirable than seed-raised plants. The word clone does in itself carry increasing negative connotations as 'shock horror' articles on human cloning proliferate in the media. As with the debates about natives and exotics, whether a clonally-maintained cultivar is more or less appropriate than variable seedlings depends very much on the context in which the plants are being used rather than some immutable higher law. A valid objection to cultivars is that for some species they are more expensive to purchase than seed raised plants. For example, seedling-grown *Betula* typically have lower production costs than grafted or chip-budded cultivars. Increasingly however objections to cultivars are more philosophical and often tied up with bio-diversity ideas.

One of the most commonly encountered of these is essentially an economic-rationalist one: plantings (i.e., cultivated populations) of cultivars are less able to withstand outbreaks of virulent pests and diseases. This may be true if a particular cultivar is highly susceptible to a given pest or disease, but again it depends on context. In a ground cover planting in a prestige urban context it may be just as bad to lose fifty per cent of seedling grown plants as one hundred per cent of a clonal planting. In woodland edge and other naturalistic plantings, the loss of half of the planted seedlings would not be such a visual problem and would be preferred over total loss of cultivars. Because of their inherent genetic variability, a stand of seedling trees may enter decline over a longer time period than clonal trees of the same species, but is this advantageous? In an urban street the answer is probably no. In a woodland situation variable decline is desirable. Of course the pest:disease argument often ignores the fact that with really virulent organisms (the real problems) there often is not enough genetic variation in the entire genome of the plant species in question to avoid a catastrophic epidemic. This proved to be the case with Chestnut Blight in the USA, and Dutch Elm Disease in the USA and Europe.

Another argument against cultivars is that because they are clonal, plantings of cultivars do not support as much associated biodiversity as do plantings of seedlings, each of which contains different DNA. Clearly it is going to be very difficult to generalise on this; it will depend on the organisms in question, whether their needs are well met by that particular cultivar and so on. A key factor underpinning all of the considerations is the scale of planting in question. These considerations are potentially more significant with cultivars that might be used on a very large scale, across whole cities or regions, compared with those which are used on a small scale, forming part of a patchwork or mosaic of plant types.

With exotic species (most cultivars are selections of these; there are relatively few selections of native species) we do not generally require, indeed in most cases definitely do not want individuals to reproduce successfully by seed. As a result, the greater genetic variation found in seedlings that may enhance reproductive success is undesirable in many situations, making cultivars a potentially more desirable commodity. Reproductive success in native species, especially in naturalistic contexts, is a different issue and is addressed later in this chapter.

Local populations, ecotypes and provenances

These have become the source of much anguish in plant specification, particularly with native species, which as a general principle are used in situations where it is expected they will reproduce sexually from seed at some point in their lives. The words 'population', 'provenance' and 'ecotype' are used very loosely and not always very helpfully in this debate. Population and provenance in common usage are more or less synonymous, and refer to a geographical location within a species' natural or semi-natural range from which collections of seed may have been made. For example, there is a Pennines (Derbyshire to Cumbria) population of the Globe flower, *Trollius europaeus*, as well as discrete populations in south-west Scotland, Perthshire and the Northern Isles. Population also has a more specific use for plant demographers and geneticists, who refer to popu-

lations in terms of the likely flows of genetic material between a large number of individual plants within a portion of the range of a species. Depending on the pollination and dispersal biology of the species in question, populations in this sense may either be very extensive and only interrupted by major topographic features, or alternatively highly fragmented into distinctly localised populations that do not normally exchange genes with other populations.

Ecotypes may sometimes be populations or simply parts of populations; the critical issue is that they have evolved in response to a set of localised conditions, resulting in morphological or physiological traits that make them distinct. These may exist between two distributions but may not be obvious; for example are there distinct differences between Cumbrian *Trollius* and Perthshire *Trollius*? Probably not, since they occupy relatively similar cool, wet habitats in both locations, but as yet no one knows, because no tests have been carried out on populations of this species.

Clear examples of ecotypic variation are often found in species that have wet and dry distributions. In some North American oaks for example, populations are found both in wet valleys along flood plains, and on dry skeletal soils on ridges (Santamour *et al.*, 1980). It would be surprising if differential tolerance of soil de-oxygenation and summer drought had not evolved in these ecotypes. Significantly different ecological traits are often best-correlated with different ecological conditions in the range rather than actual distance between two populations (Millar and Libby, 1989). Studies into how geographical distance between populations correlates to differing genetic make up provide conflicting results (Wendel and Parks, 1985; Leeton and Fripp, 1991). However populations that are found at considerable distances from one another will, by virtue of the different ecological conditions resulting from this, have a higher-than-average chance of possessing different environmental tolerances.

Non-native 'natives'

Britain has a very low level of endemism (plants occurring here and no where else). Most of the species in our flora extend across Europe, in some cases into Eastern Europe. Consequently many British natives are also the natives of many other European nation states. As the use of native plants has increased in the past two decades, conservationists have become increasingly aware that seed and plants of some 'native' species sold in Britain are imported and are most likely derived from populations that naturally occur in central Europe. With wildflower seed this issue was most clearly demonstrated by tall agricultural selections of *Lotus corniculatus* (Ackeroyd 1994) and more recently hawthorn transplants from central-Eastern Europe.

A variant on this issue involves the native grasses that are used in wildflower seed mixes. These are generally derived from either agricultural or sports turf selections rather than wild collected populations. Some of these seed strains are harvested from plants growing outside Britain (for example New Zealand, in the case of crested dogstail, *Cynosurus cristatus*) from plants originally exported from Britain for agricultural use. Grasses grown from such seed are often more vigorous than forms found in old meadows in Britain because they have been selected for feeding livestock or standing up to intensive wear.

These issues raise strong passions, partly because of some of the philosophical issues previously raised, but more significantly because of the fear that such plants lie outside the morphological, biochemical, and phenological ranges associated with British populations of these species. As a result it is feared that they will prove unsatisfactory as habitat or fodder for invertebrates that have evolved to co-exist with these species; that they will fail to reproduce-persist satisfactorily; and that they will just look different, be more or less aggressive, or will simply 'dilute' native British bio-diversity. These risks are difficult to quantify given the limited data available. It has been suggested that continental forms of *Lotus corniculatus* are less attractive to butterflies than native forms. However there appear to be no specific, peer reviewed studies that confirm this. If you want to use native species it seems eminently sensible to try to source British genomes, but on a

philosophical level the issue is really quite grey, especially with some woody species.

For British trees and shrubs that have been widely planted during the last 500 years, the question is what is a British population? There has been an active pan-European trade in oak, beech, ash, etc., for centuries and as financial receipts in eighteenth century archives show, many fine 'British' stands of trees on country estates are in fact Continental European stands. There has therefore been ongoing introduction of continental genes for a long time, which have inevitably been incorporated into the genomes of at least some British populations. It is hard to believe that the enormous upsurge in the use of hedges after the Acts of Enclosure was not fuelled in part by imports from continental nurseries.

How poorly fitted are European forms of 'British' species?

Most of the data that is available is drawn from forestry, and deals with survival post transplanting and growth volume per unit time, rather than habitat value to native invertebrates etc. There is clear data that birch from Finland are less well fitted to growth in Scotland than are genotypes of British origin, due to their early flushing and sensitivity to late frosts (Worrell *et al.*, 2000). This would perhaps be expected given the significant climatic differences. Studies on genetic distribution suggest lack of fitness is most strongly developed when the conditions between the donor site of genes and receptor site (where the plants are to grow) are markedly un-alike. Key factors in this include day length, winter temperatures, summer temperatures, rainfall, solar radiation, soil moisture storage, pH and predation regimes.

Poland has a significantly different climate from lowland Britain and one would expect reduced 'fit' in genetic terms, but what about the Netherlands, Denmark, Western Germany and Northern France? Climatic differences between lowland Britain and the latter are often no greater than comparisons within Britain itself. It is very difficult to model or predict the outcome of these introductions, and in practice application of the precautionary principle is no bad thing. It is however important not to confuse pessimistic speculation with factual knowledge of cause and effect.

The current controversy tends to be based on the notion that the flora of Britain has never received genes from the European mainland and that if this happens, it will inevitably have some significant adverse effect. No one actually knows whether this is so, but there is no compelling evidence from the past few hundred years of woody plant introductions having adverse effects. All one knows for certain is that there will be additional sets of genes in circulation which may be dissimilar to those originally present. One of the purposes of bio-diversity action plans is to conserve native bio-diversity, but does this mean no further change in genetic make-up can occur? Is this what was intended by those people originally conceiving this policy?

One could argue that with the advent of global warming, genes from plants which have evolved in climates where the mean temperatures of the summer months are on average 1–3°C higher than Britain may well prove to be a useful thing. Whatever policy makers believe, the reality is that the environment will change, and so must plant genomes.

Local versus non-local natives

As the conservation movement has evolved, so too has consideration of the plant materials used in the landscape. The notion that conservation is about maintaining species within a given geopolitical unit has shifted to seeing species as groupings of populations, some of which have evolved distinctive genetic characteristics in response to local conditions. Conservation is primarily about the conservation of genes rather than organisms as individuals. The debate emanating from this change in conservation thinking has perhaps become most marked in relation to the use of seed of native herbaceous species as part of wildflower sowing mixes. From a landscape practitioner's perspective there are essentially two polar positions that one can hold; the conservative (i.e. pes-

simistic) versus the liberal (i.e. optimistic) viewpoint. There are of course many intermediate positions between these poles.

The pessimistic position strongly reflects the 'precautionary principle' – we do not know a great deal (particularly in the case of any given species) about how the genomes of a species differ either within a population or across the UK. As a result it is best to assume that introducing genes from outside a population will change the status quo and this change is likely to be harmful. This attitude has led to the use of terms such as 'genetic pollution' to describe the process of genes being incorporated into a population from another population of that species. Another important tenet is that the genome of a local population represents something unique – in this case the product of evolution ongoing in Britain since the end of the last Ice Age – and therefore is of intrinsic merit and worthy of preservation.

The optimistic perspective can simply be based on ignorance of all of the above. In more informed persons it may however reflect understanding that the genomes of individuals within a plant population are not fixed commodities (like an ancient building) but are the product of continuous change driven by natural selection. Genetic change is ongoing as you read this text, and is regulated by the process of natural selection which favours individuals that are better fitted to an environment and leads to the elimination of those that are poorly fitted. Natural selection will eventually fix it if it can be fixed! Optimists argue that outside of nature reserves (or other scenarios where there is clear evidence that introducing genes from other populations into an area may be harmful) using native, but non-local populations is unlikely to lead to the negative consequences feared by the pessimists.

These two positions are difficult to reconcile, and to some degree, they mirror debates in theology and philosophy from earlier times, with both sides claiming truth to be on their side. For landscape practitioners who are contracted to do things rather than philosophise, the bottom line is to have some idea as to what is acceptable or not acceptable and where and when. Which of these positions is best supported by the available scientific evidence?

Some of the key considerations for specifiers to take into account are as follows.

Rarity of the species in question

Scientists involved in the use of native species in habitat restoration works (for example Wells *et al.*, 1981) have tended to shy away from uncommon species since these have been the accepted focus for conservation agencies. Species that are uncommon may be so for a variety of reasons, but simply by virtue of their relatively small numbers, they are the species most likely to suffer following the introduction of 'harmful genes'. This is clearly paradoxical: establishing rare species by sowing and planting is likely to increase both their population size and genetic diversity, thus meeting typical goals of conservation programmes. Conservation groups are generally much less concerned about introducing non-local genes into common species as it is generally assumed that because these are common, they will contain a more catholic mix of genes which will buffer change.

Genetic structures of plant populations

Relatively little is known about the way in which genetic variation is distributed across local and national populations of British plants. It is generally assumed that species that are rare and more isolated in the landscape will possess less genetic diversity than species that are common and which exchange genes with a wide range of individuals. Quantitative studies do not always support this however (Moran and Hopper 1987). Common species will often have been moved around more through agriculture than will rare species. DNA profiling is currently in vogue and while valuable in terms of deciding whether population A is similar or dissimilar to population B, it tells you little about what this means in terms of fitness for an ecosystem.

The pollination biology of plants is a useful guide as to how widespread genes are likely to be across plant populations. Plants that are wind pollinated (such as grasses and oak trees) are likely to exchange genes over considerable distances (Centre for Plant Conservation, 1991). In such cases local and distant populations may share many genes and therefore arguments for not using seed derived from say 300 kilometres away may be difficult to substantiate other than on emotional grounds. Conversely, species that are significantly self-pollinated are more likely to develop local populations with a distinctive genetic structure. As previously stated, the most significant differences in plant genomes are likely to be correlated with ecological differences rather than geographical distance between sites. Consequently in terms of plant fitness for a site with relatively wet soils, it may be better to use a non-local seed source involving plants that also occur on wet soils, than a local seed source drawn from drier sites.

Species selection through understanding the proposed use and context

Most of the species used in meadow and woodland mixes are widespread species which (as previously discussed) are presumed even by pessimists to be less likely to have adverse effects on local populations. Very few landscape projects involve rare species. Where they do, there is a much stronger argument for the use of seed collected from local populations, if these exist. Context is also important; for example if the landscape project is in a highly urban location with no remnant populations of the species in question nearby, then local seed sources are clearly neither available nor necessary. Sites in rural landscapes adjacent to existing populations of species require much greater consideration as to the source of the plant material to be used.

Perceptions of genetic pollution

Genetic pollution is a highly emotional concept that is primarily based in the anthropomorphic notion that plant genomes are fixed and must be kept 'pure'. Many species that are rare or declining may be in this predicament because of isolation from other individuals of that species. This leads to diminishing genetic diversity and reduced capacity for natural selection to promote fitness, especially in rapidly changing environments. Conservation programmes frequently aim to increase genetic diversity, with the proviso that new genes are derived from populations occurring in broadly similar environments. Advantageously selected new genes entering a population may lead to changes in the plants themselves; this cannot be considered as pollution, merely the ongoing process of natural selection. Studies in forestry show that even when poorly-fitted species are planted, a percentage of the offspring of those trees that survive sufficiently long to reproduce are well-fitted to the site (Bennuah, 1992). In one generation natural selection may dramatically improve ecological fit of offspring.

Concerns remain however that introducing genes from distant populations can reduce fitness of local plant populations. The impact of 'outbreeding' depression is a matter of some controversy in the conservation genetics area of study with for instance a recent study (Keller *et al.*, 2000) found that crosses between Swiss cornfield annuals and populations of the same species from elsewhere in Europe reduced fitness. As has previously been discussed these effects are likely to be most marked when populations are drawn from substantially different ecological conditions. A study by Fenster and Galloway (2000) found that with a North American legume there was no evidence of reduction in fitness after crosses between populations hundreds of kilometres apart.

While the concept of genetic pollution is widely discussed by landscape practitioners, its application to plant materials over the geographical scale of Britain is in many cases deeply flawed. From a conservation perspective, ensuring sufficient genetic diversity to maximise the opportunities for natural selection and maintain fitness within changing environments (rather than trying to hold plant genomes in an unachievable state of suspended animation), is likely to be the most successful strategy. To quote from Frankham (1999):

'Currently an extremely cautious approach is taken to mixing populations. However, this cannot continue if fragmented populations are to be adequately managed to minimise extinctions'.

2.3 Plant quality in terms of the nursery product

Thus far this chapter has considered plant selection primarily in terms of the genetic constitution of difference species, and sub-specific variants. Once the choice of genotypes has been made it is then necessary to try to procure the plant material. While some plants may be collected as seed from wild populations, most material will be obtained from the nursery stock industry. As is particularly evident with trees, some species are available as a very wide range of nursery products. The impetus behind the National Plant Specification Project (HTA, 1997) was to help plant specifiers to improve their understanding of this range of products.

While most plant specifiers vigilantly inspect newly-purchased stock for obvious defects, such as broken branches, pest or disease infestations, they are often less aware of how different nursery production techniques can affect the capacity of species to establish successfully in the landscape. Specific information on this aspect of plant quality is given elsewhere in this book; however, some of the issues that all specifiers need to be aware of are as follows.

Plant size/age

There is a trend in the nursery stock industry towards offering larger, more mature plants. Traditionally in Britain we have used smaller plants than has been normal practice in the USA and in some parts of Europe. This current trend is driven by the desire of clients to have an instant landscape, and the need for growers to maintain market share through new products. Large plants cost more than smaller plants, but have the added advantages of greater resistance to post-planting vandalism (i.e. with advanced trees) and in some cases rough handling during planting. From the perspective of establishment however, are large plants more able to cope with the sub-optimal site conditions and post planting maintenance that are common to many public and commercial landscape sites?

Perhaps rather surprisingly there has been relatively little research into this issue. What research there is (for example Whitham *et al.* 1986), plus much observational data, suggests that in general terms as woody plants get larger, they are less able to establish satisfactorily. This is not to say that large, mature plants are more prone to dying post transplanting, but rather that their likely growth rates after transplantation are inversely correlated with the age of the transplant. This relationship is strongly influenced by the form of production, with some techniques more problematic than others.

Whether slow 'take off' post planting is a problem or not depends to what extent transplanted stock is expected to grow. Slow growth post planting is unlikely to be a problem with specimen *Hebe* in 20 litre pots. With extra heavy standard oak trees, which are expected to grow at 300–450 mm per year post transplanting, it may be. To put this into context a 1 + 1 birch seedling is likely to overtake a 3 m standard tree within five years. Species that are difficult to transplant, such as oak and birch, catch up advanced planting stock faster than easy-to-transplant species such as *Tilia* and *Acer*.

The stunting or 'check' observed in much advanced woody nursery stock post transplanting is generally due to the almost inevitable suboptimal root : shoot ratios of large stock, whether field grown and lifted or grown in containers. These take time to correct; the plant must photosynthesise effectively and use the resulting carbohydrates to make additional root tissues before it can return to producing typical shoot growth. Under hostile site conditions, severe water stress induced by competition with turfgrass or weeds, or compacted soil restricting root growth often restricts the development of adequate root : shoot ratios, resulting in many years of 'dwarf shoots'.

By providing appropriate site preparation (alleviation of compaction) before planting and good post-planting husbandry (effective management of competing herbaceous vegetation, mulching, irrigation where essential etc.) advanced nursery stock can be 'nursed' through and out of transplant check. Such a level of care is however uncommon, especially for trees that are planted in mown turf on prestige sites.

Form of plant production

This has a particularly major impact on the root characteristics of trees.

Container growing

This is seen by most specifiers as a desirable technique because it involves no loss of roots at planting, and therefore should avoid post-planting check. But is this so? Plants in containers inevitably have access to a relatively small, finite volume of moisture supplying compost. The goal of quality nursery stock growers is to replace that moisture by irrigation before its absence induces severe moisture stress in plants. As a result good quality stock grows quickly and looks leafy and healthy because it has not experienced severe moisture stress. However in the absence of moisture stress episodes, the root:shoot ratio of the plant declines. Rogers and Head (1969) reported that apples grown in irrigated containers had a root:shoot ratio of 1:7. Mature apples growing in sandy soils had a root:shoot ratio of 1:1. Good quality nursery stock inevitably has a sub-optimal root:shoot ratio for planting into un-irrigated landscapes, and the larger the plants at planting, the worse this relationship becomes.

The other problem with container-grown plants, and to a lesser degree 'containerised' stock, is root spiralling. Again this is most problematic with advanced specimens as these will often have occupied the final pot (as well as some of the intermediary pots) for longer, increasing the likelihood of roots having been deflected round and round by the internal walls of the pot. The problem can be reduced to some degree by pot design with internal flanges, but is difficult to eliminate altogether. When transplanted into a landscape site, trees with severely spiralled roots often show ineffective root exploration of the surrounding soil, resulting in

Fig. 2.6 The root ball of a container-grown standard tree five years after planting (after it blew over). Very few roots have grown out of the strongly-spiralled root ball, a result of stock remaining in the container for too long. (Photo: James Hitchmough)

a thickening of the existing spiralling roots (Fig. 2.6). In a percentage of trees this leads to short term instability and as the trees become larger and the length of the lever increases, a tendency to heave or blow over under storm conditions. Root spiralling and similar root malformations resulting from nursery production appear to be most problematic with fast growing and ultimately large species.

Plants grown in containers of composts derived from organic debris such as bark and peat also suffer from the hydrophobic (water repelling) nature of these materials. As these media dry out due to plant transpiration, they shrink and become increasingly hydrophobic. This is particularly serious when stock in large containers are planted with dry root balls, especially under climatic conditions conducive to high evapo-transpiration. Root balls dry out before roots can tap into water stored in the surrounding soil and the plant becomes stressed. With large root balls it is very difficult to rewet the compost *in situ*, as water applied tends to run off the ball and around the sides. Specifiers should also insist on soaking of root balls prior to planting. Without close site supervision this is often difficult to achieve.

Container/field-grown hybrids

Many of the problems associated with growing advanced trees in containers are alleviated by transplanting field grown stock into above ground containers for the year before sale. In many cases the walls of the containers are made of a semi-rigid plastic with a profile similar to that of an egg tray. Roots that reach the walls of the container are channelled into the concave cups which are perforated at the end. Roots are ultimately air-pruned and spiralling eliminated. This system probably produces the best quality root system possible to date.

Bare root

In common with root-balling methods, this involves direct loss of roots at lifting. Bare root stock is often grown to a relatively small size prior to lifting, is low cost to purchase and if correctly handled to minimise root desiccation, is a biologically dynamic product. This is to be preferred where its use is appropriate. Root loss is often quite low when transplants have been undercut or lifted at least once in the production cycle in the field. Spiralling does not occur with this product, and since the roots are immediately in direct contact with the site soil, problems of hydrophobic potting compost are avoided. Clearly the planting season is restricted for bare root trees, and they often have low initial impact. Plant handling protocols that avoid root desiccation are essential when purchasing bare root material (Kendle *et al.*, 1988).

Root-balled

This is normally reserved for advanced trees, conifers such as specimen *Chamaecyparis* and *Rhododendron*. Most really large, advanced trees are grown in this way. This technique has the advantage of avoiding spiralling and other problems of container growing, but often captures a relatively low percentage of the tree roots present prior to lifting. With really large stock root capture can be as low as ten per cent (Watson and

Himelick, 1982). Quality growers undercut and side cut the roots of root-balled trees in the years prior to final transplanting. The purpose of this is to sever roots and initiate new roots to form a more branched root system within the root ball. The problem is however that many species initiate new roots chiefly at the cut ends of the roots, rather than closer to the bole of the tree (Gilman and Yeagher, 1988). As a result, many of the new roots are eventually left in the field when trees are finally lifted. One only has to inspect the stumps of cut roots within the hole created by lifting to appreciate that root loss is often appreciable. Clearly this has a significant impact on the plant's capacity to re-establish through vigorous growth, especially following transplanting into sub-optimal soils.

Signs of past stress

In plants, stress can be defined as a shortage or excess of a resource required for growth. The most common sources of stress are too little or too much water (i.e. insufficient soil oxygen), and too few nutrients. All of these factors result in plants with a similar appearance, often yellowish foliage, red tinted at times, reduced shoot inter-node length (dwarf shoots), and smaller foliage than normal. These symptoms are much more likely to be exhibited by plants grown in full sun than those grown under protection in netting tunnels etc. Nursery stock grown under protection without exposure to wind and sun can exhibit the opposite characteristics, large leaves composed of thin walled cells and atypically long, leggy shoots.

Material with either of these types of appearance should be avoided. Over-protected material is more likely to experience wind and sun scorch, plus mechanical wind damage, after planting out in unprotected locations. It is important that plants grown under protection are gradually exposed to unprotected conditions on the nursery, via a hardening off process, before being planted on landscape sites. Plants that have been severely stressed in the past often have very slow growth

rates post planting, even when planted in good soil under optimum growing conditions.

Growth form

To some degree this is a culturally-defined characteristic, rather than necessarily a question of right or wrong. This is discussed in greater detail for advanced trees in Chapter 10. Branching density is a useful general measure of quality for use with shrubs, woody and herbaceous ground covers and some climbers. These plants are often grown either to block or screen a view, to define a route, or to cover the ground or a structure. High branching density generally contributes to achieving these goals. There are of course exceptions to this, for example where shrubs have a sculptural 'see through' role, in which case high branching density is undesirable.

Pest and disease status

When accepting or rejecting a consignment of plants, plant specifiers need to be able to put the presence of some pests and diseases into some kind of context. For example, rejecting a consignment because of the presence of aphids would in most cases be inappropriate as these insects are widespread and are only a significant problem with some highly sensitive species. On the other hand, plants showing evidence of wilting and foliage browning associated with catastrophic diseases such as *Phytophthora* root rots should be rejected immediately. A useful plant pathology text to help identify common pathogens and insect pests is Buczacki *et al.* (1998).

2.4   Summary

Plant selection is a key process in developing landscapes that are functional, sustainable and yet provide meaning and richness for human beings. There is considerable evidence that many plant specifiers do not utilise plant selection as effectively as they might. Increasing environmental pressures require contemporary plant specifiers to have much greater understanding of the philosophical and scientific issues that underpin decisions on plant selection. Understanding these issues allows specifiers to feel more confident, and able to make decisions on a considered basis rather than in response to current fashion or orthodoxy. More practical but of no less importance is the need for plant users to be aware of the characteristics of different types of nursery stock in order to make effective decisions on plant procurement for a given project.

References

Ackeroyd, J. (1994) *Seeds of destruction*. Plantlife, London.

Bennuah, S.Y. (1992) Provenance variation in Grand Fir, *Abies grandis* Lindley. Unpublished MPhil Thesis, University of Edinburgh.

Buczacki, S.T., Harris, K., & Hargreaves, B. (1998) *Collins Photoguide; Pests, Diseases, and Disorders of Garden Plants*, 2nd edn. Collins, London.

Centre for Plant Conservation (1991) Genetic sampling guidelines for conservation collections of endangered plants. In: Falk, D.A. & Holsinger, K.E. (eds) *Genetics and Conservation of Rare Plants*. Oxford University Press, New York.

Clement, E.J. & Foster, M.C. (1994) *Alien Plants of the British Isles*. Botanical Society of the British Isles, London.

Dirr, M.A. (1997) *Dirr's Hardy Trees and Shrubs, an Illustrated Encyclopaedia*. Timber Press, Portland, Oregon.

Fenster, C.B. & Galloway, L.F. (2000) Inbreeding and outbreeding depression in natural populations of *Chamaecrista fasciculata* (Fabaceae). *Conservation Biology*, **14**, (5), 1406–12.

Frankham, R. (1999) Quantitative genetics in conservation biology. *Genetical Research*. **74**, (3), 237–44.

Gilman, E.F. & Yeagher, T.H. (1988) Root initiation in root pruned hardwoods. *HortScience*, **23**, 351.

Hansen, R. & Stahl, F. (1993) *Perennials and their Garden Habitats*. Cambridge University Press, Cambridge, UK.

HTA (1997) *National Plant Specification*. HTA/JCLI, Reading.

Jellito, K. & Schacht, W. (1990) *Hardy Herbaceous Perennials*. Batsford, London.

Keller, M., Kollmann, J., & Edwards, P.J. (2000) Genetic introgression from distant provenances reduces fitness in local weed populations. *Journal of Applied Ecology*. **37**, (4), 647–59.

Kennedy, C.E.J. & Southwood, T.R.E. (1984) The number of species of insects associated with British trees. A re-analysis. *Journal of Animal Ecology*, **53**, 455–78.

Kendle, A.D., Gilbertson, P., & Bradshaw, A.D. (1988) The influence of stock source on transplant performance. *Arboriculture Journal*, **12**, 257–72.

Kendle, A.D. & Rose, J. (2000) The aliens have landed! What are the justifications for 'native only' policies in landscape plantings? *Landscape and Urban Planning*, **47**, 19–31.

Leeton, P. & Fripp, Y.J. (1991) Breeding system, karyotype, and variation within and between populations of *Rutidosus leptorrhynchoides* F. Muell. (Asteraceae:Inuleae). *Australian Journal of Botany*, **39**, 85–96.

Millar, C.I. & Libby, W.J. (1989) Disneyland or native ecosystems: Genetics and the restorationist. *Restoration and Management Notes*, **7**, (1), 60–67.

Moran, G.F. & Hopper, S.D. (1987) Geographical population structure of eucalypts and the conservation of their genetic resources. In: *Nature Conservation; The role of remnants of Native Vegetation*, pp. 151–62, Surrey Beatty, Chipping Norton, NSW, Australia.

Owen, J. (1991) *The ecology of a garden: the first fifteen years*. Cambridge University Press, Cambridge.

Rich, T.C.B. & Woodruff, E.R. (1996) Changes in the vascular plant floras of England and Scotland between 1930 to 1960 and 1987–1988: the BSBI monitoring scheme. *Biological Conservation*, **75**, 217–29.

Rogers, W.S. & Head, C.G. (1969) Factors affecting the distribution and growth of roots of woody perennial species. In: Whittington, W.J. (ed.) *Root Growth*. Butterworths, London.

Santamour, F.S., Garrett, P.W. & Peterson, P.B. (1980) Oak provenance research: The Michaux Quercetum after 25 years. *Journal of Arboriculture*, **6**, (6), 156–9.

Southwood, T.R.E. (1961) The number of species of insects associated with various trees. *Journal of Animal Ecology*, **30**, 1–8.

Thompson, K. (1995) Native and alien invasive plants: more of the same? *Ecography*, **18**, 390–402.

Watson, G.W. & Himelick, E.B. (1982) Root distribution of nursery trees and its relationship to transplanting success. *Journal of Arboriculture*, 8, 225–9.

Wells, T.C.E., Bell, S.A. & Frost, A. (1981) *Creating Attractive Grasslands using Native Plant Species*, Nature Conservation Council, Shrewsbury, Shropshire.

Wendel, J.F. & Parks, C.R. (1985) Genetic diversity and population structure in *Camellia japonica* L. (Theaceae). *American Journal of Botany*, **72**, 52–65.

Whitham, A., Young, R., & Moloney, D. (1986) The effect of container size on growth of some natives in the field. *Australian Horticulture*, October Edition, 75–9.

Worrell, R., Cundall, E.P., Malcolm, D.C., & Ennos, R.A. (2000) Variation among seed sources of silver birch in Scotland. *Forestry*. **75**, (5), 419–35.

3 Procuring Plants for Landscape Projects

*Nick Coslett, Tom La Dell and James Wilson
with contributions from Mike Smith, Mike Browell
and John Parker*

3.1 Introduction: plant provenance

Contemplating the magnificence of a two-hundred-year-old oak tree, it is tempting to ask if it matters whether it was planted as a locally found acorn, bought as a small tree from a nearby nursery or transplanted as a root-balled specimen tree. What is important is the significance of the tree today.

Perhaps two hundred years ago it did not matter, and guidance on the selection, procurement and purchase of plants was not necessary. Others might argue that, whilst inert materials such as bricks, paving, etc., can be made to specified sizes and consistent colours and textures, plants are not manufactured and no two are the same. This, to many, is part of their charm and, added to their ever-changing nature, does beg the original question:

'What does it matter what we buy as long as it grows?'

However this inconsistency and variability is one of a number of reasons why a plant specification guide is so important. It is easy to buy bricks; it should be as easy to buy quality plants.

Two hundred years ago a relatively narrow range of species were grown, although imports of plants have been part of our landscape heritage since the Romans and before. After the voyages of Captain Cook in the 1760s the volume of imports accelerated dramatically as botanical adventurers returned with new species for commercial and botanical interest. The founding of the RHS in 1804 with the purpose of the 'improvement of horticulture' coincided with the interest in plants and funding of expeditions. Today tens of thousands of taxa can be purchased, from UK sources and elsewhere. Those specifying plants need guidance on how to select plants from this ever expanding range of choice. Which cultivar is appropriate? Will the hybrid be hardy and/or subject to disease? Should a particular clonal form be specified? Are seed raised plants available?

Provenance and origin

'Provenance' and 'origin' are two topical issues which relate to the range of plants available. It is often assumed that these would not have worried the plant purchaser two centuries ago; however there is evidence that by the early eighteenth century there was discussion amongst horticulturists as to which forms of widespread European trees did best in Britain (Miller, 1731). Modern economics often result in seed for 'English' oak (*Quercus robur*) being collected in the Czech Republic and then grown in the UK. This may be the same species, but from a different part of its natural range. Where climatic patterns are significantly different this is likely to result in genetically controlled differences in plant growth; possibly in vigour, time of bud break, flowering etc. This may have an impact, albeit subtle, on the ecosystems associated with oak woodland.

The decreasing use of local sources and an increasing use of selected and vegetatively propagated forms, often grown for varying periods in different locations, are bound to raise issues such as these. These concerns are linked to the expanding use of national and international sources of supply. Should plants grown in Eastern Europe from local sources be planted in the UK? Philosophical aspects of this question are discussed in detail in Chapter 2; however in practical terms there is evidence that, if plants are travelling long distances between lifting and replanting, then there is increasing opportunity for damage to occur in handling and transit. Guidance on lifting, storage, protection, handling and transporting plants is an essential part of their procurement.

Definitions for origin and provenance have been established for forestry use and these are equally applicable for amenity use, especially as the revised *Forestry Reproductive Materials Regulations* (FRM Regs) coming into use in 2003 will classify plants for either forestry or amenity use (Forestry Commission, 2001). However in terms of these regulations, provenance and origin are only important when referring to native or naturalised species.

Box 3.1   Provenance jargon demystified (after Aldhous, 2002).

Examples of use of these terms:
- *Pinus sylvestris* seed collected from a native stand in Glen Tanar would be of Glen Tanar origin and Glen Tanar provenance;
- *Fagus sylvatica* seed collected in Cirencester Park, Gloucestershire, in plantations known to have been planted with seed originating from the Forêt de Soignes in Belgium would be of Belgian origin and Cirencester Park provenance;
- *Quercus robur* acorns collected in Hampshire in an oak plantation of unknown origin would be of Hampshire provenance, origin unknown.

Amenity plants raised from seed
'Origin' and 'provenance' are defined for amenity planting in the HTA National Plant Specification, (NPS) Section T10.2. These definitions are repeated in sections covering shrubs and herbaceous species raised from seed.

While the exact wording differs, the meanings of the definitions of 'origin' and 'provenance' in the NPS and in the EC Directives, old and new, are the same.

Amenity plants – 'country of origin'
In Section T10.2 the NPS cites a 'British Standards' definition of 'Country of origin' as 'the country where plants have been growing in the latter half of the most recent growing season'. This definition may be relevant to vegetatively propagated ornamental cultivars but must not be applied to forestry stock raised from seed.

Local seed zones and regions of provenance
Seed sources from adjoining areas with similar site and climate can be grouped together as coming from a '**local seed zone**'. The size of any such grouping may vary by locality.

Local seed zones may in turn be grouped together to form '**regions of provenance**'.

Figure 3.1 shows a Forestry Commission map of 'local seed zones' and 'regions of provenance' for native trees and shrubs in Britain (Herbert *et al.*, 1999). The four regions of provenance are differentiated on the basis of 'accumulated summer heat' and 'total annual rainfall'. They have been divided into 24 local seed zones, using ecological and natural physical boundaries. These are the zones and regions recommended when specifying origins of most native species for forestry purposes.

Seed from any seed source should be suitable for sites of similar soil and climate elsewhere in the same local seed zone. If seed is not available from within a preferred local seed zone, the next choice should be from among stands of good form and vigour growing at similar elevations in the same 'region of provenance'.

Historical descriptors
Historical descriptors are important in Britain because of the scale on which native vegetation has been destroyed and species have been moved, being planted often many hundreds of miles from their original seed source.

Box 3.1 *Continued.*

The terms 'authochthonous', 'indigenous', 'native', 'alien' and 'naturalised' may each be used to describe an aspect of the history of the seed source. The term 'autochthonous' is likely to be unfamiliar to plant users but is incorporated in the revised EC FRM directive.

autochthonous (synonym site-native)
an autochthonous seed source is one which has been continuously regenerated naturally. However, a seed source may also be considered autochthonous if regenerated artificially from seed collected from the same source or from autochthonous stands in the near vicinity .

indigenous
an indigenous seed source is an autochthonous seed source, or is a source raised from seed, the origin of which is in the same region of provenance .

The **range** of a species is the geographical area over which a species occurs (or occurred before clearance by man); **natural range** is that part of the range where the species occurs/occurred naturally, without intervention by man. A species is native within that range. A species' natural range may change in response to a natural change in climate; it is dynamic, not static. **Extended range** is the additional area where a species occurs as a result of introduction by man, whether deliberate or inadvertent.

A species is **introduced** (synonyms alien, exotic) within its extended range. If an introduced species is able to grow, reproduce and colonise, it is **naturalised**. A species such as *Fagus sylvatica* (beech) which, in Britain, occurred naturally only in central and southern England, is native there and introduced/naturalised elsewhere.

Table 3.1 Descriptors of seed sources for forestry and amenity planting stock (Aldhous, 2002).

Class of descriptor	Frequency of use for forestry and amenity planting stock		
	Commonly	Sometimes	Rarely
Botanical	Genus, species, cultivar, common name	Clone, variety, hybrid	Subspecies, forma
Geographical	Provenance, origin, source, stand, local seed zone, region of provenance		
Historical/geographical	Native, alien, exotic, introduced, naturalised	Natural range, indigenous	Autochthonous, extended range
Ecological		National vegetation classification, woodland type	Forest type
Qualitative	Selected, source-identified, qualified, tested		

When is it important to consider provenance? Table 3.1 lists the seed sources likely to be available, and Table 3.2 gives priorities of importance against the vegetation type of the site.

Work by the Forestry Commission's Roger Herbert has identified the regions of provenance (seed zones) for trees and shrubs within the UK (Fig. 3.1). Principally for forestry use, the classification is also of value when used for amenity planting.

Biological truths

Although it is well known that oaks establish best when planted as acorns, clients increasingly expect to see 'value for money' after a landscape is planted and are less content to wait for plant growth. The industry has responded by producing plants of ever-increasing size, which contradicts the biological and economic truth that small plants are much easier and cheaper to procure, transport,

Table 3.2   Matching seed source to site for amenity and forest planting (Aldhous, 2002).

Seed source	Restoration of ASNW# Native woodland fragments	General woodland planting	Land restoration Open landscapes	Urban landscape
Local seed zone+	****	***	**	*
Local region of provenance	***	****	****	***
Source in Britain	**	**	**	**
Near-European origin++	X	*/**	*/**	*/**
Other origin	X	Use dependent on origin and circumstances of site		

**** *** ** * Decreasing order of preference.
# Ancient semi-natural woodland.
+ Where local seed sources are essential, sufficient time may have to be allowed for stock to be raised under a 'contract grow' or similar arrangement.
++ Alternatives that may be appropriate for C and SE England.

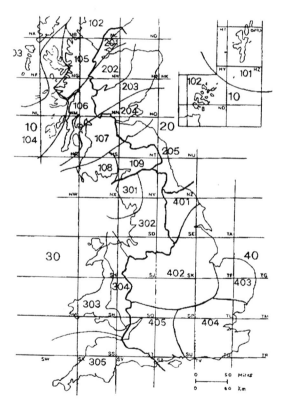

Fig. 3.1 Seed provenance regions for trees and shrubs in the UK. (Crown copyright, reproduced in Herbert *et al.*, 1999)

handle and establish. Use of these larger plants requires knowledge of their particular procurement procedures to ensure successful establishment and growth. They are also likely to require special attention to their cultivation requirements as larger plants will take longer to establish and grow away in their new locations.

During the last forty years competitive tendering has been used increasingly for purchasing the quantities of plants required for the majority of the large landscape projects. For almost as long, wholesale nursery suppliers have been complaining about the lack of specifications and standards universally accepted and used throughout the industry. Whilst grades and standards have been introduced since the 1970s, methods of growing are constantly changing and the range of sizes is increasing, both of which factors tend to compromise out-of-date standards.

An excellent example is the phenomenal rise in container growing. In the 1950s the majority of plants were supplied bare-root or root-balled. Container growing gained popularity during the 1960s and at this time a plant might be specified by height and as p.g. (pot grown). In the 1970s the size of the container was included. In the 1980s an indication of the 'number of breaks' and the 'habit' of the shrub was added. This is just one example of how the increasing use of a range of criteria allows the visual quality of the plants to be specified more exactly and improves the tendering process. The co-operation of a group of nursery-men established the European Nurserystock Association (ENA) and established standards for the procurement of plants throughout Europe. This was in part interpreted within the UK by the Horticultural Trades Association, who produced the *National Plant Specification* (NPS) (HTA, 1997 and 2002).

The supply chain

How to propagate, grow, buy, lift, transport, handle, plant, establish and maintain plants has been known for many years. In the past these actions might have been carried out by a limited number of skilled craftspeople. In recent years more people have become involved, and the term 'the supply chain' has been coined. Nowadays not only do plants spend longer in the process of supply but they are handled by many more people, some of whom may not appreciate how perishable they are. Again guidance is needed through this stage of the procurement process.

During the last three decades considerable changes have taken place in the production, supply and use of plants. It is important for everyone involved to keep up-to-date with the development of new techniques and the improvement of standards and information. At the same time the simple but essential physiology of plants must not be forgotten. The sections which follow highlight the importance of careful plant specification and selection and the significance of those involved in the supply chain.

3.2   The plant

There are two aspects to selecting plants for landscape and design sites.

The first is to select plants suitable for the site, taking into account the following factors (among others):

- soils
- aspects
- hardiness
- height
- width
- habit

- root system
- rate of growth
- ease of establishment and
- maintenance.

The second is the specification of the chosen plants, based upon the following criteria:

- size
- height and spread
- stem development
- branch development
- the way it grows naturally
- the nursery growing regime
- open ground, root-balled or container grown
- growing medium
- growing conditions
- artificial protection
- fertiliser regime
- plant handling from the nursery to the final position on site.

This list is not comprehensive, but it gives an idea of the complexity of plant selection and specification. There is a regrettable tendency in the landscape industry to make standards for plants as narrow as possible. The further this proceeds, the less the plant material will be suitable for the wide variety of landscape schemes and site conditions that exist.

There is usually an assumption by clients, specifiers, suppliers and contractors, that there will be expensive soil amelioration and that the job of the landscape architect and amenity horticulturist is to accommodate whatever plant material the nursery produces. This is a serious distortion of the professional responsibility of these practitioners. Even greenfield sites vary greatly, with soil from clays to coarse sands. It is the handling of these soils through the site development process which is more important than soil amelioration. For some denatured soils, amelioration may even worsen the conditions for plant establishment. The increasing use of derelict and contaminated (brownfield) sites for development is an entirely welcome change with many benefits, but the advantage can be lost if an attempt is made to re-create greenfield site planting conditions. It is soil preparation – creating a medium which plants can establish into – which is crucial. It is also vital that the selection of plants is made in the light of site conditions.

This may entail selecting plants which have been cultivated appropriately in the nursery.

Suitable plants

The only guidance which is exclusively for the selection of landscape plant material in the United Kingdom is in the Joint Council of Landscape Industries' tree, shrub and herbaceous plant lists. These are checklists and give no assessment of plant performance in particular site conditions. The choice of plants for the lists is based on a compromise between nurserymen and plants users on the JCLI. Although many of these commonly grown plants are known performers, no attempt has been made to evaluate or rank their performance in comparative terms. The lists omit many invaluable plants that are not commonly grown. They also give a relatively uncritical indication of commonly available plants, and thus are limited in their value in plant selection.

Many nursery catalogues have selection lists for plants suitable for a wide variety of site conditions. These are usually based on data for gardens and are often helpful in drawing up initial lists of plants suitable for a site but they may not be a reliable guide to the plant's overall performance in landscape conditions.

Selection lists are increasingly common with plant software packages, and these offer the best possibilities for bringing together plant selection and essential data on the plants themselves in a convenient form. The format may be convincing but the quality of the package is only as good as the data – in some cases this is fairly poor. With certain packages (HELIOS for example) there is an ability to add plants and data to refine the lists and selection process.

Viewing plants in the nursery can provide an understanding of how they are produced and also gives the opportunity to see them correctly labelled. However young plants are little or no guide to future growth and form – nursery production is geared to producing an attractive plant in the container which may or may not mirror the true growth form. Nurseries, quite understandably, often do not know how plants perform on landscape sites, and this can lead to unsuitable plants being promoted for landscape use. Some nurseries that supply retail outlets (where an attractive young plant is paramount) may use the landscape industry as a sink for their second quality plants. Therefore care needs to be exercised when selecting a nursery to visit. The most reliable way to assess plant performance is to observe it on a wide range of landscape sites.

Plants can also be viewed in gardens with recognised plant collections and in botanic gardens. However these are grown in ideal conditions, either available on the site or specially created for them. They may give little more than an idea of the form of the plant in ideal conditions. A botanist would observe that you really find out about a plant's tolerances when you find out why it fails on a particular site. Demonstration gardens of good landscape plants can be helpful in showing them mass planted in an area with known soil and climatic conditions. The Professional Plant User Group is encouraging these demonstration gardens as a good way to broaden plant knowledge and choice in the professions. The first was opened in 1997 at Ryton Organic Gardens, near Coventry. There are shrub and tree plantings together with an adventurous mass planting of herbaceous perennials. It is hoped that at least one landscape and horticulture college will soon start a new demonstration planting and that others with different soils and climate will follow.

Specification of plant material

Generally plant specifications are mostly concerned with the appearance of the plant and are little to do with the suitability of the plant for its intended site. Other countries (for example Germany) have standards that are also concerned with how the plant is grown and therefore relate to how it will establish in its final site. This is the next essential step for the development of the plant specification in the UK.

British Standards

The baseline specifications most commonly used within the UK landscape industry include BS 3936.

Part 1: 1992 – covers specification trees and shrubs.

Part 2: 1990 – covers specification for roses.

Part 3: 1990 – covers specification for fruit plants.

Part 4: 1984 – covers specification for forest trees.

Part 5: 1985 – covers specification for poplars and willows.

Part 7: 1989 – covers specification for bedding plants.

Part 9: 1998 – covers specification for corms and tubers.

Part 10: 1989 – covers specification for ground cover plants.

Part 11: 1984 – covers specification for container-grown culinary herbs.

Part 1 comprises a short general specification and defines the terms used in describing plants and their forms in the nursery – for example, standards, whips and shrubs. However the level of specification is so general that it can hardly be applied and has no measurable indicators. For example,

> 'Root system: the root system shall be alive and healthy, balanced in relation to the whole plant and in a condition conducive to successful transplanting and establishment'.

The lengthy appendix has lists of climbers, conifers, trees and shrubs and specification standards for a wide variety of forms of trees.

Part 10 is for ground cover plants and follows the same format, including many shrubs in Part 1, together with some herbaceous plants.

Larger trees are covered by BS 4043: 1989, 'Recommendations for transplanting root-balled trees'. This is a little more comprehensive than other British Standards for plants. The cultivation, lifting and handling of the trees is specified. Planting and aftercare are well covered, together with detailed guidance on staking and guying. There is no list of trees, however, nor an indication of the variation of tolerance to transplanting at these larger sizes. The more comprehensive approach (including cultivation) should be expanded to all

plant material. The JCLI (Joint Council of Landscape Industries) are due to publish a best practice guidance note which supplements this BS in the near future.

National Plant Specification

The *National Plant Specification* (NPS) was published in 1997 by the Horticultural Trades Association and revised in March 2002 (HTA, 2002) and it is considered to have superseded BS 3936. It came about after cross industry concern that a lack of rigour in the use and monitoring of specifications had led to an abuse of the tendering procedure where like was not being compared with like.

Developments in production practice throughout the industry and in Europe were making the British Standards out of date. The NPS listed a wider range of plants based on the JCLI approved plant lists of trees and shrubs and includes herbaceous perennials for landscape use. Specification of different production sizes, habit and form with an indication of branching and method of propagation were included, with indicators to likely availability across the industry.

The NPS includes the following plant categories:

* trees
* shrubs (including rhododendrons and roses)
* bamboos
* climbing plants
* conifers
* herbaceous perennials (including grasses, sedges, rushes, bulbs, corms, marginal and aquatic plants)
* British native origin plants / wildflowers.

NPS also includes:

* The CPSE code for Handling and Establishing Landscape Plants
* Specification of Origin and Provenance for Amenity and Forestry Planting
* Specification for Root-balled Trees
* Glossary of Terms

Each category specification gives illustrations and a summary of information. Details on each plant are given and although it cannot include all taxa grown, it does include those most widely grown and is far more inclusive than the previous BS appendix.

References to the National Plant Specification are included in the National Building Specification (NBS), along with details of the Nursery and Contractors Certification Schemes (NCS and CCS) and the companies who have been inspected and accredited as members of these schemes. These companies agree to conform to a specification according to NPS and not to substitute without written authorisation; they are rigorously inspected bi-annually to ensure that their businesses meet the standards of the scheme. NPS is also included in the HELIOS software package and has a plant search and plant palette building facility for projects.

NPS is a significant step forward from the British Standard and has strong industry backing. Its first few years have shown a slow uptake as practices are slow to adapt or update their established 'in house' systems. Its comprehensive use by designers and specifiers in both public and private sectors and its inclusion in all landscape work will lead to improvements in the quality of planted landscape. It is beginning to influence how plants are grown on the nursery, mainly in order to achieve the plant habit and branching structure advised within the specification. However, it does not yet address the issue of how the plant will establish in its new location. Nor does it address the issue of growing media.

At the time of writing the HTA is working with BSI to develop the NPS into a National British Standard. The aim will be to incorporate the NPS chapters on trees, shrubs, bulbs, corms and tubers into BS 3936, and to develop the remaining NPS chapters into supporting Publicly Available Specifications (PAS), accredited and marketed by BSI. Work on the PAS documents may be completed by spring 2004, but the revision of BS 3936 may take a little longer.

Other matters, essential for plant specification and survival, are not generally covered by standard specifications. There is extensive evidence that cultivation and handling in the nursery is critical in determining the following:

- Survival of the plant in transit.
- Establishment on site.
- Speed of establishment, particularly the period over which watering is required.
- Rate of growth.
- The form of the developing plant, the size and habit of the mature plant, especially trees.

However it has also to be recognised that each site will have individual conditions and no plant specification can compensate for inadequate site preparation prior to planting. The largest cause of plant failure outside poor handling is lack of site soil cultivation to provide a medium that will drain and allow new roots to penetrate. Good contact between site soil and root ball is important. Small gaps due to lack of appropriate soil cultivation or consolidation or differences in soil expansion and shrinkage in varying moisture conditions can lead to a barrier to water migration between local soil and root ball soil. Dry root balls in wet planting pits will cause plants to fail.

Open ground plants

In general, open ground plants of suitable species are larger, healthier and cheaper than equivalent container grown material (Fig. 3.2). There are two disadvantages.

- Bare roots are susceptible to drying if left exposed, and this rapidly reduces survival rates.
- The current demands of construction projects often insist on planting outside the dormant season, which excludes use of open ground plants.

Poor handling of open ground material in the nursery, in transit and on site are the main causes of these drying out problems. This has reduced the use of these plants despite the evidence on many sites that they establish and grow better than container-grown material.

The Committee on Plant Supply and Establishment's *Plant Handling and Establishing Land-*

Fig. 3.2 High quality bare root trees transplant very well in species that tolerate this practice. (Photo: James Hitchmough)

scape Plants (1996) has established set standards for plant handling. Although this document was revised in 1996 the standards are still not high enough and there is no means of enforcement. An additional precaution in specification should require that all bags for root protection be made of co-extruded polythene (black on the inside and white on the outside). These are used by the better nurseries although they are more expensive than the usual black, white or transparent polythene bags, which can heat up in winter sunshine to the detriment of the roots inside.

Also it may be desirable to specify that the supplying nursery grows the plants, unless otherwise agreed, so that the handling period is reduced.

However few nurseries will be able to offer all plants, often because of specialisation and economies of scale, and most will 'buy in' to some degree to make up customer orders. The specifier must demand to be told which items are subject to a longer supply chain and therefore more exposed to handling problems. Clear insistence on the CPSE code will minimise but not remove problems. Those nurseries which belong to a certification scheme or are quality assured will be better able to track the plant and give evidence on handling.

Open ground plants can be coldstored at around 1°C and safely planted up to the end of May. A high humidity store is needed with suitable root protection. The plants must be placed in the coldstore by the end of December. Coldstored plants have, from experience, established better at the end of May than conventionally-stored plants which were planted in late March on an adjacent site.

Container-grown plants

Container growing produces other problems that are not dealt with in standard specifications. It is itself an environmentally rather wasteful method of cultivation as the pots use large quantities of plastic. The use of polythene 'bag style' pots as opposed to rigid pots would reduce this waste. Some form of recycling may be required under current waste legislation.

However the nursery industry has adopted the rigid pot; it has both production and on-nursery handling benefits but is more difficult to handle in transit and on site. Pots are now classified as packaging, and the larger nurseries are now taxed on them as part of new taxation on packaging waste. There have been attempts to re-cycle used pots but these have not been sustained and have been uneconomic. Some nurseries will offer their customers the chance to return pots, for re-use, though phytosanitary implications and costs have to be accounted for.

Second-hand pots have to be cleaned, and this cleaning can cost more than a new pot. At present economic factors are against this recycling. Recent developments in Europe, and specifically in Dutch nurseries, have involved biodegradable pots which break down after 18 months, but viability has not yet been proven.

Container growing also uses compost, bulky organic matter. This is usually peat although in some instances it is material (coir) imported from tropical countries where it should be used as a much-needed soil ameliorant. Transport costs are also increased for container-grown plants as they are heavier and bulkier than bare root stock.

During the 1990s there has been much campaigning by environmentalists on the peat issue. In Britain the low land peat mire is a rare habitat but all commercial horticulture uses non-British peat sources, either Irish (where 66 per cent of extracted peat is burnt in power stations) or from the Baltic States.

There are also wide-scale current research and trials on composted organic matter (much resulting from domestic garden waste) as a diluter for peat or as an alternative. Problems that have been identified so far involve consistency and nutrient levels. Specification standards are being developed by the Waste and Resources Action Programme and will be available soon. Developing the markets for recycled products is an important facet of sustainable development.

There is little scientific evidence on the effects of container plant cultivation on plant establishment. It is known that the root system is influenced by the compost and cultivation methods. Most composts are all organic matter (usually peat and bark), with added nutrients. There is no nutrient storage within the media so when nutrients run out the plant starves. This has been called premature senescence, and it severely affects the success of establishment on site. A percentage of sterilised soil in the compost reduces its severity and may also lead to the development of a root system which is better adapted to root out of the pot and into the surrounding top soil. It appears from preliminary grower trials that inclusion of some composted green waste may have a similar effect to soil.

Container-grown plants are more susceptible to frost or drought damage than open ground plants. They are often grown in glasshouses or polythene tunnels, and the root and shoot growth is softer and more frost sensitive. In order to come this, container plants should always be specified as being grown in the open (hardened off) for at least two months before being supplied to site. An added advantage is that plants supplied in spring will not have had their roots killed off in a previous severe winter.

Container-grown plants (Fig. 3.3) must be well established in the pot, but not too long within it or the root system becomes too dense. In both cases successful establishment is reduced: in the first case the plant rocks in the compost and is slow to root out into the surrounding soil, and in the second the plant lacks juvenile vigour and may also be more prone to drying out.

Trees have more cultivation requirements than shrubs, both between different species and in the sizes they are offered. They are usually grown on the nursery for a longer period and nursery practices will be more significant in shaping their future development. Formative pruning in the nursery affects the growth and shape of the tree throughout its life (see Chapter 16). A strong leading shoot and well-spread, even branched crown are essential for future growth. If trees develop from a bushy head without a leading

Fig. 3.3 High quality container-grown stock. (Photo: James Hitchmough)

Fig. 3.4 Root-balled heavy standard trees. (Photo: James Hitchmough)

shoot, a weak forking branch structure will develop and the tree may split in later life.

Rootballed plants

Some plants can only be container grown, and most others can be rootballed to protect the root system. This allows planting throughout the year (apart from periods of flush growth) and reduces the risk of damage during handling (Fig.3.4). However rootballs are heavier and bulkier and their aftercare demands, if summer planted, are significantly higher. There is evidence from planting trials that up to certain nursery stock sizes (depending on the species of tree) rootballing has no advantage over properly handled and protected open ground trees. The rootballing sizes in the NPS should be used as minimum size in specifications. Rootballing should not be regarded as a substitute for high quality protection of roots from lifting to planting. With proper handling on the nursery to protect roots from drying out, more open ground plants could be used in landscape planting, with useful cost savings.

Genetic variability

In general, provenance has less effect on plant establishment than cultivation, with one exception: the considerable genetic variability in most species throughout their natural geographic range. This is of great concern with native plants, for example where importation of hawthorn grown from southern or eastern European seed introduces a new gene pool into the local population. Some have argued that this reduces native genetic variation within an area. There is also the cultural argument that non-local populations of native species may lead to a change in landscape character; central European hawthorn leaf out a month before native stock.

This is a complex matter with no easy resolution. There has been a strong move by some ecology professionals to ensure that only stock grown from a very local area is used. The counter view from others has been that you can mix any provenances and nature will sort it all out. Both are extreme views and we should generally follow neither. The professional approach is to use a balanced judgement that assesses the appropriate genetic stock for each site. This will be:

Native plants

- Is the site in an area where the stock should be of British origin?
- Are there local conditions that justify using stock of more local origin?
- Can plants be used (for example in a town) where the seed origin does not matter?

- Is the plant for timber production, and so the seed origin should give the highest timber yield?

Introduced plants

- Does the nursery plant come from a location in the wild where it will tolerate the climate of the site?
- Are all plants from the species' range hardy everywhere in Britain?

All our native vegetation is, at best, semi-natural and there is continuous variation within this from, say, a National Nature Reserve to an urban bedding scheme. Native plants are the foundation of our indigenous ecosystems. In general they support the most wildlife. Many wildlife areas need to be protected from introduced species that may be lifeless 'padding' in the ecosystem, or may get out of control and take over. Visually, the rural landscape is dominated by relatively few native woody species, with introduced species in forestry or parks and gardens making a varying impact. In general the natives maintain the ecological and visual diversity of the landscape.

The cultivation of introduced, exotic species is part of all human history. All plants need an agent to move their seeds or spores around. People have been very good at it, whether they move food plants, (most of our food plants come from introduced plants) or ornamentals. Introduced species can be used whenever they are appropriate. Both the rural and urban landscapes are in need of improvement, and a return to the use of only native species in all situations would be retrogressive.

The quality of wildlife habitats depends on the type of management they receive as well as the plants and animals present. Native plants should be used where they bring real wildlife benefits or local distinctiveness. They should not be used as a 'political' statement when introduced plants would be more effective or appropriate.

The geographic selection of exotic species can also affect their suitability for our temperate climate. Those seed sources selected from altitude are likely to be the hardiest available and therefore more adaptable to UK conditions. If plants are sourced from regions with milder winters, for example, southern Europe, they may not initially be well fitted to winter cold in Britain, as they may not have been adequately exposed to the acclimation stimuli that increase winter hardiness in plants. These plants will however become hardy when exposed to the next autumn acclimation cycle in Britain, providing that they are genotypes that physiologically have the capacity to become cold tolerant. For example some named cultivars of the North American *Magnolia grandiflora* that are popular in Italy may originally be derived from wild populations in Florida, and are unproven for the UK conditions and may not be suitable apart from sheltered areas.

The increased use of imported specimen plants from southern Europe is currently very fashionable and confidence in their hardiness is possibly fuelled by the effect of global warming. However a hard winter may cause significant losses of these imported plants. Their suitability in more northern areas carries a risk, which should not be ignored. These plants need care in site preparation and planting to ensure that they root out quickly into the surrounding soil and develop a frost resistant root system.

The advent of the 'plant passport', as a European directive has created a free market in European plants, so that here is an even greater need for increased awareness of plant suitability and quality by the professions which use and specify plants. This increases the need for greatly improved plant specification with a large input from the consumer.

Without this awareness of where the plant comes from and supply chain implications there is a risk that plants selected will be less suitable for establishment in landscape conditions. The development of contract growing (see below) may be a result of the unreliability of plant quality when plants have been obtained from the open market. Although contract growing can appear to have significant benefits for the customer it is in conflict with the creation of an open market in landscape plant supply. The development of more precise plant specification in the industry will ensure a more even quality of plant supply. It should be considered that there is a government policy to reduce the cost of construction in delivering new development.

Professional plant users should be able to specify plants with confidence, knowing that they are grown to a previously agreed standard. Nursery visits to inspect plants regularly should be unnecessary, as the issues of quality and suitability for landscape use go far beyond a brief visual inspection of plants in pots or in the field at the nursery. Plant performance must be assessed in landscape conditions and plant producers must concentrate on growing and supplying plants of suitable quality for landscape and amenity use.

3.3 Securing plant supply

The single objective of assuring a quality product at a reasonable price underpins all the various systems of plant procurement. They can broadly be divided into six forms:

- open tendering in a main contract where plant supply is part of the works
- nominated tendering in the main contract
- open tendering for nomination in a main contract before it is put out to tender
- open tendering for supply organised by a project manager
- nomination without tendering
- advance ordering and contract growing.

Open tendering in a main contract

This is the traditional method of tendering against a specification where the entire responsibility for sourcing the plants is in the hands of the landscape contractor. The landscape architect should then check the plants to ensure they meet the specification.

This method works well when the plants are available on the open market but is liable to abuse through undeclared plant substitution when plant shortages occur. Changes to selected plants can have an impact on the final outcome of a project and implications for maintenance liabilities. The Horticultural Trades Association have developed a Nursery Certification Scheme where registered nurseries are bound to use the National Plant Specification (NPS) and follow clear and open procedures when plant substitution occurs. Use of these registered nurseries is a more assured route to supply of quality plants.

Further problems can occur with the landscape contractor sourcing the plants, if there is a dilution of specification either by main contractor or landscape sub-contractor. In many instances the supplying nurseries will be bidding for plant supply on a truncated version of the specification and thereby attract the cheapest price. Also the time-scale for supply can be foreshortened to just a few days, limiting the time to communicate changes and carry out quality checks, and making the available stock a *fait-accomplis*.

Most nurseries supplying the landscape market both grow their own plants and buy in plants on the open market. This has developed as contractors prefer to purchase from one nursery to reduce their administrative costs. Nurseries should make reasonable efforts to secure the specified plants. It is reasonable to ask for evidence of how many nurseries have been asked to supply a plant and a few calls to other nurseries will easily settle if a plant can or can not be supplied that season.

However plant procurement has often been subject to abuse by nurseries because of the limited plant knowledge of landscape architects. The profession often has limited training and experience of plant selection and inadequate enforcement of the specification. With NPS, better training in plant selection and the closer inspection of schemes at their critical times, soft landscape problems can be reduced to minimal levels.

The key elements to follow in open tendering are:

- Ensure species, precise cultivars and numbers are available in quantities required. Discuss this with growers pre-tender if this is in doubt.

- Use a precise specification (preferably the NPS) in respect of species, form, height, root condition (size and condition of container/root ball etc.), breaks (minimum number of breaks/branches), packaging, delivery, inspections.
- Write into the specification what plant supply must be secured by the contractor by a certain date, well before planting. This avoids last minute plant shortages.
- Ensure that the specification is enforced at all stages. Critical stages are to ensure the tenders are compliant, that plants are checked if necessary at the nursery before delivery to site, and on delivery.

Whilst this method is most widely used, and even if it produces competitive prices, there can in the end be disappointment in the quality of the plants delivered to site. This is usually because the above key stages are not thoroughly followed. Firm enforcement of the contract by landscape professionals will lead to higher standards and more reliable supply.

Nominated tendering in the main contract

A list of nurseries can be provided in the contract and the tenderers have to seek competitive quotations from these nurseries to include the chosen one in their tender prices. It is usual to check with each nursery that they wish to be on the tender list. This can be for all the plants in the contract or some selected plants.

Open tendering for nomination in the main contract before it is put out to tender

It may be desirable to nominate supplying nurseries in the main contract. This may be for example for larger, specimen plants or to ensure that open ground plants are grown by the supplying nursery. The nursery for nomination in the contract will have been selected by tendering for these plants before the main contract is put out to tender.

Open tendering in project management

In a broader and developing form of procurement, the landscape professional may be the project manager, securing individual contractors and suppliers for a project. Plant supply can be tendered to one or more nurseries in the interests of securing the appropriate quality at the best price for the client. The project manager then determines delivery dates and coordinates these with the work stages on site and the contractor undertaking the planting.

Nomination without tendering

There may be reasons to nominate a nursery in the contract for some or all of the plant supply. This may, for example be for some specimen plants or that the client wishes to use a particular nursery or the landscape professional advises the use of a nursery. This may involve selection of plants at the nursery. The plants may or may not be contract grown.

Advance ordering and contract growing

The landscape professional may act as partial project manager by securing all the plants from one or more nurseries, specially grown for the contract. If there is a long contract period it may be possible to include some quicker growing herbaceous plants and shrubs for the contractor to tender for supply at the start of the contract. Generally though, contract growing is directly secured by the landscape professional on behalf of the client. This may be for one large project or a client with several similar schemes may wish to secure the same plants for all sites. This, of course, raises issues of local diversity and appropriateness of plants for the designer.

In principle, any plants can be grown and supplied by a whole range of nurseries, so it is necessary to look at the advantages and disadvantages of contract growing.

The advantages are that plant supply can be secured in full at the correct quality. Large quantities of plants can be supplied without disrupting the market. The price of the plants is known and secured at an early stage of the work process.

The disadvantages are that the client is involved in two tender processes and will have to fund at least part of the cost of the plant supply long before this is required in a single contract process. Contract growing is more time consuming for the professional than normal supply (even allowing for reduced time in checking plant quality) and will have to be funded. A fuller plant specification is needed which will go into some details of how the plant is grown at the nursery. This may include the type of container, the type of growing medium, if the plant is grown out in the open or under protection, and the available nutrients in the compost when the plant is delivered. As many landscape professionals have little knowledge of this, it can lead to insufficiently precise specifications or even dependence on a single nursery that has the confidence of the professional. Either situation does not deliver the most competitive result for the client.

There can be problems if a batch of plants fail in the nursery or if a contract is delayed and plant supply with it. Nurseries have to be paid for holding the plants longer and maintaining nutrient levels in the compost. At the end of the day equivalent plants may simply be cheaper if they are supplied when they are needed.

The publication and increasing uptake of NPS makes contract growing on quality grounds less justifiable. However, it is useful to ensure the supply of less commonly grown plants or advance purchase of trees while on the nursery, some years before they are needed.

A JCLI guidance note *The Advance Ordering and Contract Growing of Hardy Nursery Stock* has been produced to set standards and guide contract growing agreements (Committee on Plant Supply and Establishment, 1998 and revisions).

3.4 The plant supply chain

The supply chain is based on a sequence of confidences. The client places confidence in the landscape architect to design, specify and supervise to achieve a mutual objective. The landscape architect places confidence in the plant producer to meet the specification, and in the contractor to carry out satisfactory planting. The project manager, where present, places confidence in all the players to perform diligently to the agreed time-scale and cost plan.

In recent years the arrival of the non-technical project manager to cost-manage the project has caused an erosion of the landscape architect's traditional role to check and approve work on site. Without the designer's technical verification of standards, a wide loophole exists for specification cheating. Blatant specification cheating is common in landscape work, particularly in plant specifications. Few project managers are able to differentiate between 1 + 1 transplants and cell grown plants, especially after planting.

Chains

A good starting point is to acknowledge that all players in the supply chain are inter-dependent and need each other to enable the chain to exist. None would be there without the others, and a respect for the other players' roles and strengths is fundamental to a successful scheme.

A weak link in the chain, a participant who does not perform correctly, is a burden to the plant supply chain and causes costs to the other players. There is also a wider impact outside the chain that affects the entire marketplace. Those excluded from taking part because of honest pricing are unable to find work and may go out of business for no reason other than their integrity.

A chain breakage wastes time and money to the other participants and this can be very costly. At the very least it means that someone has to stand the cost of extra time, replacement of plants, or a sub-standard job. At the worst it means a widespread chain reaction affecting a much wider group of people; honest tenderers who are usurped by unscrupulous cheats, a loss of credibility for honest designers and specifiers, loss of confidence in plant producers and planting contractors and dissatisfaction from clients.

Certainties

Some simple proposals for a successful plant supply chain are as follows:

- Recognise the common objective – a satisfactory scheme as designed.
- Respect the roles and duties of other players.
- Co-operate and assist the other players to achieve the objective.
- Resolve problems rapidly and positively.
- Achieve the specified standards as a minimum.
- Ensure certification, verification and robust policing of standards.

The common thread should be that all parties want to achieve a satisfactory outcome. Each link in the chain needs the others to do this, and respect for the roles and duties of other players is essential. Typically problems will occur when roles become blurred and one player attempts to take on the role of another. For example, a plant producer should not be tempted to substitute/specify different plants without consultation.

The plant producer's position may be within or alongside the plant supply chain. If pre-selected or nominated, the plant suppliers will have a standard role in line with the other players. However, where selection of the plant producer is left to the planting contractor, there is a potential weakness in the chain caused by a sub-group of competitive tendering, which will be beyond the specifier's control. Where the plant producer is not linked into the end objective of the chain there is a real risk of detachment, as they will not share the goals/objectives of the other participants.

The aim of plant specification should be to encourage a spirit of mutual co-operation and to assist other players in achieving the common goal. It should be made impossible for any player to deceive another for individual advantage through the specification. Universal adoption of a single recognised standard, the NPS, is an ideal means to safeguard against this. When a problem occurs, the specification must make it easy to resolve positively, rapidly and amicably, not to facilitate wriggling through loopholes or cheating. Any delay in resolving problems is expensive

to other participants, and the best approach is to encourage a positive attitude.

The specification is a written model and, like all models, it imitates the real thing: it cannot be perfect. There should be a well-recognised common understanding of the specification. A situation should not arise where one player offers plant material that is wide of this 'well-recognised' specification. If that occurs it is almost certainly due to an attempt to deceive other players, causing a waste of time and money to all.

The NPS and The Horticultural Trades Association's Nursery Certification Scheme (NCS) are key improvements recently brought to the plant supply chain. Landscape architects can play a leading role by adopting and using the NPS and by encouraging the use of Certified Nurseries. It is an opportunity for the profession to improve its collective image and re-establish integrity in the supply chain by a more diligent approach to specification, certification, verification of standards and careful project management (see Table 3.3).

3.5   Future developments

Young plants are perishable goods and they commonly pass through several different hands before the full process of establishment is complete. This has a number of disadvantages.

- It is difficult to establish responsibility for any failure.
- The disjointed supply chain can cause further stress to the plants.
- New developments and techniques will only emerge if they are in the interests of everyone in the chain.

Furthermore, there is an almost unhealthy concentration on cost cutting and economy at each stage of establishment, with the consequent potential for ruining the entire venture for the sake of a small saving. The plant material, for instance, will rarely be more than 50 per cent of the total establishment cost. In the case of forestry transplants, perhaps less than ten per cent of planting and three years of aftercare costs.

Table 3.3 The duties, roles, typical skills and weaknesses of the various participants in the plant supply chain.

	Duties (responsibilities)	Roles (tasks)	Skills (needs to know)	Typical weaknesses
Specifier: landscape architect	Professional responsibility to client Supervision of contract	Select appropriately Ensure availability Specify correctly Avoid ambiguity Ensure fair competitive tendering Approve materials Check quality and certify completion	Design Plant selection Specification Tendering Contract administration Quality control	Poor specification Inadequate checking
Plant producer – nursery	Commercial supplier to contractor	Grow appropriate plant material Notify availability to specifier/purchaser Ensure compliance with specification Tender competitively on fair basis Deliver in good condition Secure payment and profit	Plant knowledge Specifier's needs	Non-compliance with specification
Planting contractor	Contract to carry out scheme	Notify specification to supply nursery Ensure compliance with specification Receive and handle plant material Carry out planting Secure payment and profit	Plant selection Contract administration Plant handling Planting Quality control	Non-compliance Poor handling Poor work offered for approval specification Quality control
Project manager	Professional responsibility to client Supervision of contract	Contract management Cost control	Contract administration	Assumes responsibility for quality control Seeks cost saving Allows poor policing of specification
Client	Relationship to design team Contract	Payment for professional services Payment for contract	Scheme as designed	Seeks cost saving

Despite the apparently disorganised state of the industry, the majority of the results seem to satisfy the public's expectations. Also (to its credit) the industry satisfies an enormous variation in demand, both in volume as well as variety.

- It copes with the timescales and delays of the building and construction industries.
- It has steadily improved the range and quality of stock that is available.
- It has developed a 'long distance' trade with

Europe, which gives it a greater resilience of supply.

Problematic issues

Those engaged in the industry tend to have a more critical eye. Typical complaints include:

- a poor choice of species and cultivars;
- occasional supply of inappropriate provenance;
- lack of knowledge on behalf of purchasers with regard to what they actually need;
- unreliable plant deliveries in terms of quality and time and
- little attention given to the basic horticultural techniques of soil preparation and aftercare.

Complaints also revolve around the competitive tendering for plants, where it is not matched by good quality control and so too much inferior stock is planted. The demand for 'instant effect' encourages over-stocking and the use of oversized stock. Clients may not seem to appreciate good quality planting: for example, a planting condition is satisfied by plants that barely survive rather than those that grow well from the first season.

Although these complaints are anecdotal, they are repeated frequently and seem to have at least some basis in fact. There is, for instance, evidence that many large-scale planting schemes regularly suffer failure rates of 25 to 50 per cent and, worse still, that this order of losses seems to be expected.

It is possible to speculate on the reasons for the poor performance of the industry. It is often suggested that plant knowledge and basic horticulture are poorly taught in landscape design schools. Architects, engineers and surveyors will also take on the design of a scheme without any specialist advice or training, and where a landscape professional is appointed, he or she often does not have a sufficient 'say' in the outcomes, or monitor the scheme effectively to ensure proper planting arrangements.

Landscape design is sometimes an afterthought, and frequently starved of cash by other demands in a development project. Overall it may be that public and customer expectations are far too low:

planning authorities, for example, are often satisfied by poor planting to fulfil the landscape conditions on planning consents. The fragmented supply chain and lack of overall responsibility for outcomes makes efficient quality control virtually impossible.

The Joint Council for Landscape Industries and the CPSE have done much to encourage improvements by publishing codes of practice and standards such as the JCLI Select List of recommended plants and the Code of Practice for plant handling and establishment; but it is clear that this is not enough. Nor does it seem likely that further biological research will provide a remedy for all the industry's problems. Horticultural and technical requirements are well known and researched, but the industry is not sufficiently organised to use the knowledge properly.

Improvement is only likely to stem from better-educated clients demanding higher standards: for example, plants which are thriving at the end of the first season, rather than just surviving. Local authorities should enforce better compliance with landscape conditions on development approvals. There should be greater vertical integration within the industry; for example, nurserymen could take responsibility for planting and aftercare, and also possibly embrace the detailed design. Clients could be persuaded to buy on the basis of quality rather than price (this may be an unrealistic hope), and there should also be self-regulation within the industry to encourage higher standards and less wastage.

Some clients such as supermarkets are beginning to demand better performance from their industry. The government is also placing more emphasis on good design for new development in the countryside and elsewhere. However, it is the industry in all its different guises that has to regulate, develop and positively demonstrate what can be achieved with good client support.

3.6 Conclusions

This chapter has focusesd on the selection and purchase of plants for landscape sites. Considerable changes have taken place within the landscape industry during the last few decades, and it is important to be aware of their significance for the nurseryman, landscape architect, contractor and all others involved. Increasing sophistication of growing techniques, purchasing procedures, project management and contract implementation, can all complicate the simple task of procuring plants. These problems are identified here, and some indications given of how current initiatives are trying to improve the quality of this, the central activity in the successful establishment of planted landscapes.

References

Aldhous, J. (2002) *Specifying Seed Sources for Trees for Large Scale Amenity and Forestry Planting: Recommendations for Best Practice*. JCLI/CPSE, London.

Committee on Plant Supply and Establishment (1996) *Plant Handling and Establishing Landscape Plants*. JCLI/CPSE, London.

Committee on Plant Supply and Establishment (1998) *The Advance Ordering and Contract Growing of Hardy Nursery Stock*. JCLI/CPSE, London.

Forestry Commission (2001) *Forestry Reproductive Materials Regulations*. Forestry Commission, Edinburgh.

Herbert R., Samuel, S., & Paterson, G. (1999) *Using Local Stock for Planting Native Trees and Shrubs*. Practice Note 008, Forestry Commission, Edinburgh.

HTA (2002) *National Plant Specification*. Horticultural Trades Association, Reading. (Available in ring-binder or CD-Rom form)

Miller, P. (1731) *Gardener's Dictionary*. Rivers, London.

II Managing Plant Growth on Landscape Sites

4 Amelioration of Underperforming Soils

Tony Kendle and Bob Sherman

The most basic piece of research anyone trying to grow plants must begin with is to look at the soil type, to decide which plants to grow, or even whether it is worth growing plants at all. In landscape work, sometimes even this is impossible: soils are likely to be fundamentally altered during construction, or even sold and later replaced. Fortunately the plants that landscape professionals select are not usually as demanding of high quality soil conditions as agricultural crops, and growth rates are seldom as critical. Even so, close attention to the soil and its treatment should be a basic tenet of good landscape construction and maintenance. Plant growth is, for good or ill, intimately linked to the soil. Whether we ignore it or not, the drainage, fertility, pH and other characteristics of the site will have their effect on the performance and appearance of the plants growing there.

4.1 Soil problems on landscape sites

The soils encountered in landscape work have tremendously variable and sometimes unpredictable characteristics. Because we work where man's activities are most highly concentrated, the substrate materials may exhibit extremes of behaviour that far exceed those of normal agricultural soils. The pH may range from 2–12; the nutrient content may range from excess to almost non-existent; there may be little or no buffering capacity; almost no organic matter; many sites may even carry a pollutant load. Every textural class and soil classification can be encountered, including some that have never been properly described. The profile may be extremely complicated, with mis-matched soil types overlapping, and sometimes buried obstacles. Large areas of the soil may be covered with variably permeable hard surfaces. Often there is very great variability on just one site. This may not appear a very promising beginning, but the situation can be made even worse by deep soil compaction and denaturing during development.

Soil compaction affects plant growth in many ways. It can lead to poor water use, restricted nutrient uptake, lack of oxygen, accumulation of carbon dioxide, or root impedance. Compaction is not invariably damaging (Plate 2). In certain soils a small amount of compaction may actually increase plant growth by producing a better balance between air space and water retention. However the scale and severity of the damage caused by heavy machinery on landscape sites means that the effects are nearly always detrimental. Direct damage may take the form of plant losses through drought or waterlogging, poor plant or seed establishment or a general reduction in plant vigour. There are also many possible forms of indirect damage, including increased aggressiveness of certain diseases, or increased susceptibility to disease where plants are growing poorly; increased likelihood of unintentional herbicide damage because of low vigour and surface rooting; and possibly increased susceptibility to climate extremes. Managerial problems can include greater difficulties in working the soil, greater time required for irrigation, and a requirement for greater inputs of water and nutrients.

Plant survival and growth can be dramatically effected, and traditional remedial solutions may

Direct	Indirect
Waterlogging	Weed competition
Drought	Increased likelihood of pathogen attack
Major toxicities	Increased susceptibility to climatic
Salinity	extremes
Nutrient deficiency	Shallow rooting and susceptibility to
Impenetrability	erosion, trampling, herbicide damage

Fig. 4.1   The ways in which soil conditions can lead to plant failure or poor growth.

not prove adequate (Fig. 4.1). Unfortunately most soil science research has taken place on the high quality soils found in agriculture, exposed to the relatively sane cultivation operations practised by agronomists. Some of the basic concepts of soil management may need to be revised to cope with the extreme substrates and extremes of poor handling found on landscape sites (Fig. 4.2).

The likelihood of compaction depends on many things, in particular soil type. Good topsoil should contain well-structured crumbs that are relatively stable. Topsoil is therefore more resistant to light compaction damage than subsoil. However the organic matter bonds which help to create this structure can be broken fairly easily by cultivation when wet, and topsoil has, in a sense, more to lose than subsoil. The latter can be brought back to its original state more easily when it is damaged.

When topsoils are lifted and stacked for long periods, anaerobic conditions present in the heap can lead to a breakdown in the organic matter that helps to stabilise the soil crumbs. This can in turn lead to an increased likelihood of compaction and denaturing during re-spreading.

There is also an important difference between clays and 'light' soils such as silts and sands. Sands are easier to compact than clays, and compaction can happen at any soil moisture content. Clay soils

Fig. 4.2 Soils may sometimes be composed largely of engineering substrates such as crushed rock. (Photo: James Hitchmough)

Fig. 4.3 Waterlogged compacted clay soil destroyed by machine trafficking during the building construction phase. This is the norm on many landscape projects. (Photo: James Hitchmough)

are relatively tough when dry and resist damage well. Compaction is only likely when the soil is wet and therefore the particles are well 'lubricated'. When compaction does occur, though, the damage to clay soils will be more dramatic and will lead to the maximum deviation from their behaviour in an undamaged form (Fig. 4.3). Water and air infiltration, and drainage, will still occur in compacted sandy soils, though at a reduced rate.

Silts or very fine sands can be the hardest to manage because they do not easily form crumbs but at the same time the diffuse pores are too small to allow water to drain. Once their initial structure has been lost, it can be extremely difficult to carry out successful remedial treatments.

For most of the twentieth century the challenges posed by urban and development site soils were completely ignored by soil scientists. Some significant and important texts have now appeared, but these still largely focus on identifying the characteristics and range of issues associated with urban soils, rather than giving specific cultural guidance and options for soil improvement. One reason for this is that the objectives of landscape work are often more complex than found in crop production (discussed below). However the most important issue may be that the solutions to landscape soil problems are only partly technical – the

biggest challenge may be to change the common procedures and practices of landscape professionals to make successful soil manipulation possible.

4.2   Soil ameliorants – improving poor soils for plant establishment

Assuming that we are able to define the characteristics a 'good soil' should have, it should be possible to manipulate poor soils to meet these objectives. We have the technology to undertake manipulation of the soil environment with a great deal of sophistication. With the above discussion in mind, it is not surprising that the choice of ameliorant or remedial treatment can be complex, but a more serious problem is that in practice the scope for amelioration of the site soil often remains completely unaddressed in landscape schemes. There are always a few hopeful phrases in the specification along the lines of:

'. . . the contractor shall ensure good drainage at all times'

but the landscape practice often shies away from a targeted programme of amelioration.

This chapter looks at the specification and use

of chemical and physical amendments that can improve soil performance. There are two particular groups: amendments that are primarily chosen to target nutritional problems (fertilisers) and those that tackle other chemical or physical soil characters (soil conditioners). Surface treatments such as mulches, and physical modifications that are made through cultivation and drainage are not considered here (see also Chapters 5 and 8).

Of course the separation between physical and chemical effects is sometimes arbitrary. Soil physics and nutrition are often interdependent: for example a plant that has its roots restricted by waterlogging may suffer from nutrient shortages. Similarly many additive materials such as bulky organic manures influence both physical and chemical characters. Nevertheless there is still a broad *de facto* recognition in the horticultural and landscape trades of a difference between primarily nutrient boosting materials and those that have other effects.

By definition, 'amelioration' implies that some perceived target characteristics are desirable and that the ameliorant chosen has some perceptible benefit. In practice we still only have a basic understanding of the way that ameliorants can change soils, which ameliorants to use to resolve which problems, and what the relative cost effectiveness of different inputs are.

There is often disagreement about whether ameliorants work or not. The technical literature is littered with results of research trials that present conflicting findings about whether a given additive does or does not work. The authors of the reports rarely seem able to resist drawing sweeping conclusions from their findings; the basic problem with any soil additive, whether it is organic matter, lime, fertiliser or whatever, is that you can never separate the effect that it has from the original soil type that you are working on. Some ameliorants that work under one set of conditions will be useless or may even have a negative effect if used in the wrong way, or on the wrong soil.

The value of *some* amelioration practices is well proven. For example, on many derelict land sites and subsoils, nutrient-rich organic matter is essential unless only nitrogen fixing plants will be grown, or a prolonged fertiliser programme is planned. However the situation is usually less clear. A crumb former will not work particularly well on a soil that is unable to develop such a structure, such as a sand; a material with a good buffering capacity would be extremely valuable on a sand but not necessarily on a clay.

Some soil ameliorants may have short-lived effects, but these may produce a critical improvement in plant performance at the vulnerable plant establishment phase. Other amendments may be slow to have an effect, or may even be harmful in the short term, but could lead to significant soil improvement in the long term. Undecomposed organic matter may lead to anaerobic conditions when it is added to a soil, but after a few weeks or months the improvement in structure should exceed that from well-decomposed material. Most commonly, soil ameliorant materials are used as 'an insurance'. Like any insurance we need to accept that there will be times when they are not actually necessary and the money spent will not lead to a return. Negative results should be seen in this context.

The best way to maximise the value of these materials is to focus on the principles of soil ameliorant behaviour and rather less on empirical research, so that specifications can more accurately reflect the likely soil conditions. That is the approach taken in this chapter. For example we need to recognise that additives may have complex or multiple effects; adding lime to an acid soil is not only likely to raise the pH and possibly help to flocculate the soil into crumbs, but it will also increase the rate of organic matter mineralisation and hence lead to a flush of nutrients. Water holding gels remain as discrete particles in the soil: they will not directly improve soil structure but they can substitute for a poor structure by directly retaining moisture. 'Slimy', 'gummy' materials such as alginures hold smaller amounts of water but they may have a profound effect on soil structure that in turn can greatly improve water relations in the soil.

Unfortunately at the moment manufacturers of soil ameliorants do not generally encourage clarity. The industry is increasingly dominated by waste companies driven by their need to meet government recycling targets, and a greater understanding of performance criteria is not in their interest. 'Soil conditioner' in particular is now a generic term for any bag of brown stuff that no-one can find a use for, sold on the back of mystique, the modern equivalent of snake-oil!

4.3 Plant fertilisers and nutrients

Nutrients are minerals needed to create proteins and other compounds necessary for plant growth. Gardening folklore suggests that different nutrients favour certain plant parts – 'nitrogen for leaves, phosphorus for roots, potassium for fruits'. This belief relates to the likelihood of high demands for certain types of compounds in different organs. These unbalanced demands are usually only found in high productivity crops that carry disproportionate amounts of some types of growth. In most plants, particularly on impoverished soils, all nutrients are needed to support any type of growth. So on a very nitrogen deficient site, nitrogen fertiliser will boost both roots and shoots.

Plants may require such tiny amounts of some nutrients (micronutrients) that they get all they need from any soil or even rainfall. Micronutrient deficiencies are usually only seen on acid sandy soils in wet areas. However deficiencies are sometimes caused by poor root growth or by pH extremes, which can make the nutrients unavailable. Excess phosphorus can also bind with the micronutrients and make them unavailable.

Some nutrients (macronutrients) are required in large amounts but most of them are readily supplied by soils and deficiencies are uncommon. Of all of the nutrients that plants need, only three or four are commonly encountered as fertilisers.

Do fertilisers really work?

The plant's need for some fertilisers is greatest in the period before real establishment. Young transplants can more than triple their biomass over the first growing season and that new growth cannot be produced without nutrients, but at the same time the efficiency of the root system is less than that of established plants. Nevertheless, only about half of experiments carried out on newly planted trees show positive responses to fertilisers. Why is this?

Fertilisation is only necessary for those nutrients where supply does not match requirements. The need for fertiliser is therefore determined by:

- plant nutrient requirements
- nutrient levels in the soil
- soil qualities, such as pH or water level
- root health and efficiency
- weed competition.

Even on very infertile soils a response may not occur if the plants have very low nutrient demands, are in poor health or if weed competition or drought are severe.

When not to fertilise?

Sometimes fertiliser applications can be counterproductive.

- High levels of available nutrients will reduce diversity in wildflower-rich swards, and poor soils are usually an advantage (see Chapters 19, 20 and 22). If fertility is extremely low then adding nutrients will help establishment, but research suggests that slow release organic manures are preferable to soluble fertilisers.
- Most newly-planted trees that fail quickly do so because they suffer from waterlogging or drought. To reduce drought effects, weed control is essential. Weeds also take nutrients but an attempt to compensate by adding fertiliser will lead to more vigorous weeds and more severe drought.
- Excess amounts of some nutrients can cause toxicity. Common soil contaminants, such as zinc, boron or copper, are essential plant nutrients at lower doses. Even where direct toxicity is not seen, too much of one type of fertiliser can prevent the uptake of other nutrients. Excess nitrogen can cause reduced hardiness or lush, weak growth.
- Toxicity symptoms can also arise from poor

application rather than the use of excessive amounts. Sudden high doses of very soluble material can cause salinity damage. (This can even occur with some organic materials such as poultry manures.) Some fertilisers are damaging if spread on leaves.

- Sandy soils have water and nutrient shortages. In wet seasons the response to nutrients is usually positive but in dry summers even slow release fertilisers can aggravate drought. Wherever possible, bulky organic manures should be used instead of artificial fertilisers as they improve water holding.

The role of different nutrients

Usually only three nutrients, Nitrogen (N) Phosphorus (P) and Potassium (K), are worth adding to soils. Some fertilisers have a wider range of nutrients present including many trace materials, and advertisements frequently imply an advantage that only rarely pays off.

Calcium (Ca) is a plant nutrient but it also controls soil pH. Liming is usually carried out to modify acidity rather than because of any deficiency. Actual calcium deficiency is rare. Symptoms are sometimes seen in fruit crops or container plants, but the problem usually arises from soil moisture problems rather than shortage of the mineral.

Magnesium (Mg) deficiency is not typical on most soils but can occur on light, acid, sandy soils in areas of frequent rain or where root growth is poor. Adding too much potassium to soils can also induce Mg deficiency. Magnesium is now added as a standard component of some fertiliser formulations.

Potassium is moderately soluble but is fairly effectively held by clays and becomes available to plants if the levels in the soil solution fall. Deficiencies arise primarily on poor, sandy soils in high rainfall areas. Addition of potassium fertiliser is generally very straightforward and effective.

Potassium is not held within complex organic molecules and it can leach from bulky organic remains so composts that have been left in the open may be poor potassium fertilisers. Ashes from burnt organics contain high proportions of potassium.

Phosphorus is highly immobile in soils. Often the plants only take up a small proportion of the added fertiliser and many agricultural soils have built up high P levels over the years.

Phosphorus solubility is decreased in extreme pH conditions and on alkaline soils it may be hard for plants to obtain the amounts they need. Soil contaminants can also bind with the phosphorus and so deficiencies are sometimes seen on polluted sites.

The low mobility of this element also means that the roots must go to the nutrient, not vice versa. The efficiency of phosphorus uptake can be limited when the root system is not performing adequately. Mycorrhizal fungi can be particularly important in boosting phosphorus nutrition as they help plants reach additional reserves.

Some phosphorus is also stored in an organic form and this can be very important in extreme conditions when inorganic phosphorus is made unavailable. Addition of bulky manures can therefore be a valuable method of fertilisation on high pH soils.

Nitrogen nutrition is particularly complex. Nitrogen is required in the greatest amount by plants but unlike the other elements mentioned, this usually has no geological source in the soil. It can only be stored as organic matter that has to be mineralised by soil bacteria to become available to plants. This mineral nitrogen is very mobile in soils.

In early spring soil mineral reserves of nitrogen will have been leached by rain, and because of low soil temperatures bacterial activity will be low. Plant demands therefore outstrip supply, and soluble nitrogen fertiliser may be useful. However excess applications on sandy soils can cause serious nitrate pollution.

Under waterlogged or anaerobic conditions the mineralisation process is again inhibited, or even substituted by a process that loses nitrogen to the air. Nitrogen shortage is therefore a symptom of poor soil drainage, or can arise if topsoil has been stored for long periods in large heaps. Conversely following soil disturbance or cultivation, mineralisation rates are speeded up and a flush of nitrogen can result. This can mask longer term deficiency problems.

Any soil that is low in organic matter will exhibit nitrogen deficiency. Some sub-soils and industrial wastes may have such serious problems that almost nothing will grow. Adding fertiliser is not always successful, since leaching losses can be high on these soils. Even assuming that the nutrients are all retained, it is impossible to add more than a small fraction of the reserves normally present in the soil and deficiencies rapidly reappear. More sustainable solutions come from the addition of organic matter that directly replaces the missing reserves, or the use of nitrogen fixing plants that are able to provide a green cover while building up soil reserves.

4.4 Problems of nutrient availability

Sometimes problems to do with the soil or the plant root system mean that the nutrients cannot get to where they are wanted. The plant will show deficiency symptoms even though the soil has adequate reserves.

Micronutrient availability problems are nearly always linked to soil pH. For example extreme alkalinity makes many nutrients insoluble and added fertiliser may also become unavailable. When plants show intolerance to pH extremes it is rarely direct acidity or alkalinity that causes problems but rather the induced shortage (or excess) of minerals.

Complex fertiliser formulations such as sequestered nutrients can maintain nutrient solubility in high pH. For example sequestered iron is available as a fertiliser from specialist suppliers. The 'blueing compound' used to treat hydrangeas on alkaline soils is a sequestered form of aluminium. (Aluminium is not classified as a 'necessary' plant nutrient because a deficiency will not stop growth. However the element affects some flower colours.) Foliar feeding bypasses soil problems and may also be useful for getting nutrients into young transplants with limited root systems. Large plants cannot easily be treated.

However direct treatment for pH induced problems is rarely sustainable. It is more cost-effective to modify the pH itself through liming or the addition of sulphur. The best solution is obviously to select plants adapted to the soil acidity levels but sometimes because of soil movements and practices such as topsoil importation it can be difficult to predict the final site pH at the design stage. This is why many commonly chosen landscape plants have a wide pH tolerance.

A more common problem when dealing with landscape plant establishment occurs when the root system of transplants cannot meet the demands of the plant. Given that phosphorus is very immobile, phosphorus deficiency can occur in small transplants when the soil reserves are adequate for much larger, established, plants. Application of phosphorus fertiliser close to the roots of new transplants may be valuable even where soil analysis indicates no deficiency. Use of mycorrhizal fungi additions has given good results in research, but it is hard to translate this to a reliable practice where the range of plant material is diverse, and where not all species will definitely form such associations.

Nutrients in containers

Although mineral soils usually produce more than enough trace nutrients for plants, the same may not be true for container composts composed of composted bark and other organic debris. Fertiliser formulations for these may need to contain a complete range of elements.

Plants in containers have to survive within a fraction of the normal rooting volume. Even when irrigated frequently the plants undergo rapid swings in moisture availability. Soluble fertilisers are rapidly leached while, as the pot dries, high salt concentrations can increase drought damage. Enormous advances in the quality of container plant production were made following the development of high tech slow release fertilisers such as Osmocote®. However plants obtained from overwintering standing grounds or garden centres may have no reserves left in the pots and will rapidly show growth decline.

The hydroponics growing system used for some

interior planting utilises an ion exchange resin that mimics natural soil processes by releasing nutrients into solution when levels are low, but taking them back again if levels rise.

How to recognise a nutrient shortage

Nutrient deficiency symptoms are widely discussed in horticultural literature. These can be supplemented by chemical analysis of leaf tissue. However these techniques are only useful for long-term maintenance and clearly cannot help predict a deficiency before plant establishment. The methods are also unreliable for some plants, which can adjust their growth to reach a balance with site conditions – their productivity is restricted but the leaves may not show deficiency symptoms.

If a site has been vegetated before development then the nature and health of the plants that grow there are indicative of soil fertility. Very fertile soils support characteristic species such as nettles and docks.

Soil analysis should follow a standard methodology that can then be interpreted in the light of previous experience of plant demands. Many soil analysis companies use the established Agricultural Development Advisory Service (ADAS) fertility index. Soils are given a rating for nutrient content on a simple scale of 0–5 and fertiliser recommendations made accordingly. However there are a few difficulties when applying these principles to landscape sites. They can show extremely variable soil fertility and so the sampling methods may need to be modified. A large number of samples can be required to get a complete picture and it may be important not to mix sub-samples together.

Direct soil analysis is often regarded as unsuccessful for soil nitrogen. Measures of total nitrogen are easy, but the levels may not bear any relation to the actual amounts available to plants. Mineralisation of available nitrogen is affected by variables such as temperature, soil moisture, pH etc. Once the nitrogen is released it may leach or be taken up. Any analysis of available levels is therefore just a 'snapshot' of a moving figure. ADAS assess nitrogen status by considering the soil type and the previous land use and making

an intelligent guess. In practice an ADAS index of 0 is often assumed for nitrogen on landscape sites because soil of poor quality is frequently encountered.

In landscape situations a measure of total nitrogen can be valuable despite these problems. This will at least show any absolute and fundamental deficiency that must be corrected. However we can also take a leaf out of the agriculturists' book and make a guess that nitrogen shortage in new landscape plantings is more common than is generally recognised.

Whatever systems are used to measure nutrient levels, there is the complication that we often have no idea of what condition the soil will be left in after development has finished. Topsoils may be imported from areas with different nutrient status from the original site or may have degenerated in store. It makes sense to anticipate from first principles what nutrient problems are likely, which in practice will be phosphorus or nitrogen.

4.5   Fertiliser formulations

If fertiliser formulations provide NPK in combination they are referred to as compound or 'complete' fertilisers. 'Straight' fertilisers provide one nutrient only.

The majority of fertilisers are relatively simple chemicals, such as potassium chloride. The useful nutrient may only make up part of the compound so the actual fertiliser value is less than 100 per cent by weight. However sometimes salts are manufactured which are made up entirely of useful nutrients and these provide very concentrated nutrient supply. For example ammonium nitrate (sold as Nitram) is a combination of two nitrogen ions that both have a fertiliser value.

These simple salts are generally easy and cheap to manufacture. They often provide the nutrient in a soluble form that can give rapid effects but some, such as the nitrogen ions mentioned above, can leach easily from light soils especially if applied to bare ground in wet weather. This is wasteful and can cause pollution. Very soluble fertilisers can also be highly disruptive to soil organisms. Not surprisingly these materials are unpopular with organic farmers.

Some fertilisers are made of much more complex chemicals that can be less reactive and so provide a slow release effect. These are also safer to handle. Not all are artificially manufactured: some are waste products and others are derived from rock sources.

High tech slow release formulations control fertiliser availability in much more precise ways. These often work by coating simple soluble fertilisers with a material that prevents them from becoming instantly available, such as a slowly dissolving outer layer. By varying the nature or thickness of these outer layers the manufacturers can produce mixtures that release nutrients in whatever pattern seems useful. Formulations that last weeks or months are available.

These formulations can have significant advantages over other materials because the rate of release is not necessarily influenced by temperature or biological activity. Therefore compounds do not suddenly flush too many salts or fail to supply nutrients when the plants need them.

Organic fertilisers would be expected to be those that come from animals or, rarely, plant wastes. However some materials that chemists would classify as 'organic' such as urea are manufactured artificially and would not be acceptable to organic growers. Organic materials usually have to be converted to an inorganic form by bacteria before they can be taken up, although manures may also contain ureas and other salts that are immediately useful to plants. An important distinction needs to be made between concentrated and bulky organic fertilisers. Concentrated materials derived from an organic source include hoof and horn or blood, fish and bone. These are comparatively costly but easy to apply. Manures are bulky and application or transport costs can be high. Concentrated nutrient sources approved by 'organic' horticulture and agriculture agencies such as the Henry Doubleday Research Association in the UK (HDRA) are shown in Table 4.1.

Bulky organic materials can have very beneficial effects on soil structure and soil organisms as well as providing nutrients. They also have certain disadvantages compared to artificial fertilisers. They often have very variable nutrient content, and there is little opportunity to modify the nutrient balance in order to target specific deficiencies. The majority of the nutrient content of organic materials will also not be available until bacterial mineralisation occurs. They are therefore sometimes seen as 'inefficient'. These problems are more significant for crop producers who need to produce high yields on precise schedules. However on many landscape sites nutrient efficiency is not critical, and the multiple beneficial effects of organic matter may be important.

Inevitably some organic materials have such low levels of available nutrients that they cannot realistically be regarded as having any fertiliser value. These are therefore discussed below as soil conditioners.

The value of a bulky organic material as a nitrogen fertiliser is dependent on the ratio of carbon and nitrogen (Table 4.2). High carbon materials (e.g. bark chips) mineralise slowly and can even take nitrogen from the surrounding soil as the bacteria that decompose them struggle to find the elements they need.

Organic fertilisers can contain quite high levels of trace elements and may provide the nutrients in a more readily available form on difficult soils.

Calculating dose rates

The recommended figures on the side of the packet represent the manufacturer's guess about the levels appropriate for most plants on most soils. Of course different fertilisers have different proportions of each nutrient. These allow particular balances to be specified for those few ornamentals which we know have atypical demands; for example increasing potassium levels for floriferous plants such as hybrid roses, or providing higher nitrogen for turf. Sometimes differences in fertiliser nutrient content reflect the origins of the material rather than a deliberate philosophy of formulation and are little more than a form of brand differentiation (Table 4.3).

The vast majority of people using fertilisers have no idea of whether the soil is deficient or not, and are applying the fertiliser as an insurance. A more sophisticated approach is to look at the fertiliser content of the soil that is to be used, and compare

Table 4.1 Nutrient sources recommended for 'organic' cultivation.

Name	Nutrient content	Use
Hoof and horn	N: *major* P: *minor* K: *minor*	• To correct nitrogen deficiency. • Soil preparations where strong initial growth is required. • Under bark and woodchip mulches applied directly after planting to eliminate nitrogen robbery.
Fish meal	N: *major* P: *minor* K: *minor*	• To correct nitrogen deficiency.
Natural rock phosphate	N: — P: *major* K: —	• To correct phosphorus deficiency. • Ensure cadmium content < 90 mg/kg of P_2O_5.
Poultry manure pellets (deep litter)	N: *major* P: *major* K: *major*	• As general fertiliser in 'cropped areas'. • As base dressing on soils with very low nutrients.
Seaweed meal (not calcified seaweed)	N: *major* P: *minor* K: *major*	• As part of general base dressing on soils with very low nutrients (usually mixed with hoof and horn and bonemeal). • To raise potassium levels if necessary.
Pelleted wool	N: *major* P: *major* K: *major*	• As general fertiliser in cropped areas. • Slow release nutrients, especially potassium. • As a base dressing, similar to poultry manure pellets. (Mixtures of the two are now available.)
Basic slag	N: — P: *major* K: —	• To correct phosphorus deficiency.
Calcined aluminium *Phosphate rock*	N: — P: *major* K: —	• To correct phosphorus deficiency.
Kali vinasse	N: *minor* P: *trace* K: *major*	• To correct potassium deficiency.

Note: Organic standards are under constant review. This is not a definitive list but represents the range of products currently offered for use.

Table 4.2 Typical nutrient contents of bulky organic manures.

Type	Moisture content range (%)	Mean moisture content (%)	Nutrient content range (dry weight %)	Mean nutrient content *(dry weight %)
Farmyard manure	8–85	76	N 0.3–2.2P 0.04–0.9K 0.08–1.4	N 0.6P 0.1K 0.5
Poultry litter	6–90	40	N 0.3–4.5P 0.04–2K 0.1–3	N 1.75P 0.9K 1.0
Sewage sludge	5–94	55	N 0.2–1.7P 0.04–1.0K 0.08–1.9	N 1.0P 0.3K 0.2

* Nutrient concentrations can depend very much on storage conditions, because fertility can be leached from these materials. Where material is stored in a well-covered place figures can be towards the higher end of the range.

Table 4.3 Nutrient content of concentrated fertilisers.

Type	Major nutrient content (% by weight)
Fish meals	N 7–14 P 9–16
Hoof and horn	N 12–14
Calcium nitrate	N 15.5 Ca 20
Sodium nitrate	N 16
Ammonium sulphate	N 21
Ammonium nitrate	N 34
Urea	N 46
Superphosphate	P_2O_5 18–20 (P 9) Ca 20
Triple superphosphate	P_2O_5 47 (P 20) Ca 14
Basic slags	P_2O_5 9–16 (P 4–7)
Rock phosphate	P_2O_5 29–36 (P 12–15)
Potassium chloride	K_2O 60 (K 50)
Potassium nitrate	N 13 K_2O 44 (K 37)

that with what is known about the requirements of the plants to be grown, such as the ADAS index discussed above. Yet even these recommendations make assumptions about the nutrient load required based on experiences with farm or forestry crops rather than landscape plantings.

In practice we are ignorant of the specific nutrient demands of most established ornamental plants and complex, mixed, plantings can never be treated with precision. Fortunately most plants have broadly compatible requirements, and in a landscape context we may not want too much productivity if it will increase maintenance. Also we may prefer to choose plants that match the soil rather than changing the soil to match the plants: the 'Genius of the Place' refers to soils as much as setting.

Fertiliser formulations carry a statement of the percentage of each nutrient that is contained in the mix. British fertilisers express the phosphorus content as P_2O_5 and potassium as K_2O rather than as the percentage of the pure nutrient. This will not matter where fertiliser rates are recommended following soil analysis, as consultants will use the same terminology. However different systems are in use outside the UK.

Almost all fertiliser recommendations, however they are calculated, will only provide one year's nutrient requirements. Many landscape plantings only receive inputs during establishment. Maintenance contracts usually only specify regular fertilisation for roses, herbaceous borders, annuals and turf. This focus on early inputs is okay when the deficiency problems are temporary (e.g. problems of P supply arising from a limited root system), but fundamental and chronic nutrient shortages may require applications over a longer term or different approaches, such as adding organic matter.

Fertiliser application

The most common method of fertiliser application is broadcasting. Obviously this is the best option for general site deficiencies or for features such as turf. Very soluble fertilisers are best applied in spring rather than autumn to minimise leaching, and top dressings after planting may be required.

However for establishment problems related to immobile nutrients, localised additions close to the plant may work better. The roots must be protected from high concentrations of fertilisers. For example phosphorus added to the base of a planting pit must be covered with soil before planting. Fertilisers can damage seedlings and should be applied either well before sowing or after the seed has established. Where damage (or indeed leaching) may occur multiple applications of small amounts of fertiliser will be preferable to one large application.

4.6 Soil conditioners

Soil conditioners are regarded here as those additives which have at least some potential physical or chemical effect other than boosting the levels of available nutrients. Materials recommended by HDRA are shown in Table 4.4. In some cases products are not widely available but are locally available in bulk. A typical example is hop waste, not commonly available outside hop-growing areas but stockpiled in large quantities in Kent. As discussed above, different soil additives can in fact do several different things and part of the inconsistency in performance can be due to a poor match between the material chosen and the needs

Table 4.4 Characteristics of some bulky organic soil conditioners recommended by HDRA.

Description	Analysis	Availability
Municipal compost Available in two forms: green waste and green waste plus kitchen waste. The latter contains source-segregated kitchen waste which will cause a degree of variability in each batch. Ask for individual batch analysis. Green waste compost contains mainly trimmings, prunings and grass clippings, composted and screened according to client requirements.	N: 0.5–2.4 (medium to high) P: 0.1–0.7 (medium to high) K: 0.2–1.9 (medium to high)	Widespread.
Hop waste Waste product from brewing industry. Preferable composted but not always available as such.	N: high P: high K: very low	Locally abundant. Contact a local brewer or hop farm.
Composted bark Bark from forestry operations composted with a suitable source of nitrogen, for example, poultry manure.	N: 0.1–0.4 hardwood (low) N: 0.04–0.4 softwood (low) P and K: negligible	Widespread.
Bracken Harvested and composted common bracken.	N: not specified P: not specified K: high	In the UK sources include the Forestry Commission and the Royal Society for the Protection of Birds.

Note: Analyses are quoted as percentage of dry matter.

of the soil. It is important therefore to identify the modes of action by which a soil ameliorant improves a soil.

Crumb forming

Some organic molecules act as 'glues' that help to bind soil particles together into stable crumbs with pores in between. The resulting structure is the key to good growth, particularly on heavy soils. The ameliorants should be reactive organic materials, which provide good food for soil micro-organisms but are not necessarily well structured themselves (e.g. farmyard manure).

Flocculant

Adding lime-rich materials to a clay soil can improve its structure by the chemical process known as flocculation, which binds the particles into larger, stable, blocks.

Textural modifiers

Soil texture refers to the balance of sands, silt and clays in a soil, which has a fundamental effect on properties such as drainage, water retention, etc. In the strict scientific sense, soil texture is determined without reference to the organic matter content but some materials (such as milled bark) can behave in a similar fashion to grit, altering drainage properties.

Resource-holding sponges

On sandy soils, peat particles are said to improve moisture retention by acting as 'sponges', trapping water that would otherwise have drained away. Even on heavy soils, peat particles can perform a similar role after drought, because clays can be slow to rewet (although for peat to be successful at collecting water, a wetting agent should be incorporated). Agripolymers may do this job more effectively than peat.

Similarly, fertility can be improved by increasing the ability of the soil to hold onto nutrients that would otherwise have leached away, i.e. improving the cation exchange capacity (CEC). Adding clays or some organic materials to light soils will also improve the CEC.

Buffering capacity

A rise in the CEC of a soil also tends to lead to improved buffering. This protects the soil from sudden chemical imbalances, e.g. salinity following fertilisation, or deficiency following heavy rain. Excess chemicals are temporarily immobilised and slowly made available again as the CEC level in the soil water falls.

Soil separator/bulking agent

Where substrates are essentially structure-less, i.e. without stable crumbs, soil masses can still be separated, and drainage fissures kept open and aerated, by the addition of a bulky material such as peat. Physical treatments such as ripping often work much better if such material is incorporated at the same time to reduce re-compaction.

Ideally, any organic matter used should be resistant to rapid decay by micro-organisms and should be rich in lignin and celluloses. Coarse sands and gravels have also been used to keep open drainage and aeration channels in otherwise heavy soil, which can be compared with the sand slitting of football pitches, and also the use of French drains.

Humus source

Humus, in the sense of the most stable organic matter produced after the breakdown of more reactive compounds, can strongly bind with clay, changing the physical properties and in particular making it less sticky and less prone to compaction. Humus can also form long-term bonds with some soil contaminants, making them less available to plant roots.

4.7 Possible problems from ameliorant addition

'Insurance' applications of ameliorants could be misguided if the materials used should prove to be harmful. Although not all have been proven, there are several possible problems which have sometimes been attributed to soil ameliorants.

- Increased **Waterlogging** can result from the use of organic material in planting pits on poorly drained land.
- Temporary **Salinity** problems can result from the use of certain materials, particularly composted nutrient rich organic matter.
- **Rewetting** can be very difficult with some ameliorants, particularly peat. This can make them less effective at retaining periodic water supplies, e.g. summer rain.
- **Shrinkage** and instability is sometimes seen when pits are filled with a very high percentage of organic matter. This can lead to poor rooting and drought, even when the surrounding soil is moist.
- A slightly different point concerns the presence of **Rooting barriers,** even where shrinkage does not occur. It has been suggested that plant roots can find the interface between rich organic matter and mineral soil difficult to cross. There is no clear evidence as to whether this is a real phenomenon or the circumstances under which it could occur.
- **Nutrient immobilisation** occurs when carbon-rich organic matter is broken down by bacteria. To achieve the correct balance of chemicals that they require, these micro-organisms can take free nitrogen and phosphorus from the soil, which leads to temporary nutrient deficiency symptoms in the plants.
- A more subtle problem is **Nutrient imbalance,** which can occur when the proportions, not the total levels, of nutrients in a soil become less favourable. For example, adding extra nitrogen to a soil that is already deficient in phosphorus can increase the severity of the phosphorus deficiency. These effects are sometimes called nutrient antagonisms and other

examples include N/K; K/Mg; Mg/K; P/K; P/Zn; Na/Ca; K/Ca; Mg/Ca; Ca/Mn; Mn/Cu; Zn/Co and Ni/Fe.

It is impossible to generalise about the risk of such problems, as it depends on the nutrient status of the soil and the ameliorant. The effect is less likely with good all round fertilisers such as farmyard manure.

- **Oxygen depletion/methane generation** may occur when reactive organic matter is buried under waterlogged or anaerobic conditions, aggravating conditions for plant roots.

- **Toxins** arising from industrial pollutants are a major problem in domestic refuse and particularly in sewage (see below). Natural toxins in bark require correct composting.

- Many organic materials carry **Plant pathogens** and some, such as sewage sludge, also present concerns about human health. Fungi, nematodes and bacteria are usually killed by composting/ digestion if this is well done. However, it is not uncommon to see weed seeds like tomatoes surviving on sludge, which has been digested, which suggests that other organisms may escape in cold spots. Virus death is harder to ensure and the spread of Tobacco Mosaic Virus from compost has been recorded. There are some concerns that 'matured' rather than composted wood products may contain fungal infections such as *Armillaria*.

- The situation as far as **Human pathogens** are concerned is complicated by a lack of knowledge of the possible vectors and levels of contamination likely to present a risk, but it is widely recognised that gardeners need tetanus inoculation in case cuts should come into contact with soils or manures.

- **Weeds** are most commonly seen in topsoil (and no specification clause will ever prevent them from being there). The use of topsoil as a planting pit backfill is often obvious from the huge crop of arable weeds that appears at the tree base.

- **Compaction/slumping** can occur with fine textured soil materials if they are mishandled.

Quality control

Careful control is needed over the source and quality of organic materials used as ameliorants. Some materials, such as domestic refuse or animal wastes, vary enormously with supplier and also with season. Barks and leaf moulds vary with species. Even so called 'uniform' materials such as peat only achieve their reliable reputation because of exhaustive research and experience of the qualities of different sources, ages and heavy investment in harvesting and milling equipment.

Quality control is of most importance with regard to materials that can sometimes contain toxins, such as sewage sludge. Unfortunately, the reputation of sludge-treated composts and soils has been tarnished by rather cavalier attitudes towards the risks of phyto-toxicity that have been shown in the past by some water authorities.

If a given sample of soil has contaminants below ICRCL trigger levels it is regarded as completely uncontaminated. However, a figure above the trigger level does not mean that problems will definitely occur. The effects of given levels of a contaminant may or may not be harmful depending on the species, the soil textures, the pH, etc. Many robust plants, grasses and vigorous native shrubs and trees in particular, are relatively tolerant of pollutants but of course there are thousands of taxa from which a landscape architect may choose, and for the vast majority the tolerance to individual toxins, let alone cocktails, is totally unknown.

This leads to a situation where the published trigger levels are regarded as the *de-facto* limits for acceptable contamination. Anybody who chooses deliberately to overstep them makes themselves vulnerable in the case of a contractual dispute. Even where there is no dispute about target levels, regular sampling is essential to ensure that loads are falling within the agreed guidelines.

4.8   Common soil additives

It is worth re-emphasising that many organic materials are inherently variable and that the tables presented in this chapter must be interpreted as a guide only. For example, organic materials that contain nutrients may still be lacking in certain minerals, and may even take others out of the soil. Some may be a long-term nutrient source but in the short term deplete available nitrogen because of high carbon ratios.

Treatment also affects characteristics. The degree of composting a material undergoes affects longevity, salinity, physical structure, nutrient release and uptake, pathogen presence, etc. Milling can alter the physical properties of some materials such as bark. Wetting agents will affect the water holding profile. New technology is appearing, such as worm working of organic wastes. This can improve their physical characteristics enormously but at present the economics look poor and there may be more pathogen problems because no heating occurs in this process.

Soil additives for ecological plantings

Soil additives can be used in more adventurous ways in order to 'design' soil conditions. In theory we could use additives to make soils drier or wetter, more fertile or more impoverished, more acidic or more alkaline—the full potentials have rarely been explored but may be particularly useful for habitat creation.

Many of the activities that we undertake as part of 'horticultural vegetation management' – such as feeding, watering plants etc. – are exercises aimed at overcoming the limitations to growth imposed by the environment. In other words, we deliberately minimise stress. However stress is one of the factors which limits the growth of dominant, competitive, monocultures and stress is therefore a key to the development of diversity in freely-competing plant communities. For naturalistic landscapes therefore we need to create it deliberately. This was identified by Roberts and Roberts (1986) but the principles have only been slowly adopted since then.

A notable exception is work by the Groundwork Trust of St Helens in Lancashire on how overly-productive soils could be 'ameliorated' by the addition of large quantities of hostile material such as brick rubble, pulverised fuel ash or colliery spoil, in order to make conditions less suitable for the competitors and more suitable for other flowering species (Bloomfield et al., 1981).

Specifying ameliorants

It is obviously impossible to provide general-purpose specifications for soil ameliorants in a way that avoids the need for site assessment and professional judgement. Their use and rates of application must be decided in the light of soil conditions encountered, the species to be planted and the availability of other site treatments such as ripping. Even so, some general points can be made.

- Soil amelioration is not a substitute for critical practices such as good weed control.
- Organic ameliorants should not be used on waterlogged soils without some attempt to improve site drainage by ripping, French drains, etc.
- Reactive, i.e. uncomposted or undigested organic matter should not be used at depth.
- Most undecomposed or unstabilised organic matter should not be used without the addition of nitrogen.
- Backfills made up of 100 per cent organic matter are unnecessary and may lead to problems of instability, shrinkage, etc. 20 per cent by volume mixed with the site soil is a good rule of thumb.
- Where possible, produce a uniform tilth by incorporating organic matter across the entire site; sharp divisions in soil type should be avoided.
- Quality control must be specified and enforced by regular sampling, especially with regard to salinity and pollutants.

For maximum benefit, ameliorants should be chosen by matching their effects to the soil type or soil problems encountered. The following list shows which types of material are best suited to certain problem soils.

Clay soils
Use ameliorants that have a humic, bulking, crumb forming or flocculant effect.

Silt soils

Use ameliorants that are bulking, crumb forming or textural modifiers.

Sands

Use ameliorants that are colloidal, textural modifiers, nutrient sources, resource storage improvers or have a high buffering capacity.

Organic matter, deficient wastes and subsoils

Use ameliorants that are humic and nutrient sources.

Compacted soils

Use bulking, crumb forming, resource storing ameliorants.

Structureless land

Use bulking, crumb forming and flocculating ameliorants.

Contaminated land

Use humic and buffering ameliorants, those that are nutrient sources (if high in P) and calcium (for pH effects).

Droughted land

Use ameliorants that improve water storage or are crumb forming to improve rooting depth.

4.9 Summary

Landscape soils are usually more diverse than agricultural soils, and can encompass wider extremes of behaviour. Many construction processes will inevitably degrade or radically change soil quality, making pre-design soil assessment of limited value. Frequently the only major option open to landscape professionals is the remediation and amelioration of the soils after construction.

Ameliorants lead to physical and chemical changes in soil character that need to be matched against the initial soil conditions and the design and management objectives. Predicting the behaviour of ameliorants in different soils is not a perfect science, but remediation can be greatly improved by having some basic understanding of the likely modes of action of different additives in different conditions.

Although there are signs that soil scientists are beginning to be interested in these issues, significant practical advances are only likely to come when we have professional procedures that allow for soil assessment and choice of remediation after degradation has occurred, as well as monitoring procedures that identify when additives have been successful.

References

Bloomfield, H.E., Handley, J.F. & Bradshaw, A.D. (1981) Topsoil quality. *Landscape Design*, **135**, 32–4.

Roberts, R.D. & Roberts, J.M. (1986) The Selection and Management of Soils in Landscape Schemes. In: Bradshaw, A.D., Goode, D.A. & Thorp, E. (eds) *Ecology and Design in Landscape*. The 24th symposium of the British Ecological Society. Blackwells, Oxford. 99–126.

Further reading

Ash, H.J. (1991) Soils and Vegetation in Urban Areas. In: Bullock P. & Gregory P.J. (eds) *Soils in the Urban Environment*. Blackwells, Oxford.

Ash, H.J. (1992) *Flowers in the Grass*. English Nature, Peterborough.

Craul, P. (1992) *Urban Soils in Landscape Design*. Wiley, New York.

Gilbert, O.L. (1989) *The Ecology of Urban Habitats*. Chapman & Hall, London.

Harris, J.A., Birch, P., & Palmer, J.H. (1996) *Land Restoration and Reclamation: principles and practice*. Longman, Harlow.

Henry Doubleday Research Association. *Organic Grounds Maintenance Manual*, European Council Regulation 2092/91.

Marrs, R.H. & Gough, M.W. (1990) Soil Fertility – a Problem for Habitat Restoration. In: *Biological Habitat Reconstruction*. G.P. Buckley (Ed). Belhaven, London. pp 29–44.

Further sources of information

There are numerous suppliers of 'organic' composts etc. For information on suppliers within a local area please contact HDRA Consultants, tel: 024 7630 8202.

5 Soil Drainage

Gordon Spoor

Good soil drainage is essential for most efficient and successful forms of plant growth and productivity. All plant roots require oxygen for active growth (with the exception of aquatic and some wetland plants) and their oxygen supply must come from within the soil itself. Under good growing conditions, the soil oxygen reserves will only provide a one-to-two day supply, and hence there is a continuous need for replenishment from the atmosphere. This replenishment can only take place through air-filled soil pores and drainage is needed to provide these by removing excess soil water. Aquatic and some wetland species have the ability to transfer oxygen to their roots through their aerial parts, so that the degree of soil aeration and drainage needed may be reduced, or even zero. Nevertheless, even in such situations some degree of water control is usually needed to provide the required levels of wetness and dryness.

Good drainage is also useful in helping control soil erosion and necessary for maximising soil support for traffic and public access. Soil erosion occurs through surface runoff and drainage can reduce the risk of this by assisting water infiltration into the soil and so controlling the rate of runoff (Fig. 5.1). The ability of soils to support loads without significant sinking or soil damage is very dependent upon the moisture content. This 'support capacity' is much reduced under wet conditions. Improving drainage to remove excess water and lower water tables to below about 0.5 m increases the support strength considerably and allows satisfactory trafficking and access over much longer periods.

Drainage cannot cure all soil ills, and it is limited in terms of the quantities of water it can remove, but it has a very important part to play in the management of soils for turfgrass, sportsfield, planting beds and trees.

The strategy for achieving an effective drainage system can be summarised as follows:

- identify, through site and soil surveys, the nature of potential drainage problems and the soil drainage properties and characteristics
- identify the optimum type of drainage system considering not only the soil but also whether changes to the growing system, to surface levels or to the soil condition may be possible, to improve drainage efficiency and reduce costs
- design the optimum drainage system and identify the installation requirements
- identify any necessary soil treatments to maximise drainage efficiency
- plan and schedule future maintenance requirements.

5.1 The nature of drainage problems and water flow routes

Drainage problems arise in a number of different forms, depending on the soil, climatic and local site conditions. The problems can be divided broadly into four types:

- surface,
- groundwater,
- perched water and
- seepage.

These are all illustrated diagrammatically in Fig. 5.2.

Fig. 5.1 A swale in a large landscape project designed to receive drainage water and retain it whilst it slowly permeates into the soil. These swales can be sown or planted with attractive vegetation. (Photo: James Hitchmough)

Surface drainage problems (Fig. 5.2a) arise when rainfall rates exceed soil water infiltration rates. These are common on all soils where surface compaction has occurred, and a good example would be surface waterlogging on sportsfields after heavy use under wet conditions. Some soils which are low in organic matter content and high in fine sand and silt particles tend to collapse and are very prone to natural compaction and runoff.

Groundwater problems arise as a result of excessively high water tables and subsurface drains are needed to hold these down (see Fig. 5.2b). They are common on deeper permeable sandy and gravelly soils. However when subsoil permeability is very low, as in poorly structured

clay soils or severely compacted subsoils, water tends to pond on top of the subsoil within the more permeable surface layers and 'perched' water table problems arise. Failure to alleviate subsoil compaction on re-instated sites often produces this condition. Drainage in these situations has to be through lateral water movement either through the topsoil or over the surface, both possible on slopes. The alternative is through subsurface drains which are backfilled with a very permeable material. The permeable backfill allows rapid downward water flow from the permeable surface layers into the drain (see Fig. 5.2c).

Seepage situations arise when water enters from the surrounding areas, either upwards in artesian situations or laterally from spring lines or from sloping areas (Fig. 5.2d). In the first situation, water pressures have to be relieved, often through groundwater pumping, and in the case of lateral inflow, the incoming water must be intercepted before it reaches the area to be protected. For effective interception, the drains must be placed at the bottom of the permeable layer through which the water is flowing, otherwise little water is intercepted.

5.2   Site investigations

Careful site investigations are essential before embarking on any drainage works, to ensure that potential problems, if any, are clearly recognised and to collect the necessary information for system selection and design, and efficient installation. Particular attention needs to be paid to the soil type and its structural condition, the likely sources and quantities of water to be dealt with, the topography of the site and location of a satisfactory drainage discharge point or outfall. This information needs to be considered alongside possible variations in plant husbandry systems, such as the use of mounding or raised beds, in the plant species selected (based upon their wetness tolerances), and in chosen final surface levels, all of which can assist in reducing drainage need in difficult or expensive drainage situations.

The ease of water flow into soil (infiltration) and through it (permeability) is very dependent upon

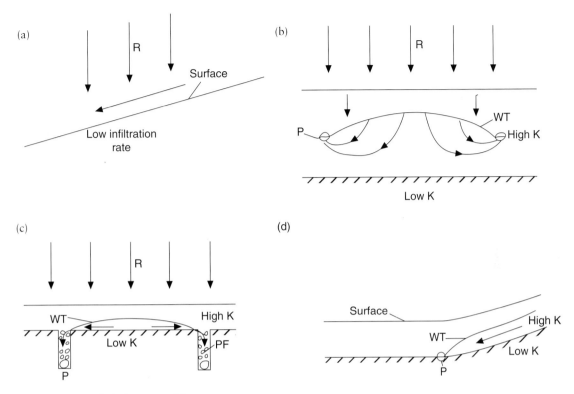

Fig. 5.2 Types of drainage problem.
(a) Surface   (b) Groundwater table   (c) Perched water table   (d) Seepage
K – Soil permeability   R – Rainfall input   P – Pipe   WT – Water table   PF – Permeable backfill

the size range of soil particles present and how they aggregate together. The particle size distribution, comprising specific percentages of sand, silt and clay particles, defines what is termed the soil texture. The nature of soil particle aggregation, and the shape and size of the aggregates, define the type of soil structure. Whilst coarse sandy and gravelly soils are always very permeable with high infiltration rates, the permeability and infiltration characteristics of the other soil types are very dependent upon their structure.

Soil texture can be readily identified in the field by taking a handful of soil, wetting and working it well to break down any structure, wetting and drying it until it achieves a state of maximum stickiness and then assessing the predominant feel. If it feels predominantly gritty it is a sandy soil; if soapy, a silt; if predominantly sticky, a clayey soil and if a combination of all three, a loam. Having

established the basic textural class, the texture can be defined in more detail, again in terms of feel. For example, a definite loamy soil with a little more stickiness would be a clay loam, or a definite clayey soil with a significant soapy feel would be classified as a silty clay. Common texture classes are identified in Table 5.1.

Subsoil structure is particularly important in the context of drainage. This can only be assessed satisfactorily by opening up a soil pit, examining the soil profile and taking out undisturbed spadefuls of the subsoil to be broken apart by hand, to assess the size and shape of the structural units present. The common shapes and sizes of structural unit found in subsoils are shown in Fig. 5.3, together with indications of how these influence soil permeability. The smaller the size of the structural units and the closer they approach the blocky shape, the better the structure and the higher the

Table 5.1 Permeability (saturated hydraulic conductivity) values of different soil types.

Saturated hydraulic conductivity (m day^{-1})

5.0	1.0	0.5	0.1	0.05	0.01	0.005	0.001	0.0005

Sandy loam

Clay loam

Silt loam | Silty clay loam | Silty clay

Peat

Clay	Clay		Clay		Clay
(Good structure)	(Moderate structure)		(Poor structure)		(No structure)
Blocks/prisms 20 mm	Blocks/prisms 20–50 mm		Prisms 50–100 mm		Prisms 100 mm

20–50 mm: Minimum dimension of prism.

soil permeability. Severely damaged and compacted subsoils (common in reconstituted situations) often have almost no recognisable structure; they are effectively structureless and have almost zero permeability. The profile pit also allows changes in soil texture with depth to be identified, assisting in the identification of the type of drainage problem likely to arise. A critical factor in dealing with seepage is to determine the location of the very low permeable layer at depth, to ensure that the required interceptor drain depth can be identified accurately.

Table 5.1 provides a guide to the magnitudes and relative permeabilities of the different soil types and structural conditions. It can be seen that a well structured clay subsoil can have a permeability more than 100 times greater than a poorly structured one, the permeability of the former

being close to that of a sandy loam. The observed soil profile conditions together with knowledge of the likely sources of water (rainfall, seepage inflow) will give a very good indication of the type of drainage problem to be addressed.

The volume of likely seepage or spring line water quantities are often very difficult to estimate, but information on rainfall inputs and required drain discharges for the other drainage situations are available. The most useful source of such rainfall data for England and Wales is MAFF Technical Bulletin 34, *Climate and Drainage*, published by HMSO. Although currently out of print, library copies are available; the alternative source would be the Meteorological Office. Due to the uncertainties in the seepage case, it is usual in design to over-estimate seepage quantities.

Topographic information and possible outfall

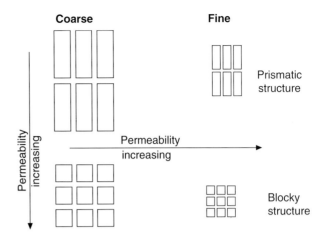

Fig. 5.3 Types of soil structure and influence on soil permeability.

locations are needed to assist in drain layout design. In ground water table control situations, varying topography can have a major influence on water table depth relative to the actual soil surface, some areas being wetter than others. Where a number of options exist with respect to plant or tree selection, choices can be made for the different locations based upon the plant tolerances to different degrees of wetness.

5.3 Types of drainage system

From a drainage point of view, there is no fundamental difference between open ditches and subsurface pipes; the choice is dependent upon whether ditches would provide interesting features or wildlife habitats in themselves or would be unwanted surface obstructions. Both ditch and pipe systems can be designed to function satisfactorily in the different drainage situations, although permeable backfill material will be required with pipes in certain situations, to ensure that water can get rapidly from the source into the pipe itself for removal. Figure 5.4 illustrates how ditch and subsurface pipe systems can be used interchangeably to overcome the different types of drainage problem.

In situations where there is a risk of pipe drains becoming blocked with iron ochre, or through siltation in unstable soils, there are advantages in using ditches only or a combined system. In the combined system the pipe drains discharge directly into an open ditch, allowing easy pipe flushing and cleaning.

In poorly-structured low permeability clayey soils with perched water table problems, drain spacing requirements may be too close for pipe or ditch systems to be economic or feasible. Mole drains are often a viable alternative in these situations, as they are relatively cheap and very satisfactory when used in combination with a widely spaced pipe system. The mole drains are pulled across the line of the widely spaced subsurface pipes, connecting with the permeable backfill above the pipe (see Fig. 5.4c). Water collected by the mole drain is discharged into the permeable backfill and so downwards into the pipe. The disadvantage of mole drains is that they may have to be renewed every three to five years, depending upon the suitability of the clay; however, this is a small inconvenience for achieving effective drainage under difficult circumstances.

In situations such as sportsfields, where surface water ponding can be a problem, closely-spaced sand slits connected to more widely-spaced subsurface pipes can provide a permeable connection between the surface and the pipe to allow for rapid surface water removal (see Fig. 5.4a). One problem with these systems on the heavier cracking clayey soils is that shrinkage is likely to occur during dry periods, opening up the slits. This can introduce potential safety risks on sportsfields,

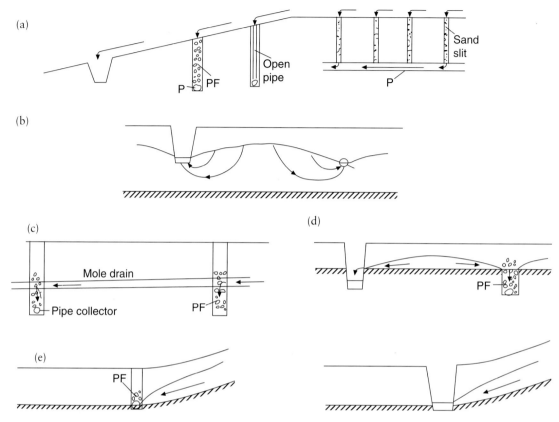

Fig. 5.4 Application and inter-changeability of ditch and subsurface pipe systems in different drainage situations.
(a) Surface drainage (b) Groundwater table control (c) Mole drainage (d) Perched water table control   (e) Seepage water interception
PF – Permeable backfill P – Pipe

unless the slits are filled or they close naturally on re-wetting, before play resumes.

To avoid soil erosion, surface drains need to be grass covered, particularly when running down-slope. Water can be discharged from them either directly into ditches or through permeable backfill above pipe drains. In situations requiring high surface drain discharges into subsurface pipes, a vertical open inlet pipe can be used connecting the surface directly to the pipe below (see Fig. 5.4a).

5.4   Drainage system design

Drain layouts

There are two guiding principles in designing drainage system layouts:

- First, to make best use of the surface topography to achieve the desired water flow routes and drain gradients and
- second, to intercept flowing water as soon as possible.

In landscape situations there will often be opportunities to form surfaces to the desired levels and slopes, to achieve maximum drainage efficiency. The need for interception arises under surface and perched water table conditions, when water tends to seep laterally downslope over the surface or through the upper soil layers. Aligning the drainage system to intercept this flow, with drains running on the appropriate grade close to the contour, will produce the best results. Parallel drainage systems (Fig. 5.5a) are very appropriate

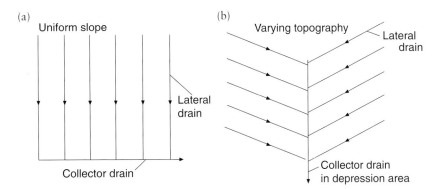

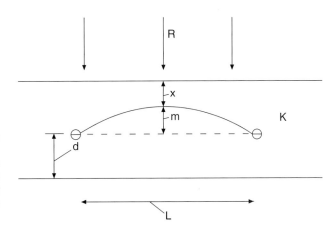

Fig. 5.5 Drain layouts.
(a) Parallel system
(b) Herringbone system

Fig. 5.6 Design parameters in groundwater control situation.
R – Rainfall input K – Soil permeability
L – Drain spacing m – height of mid-drain water level above drain d – depth to layer of low permeability x – desired depth to water table below soil surface

for uniform sloping areas, and herringbone systems where the main collector drain can be routed down a depression area (see Fig. 5.5b). As drainage systems are most susceptible to failure at pipe junctions, there are advantages in keeping the number of junctions to a minimum.

Depths and spacings

Drain depths are dependent upon site conditions and the nature of the particular drainage problem. Shallow systems are obviously appropriate for surface drainage, whereas drain depth can have a significant influence on drain spacings in ground-water table control sites. In these latter situations, the deeper the drains are, the wider the spacings can be to achieve the same control over water table depth. An approximate relationship linking water table depth and spacing in the groundwater case

(and useful also for estimating the required drain spacings) is as follows:

$$L^2 = \frac{8 K m d}{R}$$ (see Fig. 5.6)

Where L = drain spacing,
K = permeability,
m = height of mid-drain water level above drain,
d = depth to layer of low permeability,
R = design rainfall input. (all units in metres)

The design water table depth ('x' in Fig. 5.6; Table 6.2) depends on plant and surface support requirements at the critical time of year for drainage, in the UK usually in winter and spring.

Permeability values (K) can be estimated from Table 5.1, and values of the winter rainfall input R obtained from MAFF Technical Bulletin 34, *Climate and Drainage*. It is common practice to design on a basis of the upper quartile rainfall

Table 5.2 Guideline minimum water table depths.

	Water table depth (m)
Winter/spring	
Grassland to be trafficked by people/machines	0.5
Wet grassland for bird habitat	0.1–0.3
Deeper rooted plants/trees	0.5–0.6
Summer	
Grassland to be trafficked	0.5–0.6
Deeper rooted plants/trees	0.8–1.0

values, which are estimates of the rainfall expected during wet winters. A rule of thumb alternative is to design on approximately twice the average monthly winter rainfall. As a general guide, values of between 0.007 and 0.009 m/day are commonly used depending on the rainfall. Common spacings used for groundwater table control in the more permeable soils are of the order of 20–25 m.

Drain depth has little effect on drain spacing in the perched water table situation as the drain is usually in the low permeability layer. Spacing requirements are now dependent upon the depth of the more permeable upper soil layer, and this depth can sometimes be usefully increased by subsoiling. There can be a major disadvantage in draining unnecessarily deep in this situation, as it increases the quantity of expensive permeable backfill needed. Common drain depths are between 0.6 and 0.8 m. Collector pipe spacings in moling situations are frequently between 20 and 40 m depending upon the suitability of the soil for moling. Mole drain spacings are approximately 3 m and moling depths around 0.5 m.

In seepage situations, providing the interceptor drain extends to the low permeability layer at depth, only one drain will be required.

Backfill and envelope materials

Permeable backfill above pipe drains will be required in perched water table, moling and surface water interception situations, to ensure that water from the upper soil layers can move rapidly to the drain. It is also normally used over the interceptor drain in seepage situations to aid water entry. It would not normally be required in groundwater table situations, as water enters the pipe through the pipe bottom and sides, rather than from above through the permeable backfill. The exception is in soils with a very high fine sand and silt content, as these soils are often unstable and move into the pipe causing blockage. In these situations, an envelope/filter material rather than permeable backfill is required around the pipe at installation to prevent soil ingress. Various cocoa-fibre and synthetic envelopes for this purpose are available already fitted around the pipe from pipe manufacturers.

Pipe sizes and gradients

Pipe size requirements are dependent upon the quantity of water to be discharged (influenced by length of pipe run and pipe spacing), the design rainfall input (R) and the pipe gradient chosen. Pipe sizing charts should be available from the drainage pipe manufacturers but are also given in ADAS Land and Water Service, Reference Book 345, *The design of field drainage pipe systems*, HMSO.

Drainage materials

British Standards have been developed for pipe and envelope materials and it is always advantageous to use products which meet these standards. Purpose made pipe junctions, pipe outfall protectors, inspection chambers and control structures are readily available and should be used. A range of products are available for use as permeable backfill, including natural materials such as gravel and crushed stone and lighter products such as leca and lytag. Critical requirements are that they should be free from fines and soil, and not be easily crushed.

Numerous synthetic products are also available for use as vertical drains. These come in the form of plastic 'egg crate' types or profiled expanded polystyrene slabs, and are suitable for moving water to depth in small scale installations.

Pipe installation

No matter how good the design of the drainage system is, if the installation is poor the system will never be satisfactory. Good quality workmanship, with pipes installed under appropriate soil conditions, are critical for success. The ideal conditions for pipe installation are when soil conditions are dry. It may not always be possible to work under such conditions, but the soil should be as dry as possible and installation should never be carried out in the presence of free water or with soil being replaced over the pipe in a slurry condition. Where gravel or stone are being used the soil surface conditions need to be dry, otherwise considerable soil structural damage will occur through the trafficking of the heavy gravel/stone trailers.

Where old drainage systems are present and cut, these must be connected positively into the new system to avoid subsequent blow-outs. Trenching and hydraulic excavator installation techniques allow this, whereas trench-less methods do not. Significant deviations from the desired pipe grade must be avoided, but the worst situation is when back-grades occur along the pipe run, as these increase the risk of pipe blockage and water surcharging above the pipe.

5.5   Maximising drainage benefits

The drainage installation may be excellent, but if plants cannot exploit the new situation all the investment will be wasted. The main problems that can arise are largely associated with soil compaction, which not only retards root development but also inhibits water movement to the drains themselves. Any compaction in the upper soil layers needs to be alleviated by appropriate soil loosening. Where there is no plant or grass cover, a thorough loosening can be achieved, but it must be remembered that the greater the degree of loosening, the more vulnerable the soil will be to recompaction. Great care will be needed after loosening, keeping loads and tyre pressures to a minimum to maintain the improvement.

Where a plant cover already exists, the major effects of compaction need to be alleviated with a minimum of soil disturbance and plant damage. In grassland type situations, this can be achieved using winged subsoilers fitted with a relatively low lift height wing. The object of the operation is to induce soil to flow up and over the wings, like passing a broom handle under a carpet. As the soil flows up and over, the bending action causes

Fig. 5.7 Ripping tines mounted on the linkage of a crawler tractor to shatter compacted clay pans before topsoiling. The use of this technique is restricted to sites where services are absent or where their locations are well mapped. (Photo: James Hitchmough)

tension cracks to develop within the soil mass, fissuring through the compacted zone. The lift height of the wings or their working depth need to be adjusted so that there is sufficient lift to generate the fissures but not too much to cause excessive soil disturbance and disruption. These fissures will allow drainage, improve soil aeration and root development; the plant roots (supported by organism activity and moisture changes) will complete the remediation process. Such a technique will be successful in all but sandy soils; these have insufficient clay to swell and shrink and restructure, as the soils are wetted and dried. Greater disturbance will be required in the sands, with more care afterwards, as sandy soils are the most susceptible to compaction.

Another common situation which arises on many development sites is where the subsoil is compacted before the top soil is replaced. If this compaction is not alleviated, water will pond on top of the compacted layer forming a perched water table, and plant root development will be severely restricted. Ideally this compaction should be ameliorated before the top soil is replaced, and the topsoil placed carefully afterwards without re-compaction (Fig. 5.7).

For long-term success the drainage system needs to be well-maintained, and any compaction problems avoided or swiftly alleviated.

5.6 Disposal/utilisation of drainage water

The simplest way of handling drainage waters would be to direct them straight into the nearest watercourse, but other alternatives are well worthy of consideration.

Peak discharges soon after heavy rainfall can be very high in both surface and perched water table situations. If the discharge quantities are relatively large, direct discharge could significantly increase the risk of flooding within the watercourse, as well as increasing the risk of sediment inflows in the case of surface runoff. Where the topography allows, directing water into detention reservoirs could be very helpful in regulating the flow of a watercourse and allowing some sedimentation of the larger soil particles and aggregates. Inflows from groundwater control drainage sites are much less liable to surges, and so detention storage may not offer quite so many advantages in this context.

For all discharges, it is worth considering whether they can be utilised to create wetland habitats, whether grassland or reedbeds. Their feasibility and type would depend upon the water quantities available, distribution throughout the year, and likely seepage losses from the wetland area. Wetland habitats offer considerable opportunities for trapping sediment and improving water quality, in addition to providing wider habitat interest (Plate 3). Restricted water availability in the spring or early summer may be a problem for wet grassland habitats, but this can sometimes be reduced by storing drainage water within open water areas or reedbeds during the winter (Plate 4). The stored water can then be fed into the wetland area as required, once drain discharges have ceased. In other situations winter stored water could be utilised for irrigation purposes later in the season. Such possibilities will obviously be very dependent upon the quantities of water involved and the topography of the area.

5.7 Summary

Removing excess water from soils through drainage has an important role to play in improving soil aeration for dryland plant species, in assisting with erosion control and in increasing the soil support capacity for access and trafficking. Drainage problems and their solutions vary, depending on soil types and the specific landscape application, whether turf, sportsfield, plant bed, tree or soil management. The practical achievement of effective drainage involves not only the best type of drainage for the site, but dealing with the subsequent disposal or use of the drainage water.

References and additional reading

ADAS (1983) *The design of field drainage pipe systems.* MAFF Reference Book 345, HMSO, London.

Castle, D.A., McCunnall, J., & Tring, I.M. (1984) *Field Drainage, Principles and Practices.* Batsford, London.

Smith, L.P. & Trafford, B.D. (1976) *Climate and drainage.* MAFF Technical Bulletin 34, HMSO, London.

6 Weed Control in Amenity Landscapes

Bob Froud-Williams

Weed control in amenity landscapes poses a number of difficulties because of the diversity of situations encountered: for example, there is amenity grass (including sports turf), herbaceous and woody ornamental plantings, woodlands, aquatic and riparian habitats. All of these landscapes are generally subject to public access, which further complicates the process of weed management. There are many different reasons, too, for undertaking weed control: aesthetics, maintaining public access or sight lines, reducing damage to hard surfaces and drainage systems, promoting a desired range of plant species or lessening the effects of weed competition on planted material which could otherwise result in costly losses.

Failure to control weeds in the year when woody species are first planted may impair their growth in subsequent years, even if weeds are controlled effectively later. In addition, local authorities are responsible for the management of roadside verges for reasons of safety, while the private sector has responsibility for vegetation management beneath power lines and throughout the rail network, both for access and avoidance of fire risk.

In landscape and amenity sites there is little financial incentive for weed control, because there is no harvestable yield. Consequently, it could be argued that weed control is less of an imperative for managers and operational staff than it is in horticultural crop production. This is reflected in a relatively poor understanding of weed biology and of how control strategies can be applied in the amenity sector. An example is the low capacity to identify weed seedlings in terms of taxon and life form, clearly the starting point in developing effective herbicidal or non-herbicidal control strategies.

Herbicide use is largely restricted to non-selective products containing glyphosate. More selective herbicides to control 'bottleneck' weed problems that cannot be addressed in any other ways (such as couch grass in low shrubs) are rarely used. Herbicide development for use in amenity plantings has received negligible support from the agrochemical industry, horticulture itself being a 'poor relation' to agriculture. Occasionally, benefits can be found from 'spin-offs' such as the herbicides developed for use in oilseed rape, but subsequently registered for use in horticultural brassicas.

The low economic return associated with developing herbicides specifically for use in amenity land has resulted in few new products, many having been discovered in the 1960s and 1970s. At the time of writing all herbicides registered prior to 1993 are required to undergo an appraisal as part of a European Union review of active ingredients. For minor usage, many herbicides are not supported by the manufacturers because of the costs involved and low economic benefits and hence could lose approvals status. Examples include sethoxydim and fosamine, both of which are used in the management of amenity woodlands. Previously, several herbicides have gained support from Specific Off Label Approval (SOLA). It is envisaged that the availability of herbicides for use in amenity land is likely to decrease for reasons of cost associated with registration.

6.1 Herbicide versus non-herbicidal weed control

With one or two exceptions, herbicides available for use in amenity landscapes are of relatively low toxicity to humans and wildlife, and their mode of action and degradation pathways in the environment are well understood. Nevertheless in public landscapes, it is clearly desirable to adopt the precautionary principle and to use herbicides as little as possible. In many cases it is possible to integrate herbicidal and non-herbicidal strategies to reduce herbicide use while maintaining effective control. This does however require that practitioners have a relatively sophisticated understanding of weed biology.

If it is considered necessary to apply herbicides, consideration must be given to operator and public safety. In the UK, The Health and Safety Executive recommend Level 1 personal protective clothing (coverall, gloves, boots and faceshield) if handling concentrate, while the additional use of a respirator (Level 2) may also be required during spraying. However, having made a decision to use a herbicide it is necessary to assess the hazards of its use and the potential risk from exposure. Thus for example, a decision to use a herbicide for total vegetation control could result in a choice between glyphosate and paraquat, the latter presenting a greater hazard to health. In selecting a herbicide it is vital to choose one that presents the least environmental risk. It is essential to consult the product label and advisory notes. Nonetheless, used sensibly to the manufacturer's guidelines, herbicides pose little threat to human health or the environment.

Application of herbicides should take into consideration the risk of drift and so should not be applied at wind speeds greater than two to four miles per hour. However, vapour drift may occur if conditions are too still. Care must also be exercised with regard to disposal of surplus chemical and containers, details of which are available in the most recent *Pesticides: Code of Practice* (HMSO, 1990) If spray equipment is calibrated correctly for the area to be treated, there should be little surplus for disposal after treatment, but

in such circumstances excess chemical may be sprayed into an approved soakaway or collected by a disposal company. Containers may be buried at appropriate sites at a minimum depth of 0.8 m or in some instances burnt, but this excludes many herbicides for amenity use. Herbicides should be stored in accordance with guidelines issued by The Health and Safety Executive as contained in Guidance Note AIS16 *Guidance on storing pesticides for farmers and other professional users*. Records of storage, usage and disposal of herbicides should also be kept.

6.2 Why use herbicides?

Applied correctly, herbicides may be more effective than other methods of control which are more laborious and time-consuming. Furthermore mechanical methods such as mowing and hoeing may allow roots and cut fragments to regenerate, and for stoloniferous or deeply rhizomatous weeds there are often no other effective control measures available. This is more evident in amenity landscapes than in commercial horticulture and agriculture, where it is often possible to plan long-term weed management options. In the amenity area (in site preparation for planting for example) works often have to be undertaken and completed to contractual timescales that make mechanical control of weeds impossible. There is also the dilemma of disposal of cut herbage material, when nonherbicidal techniques such as cutting are employed. This may be particularly important in aquatic environments where there could be environmental damage from the decomposition of cut floating vegetation.

Herbicidal weed control greatly reduces the risk of physical damage to trees and other woody plants compared with the use of mechanical weed control devices such as strimmers and brush cutters. Indeed there is less risk of injury to the operator provided that manufacturers' instructions are adhered to. In terms of energy expenditure, herbicides are generally a more energy efficient means of controlling weeds than using petroleum-powered cutting or cultivating implements. It is very common for herbicides to be considered as 'unsustainable' because they involve industrially synthesised organic molecules, yet to see frequent mechanical cultivation via hand-held hoes as sustainable. This comparison generally fails to include the diesel fuel used to ferry maintenance staff back and forward to landscape sites to do this work.

Herbicides can be problematic for amenity managers. For example, given that one of the objectives for weed control is to maintain visual appearance, the presence of dead and dying vegetation may be unacceptable, precluding the use of such products. It may be visually more tolerable for example to have mown vegetation than vegetation which appears contorted in growth or desiccated. The necessity for spray applicators to hold certificates under the *Control of Pesticide Regulations* (1986) also restricts the number of employees with the necessary training for herbicide application, sometimes creating logistical problems. Similarly the requirement to place signs informing the public of areas that are to be, or have been sprayed, can pose problems for managers.

6.3   Alternatives to herbicides

Germany is an example of a country that has more or less stopped using herbicides in the management of amenity landscapes. It is possible to do this, but to maintain the same standard of management without herbicides requires the input of more money and labour. Until recently this has been possible in Germany because of their tradition of well-funded urban greenspace agencies. This is no longer the case and consequently much of this greenspace is now under severe management strain. To substitute non-herbicidal strategies for herbicidal weed control with no additional funding requires a reduction in the quality of management, or a reduction in the volume of what can be managed at the previous standard. These changes have to some degree been ongoing in British amenity landscapes, and providing the landscapes still meet their functional and aesthetic requirements, this is an appropriate solution. There are still, though, bottleneck situations (such

as preparation of sites for planting that are infested with weeds such as couch grass, *Elymus repens*), that are very difficult to manage without access to herbicides.

In summary, alternatives to the use of herbicides involve the following:

- Changing the expectations of the public so that they accept the presence of weedy species.
- Increasing the use of mulching in new plantings to suppress weed seed germination. Although this is expensive, it is widely used now and is highly effective, providing the site is initially free from perennial weeds.
- Using mechanical devices, for example wire brushing of pavements, to remove colonising weeds.
- Using heat to control annual weeds in pavements and plantings. This generally involves the use of propane powered flame guns. They can be effective but are relatively slow and are not very energy efficient.
- Using different types of more naturalistic plantings that can visually 'carry' weed species more satisfactorily than traditional planting designs.

Further information can be found in Hitchmough (1994).

6.4   What are herbicides?

Herbicides are chemicals designed to disrupt plant growth resulting in mortality. They can be classified in various ways based on their type of activity, time of application, usage and chemical structure.

Herbicide activity may be considered as:

- contact acting, translocated (systemic) or residual
- selective/non-selective
- foliar or soil-acting.

Contact herbicides cause localised damage and need to achieve good deposition on the target to achieve control. As such they are unlikely to be effective against perennial vegetation and their application is dependent on a foliar target. Examples are diquat, paraquat and glufosinate ammonium, although the latter two have some limited translocated activity (paraquat more so if applied at night-time).

Translocated herbicides are usually applied to the foliage and are transferred either within the xylem or phloem to the site of action. Time of application may be important: those that are phloem mobile are likely to be translocated from the leaves to the roots or perennating structures (together with photosynthesised assimilate) later in the lifecycle of the plant. Examples include glyphosate and picloram.

Residual herbicides are applied to the soil and are taken up either by germinating seeds or through the roots of established plants. Examples of the former include propachlor and of the latter amitrole. Clearly, they may also be regarded as having translocated activity. They are dependent on sufficient soil moisture for uptake.

Selectivity of herbicides is generally considered desirable in order to remove one or more species without detrimental effects to the desired species. However there is often also a need for non-selective herbicides, for example when preparing sites for seeding or planting (e.g. glyphosate and paraquat). Other herbicides have been developed in order to maintain weed free conditions around buildings or industrial zones in the long term. These are referred to as 'totals', and an example is imazapyr.

Herbicides that are selective but still control a wide range of weeds are referred to as broad-spectrum. Narrow-spectrum herbicides may be targeted specifically against intransigent weeds, such as oxadiazon for field bindweed (*Convolvulus arvensis*).

A guide to the use and selection of herbicides for use in amenity situations is provided in the 'Amenity Handbook' (Crop Protection Association, 2001). The Crop Protection Association was formerly the British Agrochemicals Association. Table 6.1 gives some examples. The manufacture, sale and use of herbicides is stringently controlled within the UK under the *Food and Environmental Protection Act* (1985) and implemented under the *Control of Pesticide Regulations* (1986). Reference to *The Control of Substances Hazardous to Health Regulations* (1988) (COSHH) will be necessary to assess the risk of exposure to a particular herbicide and whether a more suitable one may be selected. Some herbicides such as paraquat are

Table 6.1 Examples of herbicides used in amenity horticulture.

Active ingredient	Usage	Mode of action	Symptoms
Amitrole	Translocating, foliar acting, non-selective	Inhibition of lycopene cyclase	Albinism, loss of pigmentation
Cycloxydim	Translocated, foliar acting,	Inhibition of acetyl co-carboxylase	Chlorosis, selective control of grasses
Diquat	Contact, foliar, non-selective	PS 1 inhibitor, electron diversion	Desiccation of foliage
Diuron	Residual, soil-acting	PS 11 inhibitor	Chlorosis of annual weeds
Ioxynil	Contact, foliar selective	Respiratory uncoupler	Chlorosis of broad-leaved weeds in turf
Imazapyr	Residual/foliar non-selective	Inhibits acetolactate synthase	Stunting, chlorosis in annual/perennials
Napropamide	Residual, soil-acting	Inhibition of cell division	Seedlings fail to emerge/stunting
Oxadiazon	Residual and contact activity, selective	Inhibits proto-porphyrinogen oxidase	Bleaching of annual/perennial broadleaved weeds
Propachlor	Residual, soil-acting	Inhibits cell division	Seedlings fail to emerge
Triclopyr	Foliar translocated residual	Interferes with auxin metabolism	Epinasty of perennial broadleaved weeds

subject to *The Poisons Act* of 1972 and *The Poisons Rules* (1982). Full details of herbicide active ingredients and individual products approved for use in specific situations are provided in *The UK Pesticide Guide* (revised annually) although the product label should always be referred to.

Time of application and modes of action

This is perhaps more relevant to crop situations where herbicides are applied prior to sowing, pre- or post-emergence of the crop. However in amenity situations some pre-plant treatments such as diuron, a residual herbicide may be of use. Chlorpropham and pentanochlor may be used pre-emergence (of weed seedlings) in amenity situations on herbaceous nursery stock, while propyzamide and sethoxydim may be used after the emergence of weeds. Whereas all pre-emergence herbicides will be soil-acting, post-emergence herbicides may have soil or foliar activity (napropamide and cycloxydim respectively).

Herbicides interfere with various metabolic processes in plants including photosynthesis, respiration, protein and lipid metabolism and also cell division. Many are target-site-specific, such as the triazines which are photosynthetic inhibitors that inhibit the 'Hill Reaction'. Such specificity of action has contributed to the development of resistance to some herbicides.

Selection pressure created by regular and repeated applications of certain herbicides has resulted in the appearance within horticulture of weed biotypes that are resistant to atrazine, simazine and paraquat. Resistance has mostly appeared among species which have short life-histories such as groundsel (*Senecio vulgaris*) and annual meadow-grass (*Poa annua*) which are capable of producing more than one generation per annum. Typically they are characterised by short-lived dormancy and non-persistent seedbanks. Although inbreeding within weed populations may conserve recessive genes coding for resistance, out-breeding may lead to a more rapid spread of resistance through pollen exchange.

Target sites for herbicides include receptors such as the thylakoid membrane of the chloroplast (in the case of triazines) and individual enzymes (in the case of the graminicides, grass-weed herbicides). The inability of the herbicide to bind with the target site results in *target site resistance*; enhanced detoxification of the herbicide before it interferes with the target site is referred to as *metabolic resistance*. Resistance to the triazine herbicides appears to have resulted from target site resistance, but metabolic resistance is often more frequent for other herbicides including paraquat. In order to reduce the risk of herbicide resistance, herbicides with differing modes of action should be rotated and used in combination with non-chemical methods of weed control where practicable. Many public authorities rely heavily on glyphosate because of its efficacy and very low toxicity, but such a strategy may be problematic in the longer term.

Whereas the non-selective herbicides paraquat, glufosinate and glyphosate may appear to have similarities in terms of their activity, they each have very different modes of action. Paraquat interferes with photosynthesis by interfering with electron excitation; this results in peroxidation of cells and leaf desiccation. Glufosinate inhibits the enzyme glutamine synthetase, resulting in toxic accumulation of ammonia in leaf cells. Glyphosate interferes with the enzyme ESPS synthase which is necessary for the formation of aromatic amino acids, resulting in protein deficiency and hence plant death.

6.5 Herbicide formulation and application

Herbicides may be formulated either as liquids or solids, the former as emulsifiable concentrates or suspension concentrates, and the latter as wettable powders or as granular formulations. The latter offers the potential of slow release of the active ingredient over a protracted period of time, and is also appropriate for products with a high vapour pressure such as dichlobenil. Slow release granules may provide season-long weed control and may be particularly appropriate in aquatic environments where it is not desirable for the product to dissipate rapidly. Alternatively in such situations the product may be formulated as an alginate gel, enabling its attachment to submerged leaves, as in the case of diquat alginate. Most herbicides are applied as sprays through specially designed nozzles along a spray boom which is attached to a knapsack or tractor-mounted sprayer, but it is also possible to apply far more selectively by means of a rope-wick or weed wiper.

Controlled droplet application (CDA) systems have enabled a reduction in spray volume rates. This is particularly useful in that it has enabled the development of novel spraying systems such as hand-held devices which use pre-packed oil-based formulations designed for direct application, e.g. along fence lines. These systems avoid the need for operators to have direct contact (as a result of measurement and mixing) with the herbicide.

Selectivity may be achieved through depth protection, whereby the rooting depth of the desired species is greater than that of the weed seeds and the herbicide is retained at or near the soil surface because of its limited capacity for mobility. Conversely, herbicides designed to control deep-rooted woody plants may exhibit greater mobility as a consequence of their chemical structure (e.g. picloram and tryclopyr). Clearly if they are to control deep-rooted weed species, soil-acting herbicides of greater mobility are required than those designed to inhibit germinating seedlings.

For prolonged weed-free maintenance, residual soil-acting herbicides are preferable, but their activity is highly dependent on the availability of soil moisture and they are generally inactive against already established vegetation. The use of soil-acting herbicides is more appropriate to autumn/winter, when amenity species are often dormant or least active. Conversely foliar-acting treatments generally fail to provide season-long weed control, but will remove existing vegetation, either before amenity planting or during spring/summer when the growth of both planted species and weeds is greatest. For non-selective herbicides height differentials between herbaceous

weeds and trees can provide a degree of selectivity. However, care must be taken that herbicides do not penetrate the lenticels (pores along the trunk) of desired woody species.

6.6 Principles of weed control

Any programme designed to achieve effective weed control should consider the pre-planting environment. Here the use of residual soil-acting herbicides provides the opportunity to destroy germinating weed seeds within the soil seedbank. Soil weed seedbanks are mainly concentrated in the top 200 mm of the soil, and typically range from 10 000–80 000 viable weed seeds/m^2. Many weeds have specific periodicities of seedling emergence, often with pronounced peaks in autumn and spring. Thus residual treatments should be applied prior to seedling emergence. While this will deplete seeds present in the surface horizon of the soil seedbank, subsequent soil disturbance will stimulate further seed germination. Avoiding further soil cultivation will reduce seedling emergence, as will the application of a mulch such as chipped wood bark. In practice residual soil-acting herbicides are rarely used as seed bank depleters in amenity situations before planting, because of the short timescales often associated with site development.

Where vegetative propagules (rhizomes, corms, tubers etc.) of perennial species are present, then it may prove more effective to apply a non-selective herbicide prior to planting. In many cases two applications are required at four to six week intervals to achieve close to complete control of perennial weeds. Even so, it is often desirable to employ follow-up treatments with translocated selective herbicides after planting. For effective control of many perennials (e.g. couch grass, *Elymus repens*) it is essential that the herbicide is translocated to the meristematic regions (e.g. rhizome buds). For those products that are phloem mobile (such as glyphosate) this is likely to be most effective during active growth, when photosynthetic assimilate is being transferred to these perennating structures which also serve as storage organs.

Not all translocated chemicals move in the

phloem; some are transported within the xylem following uptake by the roots. For such applications it will be desirable to treat earlier during vegetative growth when transport is primarily from the roots to meristematic shoots. Similarly selective herbicides may be applied at appropriate times during the plants' life cycle. One of the first specific graminicides, alloxydim sodium (now superseded) was developed for selective control of couch grass in ornamentals, being translocated to the meristematic shoots. Conversely, clopyralid (developed specifically for control of creeping thistle *Cirsium arvense*) is translocated to the growing points of the creeping roots. Again, soil cultivation may prove counter productive, for unless it is repeated regularly to deplete the bud bank, it will fragment and disperse these propagules and stimulate regeneration. Fragmentation will also reduce the efficacy of those herbicides with systematic activity. It can, however, improve the performance of contact-acting herbicides such as paraquat and glufosinate ammonium.

Regular mowing may also enhance herbicide performance by providing young foliage that takes up more of the active herbicide ingredient than older, mature foliage. In the case of foliar acting products, sufficient leaf area needs to be present for the interception of spray deposits. Some weed species offer an insufficient target for herbicide retention: horsetails (*Equisetum* spp.) are an example of this. They also have silica deposited within their cell walls, which renders herbicide uptake problematic. The presence of both rhizomes and dormant tubers makes this a particularly difficult weed to eliminate; however propyzamide is effective against it. Repeated cultivation may contribute to its susceptibility to herbicides, but other factors such as improved drainage may help to reduce its competitiveness

with other species. A key objective of amenity planting should be to select those species most likely to suppress weed growth rather than rely heavily on the use of herbicides or other long-term weed control inputs.

Weed control in amenity grassland

Other than through mowing, weed control in amenity grassland in parks and other public landscapes is generally non-existent. This is an entirely satisfactory situation that is possible because many weeds are suppressed by mowing, and because of the low functional and visual requirements of this type of grass sward. By contrast, sports turf is more intensively managed for uniformity of appearance and consistency of performance. The use of herbicides is essential to achieve a playing surface free from broadleaf and grass-weeds. Weed control measures will need to be employed throughout the life of the turf and especially during its establishment. Table 6.2 gives some suitable herbicides.

Soil sterilisation (using methyl bromide or dazomet) prior to sowing may be undertaken in prestige situations, to eliminate perennial weed fragments and the weed seed bank. Methyl bromide is being phased out and will not be permitted after 2005, while dazomet is more costly.

In less intensively-managed sports turf, existing vegetation may be controlled with either contact or translocated non-selective herbicides. During the establishment of sports turf, fluroxypyr, isoxaben and mecoprop-P may be used for broad-leaf weeds. Use of ioxynil is restricted and application by hand-held applicator prohibited.

Weed control needs to be continued on established sports turf, particularly to prevent ingress of weeds into gaps created by turf wear. The major-

Table 6.2   Herbicides approved for use in turf (restrictions may apply).

2,4-D + dicamba	Clopyralid + fluroxypyr + MCPA	Ethofumesate
2,4-D + mecoprop-P	Chlorthal dimethyl	Ioxynil
2,4-D + picloram	Dicamba + dichlorprop + MCPA	Isoxaben
bifenox + MCPA + mecoprop-P	Dichlorprop + ferroussulphate + MCPA	Picloram
Clopyralid + diflufenican + MCPA	Diuron	

Table 6.3 Herbicides approved for use in amenity grass (restrictions may apply).

Asulam
2,4-D + picloram
MCPA + mecoprop-P
Bifenox + MCPA + mecoprop-P
Dicamba + MCPA + mecoprop-P
Dichlorprop + MCPA
Clopyralid + triclopyr
Fluroxypyr + triclopyr
Isoxaben

Fig. 6.1 Bracken (*Pteridium aquilinum*) encroaching on heathland to which the public has access. (Photo: R.J. Froud-Williams)

ity of broad-leaved weeds are controlled by 'broad-spectrum' mixtures of herbicides involving 2, 4-D, MCPA, mecoprop-P, and dicamba. Slender speedwell (*Veronica filiformis*) may be a problem, as it propagates from cut fragments after mowing, but it can be controlled with fluroxypyr + mecoprop. Where docks are present, asulam or dicamba may be used and thistles can be controlled by clopyralid or dicamba. Until recently there was no recommended selective herbicide for removal of annual meadow-grass, although ethofumesate is now fully approved.

Algae, mosses and rushes may be a problem in turf, and will necessitate correction of underlying drainage problems, but algae and mosses may also be affected by fertiliser treatments which affect soil pH. Both problems may be corrected by treatment with ferrous sulphate or dichlorophen.

In amenity grasslands that are not regularly cut, diversity of native flora should be a key management goal, and it is generally inappropriate to apply herbicides though some are approved (Table 6.3). In some circumstances plant growth regulators (PGRs) such as mefluidide may be useful as a means of reducing sward height. Species diversity is generally unaffected, although flowering date may be delayed.

However landowners and local authorities in the UK are obliged to comply with *The Weeds Act* (1959), necessitating the removal and prevention of spread of specified injurious weeds: ragwort (*Senecio jacobaea*), curled dock (*Rumex crispus*), broad-leaved dock (*Rumex obtusifolius*), spear thistle (*Cirsium vulgare*) and creeping thistle (*Cirsium arvense*). Attempts to revoke this act

were recently prevented. In addition it is an offence under *The Wildlife and Countryside Act* (1981) to permit the growth of or to deliberately plant Japanese knotweed (*Fallopia japonica*) and giant hogweed (*Heracleum mantegazzianum*).

Ragwort infestations may be controlled with 2, 4-D + picloram. This should not be attempted if grazing animals have access to the site or if the vegetation is to be conserved as hay, when its increased palatability will increase the risk of poisoning of ruminants through an accumulation of toxic alkaloids and irreversible liver damage. An alternative treatment is citronella oil (a natural biocide) which is more rapid in its activity and thus requires that stock are excluded for a shorter interval. In nature reserves it may be more appropriate to spot treat or weed wipe with glyphosate (this is extensively utilised by English Nature) or alternatively to pull mechanically from the ground.

For heath and moorland, management by mosaic burning is desirable to maintain species diversity, but again outside of the bird breeding season (31st March – 1st November). The main weed species in these ecosystems are bracken (*Pteridium aquilinum*, Fig. 6.1) and purple moor grass (*Molinia caerulea*). Fire can sometimes restrict the spread of these species, but other forms of control are also necessary. Mechanical flailing may be used for purple moor grass. Suitable herbicides for control of purple moor grass include sethoxydim, whereas bracken may be treated with asulam. It may also be necessary to prevent the process of ecological succession resulting in domination by birch and pine. The latter may be removed mechanically as it does not regenerate from cut stumps. However, birch will regenerate after cutting unless the stumps are chemically treated.

Weed control in amenity woodlands, and specimen trees in grass

A number of herbicides are registered for use pre-planting and throughout the establishment phase of woodlands. Initial vegetation clearance may be achieved with contact or systemic non-selective herbicides (see Table 6.4). The prevention of seedling emergence around planted trees may be achieved with residual soil-acting treatments of diuron, propachlor and propyzamide. Alternatively oxadiazon may be used in newly-planted woodlands and dichlobenil in established plantations. Sheet mulches (such as black polythene, woven weed mat fabrics or chipped bark) are an alternative. These mulches do however need to be able to withstand penetration by emerging perennial weeds.

Brushwood (unwanted woody plants) may be controlled by mechanical methods, though

Table 6.4 Herbicides approved for use in amenity woodlands.

Diclobenil:	annual & perennial weed control in established plantations.
Diuron	residual weed control.
Oxadiazon:	residual weed control and use in newly planted wooded areas.
Propachlor:	pre-emergence residual weed control.
Propyzamide:	residual control of annual & perennials.
Glyphosate:	pre and post planting weed control.

deciduous species tend to regenerate by means of suckers. Herbicides alone are unlikely to be acceptable because of the aesthetic appearance of treated plants. A combination of mechanical and chemical treatments generally proves most successful. Stumps may be treated with 2, 4-D + dicamba + triclopyr, or glyphosate applied immediately after cutting. Scrub vegetation may be removed with fosamine ammonium or tryclopyr. The former may be applied to conifer plantations for brushwood control during August-October, but symptoms fail to develop until the subsequent spring. Although use of the triazines (atrazine and simazine) in amenity situations is no longer approved, both are recommended for use in forestry.

In forest picnic and recreation sites it may be necessary to restrict the encroachment of scrub vegetation such as brambles and gorse. Although it is enjoyed for its appearance during flowering, Rhododendron (*R. ponticum*) is a noxious weed of forests (Fig. 6.2). Introduced in 1765 from the Iberian Peninsula, it has proved to be an invasive weed that excludes native ground flora species such as bluebells and primroses. Each flower has

Fig. 6.2 Invasion of amenity woodland by rhododendron (*R. ponticum*). (Photo: R.J. Froud-Williams)

the potential to produce around 5000 seeds which are wind-borne and require light for germination. Cutting facilitates proliferation, as does burning, while the presence of phenols within the leaves deters herbivores. Application of lime to the soil may destroy germinating seedlings. Herbicidal control may be achieved through application of ammonium sulphamate.

Weed control on roadside verges

Roadside verges form a network of semi-natural vegetation covering approximately 180 000 hectares of the UK. Nature conservation is a key management goal for this vegetation. Periodic mowing is the traditional method of vegetation management, but is costly and may require more than one cut per annum. Use of growth regulators such as maleic hydrazide suppresses growth of grasses and even affects species composition in favour of fine-leaved grass species and forbs rather than coarse tussock grasses. Spot application of herbicides such as 2, 4-D provides control of noxious broad-leaved species. Road verges are an increasingly important habitat for native wild-flower species and broad-leaved herbicides should never be applied as an overall application.

Weed control in riparian corridors

Three invasive, alien weeds are acutely evident along riparian corridors. They are Giant hogweed (*Heracleum mantegazzianum*), Japanese knotweed (*Fallopia japonica*) and Himalayan balsam (*Impatiens glandulifera*) (Plates 5, 6, and 7). All were introduced as ornamentals and have subsequently escaped from cultivation.

Japanese knotweed was introduced in 1825 and was naturalised by 1886 (Child and Wade, 2000). It is a clonal perennial, flowering but failing to produce viable seed under UK conditions. The plant is dioecious and only the female of a single clone appears to have been introduced. Despite failing to produce viable seed, it propagates by an extensive system of rhizomes. Although the stems die back in winter, the presence of a dense litter precludes other vegetation other than geophytes. Spread is most likely to occur through 'fly tipping' of rhizomes, the transporting of contaminated soil and inappropriate use of flails and strimmers.

It can regenerate from cut stems, which may also be further dispersed if deposited in waterways. Cultural control may suppress Japanese knotweed, but needs to continue for many years in order to prevent further rhizome regeneration. Chemical control options will be dictated by the location of the weeds; for only 2, 4-D amine and glyphosate may be applied in riparian habitats (Environment Agency, 1996). Elsewhere triclopyr, imazapyr and picloram provide alternative approaches, but have considerable persistency: six weeks, nine months and two years respectively.

Giant hogweed is a native of the Caucasus Mountains and was introduced as an ornamental in 1893 (Tiley *et al.*, 1996). Since then it has escaped from cultivation and invaded river valleys, particularly in South-eastern Scotland. It is a highly competitive forb attaining a height of up to five metres. It is a monocarpic species that dies after flowering and may take four years to flower, producing more than 50 000 seeds which may remain viable for fifteen years. Seeds are dispersed up to ten metres by wind and over much longer distances by water. Although the plant is undesirable because it is invasive and impairs public access to footpaths, it is also a noxious weed due to the furano-coumarins in its sap, which are highly photosensitising. In the presence of ultra-violet (UV) light, contact with human skin may result in severe blistering necessitating hospitalisation. Cultural control by strimming is strongly inadvisable without protective clothing. Cutting rarely provides effective control but will prevent seed production. As for chemical control, the choice of herbicide is dependent on location. Riparian infestations may be treated with glyphosate either as a spray or spot treatment. Otherwise tryclopyr may be used selectively in grassland or imazypyr for non-selective removal in non-cropped land.

Himalayan (or Indian) balsam, a native of western Himalayas, was introduced in 1839

(Beerling and Perrins, 1993). It is the tallest annual forb in the British Flora attaining a height of 2.5 m. Dispersal involves a ballistic mechanism of seed dissemination. It produces about 800 seeds per plant, which rarely persist more than twelve months in the soil seedbank. Unlike giant hogweed, it is frost sensitive. Cultural control may be achieved by cutting before the end of June (prior to flowering and seed set) but too early a defoliation will facilitate regrowth and flowering. Chemical weed control may be achieved with glyphosate either as a spray or as a weed wipe in areas of conservation value.

Weed control in aquatic vegetation

It has been estimated that there are in excess of 2400 km of standing water (lakes and reservoirs) in England, Scotland and Wales; 30 800 km of river channels in England and Wales managed by the Environment Agency; 32 300 km of drainage ditches managed by the Internal Drainage Boards and 100 000 km managed by individual landowners, and 3200 km of canals managed by British Waterways.

Aquatic vegetation may prove a nuisance for recreational and leisure activities associated with waterways. Not only do weeds present a risk of flooding and interfere with irrigation and pumping systems, but they may also impede water flow, increase silting-up and so interfere with navigation, foul propellers, snag fishing lines and impair the suitability of the waterway for angling. In addition they can pose a health and safety risk through the growth of blue-green algal blooms in reservoirs. These result in the production of toxins and so deny access to the public for recreational water sports.

Uncontrolled algal blooms and weed mats may obscure the water surface posing a risk to both humans and animals alike. As with all large-scale weed management in amenity landscapes, a balance needs to be struck between the visual and functional qualities of the landscape in question and habitat conservation.

Weed problems associated with aquatic habitats may be considered in four categories: emergent,

sub-merged, floating and algal. Examples of the first three categories are common reed (*Typha latifolia*), mares-tail (*Hippurus vulgaris*) and duck-weeds (*Lemna* spp.). Their control may be achieved through mechanical (Fig. 6.3) chemical and biological means. Mechanical control includes the use of weed-cutting boats, but it is essential to remove cut vegetation to avoid de-oxygenation. On non-navigable stretches the use of tractor-mounted buckets and dredging may be practised, but may not be environmentally acceptable. Mechanical methods are not particularly suitable for algal problems, with the exception of filament-ous algae which form areas of blanket weed or cott.

The use of barley straw has been found to have a phytotoxic effect on algae and is applied to

Fig. 6.3 Aquatic weed control in a drainage channel using the 'Berkenheger Spider' weed cutting machine. (Photo: R.J. Froud-Williams)

Table 6.5 Herbicides approved for use in and near water.

Asulam	docks, bracken
2,4-D	emergent broad-leaved weeds
Dichlobenil	aquatic weeds
Diquat	floating weeds and algae
Fosamine	ammonium: woody weeds
Glyphosate	water-lilies, reeds and emergent weeds
Terbutryn	floating and emerged algae
Maleic hydrazide	grass suppression

reservoirs and lakes in the form of floating pontoons. Biological control through selective grazing by herbivorous fish may be suitable in contained water bodies such as lakes and reservoirs. Elsewhere in the world both fungal pathogens and phytophagous arthropods have been used to control aquatic weeds selectively.

Chemical control in or near water is problematic because of the risk of pollution and the need to prevent the movement of compounds within the waterway. This may be addressed through the use of formulations such as slow release granules, notably dichlobenil. In the UK only seven herbicides and one growth regulator are approved for use in or near water (Table 6.5), their application being possible by knap-sack, long-lance or boat-mounted sprayer. However, before herbicide use in or near water, the appropriate regulatory body must be consulted.

A number of alien aquatic plants have been introduced accidentally into the British Isles, often from aquatic nursery supplies. These include Australian stonecrop (*Crassula helmsii*), Parrots feather (*Myriophyllum aquaticum*) and Floating pennywort (*Hydrocotyle ranunculoides*). The latter is a highly invasive species introduced by the aquatic nursery trade during the 1980s. Mechanical control tends to release nutrients, enables regeneration and is detrimental to banksides. Of the approved herbicides, it is not susceptible to glyphosate in any of the permitted formulations and use of diquat is not considered sustainable, as it is only effective at high dose rates. At the time of writing use of diquat in or near water

has been rejected by the EU review of pesticides, although an appeal against this ruling is likely.

Weed control in ornamental plantings

The very nature of ornamental plantings is that for aesthetic purposes they often involve a mixture of species, each differing in their susceptibilities to the various herbicides registered for use in such situations. The diversity of plants (including annuals, biennials, herbaceous and woody perennials, bulbs and corms) presents particular difficulties for chemical weed control as the range of herbicides is very restricted: some were discovered more than forty years ago, including chlorpropham and pentanochlor.

There are exceptions, however: the relatively recent introduction cycloxydim (a graminicide) is registered for use on bulbs and corms, as well as having 'off label' approval for use in non-grassy amenity vegetation. Guidance on weed control in specific amenity plantings is provided in *The UK Pesticide Guide*.

Site preparation for planting

Decisions on pre-planting weed control need to be taken in response to assessment of the weed flora of the site, and the objectives of the planting. Where perennial weeds are absent or only represent a small percentage of the standing herbage, sufficient weed control may be achieved by cultivation. In most situations this will not be the case, and applications of glyphosate at four to six week intervals at some point between early summer and autumn are likely to be required.

In addition to weeds found on the site itself, the growing of ornamental plants in containers has contributed to the creation of an additional weed loading, for some weeds are readily dispersed by this type of nursery product. These include hairy bitter cress (*Cardamine hirsuta*) and groundsel (*Senecio vulgaris*). These weeds can generally be pulled off containers at planting but inevitably some plants survive or new plants develop from the seedbank within the planted container. Hairy bitter cress is susceptible to isoxaben, groundsel to napropamide, annual meadow-grass and smooth sow-thistle (*Sonchus oleraceus*) to a mixture of isoxaben + trifluralin. Serious consideration should be given to rejecting consignments of container grown nursery stock that are infested with these weeds.

Control of seedling weeds immediately post planting

Judicial selection of plant material, combined with sensible design, can achieve effective ground cover and so suppress weed emergence in the longer term. Immediately after planting a pulse of weed germination will always occur that must be controlled. This can be achieved most effectively by mulches of organic debris such as bark chips or by woven fabric sheets. Deterioration of these sheets through exposure to UV light can be reduced by a superficial covering of organic debris. These are, however, relatively expensive treatments and will not be options on all sites.

Control of established weeds later in the establishment period

When mulches are not available (and even when they are) some weeds will always establish and begin to spread. Given abundant skilled labour these can be managed by traditional means such as handpulling, although in the absence of a mulch layer, the disturbance associated with this practice will in itself simply lead to additional germination pulses. Where labour is not available, in woody ornamentals weeds can often be controlled at the end of first growing season by the overall application of selective herbicides (see Table 6.6). Infestations of perennial grasses, sedges and horsetails can be controlled in shrub plantings by an autumn application of the residual herbicide propyzamide; dichlobenil is more appropriate for control of perennial broad-leaved weeds. Not all woody plants tolerate dichlobenil, and an appropriate source of reference such as the *UK Pesticide Guide* must be consulted.

In established woody ornamentals, cleavers (*Galium aparine*) and field bindweed (*Convolvulus arvense*) may present a problem. Because of their growth habit it is generally difficult to apply foliage-absorbed herbicides without damaging the surrounding ornamentals. Application of oxadiazon as a granular formulation is useful, but care should be taken as not all ornamentals are equally tolerant.

Other problematic weeds that sooner or later invade ornamental plantings include couch grass (*Elymus repens*), cow parsley (*Anthriscus sylvestris*), docks (*Rumex* spp.), creeping thistle (*Cirsium arvense*), perennial sow-thistle (*Sonchus arvensis*) and stinging nettle (*Urtica dioica*). Some of these are effectively controlled by herbicides such as propyzamide and dichlobenil, but sometimes repeat spot applications of glyphosate are necessary.

Table 6.6 Examples of herbicides approved for use in ornamentals.

Herbicide	Bulbs/corms	Hardy ornamental nursery stock	Trees and shrubs
Bentazone	Yes	No	No
CIPC	Yes	No	No
Cyanazine	Yes	No	No
Diuron	No	Yes	Yes
Dichlobenil	No	Yes	Yes
Isoxaben	No	Yes	Yes
Metazachlor	No	Yes	No
Napropamide	No	No	Yes
Pentanochlor	Yes	Yes	No
Propyzamide	No	No	Yes
Oxadiazon	No	No	Yes

Selective control of weeds in herbaceous plantings is much more difficult, because in many cases there are close botanical relationships between the ornamental species and the invading weeds. Grass colonisation can however be very effectively controlled in herbaceous plantings that consist only of forbs (non-grasses) by overall applications of selective graminicides such as sethoxydim. Many of these uses of herbicides are however in the 'off label' category.

Total vegetation control

Non-selective herbicides may be used on paths and other hard surfaces. Typically, such treatments tend to be residual soil-acting herbicides providing prolonged weed control. Specifiers need to be careful when dealing with these situations; desirable woody vegetation may be rooting into areas onto which it is proposed to apply total herbicides, potentially leading to severe damage. Both atrazine and simazine were commonly used for total vegetation control on hard surfaces, but industrial and amenity use of these chemicals was withdrawn in September 1993. Other alternatives include dichlobenil and diuron (see Table 6.7), although use of the latter in amenity situations is restricted from the beginning of February until May. It is essential to be aware that there is greater risk of herbicide pollution from run-off from hard surfaces and care should be exercised not to spray over drains. Non-residual treatments are restricted to paraquat, glufosinate and glyphosate.

Non-chemical approaches for weed control on pathways include the use of path sweeping

Table 6.7 Examples of herbicides for total vegetation control.

Amitrole
Bromacil
Dichlobenil
Diuron
Glyphosate
Glufosinate ammonium
Imazapyr
Picloram
Sodium chlorate

machines equipped with contra rotating steel brushes. These are increasingly widely used, often in conjunction with applications of glyphosate to control perennial species. The economic cost associated with Japanese knotweed is of particular concern: the emerging shoots may seriously damage pavements and other hard surfaces. *Buddleja* spp., which are frequently associated with industrial sites, are also becoming a problem (Plate 8).

6.7 Future directions

The lack of financial gain from vegetation management on amenity land, coupled with the prohibitive cost of herbicide development and public anxiety regarding the use of agrochemicals, makes it likely that there will be a greater emphasis on non-chemical weed control methods in the future. There has already been a commercial patent to utilise steam and infrared radiation for non-selective weed control in urban areas. It is likely that more attention will be given to the use of natural products and biological agents for weed control, particularly where conservation issues are foremost. Invasive alien species such as Japanese knotweed are potential candidates for such an approach.

An increased reliance on non-chemical methods is becoming evident; a mechanical weed puller suitable for removing tall growing weeds has been introduced commercially. The demand for cut flowers, herbaceous and woody ornamentals and high quality sports turf continues to increase, and is likely to increase pressure for new developments in weed control in these economically attractive sectors of the industry. Some of these in time may feed through into the amenity sector.

References

Beerling, D.J. & Perrins, J.M. (1993) Biological Flora of the British Isles. No.177: Impatiens glandulifera Royle (Impatiens roylei Walp) *Journal of Ecology*, **81**, 367–82.
Child, L.E. & Wade, P.M. (2000) *The Japanese Knotweed Manual*. Packard Publishing Ltd, Chichester, UK.

Crop Protection Association (2001) *Amenity Handbook: a guide to the selection and use of amenity pesticides*. Crop Protection Association, Peterborough, UK.

Environment Agency (1996) *Guidance for the control of invasive plants near watercourses*. Environment Agency.

Hitchmough, J.D. (1994) Minimising herbicide use. *The Horticulturist*. 3, (3), 2–8.

Tiley, G.E.D., Dodd, F.S. & Wade, P.M. (1996) Biological Flora of the British Isles No.190. Heracleum mantegazzianum Sommier & Levier. *Journal of Ecology*, 84, 297–319.

Whitehead, R. (2003) *The UK Pesticide Guide 2003*. CABI Publishing, Wallingford, Oxon.

Further reading

Anon (1996) *Using Pesticides: a complete guide to safe effective spraying*. British Crop Protection Council.

Davison, J.G. (1983) Effective weed control in amenity plantings. *Scientific Horticulture*, 34, 28–34.

Hance, R. & Holly, K. (Eds) (1989) *Weed Control Handbook. Principles*, 8th Edn. Blackwell, Oxford.

7 The Long-term Health of Plants

Tony Kendle

Plant health problems can arise at any time and can affect most species. There are vast numbers of pests and diseases that can attack; this is shown by even a brief look through any of the available pest and disease textbooks(such as Buczacki and Harris, 1998). However, most of these problems are uncommon, and attacks can be seen as really little more than bad luck. Identification of the problem may satisfy curiosity – but it rarely allows us to find a remedy and almost never helps in future strategic planning.

Some diseases are of course encountered quite commonly. Amateur gardeners are sometimes able to put in the effort required to nurse ailing plants – in fact at times success against all odds becomes part of the fun. But when health problems are regular and recurrent, landscape professionals normally use a highly flexible strategy: they avoid disease-susceptible plants. This is one of the key criteria for plant selection – we rely on plants that are robust, and when a pathogen (an organism like bacteria, fungus or a virus that causes disease) begins to be seen with regularity, the plant soon disappears from new designs. An example is groundcover juniper, which was used much less widely once *Phytophthora* root rot attacks became widespread (Plate 9).

Many very damaging pests and disease outbreaks are not random events, but are linked with environmental conditions. Such health issues manifest themselves as pathogen attacks, but in fact reflect other problems, such as poor site conditions or plant material handling. This means that specifications and sound cultural techniques can be used to reduce the likelihood of such attacks recurring.

7.1 Quality of supply

There are many problems that can arise, depending on where and how plants are purchased. Nurseries can of course sell a wide range of different diseases with their stock and anyone can be unlucky at some time, but there are two sources of problems that are common enough to merit more detailed discussion.

Water-borne fungal infections

Firstly, there are some diseases that become endemic within nurseries due to their growing methods. The most typical are those with water-borne fungal spores such as *Phytophthora* that can build up in irrigation systems – especially where water is recycled and not adequately treated. These spores are sometimes present in the growing media of containerised plants and can lead to infection later on site, particularly if planting takes place in wet conditions.

It is easy enough to identify the problem, but solving it can be difficult. Landscape professionals can write a clause in a specification which demands that plants are healthy, but infection may not be apparent until the plant is on-site and liability is difficult to prove at this stage. It is probably better to develop a select list of known and trusted suppliers, and to pay attention to effective site drainage – especially when working on heavy soils. Susceptible species are best avoided on such sites.

Imported soil ecosystems

The second problem that is starting to appear is more subtle, and relates especially to field-grown specimens imported from overseas. Movement of plants with associated soil has become much easier with changes in European Union regulations that favour a single open market. In the United Kingdom, we are now able freely to import root-balled or containerised field-grown plants from other EU countries (Fig. 7.1).

DEFRA does of course have a system that safeguards against the uncontrolled movement of pests and diseases – the plant passports scheme – but evidence is accumulating that these controls do not (and could not be expected to) deal effectively with the full range of problems that may be imported when large blocks of a 'foreign field' are brought into the UK. These soil balls are complex ecosystems that teem with thousands of organisms, impossible to test. The same is of course true when we move any root-balled plant, even if it is only travelling between counties not countries. However for imported plants, we are faced with a range of organisms that are not typical or indigenous to the region, and any outbreaks are more likely to attract concern because of this. Again solutions are not easy to find, but the situation

Fig. 7.1 'Exotic' nursery stock such as palms are increasingly imported from Northern Italy and used in landscape schemes. (Photo: James Hitchmough)

needs monitoring. Imported stock may not always be the great value that it seems.

Another aspect of stock origin that is often discussed is the idea of buying from nurseries that grow plants in stressed conditions, in the belief that they are tougher or 'more hardy'. The actual evidence that this is true is slim, while there is an unquestioned relationship between stress and disease – particularly with regard to insect attack. Nurseries that grow plants under difficult conditions may actually be pre-disposing them to disease.

Of course it is well known that excessively soft growth is more susceptible to winter cold or fungal attack, but to avoid this the most important thing is for nurseries not to force plant growth late into the growing season. This means they should not fertilise with large doses of nitrogen late in the summer, and they should remove plants from protected tunnels or glasshouses early enough for them to harden off in late summer. A specification clause that the plant material must be adequately hardy will give some opportunity for recompense, but the best way of avoiding the problem is by working with nurseries that you trust.

An area that has received relatively little attention is the relationship between nursery root development and subsequent tree health and vigour. New container designs, such as spring-rings, offer the potential to avoid problems like root spiralling, and may be fundamentally important for species prone to the problem (see Chapter 10). However there are costs to nurseries that use such containers, and the benefits do not materialise until some time after planting. Landscape professionals need to be prepared to specify these container types and to pay extra for them.

7.2 Quality of handling

There are various ways in which poor handling can affect plant health. Well-recognised issues are root desiccation on bare-root stock, and high or low temperature damage to roots if the plants are packaged and stored incorrectly. Most reputable nurseries will implement handling and storage systems to reduce such risks.

More problematic can be simple rough handling, that has been shown by research to increase the likelihood of pathogen attack on bare-root trees. This handling damage can easily happen in transit, and even good nurseries may have a poor delivery driver. Inspect the stock at arrival and, if time allows, reject stock that shows many broken roots and shoots. It may be worth a clause in the specification that requires contractors to trim the damaged areas of plants.

7.3 Site characteristics

For 'trouble-free' taxa normally used in landscape plantings, the vast majority of disease problems that arise do so because of site conditions. The stresses caused by problems such as poor drainage or poor nutrition are rarely sufficient to cause plant death directly: the failure is 'caused' by pathogenic infection. The most common problem is compaction from mishandled soil – leading to poor soil structure, impeded rooting, poor drainage and low aeration. The risks are highest on heavy soils that need good structure to perform well.

Mishandling and quality deterioration often occur during lifting, storing or re-spreading. Where there is the option to specify imported soil, it is wise to select soil texture classes that do not depend on good structure in order to drain: specifically sandy loams. When soils are to remain in situ and can be damaged by heavy traffic, then it is worth taking every precaution to prevent structural collapse, such as specifying low ground pressure vehicles and above all restricting site traffic to a minimum.

Because structural problems occur at or close to the surface of the soil, it can be possible to see waterlogging even when a subsurface drainage system has been installed. Remedial actions therefore include the use of surface drainage techniques, such as sloping and mounding the site, together with ripping. On heavy soil, it may again be worth anticipating the problem by using a design that incorporates surface falls to drains or soakaways.

7.4 Soil ameliorants

Adding organic ameliorants to the surface of the soil will have no effect if barriers to the downward movement of water are not resolved. Decomposing organic matter in wet soils may in fact increase the risk of oxygen shortage, or even susceptibility to disease.

In general there are some potential health issues to consider regarding the use of organic ameliorants. For example, there are some concerns that the use of uncomposted wood chips – particularly those that have been 'home made' using a shredder – may be a possible means of spreading *Armillaria* (honey fungus) or other fungal problems. In practice, examples seem to be rare, relative to the amount of woodchip used.

One factor that may be important in determining the expression of *Armillaria* is the size of the woodchip particles. The risk is greater with large particles that can act as a food reservoir for the disease. It may also be less likely that the disease will spread if the site is dry and the woodchip is not incorporated into the soil, but there is no research to confirm this.

7.5 Soil problems

Soil chemical extremes, such as nutrient deficiencies, pH and even contamination, can also lead to plant performance problems. For imported soils, keeping to the specifications of the British Standard BS 3882 will provide for adequate quality.

In situ soils are potentially more problematic; for remedial options for different extremes see Chapter 4. If the site soil has a suspect history or departs radically from the parameters of BS 3882, it would be worth seeking specialist advice.

7.6 Regional susceptibility

Although the British Isles is a small landmass, its geographical regions have markedly different weather. Even a cursory glance at a crop distribution map will show striking regional differences, often based on disease susceptibility influenced by local weather. The same risks hold good for ornamental plants: for example, decorative *Malus* and *Prunus* are as disappointing as the commercial fruit species in the South-West, because of wet weather and high-humidity-linked diseases. Many landscape designers find themselves working far away from the areas they know best. It is always advisable to check with local experience as to what does best under local conditions.

7.7   Strategic planning

For the most strategic approach to landscape disease control, it is worth considering the implications of plant choice and planting pattern on the regional likelihood of disease spread. It has often been suggested that the selection of a genetically diverse population of plants is an important disease prevention strategy, whereas reliance on a few clones makes the rapid spread of infection more likely. This principle is accepted for crops by those who are interested in low-input or organic systems, but the evidence supporting this idea on a landscape scale is weak.

There may have been greater susceptibility of elm to Dutch elm disease because the plant spreads vegetatively and was actually largely clonal. Nevertheless, many clearly genetically distinct forms were destroyed. Certainly other major epidemic tree disease problems that have struck in the UK in recent years have attacked or threatened widespread populations of genetically diverse native plants. Conversely there are some ornamental plants that have existed in the country as limited clonal forms for centuries and that remain robustly healthy. The reality is that we have a very poor understanding of how much diversity is enough to prevent disease epidemics. We also rarely have the information for strategic choices of plant material on a regional scale, although some local authorities have adopted policies that avoid over-reliance on a few species in street tree plantings.

Nevertheless, the concept seems logical and there is a good argument for a precautionary approach, and therefore for using a wide range of varieties. The problem in landscape work is that we actually use very few taxa, because we trust very few taxa to be disease resistant. This is a Catch-22 of professional landscape work: by reducing short-term disease risks we may be increasing the chance of long-term problems.

References

Buczacki, S. & Harris, K. (1998) *Pests, Diseases and Disorders of Garden Plants*, 2nd edn, HarperCollins, London.

BSI (1994) BS 3882 *Specification for topsoils*. British Standards Institute, London.

III Establishment and Management of Trees

8 Establishment of Planted Nursery Stock

James Hitchmough

This chapter deals with maximising the successful establishment of transplanted nursery stock through the use of effective planting practices and post planting weed management. Although many of these inputs might appear to be essentially matters of common sense, it is all too common to find that transplanted stock establishes poorly or even fails because these issues are neglected. To help landscape practitioners develop greater understanding of the factors underlying effective establishment specification, the research evidence behind many widely used horticultural techniques is reviewed. This chapter should be read in conjunction with Chapter 4, 'Amelioration of Underperforming Soils' and other chapters dealing with specific plant types.

The alternative to planting nursery grown stock is direct seeding. This is taken for granted for lawns and the selection, sowing and cultivation of grass seed is covered in Chapter 26. Forbs (herbaceous plants other than grasses) can be sown with grasses to establish flowering meadows (Chapter 22) or annuals can be sown instead of bedding plants (Chapter 23). Woodlands and scrub can also be established by sowing tree and shrub seed directly onto a landscape site. The technique is not covered here in detail, however sources of further information are identified.

For thousands of years, woodlands have been established and re-established by seeding to speed up natural regeneration for forestry and a timber crop. Direct seeding to establish woodlands primarily for amenity and wildlife is more recent. Robinson (1911) describes the establishment of oakwoods at Gravetye by sowing acorns. Direct

seeding was used in Germany and the United States on sites without topsoil (Neef, 1976; Plas, 1976). In the 1980s the technique was developed in Britain for topsoil sites (where weed control is fundamental to success) (La Dell, 1983, 1987 and 1988; Putwain, 1998) and quite large tracts of woodland were established (Figs 8.1, 8.2). The design of a direct seeding scheme is specific for each site and the desired type of woodland or scrub. Both the ecological and horticultural requirements have to be understood for a scheme to be a success. The sowing techniques are based on simple adaptations of agricultural equipment.

The use of direct seeding did not become widespread as it was often misapplied; the Forestry Commission reported some problems in using it to establish commercial forestry crops. There is renewed interest by the Commission, ecologists and others in the technique for the establishment of natural and diverse woodlands for amenity and wildlife. The development of equally sophisticated and effective techniques for direct seeding woody species on an extensive scale is discussed in relation to South Eastern Australia by Hitchmough (1994) (Fig. 8.3).

8.1 Planting practices

Timing of planting

This is typically determined by the form of nursery production and the degree of root damage, but often by contractual and other abiotic factors. Despite these outside pressures, it is important to do everything possible to avoid planting at times

Fig. 8.1 Maturing oak wood; tree and shrub seed sown in 1980. (Photo: Tom La Dell)

Fig. 8.2 (*below*) Alder Carr, seed sown in 1978. One of the parent alders is shown in the foreground. (Photo: Tom La Dell)

when it is biologically undesirable to do so. Decisions on planting time require a good understanding of local conditions, as these have an overriding influence on the outcomes.

Container and containerised stock

These can be planted in any month of the year, although the best establishment generally results when this is undertaken during the cooler months of the year. During the warmer months keeping the root balls of planted stock supplied with water whilst the roots colonise the surrounding soil is more maintenance intensive. This is particularly so with stock grown in peat-bark composts, which shrink and become hydrophobic on drying out.

Autumn is generally the optimal time for planting most species: autumn soil temperatures are usually high enough for some root establishment before severe moisture stress is encountered in late spring. Whitcomb (1987) found six out of seven

Fig. 8.3 A sophisticated direct seeding machine for establishing large areas of new woodland or shelter belts. A herbicide nozzle on the front of the machine sprays out a band of turf, a coulter cuts a sowing slit into which seed is delivered at a predetermined rate, which is then closed by a rear pressure wheel. This technology is widely and successfully used in Australia. (Photo: James Hitchmough)

species of evergreen and deciduous shrubs and trees investigated had made significant root growth by the spring, following an autumn planting. An earlier study (Whitcomb, 1984) found that the capacity to survive a dry summer without irrigation was significantly greater for nursery stock planted in autumn as opposed to spring. Autumn planting was least beneficial in the case of extremely drought tolerant species. On sites prone to waterlogging during the winter, and with species that typically make some growth during this period, root systems may be severely damaged before the onset of spring, and planting at the latter time may prove more successful. Soil deoxygenation is most damaging to root systems that are growing actively and have a high oxygen requirement (Kozlowski, 1985).

In cold areas, frost-sensitive species are best planted in spring to allow a full growing season to elapse before they are exposed to potentially lethal temperatures. Cold tolerance increases with age in many woody plants (Larcher, 1983), and the most

cold sensitive parts (the leaf canopy) grow out of the layers of air closest to the ground.

Bare-root and root-balled stock

In these types of nursery stock, the extent of root damage and resulting water balance difficulties largely restricts planting to the autumn to early spring period. In North America there has been considerable research into the optimal time for planting this stock during the dormant season (Watson, 1986a; Whitcomb, 1987; Witherspoon and Lumis, 1986). Because of low winter soil temperatures in the USA, most of these studies involve comparisons of autumn and spring. The results are sometimes contradictory, and suggest that responses are species and climate specific. After five years growth, Watson (1986a) found no difference between advanced trees planted in spring, summer or autumn.

Better performance in a particular season seems to relate strongly to carbohydrate storage and mobilisation patterns at the time that the roots were severed for lifting. In deciduous species carbohydrate levels in the roots decline in spring as leaf buds begin to open, restricting carbohydrate availability for root development (Witherspoon and Lumis, 1986). This suggests spring is not an optimal time for planting. In the maritime climate of Britain, autumn-planted *Betula pendula* and *Acer pseudoplatanus* had made twice as much root growth by leaf expansion, as had spring-planted stock (Gilbertson *et al.*, 1987). The increasing winter coldstorage of autumn lifted bare-root stock may influence these responses. Stock treated thus and planted in spring may contain higher levels of stored carbohydrate than similar stock lifted from the nursery row in spring and then replanted in the landscape.

Planting hole construction

On extensively cultivated/amended soils, planting is largely a question of making a hole large enough to accommodate the root system. Planting hole characteristics are most critical when pit planting advanced trees in paved streets on clay soils where the surrounding soil cannot be cultivated or amended prior to planting. The discussion that follows primarily refers to these difficult situations.

In traditional decorative horticulture, planting hole construction has often been directed towards depth, rather than width. The realisation that woody plant root growth in soils is primarily horizontal and close to the surface (Perry, 1982) has led to a reappraisal, and to the use of relatively shallow, broad holes (Watson, 1986b). On uncultivated soils the purpose of hole construction should be to produce a well-aerated, non-compacted ring of soil into which plant roots can readily elongate. On sites prone to waterlogging, cultivation of the soil beneath the root ball is counterproductive as this frequently becomes a sump due to the large soil pores that result. Planting holes on non-cultivated sites should ideally be two to three times the diameter of the root ball, and no deeper than the root ball. Where the soil beneath this is smeared or compacted, fracturing of this layer in situ with a fork may be useful. Watson suggests that on soils prone to severe spring waterlogging, trees perform better when planted on gently contoured mounds 10–20 cm above original ground level.

Glazed or smeared planting hole walls can reduce the number of roots which grow from the planting hole backfill into the surrounding uncultivated soil (Table 8.1). Observation suggests that some species are more able to do this than others. High vigour species appear most successful.

On clay-based soils the most appropriate tools for hole construction are spades and forks, the latter being desirable on heavy clay soils. Large planting holes for advanced trees can be dug by mechanical bucket excavators providing that on wet clay soils the walls of the holes are then loosened with a fork prior to planting. On sandy and silty soils these interface problems are generally far less significant.

Planting

Planting is the most critical event in the life of nursery stock, and attention to detail is important to maximise the chances of successful establishment.

Container-grown and containerised

It is particularly important to soak the root balls in preparation for planting when container stock is in soil-less composts that shrink and become hydrophobic on drying. Stock planted with dry root balls is extremely difficult to re-wet in situ, even with irrigation, and will suffer severe moisture stress or even death. In overmature container stock grown in soil-less media, the only reliable means of wetting the root ball is to immerse the containers for several hours in a shallow temporary water bath constructed on site with sleepers and heavy duty polythene. These practices are particular critical for container stock planted between late spring to autumn. Where pre-soaking and subsequent irrigation is not possible, planting container stock during the warmer months in the drier parts of Britain often leads to poor establishment and even death.

The exterior of container-grown root balls may be roughened to ensure some roots are in direct contact with backfill. As with many transplanting issues this appears to be a worthwhile input, but there is little scientific evidence to confirm this (Gilman, 1990). Roughening is sometimes recommended as a means of increasing root ball surface area in contact with the surrounding moist soil. However as water movement is nearly always from root ball to the finer textured backfill this practice is questionable.

Traditional horticultural 'good practice' dictates

Table 8.1 Influence of smearing of planting hole walls on root escape into the surrounding soil (adapted from Nicolosi and Fretz, 1980).

Treatment	Number of roots per core of soil
Wall of planting hole loosened prior to backfilling	3.3
Wall of planting hole smeared at backfilling	1.2

that the top of the root ball is placed at the same level as the finished soil surface. Under most soil conditions this specification is highly satisfactory. On poorly drained, compacted soils researchers (Ruark et al., 1982; Watson, 1986b) have shown that tree establishment may be improved on poorly drained, compacted soils by planting on low mounds or even allowing the top few centimetres of the root ball to project above finished soil level (Watson, 1986b). These practices increase soil oxygen levels in the root ball, but also increase the risk of desiccation, and are most effective when combined with coarse organic mulches to reduce the latter risk.

On soils subject to marked soil moisture stress, planting slightly below the finished soil grade is sometimes practised. Saucer planting is useful on soils that have low infiltration rates, are hydrophobic when dry, and where effective capture of precipitation is important. Saucers should be shallow, and used with discretion when dealing with species naturally found on well drained soils when planted on clay soils, in climates with seasonally high rainfall.

On clay soils, deeply-planted container stock may suffer unnecessary moisture stress. Water cannot move from the narrow pores in the clay backfill overlying the root ball, into the large pores of the container root ball, until the soil is saturated. This leads to plants experiencing severe moisture stress even after irrigation or rainfall. On well-drained soils, deep planting of container stock is less disadvantageous, but as a general principle is best avoided.

Root-balled stock

Much of the discussion on planting container-grown stock is relevant to root-balled stock. Root ball collapse during planting is a practical hazard with this type of stock, and deliberate roughening of the root ball is undesirable. To minimise risk of ball disintegration, only the burlap on the base of the root ball is cut away prior to planting. Plants are then planted and when surrounded by lightly firmed backfill, the remaining burlap is cut away from the root collar and pulled out from around the walls of the partly-buried root ball. Hessian (but not polypropylene) burlap rots fairly quickly in moist soil but as it may present a short-term barrier to root elongation (for example, where doubled over) it is best removed whenever possible.

Planting bare-root stock

Woody plants

Most of the principles and practices of planting bare-root stock are similar to those employed with container-grown stock. It is most important that root systems, and fine textured root systems in particular, are not exposed to drying air prior to planting. Root initiation largely occurs from or immediately adjacent to the cut surfaces of roots (Watson and Himelick, 1982). Planting holes for such stock should be sufficiently wide to ensure that these new roots do not immediately encounter a wall of uncultivated, potentially compacted, and poorly oxygenated soil.

Given the three-dimensional form of the root system of larger bare-root trees and shrubs, care is required when backfilling to ensure adequate root-soil contact. Backfilling in stages is a good practice, followed by a light shaking of the plant and light firming to settle soil between the roots with larger bare-root stock. This is often difficult to achieve on wet, compacted clay soils. In the case of small one or two-year-old bare-root trees and shrubs, this procedure can generally be reduced to one cycle. Much less care is required with the spatially less complex roots of transplants such as 1 + 1s and whips.

Herbaceous plants

In contrast to woody plants, the bulk of herbaceous plants are best planted slightly deeper than they were growing in the nursery. There is a tendency in many herbaceous plants for the overwintering vegetative buds to gradually ascend the basal stem as the plants age, and in doing so 'grow out' of the ground. In some cases deeper planting seems to encourage the re-invigoration of the plants, and does not appear to cause the deoxygenation problems it might in trees or shrubs; in herbaceous species the root systems quickly adjust to the new conditions.

There are exceptions to the deeper planting principle. *Iris × germanica* cultivars perform better when the rhizomes are exposed to sunlight. Herbs which overwinter as leafy buds or evergreen leaf rosettes are often sensitive to deep planting and frequently die if these photosynthetic structures are covered by soil or deep mulches.

Bulbous plants (bulbs, corms and tubers)

These plants need to be placed in the soil at an appropriate depth. A useful rule of thumb is to plant at depths of two to three times the diameter of the bulb. On heavy soils bulbs are planted more shallowly, and on light soils more deeply. In most cases this works acceptably well, even though within their natural habitats it is not uncommon to find small bulbs placed very deeply in the soil, even on heavy clay (Rix, 1983). When in doubt plant shallowly, as the worst that is likely to happen is that the flower stems will fall over due to the lack of basal support. Some species have contractile roots that pull the bulbs down into the soil.

Bulbous plants are sensitive to polarity and must be planted with the apex of the bulb, corm or tuber facing upwards or at least not downwards. With some species the top is not always obvious, in which case bulbs should be planted on what appears to be their side. Planting is discussed further in Chapter 24.

Backfilling

In most cases the most appropriate backfill for newly planted stock is the soil excavated from the planting hole. Where the excavated soil is heavily compacted, any clods should be broken up with a fork or similar implement prior to backfilling, to ensure the root ball is surrounded by an oxygenated, root penetrable substrate.

Pit planted trees are often specified as requiring amendment backfills with composted bark, green waste or similar. Whitcomb (1987) found that peat and other organic amendments to clay and sandy soils of average-to-good physical condition were generally not advantageous. Whitcomb has suggested that the reason for this is that the direction of water movement in unsaturated soils is from coarse textured substrates (the amended backfill soil) into finer textured soils (the unamended soil surrounding the planting hole). This could lead to plants in the amended backfills experiencing more moisture stress than those in unamended backfills. Nelms and Spomer (1983) estimate that soilless container media lose up to 85 per cent of their available water a few hours after transplanting, as a result of particle size gradients and evapotranspiration. Peat and similar materials in backfills may act as a wick and remove water by evaporation.

In a study of the establishment of bare-root deciduous trees, Davies (1987a) found that backfills amended to varying percentages with peat were beneficial at one site, detrimental at another and had no effect either way at a third. Rootballed stock would seem to be the least likely to be adversely affected by amended backfills; in some cases the texture of the soil root ball may be finer than the surrounding soil, leading to a simultaneous movement of water out of the backfill into the root ball and into the surrounding unamended soil.

Carnell and Anderson (1986) found that there was no improvement in the oxygenation of tree planting pits in heavy clay soils following backfill amendment with peat. Additional organic matter can also contribute significantly to local soil deoxygenation (in the short term) by virtue of the oxygen consumed by decomposer microorganisms (Kopinga, 1985).

Organic amendments are likely to be most useful on extremely coarse, highly-oxygenated soils such as brick rubble, where water unavailability is a dominant cause of poor establishment. In old slate quarries, vegetation establishment is greatly facilitated by pumping of organic slurries into the pore space between the massive slate particles (Bradshaw and Chadwick, 1980). On machine-destroyed clay soils, there is often no alternative but to add organic materials in an attempt to produce a material that has capacity to drain and allow root penetration. The other materials that are sometimes added to backfills are the high molecular weight polymers collectively referred to as superabsorbents. These materials are strongly hygroscopic and when mixed with water swell up into gels that hold, at low tensions, many times their own weight in water. The literature of superabsorbents as backfill amendments is contradictory, with some research showing significant benefits (Callaghan *et al.*, 1989) while other studies (Hummel and Johnson, 1985; Davies, 1987b) show no significant effects.

Until unequivocal evidence of the efficacy of planting hole amendments in the field is available, they are probably best avoided in all but the most hostile of planting environments; resources should transferred to more proven means of reducing establishment moisture stress, such as weed control and mulching.

Once the backfill is replaced it should be lightly firmed to ensure good physical contact between the root mass and the surrounding soil, to minimise drying out of the root ball through evaporation, and restrict wind rocking. Firming must not be excessive or the resulting localised compaction and poor aeration may have detrimental effects on root establishment. The wetter the soil at the time of planting the less the soil should be firmed, especially in clay soils.

When planting takes place between spring and autumn the backfilling process is ideally completed by watering in the stock. Landscape practice and scientific studies (for example Clemens and Radford, 1985) support the importance of this activity, especially with container grown stock which is prone to desiccation before the roots can colonise the backfill. The volume of water applied should be related to root ball size, with five litres the minimum per plant for stock in half to one litre pots. On sites where watering immediately after planting is not feasible, great care must be taken in the timing of operations to ensure a high likelihood of rain in the week following planting, and root balls must be soaked thoroughly before planting.

8.2 Staking and tree protection

This is generally only necessary with advanced trees, although freestanding stakes may indirectly aid the establishment of smaller stock in urban grasslands by reducing mower damage. It is well established that staking woody plants increases the height to girth ratio, leading to trees that are tall and thin, and inclined to be less stable following stake removal (Jacobs, 1954; Harris and Hamilton, 1969; Harris *et al.*, 1972; Patch, 1987). It is also suspected that staking restricts the thickening of tree roots (Fayle, 1968). Despite this, staking is still required for advanced trees to provide initial support until the roots colonise the surrounding soil. This support is particularly important in situations where trees are subjected to a high level of contact with the public. To minimise the adverse effects of staking, trees should be staked at or below one third of their height and the ties and stakes removed after one year whenever possible. Staking of advanced trees is discussed further in Chapter 10.

Plastic treeshelters have become a standard specification item on many urban fringe and rural tree and shrub plantings. They can improve survival and early growth rates (Potter, 1991), but they represent a substantial cost and local knowledge is often required to assess whether they are absolutely necessary. Where browsing and grazing is unlikely to be intense, the funds that might be used to supply treeshelters may be more effectively employed on improving weed control around young trees. Kerr (1995) points out that tree shelters do not remove the need for weed control.

8.3 Control of weeds around newly planted nursery stock

In establishing vegetation, the main reason for controlling weeds is that they compete for resources with the desirable plants, leading to a reduction in growth or even death in newly-planted stock. Weed control is one of the most important, if not the most important of inputs into the establishment of landscape vegetation.

Competition from weeds involves the following resources.

Water

Due to their rapid growth rates weeds are generally extremely effective at utilising supplies of soil moisture. Water is taken up from a soil surface covered in weeds at approximately two to three times the rate of water loss from a bare soil surface (Winter, 1974). The ensuing moisture stress increases the frequency of stomatal closure in the planted species, leading to dramatic reductions in photosynthesis and growth (Davies, 1987a).

Mineral nutrients

Given their high growth rates and capacity to utilise soil water, weeds are very efficient competitors for mineral nutrients and in particular nitrogen. In agricultural situations weeds have been shown to be capable of capturing twice as much nitrogen from a soil than the planted crop (Hewson and Roberts, 1973). Fales and Wakefield (1981) found that turf grasses significantly reduce nitrogen levels in the tissues of establishing woody plants.

Light and physical space

The abundant growth that weeds produce can cast damaging shade on vegetation that requires high light levels. The damage, while potentially serious, is only a short-term problem with trees and other tall-growing plants. With low-growing plants such as prostrate and semi-prostrate ground cover species, weeds constitute a continual threat to survival.

Allelopathic interactions

Allelopathy is the phenomenon whereby biologically active chemical compounds are liberated from plant parts into the soil. These chemical compounds may be damaging either to the plants themselves, their offspring (seedlings germinating around the parent plant), or other species of plants adjacent to the alleopathic species.

Studies into the affect of mown turf on the growth of newly-planted trees and shrubs (Fales and Wakefield, 1981) show that even when the soil profile is maintained at field capacity and nutrients are not limiting, significant growth depression still occurs, compared with the same species under turf-free conditions. Walters and Gilmore (1976) found that leachate resulting from dripping water through *Festuca* leaf litter reduced the growth of *Liquidambar styraciflua* seedlings by 60 per cent. Smith *et al.* (2001) found similar responses in hickories, *Carya* spp.

Growth increases in establishing trees and shrubs where there is a programme of post planting weed control are commonly in the range of 150 to 400 per cent (Fig. 8.4, (a) and (b)). Actual data from a range of weed control studies are shown in Table 8.2.

Factors influencing the severity of competition

The degree of growth reduction in planted species varies according to:

- the characteristics of the weeds,
- characteristics of the planted vegetation,
- timing of competition,
- size of the weed-free area, and
- the effect of other plant husbandry practices.

Characteristics of the weeds

Species that grow rapidly are potentially highly competitive. Competitive capacity is particularly high in annual species and herbaceous species in general. It is generally lowest in woody species, although in time the stature of many woody plants and their capacity to shade lower growing plants compensates for this lack of fundamental competitiveness.

Competitive capacity is also influenced by the time of the year and by the stage of growth of both weeds and desirable plants. In the absence of allelopathic effects, weeds exert little competition when dormant, especially if this involves a period of leaflessness. A more subtle interaction is that of

(a)   (b)

Fig. 8.4 The effect of weed competition on the first-year growth of birch transplants: (a) shows a typical seedling grown without weed control; (b) shows the same, with weed control from spring to mid-summer. (Photo: James Hitchmough)

Table 8.2 Effect of weed control on the post planting growth of a number of woody species.

Planted species	Growth increases as a % of weedy controls				Years post planting at which assessed	Reference
	Height	Girth	Basal area as m²/ha	Total branch length		
Cornus florida	–	125	–	–	1.5	Fales and Wakefield 1981
Forsythia spp.	–	–	–	927	2	Fales and Wakefield 1981
Pinus radiata	172	–	522	–	7	Cromer _et al._ 1977

mown and unmown turf with newly planted trees. Despite the fact that a large number of authors (Fales and Wakefield, 1981; Ryan and Lewty, 1984; Insley and Buckley, 1986; Davies, 1987a) have shown that mown turf grass has a significant depressant effect on growth in newly planted trees and shrubs, many landscape practitioners continue to believe that regular mowing largely alleviates any adverse effects. Mown turf does have a smaller root and shoot volume than unmown turf, but in terms of water use this is more than compensated for by the presence of actively growing leaves and tillers in the former. Unmown turf tends to become reproductive and produces flowering culms at the expense of rapidly transpiring vegetative growth. At the species level, grasses (and presumably other herbaceous taxa) vary in their capacity to utilise soil water. Lombard *et al.* (1988) found that daily water consumption to be 2.5 mm per day in *Festuca rubra* var. *commutata* and 3.0 mm/day in *Lolium perenne* 'Derby'.

Woody and herbaceous ornamental ground covers also compete for resources with newly-planted trees and shrubs. Given the relatively low growth rates of the predominantly woody plants involved, they are however generally far less damaging than herbaceous weeds or turf (Shoup and Whitcomb, 1981).

Characteristics of the planted vegetation

Few studies have examined the relationships between planted vegetation of varying vigour and the growth depressant effects of weeds. Observation suggests that vigorous planting stock has greater capacity to compete with adjacent weeds. Vigour in planting stock has both a genotypic and phenotypic base. *Platanus* and *Populus* are inherently more vigorous than most *Fagus* and *Quercus*. These observations are broadly supported by growth rate data (Jarvis and Jarvis, 1964). Overlying these genotypic differentials in vigour is the phenotypic nature of the plant as determined by nursery practice and the environment of the planting site.

Young, vigorous planting stock of inherently vigorous species, well suited to the environment of the planting site, are likely to have the highest capacity to tolerate weed competition. Stressed plants of semi-mature nursery stock, of species that are naturally slow growing, or made so by poor environmental fit, are likely to be the most adversely effected.

Timing of competition

Weed competition is most damaging when it occurs at a time when supplies of a resource are becoming limited. For example, competition for water is likely to be least damaging during the winter months when rainfall is often abundant and evaporation is low. As transpiration increases in spring, supplies of water will become limiting and competition for this resource increasingly intense. The water demands of desirable and weed species are likely to be greatest during periods of active extension growth. It is likely that competition during these growth flushes is particularly critical. Competition for resources between active growth flushes may of course affect later growth flushes by causing a stress-induced physiological check.

In planted woody nursery stock, the critical time for competition is the first growing season after planting (Ryan and Lewty, 1984). During this time transplanted stock generally needs to redress root: shoot ratios that are generally inappropriate for the planting site. The photosynthesis necessary to do this is seriously restricted by the presence of weeds. Within the first growing season, the critical time for weed control is often the first three months.

For trees and shrubs planted in mown turf, whether weed control needs to continue beyond this initial period to achieve maximum or at least significant benefits, depends very much on the objectives of the planting. Many of the longer-term studies on the duration of weed control involve fruit trees. Welker and Glenn (1989) suggest growth benefits are clearly discernible from ongoing weed control for at least four years post planting. From a management perspective, deciding whether to continue weed control around trees in turf beyond the first year involves balancing a variety of resource issues. In most cases weed control beyond two years is unlikely to be justifiable, except in the case of advanced trees which require an extended period to re-establish appropriate root:shoot ratios.

Size of the weed-free area

The size of the weed-free area necessary to provide an acceptable level of growth varies according to the size of the nursery stock being planted and the nature of the surrounding weeds (Table 8.3). For a given weed-free area, the wider the root ball

Table 8.3 The influence of the diameter of weed-free area on the first season growth of planted trees (from Davies 1987a) as dry weight of above ground parts after three years growth.

Plant species	Increase in growth of trees in various weed-free areas (in m²) as a percentage of the weedy control		
	0.25	0.5	1.0
Acer pseudoplatanus	204	727	909
Quercus robur	340	660	1000

being planted, the closer the zone of root development will be to the roots of weeds. Hence the larger the planted stock, the larger will be the area of weed control required to deliver the same level of growth benefit. The larger and/or more vigorous the surrounding weeds, the further their root systems are likely to extend, and the greater the diameter of the weed-free area required. Laterally spreading stoloniferous weeds such as couch grass (*Elymus repens*) are adept at recolonising weed-free areas from the periphery.

Weed-free areas used in landscape management are generally far too small. A desirable weed-free standard for 1 + 1 transplants would involve a minimum diameter of 1.0 m, and a minimum of 2.0 m for advanced trees with a 450–600 mm root ball.

Effect of other plant husbandry practices

The two most important factors to consider here are irrigation and nutrient regime. Whitcomb (1981) demonstrated that incremental applications of nitrogen did not alleviate the effects of turf competition on *Ilex cornuta*, *Juniperus* 'Hetzii', *Ligustrum* 'Vicaryi' and *Pinus thunbergii*. Similarly, Goode and Hyrycz (1976), Nielson and Wakefield (1978), Fales and Wakefield (1981) and Davies (1987a) report no significant alleviation of the effects of turf competition on establishing woody plants following a surface application of fertiliser.

Even if irrigation and nutrient placement can alleviate some of the negative effects of weed competition in some species to some degree, it is far more resource efficient and environmentally desirable to eliminate the source of the problem. A study by Cromer *et al.* (1977) on the establishment of *Pinus radiata* shows that growth rates achieved with weed control in the first year, followed by occasional control of woody weeds, required the addition of 807 kg/ha nitrogen, 202 kg/ha phosphorus and 232 kg/ha potassium in the presence of weeds.

8.4 Mulching as a method of post planting weed control

The means by which weeds can be controlled after planting include: cultivation, selection of taxa with appropriately dense leaf canopies, chemical control via a range of herbicides, and mulching. As herbicidal weed control is discussed in greater detail in Chapter 6, this chapter deals exclusively with mulching.

Mulches as weed control agents

The declining use of cultivation and herbicides to control weeds in public landscapes has made mulching the ubiquitous treatment (Fig. 8.5). In

Fig. 8.5 Mulching is a valuable weed control technique. Here, deep mulches of composted materials have been spread in late winter over extensive herbaceous plantings. Many species will tolerate this treatment. (Photo: James Hitchmough)

most cases mulches are extremely valuable aids to plant establishment but in order to maximise their effectiveness it is necessary to understand their properties. Mulches not only control weeds but provide other growth benefits. Table 8.4 illustrates the positive effects of mulching on the growth of a number of species during the establishment period.

The effectiveness of mulches in controlling weeds is heavily dependent on the nature of the weed source. Weeds may colonise from one or a combination of the following:

- an existing soil weed seed bank
- weed seeds deposited on the site from adjacent weeds via gravity, wind, water, or animal vectors
- a standing crop of vegetative annual and perennial weeds
- viable vegetative fragments of rhizomes, stolons etc. buried in the soil following cultivation
- stolons and rhizomes of vegetative weeds immediately outside the site (yet to arrive).

Mulches and weed seed germination and establishment

Almost all mulches are capable of restricting the germination of weed seeds that are present on the surface or in the top few centimetres of the soil before the mulch is applied. Mulches inhibit weed germination and establishment from the soil seed bank in three main ways.

- They insulate the underlying soil from the diurnal temperature fluctuations that are often a trigger in promoting the germination of many species of weeds (Thompson *et al.*, 1977). This occurs chiefly with plant debris and mineral gravel mulches.
- Mulches prevent light from reaching weed seeds at the soil surface. Weed species such as *Holcus lanatus*, *Poa annua*, and *Stellaria media* (Grime, 1979) require light for germination, and providing a mulch is either sufficiently opaque or applied thickly enough to intercept light, the germination of seeds on the soil surface will be inhibited.
- Where germination does occur beneath a mulch, many germinants will exhaust their carbohydrate reserves in growing through the mulch to reach the light. With impermeable synthetic mulches such as black polythene or weedmat all the seedlings will die. The larger the weed seeds are, the greater the risk is that mulches will fail to suppress the seedlings. Successful weed seedling emergence in mulched areas is inversely proportional to mulch opacity, depth, and physical resistance to the weed seedlings.

Table 8.4 Comparison of the growth of a number of tree species under mulched and unmulched (bare soil surface) soil conditions.

Species	Growth of plants in mulch treatments as a percentage of a bare soil control			
	Pine bark / wood chips	Hay	Black polythene	
Acer rubrum	240	–	–	Fraedrich and Ham 1982
Acer saccharinum	650	–	–	"
Acer saccharum	188	–	–	"
Alnus cordata	–	–	182	Davies 1987a
Magnolia grandiflora	116	–	–	Hensley *et al.* 1988
Prunus persica	–	155	–	Cockcroft 1966
Salix fragilis	–	–	223	Davies 1987a

Another important issue is the capacity of the mulch to inhibit the germination of weeds from seed rain onto its surface. This is an ongoing process in all landscapes, and in the absence of maintenance eventually leads to the colonisation of mulched surfaces by weeds. The rate at which weeds can colonise the surface of mulches depends in large part on the choice of mulch. The observations of most landscape practitioners (for example, Baines, 1982) suggest that mulches composed of relatively massive particles such as coarse wood chips are most resistant to weed seed invasion. The surfaces of these types of mulch dry quickly after rain or irrigation, presenting a hostile site for seed germination. With plant debris mulches, their capacity to resist this source of invasion declines with age, as decomposition leads to smaller particles that retain moisture more readily. The most effective mulches for restricting colonisation via weed seed rain are synthetic materials such as polythene woven weedmats, followed by very coarse grades of bark, wood chips, and coarse mineral aggregates.

Mulches and vegetative weeds

With a few exceptions, the control of standing weeds, perennial weed fragments in the soil, and vegetative invasion from outside via stolons cannot be achieved satisfactorily by mulching. Unless there are compelling reasons against this, standing weed vegetation should be killed by a non-residual translocated herbicide such as glyphosate before cultivation and mulching. Annual weeds lack a subterranean carbohydrate store and are more readily controlled by mulch application than are rhizomatous-stoloniferous perennials. Synthetic sheet mulches can only be used as a form of pre-planting weed control with closely-mown non-stoloniferous weeds. Even with synthetic sheet mulches, some follow-up weed control is necessary to eliminate the regrowth that emerges through the planting holes.

Controlling invasion by stoloniferous weeds from the margin of the mulched areas is most critical when dealing with discrete areas of mulching around trees and shrubs in urban grasslands.

Where the turf contains stoloniferous species such as couch grass (*Elymus repens*), or creeping bent (*Agrostis stolonifera*) mulches of plant or mineral origin are very quickly colonised, and the water conservation benefits of the mulch are lost.

Mulches as soil moisture control agents

Mulches reduce the rate of moisture loss from soils by a combination of the following processes:

- Restricting weed colonisation that would otherwise compete for available water.
- Insulating the soil, reducing soil temperature and the rate of evaporation. Soil temperature is determined by mulch colour, depth and thermal characteristics. Transparent polythene mulches and dark mulches of low insulative capacity significantly increase soil temperature.
- Breaking the continuity of water films between the soil water phase and the atmosphere. This commonly occurs with mineral and plant debris mulches where the average size of the mulch particles is many times greater than those of the underlying soil particles. Under these conditions the water films around mulch particles are eliminated by evaporation and cannot be replaced by capillary lift from the underlying soil. Handreck and Black (1989) suggest that heavily-mulched soil loses approximately one third of the water evaporated from an unmulched surface. Other studies (for example Shearman *et al.*, 1979) report more dramatic examples of soil moisture conservation.

Sheet polythene (and to a lesser degree woven weedmats) provide a relatively impermeable barrier to soil water evaporation. Finely textured mulches such as decomposed mushroom compost, or those with a spongy internal structure such as peat, are less effective in controlling moisture loss because they help to maintain a continuum of water films between the soil and the atmosphere. The beneficial effects on plant growth that result from mulches maximising soil water availability have frequently been observed in the field, but it is difficult to separate the improvement that is due to soil moisture from growth improvements because of other factors such as more equable soil temperature. Many authors (for example Zahner, 1968; Fraedrich and Ham, 1982) believe the former to be the key factor.

Mulches as a means of moderating soil temperature

Mulches can affect plant growth by significantly modifying the temperature of the surface layers of the soil. Most mulches insulate the soil from the dramatic fluctuations that occur in air temperature (Appleton *et al.*, 1990). Mulched soils tend to be warmer in winter and cooler in summer than non-mulched soils, extending the growing season for plant roots. The optimal soil temperatures for root growth, and the effect of temperatures outside these ranges, are only understood for a small number of taxa used in the urban landscape (other than turf grasses). Most woody species appear to perform best at soil temperatures of 20–30°C, with cool temperate species at the lower end of the range (Kozlowski, 1985). In cool climates the growth of some taxa may be improved by soil heating mulches such as black polythene and weed fabrics.

The effect of mulches on the availability of soil nutrients

In addition to providing some nutrients as they decompose (plant debris mulches only), mulches can also make the nutrients already present in the soil more available. This applies in particular to potassium, phosphorus, calcium and magnesium (Russell, 1973; Litzow and Pellet, 1983; Robinson, 1988). The improvement in the availability of these minerals is primarily due to the effect that mulching has on soil moisture availability.

The effect of mulches on soil compaction and physical properties in general

The increased density of soil that results from surface trafficking by pedestrians or vehicles is detrimental to root growth. In permanently mulched soils that are subjected to occasional trafficking, the higher moisture content and correspondingly-reduced penetrative resistances will facilitate root development, even in relatively compacted soils. Whether plants can take advantage of this depends on their tolerance of the reduced levels of oxygen that are associated with these circumstances. The increased populations of soil animals such as earthworms which are commonly associated with mulching (Tisdall, 1978) appear to have a positive (albeit relatively gradual) impact on the recuperation of previously-compacted soils. Synthetic mulches such as weedmat also encourage large populations of soil macrofauna, which improve the aeration of the soil surface via their tunnelling activities. Mulches also have a significant capacity to restrict soil erosion, both during and after the establishment period. This is particularly important on erosion-prone soils on sloping sites.

Plant debris mulches contribute substantial quantities of organic matter to the soil as they decompose. This is particularly so with lignified materials such as wood chips that decompose relatively slowly. This organic matter benefits soil structure and also increases water and nutrient holding capacity. Non-lignified material such as green manures may also add substantial quantities of nutrients to soils as it decomposes, although there is a risk with such materials of transient nitrogen deficiencies, when soil bacteria utilise the soil nitrogen as they decompose the mulch. In practice this rarely appears to be a problem.

Choosing mulch products

A wide variety of fabric and woven mulch products are available commercially, together with a range of bark and other organic debris. Some of the latter are produced to have predictable and reliable physical properties, and are valuable in many situations. Other organic materials are often locally available, and may be useful but they require careful inspection and consideration of their physical and in some cases chemical properties. The same is true of mineral mulches such as crushed rock and gravels of varying coarseness. Apart from the basic physical properties of the mulch such as water penetrability and durability, a factor in selecting mulches for discrete tree planting is the diameter of the mulching sheet. Minimum effective sizes have previously been discussed. The other factor that is important in mulch selection is its appearance in relation to the visual character of the location and the planting itself.

Problems with mulches

Restriction of oxygen and water movement into underlying soils

If they are applied too thickly, or used to blanket black polythene, plant debris mulches can interfere with oxygen diffusion from the atmosphere into the soil and lead to root damage. This situation is most common on poorly-drained, fine textured soils (Davies, 1983). Mulch-induced soil deoxygenation can be observed in newly-established landscapes where there are deep mulches of plant debris containing a high percentage of fines, on top of poorly drained soils in a high rainfall climate or with frequent irrigation. The mulch layer immediately above the soil surface becomes saturated and fails to dry out by the next rainfall or irrigation event, substantially slowing down the rate at which oxygen can enter.

There is relatively little quantified information on threshold depths for mulching to avoid these problems. Watson and Kupkowski (1991) found no significant difference in oxygen levels between bare soil and that mulched with a 450 mm layer of coarse wood chips! For fine to medium textured plant debris mulches, it is proposed that 50–75 mm should be seen as the maximum depth, and 75–100 mm for coarse plant debris or mineral mulches. The reduction in soil oxygenation that may be associated with deep mulches potentially counteracts the growth benefits that arise from superior weed control. Because of their capacity to restrict water access to the underlying soil, mulches should ideally be spread when the soil is at or close to field capacity.

Greater risk of frost damage to establishing plants

Because of their insulative capacity, plant debris mulches (and to a lesser degree mineral mulches)

restrict both soil heating during the day and the escape of heat from the soil at night. Under nocturnal conditions, net radiation loss from the mulch surface occurs, and this heat is not readily replaced from the underlying soil. On clear still nights the air in contact with the top of the mulch also cools, and if sufficient heat is lost, sub zero temperatures may occur. Nocturnal temperatures above a mulched surface may be 2–4°C colder than above an adjacent bare soil surface (Creech and Hawley, 1960). During winter or early spring these temperature differentials may result in damage to plants in mulched areas whilst the same taxon surrounded by bare soil is unaffected. In cold climates organic and mineral mulches should be scraped away from young plants of frost-sensitive species during the coldest months of the year. Mown turf and ground cover plants, or indeed any insulative ground surface, have a similar or greater effect. Nocturnal air temperatures in winter above synthetic sheet type mulches are relatively similar to those above a bare soil surface.

Increased incidence of damage from slugs, vascular wilt and root rotting fungi

The moister soil conditions that result from mulching may pre-dispose some plant species to increased damage from these sources; this applies particularly to herbaceous plants. Unfortunately there are few published studies that have addressed this issue in the context of landscape plantings. Fraedrich and Ham (1982) found no evidence of increased *Fusarium* and *Pythium* under mulched soil.

Summary

Over the past thirty years there has been a considerable amount of research into the establishment and planting of nursery stock, giving an independent review of the efficacy of various techniques used in practice. This can help practitioners to draw up more effective specifications. Perhaps the most important activity that can affect establishment is the control of weeds after planting. The reasons for its importance are well established, but in spite of this it is all too common for landscape projects to perform poorly because inadequate attention is paid to this. One of the most effective techniques for achieving post-planting weed control and successful establishment is mulching.

References

Appleton, B.L., Derr, J.F., & Ross, B.B. (1990) The effect of various landscape weed control measures on soil moisture and temperature, and tree root growth. *Journal of Arboriculture*, **16**, (10), 264–8.

Baines, C. (1982) Shrub planting techniques for establishment. In: C. Addison, & P. Thoday (eds) *Cost Effective Amenity Landscape Management*, HEA Conference Proceedings, Cannington College, Somerset.

Bradshaw, A.D. & Chadwick, M.J. (1980) *The Restoration of Land*. Blackwell Scientific Publications, Oxford.

Callaghan, T.V., Lindley, D.K., Ali, O.M., Abd El Nour, H., & Bacon, P.J. (1989) The effect of water absorbing synthetic polymers on the stomatal conductance, growth and survival of *Eucalyptus microtheca* seedlings in the Sudan. *Journal of Applied Ecology*, **26**, (2), 663–72.

Carnell, R. & Anderson, M.A. (1986) A technique for extensive field measurement of soil anaerobism by rusting of steel rods. *Forestry*, **59**, (2), 129–40.

Clemens, J. & Radford, S.P. (1985) Field establishment of container-grown plants: II. Effects of potting medium, stock size, hole type and irrigation. *Journal of Environmental Management*, **21**, 262–70.

Cockcroft, B. (1966) Soil management of peach trees in the Goulburn Valley, Victoria. *Australian Journal of Experimental Agriculture and Animal Husbandry*, **6**, (20), 62–5.

Creech, J.L. & Hawley, W. (1960) Effects of mulching on growth and winter hardiness of evergreen azaleas. *Proceedings of the American Society of Horticultural Science*, **75**, 650–57.

Cromer, R.N. (1977) Fertiliser trials in young plantations of Eucalypts. *Australian Forest Research*, **5**, (2), 1–10.

Davies, R.J. (1983) Transplant stress. In: P.R. Thoday (Ed.) *Tree establishment*. pp 40–50. Symposium Proceedings, University of Bath.

Davies, R.J. (1987a) Trees and weeds; weed control for successful tree establishment. *Forestry Commission Handbook 2*. HMSO, London.

Davies, R.J. (1987b) Weed competition and broadleaved tree establishment. In: D. Patch (Ed.) *Advances in Practical Arboriculture*. pp 91–9, Forestry Commission Bulletin 65, HMSO, London.

Fales, S.L. & Wakefield, R.C. (1981) Effects of turfgrass on the establishment of woody plants. *Agronomy Journal*, **73**, 605–10.

Fayle, D.C.F. (1968) *Radial growth in tree roots*. Technical Report No. 9, Faculty of Forestry, University of Toronto.

Fraedrich, S.W. & Ham, D.L. (1982) Woodchip mulching around maples: effects on tree growth and soil characteristics. *Journal of Arboriculture*, **8**, (4): 85–9.

Gilbertson, P., Kendle, A.D., & Bradshaw, A.D. (1987) Root growth and the problems of trees in urban and industrial areas. In: D. Patch (Ed.) *Advances in Practical Arboriculture*, pp 59–66, Forestry Commission Bulletin 65, HMSO, London.

Gilman, E.F. (1990) Tree root growth and development: II. Response to culture, management and planting. *Journal of Environmental Horticulture*, **8**, (4), 220–27.

Goode, J.E. & Hyrycz, K.J. (1976) The effect of nitrogen on young newly planted apple rootstocks in the presence and absence of grass competition. *Journal of Horticultural Science*, **51**, 321–7.

Grime, J.P. (1979) *Plant Strategies and Vegetation Processes*. John Wiley, Chichester.

Handreck, K.A. & Black, N.D. (1989) *Growing Media for Ornamental Plants and Turf*. Revised edn. New South Wales University Press, Kensington, NSW.

Harris, R.W., Leiser, A.T., Neel, P.L., Long, D., Stice, N.W., & Marie, R.G. (1972) Tree trunk development: influence of spacing and movement. *Combined Proceedings of International Plant Propagators Society*, **21**, 149–61.

Harris, R.W. & Hamilton, W.D. (1969) Staking and pruning young *Myoporum laetum*. *Journal of American Society of Horticultural Science*, **94**, 359–61.

Hensley, D.L., McNeil, R.E., & Sundheim, R. (1988) Management influences on growth of transplanted *Magnolia grandiflora*. *Journal of Arboriculture*, **14**, (8), 204–7.

Hewson, R.T. & Roberts, H.A. (1973) Some effects of weed competition on the growth of onions. *Journal of Horticultural Science*, **48**, 51–7.

Hitchmough, J.D. (1994) The establishment of urban landscape vegetation, *Urban Landscape Management*, Inkata, Sydney, Australia.

Hummel, R.L. & Johnson, C.R. (1987) Does pruning at

transplanting improve sweetgum growth? *American Nurseryman*, **165**, (3), 99–105.

Insley, H. & Buckley, G.P. (1986) Causes and prevention of establishment failure in amenity trees. In: A.D. Bradshaw, D.A. Goode, & E. Thorp (Eds) *Ecology and design in landscape*, pp 127–41, Blackwell Scientific Publications, Oxford.

Jacobs, R.M. (1954) The effect of wind sway on the form and development of *Pinus radiata. Australian Journal of Botany*, **2**, 33–51.

Jarvis, P.G. & Jarvis, S.J. (1964) Growth rates of woody plants. *Physiologica Plantarum*, **17**, 654–66.

Kerr, G. (1995) *The use of treeshelters: 1992 Survey.* Technical Paper 011, Forestry Commission, HMSO, London.

Kopinga, J. (1985) Research on street tree planting practices in the Netherlands. In: *Metria 5: Preparing and Selecting Sites for Urban Trees.* Proceedings of the Metropolitan Tree Improvement Alliance, Penn. State University.

Kozlowski, T.T. (1985) Tree growth in response to environmental stresses. *Journal of Arboriculture*, **11**, (4), 97–111.

La Dell, T. (1983) An introduction to tree and shrub seeding. *Landscape Design* **144**, 27–31.

La Dell, T. (1987) Tree and landscape seeding. *Landscape Design* **168**, 53–4.

La Dell, T. (1988) The establishment of amenity trees and shrubs by direct seeding: weed control and management, *Aspects of Applied Biology*, **16**.

Larcher, W. (1983) *Physiological Plant Ecology*, 2nd edn. Springer-Verlag, New York.

Litzlow, M. & Pellet, H. (1983) Influence of mulch materials on growth of green ash. *Journal of Arboriculture*, **9**, (1), 7–11.

Lombard, P., Price, S., Wilson, W., & Watson, B. (1988) Grass cover crops in vineyards. In: *Proceedings of the Second International Cool Climate Viticulture and Oenology Symposium*, Aukland, New Zealand. pp 152–5.

Neef, G. (1976) Geholzansaat auf Rohbaschungen. *Neue Landschaft* **9**, 520–26.

Nelms, L.R. & Spomer, L.A. (1983) Water retention of container soil transplanted into ground beds. *HortScience*, **18**, 863–6.

Neilson, A.P. & Wakefield, R.C. (1978) Competitive effects of turfgrass on the growth of ornamental shrubs. *Agronomy Journal*, **70**, (1), 39–42.

Nicolosi, R.T. & Fretz, T.A. (1980) Evaluation of root growth in varying medium densities and through dissimilar soil surfaces. *HortScience*, **15**, (5), 642–4.

Patch, D. (1987) Trouble at the stake. In: D. Patch (Ed.) *Advances in Practical Arboriculture*, Bulletin 65, pp 77–84, Forestry Commission, HMSO, London.

Perry, T.O. (1982) The ecology of tree roots and the practical significance thereof. *Journal of Arboriculture*, **8**, (8), 197–222.

Plas, W.T. (1976) Direct seeding of trees and shrubs on surface mined land in West Virginia. In: K.A. Utz (Ed.) *Proceedings of the Conference of Disturbed Surface Areas*, pp 32–42.

Potter, M.J. (1991) *Treeshelters.* Handbook 007. Forestry Commission, HMSO, London.

Putwain, P. (1998) *Direct Sowing of Trees and Shrubs on Roadside Embankments*. Plantech Research, University of Liverpool, Liverpool.

Rix, M. (1983) Growing Bulbs. Croom Helm, London.

Robinson, W. (1911) *Gravetye Manor*. John Murray, London.

Robinson, D.W. (1988) Mulches and herbicides in ornamental plantings. *HortScience*, **23**, (3), 547–52.

Ruark, G.A., Mader, D.L., & Tattar, T.A. (1982) The influence of soil compaction and aeration on the root growth and vigour of trees – a literature review. Part I. *Arboricultural Journal*, **6**, 251–65.

Ryan, P.A. & Lewty, M.J. (1984) How to grow hoop pine on farms. *Queensland Agricultural Journal*, **110**, (1), 54–8.

Shearman, R.C., Steinegger, D.H., Kinbacher, E.J., & Riordan, T.P. (1979) A comparison of turfgrass clippings, oat straw and alfalfa as mulching material. *Journal of American Society for Horticultural Science*, **104**, (4), 461–3.

Shoup, S. & Whitcomb, C.E. (1981) Interactions between trees and ground covers. *Journal of Arboriculture*, **7**, (7), 186–7.

Smith, M.W., Wolf, M.E., Cheary, B.S., & Carroll, B.L. (2001) Allelopathy of bermudagrass, tall fescue, redroot pigweed, and cutleaf evening primrose on pecan. *HortScience*, **36**, (6), 1047–8.

Thompson, K., Grime, J.P., & Mason, G. (1977) Seed germination in response to diurnal fluctuations of temperature. *Nature*, **67**, 147–9.

Tisdall, J.M. (1978) Ecology of earthworms in irrigated orchards. In: W.W. Emerson, R.D. Bond, & A.R. Dexter (Eds), *Modification of Soil Structure*. p. 297, John Wiley, London.

Walters, D.T. & Gilmore, A.R. (1976) Allelopathic effects of fescue on the growth of sweetgum. *Journal of Chemical Ecology*, **2**, 469–79.

Watson, G.W. (1986a) Twig growth of eight species of shade tree following transplanting. *Journal of Arboriculture*, **12**, (10), 241–5.

Watson, G.W. (1986b) Cultural practices can influence root development for better transplanting success. *Journal of Environmental Horticulture*, **4**, 32–4.

Watson, G.W. & Himelick, E.B. (1982) Root regeneration of transplanted trees. *Journal of Arboriculture*, **8**, 305–10.

Watson, G.W. & Kupkowski, G. (1991) Effect of a deep mulch layer on the soil environment and tree root growth. *Journal of Arboriculture*, **17**, (9), 242–5.

Welker, W.V. & Glenn, D.M. (1989) Sod proximity influences the growth and yield of young peach trees. *Journal of American Society of Horticultural Science*, **114**, (6), 856–9.

Whitcomb, C.E. (1984) Another look at fall planting. *Oklahoma Agricultural Research Reports*, **855**, 28–9.

Whitcomb, C.E. (1987) *Establishment and Maintenance of Landscape Plants*. Lacebark Publications, Stillwater, Oklahoma.

Winter, E.J. (1974) *Water, Soil and the Plant*. Macmillan, London.

Witherspoon, W.R. & Lumis, G.P. (1986) Root regeneration, starch content, and root promoting activity in *Tilia cordata* cultivars at three different digging-planting times. *Journal of Environmental Horticulture*, **4**, (3), 76–9.

Zahner, R. (1968) Water deficits and the growth of trees. In: T.T. Koslowski (Ed.) *Water deficits and plant growth Volume 2*. Academic Press, New York.

9 Tree Roots and Buildings

Glynn Percival

One of the most litigious areas of arboriculture must be the relationship between tree roots and buildings. In urban and suburban landscapes, trees grow in close proximity to buildings and infrastructure: consequently, the potential for conflict is great. Similarly, the process of developing land for buildings and infrastructure can be devastating to existing trees. Post-development soils are often so destroyed by machine trafficking that newly planted trees have difficulty surviving. If trees manage to establish and mature they may eventually be viewed as responsible for damages to buildings. If pavements, sewer lines or foundations need repair is it a tree problem, a problem of poor management or tree vulnerable construction? Finding answers requires a multi-disciplinary approach to minimise these conflicts (Watson and Neely, 1995).

Many of these tree management problems have their origins in a lack of information to guide important decisions. Most members of the public, architects, planners, builders and contractors have a poor understanding of tree biology, and especially root biology. Even among landscape professionals, understanding of root system biology is often restricted and in many cases misunderstandings are common. Without an up-to-date, scientifically based understanding of the situation it is difficult to avoid unintentional damage to trees during construction works, to assess what can be done to provide remedial action and whether trees will recover. Ample evidence exists that given this understanding, and with sensible species selection (taking into account ultimate size and potential danger to buildings) attractive urban environments can exist with trees and buildings in harmony.

9.1 Root function

Roots have been described as the 'invisible' or 'hidden' part of a plant. However, about 80 per cent of problems relating to amenity trees are root related. Major functions of tree roots include:

- Acquisition and translocation of essential nutrients and water from the soil.
- Synthesis of growth controlling substances or their precursors (cytokinins).
- Stability and anchorage.
- Deposition of carbon in the soil through
  (a) the death and decay of roots during the growing season,
  (b) the release of root exudates.
- Storage organ for carbohydrate reserves (glucose, fructose, sugar alcohols) (Eissenstat et al., 2000).

Current views on tree root architecture

It is a widely held misconception that trees possess many strong vertical 'tap' or 'anchor' roots extending deeply (up to two metres) into the soil, with limited lateral root development beyond the canopy (Fig. 9.1). A more accurate description is that:

- The diameter of tree root spread is roughly two to three times the height of the tree, i.e. root growth extends well beyond the canopy.

Figure 9.1 The root system of a ten-year-old plane tree (*Platanus* x *acerifolia*), after its roots were excavated from the soil using high-pressure hoses. There are no tap roots, and indeed the roots are rarely deeper in the soil than 45 cm, but the root ball has a radius of 6 m. The tree was approximately 5 m tall when excavated. (Photo: James Hitchmough)

- The bulk of root growth is predominantly lateral in soils, parallel with the surface.
- Under most conditions of soil and climate in the United Kingdom about 95 per cent of roots are found in the upper 600 mm of soil.
- All roots contribute to the moisture supply and stability of trees, and there is no meaningful distinction between 'feeder' and 'support' roots.
- Tap roots are uncommon in transplanted trees, probably surviving only for the first few years in a tree's life.

Table 9.1 Root depth categories for all trees (Cutler, 1995).

Depth	Number of trees	%
<0.5 m	528	15.2
0.5–1.0 m	1083	31.2
1.0–2.0 m	1737	50.1
>2.0 m	121	3.5
TOTAL	3469	100.0

- The ratio of root:crown is determined by a combination of species and site conditions, and varies from 0.15:1 to more than 1:1.
- The roots of most healthy trees grow seasonally without dying back, but will be prevented from growing in a fixed direction by any inhospitable buffer.
- Roots do not grow towards anything in particular, but branch profusely when favourable moisture/nutrient conditions allow.
- Root penetration to four or five metres depth may occur, particularly in dry areas with a low water table or where an obstacle to normal root growth exists. However this is rare.

Data from the Kew root survey (a survey of wind-blown trees carried out after the storm of 1987–1988; Table 9.1) supports this model with 45–50 per cent of tree roots occupying the top metre of soil; the remaining 50 per cent extend down to two metres. No more than four per cent of root plate measurements showed roots at a depth of more than two metres. This model emphasises the point that ploughing, trenching, raising or lowering the soil level, even the top 200 mm, can destroy a major proportion of a tree root system.

9.2   Urban soil

Unlike forest or field soils, in urban landscapes the soil often suffers deoxygenation as a result of excess water application, impeded drainage, mechanical compaction or impermeable surface coverings (Fig. 9.2). This almost ubiquitous factor results in the physical impedance of root growth

Figure 9.2 Impermeable surface coverings reduce soil aeration and are a physical barrier to root growth. (Photo: Glynn Percival)

Table 9.2 Soil attributes, by soil texture class, where root growth becomes significantly limiting (after Morris and Lowrey, 1988).

Soil texture	Root-limiting bulk density (g/cc)	Root-limiting % pores normally filled with air
Sand	1.8	24
Fine sand	1.75	21
Sandy loam	1.7	19
Fine sandy loam	1.65	15
Loam	1.55	14
Silt loam	1.45	17
Clay loam	1.5	11
Clay	1.4	13

and reduced levels of aeration. The natural resistance of soil to root penetration influences the volume of soil explored, the intensity of the exploration and the form of a root system (Pregtizer *et al.*, 2000). Tree roots have difficulty penetrating soils with bulk densities greater than $1.7\,g\,cm^3$ and when air pore space is less than 15 per cent. Specific root-limiting bulk densities by soil texture class are given in Table 9.2.

Increased soil temperature in urban environments affects root initiation, branching, orientation, direction of growth and lifespan. Soil temperatures greater than 35°C generally result in root death; the maximum ranges from 25–30°C, optimum from 10–30°C and minimum between 0–7°C (McMichael and Burke, 1998).

A tendency to winter waterlogging because of slowed water infiltration, and summer drought due to low moisture-holding capacity results in significant root death, particularly when the soil water content is rapidly replenished after a period of drought.

Reduced nutrient availability, caused by impaired root uptake and slower nitrogen mineralisation, can influence root turnover. In forest trees for example, fine root turnover increased exponentially with nitrogen availability (Majdi and Kangas, 1997).

There is a reduction in arbuscular mycorrhiza at or around the root zone and an increased susceptibility to pathogenic root fungi. In addition, decaying tissue resulting from construction damage may permit the build-up of pathogens in the rhizosphere. Fungicide application may alleviate this problem (Wells, 1999), but is not practicable in most situations.

Anaerobic conditions resulting in the production of gases such as methane can displace oxygen from the soil atmosphere, either through physical means or through the development of bacteria which are able to metabolise methane. Carbon dioxide and several trace gases such as ethylene are toxic to roots at low concentrations (about two per cent). Species suitable for soil conditions with varying levels of aerobic substrate have been identified by Crook (1992; see also Table 9.3).

Root responses to urban soils

Tree roots require about 15 per cent oxygen within soil pores in order to function effectively (the

Table 9.3 Recommended trees for various levels of aerobic substrate.

Substrate aerobic for at least 1 m	Substrate aerobic for at least 0.5 m	Substrate aerobic for less than 0.5 m
Ash (*Fraxinus excelsior*)	Sessile oak (*Quercus petraea*)	Silver birch (*Betula pendula*)
Bird cherry (*Prunus padus*)	Pedunculate oak (*Q. robur*)	Downy birch (*B. pubescens*)
Gean cherry (*P. avium*)		Alder (*Alnus glutinosa*)
Lime (*Tilia spp.*)		Grey alder (*A. incana*)
Beech (*Fagus sylvatica*)		Willow (*Salix* spp.)
Hornbeam (*Carpinus betulus*)		
Horse chestnut (*Aesculus hippocastanum*)		
Silver firs (*Abies spp.*)		
Spruces (*Picea spp.*)		
Southern beech (*Nothofagus spp.*)		
Larches (*Larix spp.*)		
Pines (*Pinus spp.*)		
Douglas fir (*Psuedotsuga menziesii*)		

atmosphere is approximately 21 per cent oxygen). Concentrations below this threshold affect numerous physiological and metabolic processes. These include disintegration of leaf ultrastructure, leading to wilting, chlorosis, abscission and reduced photosynthetic capacity, as well as stem hypertrophy, blackening of roots and death.

Cytological investigations conducted in woody plant roots indicate that water stress damages the cellular membranes of root tips. At different development stages, damage such as lack of protoplasm, formation of membrane vesicles and coagulation of cytoplasmic content has been demonstrated (Chiatante *et al.*, 2000).

Tree species adapted to thrive in areas of periodic waterlogging (swamps, marshes, bogs) have inherent survival mechanisms to alleviate these stresses. These include oxygen transportation from shoots to roots and the subsequent release of oxygen into the soil environment; production of lenticels on roots and submerged stems to improve gaseous exchange; and formation of aerenchyma tissue and adventitious roots. In addition carbon metabolism can be adjusted to avoid accumulation of toxic compounds and a low metabolic rate maintained over long periods (Kozlowski *et al.*, 1991). Ware (1994) suggests species with these adaptations should be more widely utilised to

reduce the high mortality rates common in plantings associated with urban development.

Urban soil management

Site analysis should aim to identify situations where deoxygenation is a likely occurrence i.e. low lying sites, naturally impermeable soils such as heavy clays, soils with impermeable layers below the surface, past site usage that has resulted in surface or sub-surface compaction, and excess water application through existing irrigation systems. Methods for the detection and alleviation of soil compaction and deoxygenation include:

- Assessing the nature and condition of pre-existing vegetation on the site, to get an idea of conditions over a longer period of time than on the day of the site visit. Smaller, stunted plants with yellowing necrotic leaves are indicative of long-term problems whilst the presence of, for example, wetland plants such as rushes, *Juncus* spp., and *Phragmites* indicates long-term periodic waterlogging.
- Observation of the topography i.e. the presence of standing water, and noting grey mottling in the walls of a hole dug in soils (a result of the oxidation-reduction of iron compounds).

- Assessing soil oxygen status directly by the use of oxygen measuring meters.
- Inserting steel rods into the soil profile and relating soil oxygen content to the rate of rusting (Hodge and Knott, 1993).
- Puncturing soils with an auger to make 37 mm diameter holes, 300–500 mm deep, at 450 mm intervals singly or in combination with soil aeration machines (Day and Bassuk, 1994).
- Recording penetration resistance to determine the physical properties of the soil such as bulk density and pore volume.
- Using oxygen-permeable and/or smaller, thicker unit paviours with crenellated edges to increase water and air movement between the soil surface and atmosphere.

Useful discussions on the merits and disadvantages of each system can be found by reference to Hitchmough (1994).

Perhaps the simplest approach, though, is to be aware of the relative degrees of tolerance which different species and genera have for development impacts, and to select the appropriate species (Table 9.4).

'Ideal' urban soils

Although differences in tolerance between species exist, and 'pioneer species' such as alder are able to tolerate extremes of drought or waterlogging, favourable soil conditions can be defined as:

- soils with bulk densities (penetrative resistances) <1.7 g/cc
- soil oxygen concentrations >15%
- soil moisture and temperature between 0.03–0.2 Mpa and 10–30°C, respectively
- pH between 5.5–6.5
- carbon dioxide concentrations <5%
- soluble salt <200 ppm
- clay/silt content <15%.

Soils should also be tested for macro and micronutrients, organic matter, and any toxicity before transportation to the site as it is relatively easy to correct serious discrepancies before or during spreading. Nutrient sensitivity varies between species and where soil has been tested previously, suspected deficiencies can be further determined through foliar analysis. Nutrient analysis forms part of a commercial service offered by many reputable laboratories: deficiencies are identified and recommendations given on the type and concentration of fertiliser to apply to remediate these problems.

Root distribution patterns

Tree root systems exploit channels of low-density, adequately oxygenated soil. Consequently, in hostile urban sites, lateral root spread occurs not as a uniform expanding front but rather as irregularly-located wedges of root growth in favourable volumes of soil. Research on tree root distribution patterns is primarily based on data derived from forest and field sites. It is not clear that these patterns are especially useful for urban trees where the variety and specificity of urban factors (compaction, soil infertility, impervious paved surfaces, etc.) differ radically from those in a forest. Knowledge of root location and prediction of probable root distribution is critical in investigating and assessing the impact of infrastructure prior to construction. For example, it is important to understand how the root architecture of existing trees will alter, following the laying of roadways and paved areas which negatively-influence the physical properties of soil around them (Fig. 9.3).

With this information, changes in project design can be made that are less destructive to existing trees, and more effective protective methods can be specified. Although research into these problems is limited, a model of root development underneath road surfaces has been proposed by Kopinga (1995). In summary, it suggests that roots are initially attracted by the comparatively high degree of humidity of the soil underneath the road surface. Root development is, however, usually restricted to the interface between the sand and road surface due to soil compaction. The small quantity of water present is quickly absorbed by the arriving roots, in turn creating a gradient of soil humidity which then stimulates apical root

Table 9.4 Relative tolerance of selected species and genera widely planted in the UK to development impacts. (Adapted from Matheny and Clark (1998); information concerning the relative tolerance to development impacts of many more species can be found within this publication.)

Common name	Scientific name	Relative tolerance	Comments
Box elder	*Acer negundo*	Good	Tolerant of root loss and saturated soils. Select superior individuals for preservation
Norway maple	*Acer platanoides*	Moderate-good	Moderately tolerant of root pruning
Sycamore	*Acer pseudoplatanus*	Moderate	
Alders	*Alnus spp.*	Good	Considerable resistance to 'contractor pressures'
Birch	*Betula spp.*	Poor-moderate	Intolerant of root pruning. Mature trees are particularly sensitive to development impacts
Deodar cedar	*Cedrus deodara*	Good	Tolerant of root and crown pruning. Intolerant of excess soil moisture
Hawthorn	*Crataegus spp.*	Moderate	Intermediate tolerance to root loss and saturated soils
Beech	*Fagus sylvatica*	Poor	Mature trees particularly susceptible
Ash	*Fraxinus spp.*	Moderate	Moderately tolerant of root pruning
Gingko	*Gingko biloba*	Good	Tolerant of root pruning
Holly	*Ilex spp.*	Good	
Walnut	*Juglans regia*	Poor	Intolerant of root loss and mechanical injury (poor compartmentalisation)
Tulip tree	*Liriodendron tulipifera*	Poor-moderate	Intolerant of root pruning and mechanical injury
Apples	*Malus spp.*	Moderate	
Norway spruce	*Picea abies*	Moderate	Often windthrows. Intolerant of root loss
Scots pine	*Pinus sylvestris*	Good	Tolerant of root loss. Intolerant of saturated soils
London plane	*Platanus* x *acerifolia*	Poor or good	Response appears to be location-dependent. Benefits from supplementary irrigation
Lombardy poplar	*Populus nigra* 'Italica'	Moderate-good	Tolerant of minor amounts of fill. Intolerant of changes in soil moisture. Decays rapidly.
Douglas fir	*Pseudotsuga menziesii*	Poor-good	Tolerant of fill if limited to 25% of root zone
False acacia	*Robinia spp.*	Poor	Intolerant of root injury
Willow	*Salix spp.*	Moderate-good	Moderately tolerant of root pruning. Considerable resistance to 'contractor pressures'
Rowan	*Sorbus aucuparia*	Moderate	Tolerant of root loss. Intermediate in tolerance to saturated soils
Bald cypress	*Taxodium distichum*	Good	Adapts readily to a wide range of soils: wet to dry, sandy to heavy. Tolerant of alkaline soils
Lime	*Tilia spp.*	Moderate-good	Moderately tolerant of root pruning. Considerable resistance to 'contractor pressures'
Elm	*Ulmus spp.*	Good	Tolerant of root pruning

growth. This, combined with the low level of fertility, is probably the reason that roots under hard surfaces form few branches and fine lateral roots. Once roots reach the soil on the other side of the road they explore in a normal rooting pattern. This induces an increase in the diameter of roots underneath the road, which with time can result in the formation of surface cracks.

Figure 9.3 Roads and pavements will affect the root distribution of trees by altering the physical properties of the soil around them. (Photo: Glynn Percival)

Although this model cannot be used to predict how all tree species will respond universally, work by Lindsey *et al.* (1995) on the root distribution pattern of mature cork oaks under a range of substrates generally supports this model, as does that of Nicoll and Armstrong (1998). Further information concerning the influence of soil type and root interactions on pavement damage is presented by Sydnor *et al.* (2000).

9.3   Forms of damage to trees

Trees require adequate protection on development sites from the earliest stages until final completion. Without protection they are vulnerable to various forms of damage, such as root compaction caused by the laying of tarmac and concrete surfaces (Plate 10), as well as by machinery moving over the soil surface, and increased soil level caused by the dumping and tipping of building materials and debris. In addition, fuel and sump oil seepage can be directly toxic to tree roots, and accidental damage caused by the removal of bark and branches by machinery leads to exposure and pathogen attack. Finally buildings and paving can reflect sunlight onto bark which can 'scald' thin barked trees such as beech.

Protecting trees

Guidelines for the protection of trees during construction have been published by Helliwell (1985) on behalf of the Arboricultural Association and British Standard 5837 (1991). Salient points include:

- Erect a stout fence, about 1.3 m high, around the tree to keep the area free of dumping and vehicles.
- Inform the contractor why the trees are protected. Supervision may be required.
- Designate the protected area to cover at least the spread of the crown.
- Excavation should be done by hand if close to the root system. If access is unavoidable damage can be reduced if a gravel surface or timber raft is laid.
- Inspect the site frequently during construction and at an appropriate time after development.
- Have a long-term management programme to ensure tree cover, involving the residents/occupiers of the site.

Tree Protection Zone (TPZ)

The key to survival during development is identification of a Tree Protection Zone (TPZ), i.e. the erection of a fence to enclose the entire root area. In practice, however, this is unfeasible as root systems normally extend well beyond the crown periphery. Root spread may also be greater in one direction than another, depending on the presence of other trees, buildings, soil fertility and soil structure. The most widely-adopted technique to identify a TPZ is the drip line method i.e. protect the area within the drip line for broad-canopied trees, or up to 1.5 times the drip line for narrow canopied trees. This method suffers from a number of disadvantages: leaning trees have many support roots away from the lean and beyond the canopy; columnar shaped trees such as *Populus nigra*. 'Italica' and *Fagus sylvatica* 'Dawyck' would not be adequately protected, nor narrow crowned closely-spaced trees growing in stands.

In recognition of these weaknesses Matheny and Clark (1998) have developed a system based on trunk diameter, age, vigour and tolerance to development impacts (see Table 9.4).

Calculating the tree protection zone

(1) Evaluate the tolerance of the tree to development impacts in terms of good, moderate or poor (Table 9.4).

(2) Identify the age of the tree i.e. young, mature or overmature (Table 9.5).

(3) Using Table 9.5 find the distance from the trunk that should be protected per 2.5 cm of trunk diameter.

(4) Multiply the distance by the trunk diameter to calculate the distance for the tree protection zone.

Example 1:

A healthy 60-year-old 75 cm diameter walnut (*Juglans regia*) (poor tolerance, mature age)

$$37.5\,cm \times 75\,cm = 28.13\,m/2.5\,cm$$

$$= 11.25\,m \text{ tree protection zone}$$

Example 2:

A 15-year-old, healthy 32.5 cm diameter Alder (*Alnus* spp.)

$$15\,cm \times 32.5\,cm = 4.88\,m/2.5\,cm$$

$$= 1.95\,m \text{ tree protection zone}$$

Retention of existing trees

The result of poorly thought out retention efforts is a legacy of failed designs, lost opportunities and an ecologically impoverished landscape. However, tree retention is pointless if there is not a high possibility that the tree will (a) survive, and (b) not result in additional costs for the house/building owner at a later date for tree removal or remedial pruning. Decisions on retention have to be objectively, not emotionally, based, and must consider the significance of the tree, in terms of cultural, historical, environmental, aesthetic and botanical factors. Similarly, collection and presentation of information in an easily understood form is essential if designers are to interpret it effectively when producing layout proposals. Two important systems to aid in this decision process are those of Helliwell (1990) and Barrell (1993).

The Helliwell system, later revised by Coombes (1994), is used to assign a non-timber monetary value to amenity trees. In brief, seven factors are identified for each tree, namely size, useful life of tree, importance of position in the landscape, presence of other trees, relation to the setting, form and special factors. For each of these factors the tree is given a score of up to four points and the scores for all the factors are then multiplied together. A conversion factor (£1200) is then used to arrive at a monetary amenity value. This system has been adopted by estate agents, insurance brokers and building firms throughout the UK.

Another major problem is how long a tree can be expected to remain on site with an acceptable degree of safety. Use of the Safe Useful Life Expectancy (SULE) rule developed by Barrell (1993) is one of the most effective ways of pro-

Table 9.5 Guidelines for optimal tree preservation zones (adapted from Matheny and Clark (1998) and BS 5837 (1991)).

Species tolerance	Tree age	Distance from trunk (per 2.5 cm trunk diameter)
Good	Young (<20% life expectancy)	15 cm
	Mature (20–80% life expectancy)	22.5 cm
	Overmature (>80% life expectancy)	30 cm
Moderate	Young	22.5 cm
	Mature	30 cm
	Overmature	37.5 cm
Poor	Young	30 cm
	Mature	37.5 cm
	Overmature	45 cm

viding this information. Trees are assigned a SULE category between one and five. For example 'one' equates to a long SULE, (trees that appear to be retainable with an acceptable level of risk for more than 40 years) whilst 'four' means a tree has a high level of risk that would need removing within five years. Within each category trees are then assigned a letter identifying the reason why they were placed within each numerical category. For example 'four-A' equals a dead tree, hence the need to remove it within five years.

Individuals should be aware of both systems and adopt them when involved with decisions relating to tree retention.

9.4   Managing root growth

Roots crack and plug sewer lines; they lift and break kerbs, sidewalks, pavement and building foundations. When roots dry the soil under pavement and buildings, certain soils shrink and settle resulting in structural damage. Shallow roots in lawns can be unsightly and difficult to mow around. Root suckers in lawns and planting beds are a nuisance. The economic consequences of such damage can be high. For example total annual costs are estimated to average $4.28 (about £2.85) per tree according to a survey undertaken in fifteen American cities (McPherson and Peper, 1995). Information available points to a similar cost in UK towns and cities (Harris *et al.*, 1999).

Rootspread in relation to planting distances from buildings

One of the major factors involved in tree root damage is the safe distance of trees from the buildings in question. The Royal Botanic Gardens Kew have played a key role in this area, having made intensive efforts to accelerate the synthesis of results from various field investigations, questionnaires and surveys into sound practical guidelines (Gasson and Cutler, 1998). Table 9.6 gives details of the distances within which 50, 75, and 90 per

Table 9.6   Root spread data: distance from buildings at which damage was recorded.

Genus	No of cases	% on shrinkable soils	% in drains	Distance from buildings % damage recorded (m)			Max root spread (m)
				50%	75%	90%	
Acer	1098	99	9.6	6.0	9.0	12.0	30
Aesculus	386	98	11.0	7.5	10.0	15.0	23
Betula	217	100	5.5	4.0	7.0	8.0	10
Crataegus	615	99	1.6	5.0	7.0	8.7	11.5
Cupressus	407	100	2.5	2.5	3.5	5.0	20
Fagus	154	100	>1.0	6.0	9.0	11.0	15
Fraxinus	1007	99	4.5	6.0	10.0	13.0	21
Malus, Pyrus	80	96	2.0	4.0	6.0	8.0	10
Platanus	1467	100	7.5	5.5	7.5	10.0	15
Populus	1165	99	24.0	11.0	15.0	20.0	30
Prunus	860	100	4.5	3.0	6.0	7.5	11
Quercus	1546	100	3.5	9.5	13.0	18.0	30
Robinia	411	100	>1.0	7.0	8.5	10.5	12.4
Salix	787	100	18.5	7.0	11.0	18.0	40
Sorbus	303	96	>1.0	5.0	7.0	8.5	11
Tilia	1112	100	1.0	6.0	8.0	11.0	20
Ulmus	316	100	>1.0	8.0	12.0	19.0	25

Note: If trees already exist within the distances given, these figures must not be taken as an indication that they are a risk to buildings, until all other factors, including soil type and past history of the site have been considered.

cent of all damage was reported for eighteen common tree genera widely planted in the UK. To avoid detrimental interactions between trees and buildings, adoption of the 75 per cent figure as a guide to safe planting is suggested, if the tree is expected to grow to its maximum size. For most Rosaceae, *Betula*, small *Acer*, *Cupressus* and *Chamaecyparis*, the 50 per cent figure could be more suitable. In the case of potentially very large trees, which normally grow in parkland or woodland, the 90 per cent figure is more appropriate. On non-shrinkable soils it may be possible to have trees closer than these indicated distances without structures suffering root-induced damage.

Root loss – how much can a tree tolerate?

There is no convenient answer to this question. Species, age, physiological condition and the level of aftercare available are all factors that have to be considered. As a guideline, young nursery trees can lose up to 75 per cent of their roots when lifted and survive. A fully mature tree which loses 5–10 per cent of its roots will suffer some crown die back, be more susceptible to pests or may even die. As a useful rule of thumb, a healthy vigorous tree that is still growing will be able to stand the loss of up to 30 per cent of its root system without showing any ill effects and up to 50 per cent without dying. There may, however, be problems of stability if all the roots on one side are severed.

9.5 Shrinkable soils

British soils vary considerably in their potential for volume change, with clay soils most vulnerable to shrinkage upon drying and swelling following re-wetting. Indeed, virtually all cases of alleged damage to building foundations by tree roots in the UK are recorded on shrinkable clay soils. Damage resulting from soil shrinkage and expansion includes the cracking and subsidence of pavements, foundations, masonry and walls. Doors and windows commonly stick due to such building movement. Surface cracking of a soil indicates its susceptibility to shrinking and swelling.

However, not all soils shrink to the same extent. A simple test to determine the plasticity and make up of clays involves cutting, shaping and measuring a block of clay, leaving it in a warm room for two to three weeks and then measuring it again (BS 1377, 1990). The Building Research Establishment has published a number of useful digests dealing with the nature of clay soils and the occurrence and identification of shrinkable clays in the UK.

In summary the clays of Britain fall into three groups: older marine sedimentary deposits of the Eocene, Lower Cretaceous and Upper Jurassic vintage; glacial clays derived from the last ice age; and the more recent Quaternary deposits of alluvial clays. The Eocene clays of the South-East of England are highly plastic compared to the very sandy boulder clays of the North, and it would appear that the areas with the highest soil moisture deficit have the most highly expansive clays (see O'Callaghan and Lawson 1995, Arboricultural Association 1997 for useful information and references).

Minimising shrinking and swelling problems

The only guarantee on shrinkable soils that trees will not cause damage to structures with shallow foundations is to ensure that the tree-to-building distance is greater than the maximum tree root radius. Although this is a logical approach, if adopted it would almost eliminate trees from the urban environment.

More commonly used methods include to provide buildings with deep, strong foundation footings. Short-bored pile foundations (augered holes filled with concrete so they are integral with the foundation) 3 m long can provide stability at reasonable cost. Other solutions are to plant moderately vigorous trees that will grow to a small or medium size. Avoid larger trees, (oak, poplar, willow, elm, horse chestnut), particularly if building foundations are inadequate. If trees begin to cause damage around existing buildings, consider removing them. Do not repair settling cracks in buildings or pavement until the soil has had a chance to rewet and the cracks partially close.

While a tree is young, or before planting, improve the structure, fertility, and moisture conditions of half the soil under what will be the mature canopy away from the building. This should increase root branching in the improved soil and minimise root growth toward the building. Crown lifting (reducing or thinning) will reduce water demand and root growth. Ensure trees are adequately watered so that the soil does not subside or expand unduly (Arboricultural Association, 1997).

Root barriers

Over the past few years numerous root barriers have become commercially available. Most consist of heavy gauge black polythene with internal vertical ribs designed to deflect root growth laterally and/or downwards and concomitantly reduce root spiralling. Other synthetic fabric barriers combine a geotextile fabric with a time-released herbicide, while a square polyethylene planter, wider at the base than at the top, is also available. Similarly, incorporation of a root herbicide into the trench back fill to kill roots entering the trench area has been shown to control tree roots effectively when applied singly or in combination with a root barrier, but has raised political and environmental concerns. Extensive trials in the USA have shown root barriers to be quite effective in reducing damage to man-made structures (Nicoll and Coutts, 1997).

Contrary to this, a number of disadvantages of root barriers have been highlighted by Gilman (1996). These include that roots may be confined within the device and trees become unstable as they increase in size; as roots enlarge, they can occasionally lift the barrier out of the ground, or if the devices are set too low, roots will often grow over the top. Root barriers can potentially limit the capacity of trees to develop into large effective specimens.

Is building damage the fault of the tree?

Most examiners tend to become preoccupied with the effects of trees on foundations in clay soils, but it is important to remember that any agency that sponsors local drying and wetting of soil can cause differential soil movement. These include leaking drains and rainwater pipes, overflows, paving diverting rainwater to one part of a building and boiler bases and hearths. In addition it is always wise to consider that differential settlement may also be caused by inherent building design defects. These include:

- ill prepared foundation trenches
- parts of buildings of different weights being founded at the same level
- interaction of different types of foundation close to each other
- failure to take account of features nearby which may affect subsoil performance, such as open land and paving
- installation of underground central heating pipes resulting in soil shrinkage.

Recorded cases exist of action being recommended which has the opposite effect to that desired, for example pruning will reduce the water demand of the tree in the short term, but complete removal can lead to the expansion of a shrinkable clay soil and resultant heave (Harris et al., 1999). It is important to remember that plastic clays, which are most associated with building damage, are unlikely to support root growth of species other than those with adaptations to tolerate deoxygenation below 1–1.5 metres. In many instances subsidence damage cannot be attributed solely to a tree or trees, and in some cases the building would have failed even in the absence of trees.

Water demand

Guidance on assessing the risk of foundation damage due to water absorption by trees causing shrinkage of clay soils can be found by reference to McCombie (1995). He argues the problems of soil shrinkage, and the allowance currently recommended is too simplistic and inadequate. Based on his research (McCombie, 1993) and that of others (Biddle, 1983) modifications are proposed to the UK National House Building Council's current guidelines which allow the correct assess-

Table 9.7 Water demand of commonly planted UK species; see McCombie (1995) for full details and derivation of equations.

Species	K95	Water Demand	d/h for 0.5 m foundation with tree h = 2 hmax/3	D/H required
High water demand				
Willow (*Salix*)	1.92	H	1.45	
Apple/Pear (*Malus/Pyrus*)	1.9	H	1.43	1.5
Cherry/Plum (*Prunus*)	1.85	H	1.38	
Poplar (*Populus*)	1.69	H	1.22	
Hawthorn (*Crataegus*)	1.65	H	1.18	
Oak (*Quercus*)	1.64	H	1.17	
Whitebeam/ Rowan (*Sorbus*)	1.42	M	0.95	
Moderate water demand				
Lime (*Tilia*)	1.41	M	0.94	1.02
Elm (*Ulmus*)	1.41	M	0.94	
Horse chestnut (*Aesculus*)	1.41	M	0.94	
Maple/Sycamore (*Acer*)	1.4	M	0.93	
Beech (*Fagus*)	1.38	M	0.91	
Low water demand				
False Acacia (*Robinia*)	1.28	L	0.81	
Common Ash (*Fraxinus*)	1.26	L	0.79	0.82
Birch (*Betula*)	1.24	L	0.77	
Plane (*Platanus*)	1.17	L	0.76	

Notes:
K95 = A value derived from re-assessment of the Kew data to take into account tree height and distance from the building where actual damage was recorded.
H = High, M = Moderate, L = Low.
d/h = The maximum distance to damage for 95% of cases (d) divided by the height of the tree (h) compared with the height of the tree divided by the maximum height for the species (hmax).
D/H = The actual distance required for planting on high plasticity soils, expressed as a multiple of tree height.

ment of common species, taking into account their water demand (high, moderate or low), height, and soil shrinkability (Table 9.7).

Roots blocking drains

Tree roots are frequently blamed for blocking drains, but in reality these form only a small proportion of the total number of root-related enquiries (Table 9.2). Drains almost certainly need to be leaking before roots are attracted to and proliferate within them. Drain damage usually occurs on shrinkable clays, where there is more likelihood of relative movement between buildings and drains than on stable soils. If the pipes carry water that is cooler than the surrounding soil, water may condense on the outer surface. This could be attractive to roots, and give a false impression that roots were 'attacking' the drain.

A range of measures exist to prevent or delay the invasion of drains, including selection of appropriate tree species for the site, water-tight flexible telescopic joints, and wrapping sewer joints with copper wire screen, which although toxic to small roots does little to prevent cracks caused by enlarging roots. Penetryn is used to seal leakages utilising a liquid dual component acrylic gel that is pumped into the joints. Pipe sliplining involves a 10–12 m long plastic pipe which is welded together and either drawn or pushed through the existing defective pipe. Alternately, a liner of acid-resistant polyester fibre impregnated with resin can be placed into the defective pipe and when in position cured with hot water to produce a rigid and hard wearing pipe. All of these techniques have their advantages and disadvantages (Groninger *et al.*, 1997).

9.6 Avoiding conflicts between urban trees and people

A diverse range of participants are involved in the development process, including developer, builder, civil engineer, service engineer, soils engineer, architect, landscape architect, general contractor, demolition contractor and city/county planner. Their understanding of root physiology will range from good to non-existent. To avoid conflicts before, during and after site development, the role of the scientifically-literate arboriculturist is to provide the best information possible and to convey that information to all interested parties in an appropriate and understandable format. Tasks should include:

- Identifying the goals of the project and assessing how trees are involved.
- Knowing the community's restrictions and requirements regarding trees and ensuring compliance.
- Assessing the composition and condition of the tree resource, i.e. listing species by number and percentage of total population; preparing a profile of trees based on diameter, height, and crown spread; listing trees showing specific insect and/or disease problems etc.
- Compiling all site information significant to trees (location of trees, species, crown spread, height, girth of stem, overall condition, health, stage of maturity etc.).
- Appraising the value of trees when required.
- Evaluating the impacts that development will have on the trees and how the trees are likely to respond.
- Suggesting alternative designs to minimise impacts.
- Recommending trees for retention or removal.
- Assisting in securing necessary permits and approvals relative to trees.

- Determining how work should proceed to protect trees from damage.
- Preparing necessary drawings, reports and specifications.
- Communicating with all parties involved with the project.
- Educating people involved in the project.
- Responding to tree-related issues throughout the development process.
- Maintaining records of actions and decisions regarding trees.
- Monitoring construction activity and tree response to site changes and determining appropriate action.

These issues are discussed in greater detail by Matheny and Clark (1998) and Weinstein (1984).

References

Arboricultural Association (1997) *Subsidence Risk Assessment for Buildings Near Trees*. Arboricultural Association, Ampfield House, Ampfield, Romsey, UK.

Barrell, J.D. (1993) Pre-planning tree surveys: Safe Useful Life Expectancy (SULE) is the natural progression. *Arboricultural Journal*, **17**, 33–46.

Biddle, P.G. (1983) Patterns of soil drying and moisture deficit in the vicinity of trees on clay soils. *Geotechnique*, **33**, 107–26.

British Standard 5837 (1991) *Guide for Trees in Relation to Construction*. British Standards Institution, Park Street, London.

British Standard 1377 (1990) *Methods of Testing for Soil for Civil Engineering Purposes (Part 2)*. British Standards Institution, Park Street, London.

Chiatante, D., Di Iorio, A. Maiuro, L., & Scippa, S.G. (2000) Effect of water stress on root meristems in woody and herbaceous plants during the first stage of development. In: A. Stokes (Ed.) *The supporting roots of trees and woody plants: form function and physiology*, pp. 245–58. Kluwer Academic Publishers, Netherlands.

Coombes, S.A. (1994) Amenity valuations: the Helliwell system revised. *Arboricultural Journal*, **18**, 137–44.

Crook, C.S. (1992) The feasibility of tree planting on landfill containment sites. *Arboricultural Journal*, **16**, 229–41.

Cutler, D.F. (1995) Interactions between tree roots and buildings. In G.W. Watson & D. Neely (Eds), *Trees* and Building Sites: Proceedings of an International Workshop on Trees and Buildings, pp 78–87. International Society of Arboriculture, Illinois, USA.

Cutler, D.F. & Richardson, I.B.K. (1989) *Tree Roots and Buildings*, 2nd edn. Longman Scientific and Technical, Harlow.

Day, S.D. & Bassuk, N. (1994) A review of the effects of soil compaction and amelioration treatments on landscape trees. *Journal of Arboriculture*, **20**, (1), 9–17.

Eissenstat, D.M., Wells, C.E., Yanai, R.D., & Whitbeck, J.L. (2000) Building roots in a changing environment: implications for root longevity. *New Phytologist*, **147**, 33–42.

Gasson, P.E. & Cutler, D.F. (1998) Can we live with trees in our towns and cities? *Arboricultural Journal*, **22**, 1–9.

Gilman, E.F. (1996) Root barriers affect root distribution. *Journal of Arboriculture*, **22**, (3), 151–4.

Groninger, J.W., Shepard, M.Z., & Seiler, J.R. (1997) Herbicides to control tree roots in sewer lines. *Journal of Arboriculture*, **23**, (5), 169–72.

Harris, R.W., Clark, J.M., & Matheny, N.P. (1999) *Arboriculture: Integrated Management of Landscape Trees, Shrubs and Vines*, 3rd edn. Prentice-Hall, Englewood Cliffs, New Jersey.

Helliwell, D.R. (1985) *Trees on development sites*. Arboricultural Association, Ampfield House, Ampfield, Romsey, UK.

Helliwell, D.R. (1990) *Amenity valuation of trees and woodlands*. Arboricultural Association, Ampfield House, Ampfield, Romsey, UK.

Hitchmough, J.D. (1994) *Urban Landscape Management*, pp. 114–21. Inkata Press, Sydney, Australia.

Hodge, S.J. & Knott, K. (1993) A practical guide to the use of the steel rod technique for the assessment of aeration in urban soils. *Journal of Arboriculture*, **19**, (5), 281–8.

Kopinga, J. (1995) Aspects of the damage to asphalt road pavings caused by tree roots. In: *The Landscape Below Ground: proceedings of an international workshop on tree root development in urban soils*, International Society of Arboriculture, Illinois, USA.

Kozlowski, T.T., Kramer, P.J., & Pallardy, S.G. (1991) *The Physiological Ecology of Woody Plants*, p. 136, Academic Press, San Diego.

Lindsey, P.A., Gross, R., & Milano, B. (1995) An investigation to assess the impact of street infrastructure improvements on the roots of adjacent cork oak trees. In: G.W. Watson & D. Neely (Eds) *Trees and Building Sites: Proceedings of an International Workshop*

on *Trees and Buildings*. International Society of Arboriculture, Illinois, USA.

Majdi, H. & Kangas, P. (1997) Demography of fine roots in response to nutrient applications in a Norway spruce stand in southwestern Sweden. *Ecoscience*, **4**, (2), 199–205.

Matheny, N. & Clark, J.R. (1998) *Trees and development: a technical guide to preservation of trees during land development*. International Society of Arboriculture, Illinois, USA.

McCombie, P.F. (1993) The relative water demand of broad-leaved trees – a new analysis of the Kew Tree Root Survey. *Arboricultural Journal*, **17**, 4.

McCombie, P.F. (1995) The prediction of building foundation damage arising from the water demand of trees. *Arboricultural Journal*, **19**, (2), 147–60.

McMichael, B.L. & Burke, J.J. (1998) Soil temperature and root growth. *HortScience*, **33**, (6), 947–51.

McPherson, G.E. & Peper, P.J. (1995) Infrastructure repair costs associated with street trees in 15 cities. In: G.W. Watson & D. Neelyn (Eds) *Trees and Building Sites: Proceedings of an International Workshop on Trees and Buildings*. International Society of Arboriculture, Illinois, USA.

Morris, L.A. & Lowery, R.F. (1988) Influence of site preparation on soil conditions affecting stand establishment and tree growth. *Southern Journal of Applied Forestry*, **12**, (3), 170–78.

Nicoll, C. & Coutts, M.P. (1997). Direct damage by urban roots: paving the way for less damaging street trees. In: *Arboricultural Practice Present and Future*, pp 77–84. DoE, Norwich, UK.

Nicoll, C. & Armstrong, A. (1998) Development of *Prunus* root systems in a city street: pavement damage and root architecture. *Arboricultural Journal*, **22**, (3), 259–70.

O'Callaghan, D. & Lawson, M. (1995) A critical look at the potential for foundation damage caused by tree roots. In: G.W. Watson & D. Neely (Eds) *Trees and Building Sites: Proceedings of an International Workshop on Trees and Buildings*. International Society of Arboriculture, Illinois, USA.

Pregtizer, K.S., King, J.A., & Burton, A.J. (2000) Responses of tree fine roots to temperature. *New Phytologist*, **147**, (1), 33–42.

Sydnor, D.T., Gamstetter, D., Nichols, J., Bishop, B., Favorite, J., Blazer, C., & Turpin, L. (2000) Trees are not the root of sidewalk damage. *Journal of Arboriculture*, **26**, (1), 20–25.

Watson, G.W. & Neely, D. (1995) *Trees and Building Sites: Proceedings of an International Workshop on*

Trees and Buildings. International Society of Arboriculture, Illinois, USA.

Ware, G.H. (1994) Ecological bases for selecting urban trees. *Journal of Arboriculture*, **20**, (3), 98–103.

Weinstein, G. (1984) Central Park, New York – A management survey of an urban forest. *Arboricultural Journal*, **8**, (4), 321–30.

Wells, C.E. (1999) Advances in the root demography of woody species. Unpublished PhD thesis, The Pennsylvania State University, USA.

10 Semi-mature Trees

James Wilson, Caroline Swann and Peter Thoday

Using semi-mature trees is not a new activity. It is likely that large palms were transported in the creation of the Hanging Gardens of Babylon and the use of semi-mature trees in Britain during the 19th century and earlier is well documented.

However, during the first half of the twentieth century the use of semi-mature trees declined. It is really only during the last thirty years that they have regained their popularity throughout Europe and the United States. The first standard for transplanting semi-mature trees in Britain was produced in 1966 (British Standards Institute, 1966). Biologists would argue that small trees generally establish and grow more quickly than their older, larger counterparts. Within a few years a vigorous 1.8 m feathered birch can grow taller than a semi-mature tree of the same species. While this is undoubtedly true, in some landscapes the high vulnerability of small planting stock to vandalism and mower operators will negate the advantages of more rapid establishment and growth. When making decisions on the size of tree planting stock for a project, the key factor is to match planting stock size and maturity with the site conditions and maintenance regime. Where site conditions are biologically hostile and post planting maintenance likely to be poor, small planting stock will generally be the better option. Where site conditions can be satisfactorily ameliorated and post-planting weed control and irrigation can be guaranteed, semi-mature trees are worth considering.

The obvious advantage of a semi-mature tree is the visual impact of the size and scale of the plant in the development, particularly as a mass of leaves and branches. Thriving semi-mature trees can screen and complement buildings, cast shade, provide the largest replacements for lost trees and make a highly significant contribution to new landscapes immediately after planting.

By using large trees, landscape architects can make their design vision a reality as rapidly as possible. The immediacy of this impact may be the primary advantage of using semi-mature trees, a means of satisfying clients who lack vision or patience. Worth is also always related to financial value. While semi-mature trees are expensive in comparison to the costs of other plants, compared to other features of the development, semi-mature trees are relatively inexpensive and have the added value of increasing in worth over the years to come.

However, semi-mature trees will only provide these benefits when they recover from transplanting and re-commence normal growth, within one or two years after planting. This recovery relies on successful establishment and knowledgeable aftercare, and in particular on effective weed control and irrigation during the first two growing seasons. (Weed control is dealt with in detail in Chapters 6 and 8.) The careful selection of species suitable for the site and conditions must be followed up by good maintenance; this is important for any planting, but even more so for semi-mature trees. If ignored or neglected, they may fail to thrive and lose all the visual impact for which they were planted. Too often capital expenditure on the immediate impact of large trees is wasted because no resources have been allocated within the revenue budget to cover subsequent maintenance.

Although there are variations depending on species, size, site and maintenance regime, it may take as long as 20 years for a semi-mature tree to compensate for the trauma of transplanting at this size. This underlines the importance of including the hidden costs of aftercare.

Suppliers and contractors have responded to the poor planting and inadequate maintenance of past years by offering a full supply, planting and maintenance service. This has many advantages, principally in reducing potential conflicts over the responsibility for tree survival. As a result, landscape designers have tended to abrogate their responsibility for semi-mature trees to others. However contracts such as these are focused primarily on the survival of the trees, rather than the resumption of normal growth; in the longer term this is most important. This chapter looks at current trends and practices, to provide clearer guidance for landscape designers who are specifying the trees on what to ask for and expect.

10.1 Getting the right plant

What is a semi-mature tree? The UK *National Plant Specification* (HTA, 1997) defines semi-mature trees as 'trees with an overall height in excess of four metres and/or a stem girth measure of 20 centimetres or larger'. Typically many such trees will generally range from 4–15 m in height and will weigh between 100 kg and 10 tonnes (Fig. 10.1). In most cases they need special lifting techniques or equipment because of their spread and weight.

Species

Historically, a far more limited number of species has been available compared with smaller sizes. Better growing techniques, together with improved communication in sourcing and supplying, is increasing the range. As a result, it is even more important to consider carefully the suitability of the species for the location and also its 'transplantability'.

Different species exhibit different biological characteristics and tolerances. Most, oaks for example, are slow to initiate new root growth post planting, which is why they are often very slow to 'take off' after planting as semi-mature trees. However the pin oak, *Quercus palustris*, is an oak with vigorous root initiation (Struve and Moser, 1984), and consequently establishes rapidly even when transplanted at advanced size. Apart from species variation, success will vary depending on site conditions, the condition of the plant and the care with which it is supplied, grown and maintained.

Fig. 10.1 Semi-mature trees at the nursery. (Photo: Hillier Nurseries Ltd)

Table 10.1 Typical ease of transplanting of different genera as root-balled stock.

Readily transplanted	Intermediate	Most difficult
Acer (many)	*Alnus*	*Abies*
Malus	*Betula*	*Carpinus*
Platanus	*Buxus*	*Cedrus*
Sorbus	*Crataegus*	*Chamaecyparis*
Tilia	*Fraxinus*	*Fagus*
	Liquidambar	*Ilex*
	Populus	*Juglans*
	Prunus	*Larix*
	Pyrus	*Liriodendron*
	Quercus	*Magnolia*
	Robinia	*Pinus*
	Salix	*Picea*
		Thuja

Table 10.1 summarises the 'transplantability' of some temperate tree genera. Care must be taken in using this guide, since variations will be found between species within a genus. This information is derived from the collective experience of advanced tree nurseries, and landscape practitioners. It reflects what is easiest to grow, and thus most readily available.

Canopy forms

The majority of trees are available in 'standard' form, i.e. with a single clear stem, extending at least 1.8 m from ground level, a well-balanced crown and a central leading shoot where this is appropriate for the species. Other forms constitute only about five per cent of production: in this group are multi-stemmed and bushy trees, including species drawn from the genera *Acer, Alnus Betula, Carpinus, Crataegus, Quercus, Robinia* and *Sorbus*. Variable demand tends to undermine the reliability of supply in these forms.

Continental sources can supply a wide range of shaped trees from ready-made pleached limes to pyramids, cones, spirals, etc., in box, yew and holly. UK nurseries are now beginning to follow suit with pleached trees. It is also possible to get shaped cultivar types (e.g. *Acer platanoides* 'Globosum'), in increasing quantities and the 'natural' forms of some of the smaller trees/shrubs are proving popular, for example, *Amelanchier lamarckii, Crataegus* and *Malus* spp.

While the range is expanding, the opportunity to find the non-standard or irregularly shaped tree is diminishing. These trees, often far more irregular in form, were the 'leftovers' which improvement in production is eliminating. Now as much as ever, plant users need to talk to growers to ensure that the forms and species they would like to use will be available in the future, remembering that they take more than ten years to grow.

Production system

Traditionally most semi-mature trees have been grown and supplied as a field grown, root balled product. While this system has the disadvantage of relatively low root capture and harvest, it avoids spiralling and other root malformations common in container production. It is also cheaper to field grow and root ball than to grow in containers and this is reflected in the price of semi-mature trees. The transport of root-balled specimens is best restricted to the dormant season. In contrast well grown, container-produced trees and shrubs can be moved at any time without suffering from the act of transplanting; indeed they should immediately benefit from it. However, site conditions and husbandry inputs are more demanding during the growing season; if these factors are overlooked at that time of year, the plants will suffer more dramatic and catastrophic effects.

There is now a hybrid production system in which trees are grown in the field for most of their time in the nursery, then lifted either bare root or root-balled and transplanted into a container where they are grown on for a further year prior to sale. The leading exponent of this technique in Britain has been Hillier Nurseries.

After much testing, Hillier Nurseries now produces most of their containerised and container-grown trees in air pots constructed from a plastic sheet with a complex, concave-convex, 'egg box' form (Fig. 10.2). This method of containerisation actually prunes back the roots as they attempt to grow through the perforations into the surrounding air. The root tip withers, but behind it side roots develop, thus producing fibrous root growth. Any tendency for root spiralling to take place is prevented. The net result of all this activity is a mass of fibrous root at the edges of the circular containers that will quickly help the tree to become established once planted out on site (Fig. 10.3, Plate 11). In essence, the first year of transplant shock takes place in the nursery, where expert management and the avoidance of soil moisture stress allows substantial root regrowth to occur, to compensate for what was lost at lifting in the field.

Sources

During the last 30 years, supplies in the UK have been variable, suppliers often drawing from stands

Fig. 10.2 An air pot container opened up on the nursery. (Photo: Hillier Nurseries Ltd)

Fig. 10.3 Pines grown in air pot containers on the nursery. (Photo: Hillier Nurseries Ltd)

of trees established on old estates, nurseries and other 'one off' sources. However within the last 15 years, specialist sources have developed, although considerably more semi-mature trees are available from suppliers in Holland, Germany, Italy and France. Most suppliers trade with others, so for example, a tree growing in the UK or Germany may have been supplied from Italy.

There is considerable debate and many opinions about the use of semi-mature trees from these differing sources. A main concern has been the hardiness of stock grown in warmer climes; trees have been transplanted successfully from a range of sources. In most cases the critical issue is to assess whether that particular cultivar is suited to the climate of Britain or not. Providing they are genetically 'fitted' in the first place, any physiological 'conditioning' effects resulting from prior cultivation in a warmer climate will have disappeared completely after one season's growth in Britain.

This is just one of a number of factors which should be taken into account. Even the country of origin is difficult to determine since growers can sell trees as 'UK grown' after only one growing season in this country. There is no doubt that continental sources have higher numbers of evenly sized trees in larger size than in the UK, but supply is variable and all sources are worth considering. By personal inspection and selection, it is possible to keep up to date with supply and develop relationships with the growers. Where competitive tendering is necessary, inspection of stock also makes it easier to obtain comparative prices on the basis of accurate specification rather than more general description.

10.2   Transplanting

Successful transplanting of trees involves major disturbance of the root system. Up to 90 per cent of the active growing root system can be severed when a tree is lifted, whether bare root or with a root ball.

Trees have been transplanted for centuries but, as White (1990) says,

'The biological reasons for some of the traditional operations [in the nursery] appear to have become clouded until today their execution maybe less than ideally implemented in the interests of commerce'.

She goes on to say that,

'Nursery practices are unlikely to kill a tree which is growing in the nursery, but when that tree is used in the landscape the ability of a tree to develop roots may become the limiting factor for tree growth especially if site conditions are inhospitable'.

Current specifications call for a well-balanced root system, but this has not been defined quantitatively. In some ways it is not surprising that so little is known about root systems. Apart from the obvious difficulties of studying an extensive underground network objectively, root systems are dynamic, and vary in response to the tree's genetic make up and environmental conditions. Transplantability depends not only on these factors but also on nursery practice during production, storage and transport conditions, final planting and aftercare.

Root systems absorb water and nutrients, and physically support the tree. Lifting and transplanting inevitably results in the loss of the majority of the fine fibrous, actively growing roots. Regrowth is initiated from the remaining root system, which develops a more branched character than its undisturbed equivalent.

Transplanting success relies on the tree's root growth potential (RGP): its ability to re-root from the surviving rootsystem. Research indicates that the RGP and the extent of loss of fibrous roots vary between species. Regrowth can also be influenced by rough plant handling and seasonal factors. In order to sell large plants, trees are undercut and/or transplanted and grown on in the nursery. Through transplanting, the tree develops a more compact root system, which is beneficial in two ways:

- a more compact root system should have a higher root:shoot ratio, which should aid establishment; and
- a compact root system is easier to handle.

Transplanting or undercutting in the nursery is not however always as effective in producing a more branched root system as might be hoped. Many species only initiate new roots from the most distal portions of the cut roots (Gilman and Yeagher, 1988). When the trees are then finally root balled for sale, much of this new root growth is left behind in the field.

Root systems are easily damaged by desiccation, and this is particularly significant with plants supplied bare root. Again, there is considerable variation in tolerance of desiccation between species: those with finely branched roots (such as *Betula* spp.) are typically more sensitive than thick-rooted species such as *Tilia*. Semi-mature trees are usually supplied with a root ball to reduce desiccation. Some particularly sensitive trees are containerised (transplanted from the field into a container within the nursery) in order to ensure establishment before supply.

One of the other many factors that can affect re-growth is the influence of root mycorrhizal associations. There is currently much interest in active inoculation with these organisms to increase effective root volume, but it is not always easy to demonstrate the value of this activity except under extreme *landscape* conditions (Findlay, 1999).

Typically, by the time a tree reaches semi-mature size, it would have been transplanted at least four times. It is generally accepted that it is essential to continue to transplant every three or four years, and at each transplanting, the root ball is increased in proportion to the size of the tree. By this practice, it is assumed that the RGP of the tree is improved, drying out is reduced and mycorrhizal associations present in the nursery are transferred.

Mechanised transplanting in the nursery has

streamlined production. The French preparation method as described in BS 4043 (British Standards Institute, 1989) which required two or more growing seasons is now only used to move trees which have not been regularly transplanted. Containerisation can aid survival and is particularly useful for those that are least readily transplanted. However, the combined weight of the tree and container can either eliminate this as an alternative or restrict the size of the tree.

The range of variables affecting the physiology of root systems and their ability to re-grow is wide. Debate continues, but there is general agreement that objective data are relatively limited and current practice involves many subjective assumptions. White (1990) suggests that it is necessary to develop a definition of a root system necessary for survival and growth for each species at various growth sizes, plus a superior understanding of critical root:shoot ratios in transplanted stock. Current practice is moving towards most semi-mature trees being supplied root-balled (i.e. with most of the active root removed) while the more historic method of trenching or containerisation would re-establish a fibrous root system before supply. This suggests that expediency, rather than biology, is the main driver of nursery production methods.

10.3 Specification criteria

The appropriate specification depends on the nature of the project. Some designers justify using nominated suppliers because of the unique qualities of their trees. In this way, trees are selected by hand at a particular nursery and a price is negotiated. This figure includes planting and guaranteed costs. In this arrangement, responsibility rests solely with the supplier/contractor to ensure successful establishment. It is therefore essential that the designer selects a supplier/contractor competent to carry out the work, who understands exactly what is required.

A performance specification can thus be written which demands only that the selected trees should be supplied, guaranteed by the nursery to thrive for a specified period and planted within a set time. Once a price has been agreed, it is up to the supplier/contractor how he carries out the works. However the designer would be incompetent if he/she did not understand the work that this involved.

Where comparative prices are required for competitive tendering purposes, a more detailed specification is required. In the UK the National Plant Specification facilitates this. However there is still no substitute for personal inspection, which enables greater precision in the specification.

A range of sources can be compared throughout the tendering process. Tenderers can also provide information on other appropriate/unique trees which might not have been considered before sending out tenders. Once tenders are received, sources need to be inspected and tagged before ordering.

The following characteristics need to be specified and/or checked when using semi-mature trees.

Age

This factor is seldom used in specification but it is important. There is an optimal relationship between age and size which gives an indication of vigour. However, due to varying growth rates, estimating the age of semi-mature trees is often difficult, with the exception of species such as *Pinus* in which annual extension growth is fairly easy to interpret. As a rough guide, one continental supplier estimates that deciduous trees tend to increase in girth by 2 cm/year.

Girth

Taken as the stem circumference at 1 m height, this measure is generally accepted as a more accurate indicator of quality (in this case primarily canopy volume) than height. For semi-mature trees this is given in a series of ranges as centimetres; 25–30, 30–35, 35–40, 40–45, 45–50, 50–60 cm and so on.

Overall height

This is used as an additional qualification to girth. Although important, height often correlates less well to the mass of crown than does girth. Heights vary depending on species, for example, *Aesculus* spp. tends to be shorter and thicker in girth than *Alnus* spp. Crop densities also affect height; trees planted too close together grow taller more quickly, but without an increase in girth.

Spread

This characteristic is seldom specified although some nurseries will provide details.

Clear stem

The clear stem height can be very variable if not specified.

Transplanting

Increasingly, quality suppliers give details on the number of times trees have been transplanted. It may be worth specifying, but is difficult to check.

Root condition

Trees are usually supplied root-balled. Containerised trees are increasingly widely available. Bare root trees are generally not supplied since, for all species, they are considered too susceptible to drying out.

Root ball size

There are no UK standards. Continental sources use an approximate formula: root ball diameter = approximately 2.5 × girth, so a 40cm girth tree should have a 1m diameter root ball. UK root balls tend to be larger, although old recommendations are not dissimilar to continental sizes. Depth of root balls is less significant as roots tend to remain in the surface layers.

Digging

This factor is not usually specified, but increasingly field-grown semi-mature trees are dug mechanically, and the nature of the machine can influence transplant success. Flattened, wide root

Fig. 10.4 Lifting and root-balling semi-mature trees. (Photo: Hillier Nurseries Ltd)

balls will typically capture more roots than deep narrow root balls (Fig. 10.4). Very large trees are hand dug.

Materials

Most semi-mature trees are now wrapped in jute sacking and wire mesh. It is essential that the root ball remains rigid and does not fall apart. Wrapping materials are now usually fully biodegradable since non-galvanised wire mesh is almost universally used. If this is not the case, wrappings must be removed. Removable frames were previously popular but are now less widely used as they are too expensive to replace if lost.

Container size

Again there are no standards and a range of sizes can be found. The containers are either rigid wire mesh baskets or polypropylene pots. For container grown or containerised semi-mature trees, typical container volumes in relation to tree size are given in Table 10.2.

Time in the container

Trees should be established (rooted through), but should not remain in the same size container for

Table 10.2 Typical container volumes for trees supplied in containers.

Tree girth (cm)	Container volume (litres)
8–10/10–12	45
12–14/18–20	80
20–25/25–30	200
30–35	300
30–35/60–70	1000

more than a year. Avoid stock that is strongly pot-bound with spiralling roots, as this rooting pattern tends to persist, leading to poorer establishment and long-term instability.

Compost

Unless otherwise specified, nurseries use their own mixes, which are usually peat based, although increasingly composted bark and other organic debris are also used.

Crown form

Unless otherwise specified, a 'standard' crown form will be supplied. If another form is required, it must be described. If an irregular form is required, inspection is necessary.

Crown pruning

Generally continental sources reduce the crown quite extensively when transplanting, whereas UK nurseries reduce it less, allowing a natural crown to develop. This is discussed further on, under 'Establishment and maintenance'.

Tying in

Unless otherwise specified, tree branches will be tied in to avoid damage. Care must be taken not to tie in too tightly since breakage can occur in transit, possibly due to drying out of the branches.

Anti-desiccants

These are occasionally specified, especially for summer planting and conifers, but they may have detrimental physiological effects on the plant. Careful planting and good aftercare can eliminate the need for anti-desiccants.

Stem wrapping

This is popular in North America, where it is thought to insulate the tree and reduce transpiration. The necessity in Europe is questionable, except where considerable reflected radiation is likely. It can also protect the trunk from physical damage.

Lifting machinery

The machinery must be appropriate for the size and weight of the tree. Cranes are often required; access and timing are critical. Many suppliers provide crane off-loading, and this needs to be identified in the price.

Lifting method

Trees are usually lifted with supporting slings under the root ball, never around the stem. Ropes may be used to prevent damage to the crown. Damage can occur easily, especially in the spring when the sap is rising. Trees are either moved on special lorries with integral lifting arms or on standard 12m trailers. Ideally the trailer should be fully covered with an opaque material, or trees should be transported at night. Continental suppliers estimate transporting 50–70 trees of 25–30 cm girth on one trailer, reducing the number to 1–3 trees of 50–60cm girth.

Transporting

Ideally the time between lifting and replanting should be as short as possible, but for species which transplant easily and are well prepared and handled, delays within the dormant season should have little effect. However, it is critical to ensure an agreed delivery time, so that a crane can be hired and materials obtained in good time. No doubt those who move semi-mature trees regard all types of semi-mature trees as awkward loads.

Fig. 10.5 Container grown trees in full leaf prepared and loaded for transportation. (Photo: Hillier Nurseries Ltd)

However, in recent years considerable ingenuity in the specialist nurseries has produced efficient lifting and packing methods that should ensure that the tree arrives on site in good condition (Fig. 10.5). Those receiving such trees should pay particular attention to any damage caused to the main trunk and branches.

The odd twig broken is of no consequence compared with damage to the bark. Unloading the tree should receive the same care and attention that the loading was given in the nursery. Semi-mature transplant storage on site should be kept to a minimum. With all three categories it is permissible, for short periods, to store them lying down and is probably preferable to having them in exposed positions where they are likely to be

blown over and their canopies damaged. There is a risk of the trees drying out throughout the storage period and although this seems an obvious candidate for attention, it is surprising how many trees die through root desiccation between arrival on site and planting.

Wound paints

The efficacy of these products is questionable. A healthy tree should seal clean cut wounds on branches or roots without sealant. Small wounds heal quicker than large ones; cuts should always be made through the branch bark ridge, rather than flush with the trunk to reduce wound diameter. This will also avoid breaching the layers of toxic compounds deposited by trees within the base of branches to inhibit fungal and bacterial infections. Seriously damaged trees should be rejected.

10.4   Ground preparation and planting

Preparing the ground for semi-mature trees and subsequently planting them is basically the same as for other forms of nursery stock, except on a larger scale.

However, there is the problem of divided responsibilities. For example, on one recent site where ten trees were being established there were two clients, one main contractor, two landscape sub-contractors, one topsoil supplier, one tree supplier and one maintenance contractor. Contract arrangements like this are to be avoided because it is difficult to co-ordinate ground preparation operations, planting and aftercare. Also minor but significant requirements can be overlooked, and identifying the resulting liabilities can be very difficult.

Landscape ground preparation and planting practices are often far from ideal, and rigorous specifications are required to ensure that conditions are sufficiently benign to minimise transplantation shock and encourage subsequent establishment. The following points cover the main areas of specification.

Soil structure

The soil surrounding the root ball must be able to retain and supply moisture and air. Soils used in backfilling the tree pit should be broadly compatible in textural terms with those in the surrounding area and, ideally, with the soil within the root ball.

Soil volume

Semi-mature trees must be able to root into a suitable volume of soil outside the tree pit, if the tree is to grow to the size anticipated. This need is often ignored. Research has shown that a fairly mature forest-sized tree needs approximately $100 \, m^3$ of soil.

Drainage

It is important that measures are taken to ensure subterranean drainage, which maintains the tree pit and rooting layer in a healthy aerobic state. There are many alternative methods: the exact solution depends on site conditions.

Subsoiling/scarification

The ripping of the subsoil is now common practice where conditions allow, although methods vary.

Explosives

In the USA explosive charges have been placed below the tree pit to fracture the soil profile. This practice is not known in Europe, but does indicate the significance of creating deep fissures.

Land drainage

It is simple to insert flexible drainage, connecting the pit to the land drainage system. However, these systems may eventually become blocked by roots.

Pit drainage

A 150 mm drainage layer of gravel can assist. Others recommend mounding the base centre of the pit. These methods are only adequate if the surrounding ground is free draining. If not other measures must be taken.

Planting on raised ground

This method has many advantages but needs to be considered fully as part of the landform modelling of the site.

Pit digging

Pits should be dug immediately before planting. If dug earlier, they should be backfilled or covered over to prevent filling with water. BS 4043 (1989) recommends a pit diameter 500 mm greater than the root ball and a depth equal to the root ball. The width of the pit is more important than the depth. The base and sides of the pit must be roughened to aid root penetration, especially in clay soils.

Planting

Timing

Ideally planting should take place during the dormant season of October to March, although conifers and other less-readily-transplanted trees are best moved in late spring when root growth is active. Frozen conditions can make access to sites easier for heavy machinery, eliminating damage. Root-balled trees can be planted throughout the summer, but immediate and continuing irrigation is essential. Containerised trees may suffer less transplantation shock, but irrigation is still essential.

Orientation

Invariably trees have 'better' sides and in the UK the appearance with regard to views is considered more important than the tree's orientation in the nursery.

Depth

Many trees are killed by being planted in pits that are too deep, where the trees settle. Deep mulches tend to compound this problem.

Backfill

Ideally, excavated topsoil should have a satisfactory structure, be compatible with the surrounding area and suitable for the specified tree. Modern landscape contracts can result in incompatible soils around and within the tree pit and in the root ball. This problem can be more acute when containerised trees are used. Avoid backfilling with soils lighter than the surrounding area. There is little information on the degree to which soil incompatibilities are significant, the guidelines given here follow the precautionary principle.

Backfill should be consolidated in 150–250mm layers, and when dry, watered to soak the soil when half-filled and when complete.

Providing support

This is an integral part of planting trees and is required until the tree is capable of supporting itself. Support can be provided either below or above ground (and in certain situations both are necessary).

Below ground support methods are increasingly popular. The support is invisible, providing neither visual nor physical obstruction and avoiding vandalism problems; Appendix A of BS 4043 (1989) illustrates certain options but most specialist suppliers have developed their own methods which eliminate some of the disadvantages of the BS methods. Proprietary anchoring systems can be used but tend to be expensive and variable depending on the soil-bearing characteristics.

There are three main methods of above ground support: guying, staking and propping. Specialist suppliers now favour underground methods of guying, such as the use of fence tensioners attached to subterranean stakes buried in the mulch.

Where more traditional staking is used, the arrangement depends on the size and form of the tree. In Germany, stakes are often used with natural fibre ties, rather than rubber or plastic ones, and are designed to support but allow movement.

Propping is a popular method in the German Bundesgartenshauen and is excellent for disturbed ground that might not support other methods. It is very easy to install and remove and is suitable for a wide range of tree forms. However, it is visually intrusive, obstructive and easy to vandalise. Ideally propping should be removed after two years.

10.5   Establishment and maintenance

Current contract arrangements imply the finish of the works at 'practical completion'. In fact for semi-mature trees, although they are usually planted for their early impact, it is really only the beginning of the development of their long-term effect in the landscape.

Unlike smaller, more fragile plants, that may die rapidly if not maintained, there is considerable 'residual life' in large trees. This means it might be sometime before inadequate aftercare is obvious, and by this time the tree can be irreversibly weakened and incapable of regaining its original vigour.

In this awkward situation, the visual impact of the tree is less than optimal but it is not dead. At what point is a replacement required and who is liable for the failure? If failure is judged to have occurred after two years, any replacement will be smaller, which is a particular problem if the failed or declining trees are part of a formal arrangement, group or avenue. In this case, should a replacement be equal to the remaining trees?

The best solution is to ensure that all the necessary considerations and specifications have been covered in the selection and planting of the trees, and that the allowance for establishment and maintenance is adequate to ensure that slow, long-term failure does not occur. The following maintenance criteria need to be considered.

Irrigation

This is the most essential operation. It is better to require the regular (e.g. weekly) application of a set amount of water (e.g. 20 litres) per tree than to leave this requirement more open-ended. Installing a coil of land drainage pipe around the root ball makes it easier to get the water to the right place, otherwise superficial watering needs to be applied slowly to ensure percolation.

In hotter climates where irrigation is a regular activity, it is typical to form 'saucers' round the base of the tree that hold irrigation water, allowing it to seep into the root ball. Automatic irrigation systems are often worth installing for high value items such as semi-mature trees. Rings of drip emitters or bubblers can be ideal for providing regular watering at night when evaporation is less.

In recent years after dry winters and springs in the UK, significant soil moisture deficits have been recorded in March/April. Irrigation is essential to saturate the total soil volume at the time of planting, otherwise moisture can be drawn away from the planting pit by the drier surrounding soil. Many suppliers recommend daily irrigation in the first summer especially during periods of little rain. This is essential for trees planted between April and September. Care must be exercised however: on the often poorly aerated and drained, machine-destroyed soils associated with landscape sites, frequent watering can sometimes lead to anaerobic conditions and root death.

Fertiliser

Trees do not require high levels of fertility, especially during establishment. As long as the growing medium is not deficient in basic nutrients, there is no need to add any at planting time. Slow release fertilisers can be added as top dressing in April on an annual basis to promote growth if required, once the new fibrous roots are formed and the tree established. Fertiliser manufacturers should be consulted to establish acceptable rates for the size of tree, as quantities can vary considerably. On sites with poor or little topsoil, a typical fertiliser application would be 200g 20:10:10 in late February.

Mulching

Mulches extending at least 150mm beyond the tree pit greatly reduce the growth of weeds, and retain moisture. If the tree is planted in mown grass and is supported by guy wires, the mulch layer can be extended to include these supports, thereby reducing the obstruction of guy supports when mowing. Ideally granular or loose mulches should be 50–75mm thick. Mulching should be checked for depth and maintained for at least two years. The base of the tree stem should not be covered with mulch.

Weed control

This is essential for the first two years and desirable for the next three. Mulching can suppress the annual weeds, but it is better to remove perennial weeds by the careful application of systemic herbicides rather than digging in the rooting zone. On many prestige sites semi-mature trees have lawn sown or turfed across their root balls to provide a 'finished' effect for the client. This has a catastrophic impact on the recovery of semi-mature trees for reasons previously discussed.

Staking and guying

Underground support generally needs little attention. Tensioning devices fixed across the root ball can be adjusted or the stakes can be re-firmed. Guys need regular checking. Turnbuckles are not recommended where they are likely to be tampered with, although they are ideal tensioners. Fence wire tensioners are smaller and can be buried in mulch. Eye bolts and nuts, adjusted against the angle iron stake, often bend and corrode. Re-firming the posts is another option, although it is less precise. Guy wires also need to be checked to ensure that they are not chafing the stems and branches.

Stakes and ties need checking for firmness at each maintenance visit. Rubber and plastic ties can be adjusted and re-nailed, while natural fibre ties are not generally adjustable (unless re-tied). Usually they are installed so that they hold the tree secure while allowing for some lateral movement. They also allow for girth increase without constriction. Props need no adjustment but should settle firmly around the tree. They are easy to re-position if necessary.

Depending on growth rates and tensioning devices fixed within the planting position, above ground support should be removed as soon as possible, after five years at the latest. If at this time support is still needed, then the tree is not properly established and is probably best removed.

Pruning

Practical experience recommends that almost all species establish better if the crown is reduced by 20–30 per cent at the time of planting. Those involved in the UK have been reluctant to 'head back' newly planted trees although this is common nursery practice each time a plant is transplanted or re-potted. The scientific evidence for the value of this practice is rather contradictory: although branch removal reduces the area of leaf that the transplanted root system has to support, it also reduces the photosynthetic surface area of the tree. Establishment requires effective photosynthesis to allow new root tissue to be produced: however photosynthetic capacity is low in unpruned trees, where roots are unable to keep the leaves turgid. Photosynthesis is also reduced where potential leafage is pruned off post planting.

The best course of action will depend on the extent of root loss a tree has experienced during the transfer from nursery to final planting position. Pruning back is probably advantageous for trees that have suffered massive root loss, but much less so for trees that have not. This pruning requires skill and will depend on the species and the desired effect, but it is usually better to remove selected branches completely, retaining the shape of the crown, than trim all the branches a little.

Any further pruning should remove only shoots that have died back, are crossing or are distorting the form (unless a pruned shape, such as topiary or pleaching, is required). The larger the tree, the more traumatic and longer-lasting the effects of transplanting will be, particularly when these are exacerbated by poor site conditions and planting, and inadequate aftercare. A lack of appreciation of these inter-linked factors will waste the considerable financial investment in the selection and use

of semi-mature trees, and prevent the development of a valuable visual asset.

10.6   Summary

An increasing number of semi-mature trees have been grown and planted on landscape sites over the last 30 years. Production and use of semi-mature trees is still a specialist activity, but it is becoming increasingly popular. Research and skilled knowledge need to be united to provide guidance to ensure satisfactory inclusion of these trees on landscape sites.

Although transplanting semi-mature trees is not new, current practices are very different from historical methods. This raises questions about how the physiology of the tree is affected in transplanting. Over a century ago, local trees were prepared, probably over several years, speedily transplanted and then diligently maintained. Few people were involved and no questions needed to be asked about provenance (the genetic origin of the tree), its hardiness, soil compatibility, desiccation, transport and lifting methods, or all the many issues that are of concern today.

Nowadays, a wide range of species of trees are grown in many climates and soils and then transplanted to a wide range of soil types and situations, frequently many hundreds of miles from the nursery. Furthermore, many agencies may be involved and jointly responsible for the success of the operation. It is now even more important for those using these trees to understand the inter-linked requirements of this process, so that correct procedures can be carried out at all stages.

While the successful use of semi-mature trees has resulted in this growth in supply, there are many examples that have been less than satisfactory. Practices have changed, streamlined by economies of production and demands of market forces. Without skilled and knowledgeable supervision at all stages, essential corners within the process are cut, jeopardising the long-term successful establishment of semi-mature trees.

Ideal horticultural requirements are generally well known, but few landscape sites and circumstances correspond to ideal practice. Not enough is known about the adaptation of the ideal to the more realistic constraints of typical sites, skills and supervision levels. In some instances, research could provide better understanding. In other cases, pooling the wide range of experiences achieved over recent years may help to make it easier to make better judgements. The following areas require further debate or study.

Source selection

Semi-mature trees are successfully grown and transplanted in many climates across Europe. However, increasing knowledge is available of the variable growth cycles in these different climates. Do these have any effect on the selection of the source of trees? Do we know how readily trees from, for example, North Germany, South Holland or Western England will adapt to different climate and conditions?

Provenance

Should we concern ourselves with the provenance of the selected trees? There is increasing concern about the trading of plants between countries. It should be possible to obtain documentation indicating the country of origin of a tree and its movements from first nursery to point of final planting.

Nursery practice

Do we know enough about the practices of the supply nurseries? Has the tree been transplanted regularly? Has undercutting been carried out at the right time of year to coincide with active root growth? Have the trees been grown at appropriate spacings in the nursery, and what are the appropriate spacings for the species? How do these varying practices affect our choice and the ability of the tree to re-establish on the site? Serious specifiers should consider all these factors.

Root ball sizes

The current practice of regular transplanting results in the supply of a well-branched root system from which the majority of the actively growing root has been severed. Establishment depends on fast root regrowth from the root system within the root ball. White (1990) suggests that 'root regeneration capacity, both potential and actual, is probably more important in terms of survival than the initial size of the system lifted from the nursery'.

Do we worry about root ball sizes unnecessarily? Under what conditions could root balls be reduced – are there instances when they should be increased?

Soil compatibility

Considerable research has been undertaken into the mechanics of water movement through composts and sand beds in container plant production. Little investigation has been carried out into the relationship between the soil within the root ball, in the planting pit and the surrounding site soil. Experience gives some guidance but this should be supported by more specialist research.

Choice of species

It was reasonably easy to establish semi-mature trees when the range of species available was typically the surplus of popular, easily transplanted lines. Now that a wider range is available we need more specific information. Focused research, or the pooling of experiences, might make it easier for the specifier to avoid choosing species that require particularly unique or costly measures to transplant successfully.

Acknowledgement

The following individuals provided advice on the original version of this specification:
T.L. Nelson, Pixton Woodlands, Dulverton, Somerset.
R. Inwood, Specimen Trees, Knutsford, Cheshire.
R. Tuff, Hillier Nurseries, Ampfield, Hampshire.
P. Flugge, Pflanzenhandel, Lorenz Von Ehren GmbH, Hamburg, Germany.

J. Van Vechel, Gebr.van denBerk bv., Sint-Oeden-rode, Netherlands.

References

British Standard (1966) BS 4043: Confirmed Sept. 1978; *Recommendations for transplanting semi-mature trees*. HMSO, London.

British Standard (1989) BS 4043: *Recommendations for transplanting root balled trees*. HMSO, London.

Findlay, C.M. (1999) The role of arbuscular mycorrhizal fungi in the early growth of rowan (*Sorbus aucuparia*

L.) Unpublished PhD Thesis, School of Landscape Architecture, Heriot Watt University.

Gilman, E.F. & Yeagher, T.H. (1988) Root initiation in root pruned hardwoods. *HortScience*, **23**, pp 251.

HTA (1997) *National Plant Specification*. HTA, Reading.

Struve, D.K. & Moser, B.C. (1984) Root system and root regeneration characteristics of pin and scarlet oak. *HortScience*, **19**, 123–5.

White, J.J. (1990) *Nursery stock rootsystems and tree establishment: a literature review*, Forestry Commission Occasional Paper 20, HMSO, London.

11 Trees in Paving

Tony Edwards and Tim Gale

Expenditure on the planting, establishment and management of amenity trees in the UK is very considerable, certainly in excess of £250 million per annum. In spite of this investment, there is still a pressing need to improve the management of urban trees – the 1989 Forestry Commission survey of urban trees (Hodge, 1991) found many were in a poor state of health. Trees are planted in many different situations within the urban environment; this chapter concentrates on the needs of urban trees planted in paved areas.

Many urban trees are planted in paved areas where they have a valuable role in improving the amenity of spaces dominated by concrete, brick and asphalt. It is only the adaptability of many tree species that allows us to put them into this alien environment and still achieve a high probability of survival. The mean shoot extension of urban trees is on average just over half that of similar trees in a nursery or arboreta (see Table 11.1). The Forestry Commission Survey found 34 per cent of trees under 15 years old were in less than good condition. Of the 15 per cent of trees recorded as 'damaged', only 1.5 per cent of this was due to vandalism: the remainder resulted from hostile site conditions, bad detailing or poor maintenance (Fig. 11.1).

In the same survey, over 30 per cent of trees less than ten years old were planted in paving. However, after 40 years there is a sudden drop in the number of trees in paving, which may reflect the removal of trees because of problems with their size and with associated root-induced paving and kerb damage (Fig. 11.2).

Estimates of the survival rates for urban trees start from as low as 50 per cent. A survey of standard trees planted on Scottish Development Agency sites concluded that an average success rate for the schemes studied was 54 per cent with only 33 per cent of this percentage recorded as being in good or excellent condition (Forestry Commission, 1987).

11.1 Choosing the right tree

In the 1989 Forestry Commission Survey, five genera made up 70 per cent of trees surveyed. In the Countryside Commission's Tree Survey of London (Cobham Resource Consultants, 1993), twelve genera constituted 73 per cent of trees. Both these studies suggest that relatively few genera are widely planted in urban areas, and that there is an opportunity to identify and utilise tree taxa better fitted to urban conditions. The final column of Table 11.1 clearly shows that there are considerable differences between genera in terms of their tolerance of urban environments.

Trees planted in paving may enjoy some benefits, as well as disadvantages. Some pavings may act as a mulch over root systems, allowing water and oxygen penetration while competing vegetation is excluded. Some tree pits may provide trees with relatively large volumes of fertile root-penetrable soil that are not available in other urban situations.

The *London Tree Survey* shows that the most commonly recorded street trees found in paving were sycamores, followed by ash, plane, cherry, birch, hawthorn and lime. In the earlier Forestry Commission study the most abundant urban trees

Table 11.1 Mean shoot extension and percentage in good condition of major species in relation to location; adapted from Hodge, (1991).

Species	Trees in paving		Trees in grass		Trees in shrub planting		Mean extension growth of urban trees as a percentage of trees in arboreta and nurseries
	Mean shoot extension (cm)	% of trees in 'good' condition	Mean shoot extension (cm)	% of trees in 'good' condition	Mean shoot extension (cm)	% of trees in 'good' condition	
Acer	10.4	74	9.7	82	15.2	86	51
Betula	10.7	79	11.3	82	9	77	67
Fraxinus	7.3	68	11.6	76	17.7	93	44
Platanus	15.2	87	17	95	13.2	75	62
Prunus	10.4	83	14.1	78	11.4	90	70
Robinia	24.9	84	17.3	75	19.2	87	96
Sorbus (aria types)	15.5	82	8.4	92	14.8	83	70
Sorbus (aucuparia types)	15.4	82	12.7	61	13.9	73	56
Tilia	9.6	82	11.1	89	12.4	87	69

were maple species, cherry, rowan, birch, whitebeam, lime, sycamore, ash, plane and hawthorn. Interestingly, the Forestry Commission survey showed that the (then) relatively uncommon species, *Alnus cordata*, *Zelkova serrata*, and *Robinia pseudocacia* all outperformed the ten most common trees in terms of shoot extension.

The size of the tree at planting is important in relation to its chance of survival in a paved area. While there is little protection against the vandal who systematically strips the bark around mature trees, a more frequent cause of loss is snapping of the upper part of the tree, usually above a tree tie. The ability of the tree to protect itself against the forces exerted on it depend on its girth. If it can resist the bending moment exerted on it by external forces, it will not snap. This is shown by a decreasing percentage of snapped trees as age (and therefore girth) increases. The moment of inertia (lxx) of a section of circular shape is

$$0.0491 \times d4$$

(where d = diameter)

From this it can be calculated that a tree with a girth of 17 cm is 35 times stronger than one with a 7 cm girth.

In vulnerable public areas, the improvement in terms of amenity and increased resistance to vandalism may well support the extra costs of specifying a larger tree. The use of semi-mature trees is discussed in Chapter 10.

11.2   Tree grilles and pavings

The fundamental problem with planting in paving is the need for the tree to obtain sufficient water, oxygen, nutrition and anchorage to thrive. Placing surfaces impervious to the movement of oxygen over existing tree roots rapidly induces anaerobic conditions, root damage and tree decline (Table 11.2).

The greater the volume of topsoil provided to the newly-planted tree, the greater the risk of settlement as the soil settles and organic amendments oxidise and disappear. To avoid uneven settlement for paved surfaces subsoil needs to be compacted, thus eliminating many of the voids that could contain soil oxygen. This chain of events is clearly antagonistic to the requirements of the tree.

Tree grilles can accommodate the inevitable soil movement that occurs in planting pits, while allowing water and oxygen to get to the root

Fig. 11.1 Surface rooting resulting from concrete haunching and compacted ground; note the damage that the guard rail is causing. (Photo: Edwards Gale)

Fig. 11.2 Root-induced paving damage is one reason for the decline of urban trees in paving. (Photo: Edwards Gale)

Table 11.2 Typical impermeability of various ground surfaces to water and air movement.

Finish	Impermeability factor
Asphalt or concrete	0.85–0.95
Paved with cemented joints	0.75–0.85
Paved with open joints	0.5–0.7
Blocks with open joints	0.4–0.5
Macadam roadways	0.25–0.6
Gravel roadways	0.15–0.3
Grassed areas	0.05–0.25
Wooded area	0.01–0.2

system (although in established trees this will only be to a small portion of the roots). Some grilles come as a two-part system with an inner circle that can be removed as the girth of the tree develops to its maximum size. The essential requirement is that a strong frame to support the various elements of the tree grille is positioned outside the potential settlement zone. This will need to be supported on a ring beam or haunching around the edge of the paving, otherwise the frame will twist and fail to support the grilles.

Cast iron tree grilles are popular because of the attractive patterns available and their ability to withstand harsh treatment within the pavement. As well as their natural deadweight they can have locking mechanisms to prevent removal. The cast iron generally sits in a mild steel frame which provides an accurate bed for the elements of the grille. An additional benefit of cast iron is that the tree can be linked to a mild steel tree guard; this may be useful in areas where vandalism or car damage is likely. The grilles may be coordinated aesthetically with associated bollards, light columns, signage and seats.

A new product in the tree grille market is made from recycled heavy-duty plastic, which comes in a variety of colours and will not rust or corrode. These are lighter and can be lifted by one person: this overcomes the problem of lifting iron or concrete to top up soil or gravel.

Concrete has also been used in grille systems, but its thickness and the relatively large amount of concrete needed for structural requirements limit its use. It is often found as part of a paving system to provide a consistency in finishes, rather than as a satisfactory grille solution.

A more expensive but ultimately more reliable method of siting trees in paving is to suspend the paving surface slightly above soil level. The paved surface may then be treated as a floor slab over the tree pit. A reinforced concrete slab may extend from the surround of the tree so that even if the ground settles the slab will not be resting on the ground. The paving will continue to be supported without showing any surface deformation and no load will be on the tree pit. To be able to carry sufficient load in this design, the edge of the slab is likely to need either an upstand or downstand beam on its edge and loading may have to accommodate vehicle as well as pedestrian traffic.

To avoid the need for a reinforced slab to be able to span an indeterminate distance, an alternative solution is to have a perforated wall the full depth of the tree pit, bearing on the subsoil at the base of the pit. A perforated wall will allow air, drainage and roots to penetrate into the area outside the tree pit.

The soil level can finish below the top of the wall, with a concrete lid placed over it. The necessary grille can be fixed to the edge of the concrete lid with the surface of the topsoil below. In the event that a tree dies or is vandalised, the tree may still be removed without destroying the integrity of the paving by removing the tree grille.

In an avenue situation, it is preferable to create a planting trench rather than individual tree pits. This enables a greater volume of selected soil to be provided and available for each tree. The concrete

slab would then span across, and be supported by the side walls. Within the linear tree pit it is easy to make provision for irrigation and drainage under the slab, should this be necessary. This procedure makes available a soil that is well supplied with oxygen and moisture. In natural well-structured soils oxygen can account for 15–20 per cent of total soil gases. Handreck and Black (1989) report that the bulk density at which root penetration is inhibited is about $1.5\,\mathrm{g/cm^3}$ in fine textured soils and $1.75\,\mathrm{g/cm^3}$ for sandy soils. Under most urban conditions the tree will often find itself constrained to the soil within its tree pit because the surrounding soil is often compacted to such a degree that it does not contain sufficient oxygen to support root growth (Fig. 11.3).

Paving finishes are generally considered as part of a 'pave and pipe' system which assumes that the majority of rainwater will run off from the surface into gulleys and into a surface water system. In the urban context this system is usually closed, with no water leaving the pipe to percolate into the ground. The ground below paving can therefore be drier than would be the case in an open field situation, with little chance that the root ball can

Fig. 11.3 Unusually generous pit planting provision for street trees. Unfortunately no grille provision was made when the trees were planted, and in this busy street pedestrian compaction of the soil surface resulted in this being less successful than initially anticipated. (Photo: James Hitchmough)

Fig. 11.4 Best practice situation in Holland. Unit pavers are laid on a sand base, both for the pathways and the road surface; this maximises penetration of water and oxygen into the underlying soils. (Photo: James Hitchmough)

obtain sufficient moisture from rainfall even in a temperate situation.

There is also considerable variety in the degree of porosity in paved finishes. Both macadam and concrete paving can be designed to be relatively porous. Porous paving will assist the tree roots so that they need not be dependent on capillary action to draw soil moisture from the water table. As the size of the tree pit is related to the field capacity of the soil, the porosity of the paving will have a direct influence on the size of tree pit required.

Finishes with open joints can be twice as permeable as sealed paving finishes (Fig. 11.4). In addition, the colour of the paving and the wavelength of light it accepts will affect the heat build-up and reflection from the surface (Forestry Commission, 1987). Together they can create an almost desert-like environment. Conversely the radiated heat from paving may improve the growth of warmth-demanding trees such as *Ginkgo biloba* when these are used as a street tree in Britain.

11.3 Services and trees

The soil beneath paving can be a battleground between roots and public utilities. Trees are blamed for indirect damage to services by causing subsidence, and for direct damage where roots enter ducting etc. (or even in extreme cases, where falling trees lift services as they fall). *Best Practice in Street Works and Highway Works* (DETR, 2001) points the way forward for the minimisation of disturbance to the highway, including trees. This makes reference to the NJUG guidelines (1995) regarding services in proximity to tree roots and routes, and the DETR (1999) guidelines on highway works and trees.

The deoxygenating damage caused by escaping gas from leaking joints is well known (Pankhurst, 1980). Unlike town gas, natural gas is not directly poisonous, but it has a harmful effect on vegetation because it displaces soil oxygen. Non-porous paving up to the bole of the tree may prolong the damage, even after a leak is repaired, through slowing down the diffusion of gas out of the soil. Trees and gas services are therefore capable of damaging each other. In the past, the National House Building Council's *Practice Note 3* gave unrealistic guidance on the position of gas mains and other services in relation to trees; this was founded on the general concern about clay soils and settlement which followed the 1976 drought. This has now been revised in more recent standards (Volume 1, Chapter 4.2 of the NHBC (2001)) which provides a more realistic guide to good practice.

Tree roots are concentrated in the top 600 mm of soil (BS, 1991) and the root system typically comprises between 20 and 50 per cent of the mass of the whole tree. Only a small percentage of the root system extends below one metre, due to declining levels of soil oxygen. The shape of a conventional tree is that of a thick-bottomed wine glass. Unfortunately, most of our service infrastructure is in the zone 0.5–1 m.

To avoid problems when planting, ensure that roots are contained where necessary to avoid root trespass into primary service areas. Root barriers can act as a physical obstacle to the most active root zone. If the barrier does not extend down far enough into the soil, roots will pass under the barrier. A root deflected deeper to pass under a barrier will not stay at this level, and will attempt to regain an optimum level, making its way to the surface on the other side. An alternative is the root control bag, which only permits small roots (up to 3 mm) to escape from the containment, with approximately 75 per cent of all roots contained in the bag. Roots in relation to built structures and services are discussed in more detail in Chapter 9.

BS 5837 (1991) covers all aspects of tree planting in relation to construction and the 1991 edition updates guidance originally published in 1980. The ideal solution should be trenchless excavation whenever possible. Trenching is often warranted when excavations are within a distance that is two and a half times the trunk circumference of the tree. When planting trees in sites such as business parks, in circumstances where the rate of technical change is likely to require new or updated services to be provided (e.g. the service corridors) it is prudent to leave a number of blank ducts at distances from 0.5–1 m from the tree. In the event of disturbance being necessary, routes are already designated and no further excavation is needed.

The damage caused by tree roots will not only affect services, but will also damage surface finishes and properties (Plate 12). Claims for tree damage in London made between 1986 and 1992 were in excess of £20 million, and repairs to a single property generally exceed £20 000. Tree pruning to restrict a tree's water demand and consequent root activity costs in the range £250–£500 per tree. It is a wise investment to manage public trees, which are often in paved areas, to prevent damage. The reality is that it is often beyond a local authority's budget allocation to prune every tree (there are approx. 1.3 million trees in public ownership in London alone) and tree officers have to be alert to potential risks from the largest trees and those with the highest water demand.

In a recent case (2001) in the House of Lords (Delaware Mansions Ltd and another v. Westminster City Council) underpinning costs of £570 000 were awarded, due to damage by an 80-year-old plane tree. This case has caused great concern about the potential level of damages. It has also established that the cost of remedial works to repair damage caused by trees is recoverable, but the tree owner must first be given the chance to remove the tree. A five-year research project is currently being carried out by Dr Neil Hipps at Horticulture Research International with backing from the insurance industry, government and academics; the project will determine the effect of pruning on water uptake, so that management practices can be linked directly with water demand.

11.4 Getting the tree pit right

Where root growth is not restricted by compaction or low soil oxygen, a 20 m tall parkland tree is likely to have a root plate diameter of at least 20 m, exploiting a depth of soil of 1 m. This corresponds to a soil volume potentially occupied by the roots of 400 m^2.

Trees in paved areas are unlikely to enjoy unconstrained root development, and the soil initially provided in the planting pit will be the primary and maybe the only source of nutrients and water to sustain the tree as it grows. It has been assessed that on degraded soils, trees planted in pits of appropriate size for their root ball will have barely enough nitrogen to ensure full leafing out. If the tree is competing with grass, the growth may even regress to the point of a negative shoot extension (Davies, 1987). Both research and observation suggest that the larger the tree pit, the greater the likelihood of success. Preferably the pit should be so large that it is an island of soil in a paved area which can support several trees, as for example in London's Berkeley Square where plane trees are still surviving and prospering more than 200 years after planting.

In a study by landscape architect James Urban in the USA (Urban, 1991), more than 1300 mature trees in intensively developed urban areas were assessed and he concluded that in general,

'those trees planted in 200 cubic feet (22 m^3) or more of soil were in better condition than nearly all their counterparts in smaller volumes. Below this soil volume, tree vigour and condition generally – but not always – decreased with decreasing amounts of soil.'

Guidance on sizing of tree pits is usually vague and focuses on simply accommodating the root ball. However Lindsey and Bassuk (1991) have developed a formula for calculating tree pit volume based on the water demand of the trees. The calculations below are derived from Hitchmough's (1992) adaptation of Lindsey and Bassuk's work. The formula used in these calculations is rather simplistic and does not take into account the inevitable extremes in site variation. However it uses information that is readily available, and at worst provides a useful guide to the adequacy of planting pit provision to support a tree of a given mature size.

11.5 Calculating the volume of soil required to support varying tree sizes

A. Estimate the daily water use of the tree in litres

Assuming a leaf index of 4 (a typical value for deciduous trees), and an evaporation ratio of 0.25 (tree leaves typically evaporate a quarter of the water that is lost from a water surface of the same area), then the two remaining variables necessary to compute tree daily water use are the canopy size (surface area of the ground enclosed by the perimeter in cm^2) and the mean daily evaporation rate for the site in the peak demand period. For example London is 0.33 and Glasgow 0.28.

For a tree with a canopy radius of 4m growing in London the calculation is

$$\frac{(400\,cm \times 400\,cm \times 3.14 \times 0.33 \times 0.25)}{1000}$$
$$= 165.8\,litres$$

B. Calculate the soil volume required

Given the tree's daily water use, the soil volume to hold that daily supply can be estimated from the water-holding capacity of the soil, a factor that varies widely.

Available water (AW) is defined as the amount of water in the soil between permanent wilting point (PWP) and field capacity (FC), and can be measured in the laboratory. Saturated soil, where all the soil voids are filled by water, must be avoided as it leads to anaerobic conditions. Oxygen is also essential to healthy growth and therefore the amount of air voids is also important.

Table 11.3 indicates the percentage of air-filled voids in a soil when it is at field capacity. It can be seen that sandy loam, which has the same available water capacity as silty clay, is to be preferred for its greater air holding capacity. It is possible to increase water-holding capacity by textural modification, addition of organic materials or water-holding polymers. Research on the efficiency of water-holding polymers varies widely but perhaps Kendle's advice is the most useful.

'Where irrigation or rainfall is infrequent but not absent, they can make a substantial difference. Where there is plenty of water, or none, they will not make any difference.' (Kendle, pers. comm.).

Using figures for silt loam the calculation below shows the volume of soil required to support the tree if the soil is returned to field capacity every day.

Soil volume required to provide one day's water supply to a tree
$$= \frac{daily\ water\ use\ (165.8\ litres)}{available\ water\ holding\ capacity\ (20\%)}$$
$$= 829\ litres\ (0.829\,m^3).$$

To complete the calculations for the total volume of soil required, the rainfall interval, which is defined as the typical number of days without significant rainfall (or irrigation), must be inserted:

Total soil volume required
= Soil volume that provides one days supply of water (0.829 m^3) × Rainfall interval (10)
= 8.29 m^3.

This value illustrates the large volumes of soil that are necessary to maintain trees in an actively growing, stress-free condition. The calculation above is rather optimistic, in that it assumes a high soil AW (20%), and also that rain will rewet the profile on average every ten days during the period of greatest moisture stress, generally May to August. In London, for which the calculation has

been undertaken, this is very unlikely to happen. If a more conservative and realistic assumption is made, that soils will not be rewetted by rain during this period (given low pavement permeability etc.) more frequently than once every 30 days, the soil volume required expands to almost 258 m³. This volume of good quality soil is unlikely to be provided for trees in paving in all but a few prestige developments. As a result one has to expect most trees in paved surfaces to be under soil moisture stress for considerable periods during the summer months. Consequently, as trees mature they will tend to show slower growth than might be expected, unless it is possible for roots to escape from planting pits into the adjacent soil.

The soil volumes shown in Fig. 11.5 assume the tree pit to be a closed system without access by the roots to water outside the tree pit. A tree with an 8 m diameter canopy is shown to require a tree pit 4 × 4 m on a loamy sand, less on a soil with higher available water capacity and more on a soil with a low available water capacity.

It is evident from casual observation that most large and established trees in paved areas must

Table 11.3 Available water and air-holding capacity of various soils (on a volume basis) of different soil textural classes (adapted from Craul, 1992).

Soil class	% Available Water (AW)	% Air
Loamy fine sand	5.4	27.2
Sandy clay	7.8	11.6
Coarse sandy loam	8.7	15.8
Loamy sand	10.1	26.9
Sandy clay loam	11.9	13.4
Silty clay	12.3	9.1
Sandy loam	12.3	18.6
Clay loam	12.7	13.0
Fine sandy loam	13.1	23.5
Silty clay loam	14.9	8.4
Loam	15.6	14.4
Silt loam	19.9	11.4

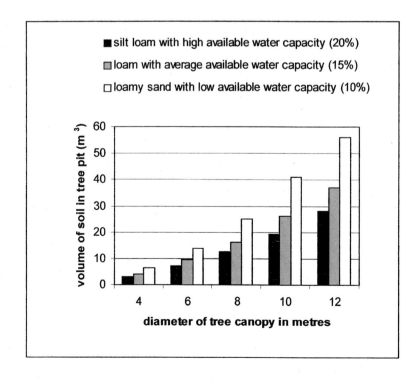

Fig. 11.5 Volumes of soil required to support typical growth on various sized trees in London. Soil volumes are calculated using the methodology of Lindsey and Bassuk, (1991).

have access to water from beyond a normal tree pit to support their substantial canopies. Species such as London Plane (*Platanus × acerifolia*) are often successful in paved surfaces precisely because they have very dynamic root systems that tolerate low soil oxygen better than most. This facilitates their escape from planting pits and increases the chances that they will gain access to volumes of soil elsewhere.

The geometry of a tree pit can have a major effect on soil volume. A square with the same diameter as a circle has a 22 per cent larger area and greater volume per unit height. When specifying a square tree pit it is important to ensure that this is what is provided, and that the value of the additional soil capacity in the corners is recognised.

Summary

Aboriculturists and landscape architects are interested in the development of healthy, vigorous trees; their aims can often conflict with the groups providing and maintaining services in the urban environment, whose only interest in trees is generally in preventing them from interfering with service maintenance and function.

One of the ways to achieve this is to intentionally restrict trees to tree pits, and prevent root escape through the use of root barriers (see Chapter 9). This approach does however require the provision of very large planting pits to maintain satisfactory tree growth. As this is generally not economically or physically possible, the only rational solution is to provide as large a planting pit as possible and to accept, and facilitate, root escape into the surrounding subterranean environment. Root/service interactions must ultimately be managed as effectively as possible by thoughtful design applied to the selection and location of service infrastructure.

References

British Standards Institute (1991) BS 5837 *Trees in Relation to Construction*. HMSO, London.

Cobham Resource Consultants (1993) *London Tree Survey*. Countryside Commission, Cheltenham.

Craul, P.J. (1992) *Urban Soil in Landscape Design*. John Wiley and Sons, Chichester.

Davies, R.J. (1987) *Trees and Weeds: Forestry Commission Handbook 2*, HMSO, London.

DETR (1999) *Roots and Routes: Guidelines on Highways Works and Trees*. HMSO, London.

DETR (2001) *Best Practice in Street Works and Highway Works*. HMSO, London.

Forestry Commission (1987) Advances in Practical Arboriculture. *Forestry Commission Bulletin 65*, HMSO, London.

Forestry Commission (1993), *Arboriculture Research Note 110/93*, HMSO, London.

Handreck, K.A. & Black, N.D. (1989) *Growing Media for Ornamental Plants and Turf*, 2nd edn. New South Wales University Press, Sydney, Australia.

Hitchmough, J.D.(1992) Calculating the Earth. *Landscape Design* September 1992, pp41–44.

Hodge, S.J. (1991) *Urban Trees, a Survey of Street Trees in England*. Forestry Commission Bulletin 99, HMSO, London.

Lindsey, P. & Bassuk, N. (1991) Specifying soil volumes to meet the water needs of mature urban street trees and trees in containers. *Journal of Arboriculture*, **17**, 6, pp141–8.

NHBC (2001) Building near Trees, *NHBC Standards* **1**, 4.2. NHBC, Amersham, Bucks.

NJUG (1995) *Guidelines for the Planning Installation and Maintenance of Utility Services in Proximity to Trees*. Joint National Utilities Group, London.

Pankhurst, E.S.(1980) The effects of natural gas on trees, *Landscape Design* February 1980, p32.

Urban, J. (1991) Big rewards from little trees grow. *Horticulture Week* 9th August 1991, pp. 21–3.

Further reading

Helliwell, R. (1990) Provision for New Trees, *Landscape Design* July/August 1990, p18.

McMillan, E. (2001) Research and Rescue. *Horticulture Week*, 26th July 2001, pp14–16.

Murdoch, J. (2001) Root of All the Trouble: Legal Note. *Estate Gazette*, 24th November 2001, p144.

12 Creating Urban Woodlands

Nerys Jones

12.1 Context

The 'urban forest' is made up of all the trees and associated open space in towns; woodlands can be a very important component of this. Where these have survived as fragments of past countryside, they have a tendency to be shadows of their former selves, and although there is a need to protect and manage such established landscape features, there is now also a great deal of interest in creating new urban woodlands.

Woodlands can be an important asset to any town or city, for their landscape and recreation value, the contribution they make to biodiversity, the way they improve air quality, the shelter they provide and the role they can play in encouraging inward investment through regeneration.

Even in very built-up areas there is often a surprising amount of additional land available. There may be scope for the creation of new woodlands on derelict wasteland and vacant development sites, in parks, school grounds, housing areas and on the open land that often lies alongside major road and rail routes.

The approach to the creation of urban woodlands described here assumes that urban greening needs to be promoted on a bold scale, in order to make a significant impact. However, this does not mean that individual woods have to be large to make a valuable contribution; many successful urban woodlands can be smaller than 0.25 ha in area. Cost-effectiveness is also assumed to be an important factor. The 'urban forestry' style of planting and management is based on a mixture of applied ecology and commercial forestry techniques and lends itself very much to community participation.

12.2 Planning

Surveys

Ownership

It is relatively easy to find out which land is in local authority ownership by applying to the council register. The Land Registry is the best source of information about land in other ownership. Neighbouring landowners can also be a useful source of ownership information.

Ground conditions

Surveys should ascertain the condition of the ground and the extent to which the land is compacted or contaminated. Techniques for relieving compaction are described later in this chapter, but urban land is rarely so contaminated that tree establishment would be prevented. Many urban soils are highly fertile, although extremes of acidity or alkalinity can result in shortage of essential minerals and slow plant growth. These issues are discussed in more detail in Chapter 4.

In most situations where long-term development of urban woodland is the aim, slow, steady growth is preferable to the soft, sappy growth which can be promoted by excess nitrogen. Urban substrates such as demolition rubble are often low in nitrogen and this makes them particularly appropriate for woodland establishment.

However, if the aim is to create a more rapid impact for short-term effect, nitrogen and other nutrients are easily supplemented. Increased fertility should be treated with caution, since it may favour weed growth. This is likely to create more competition for soil moisture that in turn may handicap the trees.

Existing habitats

It pays to begin, quite simply, by just looking at the site. The plants already growing there will give a good clue as to what new planting is likely to succeed. If certain woody species are already regenerating naturally then these will probably grow well when planted. Typical pioneers of soil-less, well-drained stony sites such as gravel pits, railway sidings and demolition land include silver birch (*Betula pendula*), goat willow (*Salix caprea*) and sycamore (*Acer pseudoplatanus*). If the site is rough grassland then typical pioneer trees may include species with larger seeds, such as oak (*Quercus petraea*) and hawthorn (*Crataegus monogyna*).

Detailed ecological surveys are also important. The local Wildlife Trust can usually advise on any habitat survey work that has been published and if none exists, they may be willing to carry out a survey themselves. Some local authorities have nature conservation officers who can also supply this information and advise on other sources of professional help. It is essential that species-rich meadows, valuable wetlands, archaeological remains and other vulnerable sites are not damaged through an overzealous drive to plant trees. It is the rich mosaic of different habitats that makes the urban forest most successful, for wildlife and for people.

Services

It is advisable to consult utility companies to ascertain the position of electricity, telephone and TV cables, gas and water pipes. Their presence above or below ground may well restrict the areas available for planting.

Community

Surveys also need to have a social dimension. It is important to understand how local people use the site, and in particular whether there are any popular desire line footpaths or serious problems of dumping or other abuse. A number of techniques can be used to ascertain the views of local people about urban forestry schemes and there should be some flexibility in the draft proposals, to allow for local knowledge and attitudes to influence the design, implementation and aftercare.

Local authorities / other agencies

How does the site fit into the Unitary Development Plan, the Local Plan, any strategy for delivering *Local Agenda 21* or enhanced biodiversity? Are there any designations such as *Site of Special Scientific Interest (SSSI)*, *Site of Importance for Nature Conservation (SINC)* or Local Nature Reserve status? Is there a plan for urban forestry at a broader strategic scale? If the site is owned by the local authority, then it is possible that several departments may be involved and there may be a need to co-ordinate planning / technical services, leisure, transport, housing and other policies.

There are a number of government agencies able to offer advice (and possibly resources) for urban woodland. The Forestry Commission operates throughout Great Britain. The Environment Agency covers England and Wales and their equivalent organisation in Scotland is the Scottish Environment Protection Agency. English Nature and the Countryside Agency in England, the Countryside Council for Wales and Scottish Natural Heritage are also useful contacts.

Is woodland the right solution?

Check that the site will actually be improved if woodland is created and that plans for urban woodland offer good value. In parks and other areas of amenity grassland, where there are steep-sloping banks, mown areas with tight corners or obstacles such as posts or scattered individual trees, then it can make very good economic sense

Fig. 12.1 There are many awkward pockets of land such as this in urban areas where woodland planting would reduce the maintenance costs and greatly improve the environment. (Photo: National Urban Forestry Unit)

to convert the landscape to new woodland (Fig. 12.1). Annual management costs of robust style urban woodland can be as little as one-eighth the cost of the annual maintenance of grassed areas where these have to be mown in part by pedestrian-guided mowers. Where land is unstable, or where sloping ground sheds storm water rapidly downstream, new woodland can be a very sound environmental and economic investment.

Check that the planned woodland will not obscure important views, or cast too much shade on neighbours.

12.3   Process

Style / design characteristics

It is important to define the objectives for the woodland clearly: this should significantly influence site preparation and the detail of design. Woodland in towns is capable of delivering benefits such as shelter and screening, air pollution filtration and stormwater moderation with a very modest commitment to management. However, where more demanding objectives are to be met, then more sophisticated design and long-term management may be necessary.

Where woodland has a specialist purpose, this is likely to have a bearing on the detailed design of the planting, the choice of species and the subsequent management. Table 12.1 provides some practical guidance.

Techniques for woodland establishment

Natural regeneration

Existing mature trees may be a good source of seeds for natural regeneration, and they should be retained wherever possible (Baines and Smart, 1991; Hodge, 1991; Fig. 12.2). Natural colonisation of a site may be speeded up by scarifying the ground shortly before seed fall, to improve potential germination conditions. With small-seeded species such as birch, whose seedlings are very sensitive to competition from vigorous grasses etc., spraying out areas of competing vegetation in winter (using a glyphosate-based herbicide) around the existing trees will greatly increase seed germination and early establishment.

Direct seeding

Tree and shrub seeding techniques have been developed on a commercial scale over the last twenty years. Sowing seeds can cost significantly less than conventional planting techniques. Tree seeding may be particularly suitable for relatively inaccessible sites such as quarries, steep embankments and road verges.

There tends to be a large amount of wastage, as many of the tree seeds germinate and establish most successfully when they are in a sheltered woodland environment. In using direct seeding techniques, the aim is to speed up natural colonisation processes. Typical mixtures may include a nurse cover of agricultural cereals, nitrogen fixing shrubs, long-lived shrubs and a mixture of pioneer and climax trees. Slower growing species will shelter amongst the faster growing nurse and pioneer species (La Dell, 1983). Where sites are inaccessible, it is particularly helpful if the resulting woodland is largely self-thinning.

Sowing is done using conventional agricultural

Table 12.1 Design criteria for new urban woodlands.

Objective	Desirable Characteristics	Design Criteria
Screening / Storm Water Moderation / Air Pollution Filtration	• Year round leaf cover	• Use some evergreen species
Public Access	• Vegetation to ground level • Rapid impact • Non-threatening landscape	• Use both tree & shrub species • Use vigorous, fast-growing species • Create clearly defined access routes with good visibility. Keep planting 3–5 m back from line of pathways • Restrict use of shrubs to areas well away from paths • Signpost routes clearly and encourage maximum public use • Use light-shade canopy species
	• Minimal likelihood of vandalism	• Ensure that local people are involved • Accommodate well used areas/desire line footpaths as open space
	• Year-round interest	• Select species for their seasonal variation (flowers, fruit, leaf colour, winter stem colour) • Introduce ground flora as woodland develops and include some evergreens
	• Robust	• Use resilient species which can withstand some physical damage
Nature Conservation (Do not let tree planting damage other valuable habitats such as established wetland, wildflower grassland etc.)	• Habitat diversity	• Manage for structural diversity (e.g. woodland glades, edges, coppice, dead wood). Include other habitats such as wetland or grassland in the design, or allow for their development
	• Wildlife food plants	• Use native species, including shrubs and herbaceous wildflowers
	• Lack of disturbance	• Make a clear distinction between access and sanctuary areas
	• Continuity of habitat	• Link the new woodland into the ecological corridor network
Education (Also see **Nature conservation**)	• Participation and monitoring	• Phase planting over several years. Involve people in growing as well as tree planting and aftercare
	• Variety	• Increase range of species, including food plants and ornamentals (but majority of planting should still conform to essential design criteria)
	• Outdoor sheltered 'classroom'	• Create teaching spaces within woodland. Provide for access and interpretation
Wood Products	• Yield regular valuable products • Readily accessible to markets	• Choose species which can yield useful products • Design access for harvesting

Fig. 12.2 This redundant railway shunting yard has been naturally colonised by pioneer woodland, mainly birch and goat willow. (Photo: Woodfall Wild Images)

seeding machinery, by hydroseeding or by hand, depending on the scale, accessibility and other circumstances. Use of a mulch is advisable to prevent the seeds from drying out and to reduce temperature fluctuations. Organic material such as chopped straw is suitable, and on steep slopes it may be advisable to bind the mulch with bitumen (La Dell, 1987). Autumn sowing is recommended, when seed is fresh and the nurse crop can be established ahead of the winter.

Planting

Planting nursery grown stock gives the most immediate initial results, but there is a greater cost involved. Care must also be taken to ensure that the young trees survive the shock of being transplanted.

The following section deals with the nature of plant material, assuming that planting is the chosen method.

Plant material

Size

Small transplants of 450–600 mm or 600–900 mm grown from seed are usually the most successful.

Young trees are relatively inexpensive and easy to handle. They also suffer less transplant shock than larger ones and so establish more easily (Bradshaw *et al.*, 1995).

'*Root trainers*' and other forms of young, container-grown seedling trees are more expensive than bare-rooted trees, but often stand a better chance of success. They can also be used to extend the period available for planting beyond the traditional bare-root planting season, November to end of March.

Provenance

Some commercial nurseries now offer a contract growing service and can supply stock of specific provenance. Very local provenance can be important when dealing with particularly localised and extreme soil conditions. For example, for a site that has very poor drainage or a high level of contamination, there may be very local populations of trees that have experienced very similar conditions. They may have evolved higher-than-average tolerances of these conditions, and their seedlings will at least inherit characteristics that enable them to perform better than general commercial stock. Provenance considerations are dealt with in more detail in Chapter 2.

Species selection

New urban sites are typically exposed and relatively free of woody vegetation. When this is the case, it is advisable to begin the initial establishment with a few pioneer species which are well suited to the local climate, aspect etc. Silver birch (*Betula pendula*), common alder (*Alnus glutinosa*), goat willow (*Salix caprea*) and aspen (*Populus tremula*) are all effective pioneers, with alder being especially well suited to sites with poor drainage and/or particularly low nitrogen availability. Where grassland is already established, oak, hawthorn and ash all act as natural pioneers, with ash tolerating alkalinity and oak being more tolerant of acidic conditions (Fig. 12.3).

Once pioneer plantations are established, or the first stages of natural colonisation are well under-

Fig. 12.3 Young nursery stock of pioneer tree species establish rapidly in the poorest of substrates, and with appropriate site preparation and establishment techniques, they can achieve closed canopy within five years. (Photo: National Urban Forestry Unit)

way, then long-lived species may successfully be introduced (Baines, 1986). In many situations their seeds will arrive unaided, carried in by birds, but if seedlings are planted, then it is advisable to promote their successful establishment and early growth through the use of weed control and tree shelters. This second phase of tree planting should reflect the dominant species in the local landscape. Oak (*Quercus* spp.), beech (*Fagus* spp) and hornbeam (*Carpinus* spp.) are three long-lived trees that are best established in this way. Guidance on appropriate regional and local plant communities can be obtained by consulting the National Vegetation Classification and through careful analysis of the neighbouring woodlands (Rodwell and Patterson, 1994).

Simplicity is the key to success. It is better to plant bold groups of trees of the same species rather than to plant randomly. Try to emulate nature, where groups of pioneer trees of the same species are often found growing together in large, simple colonies. Relate the size of the planting group to the size of the woodland.

Planting at two-metre centres gives a good balance between an effective density of planting (resulting in a closed canopy within three years) and the cost involved in achieving this. Reducing the distance between plants to one metre centres will quadruple the number of trees used, and lead more rapidly to overcrowding and the likelihood of self-inflicted early losses from intense competition for light and moisture (Black Country Urban Forestry Unit, 1991).

A typical planting mix for a pioneer woodland might be 40 per cent alder, 40 per cent birch, 15 per cent goat willow and 5 per cent wild cherry (*Prunus avium*), with groups of individual species being at least 25 in number and the wild cherry used sparingly at focal points. In the early 1980s it was the fashion to plant different species randomly on a regular grid. The grid helped to simplify mechanical aspects of maintenance, but the randomness demanded an extremely sophisticated level of management at the thinning stage. Planting in rows on a grid pattern can initially look rather formal, but it makes it easier to locate the trees during maintenance and the formality is masked within a few seasons.

There is now a much stronger commitment to a more naturalistic approach resulting in initial plantings of simple combinations. These are more robust and are easier to manage (National Urban Forestry Unit, 2001).

Site preparation

Substrate

Urban sites are very variable, with some relatively hostile to plant growth. They are often exposed and the range of substrates can vary from demolition rubble to deep, highly fertile soils. More often than not however, the existing substrate is perfectly suitable for tree establishment. Serious contamination problems are rarely encountered.

Given the appropriate choice of species, trees will grow well, even in such materials as quarry waste and demolition rubble, without the need for additional topsoil (Ruff, 1997). Planting designs should be robust enough to take account of these inhospitable conditions, and flexible enough to reflect the particular characteristics of individual sites. Topsoil is expensive to buy and moving soil from site to site is also now considered rather unsustainable. It can also introduce weeds that will need to be controlled; the drought stress caused by competition from herbaceous vegetation is a major threat to tree establishment.

Ripping

Compacted planting areas should be loosened by ripping to a depth of at least 600 mm at intervals corresponding to plant spacing (usually two metres). Assessment of compaction is discussed in greater detail in Chapter 7. A winged-tine ripper is an excellent tool for the job where access and operation is practicable (Hodge, 1991). Alternatively, where access is restricted, back-hoe excavators or tractor-mounted augers can be used to penetrate the compacted substrate. This will enhance drainage and aeration and so encourage good root growth. Beware of underground services and rip across the slope, wherever possible. Ripping up and down slopes is likely to lead to excess rainwater run off, drought stress, soil erosion and instability.

Loose tipping of material on top of the surface is sometimes preferred to ripping. This is a useful method when earth is being moved around the site anyway, but it is important to make sure that tipping does not result in a shallow layer of material overlying an entirely impervious lower layer. This will quickly become waterlogged and hostile to the growth of many trees (Dobson and Moffatt, 1993; Moffatt and McNeill, 1995).

Pre-planting weed control

Competition with herbaceous vegetation is a common cause of poor tree establishment. It may even lead to complete failure. The vegetation in an area identified for new woodlands should be cut and sprayed in advance of planting, using a glyphosate-based herbicide where possible. If this is done between late summer and early autumn, it should give ample time for effective control of any persistent weeds on the site (Baines and Smart, 1991).

Implementation

If there is a large area to be planted, it is probably simplest to use contractors. In urban areas rural forestry contractors are often overlooked, but they usually price very competitively, have appropriate skills and may be willing to travel significant distances to undertake the work.

Excellent woodland establishment can be achieved by volunteers, providing they are properly supervised. They may be slower than professionals, but each person will have a vested interest in the survival of 'their trees' and so they are likely to help protect them in the future (Fig. 12.4). Involving local people in the creation of new woodlands can be a powerful tool in developing broader ideas of stewardship and environmental care (Agate, 1998).

12.4   Maintenance and management

Weed control

Effective weed control in the first few years after planting is essential. Newly planted trees are susceptible to competition for light and particularly for moisture. It is important to keep an area of at least one square metre around each tree free of vegetation for at least the first three years after planting, in order to ensure that the tree roots become well established and that the young saplings grow vigorously (Davies, 1987).

Weed control after planting can be done in a number of ways:

Fig. 12.4 Community tree planting is a vital key to establishing new woodlands successfully in urban neighbourhoods; it increases the sense of ownership and reduces the risk of vandalism. (Photo: National Urban Forestry Unit)

- **Chemically** e.g. through further use of glyphosate (*Roundup*) applied to weeds as a contact spray early in the growing season and by using propyzamide (*Kerb* granules) applied as a residual herbicide, during the winter.
- **Physically** e.g. through the use of mulches to suppress competing weed growth. Coarse chopped bark or wood chip (100 mm layer, particle size 75 mm minimum) and sheet mulches (polypropylene or bitumenised paper) are all effective in suppressing weed seedlings. They are, however, far less effective at preventing such persistent weeds as couch grass, bindweed, mares tail and creeping thistle from regrowing from rhizome fragments in the soil.

Pest control

Post and wire fencing may be necessary to keep out ponies and horses. Rabbits and hares are unlikely to be a serious threat in urban areas. Serious vole damage can be occasionally experienced and this is much more difficult to prevent. Vole damage tends to be associated with situations where young trees are surrounded by loose mulches of organic debris, or coarse grasses and other herbaceous plants that provide cover. In all cases, tree shelters and spiral rabbit guards can offer some protection.

Thinning / longer-term management

The degree of thinning and the intensity of continuing management is influenced by the complexity of the original woodland design and this in turn needs to reflect the long-term aims for the wood itself. As a general rule, robust and simple urban forestry-style woodlands of the type described here require minimal silvicultural intervention, and resources are needed at least as much for managing people as for managing trees.

The difference between the costs of managing the simplest style of woodland and more complex, ornamental woodland planting can be as much as a factor of ten (National Urban Forestry Unit, 1998). This means that it is possible to make very significant management cost savings by adopting a simple, pioneer style of woodland.

Where thinning can be employed with skill and sensitivity it is possible to use it to produce diversity in a woodland. However, in the long term, the natural thinning which results from a lack of intervention can also produce variety since it reflects both genetic variation and the variety of growing conditions.

More orthodox thinning (within ten to fifteen years of planting and at intervals thereafter) produces trees of even size, structure and stature –

desirable for commercial timber production, but not for amenity woodland.

Six to ten years after planting, when the woodland is likely to be at the thicket stage, clearance alongside pathways may be necessary so that users feel less insecure. Thereafter visibility tends to improve quite naturally, with views opening up between the tree trunks.

By reducing or eliminating regular intervention thinning, the trees are encouraged to grow or fail in response to natural competition. This tends to produce a more varied style of woodland, with a distinctive character that reflects more fully the environment in which it grows.

Investment in local community management can bring substantial dividends and result in a more sustainable approach to long-term care (Hibberd, 1989).

Fig. 12.5 Most urban woodlands are implemented without an understorey field layer, other than what establishes from the weed seed bank. Here a six-year-old birch woodland supports a ground layer of native forbs which were established several years after the birch. (Photo: James Hitchmough)

Habitat enhancement

Herb layer introduction

Many woodland wildflowers are very slow colonisers. In the wild they mainly spread by vegetative means, so deliberate introduction in new woodlands is usually necessary.

This can be undertaken by sowing seed *in situ* or by planting pot-grown plants. Seed of many true woodland species may be difficult to obtain in quantity and relatively expensive. Planting container-grown material (pot plants or plugs) as an initial source of inoculant can provide more rapid establishment and visual impact. Seed mixes should be diluted with other material, such as silver sand, for ease of handling and sowing. Mixtures of non-woodland grasses are best avoided, as they are likely to out-compete the wildflowers. Wildflowers have been successfully established in a number of secondary woodlands in urban situations, and this has resulted in diverse, vigorous and attractive field layers (Fig. 12.5) (Cohn and Packham, 1993; Cohn, 1998).

It is important to wait until the shade canopy is established before sowing woodland wildflower seed in order to reduce the risk competition from weedy light-demanding herbaceous plants (Cohn

et al., 2000). Given limited resources it is usually sensible to establish woodland herbs in places close to points of public access, in order to ensure maximum enjoyment.

Encouraging decay

Decay is important as fungi and invertebrates are vital to the woodland ecosystem. One of the simplest ways of enhancing the habitat is by spreading leaf sweepings from elsewhere onto the woodland floor (Baines, 1995).

Dead wood is a major asset, but because of concerns over public safety, it is often difficult to accommodate in urban woodlands as standing timber. If fallen branches and rotting wood are retained at ground level then this will minimise risk to public safety whilst enhancing the habitat.

Nest boxes

Birds can be encouraged through the provision of nest boxes. These offer the same nesting opportunities afforded by hollow branches and holes in tree trunks. Special boxes can also encourage bats to roost. The manufacture and monitoring of bird and bat boxes offers considerable opportunities for community involvement.

Sanctuary areas

No-go zones, from which the public is excluded, can be useful. In these areas, dead wood can be tolerated and plants and animals that are particularly sensitive to physical disturbance can flourish. This is also a way of reducing the damage to vegetation which can be caused by trampling.

12.5 Summary

There is ample space in towns for more substantial and extensive urban woodland. Whether developed by encouraging natural colonisation or through active planting, pioneer species are best equipped to colonise hostile soils and exposed sites. Small seedlings establish more effectively than large trees, and a management regime of minimum intervention, which echoes natural succession, results in new woodlands of distinctive character.

References

Agate, E. (1998) *The Urban Handbook: a practical guide to community environmental work.* British Trust for Conservation Volunteers, Wallingford.

Baines, C. (1995) Urban areas. In: *Managing Habitats for Conservation* (Eds W.J. Sutherland & D.A. Hill). Cambridge University Press.

Baines, C. (1986) Design considerations at establishment. In: *Ecology and Design in Landscape* (Eds. A.D. Bradshaw, D.A. Goode & E. Thorp). Blackwell Scientific Publications, Oxford.

Baines, C. & Smart, J. (1991) A *Guide to Habitat Creation.* Packard Publishing Limited, Chichester.

Black Country Urban Forestry Unit (1991) *Woodland planting guidelines for the urban forest* (Poster). Black Country Urban Forestry Unit, Great Barr.

Bradshaw, A., Hunt, B., & Walmsley, T (1995) *Trees in the Urban Landscape: principles and practice.* E & F Spon, London.

Cohn, E.V.J. (1998) Woodland enhancement and forest integrity. The National Forest: from vision to reality. *East Midlands Geographer* **21**, 54–61.

Cohn, E.V.J. & Packham, J.R. (1993) The introduction and manipulation of woodland field layers: seeding, planting, timing and economics. *Arboricultural Journal* **17**, 69–83.

Cohn, E.V.J., Trueman, I.C., & Packham, J.R. (2000) More than just trees. *Aspects of Applied Biology* **58**, 93–101.

Davies, R.J. (1987) *Trees and Weeds*, Forestry Commission Handbook 2, HMSO, London.

Dobson, M.C. & Moffatt, A.J. (1993) *The Potential for Woodland Establishment on Landfill Sites*, HMSO, London.

Hibberd, B.G. (1989) *Urban Forestry in Practice.* Forestry Commission Handbook 5, HMSO, London.

Hodge, S. (1991) *Creating and Managing Woodlands around Towns.* Forestry Commission Handbook 11, HMSO, London.

La Dell, T. (1983) An Introduction to Tree and Shrub Seeding. *Landscape Design* **144**, 27–30.

La Dell, T. (1987) Tree and Shrub Seeding. *Landscape Design* **168**, 53–4.

Moffatt, A.J. & McNeill, J. (1993) *Reclaiming disused land for forestry*, Forestry Commission Bulletin 110, HMSO, London.

National Urban Forestry Unit (1998) *Trees or Turf? best value in managing urban greenspace.* National Urban Forestry Unit, Wolverhampton.

National Urban Forestry Unit (2001) *Designing Urban Woodland.* National Urban Forestry Unit, Wolverhampton.

Rodwell, J. & Patterson, G. (1994) *Creating New Native Woodlands*, Forestry Commission Bulletin 112, HMSO, London.

Ruff, A. (1997) The use of ecological principles in design solutions in urban open space. In: *Ecology and Design in Amenity Land Management*, Proceedings of Conference held at Wye College, April 1979, (Eds Wright, S.E. & Buckley, G.P.). Wye College and Research Ecology Group.

IV Establishment and Management of Smaller Woody Plants

13 Shrub Mosaics and Woodland Edge

'Natural' Models for Shrub Planting

Nigel Dunnett

The shrub is the most widely used of landscape plant types, and perhaps the most useful in terms of versatility, maintenance and durability. Yet, because of over-use and inappropriate use, landscape shrub plantings can be visually dull and have reduced ecological value. This may be for several reasons:

- Large-scale 'shrub-mass' plantings are often monotonous, and have little or no structural or species diversity; they do not reflect seasonal change, and have diminished wildlife value.
- Crude, unselective maintenance practices can again reduce structural diversity and prevent dynamic change.
- The lack of an integrated herbaceous layer further reduces the visual appeal and ecological value. Absence of a herbaceous layer also increases the need for maintenance and weed control, especially on the edge of plantings.

This chapter looks at some alternatives to the shrub plantings that have become the norm during the past 30 years.

13.1 What are shrubs?

Convenient definitions of a shrub are difficult, because the term can include plants that some may regard as trees, and others that might be regarded as being more like herbaceous perennials. However, shrubs are generally regarded as being multi-stemmed woody plants. The size of the plant has a bearing on whether it is considered to be a tree or a shrub. Small, wide-spreading trees (for example *Crataegus prunifolia*) growing on a single stem may possess shrub-like qualities, while large trees may be turned into proxy-shrubs through coppicing, burning or other practices that remove existing top-growth and encourage the sprouting of new shoots from the base. In terms of size, how does one distinguish between a large shrub and a small multi-stemmed tree, and how tall does a shrub have to get before it is regarded as a tree?

These are impossible questions to answer: in the garden plant literature, seven metres is sometimes used as a threshold height between shrubs and trees, but judgement is probably best based more upon intuition than any strict height categorisation. At the other end of the scale, some shrub-like plants (such as *Phygelius*) produce frost-tender herbaceous shoots from a woody base and are generally managed as herbaceous perennials, unless in very mild climates. Even in these areas, these 'sub-shrubs' are often more attractive when pruned back to ground level annually.

13.2 Shrubs as landscape plants

Functionally, the great value of shrubs is their human-scale and (with the exception of sub-shrubs) their permanence throughout the year. They are essential for structure plantings, dividing large spaces into smaller units and for screening unsightly or intrusive objects or views from site users. But it has been management considerations that have largely been responsible both for the dominance of the shrub as a landscape plant and for the way that shrub-based plantings have been designed.

Many shrubs are excellent landscape plants in that they are robust and will perform reliably with the minimum of maintenance over many years. They are rarely seriously affected by the herbivores (most frequently slugs and snails) which often lead to the disappearance of many herbaceous plants in landscape plantings. Once shrub canopies are established, the shade they cast will suppress many weeds, and when weed invasion does occur, and control is judged necessary, it is relatively straightforward to undertake. The separation of the shrub canopy from the herbaceous weed flora below makes it easy for maintenance staff to distinguish between what is to be kept and what is to be removed, either through cultivation or herbicides.

For designers, the most attractive thing about using shrubs is that the results of a planting can be predictable and reliable, either because of the final growth form of the plant, or because simple pruning operations can perpetuate the desired height and shape of the planting. As a result, much of the landscape shrub planting commonly encountered is undertaken primarily to fill space with undemanding vegetation in a very low-cost manner.

Of course, such 'shrub-mass', if well designed, can be extremely effective and attractive; but all too often the result is vegetation of low visual quality, lacking in any sort of distinctive character. The very restricted range of plants used in the majority of schemes, arranged in large monocultural blocks or masses, compounds this. There is great potential for an approach that is visually more interesting and ecologically sustainable, not least because these projects are the most common type of landscape planting opportunity.

In the UK, this style of landscape is a hybrid of two traditions: the garden shrubbery and continental European shrub monoculture. Shrub monoculture was a purely functional approach used on the continent by modernist designers, in effect treating plants as a material in the same way as concrete or stone to achieve uniform ground cover.

In Britain, the shrubbery developed in the twentieth century as a means of utilising the huge range of shrubby plants that had been introduced to cultivation in the nineteenth and early twentieth cen-turies, providing year-round interest. It was also a response to the need for labour-saving planting solutions to replace more intensively maintained herbaceous plantings.

Shrubs were substituted for herbaceous perennials, sometimes using the same design approach: interlocking Jekyll-style groups of the same shrub. The result was, as Graham Stuart Thomas (1992) says, an effect that was 'dull in the extreme', both in summer and winter. Such shrubberies can still be seen in some public parks.

There were, however, other traditions that were visually much richer. In *The Mixed Border* (Lloyd, 1956) Christopher Lloyd advocated the integra-tion of complex herbaceous planting and carefully chosen shrubs. This model has come to form the design basis for most garden planting in Britain, although it has generally been seen as too labour intensive for use in public or commercial landscapes.

13.3   Natural shrub communities

The design principles and management techniques for conventional shrub plantings are covered in planting design texts such as Robinson (1992). An alternative approach is to model landscape shrub plantings on their 'natural' counterparts. Such natural shrub communities tend to differ from their designed counterparts in two main ways.

Structure

Spontaneous woody vegetation develops a distinct horizontal and vertical multi-layered structure, with different levels of shrubs and usually some sort of herbaceous layer beneath. The integration of a flowering herbaceous perennial layer into designed shrub plantings is one of the key chal-lenges: imagine plantations with the vitality and richness of ancient woodlands with their carpets of spring wildflowers. How often do we find this sort of experience in our public parks and land-scapes, or even private gardens?

There is not only a distinct vertical structure but also a horizontal gradation of shrubs into sur-rounding grassland or meadow (Fig. 13.1). This

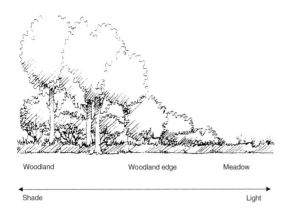

Woodland   Woodland edge   Meadow

Shade   Light

Fig. 13.1 A typical ecotone structure.

'ecotone' structure is very important, both visually and also for maximising wildlife benefit (Dramstad *et al.*, 1996).

The natural arrangement of shrubs is also often much more complex than the blocks of a standard planting. Group sizes will be much less regular, with more intricate mixing of species. An exception to this is where shrubs that spread clonally produce large suckering stands (as in Blackthorn, *Prunus spinosa*), but again there will often be an interesting interplay at the edges as suckers come up through adjacent grassland.

Development

Conventional maintenance treats shrub plantings as essentially static entities, with the main objective of keeping the shrubs within defined physical boundaries. The appearance of the planting changes little from year to year, other than by expansion and contraction in response to pruning. Looking at it in terms of the processes involved, if ecologically compatible types of plant are put together then management can be a cyclical process rejuvenating the planting and guiding a succession of growth, rather than preventing that succession happening in the first place by hard pruning.

As a basis for more ecological and sustainable ways of arranging landscape shrub plantings, *woodland edge* and *scrub mosaics* are natural models that contain a high species and structural diversity but also are characterised by an integration of woody plants with a herbaceous field layer (Fig. 13.2). In both cases this field layer contains a mixture of truly shade-tolerant woodland herbaceous species, more light-demanding woodland edge species and grassland or meadow species of open ground.

13.4 Woodland edge

This is one of the most common shrub habitats, forming the transition between the forest interior and open ground grassland or meadow habitats. Woodland edges, particularly those that are warm, sheltered and south-facing, can be composed of diverse mixes of flowering and fruiting shrubs and scrambling vines. They are both visually attractive and very valuable to wildlife. Most woodland edge habitats also contain a mix of light-demanding and shade tolerant herbaceous species growing beneath the shrubs.

The woodland edge model is particularly valuable because on many sites this represents the only real opportunity for ecologically diverse vegetation to be established. In a small urban park, for example, there may be little opportunity to establish large meadow areas but more opportunities to enhance plantation edges and boundaries by integrating meadow grassland and shrubs in an ecotone vegetation structure, as in Fig. 13.1. Woodland edge type vegetation can also be the basis of general structural shrub plantings and shrub-mass.

In design terms the beneficial characteristics of woodland edges are that they are composed of diverse mixtures of evergreen and deciduous shrubs; there are a range of seasonal highlights, from spring and summer flowering, through autumn fruiting and leaf colour to the mix of deciduous and evergreen effects over winter.

An important consideration is that detailed planting plans are rarely produced to dictate precise positions for every plant, but instead the planting is set out following a specified percentage mix. The specification will detail the species composition of a planting mixture, giving recom-

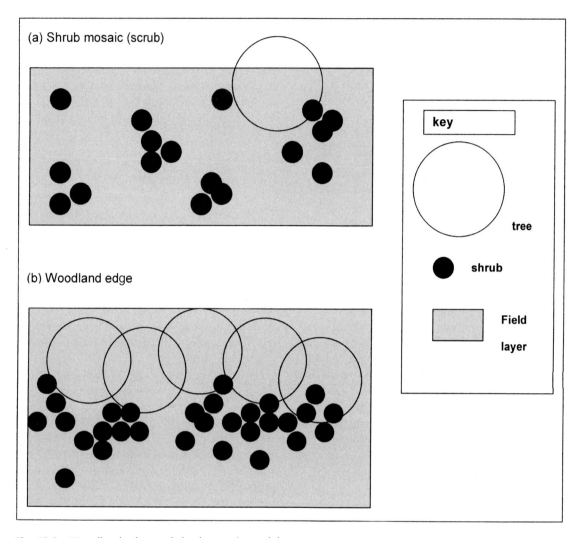

Fig. 13.2   Woodland edge and shrub mosaic models.

mended planting patterns in terms of group sizes, arrangements and planting distances. The exact positions will then be determined by whoever is implementing the planting. In many instances, locations will be given for dominant species or trees, or guidance will be given that certain species are to be planted towards the boundaries or edges of an area. In this approach to planting, the skill of the designer lies in formulating mixtures that are ecologically and aesthetically compatible, rather than spending time on deciding precisely what goes where as in traditional planting design.

These principles are well accepted for native species used in habitat creation projects. Exactly the same approach can be employed using non-native or ornamental species, where visual attributes will be as important or more so than habitat provision (Fig. 13.3). Table 13.1 gives an example of such mixtures, developed for the Sheffield Development Corporation (SDC, 1994), for use in regeneration schemes on post-industrial sites in the city.

The aim of these and other similar mixtures was to provide structural and shrub-mass planting

Fig. 13.3 Native flowering vegetation at the woodland edge: why not use exotics to produce similar effects? (Photo: Nigel Dunnett)

Table 13.1 Woody plant mixes for transport corridors around Meadowhall, Sheffield, based upon locally distinctive vegetation. Source: Landscape and Nature Conservation Strategy for the Lower Don Valley, Sheffield Development Corporation, 1994.

Thickets
15% *Betula pendula*
15% *Cytisus scoparius*
20% *Malus domestica*
20% *Salix caprea*
20% *Salix cinera*

Ornamental edge
30% *Buddleia davidii*
20% *Sambucus nigra*
15% *Cytisus scoparius var andreanus*
15% *Cotoneaster bullatus, C.salicifolius, C.simmonsii*
10% *Colutea arborescens*
10% *Ligustrum vulgaris*

Table 13.2 Shrubs that visually and biologically 'fit' the woodland edge.

Amelanchier spp.
Aronia spp.
Berberis thunbergii
Corylopsis spp.
Corylus
Cotoneaster
Euonymus (deciduous) e.g. *E. alatus, E. europaeus, E. hamiltonianus, E. planipes*
Exchorda
Forsythia
Hamamelis
Kerria
Leycesteria
Lonicera
Philadelphus
Pyracantha
Rhododendron (deciduous)
Rhus
Ribes
Rosa (species)
Rubus
Salix
Sambucus
Sorbaria
Viburnum (deciduous)

which integrated commonly-occurring species (including natives, and non-native 'garden escapes') that spontaneously colonised derelict sites in the area, but to use them in arrangements that would be aesthetically pleasing to people.

The non-native species were known to survive very well in hostile urban situations, and added extra visual appeal, as well as reinforcing locally distinctive vegetation patterns. A list of non-native genera that can be used in woodland edge mixes is given in Table 13.2.

The most appropriate shrubs to use in woodland edge plantings are those with a loose habit that will merge into each other, rather than those with a rigid and strongly stylised form. Species with very distinct appearance, for example shrubs with variegated foliage, tend to look out of place. Shrubs with abundant fruits that hang on into winter are especially valuable, while scrambling or climbing plants (e.g. honeysuckle or rose) can be integrated with shrubs. A neglected group of plants for landscape use are the shrub roses (the medium-tall types rather than the commonly planted ground cover types), but they are ideal for this type of planting. Good examples include *Rosa moyesii, R. webbiana, R. eglanteria, R. pimpinellifolia, R. xanthina*. Similar effects can be obtained

Fig. 13.4 *Rubus odoratus* in a naturalistic woodland-edge structural planting. (Photo: Nigel Dunnett)

from flowering *Rubus*, such as *R. odoratus* and *R. tridel 'Benenden'*. Suckering shrubs, which are usually avoided in formal planting schemes, are also well suited if planted amongst other more solid shrubs (Fig. 13.4).

If these types of plants are cut at a fixed height above the ground, in the same way that many standard shrub plantings are maintained, the congested mass of branches and that results will inhibit flowering. A more appropriate method is to coppice, or cut back periodically at ground level. In many cases only a percentage of the shrubs will be coppiced in any one year, on a rolling cycle for between three and ten years. Where it is a priority for maintenance to control the size of the shrubs, for example along the margins of footpaths, a shorter coppicing cycle is appropriate.

Coppicing can be used as a management technique for shrub-only plantings, but where weed control is achieved using conventional practices of mulching and/or herbicides, it also enables a flowering ground layer of bulbs (see Chapter 24) or woodland herbaceous species (see Chapter 25) to be established. Lists of shade tolerant woodland edge herbaceous plants that persist under these conditions can be found in *Perennials and their Garden Habitats* (Hansen and Stahl, 1994).

13.5   Shrub mosaics

Scrub is the general and rather unflattering name for semi-natural vegetation dominated by or characterised by the shrub form. It may often occur as a transient stage before an unmanaged site turns into woodland; but where there is some form of environmental stress or disturbance, scrub may be a much more permanent vegetation type. Scrub often occurs on free-draining, low fertility soils where there is a lack of regular management, such as over limestone, chalk or sandstones, or on more fertile soils where regular grazing or burning prevents a tree canopy forming.

There is no doubt that 'scrubby' vegetation can be amongst the most attractive of all vegetation types, particularly where shrub cover is discontinuous or rather open. Under these conditions the best qualities of both woodland edge and flowering meadows of herbaceous plants can be combined. For example, the chalk downlands or limestone dales of Britain, or their central European Steppe counterparts, combine a wide diversity of shrubs and small trees (primarily from the rose family) in a mosaic with sun-loving herbaceous perennials and grasses.

The Maquis of Mediterranean climates is an aromatic and colourful assemblage of evergreen shrubs, herbs and bulbs. By contrast the roadsides and woodland edges of the Eastern United States and the Mid-West often contain intimate mixtures of herbaceous perennials and suckering deciduous clonal shrubs, for example *Rhus glabra*, whose leaves produce visually spectacular, volcanic autumn displays.

The attraction of this mosaic model for shrub-based plantings is that it is a truly mixed planting, combining shrubs, perennials, bulbs and small trees. It also provides much more structural diversity and year-round visual interest than pure meadow, prairie, herbaceous plantings or shrub plantings on their own. Much of the design potential that is evident in the mixed border is also available, with the added advantage of reduced maintenance in the mosaic shrub planting (Fig. 13.5).

Fig. 13.5 Multifunctional shrub planting around a play area in a residential scheme in Germany; it achieves division of space, visual interest, wildlife habitat and informal play opportunities. (Photo: Nigel Dunnett)

13.6 Establishing woodland edge and shrub mosaic plantings

The essential difference between woodland edge and shrub mosaic is one of density of the woody plants: woodland edges have a higher density than shrub mosaics. For woodland edge plantings the aim will be to produce a closed canopy relatively quickly. Shrubs in native edge mixes are generally planted at 1.5–2.0 m spacings. More compact species can be planted at distances of 1.0 m, but any closer spacings will produce congested and dense twiggy masses. Very vigorous species (e.g. *Sorbaria spp.*) can be planted at 3.0 m centres. While it may be supposed that totally random mixtures give the most naturalistic effect, in practice the result can be very bitty and messy. A more realistic effect is produced if species are planted in groups (the size of which will depend on the scale of the planting), which are then randomly arranged within the planting area.

For more open shrub mosaic plantings, similar spacings can be used for the more densely planted clumps, with wider spacings of 5.0 m or more appropriate for more open parts of the planting. The aim is to achieve a naturalistic arrangement of clumping and grouping of trees and shrubs, as in Fig. 13.1. Spacing is also determined by the degree to which a particular shrub is to be repeated through a planting, to achieve pleasing rhythmical and unifying effects.

An effective natural pattern to follow is that of the 'aggregated clump with outliers', with more sparsely spaced individuals spread out into the herbaceous layer from a more densely planted clump. The main consideration in setting up such plantings is to ensure that the shrub component does not become over-dominant. Coppicing is again the main maintenance technique for this. Periodically cutting back the woody plants not only rejuvenates them, but also allows herbaceous perennials to form part of the system, because the alternating dark and light phases maximise the range of herbaceous species that can grow in the area.

Over the last decade the author has worked with shrub mosaic communities that have a very long period of visual interest because of the combination of woody plants and perennials. The most suitable woody plants to use are those that produce vigorous juvenile growth. Such species will respond strongly to coppicing, and will not suffer excessive competition from the herbaceous layer. One group of plants that can be useful are suckering or clonal shrubs (e.g. *Rhus typhina*, *Sorbaria arborea*). These species can be problematic in standard shrub plantings, but when combined with a dense perennial layer, the competition can reduce their vigour considerably, making them far more manageable (Plate 13). Most suckering species respond very well to cutting back to ground level. Table 13.3 lists a range of species that respond well to coppicing.

Herbaceous perennials

The spaces between the woody plants are then planted with herbaceous species. These can be either planted or sown, depending on what is desired, resources available, and the scale of the planting. On small-scale projects, planting may be more convenient.

There are four main types of herbaceous species that can be used in coppice systems:

- *Ruderal woodland edge species*
  These plants are typically light-demanding species, that flower quickly from seed, and reproduce predominantly by seed. They are readily established by sowing after shrub planting. Examples include *Silene dioica*, *Hesperis matronalis*, *Galium mollugo*, *Lotus uliginosus*, *Anthriscus sylvestris*.
- *Shade-tolerant species*
  These species tend to be slow growing, evergreen and reproduce by vegetative methods as well as seed. Establishment by planting is typically most appropriate for these species. Examples include *Primula vulgaris*, *Helleborus orientalis*, *Pulmonaria spp.*
- *Bulbs*
  Early-flowering species that complete their photosynthesis before the shrubs are in full leaf are generally most successful. Bulbs are discussed in greater detail in Chapter 24.
- *Meadow/grassland perennials*
  These species typically grow in scrub communities, woodland edges and semi-shaded grasslands. In trials at Sheffield, the more competitive species were most successful –

Table 13.3 Woody plants that respond well to coppice management with herbaceous field layers in shrub mosaic plantings.

Name	Clonal	Winter stem colour	Autumn leaf colour	Coloured young leaves	Flower
Acer cappadocicum			•	•	
Acer platanoides			•		
Acer saccharinum		•	•	•	
Aesculus hippocastanum			•	•	
Amelanchier spp.			•		•
Aronia arbutifolia	•		•	•	•
Buddleia davidii					•
Carpinus betulus					
Corylus avellana					
F.excelsior 'Jaspidea'		•		•	
Fraxinus excelsior				•	
Populus alba	•	•	•		
Pterocarya fraxinifolia	•				
Quercus rubra			•	•	
Rhus typhina & *R.glabra* & cvs	•		•		
Rosa spp.					•
Rubus spp.	•				•
Salix spp.		•			
Sambucus spp.			•		•
Sorbaria spp.	•				
Tilia platyphyllos 'Rubra'		•			
Viburnum opulus			•		•

Plate 1 Fashion is an important factor in plant use. Japanese cherries have been out of fashion with landscape architects for many years, despite their popularity with the public at large. (Photo: James Hitchmough)

Plate 2 Sometimes there are unexpected benefits from compacted, hostile soils: here a cultivar of the evergreen *Euonymus fortunei* regularly turns brilliant orange-red over winter. On good soil the colouring is far less pronounced. (Photo: James Hitchmough)

Plate 4 On-site drainage in Holland, where water is directed from hard surfaces into a depression; the area has been planted with wet-tolerant species to produce an attractive habitat that is rich in wildlife. (Photo: James Hitchmough)

Plate 3 The native vegetation associated with wet, poorly-drained grassland is often very attractive. (Photo: James Hitchmough)

Plate 6 Japanese knotweed (*Fallopia japonica*) is a scourge of amenity land. (Photo: R.J. Froud-Williams)

Plate 5 Giant hogweed (*Heracleum mantegazzianum*) colonising a riparian corridor. (Photo: R.J. Froud-Williams)

Plate 7 (*below*) The proliferation of Himalayan (syn. Indian) balsam (*Impatiens glandulifera*) along a riparian corridor leads to the exclusion of native species. (Photo: R.J. Froud-Williams)

Plate 8 Invasion of the urban environment by the butterfly bush, *Buddleja davidii*. (Photo: R.J. Froud-Williams)

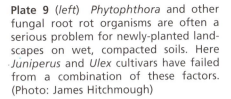

Plate 9 (*left*) *Phytophthora* and other fungal root rot organisms are often a serious problem for newly-planted landscapes on wet, compacted soils. Here *Juniperus* and *Ulex* cultivars have failed from a combination of these factors. (Photo: James Hitchmough)

Plate 11 Air pot containers of *Betula utilis jacquemontii* on a nursery site. (Photo: Hillier Nurseries Ltd)

Plate 10 Tree set in pavement: the roots will suffer compaction from the concrete surface, water stress and lack of oxygen. (Photo: Glynn Percival)

Plate 12 Root ball of a London plane (*Platanus* × *acerifolia*) raising ground levels. (Photo: Edwards Gale)

(a)

(b)

Plate 13 *Rhus typhina* and *Rudbeckia fulgida* var *deammii*. The vegetation is maintained by annual coppicing once the plants are established, combined with cutting back the herbaceous layer; both operations are carried out simultaneously in winter. (Photo: Nigel Dunnett)

Plate 14 Ground cover planting density trial. Flowering of *Erica* x *darleyensis* (**a**) is reduced as planting density increases; tolerance of drought (**b**) is also reduced. (Photo: Peter Thoday)

Plate 16 A vegetable summer house of hornbeam (*Carpinus betulus*) in a Dutch park. (Photo: James Hitchmough)

Plate 15 Cloud sculpting: beautiful cumulus hedges of box (*Buxus sempervirens*) in the garden of Jacques Wirtz. (Photo: James Hitchmough)

Plate 17 *Parthenocissus tricuspidata* is a well-known self-clinging climber, but its ability to attach itself to window frames and even glass can create conflicts. (Photo: James Hitchmough)

Plate 18 *Hydrangea anomala* subsp. *petiolaris* is also self-clinging, but has a lower shoot density per unit area of wall and its slower growth is easier to manage. (Photo: James Hitchmough)

Plate 19 *Vitis coignetiae*, grown primarily for its spectacular autumn colour, climbs by twining tendrils and needs the provision of a wire support structure or a tree. (Photo: James Hitchmough)

Plate 20 This imposing roof garden in Chicago shows that a huge depth of soil is not necessary for good landscape to be created. (Photo: Steve Scrivens)

Plate 21 A wildflower meadow in Knowsley, created by Landlife on a site stripped of topsoil. (Photo: Landlife)

Plate 22 A mixture of ox-eye daisies (*Leucanthemum vulgare*) and lupins (*Lupinus* spp.) brings colour to an inner-city housing estate in Liverpool. The lupin is widely naturalised but not native; here its use reflects its long history of association with the urban landscape. (Photo: James Hitchmough)

Plate 23 An aquatic and marginal planting scheme with habitat creation as the main objective. Yellow flag iris (*Iris pseudacorus*) and brooklime (*Veronica beccabunga*) fill the foreground, with the yellow flowers of celery-leaved buttercup (*Ranunculus sceleratus*) behind. (Photo: Kevin Patrick)

Plate 24 A recently-planted flood relief channel, with flowering rush (*Butomus umbellatus*) and branched bur-reed (*Sparganium erectum*) in mid-channel, and purple loosestrife (*Lythrum salicaria*) and fool's watercress (*Apium nodosum*) on the banks. (Photo: Kevin Patrick)

Plate 25 Direct-sown annual meadows can be effective in formal spaces; replacement of a formal bedding scheme in a Sheffield park. (Photo: Nigel Dunnett)

Plate 26 (*right*) Mixed biennials and short-lived perennials in a Sheffield park: pink foxgloves (*Digitalis purpurea*), sweet rocket (*Hesperis matronalis*) and ox-eye daisy (*Leucanthemum vulgare*). (Photo: Nigel Dunnett)

Plate 27 Three-dimensional carpet bedding in Peking. (Photo: Richard Bisgrove)

Plate 28 An inexpensive but refreshing summer bedding scheme: a central spine of *Ricinus communis* and *Nicotiana sylvestris* along a narrow bed, with blocks of green *Amaranthus caudatus* and white petunias on either side. (Photo: Richard Bisgrove)

Plate 29 Orchids (*Orchis mascula*) compete with tall grass; a thoughtful cutting regime may need to be undertaken to favour such late-flowering spring bulbs. (Photo: Fergus Garrett/Rory Dusoir)

Plate 30 The dramatic scarlet flowers and dark foliage of dahlia 'Bishop of Llandaff', contrasted with white cosmos and *Pleiobastus auricomus*. (Photo: Fergus Garrett/Rory Dusoir)

Plate 31 Steppe-inspired decorative planting, the archetypal 'German style', at Weihenstephan, near Munich. (Photo: James Hitchmough)

Plate 32 Woodland understorey planting of *Primula elatior* and violets in a Dutch nature park. (Photo: James Hitchmough)

those that form clonally spreading colonies, or have leafy flowering stems. Examples include *Geranium* spp., *Aster divaricatus*, *Crocosmia*, *Hemerocallis*, *Persicaria*, *Rudbeckia*, *Solidago*.

Establishing the field layer

The herbaceous species can be introduced through seeding, planting, or a combination of the two at the same time as woody species are planted.

A fundamental assumption is that it will require very little maintenance, and in particular very little weed control in the long term: the vegetation will develop to its own dynamic. In the early stages, if maintenance resources are limited, it is best to treat the open areas between shrub groups as a flowery meadow ground layer. Initial control of perennial weeds is essential prior to herbaceous plant establishment. On very weedy sites the preparation and establishment techniques described in Chapters 19 and 20 can be employed to prevent unattractive dominance by weeds. However, using the vigorous clonal herbaceous species discussed above, as well as using forb-only seed mixes, can be effective in minimising early weed control problems.

In the more densely planted woodland edge vegetation, the meadow will develop into more sparse, shade tolerant vegetation. However, in the mosaic plantings, the flowery meadow will persist between the shrub clumps and the more shade-tolerant species will aggregate around the woody plants. In practice, maintenance requirements are often dictated by the needs of particular clients; in locations where a more ordered appearance is required, these types of planting can be more 'gardened' to maximise display value. The field is cut back once a year in winter, and the woody plants are cut back to ground level when the canopy becomes dense. Generally the first cut will be made after three years for the more vigorous species.

Combinations of dynamic grassland plant communities can provide continuous flowering from March to November, mixing vernal woodland edge perennials with later flowering grassland species that are equally happy in sun or part-shade. The proportions of the various plant types used are important. It is best to use greater numbers of the late-flowering species, which steadily grow up through the summer and hide the remains of earlier flowering species. Fewer earlier flowering species can be used because these look attractive amongst the backdrop of fresh green foliage of the later perennials and the grasses. Because the vegetation is cut to ground level in winter, the very earliest species flower amongst very low vegetation and they can therefore themselves be short.

The great value of using shade-tolerant woodland-edge and scrub herbaceous species in these field layer mixtures is that these plant communities resemble woodland communities in themselves – the taller, later flowering species create their own shade canopy, beneath which the earlier vernal species can survive. Most of the herbaceous species that are successful in these mixed plantings tend to be vigorous and clonal, and relatively non-palatable to slugs, snails and other herbivores. The following species have been successful in the north of England:

> *Aster* 'Little Carlow'
> *Aster divaricatus*
> *Centaurea montana*
> *Deschampsia cespitosa*
> *Geranium pratense*
> *Geranium psilostemon*
> *Geranium sylvaticum*
> *Persicaria amplexicaulis*
> *Persicaria bistorta*
> *Primula vulgaris*
> *Rudbeckia fulgida deamii*
> *Rudbeckia* 'Juligold'
> *Solidago* 'Ledsham'

13.7   Summary

Promoting greater visual, structural and ecological diversity in shrub-based plantings is one of the greatest challenges for landscape designers and managers. Species selection has always tended to be rather limited, but there has been a notable tendency in recent years for very crude management of shrub plantings that reduces all to cube-like blocks and masses shaped by the sweep of a hedge trimmer. In this chapter a different approach has been put forward: one that is based upon the way that attractive 'natural' examples of shrubby vegetation fit together and function.

As with most 'ecological' approaches, the skill in creating the planting lies more in selecting balanced and compatible mixes of species than in detailed planning of visual or structural plant associations. There is an equal requirement for more enlightened maintenance practices that recognise the natural growth patterns of shrubs and respond accordingly: this is where the greatest challenge lies.

References

Dramstad, W., Olsen, J., & Forman, R. (1996) *Landscape Ecology Principles in Landscape Architecture and Land-use Planning*, Island Press, Washington.

Hansen, R. & Stahl, F. (1994) *Perennials and their Garden Habitats.* Cambridge University Press, Cambridge.

Lloyd, C. (1956) *The Mixed Border*, Dent, London.

Robinson, N. (1992) *The Planting Design Handbook*, Gower, Aldershot.

SDC (1994) *Landscape and Nature Conservation Strategy for the Lower Don Valley.* Sheffield Development Corporation, Sheffield.

Thomas, G.S. (1992) *Ornamental Shrubs, Climbers and Bamboos*, John Murray, London.

Further reading

Hilliers (1981) *Hilliers Manual of Trees and Shrubs*, David & Charles, Newton Abbot.

Phillips, R. & Rix, M. (1989) *Shrubs*, Pan, London.

14 Ground Cover

Peter Thoday

Ground cover, or more accurately plant-covered ground, has developed over the last fifty years as arguably the single most positive feature of planting design. For a variety of economic and aesthetic reasons, bare soil has gone out of fashion; indeed, some designers regard the sight of it as tantamount to indecent exposure.

As a design concept, ground cover requires the soil to be hidden beneath a canopy of stems and foliage. To achieve this it is helpful to recognise that ground cover is both a biological phenomenon and a way of husbanding plants. By nature or nurture (or frequently a combination of both) a single plant type, or more rarely a mixed community, can completely colonise an area to achieve either visual or dominant cover.

- *Visual cover* is when, from the intended view points, the planting appears to be a uniform vegetation mass screening the soil surface.
- *Dominant cover* is when a plant canopy or its debris is so dense that it prevents the growth of all other plant types within it.

Ground cover plantings have become a way of giving a finished appearance to recently planted areas. This is not necessarily biologically desirable as it requires that the canopies of the transplants should nearly touch. There are two obvious ways of achieving this: with a higher number of transplants than usual, or by using larger specimens. Both approaches result in long-term problems. Excessively close planting leads to excessive competition between individuals, which leads to premature plant failure; larger (older)

transplants frequently lack vigour and produce irregular cover.

Without going into the aesthetic aspects of ground cover at great length, the success of husbandry techniques can only be judged in the light of the effects that are intended. Inevitably the cost of ground cover varies with the species used, depending on both the number of transplants required per unit area and the variation in transplant unit costs. Plant material costs (wholesale) for ground cover currently range (at 2003 prices) from approximately £5.00–15.00 per m². However this is almost insignificant when set against the total costs of landscape works. Ground cover can be undertaken with woody and herbaceous plants and both are discussed in this chapter. Herbaceous plants are covered further in Chapter 25.

14.1 Using ground cover

The current use of ground cover can be divided into five categories.

Simple sheets

Each sheet is composed of one taxon (a species or cultivar). Sheets are typically large, and extend as a layer throughout a planted area. This is the type of ground cover planting that, when composed of low to medium evergreen shrubs, has come to be regarded as rather dull. It can however be a very effective, elegant treatment for some situations (Fig. 14.1).

Fig. 14.1 Ground cover single species sheet planting using *Stephanandra incisa*. (Photo: Peter Thoday)

Fig. 14.2 A tapestry of ground cover species in a Dutch park: ferns and *Vaccineum*. (Photo: James Hitchmough)

Patchworks

These allow large areas to be planted without the risk of monotony. The flexibility of patchwork presents a designer with a range of options. For example, groups of plants may be encouraged to fuse along their edges in a manner reminiscent of a cottage garden, or they may be planted to give the startling geometric effects so much in evidence in the works of the Roberto Burle Marx.

Tapestries

These are achieved when one plant type mingles with another. This demands skill in choosing suitable partners to give a pleasing effect, and also to ensure that a stable community of co-dominants, present in the right ratio, is attained (Fig. 14.2). The designer needs to achieve the correct initial spacing and have an understanding of the competitive form and characteristics of each type used. With woody plants, tapestries are most likely to be successful using mound-forming species with relatively slow lateral spread, such as some of the small-leaved *Hebe*, *Potentilla fruticosa* and small evergreen *Berberis*. The same is also true of herbaceous plants, clump forming species such as *Pulmonaria*, *Astrantia major* and many *Geranium*

are more successful than species that spread aggressively by rhizomes or stolons, for example *Euphorbia amygdaloides* var. *robbiae*.

Tiered plantings

These are often a three-dimensional development of patchwork ground cover plantings, and are used when the design requires the vegetation to rise from a few centimetres to a backing of considerably taller shrubs (Fig. 14.3).

Sheet with emergents

This is perhaps the most popular style in continental Europe. Ground covering taxa form a continuous understorey to both specimen shrubs and standard trees. This strategy is used on new sites and for revamping Victorian and Edwardian shrubberies. It is a practical solution for many urban sites that can also be very interesting visually. Sheets can be composed of one taxon, or of many, as in the tapestry (Fig. 14.4).

In landscape practice, 'ground cover' is often used to refer to layers of foliage that are less than 600–1000 mm tall. Layers of ground covering foliage that are composed of woody plants taller

Fig. 14.3 Tiered planting of ground cover and shrub mass with emergent trees. Ground cover edging allows the shrub masses to develop naturally without pruning. (Photo: Peter Thoday)

Fig. 14.4 *Geranium maccrorhizum*, an utterly reliable semi-evergreen herbaceous ground cover in a Swedish park. (Photo: James Hitchmough)

than this (at maturity) are often referred to as 'shrub mass'. Such definitions are largely arbitrary, as the design and management of taller ground cover (shrub mass) and lower ground cover are fundamentally subject to the same principles.

14.2 Plant selection

Plant selection is one of the most important preparatory tasks, but there is no simple way to use the morphology of a plant as an indicator of its performance as ground cover. Low growing shrubs, evergreen herbs and herbaceous perennials were among subjects evaluated at the University of Bath in the 1980s and found to be useful (Fig. 14.5).

Figure 14.6 illustrates that useful plants may spread by root suckers, layers, rhizomes or stolons.

In contrast, there are equally effective non-invasive solitary stemmed subjects. The stems of good ground cover subjects may have compressed internodes resulting in rosettes of leaves, or be heavily branched with foliage distributed over the stem length. The only common characteristic is that the aerial parts of the plant, alive or dead, are dense enough to produce a visual sward.

Traditionally, we have required 'good' ground cover to suppress weed growth. This is usually thought to be achieved by light exclusion, although it is likely that the dry mulch from dead leaves creates a hostile barrier to weeds, and in particular their seedlings. The possibility of allelopathy through chemical exudates or breakdown products from living or dead leaves cannot be ruled out. Successful subjects must maintain their stand for many years and not become open and/or prone to weed invasion. Reliable ground cover taxa are listed in Table 14.1.

This tendency to become 'open' was the downfall of many of the taxa rejected in the University of Bath trials. It is often caused by the comparatively short life of individual stems, made more extreme by the intense competition within the central area of an old woody rootstock. A similar effect rules out those herbaceous subjects which tend to produce a thriving clump perimeter, but a degenerating centre (for example *Campanula latiloba*, and *Monarda didyma*). At the other extreme there are species that produce widely-spaced growth which allows weed establishment within the 'clump'. Extensive lists of potential ground cover plants are given in Thomas (1976) and MacKenzie (1997), however it is important to recognise that many taxa discussed in these texts

Fig. 14.5 Ground cover trials at the University of Bath. (Photo: Peter Thoday)

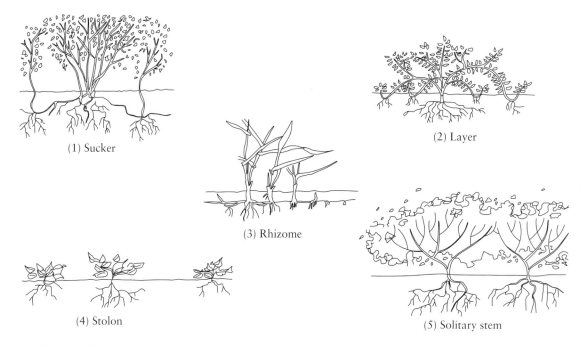

(1) Sucker

(2) Layer

(3) Rhizome

(4) Stolon

(5) Solitary stem

Fig. 14.6 Satisfactory growth forms for ground cover planting.

have not been subject to rigorous evaluation for use in the challenging conditions of the urban landscape.

Aside from design considerations, selection between plant species that have proved successful as ground cover should be based on three considerations.

- The innate vigour of the subject and its ability to match the scale of the site.
- The ability of the subject to have an economically long aesthetic life within the limitations of the maintenance programme available.
- The ability of the subject to thrive under the environmental stresses of the site: for example

Table 14.1   Some reliable ground cover plants.

Name	Growth form(s)*	Av. Height (mm)	Plants per m^2
Cotoneaster dammeri	(1) prostrate shrub	100	3
C. 'Skogholm'	(1/5) shrub	700	1.5
C. salicifolius 'Autumn Fire'	(5/1) prostrate shrub	500	0.7
C. salicifolius 'Gnome'	(5) prostrate shrub	300	3
Erica x *darleyensis*	(5) dwarf shrub	500	5
Euonymus 'Darts blanket'	(1) prostrate shrub	300	3.5
Hedera helix 'Hibernica'	(1) woody climber/trailer	250	3
Lonicera pileata	(5) shrub	800	2
Stephanandra incisa 'Crispa'	(5) dwarf shrub	600	3
Hypericum calycinum	(3) sub-shrub	300	5
Symphoricarpos x *chenaultii* 'Hancock'	(2) dwarf shrub	1000	1.5
Rubus tricolor	(4) scrambler/trailer	600	1.5
R. 'Betty Ashburner'	(4) scrambler/trailer	300	3
Juniperus communis 'Repanda'	(5) prostrate shrub	300	2.5
Vinca minor 'Bowles Variety'	(4/5) sub-shrub	250	2
Alchemilla mollis	(5) herbaceous	300	5
Bergenia x *schmidtii*	(4) evergreen herbaceous	400	5
Polygonum affine 'Darjeeling Red'	(4) evergreen herbaceous	150	5
Geranium macrorrhizum	(5) semi-evergreen herbaceous	300	5

NOTES:
Numbers given under growth form column refer to the growth categories illustrated in Figure 14.6.
Plant densities assume reasonable soil conditions, and balance long-term performance with early visual effect.

drought, nutrient status, direct sun, heavy shade, high or low pH.

14.3   Transplant size, age and condition

In establishing a sward, rather than an isolated clump, selecting small, young transplants is very important. With both lax-stemmed and clump-forming taxa, a marked difference can be observed between the success of young transplants and larger, older nursery stock. This effect is often independent of plant density. A typical demonstration of this was seen in a trial of *Cotoneaster* 'Skogholm' at the University of Bath in the 1970s.

The progress of this planting was followed from propagation through nursery cultivation to plant establishment and sward formation. Young vigorous transplants rapidly produced strongly interwoven, near-prostrate branch work. By comparison, older and larger container-grown transplants were not only slower to establish, but

produced an ineffectual sward. The bulk of their container-grown stem systems remained upright and became reproductive shoots, which failed to produce the vigorous juvenile growth necessary for an effective sward. The critical factor in developing a good framework of stems for a long-term ground cover canopy is the physiological state of the transplant. This is closely linked to the stress the plant has received in the nursery, so that nursery treatment has a direct effect on performance on site.

Plant size is also important, as a nursery-formed branch system is not so able to 'intermix' with neighbouring plants to form the framework of a sward, whereas stems produced *in situ* do this readily.

14.4   Spacing

The suitability of a species for ground cover may depend on the inherent density of its shoots and leaves. When considering the long-term effects of plant density, it is important to distinguish between those taxa that naturally produce a clone of vegetatively propagated 'daughter' plants and those that remain solitary. The clone formers do so either by producing adventitious roots from their prostrate stems or by root suckers (rhizomes or stolons). In these species the density of the ground cover swards produced is ultimately independent of the original plant number. Ground cover taxa that do not produce daughter plants are permanently influenced by their initial spacing.

Most discrete single-stemmed plants (i.e. those that are non-clone forming) respond to intra-specific competition in one of two ways. Competition results in shortages of water and nutrients which can result in a very uneven stand of different sized individuals such as that often seen in overcrowded *Brassica* seedling rows. Alternatively, typically in clonal material, it may evenly reduce the stature of all the individuals while at the same time considerably altering their morphology, particularly the number of lateral and sub-lateral branches produced.

It is essential to recognise that close planting rarely results in a mass of tightly packed stems like a bunch of watercress; on the contrary, the mature canopy is typically no denser than that formed by an isolated individual subjected to the same environmental stress.

The initial number of shoots per unit area of ground can be directly influenced by the number of shoots per transplant. Today, many specifications for nursery stock require a minimum number of basal breaks per plant. Such a requirement is well-founded, up to the number that either the individual plant or the population density of plants in a given area can sustain. Beyond that figure, shoots are only of very short-term value as any extra will be aborted within a season or two.

Plant spacing is a major concern: it not only influences the time taken for foliage to cover the ground completely, but it can also influence the long-term uniformity of the sward, and so its visual quality. It may also influence the longevity of the population, as there is some evidence that even in 'successful' close-planted swards, in which

the individuals exist in equilibrium with each other, degeneration occurs faster than with more widely spaced specimens (Plate 14(a)).

The severe drought in the summer of 1976 was responsible for a dramatic illustration of this. An established stand of *Erica* x *darleyensis* 'Darley Dale' planted in a Wellsbourne fan to provide competition data was left unirrigated. After approximately eight weeks of high temperature and drought the specimens in the closely planted apex of the fan showed severe browning (Plate 14 (b)). This condition spread progressively to the wider spacings. Although the greater part of the planting initially presented the uniform appearance of a closed canopy, resistance to drought was very different at different spacings. This was an extreme set of conditions, but it illustrates the profound effect of planting density when plants are subject to atypically severe drought stress.

Site preparation is an extremely important horticultural input: for successful ground cover, the plants must grow vigorously in their early juvenile stage. There is no need to employ novel practices; indeed satisfactory site preparation can take many forms. The most common is soil cultivation to a depth of at least 300 mm, plus the addition of bag fertilisers (typically 20:10:10 NPK at a rate of 50 g/m²) and the incorporation of bulky organic material equivalent to a 75 mm layer.

The specific cultivation technique used should depend upon the condition of the planting site. In every case the overriding consideration must be to eradicate perennial weed ramets and improve soil moisture retention for a free-draining, readily-colonised root zone. Many ground cover plantings fail because sites are planted when they are in such a hostile condition to root growth that the stress they induce makes a closed foliar canopy a biological impossibility. Site amelioration is discussed in greater detail in Chapter 4.

14.5   Establishment

This is by far the most important growth period as it determines the initial success and very often the duration and quality of the resultant ground cover. It is essential to achieve good growing conditions even on sites subject to the disadvantages of poor substrate and low budget.

The following points must not be skimped, as there is no form of planting at greater risk in the long term from transplant stress. Britain abounds in urban green space that bears ugly witness to the neglect of these key issues.

Planting

The act of planting is so basic that it should not require discussion, yet sometimes craftsmanship is of such a low standard (in terms of the planting depth and soil surface finish) that it is certain to be one of the main factors in creating stress and preventing 'rooting out'.

Pruning

Using the correct transplants on a well-prepared site, there should be no advantage in pruning at the time of planting, though claims have been made that this is beneficial when establishing woody plants of uncertain quality under adverse conditions. The likely advantage of producing vigorous juvenile shoots may be outweighed with low ground cover by their tendency to grow in a bunched upright form.

Irrigation

If site preparation has rendered the soil root-penetrable and chemically fertile, moisture availability is the major factor that will affect growth rate. In southern Britain, irrigation will have a positive effect on the growth of transplants in four years out of five. This occurs typically in the early summer period, when the difference in growth between fully irrigated and non-irrigated plantings experiencing an osmotic potential of two to three atmospheres is generally recorded as a 50 per cent increase.

Irrigation is often impractical, but surface evaporation can be reduced very significantly by mulching. The selection of the mulch material used is much more important than it is when planting trees or large shrubs. To be successful, many taxa must produce extra 'daughter' plants by adventitious means, and this inevitably involves either roots or shoots passing through the air/soil interface, so that organic materials such as wood chip must be used. The action of the mulches in suppressing weeds prevents their transpiration of water, and further aids moisture conservation. Mulches are discussed in greater detail in Chapter 8.

Weed control

This is of the utmost importance. In addition to the unkempt appearance of weedy plantings, the weeds exert a huge influence on growth by competition for water and, to a lesser extent, light and nutrients.

The form of weed control is important: in ground cover plantings, hand pulling (and, to a much greater extent, hoeing) generally causes measurable damage both below and above ground. Given the effective pre-planting control of perennial weeds, it is possible to obtain a satisfactory level of weed control by mulching, preferably to a depth of 50–75 mm with a coarse, non-absorbent material such as 15 mm diameter bark chippings.

Combining a mulch with a topical application of herbicide is even more effective, particularly if the soil is infested with perennial weeds.

Fertilising

Maintaining satisfactory fertility can be achieved simply during the two to three years of the establishment period by an annual spring application of a compound fertiliser. Granular materials are preferable, as they tend not to lodge in the developing canopy. The optimum nutritional status will depend on the planting used. Generally, herbaceous ground cover has a higher demand for, and a greater response to nutrients (particularly nitrogen) than woody taxa.

Typical annual fertiliser applications for each of the first three years of the life of a planting should be a granular preparation of $30 \, g/m^2$ of $20:10:10$ NPK mixture, applied in early spring.

14.6 Established ground cover

The closed canopy phase of a ground cover planting should require little maintenance, providing stoloniferous and rhizomatous perennial weeds have been eliminated before canopy closure. A carefully established planting will typically require no irrigation, nutrition, pruning or weed control. Nevertheless some maintenance may be necessary, if the combination of low light from the leaf canopy and leaf litter, and hostile conditions at the soil surface, fail to suppress weeds.

Any perennial weed clumps should be eradicated by spot treatment of an appropriate herbicide, e.g. glyphosate applied by glove applicator or a wick wiper. Perennial grasses such as couch grass (*Elymus repens*) can be selectively eliminated in woody ground cover plantings with a winter application of propyzamide (Kerb) following the manufacturer's recommendations carefully.

Many of the most persistent woody ground covers are low growing shrubs, adapted to tolerate stress in their natural habitats. These conditions typically favour a tight growth form. There are several techniques available which can influence the canopy density of a species during its aesthetic lifetime.

Pruning can have a positive effect by removing apical dominance and thereby allowing lateral buds to sprout, increasing the number of shoots per unit area, as in hedge trimming. However, the effects of light pruning are typically short-lived, self-correcting, and of little value in robust low maintenance designs. Chemical manipulation (pruning) to produce good ground covering is possible: growth regulators can influence apical dominance, lateral bud development and internodal length. However, as with light pruning, the effects may not persist for longer than the current season.

Those ground cover species that naturally increase their stem number will continue to do so during the established phase, if conditions allow, until they have reached their biological optimum for the site. Non-woody subjects also tend to increase their shoot number in the early years of visual cover, and in some cases, it is possible to sustain this development by extending the nutrition and irrigation programme from the establishment phase.

14.7 Over-aged ground cover

Both individual plants and plant communities can be thought of as having an aesthetic life span which is often far shorter than their biological equivalent. Many ground cover plantings show their age by canopy thinning due to a reduction in leaf size and number, shoot death or crown spread. Many herbaceous plants are good ground cover for the first three to five years but then tend to die out in patches. There are however exceptions to this: for example *Geranium macrorrizhum* and its cultivars maintain a complete cover for at least 30 years without any obvious decline. Hansen and Stahl (1993) provides a useful review of long-term herbaceous ground cover.

The consequence of ageing in herbaceous plants is, of course, a very well-known phenomenon in herbaceous borders and is variously attributed to nutrient starvation, pathogenic build-up and allelopathy. In practice there appears to be no way of reversing this condition. Symptoms associated with ageing can be delayed by growing herbaceous plants under a more spartan regime of nutrients and water; but this will often be counterproductive in ground cover-type plantings, where a complete cover of foliage is a key goal. The standard treatment is the very unattractive task of removing all the plants, cultivating the land and replanting. If this has to be undertaken, it is important to use this opportunity to clean the land of any invading perennial weeds, improve the organic matter status and, if necessary, the soil nutrition.

Replanting to achieve even ground cover should be by means of individual ramets at close spacing, typically 150 mm centres.

Many woody ground covers can be regenerated towards the end of their aesthetic life by heavy pruning, in other words coppicing. This stimulates the development and growth of basal buds, and the resultant juvenile growth quickly replaces the lost canopy if it receives the appropriate husbandry programme. Coppicing is discussed in greater detail in Chapters 13 and 16.

A one-year rejuvenation programme should start immediately after coppicing, with 100 mm mulch of coarse bark, followed in spring by a weed control fertiliser programme. Typically an application of nitrogenous fertiliser at approximately $10 \, g/m^2$ will be sufficient, followed (where possible and necessary) by irrigation.

14.8 Summary

Established ground cover is an elegant, low cost landscape feature. However, to gain its aesthetic and management benefits, the preparatory and establishment phases must not be skimped. The British climate will support this growth form in a wide range of suitable subjects, providing that the typically poor and damaged soils found on amenity sites are improved before planting, and that a simple but precise maintenance programme is strictly followed in the early years.

Regrettably, little research has been directed towards either the establishment or the long-term maintenance of ground cover plantings in recent years; however the key factors in successful specification are recognised as:

- selection of appropriate taxa in terms of growth form, vigour and longevity
- optimum spacing to produce desired appearance and longevity
- soil free of perennial weed ramets at the outset
- post-planting establishment techniques aimed at producing two years of vigorous growth.

References

Hansen, R. & Stahl, F. (1993) *Perennials and their Garden Habitats.* Cambridge University Press, Cambridge.

MacKenzie, D.S. (1997) *Perennial Ground Cover.* Timber Press, Portland, Oregon.

Thomas, G.S. (1976) *Plants for Ground Cover,* Dent, London.

15 Hedges and their Management

Tom Wright, Terence Henry and Jed Bultitude

Hedges are an under-appreciated planting form. They were probably first used by newly-agricultural people to exclude predatory animals (including other human beings) and to control the movement of domesticated animals. These roles are still important today, but hedges can also have a key aesthetic role in landscape planting: indirectly by defining lines, forming spaces and from these pleasing patterns (Fig. 15.1), and directly by providing sculptural, pleasing structures (Plate 15). Garden designers and garden owners have exploited this role across many cultures and centuries. Contemporary examples of the hedge as a visually exciting abstract structure are provided by the work of designers such as Jacques Wirtz (Plate 16).

Many of the woody plants used in hedges are potentially long-lived (the yew hedges at Crathes Castle, near Aberdeen date from the eighteenth century; Fig. 15.2), and as they mature and become structurally and botanically more complex, become increasingly important as habitats in their own right. This is clearly a very important concept in rural hedgerows, but is probably also true even with less complex types of hedges in urban landscapes. By their very nature, hedges also provide boundaries between volumes of space which are potentially attractive to some fauna. In urban gardens and allotments this is often very apparent from localised variations in the density of slugs and snails, but it is probably also true of other (less obvious) vertebrates and invertebrates.

The negative aspect of hedges is their need to be cut on a regular basis. The cost of doing this depends very much on the degree to which cutting can be mechanised, which in turn often depends on what lies next to the hedge and how this affects access. 'Buzz saw' type cutting discs mounted on a hydraulic tractor arm can provide a very good quality of cut, at a very low cost per metre of hedge length, but access for such equipment is not always practical. The current trend towards trimming all shrub mass with hedgetrimmers (see Chapter 16) suggests that no-one should be put off hedges by the cost of cutting: it is being practised routinely everywhere, but unfortunately to create the ugly sheared blobs that are beginning to dominate urban and urban fringe landscapes. In part this seems to be a response to planting free-form shrubs in spaces that are too restricted; it would be far better to recognise this at the design stage, and use elegant clipped hedges from the outset.

15.1 Hedges for garden and urban settings

Establishing formal and informal hedges

Detailed information on preparing new sites and on spacing for planting is given in Section 15.3, on rural hedgerows; much of this is also relevant to non-rural situations and planting non-native species. Spacing will often be determined in practice by the budget and the size of the plant material available. Where timescales allow, good quality hedges are most likely to result from small planting stock. The uppermost shoots should be pruned back at planting, to encourage the production of additional shoots at the base of the

Fig. 15.1 Abstract clipped hedges reflect the ground pattern of a courtyard. (Photo: James Hitchmough)

Fig. 15.2 The gigantic eighteenth-century yew hedges are still in good condition at Crathes Castle, near Aberdeen. (Photo: James Hitchmough)

plant, and ultimately form a high-density hedge. For 1 + 1 transplants and one or two litre container-grown stock, typical spacings would be 300–450 mm apart in the row. A double staggered row (300 mm between rows) provides the best result.

Time restrictions do not always permit best practice, and on many commercial sites instant hedges will be required. Some wholesale nurseries are now supplying pre-formed hedges for this market. When buying what are essentially semi-mature shrubs for this purpose, specifiers should ensure that they inspect the material before purchase, to check that basal density has not been lost during the growing process. Very few species will

'thicken up' at the base in later life without severe pruning; in the case of coniferous species, once basal density is lost, it is lost forever.

Young hedges are vulnerable to people pushing through them, and in heavily-used urban landscapes (such as car parks etc.) steel grid fencing running through the hedge as a reinforcement can be very worthwhile. In extreme cases, hedges can be planted in steel mesh cages to which they are sheared back on an annual basis (Fig. 15.3). This is expensive and only for specific locations where quality is very important, but it does ensure that the hedge can resist almost any abuse. It also allows abstract shapes to be created and simplifies maintenance.

Fig. 15.3 In a very challenging environment, hedges can be enclosed in steel structures to prevent damage by vandals and provide a framework for simple clipping maintenance. (Photo: James Hitchmough)

Fig. 15.4 Yew is remarkable in retaining its capacity to resprout along the branches when pruned severely, even when very old. (Photo: James Hitchmough)

Selecting hedge types and species

Factors to consider in selecting a hedge species could include:

- the cost of the plants
- the rates of growth and time taken to form an effective hedge
- the ultimate height required
- the routine maintenance requirements
- texture, colour, density and seasonal effects
- root competition and
- toxicity of leaves.

Evergreen hedges usually make solid, architectural barriers and backgrounds, often dark in colour, and some are suitable for shaping into sculptural forms or for topiary (Lloyd, 1995). They tend to be more expensive to buy and some are slower growing than deciduous species.

Deciduous hedges will have a variety of seasonal contrasts; they are usually lighter in texture, more permeable to light and wind, and relatively fast growing. They can be easy to establish and the initial cost is lower than for evergreens. Very old or overgrown hedges (of certain species only) can be restored to their original shape, or completely rejuvenated, by cutting back to the original trunk or trunks and then allowing new growth to develop. This is possible with deciduous hedges such as thorns (*Crataegus* spp.), hornbeam (*Carpinus betulus*) and beech (*Fagus sylvatica*), and evergreens like holly (*Ilex* spp.) and laurel (*Prunus laurocerasus*). Yew (*Taxus baccata*) is really the only conifer to be treated in this way (Fig. 15.4). With *Thuya*, x *Cupressocyparis leylandii* (now technically x *Cuprocyparis*) or *Cupressus* hedges it would be disastrous. To reduce the impact on the hedge, it is preferable to take out one side at a time, with an interval of a year or more. A dressing of fertiliser may improve the speed of recovery.

Flowering hedges require some care and understanding of the precise time to clip or prune. In general the best time for most of them is after flowering. If berries are also required, the early spring is the best option (for example, *Cotoneaster lacteus*). Guidance on hedge species and their maintenance is given in Table 15.1.

Table 15.1 Guidelines for the cutting frequency for tree and shrub species used in hedges.

Hedge species	Usual number of cuts per year	Seasons of cutting	Average range of height (m)	Rate of growth notes
Deciduous foliage hedges				
Acer campestre	One	Sept–Mar	1.5–3	Moderate Good autumn colour
Carpinus betulus (F)	One	Sept–Mar	1.5–3	Moderate
Crataegus spp.	Two	July; Nov–Mar	1.5–3	Moderate to fast

Fagus sylvatica (F)
  (also purple and copper-
  leaved cultivars)
	One	Sept–Mar	1.5–3	Moderate to slow

Prunus cerasifera (& purple leaved forms)	Two	June/July; Nov/Dec	1.5–3	Fast Some flowers
Rosa rubiginosa	Two	June/July; Nov/Mar	0.75–1.5; 1–1.5	Fast Scented foliage
Rosa rugosa pink/white	Two	July; Nov/Mar	0.75–1	Moderate Some flowers
Viburnum lantana	One	Nov–Mar	1–2	Moderate
Flowering deciduous hedges				

Chaenomeles spp. and
  cvs.
	Two	May;
		Dec/Mar
			1–1.5	All flowering hedges
				  grow quite fast and

Cornus mas	Two	June; Nov–Dec	1–2	require discerning pruning to avoid
Cotoneaster simonsii	Two	June; Dec–Mar	1–1.5	cutting out all
Forsythia x *intermedia*	Two	May; Dec–Mar	1–1.5	flowering wood

Gooseberry
(*Ribes uva-crispa*)
	Two	June; Dec–Mar	0.75–1	Produce fruit but picking
				  is tricky within the
				  hedge

Redcurrant (*Ribes*)	One	Nov–Mar	0.75–1	
Evergreen hedges				
Buxus sempervirens	Three/four	June–Sept	0.15–1	Slow *Buxus 'Suffruticosa'* is dwarf edging
Chamaecyparis *lawsoniana* and cvs	One	Feb/Mar	1.5–3	Moderate Avoid excess hard cutting into old wood
X *Cuprocyparis* *leylandii*	One/Two	July–April	2–10	Very fast One cut in March may be adequate
Elaeagnus spp (S)	One	Aug	2–3	Moderate Informal hedge
Euonymus japonicus (S)	Two	June–Sept	1.5–2	Moderate Coastal areas
Ilex aquifolium (S) and cultivars	One	July/Aug	2–5	Slow Very pollution resistant
Ligustrum ovalifolium	Four	May–Sept	1–3	Fast Needs frequent clipping
Lonicera nitida	Four/Five	May–Sept	0.5–1.5	Fast Needs regular clipping

Pittosporum tenuifolium
  (S)
	One	Aug/Sept	1.5–3	Moderate to fast
				Milder and S or SW
				  areas; cut foliage value

Table 15.1 *Continued*

Hedge species	Usual number of cuts per year	Seasons of cutting	Average range of height (m)	Rate of growth notes
Prunus laurocerasus	One	May/June	2–5	Moderate Careful hand pruning
Phillyrea angustifolia	One	May/June	2–4	Slow
Prunus lusitanica	One	May/June	2–5	Slow Not in cold areas
Quercus ilex	One/Two	Apr–Aug	1.5–5	Slow Not in very cold areas
Thuya plicata	One	Mar	2–5	Moderate Excellent conifer hedge
Taxus baccata	One	Aug/Sept	1.5–4	Moderate Best architectural hedge
Berberis darwinii	One	May/June	0.75–1.5	Slow Orange yellow flowers. Lacks density
Berberis julianae	One	June/July	1–2	Moderate Spiny barrier
Cotoneaster lacteus	One	June/July	1–1.5	Moderate Berries/flowers
Escallonia macrantha (S) and others	One/Two	Apr–Aug	1–2	Fast Seaside hedge, red flowers
Fuchsia 'Riccartonii'	One	Mar	1–2	Fast Milder SW areas
Osmanthus delavayi	One/Two	May–Aug	0.5–1.5	Slow Scented white flowers
Osmanthus x burkwoodii	One/Two	May–Aug	1–2	Slow Scented white flowers
Rhododendron hardy hybrid cultivars, e.g. 'Doncaster'	One	July/Aug	2–4	Slow-moderate Acid soils, pink-red flowers
Viburnum tinus	One	Apr/May	1.5–3	Moderate Winter flowering; pollution resistant
Olearia macrodonta (S)	One	Mar	1.5–2	Fast Seaside berries, white flowers

Key: (F) Persistent dried red/brown winter foliage. (S) Good for salt-tolerant coastal hedges.

Screens and shelter belts

Maintenance is usually much less intensive and frequent than for hedges; the majority are single or double rows of woody plants. Tree species are often allowed to grow naturally for much of their existence, with the periodic culling of laterals and topping of leaders. Even this may not be necessary for large, farm-scale windbreaks. Deciduous species used could be beeches (*Fagus* spp.), sycamore (*Acer pseudoplatanus*), birches (*Betula* spp.) and alders (*Alnus* spp.), with poplars (*Populus* spp.) and willows (*Salix* spp.) for quick effects. Evergreens would include Austrian and Corsican pines (*Pinus* spp.) and possibly Leyland cypress (x *Cuprocyparis leylandii*), although this species has been massively over-planted during the past two decades and has become an object of considerable controversy.

15.2   Pests and diseases of hedges

Pests and diseases are potentially more important for hedges than for shrubs grown as free form specimens or groups: the loss of one or more plants is visually and functionally disastrous in a hedge. Honey fungus (*Armillaria*) is prone to attack privet hedges (*Ligustrum* spp.), slowly killing a few plants each year. In prestige situations, where such drastic action can be justified, removal of the dead and infected plants should be followed by local soil sterilisation before replanting. A more realistic approach will generally involve replacing the hedge with a more resistant species such as holly (*Ilex* spp.). Yew scale can also occasionally be serious, and *Phytophthora* root rot is an increasing problem on wet soils. In the past decade box (*Buxus* spp.) has become afflicted by a serious blight disease (*Cylindrocladium* and *Volutella* spp.).

15.3   Rural hedgerows

Planting is relatively straightforward, but the importance of good aftercare to ensure successful establishment cannot be overstressed.

Site selection and preparation

Species colonisation of new hedges is a slow process; where possible these should not be planted in isolation but linked to existing good wildlife habitats, so that natural colonisation is given every chance. Exposed sites and those prone to temporary waterlogging need careful species selection and establishment methods.

On new grassy sites a metre-wide strip should be sprayed with glyphosate in late summer/early autumn; a trench 600 mm wide and 300 mm deep should be cultivated for a double row hedge. A mini-excavator can be used to invert and bury the turf as a weed control strategy. Alternatively, a deep double furrow can be ploughed, and the hedging

planted into the ridge that is formed. Fertiliser is not required on most sites, but if well-rotted farmyard manure is available it can be placed in the bottom of the planting trench; in very poor soils this will typically improve early growth rates.

Species selection

A mixture of species will give a more attractive hedge and provide a habitat for a wide range of wildlife. The emphasis should be on using native species grown from local seed – a typical mix would be of five hawthorn, two blackthorn, two beech, one hazel and the occasional holly. Species to avoid in rural hedges (some are poisonous to livestock) include box, broom, laburnum, *Rhododendron ponticum*, common elder, yew, common elm and conifers. Ideally choose species native to the area, referring to the maps in the *Atlas of the British Flora* (Perring and Walters, 1982). In many cases the local character of existing hedgerows should influence species selection.

Hedgerow trees

There is generally no advantage in planting standard trees in a new hedgerow. They are more difficult to establish and may need staking; whips or feathered trees will catch up in time. The emphasis should be on planting native species that cast a light shade, oak being a good example.

Selection and care of hedge plants

Plants should be well-rooted and about 500–800 mm high (commonly 1 + 1 or 2 + 1 transplants). On no account should the roots be allowed to dry out or exposed to frost. Specify the CPSE Plant Handling Code when ordering, and always specify co-extruded polythene bag root-wrapping. Details on plant handling are given in Chapters 3 and 8.

Planting

Hedges should be planted between November and March, avoiding frosty weather. The most practical method is to notch-plant into the cultivated soil. The soil should be worked in and around the roots, the plants firmed into the ground at the same depth as they were in the nursery. During the planting process, the roots of the bundle of plants being used should be kept in a co-extruded polythene bag and planted directly from the bag (never laid out on the soil). Where a species mix is to be planted, mix these in a cool, humid shed, so that they can be planted directly from the bags on site.

Planting distances

For a stockproof barrier, a double staggered row of plants is recommended with about 450 mm between the rows and 300 mm between plants. For single row hedges, the plants should be placed about 200 mm apart.

Weed control

Weeds compete with the hedgerow plants for light, water and nutrients; they usually pose the biggest threat to successful establishment. Mulches and some hand weeding may be necessary. For an all-hawthorn hedge, the plants can be cut back to 75 mm in late March/early April and a black polythene strip 1 m wide pushed over the top of the cut stumps. The polythene should be weighed down with stones and can be removed once the hedge has established.

For the more desirable mixed-species hedge, where hard cutting of beech and holly is not recommended, a 1 m wide strip of black polythene can be laid down both sides of the new hedge, with the hedging plants themselves mulched with bark chippings, mushroom compost or quarry dust.

The only residual herbicide recommended for use on hedges in the first season is Kerb (propyzamide). Kerb should be applied to cold soil, i.e. before the end of February. It controls grasses and other herbaceous plants except composites and legumes.

Fencing

In a grazing situation, a stockproof fence will be required. Fencing should be 2 m from the hedge to prevent stock reaching over and uprooting the plants. If rabbits or hares are a problem, appropriate netting wire should be used and buried deeply to prevent burrowing.

15.4   Management of rural hedges

Time and frequency of cutting

The best time to cut rural hedges is from early February until mid-March. Cutting between mid-March and August interferes with bird nesting, while cutting from August to early February removes berries, a valuable food source for some birds.

There is no need to cut all hedges every year. Hard cutting annually does not allow flowering, with the result that no berries or fruit are produced. A two-to-three-year cycle can be achieved by cutting one-half to one-third of hedges every year, or alternatively cutting one side of the hedge each year. Roadside hedges may need to be trimmed annually to maintain sight lines and keep the road clear. However, there is no need to cut the top and field side of such hedges every year.

To develop a hedge with standard trees, strong straight saplings should be clearly marked (e.g. by attaching strips of fertiliser bag) before the hedge is cut, and left to grow into trees. By leaving some saplings every few years this will ensure a continuity of age structure of trees.

Height and shape

Tall hedges, thick at the bottom, generally provide better shelter and wildlife habitat than shorter hedges. It is sometimes suggested that a hedge with a wide base and gently sloping sides is the ideal shape. On reasonably flat field sites this may be so, but if the hedge is growing on a bank with a rich flora, a narrower rectangular shaped hedge allows more light to penetrate to the hedge base, and may encourage establishment of desirable species.

The hedgerow bottom

If they are properly managed, the hedgerow bottom and field margin can support a tremendous range of plants, insects, birds and small mammals. For conservation purposes, hedges with field margins have the greatest species diversity of woody and herbaceous plants. High soil fertility usually leads to loss of plant species diversity. Thus slurry, farmyard manure and inorganic fertiliser should be kept well away from the hedge bottom. The hedge base and headlands should not be sprayed with herbicides: this would create bare ground conditions and encourage seed germination of annuals such as cleavers and sterile brome. Open drains and ditches adjacent to a hedgerow also increase species biodiversity, and where possible should be kept open and not piped.

Planting up gaps in hedges

Repairing gaps can be difficult: there can be severe weed competition, poor light penetration or drought, particularly if the hedge is growing on a stone/earth bank. Some authors (e.g. DANI, 1994) suggest that the soil in the gaps may need to be replaced with fresh topsoil or else enriched with well-rotted farmyard manure. Research into the best method of gapping up hawthorn hedges using the same species showed that where weed control was good and the hawthorn plants were watered during dry periods, there was no benefit in replacing soil (Henry *et al.*, 1996).

Maintenance of rural hedgerows

The common factor that determines the shape and form of the hedge will be its maintenance. The wide variety of hedge species available all have different growth rates and maintenance needs. Manual cutting of hedges is labour-intensive and rarely practised, except where special circumstances prevail. The flail may be used for hedges that are cut biennially. Flailing does encourage bud formation and helps thicken out the hedge (Fig. 15.5), but looks untidy immediately after cutting. It is not normally necessary to gather up twigs after flail cutting. Tractor-mounted circular saws are used on heavier growth.

If the hedge is cut at the same height year after year, it tends to become gappy at the bottom, and buds are not encouraged to break lower down the stems. In this case, the hedge may require coppicing using a chainsaw. The cutter bar is only suitable for trimming young shoots and its use is now largely confined to keeping garden-like hedges in shape.

15.5 'Laying' rural hedges

Where labour is readily available it is possible to pursue traditional hedge management practices, such as those used to lay the 'standard' or

Fig. 15.5 A rural hedge of field maple (*Acer campestris*) clipped with a tractor-mounted flail to provide a maze within a children's play area. (Photo: James Hitchmough)

'Midlands' hedge'. This hedge is asymmetrical in section, with the brushy ends of the cut stems (pleachers) angled out into the field. It is approximately 1.25 m tall and staked down a central line; it may be bound along the top with bindings which lock the pleachers down. The hedge will usually be laid the way it was before, otherwise uphill with the bushy or field side of the hedge against stock, and the nearside against roads, arable fields or footpaths.

Traditional techniques

The first step is to remove any rubbish from the bottom of the hedge, before trimming the nearside. Use loppers or a brushing hook to remove virtually all the brush on this face of the hedge, and try to free each tree from its neighbours. Cut the brush off the front as well as the side of the first tree. The choice of tool for cutting (pleaching) will depend on the tree size and the individual's level of skill with edged tools. Trees up to 80 mm in diameter can be tackled with a small billhook; a light axe or Yorkshire billhook is better for stems up to 100 mm, and a heavier axe for anything

bigger. If the tree is awkward to reach a small (500–600 mm, 21 or 24 inch) bow saw can be used. Inspect the tree for dead wood and broken bark near the base; these should be avoided as they will be weak points when trying to bend the pleacher over.

Standing on the nearside, with gloved left hand holding the pleacher, use the bilhook (or saw) in an ungloved right hand to make a long sloping cut down through the wood. The aim is then to bend the pleacher over until it is at an angle of about 30° from the ground, and angled about 15° from the line of the hedge into the field. Start the cut 300–500 mm up, and work down the grain until 25–50 mm from the base of the tree, trimming the stump with upward strokes of the billhook.

When about three-quarters of the way through the stem, allow the cut to become a downward split. Use the billhook as a lever and pull the tree down with the left hand, making sure as you do so that the tree is not tangled with the next one. The ideal pleacher will have a solid hold, in width about one third of the stem in diameter and about a quarter as deep. Bend the pleacher over until it is resting at right angles before knocking a

Table 15.2 Tools and equipment required for traditional hedgerow maintenance.

Laying tools	
Billhook	There are various regional styles and sizes of billhook. Choosing the right one is a matter of personal preference, although you are likely to be influenced by the size of the hedging to be cut.
Axe	A 3 lb Canadian axe is recommended for beginners.
Bow saw	A triangular 500 mm (21 inch) saw is probably the most useful.
Trimming tools	
Slasher	This is a long-handled brushing hook. A slasher with a curved hook is best as it gathers in the material to be cut.
Loppers	These come in a variety of sizes. Anvil jaw loppers tend to be more robust than scissor-action types.
Sharpening equipment	
Flat file	Used to remove nicks in cutting blades.
Knocking in stakes	
Mells, mauls and large wooden mallets	Choose the most appropriate tool for the specific circumstances.
Safety equipment	
Safety kit	All workers should have access to an up-to-date safety kit including steel-capped boots, hide-type gloves, and knee pads.

stake into the ground to hold in place. Trim off the stump, and then begin the pleaching process again.

As work progresses keep staking up. Use the line of the stakes, which should be about 500 mm apart and 200 mm behind the line of the hedge trees, as a builder would use line and level. Each pleacher should lie in front of one or two stakes before it passes through the line to the far side. Building the hedge with the pleachers is a skilled job, but the main principles are to avoid gaps, keep the hedge off the cut stumps and to keep the pleachers more or less parallel. Binding the hedge involves twisting rods of hazel or willow around the stakes to tie the hedge together.

15.6   Summary

Hedges are valuable forms of planting for both urban and rural landscapes, with many aesthetic and habitat benefits. It is important to select suitable plants and take care in their establishment, because with thoughtful management hedges can be very long-lived. In the rural environment the benefits to wildlife and conserva-

tion of traditionally-laid hedges can be considerable if such labour-intensive craftsmanship is possible.

References

Department of Agriculture for Northern Ireland (DANI) (1994) *Field Boundaries: managing gappy and overgrown hedges.* HMSO, Belfast.

Henry, T., Rushton, B.S., & Bell, A.C. (1996) Methods of interplanting gaps in existing hawthorn (*Crataegus monogyna* Jacq.) hedges. *Aspects of Applied Biology*, **44**, 327–32.

Lloyd, N. (1995) *Garden craftsmanship in yew and box.* Garden Art, Woodbridge.

Perring, F.H. & Walters, S.M. (1982) *Atlas of the British Flora.* Thomas Nelson, London.

Further reading

Brooks, A. & Agate, E. (1998) *Hedging, a practical handbook.* BTCV, Wallingford.

Maclean, M. (2000) *Resource Management: Hedges.* Farming Press, Tonbridge.

Watt, T.A. & Buckley, G.P. (1994) *Hedgerow Management and Nature Conservation.* Wye College Press, Ashford.

16 Pruning Shrubs

Tom La Dell

16.1 Shrubs in designed landscapes

Plants are much more complex design elements than inert materials. Design with shrubs, as with trees and herbaceous plants, depends on understanding their form and habit. The detail of the branching patterns, stems, leaves, flowers and fruit makes up their overall morphology. This changes with time as the plants grow. Most planting design uses the natural forms of shrubs and other plants and this needs to be followed through into management and maintenance. Where the form of plants is completely manipulated to form hedges and topiary, different pruning principles are followed. Hedges are covered in Chapter 15.

The main purpose of pruning landscape shrubs is to maintain the essential habit and character of the plant while keeping it within acceptable size limits and emphasising its seasonal highlights. It may also be undertaken to increase stem and shoot density, especially in older plants that have thinned out and lost their vigour with age and this has led to a loss of visual quality, or an increase in weed colonisation.

These pruning aims are far more thoughtful and sophisticated than the crude trimming of shrubs with hedge trimmers that has become the norm in most landscape maintenance regimes. This practice simply destroys the character and in most cases the beauty of individual shrubs and of shrub planting as a whole.

There are no excuses for this. It originates with a lack of willingness or ability to apply sound biological principles and horticultural practice to maintenance. When this is combined with the unwillingness to prepare proper specifications and tender documentation this leads to the abysmal, lowest-common-denominator results we see up and down the country. Decreasing expectations follow on from this, then loss of skills and poor workmanship by contractors. High standards must be set by the professionals who should provide their clients with a quality landscape at a reasonable cost.

The aim of this chapter is to change perceptions of what should be achieved by the maintenance of shrub planting in the landscape, and how it can be carried out. The standards set are realistic. They need to be clearly described and illustrated in contract documentation and accompanied by plans naming the plants. There should be a separate instruction for each operation at different times of the year. It should have the information clearly presented for easy use on site. The standards will only be achieved if they are supported by landscape managers, amenity horticulturists, and landscape architects representing the landscape client. Within the competitive tendering environment, contractors can not be expected to set the necessary standards.

There is a clear message that maintenance must be informed by design and is a creative part of the long-term design process. The results of what we so commonly see now are the active choice of landscape managers and amenity horticulturists and must be judged in this context. A new sense of design intent and purpose is needed if this is to change.

Where there are serious and recurring problems in pruning shrubs this is usually because the original designer selected inappropriate plants for the location. This may mean that replacement with more suitable species or cultivars is necessary. The manager should first review the situation and see if rejuvenation by coppicing is appropriate. It is certainly much cheaper than replacement and may provide a long-term solution. If replanting is unavoidable, it should be with a specific design intention compatible with current site character, and must utilise functionally-appropriate shrub species and cultivars.

Fig. 16.1 Case study: mounds separating the road and footpath were originally planted with ground cover shrubs. (Photo: Tom La Dell)

Box 16.1   Case study

Failure to understand landscape shrub pruning leads to expensive costs in removing shrubs and increased long-term maintenance costs.

Mounds separating the carriageway and footway at this site were planted with ground cover shrubs some twenty years ago. The Council took on the maintenance of these areas once they were established. Almost no routine maintenance was carried out except for lateral trimming to keep the shrubs clear of the footway and carriageway (Fig. 16.1) . The height of the shrubs built up over fifteen years or so and complaints were received that the shrub growth was too oppressive. Despite advice that the shrubs should be coppiced, the highway authority was persuaded to pay for complete removal of the shrubs and establishing grass instead. This very expensive option means that there is the continuing cost of grass cutting on relatively steep banks and between trees (Fig. 16.2). The bark of the trees has been damaged by the grass cutting, which may threaten the trees' survival. To compound the cost of the initial decision, some areas have been replanted with shrubs that do not do well on the heavy clays of the area and will never form a low maintenance cover.

A proper understanding of shrub pruning would have avoided expensive work and increased long-term maintenance costs.

Fig. 16.2 Case study: removing the shrubs completely, rather than coppicing them, means that grass cutting (on banks and around awkward trees) will be a long-term maintenance cost. (Photo: Tom La Dell)

16.2   Plant selection for long-term maintenance

Landscape architects and amenity horticulturists frequently talk about time, the fourth dimension, and one would expect that they would want their planting designs to express their design intentions

The standards set here are a start in the process of improving the quality of our designed landscapes.

Table 16.1 Examples of sprawling/ground cover shrubs with specific growth forms.

Shrubby
Deciduous
Cotoneaster horizontalis
C.h. 'Variegatus'
C. salwenensis
Deutzia kalmiiflora (after flowering in June)

Ligustrum 'Lodense'
Potentilla 'Elizabeth'
Santolina species and cvs

Evergreen
Berberis 'Amstelveen'
Ceanothus 'Blue Mound'
Erica darleyensis and cvs (spring fl.)
Ilex crenata cvs
Lonicera pileata and cvs

Prunus laurocerasus 'Schipkaensis'
P.l. 'Mount Vernon'
Senecio 'Sunshine'
Viburnum davidii
V. tinus 'Gwenllian' (spring fl.)

Self layering
Deciduous
Chaenomeles 'Jet Trail' (spring fl.)
Cornus 'Kelseys Dwarf'
Ligustrum obtusifolium 'Darts Perfecta'
Potentilla 'Longacre'
Rosa – many cvs

Rosmarinus oficinalis – prostrate cvs
Salix purpurea 'Pendula'
Stephanandra incisa 'Crispa'
Symphoricarpos 'Hancock'

Evergreen
Buxus sempervirens 'Prostata'
Calluna vulgaris cvs
Ceanothus thyrsiflorus 'Repens'
Cotoneaster 'Coral Beauty'
C. conspicuus 'Decorus'
C. dammeri
C. 'Gnom'
C. salicifolius 'Repens'
C. 'Skogholm'
Erica cinerea and cvs
E. carnea and cvs (spring fl.)
Escallonia 'Gwendolyn Anley'
Euonymus fortunei cvs
Hedera algeriensis and cvs
H. colchica and cvs

H. helix and cvs
H. hibernica and cvs
Juniperus communis 'Repanda'
J. horizontalis cvs
Lonicera pileata and cvs
Lonicera japonica 'Repens'
Prunus laurocerasus 'Low'n'Green'
Pyracantha 'Red Cushion'
P. 'Soleil d'Or' and 'Renault d'Or'
Rubus 'Betty Ashburner'
Rubus tricolor and cvs
Vinca major and cvs (spring fl.)
Vinca minor and cvs (spring fl.)
Taxus baccata Repanda

Suckering
Deciduous
Rosa nitida
Rosa pimpinellifolia

Rubus thibetanus
Sorbaria stellipila

Evergreen
Hypericum calycinum (coppice
    annually or biennially)
Mahonia aquifolium and cvs (spring fl.)
Pachysandra terminalis

Sarcococca hookeriana

Sarcococca humilis
Vinca major oxyloba

Spring flowering plants to be pruned after flowering in April/May/June are indicated by suffix (Spring fl.).

year after year. After all, this is one of the ways that distinguishes us from other design professions in the construction industry. And yet, so many planting designs seem to have no concern for their aesthetics or appearance once they are in routine maintenance.

To design for the long term it is necessary to know how a plant grows and its ultimate habit and size. These must be matched with a reasonable maintenance regime.

There are three criteria that must be met to achieve this:

- Select plants that fit the place, space and functional requirements of where they are to grow.
- Design clear and effective maintenance specifications that are realistic and achieve stated design aims.
- Design with plants for the long term, not just on the day they were planted and how they look a year later at handover.

The last point is critical as this chapter is aimed at landscape designers as well as landscape managers and amenity horticulturists. Planting design is as much about understanding, expressing and enhancing the intrinsic qualities of the plant as it is about using the superficial qualities visible in a container grown plant in the nursery or the leaf and flower detail illustrated in most textbooks and catalogues.

Design with shrubs, and indeed the associated trees and herbaceous plants in a mainly shrub planting scheme, is about the whole plant, the way it grows and how its whole form relates to neighbouring plants and the whole planting scheme.

Plant selection to suit the uses of the designed landscape is central to successful future maintenance. The first need is to understand and anticipate the growth and habit of the plant. Such understanding needs to go beyond accepting the mature sizes of a shrub as proffered in a wholesale catalogue. In many cases such dimensions are based on a very short-term view of the growth and development of shrubs, and represent a significant underestimate of their size.

16.3   Growth forms of landscape shrubs

In order to formulate effective pruning specifications for shrubs it is important to appreciate the range of shrub growth forms that exist.

Sprawling and ground cover shrubs

Usually mass planted for a ground cover shrubbery, as discussed in Chapter 14. Examples of species and cultivars of each growth form are given in Table 16.1.

Shrubby: These branch from a single short stem and the branches intermingle. (Fig. 16.3)

Fig. 16.3

Self-layering: When the branches touch the ground they will root if conditions are suitable. The stems interweave into a network of branches and twigs. (Fig. 16.4)

Fig. 16.4

Suckering: New stems are thrown up from under the soil from roots or underground stems. These are either branched and twiggy or sometimes unbranched. (Fig. 16.5)

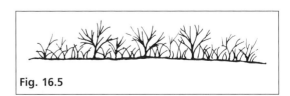

Fig. 16.5

Bushy shrubs

Usually mass planted, medium height, to create a sense of enclosure.

Domed: Each shrub naturally forms a dome of branches and foliage. When mass-planted they usually form an even height canopy. (Fig. 16.6)

Fig. 16.8   Upright and bushy with a central stem.

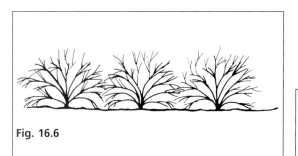

Fig. 16.6

Arching: The branches, and often the main stems too, arch over to hang down towards the ground. There may be a framework of upright stems and this creates a fountain form and an uneven outline. (Fig. 16.7)

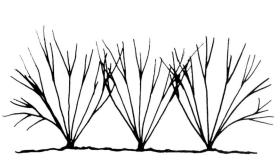

Fig. 16.9   Upright and bushy, with stems branching from the base.

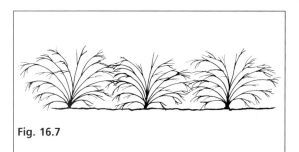

Fig. 16.7

Suckering: New stems are thrown up from under the soil from roots or underground stems. The shrubs vary from upright and even to arching and twiggy. (Fig. 16.10)

Upright and bushy

These have upright main stems with either few branches in the early years or quickly developing a mass of lateral twigs. The outline is either rather regular or uneven and feathery. (Figs 16.8, 16.9)

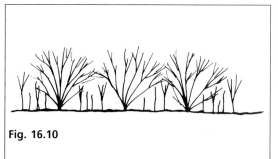

Fig. 16.10

Specimen shrubs

Planted individually or in small groups, often emerging from mass planted, lower shrubs.

Upright: Steeply ascending main branches with upright or spreading side branches. (Fig. 16.11)

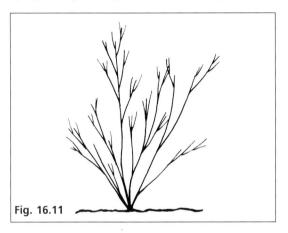

Fig. 16.11

Rounded: Fairly domed head with branching from the ground or on a short trunk. (Fig. 16.12)

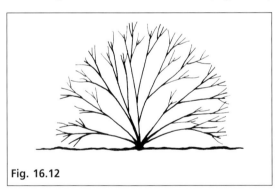

Fig. 16.12

Horizontal – tabular: Strongly horizontal branching pattern that builds up in layers. (Fig. 16.13)

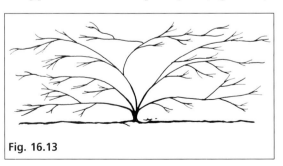

Fig. 16.13

Accent

Distinctive habit or leaf shape in contrast to most other shrubs. (Figs 16.14, 16.15 and 16.16)

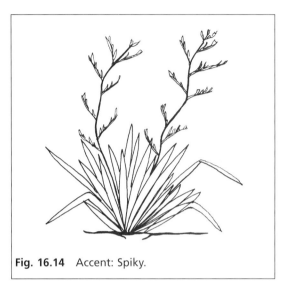

Fig. 16.14   Accent: Spiky.

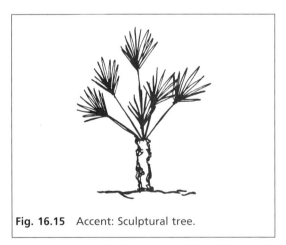

Fig. 16.15   Accent: Sculptural tree.

Fig. 16.16   Accent: Sculptural shrub.

16.4 Pruning to maintain habit and manage size

The terms 'light pruning', 'heavy pruning' and 'coppicing' are used to define the intensity of pruning. Light pruning is regular pruning to keep a shrub looking good and within bounds. It is not envisaged that this will be more than once a year. Heavy pruning is when a shrub is oversized or has too much dead or dying back wood and needs to be cut back harder to re-establish its shape. Coppicing shrubs is cutting the plant back to close to the ground so that it can re-grow to form a rejuvenated plant.

The timing of pruning is important. Late winter pruning of deciduous shrubs gives the best growth in the following growing season. Evergreens grow away best after early spring pruning when the weather starts to warm up.

Sprawling and ground cover shrubs

Objectives:

- Maintain the form and texture of the plant
- Keep the canopy dense
- Maintain a good cover of healthy, young growth
- Limit the build up of dead wood
- Enhance seasonal effects (see note on special pruning times in Tables 16.2, 16.3 and 16.4).

Light pruning

Frequency: often annual. These plants have the potential for extensive spread. Cut back in height and spread to allow for re-growth before next pruning. Optimum time: February/March. Pruning at this time ensures minimum time before re-growth, keeps berry and stem effects and is in winter low season. Dispose of clippings by removal or by concealing them under or within the canopy.

Growth form:	Recommended pruning practice:
Shrubby	Ideally, cut back strong shoots to within canopy with secateurs and leave weaker shoots to form canopy. Mechanical pruning with hedge trimmers or flails is a poor second or third best.
Self-layering	Cut back strong shoots to within canopy, using secateurs for high quality finish. Mechanical pruning is often inevitable but again a poor second best.
Suckering	Mechanical pruning.

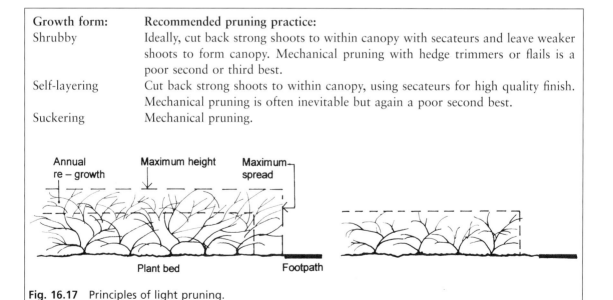

Fig. 16.17 Principles of light pruning.

Heavy pruning

Frequency: probably 3–10 years depending on plant and location. The aim is to reduce the vigour of the plant while keeping its habit and form. Optimum time: November to March. Maximise work in winter low season. Dispose of arising by pulling out entire branches from the canopy.

Chip and conceal within canopy or remove from site.

This is a simple technique to learn and very effective in maintaining a quality appearance. Trials have shown it to be cost-effective in reducing long-term problems and ugly, regularly trimmed plants. (Figs 16.18, 16.19 and 16.20)

Growth form:	Recommended pruning practice:

Fig. 16.18
Shrubby.   Cut back strong branches to near base or to weaker branch with loppers.

Fig. 16.19
Self layering.   Cut back oldest and thickest stems to ground level with loppers.

Fig. 16.20
Suckering.   Cut old stems to ground level with loppers.

Coppicing

When complete regeneration is required because plants become very sparse, with poor quality leaves and flower and fruit production. Alternatively can be used simply to manage size, or enhance a seasonal display on a chosen time cycle.

Optimum time: January to March. Cutting at other times can lead to very poor re-growth. Apply a balanced fertiliser at the end of March post

coppicing unless the soil is extremely fertile. This can be a 'green waste' compost that meets BS PAS100. These are generally naturally high in plant nutrients and are a useful product of recycling. This is particularly important for relatively low-vigour shrubs such as *Cornus alba* 'Sibirica' coppiced on an annual or biennial cycle. Dispose of arisings by chipping and spread around stumps, without covering them, or remove from site. (Fig. 16.21)

Growth form: All	Recommended pruning practice: Cut down all of the shrub to between 50 and 100 mm above ground level. Flail cutters, reciprocating blades, circular saws and bow saws can be used as appropriate for the situation. Some hand trimming may be necessary after flailing.

Fig. 16.21
Coppicing.

Bushy shrubs

Objectives:

- Maintain the habit and line of the shrub

- Maintain the form and surface texture

- Maintain shoot and foliage density for an even canopy

- Limit the build up of dead wood

- Enhance seasonal effects (See note on special pruning times in Table 16.2).

Light pruning

Frequency should be as necessary to maintain desired shape or keep the size within desired limits. Cut back frost-damaged or drought-induced dead shoots.

Optimum time: March, after winter and before new growth. For spring flowering shrubs, prune in May or June.

To maintain the growth forms the following pruning is recommended.

Growth form: All	Recommended pruning practice: Cut back frost-damaged or drought-induced dead shoots. Trim soft wooded plants to maintain dense habit

Heavy pruning

Frequency: three to five years depending on plant and conditions. Cut back to maintain form of plant as it regrows.

Optimum time: Deciduous shrubs, November to March. Evergreen shrubs, February/March. Spring flowering shrubs May.

Growth form:	Recommended pruning practice:
Domed	Cut back whole canopy to a suiable height to allow for regrowth. This usually removes most of the leaves of evergreens as the centre of the shrub or mass planting is usually bare stems. Mechanical cutting is effective.

Fig. 16.22   Heavy pruning for domed shrubs.

Arching	Cut out the most vigorous stems to near ground level leaving the shorter stems. This can only be effectively done with loppers or a pruning saw. Mechanical cutting is not suitable as it produces re-growth that has too many shoots from the base.

Fig. 16.23   Heavy pruning for arching shrubs.

Upright and bushy	These are usually coppiced for flower or bark effect.
Suckering	Cut out oldest stems to ground level. Cutting down all the stems to an even height can lead to poor re-growth and deterioration of the planting. Only loppers or pruning saws can be used.

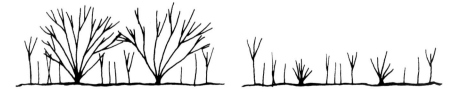

Fig. 16.24   Heavy pruning for suckering shrubs.

Coppicing

This pruning technique is valuable when complete regeneration is required because the plants are too large and the whole branch framework needs to be renewed. Alternatively it may be used where vigour is declining leading to sparse leaf cover, and reduced flowering and fruiting. Optimum time: Deciduous shrubs – November to March, evergreen shrubs – February/March.

Apply a balanced fertiliser at the end of March unless the soil is extremely fertile. This can be a 'green waste' compost that meets BS PAS100. These are generally high in plant nutrients and are a useful product of recycling. Disposal of arisings: chip and spread around stumps, without covering them, or remove from site.

To maintain growth forms, the following pruning is recommended for all categories. (Fig. 16.25)

Growth form: All	Recommended pruning practice: Note: Coppicing may be annual for upright and bushy shrubs. Cut down the entire plants to close to ground level. Flail cutters, reciprocating blades, circular saws, bow saws and loppers can be used as appropriate for the situation. Some hand trimming will be necessary after flailing.

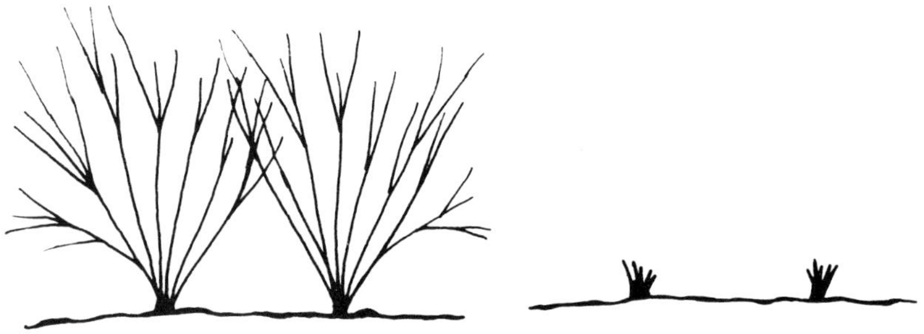

Fig. 16.25 Coppicing.

Table 16.2 Examples of bushy shrubs with specific growth forms.

Domed

Deciduous

Berberis wilsonae
Caryopteris x clandonensis cvs
  (hard prune annually)
Chaenomeles x superba cvs
  (spring fl.)
Deutzia 'Mont Rose'
  (after flowering in June)
Euonymus alatus
Forsythia cvs (spring fl.)
Fuchsia 'Riccartonii' and other cvs
Hydrangea arborescens cvs
H. macrophylla cvs

H. paniculata cvs
  (hard prune annually)
Indigofera heterantha
  (hard prune annually)
Kolkwitzia 'Pink Cloud'
Lonicera 'Claveys Dwarf'
Philadelphus cvs
  (after flowering in June)
Phlomis fruticosa
Physocarpus 'Darts Gold'
Potentilla 'Katherine Dykes'
Rhododendron (Azalea) species
  and cvs
Ribes odoratum

Ribes sanguineum cvs
Salix eleagnus
S. tsugaluensis 'Ginme'
S. purpurea 'Nana'
Sambucus nigra cvs
S. racemosa cvs
Sorbaria sorbifolia
Spiraea betulifolia var. aemiliana
S. 'Anthony Waterer'
S. *fritschiana*
S. 'Halwards Silver'
Syringa chinensis cvs (spring fl.)
S. palibin (spring fl.)
Viburnum opulus 'Compactum'
Weigela cvs

Table 16.2 *Continued*

Evergreen

Atriplex halimus
Aucuba cvs
Berberis julianae
B. verruculosa
Bupleurum fruticosum
Buxus spp. and most cvs
Choisya ternata and cvs
Choisya 'Aztec Pearl'
Cistus 'Grayswood Pink'
C. hybridus
C. platysepalus
C. 'Snow Fire'

Deciduous

Berberis x ottawensis 'Superba'
B. thunbergii cvs
Deutzia 'Rosea' (spring fl.)
D. longifolia 'Veitchii'
Fuchsia magellanica 'Gracilis'
Forsythia cvs (spring fl.)
Hydrangea quercifolia
Lonicera syringantha

Deciduous

Buddleia davidii cvs
    (coppice annually)
Ceanothus deciduous cvs
    (hard prune annually)
Cornus alba
    (coppice annually or biennially)

Deciduous

Elaeagnus 'Quicksilver'
Rosa foliolosa

C. 'Snow White'
Cotoneaster amoenus
Elaeagnus ebbingei and cvs
Erica erigena and cvs
    (spring fl.)
Escallonia 'Alice', 'Apple
    Blossom', 'Peach Blossom',
    'Slieve Donard'
Fatsia japonica
Gaultheria shallon
Griselinia littoralis
Hebe species and cvs
Hypericum 'Hidcote'
H. x moserianum

Arching

Potentilla 'Primrose Beauty'
Spiraea 'Grefsheim' (spring fl.)
S. 'Snowmound'
Tamarix ramossissima and cvs
    (hardprune annually)

Evergreen

Abelia x grandiflora
Berberis darwinii
B. x stenophylla

Upright and bushy

C.a. Elegantissima
    (hard prune or coppice
    annually)
C.a. 'Sibirica' ('Westonbirt')
    (coppice annually or biennially)
C.a. 'Spaethii'
    (hard prune or coppice
    annually)

Suckering

Symphoricarpos albus and its
    hybrids

Mahonia japonica (spring fl.)
Olearia haastii
O. macrodonta
Phlomis fruticosa
Photinia x fraseri cvs
Pittisporum tenuifolium
    and cvs
Prunus laurocerasus 'Caucasicus'
P.l. 'Ruddle Billett'
Rhododendron species and cvs
Sarcococca confusa and
ruscifolia
Skimmia species and cvs
Viburnum tinus (spring fl.)

Cotoneaster franchetii
C. hylmoei
C. 'Rothschildianus'
C. lacteus
Lonicera nitida 'Baggesons
    Gold'
Pyracantha 'Orange Glow'
P. 'Watereri'
Rosmarinus officinalis
Viburnum x burkwoodii

C.sanguinea 'Midwinter Fire'
    (hard prune annually)
C. stolonifera 'Flaviramea'
    (coppice annually or
    biennially)
Salix alba 'Britzensis'
    (coppice annually)

Evergreen

Mahonia x wagneri cvs (spring
    fl.)

Spring flowering plants to be pruned after flowering in April/May/June indicated by suffix (spring fl.)

Specimen shrubs

Objectives:

- Keep and enhance the individual character and form of the shrub
- Maintain healthy growth
- Enhance seasonal interest.

Some specimen shrubs planted in groups may need to be thinned to, say, one or three plants so that they can show their natural form in the space available. This is often the case for example with *Cotinus coggygria*, *Cotoneaster* 'Cornubia' and *Mahonia* 'Charity'. See also Table 16.3.

Light pruning

Usually limited to removing damaged or dying back

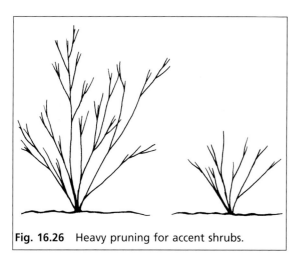

Fig. 16.26   Heavy pruning for accent shrubs.

branches. Accent plants may need to have dead leaves removed in March and possibly November.

Heavy pruning

Pruning for height is rarely effective as the shape of the shrub is spoilt. Extra vigorous shoots can be removed November to March, well back into the crown. Consider removal and replacement with a more appropriate shrub. Width control by pruning is more effective and lateral branches can be removed with loppers or pruning saws, November to March. (Fig. 16.26)

Coppicing

This is more effective than heavy pruning to reduce height as the shrub re-grows into its original form. Cut the whole shrub down to about 300 mm. This is higher than often practiced, but some plants sprout much better if not cut right to the ground. There may be too few adventitious buds left above ground level. Where surrounding canopy is likely to shade the cut stump, cut to the height of the former. Disposal of arisings: chip and spread around stumps. Apply a balanced fertiliser at the end of March unless the soil is extremely fertile. This can be a 'green waste' compost that meets BS PAS100. These are generally high in plant nutrients and are a useful product of recycling. Optimum time: February/March with bow saw, pruning saw or loppers.

Shrubs without adventitious buds

These are a special case as they do not sprout from old wood. Annual pruning is essential if they are to be kept as healthy looking plants for more than a very few years. Cut over with shears or hedge trimmers immediately after flowering, leaving a few leaves and buds at the base of each shoot.

Alternatively they can be cut back in February–March, but this is less effective in the long term. Pruning after flowering also has the advantage of producing an attractive, bushy plant through the winter months. (Fig. 16.27)

Table 16.3 Examples of specimen shrubs with specific growth forms.

Deciduous

R	*Acer ginnala*	
R	*Acer palmatum* and cvs	(only prune if essential)
R	*Amelanchier lamarkii*	(spring fl.)
U	*Aralia elata*	
R	*Cercis siliquastrum*	(spring fl.)
R	*Chaenomeles speciosa* cvs	(spring fl.)
T	*Cornus controversa*	(only prune if essential)
T	*Cornus kousa* var *chinensis*	(only prune if essential)
R	*Corylus maxima* 'Purpurea'	
R	*Cotinus coggygria* cvs	(only prune if essential)
U	*Cytisus battandieri*	(does not re-grow from old wood)
R	*Elaeagnus angustifolia*	
R	*Euonymus europaeus* 'Red Cascade'	
R	*Magnolia x soulangeana* cvs	(spring fl.)
U	*Rhus* species and cvs	
R	*Rosa* – many cvs	
U	*Syringa vulgaris* cvs	(spring fl.)
R	*Tamarix tetranda*	
U	*Viburnum x bodnantense* cvs	
T	*Viburnum plicatum* 'Mariesii'	

Evergreen

R	*Arbutus unedo*	
R	*Camellia* cvs	(spring fl.)
R	*Ceanothus* 'Autumnal Blue'	
R	*C.* 'Concha'	(spring fl.)
R	*C.* 'Delight'	
U	*Cistus laurifolius*	(does not re-grow from old wood)
U	*C. aguillari* 'Maculatus'	(does not re-grow from old wood)
A	*Cordyline australis*	(remove individual trunks to ground if necessary)
R	*Cotoneaster* 'Cornubia'	
U	*Escallonia* 'Crimson Spire'	
R	*Garrya elliptica*	
U	*Genista aetnensis*	(does not re-grow from old wood)
U	*G.* 'Golden Shower'	(does not re-grow from old wood)
R	*Hamamelis x intermedia* cvs	(only prune if essential)
U	*Hibiscus syriacus* cvs	
R	*Ilex x altaclarensis* cvs	
R	*I. x meservae* cvs	
U	*Juniperus* species and cvs	
R	*Laurus nobilis*	
R	*Ligustrum lucidum*	
R	*Magnolia grandiflora* cvs	
U	*Mahonia x media* cvs	
R	*Osmanthus* species and cvs	
A	*Phormium tenax* and cvs	
A	*P. cookianum* and cvs	
R	*Prunus laurocerasus* 'Latifolia'	
R	*P.l.* 'Otto Luyken'	
R	*P.l.* 'Mischeana'	
R	*Prunus lusitanica*	
U	*Rosmarinus officinalis* 'Miss Jessop'	
R	*Thuya* cvs	
R	*Viburnum rhytidophyllum*	
A	*Yucca filamentosa*	
A	*Y. gloriosa*	(remove individual trunks to ground if necessary)
A	*Y. recurvifolia*	

Spring flowering plants to be pruned after flowering in April/May/June indicated by suffix (spring fl.)
Key: R – Rounded, U – Upright, A – Accent plant, T – Tabular.

February–March
Chamaecyparis species and cvs
Cuprocyparis x *leylandii* and cvs

June
Cytisus x *kewensis*
C. 'Praecox'
C. *scoparius* cvs
Genista hispanica
G. *lydia*
Ulex europeaus 'Flore Pleno'

July
Ceanothus (low growing evergreen types)
Cistus dansereaui cvs
C. 'Jessamy Beauty'
C. *laurifolius*
C. *purpureus*
C. 'Peggy Sammons'
Lavandula angustifolia cvs
Lavandula intermedia cvs

September
Lavandula stoechas and cvs
Spartium junceum

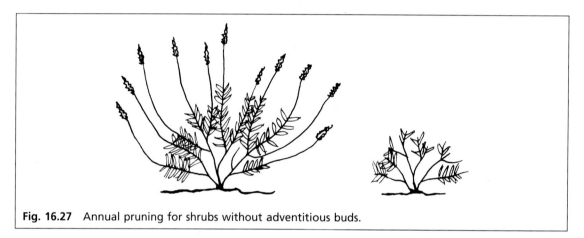

Fig. 16.27 Annual pruning for shrubs without adventitious buds.

Bamboos

These vary from tall, clump forming stands to vigorously suckering carpets of culms (main-stems) between 0.5 and 5 metres in height.

Clump forming

Remove exhausted culms to ground level. The tops can be cut out of culms if necessary and they do not increase in height. Dig out portions of over-sized clumps in April and they can be replanted if required.

Suckering

It has been found that the variegated dwarf bamboos *Pleioblastus auricomus* and *Pleioblastus variegatus* can be cut back annually to ground level. A fertiliser application is recommended after cutting. This may also apply to other low-growing species.

Lateral spread is the usual problem. The roots can be restrained by a root barrier round the clump. This should be 400 mm deep on heavy soils and about 800 mm on light soils. Any growth over the top of the root barrier is easily controlled. These are easily installed by hand digging in light soils or in trenches dug by a mini-excavator.

Usually clump forming:

Fargesia murieliae
Phyllostachys most species and cvs
Shibatea kumasasa

Usually vigorously spreading:

Chimonobambusa marmorea
Phyllostachys aureosulcata 'Aureocaulis'
Phyllostachys viridistriata
Pleioblastus auricomus

Pleioblastus pygmaeus
Pleioblastus variegatus
Pseudosasa japonica
Sasa veitchii
Sasaella vagans

Shrubs with biennial stems

Remove exhausted stems to the base in February–March. The whole plant can be cut down to near ground level. A balanced fertiliser application will be needed except in the most fertile soils.

Rubus idaeus 'Aureus'
R. cockburnianus
R. odoratus
R. spectabilis and cvs

The following shrubs are evergreen. Exhausted stems with the remains of last year's flowering still attached should be removed to the base in April–May.

Euphorbia characias and cvs
Euphorbia x *martinii.*

Table 16.4 Calendar of pruning times.

	Jan	Feb	Mar	Apr	May	June	July	Aug	Sept	Oct	Nov	Dec
Sprawling and		LP	LP									
ground	HP	HP	HP								HP	HP
cover shrubs	COP	COP	COP									
Bushy			LP									
shrubs												
Deciduous	HP	HP	HP								HP	HP
	COP	COP	COP								COP	COP
Evergreen		HP	HP									
Spring flr.			P	P	P							
Specimen			LP							LP		
shrubs	HP	HP	HP								HP	HP
		COP	COP									
Shrubs without		P	P			P	P		P			
adventitious												
buds												
Bamboos					P							
Shrubs with		P	P									
biennial												
stems												
Sub-shrubs		P	P									

Key: LP = Light pruning HP = Heavy pruning COP = Coppicing P = Pruning (all forms).

16.5   Sub-shrubs

These have a woody base and soft, non-woody shoots from the woody base each year. (The term sub-shrub is sometimes incorrectly used for a small shrub).

Cut the whole plant down to live wood near ground level in February–March.

Artemisia absinthium 'Lambrook Silver'
Artemisia 'Powis Castle'
Ballota pseudodictamnus
Ceratostigma willmottianum
Lavatera thuringiaca and cvs
Perovskia 'Blue Spire'
Phlomis 'Edward Bowles'
Teucrium chamaedrys

16.6   Summary

This chapter has assessed the aesthetic aims of shrub pruning, and based its approach to achieving these aims on the biological principles of the way shrubs grow. It is firmly based on practical experience and Table 16.4 summarises its recommendations for pruning times and methods.

We may admire the beauty of a well-pruned vineyard or orchard. They are simply the result of understanding the biological principles of maximising fruit production and sensitive craftsmanship. They are beautiful because the vine or apple tree still expresses something unique about the plant. Much of British horticulture and landscape and garden design have been devoted to finding a way to allow plants to express their character in the design. This guide shows how it can be achieved in landscapes that are based on mass plantings of shrubs. The challenge is to see this through in practical landscape maintenance. The investment in landscape design and implementation will then continue to provide delight in the lives of people who use these landscapes.

References

BSI (2002) Publicly Available Specification (PAS)100. Specification for composted materials, British Standards Institution, London.

Further reading

Cobham, R. (1990) *Amenity Landscape Management.* E & F N Spon, London.

Wright, T.W.J. (1982) *Large Gardens and Parks: Maintenance, Management and Design.* Granada, St Albans.

17 Climbing Plants

Tom La Dell

Climbing plants are the Cinderellas of the landscape plant principality, and generally receive scant attention. This chapter aims to reveal their qualities and contribute to their effective use in landscape design. There are only a few good books about them, and these are listed at the end of this chapter. Most texts on climbing plants include many 'wall shrubs'. These are non-climbing shrubs that need a wall for extra warmth, or display their flowers or fruits better if trained against a wall. These need intensive pruning and training, and so are of little use in most landscape schemes.

17.1 Climbers and their qualities

Although they are rarely seen in landscape planting, climbers have great potential: their wide variety of forms and habits are quite different from trees and shrubs, and good designers can use them to special effect. Unfortunately, their use often proves unsatisfactory. When selecting this type of plant, it is important to remember that they have evolved by exploiting specific habitats. To use them successfully, at least some of this needs to be understood.

What are climbers?

Climbers have stems that are not strong enough to support themselves and so must, in natural circumstances, use other plants for support. They are mostly woody, and either evergreen or deciduous. There are also herbaceous climbers such as hops (*Humulus lupus*) that die back to a perennial rootstock each year, and some that are annual in temperate climates, for example the cup and saucer vine (*Cobaea scandens*). Most seek out the light and need to reach the top or side of a tree or shrub to survive. Favourable conditions allow a large amount of top growth and leaf area. Their natural vigour is variable, from small scramblers to huge climbers that can reach the tops of the tallest trees. They can represent a major component of semi-natural woodland, such as tropical rain forests. Their roots are generally vigorous, seeking out water and nutrients in a large soil volume.

Why use climbing plants?

Their main use in landscape design is to provide a tall, wide-spreading cover to walls, buildings and structures. Dramatic effects can be created with flat, textured planes of green or coloured foliage in contrast to the architecture of trees and the bushiness of shrubs. Just one plant can provide a wide curtain with very little depth of branches and foliage, and consequently consume very little sideways space. Their light-seeking qualities can be used in confined spaces to provide green at higher levels. They can be used to drape over structures or down banks, as the dominant woody plant component.

The main landscape uses for climbers are:

- **As a wall or building cover:** climbers can be used to cover walls and buildings to great height and provide an architectural plane with a green, living surface.
- **On vertical and horizontal supports**, such as a pergola, to provide a plant-softened arch or

tunnel. Wire supports can be used to create the illusion that the climbers are self-supporting.

- **As a fence or trellis cover**: most climbers spread just as well along a fence as up a wall, and can be planted on one side of a fence to grow up it, over the top and down the other side.
- **As a reinforced hedge**: with occasional clipping, stem-twining climbers like Akebia, *Lonicera japonica* and ivies (*Hedera* spp.) can make an excellent hedge when grown through a metal or timber support structure (Fig. 17.1).
- **To scramble over other trees or shrubs**: this is the most natural use for climbers. Sparser-growing climbers can achieve a long-term balance of growth with the host, and co-exist successfully together.
- **As ground cover**: some climbers are quite suitable as wide spreading ground covers. They create a distinctive line and look compared to the usual sprawling shrubs. They will however hoist themselves up into any shrubs within the planting.
- **As a drape**: most climbers will cascade downwards if they are planted at the top of a wall, bank or building.
- **To reduce solar gain**: a wall clad with a climbing plant will have less solar gain in summer. Deciduous plants should be chosen if solar gain is needed in winter (although ivy, for instance, is a good insulation blanket). The tendency of some climbers to produce shrub-like growth at the top of the support structure can be used as a substitute for louvres above large areas of glazing.

17.2 Selecting the right type of climber for each situation

The 'get-up-and-go' qualities of climbers and their in-built instinct to smother and cover their hosts means that very careful selection of the right species or cultivars is essential. The climber should suit the soil conditions (often difficult next to structures) and the microclimate, which may vary sharply up and around walls and buildings. In some climbing plant genera (e.g. *Clematis* spp.) there are enormous variations in size and growth

Fig. 17.1 Climbers that maintain their basal foliage in maturity (for example many ivy cultivars) can make effective hedge substitutes when grown on a fence structure. (Photo: James Hitchmough)

rates between species and cultivars, emphasising the need to select carefully for the chosen location.

How plants climb

Plants climb by attaching themselves to their hosts, and there are many different ways of doing this. Since they are usually planted on buildings and structures in landscape schemes, the climbing method must suit the host support they are expected to climb.

The stems of most climbing plants possess high tensile strength and do not easily break. They may use the stems, the leaf stalks or the roots to climb.

Stem twining

The main stems twine around the host like a boa constrictor. The side branches may also twine, depending on the species. Once the stem thickens it is almost impossible to remove it from the host. The chosen support must be suitable for the young stems to twine around, as older stems lose their flexibility. If planted as large specimens, they must be properly tied to a post or wall. Posts and wires are generally suitable. Metal posts, especially aluminium and stainless steel, may heat up too much in full sun, and must be chosen with care. The supports must be high and extensive enough to support the full height of the plant. Once most stem twiners reach the top of the support structure, they bush out into a shrubby mass of branches. Honeysuckle (*Lonicera*) and *Wisteria* are typical examples.

Stem tendrils that twine

Tendrils are modified leaves which grip any slim support and pull the stem close to it. Vines (*Vitis*) have much-divided tendrils (Plate 19), as do *Lathyrus* spp. including sweet peas. Passion flowers (*Passiflora*) have a single coiled spring. Most of these have non-twining or weakly-climbing stems, so they usually need supporting for their whole life.

Stem tendrils with sucker pads

Some climbers are self-clinging, and the tendrils have pads that adhere strongly to a tree trunk, wall or fence. Virginia creepers (*Parthenocissus*) are the best known and fan out nicely on a flat surface (Plate 17).

Leaf tendrils that twine

Some plants have modified their leaf so that the petioles (leaf stalks) twine and grip their host. These are usually pinnate leaves (with many leaflets). *Clematis* spp. climb by this method. They tend not to form strong stems (some do, but only after many years) and easily form an unmanageable mass of foliage. They need training onto a support that the petioles can grip easily.

Adventitious roots

Ivies (*Hedera* spp.) and climbing hydrangea (*Hydrangea anomala* subsp. *petiolaris*) put out small roots from their stems when they are in contact with a suitable support. They can only grip when the roots can adhere to the support, or grow into fissures to get a proper hold (Plate 18).

They are good at naturally spreading out on a suitable surface.

Prickles

The thorns on roses (*Rosa* spp.) and blackberries (*Rubus*) help the stems to scramble over or through other vegetation. (Some species do not climb, and in these cases, the thorns take on a defensive role.) They all need careful training and usually need tying onto a support.

No visible means of support

A few plants are weak stemmed and just flop. Winter jasmine (*Jasminum nudiflorum*) is a good example. It needs to be fully supported – or given space to spread.

Each climber has its own peculiarities, and using the 'wrong' plant will give results other than those anticipated. These may be merely inconvenient, comical or just plain ugly. Floppy masses of foliage at the base of a wall which it was meant to ascend elegantly show that the wrong plant was chosen, or that nothing was provided for it to climb up.

17.3 Essential features and maintenance

In nature climbing plants need to be near their host, and consequently often compete with it for water and nutrients. The root systems are therefore well-adapted to searching out moisture and nutrient reserves in the soil, provided that the soil has the basic qualities to allow root growth in the first place. The idea that climbers need their roots in the shade may have some credibility, but if the roots have adequate moisture and there is not too much reflected heat from walls and paving (see Fig. 17.2) this can probably be overcome.

Top growth

Most climbers are adapted to growing strongly upwards to the light, and then branching out in all directions. Most are also well adapted to shade when young, and some (such as ivy) are adapted to deep shade as mature plants. Branches and leaves in the sun have a competitive advantage over those in the shade. Without a careful pruning and training, most climbers develop bare lower stems and a mass of top growth.

The natural tendency for most climbers is to rush to the top of a support and create a 'birds-nest' of interwoven stems. This can be quite ugly and often takes most of the leaves and flowers out of sight. It can only be overcome by careful training in the first few years and by avoiding planting sun-demanding species on shady walls and structures.

Vigour, coverage and height

These are largely determined by soil conditions, but also the overall suitability of the climber to the climate and microclimate of the site. Climbers from continental climates, for example *Campsis* spp., require high temperatures in summer to grow and flower satisfactorily. At the other extreme, climbers from cool temperate rainforests, such as *Berberidopsis corallina*, require similar conditions in cultivation.

Maintenance

The best way to reduce maintenance requirements is to select the plant best suited to the situation and provide it with appropriate support. Early training and pruning are the keys to success.

Training depends on the plant's growth pattern and habit. Most climbers naturally bunch their growth together, except for shade tolerant species which usually fan out. Early training involves spreading out new growth while it is still young and flexible, together with controlling the number of side shoots until the plant begins to fill its allotted space.

Climbers need some form of on-going pruning to keep them effective. Keeping to size can be a simple method of cutting back to keep it within bounds. The re-growth will be vigorous especially if the cutting back is indiscriminate. The selective removal of older stems to near their base allows

healthier young shoots to develop. Some serious untangling of interwoven stems may be necessary if this is not done regularly.

Some climbers such as wisteria have main stems that can live as long as the plant itself, like the trunk of a tree. Others (such as roses and clematis) need older stems removing periodically so that a new framework can develop. Many, such as honeysuckles, need side shoots to be removed to stop them developing into a tangled mass. Others need to be trained to form a permanent framework of large stems, and have the side shoots cut back annually. Fruiting grape vines are pruned in this manner and trumpet vines (*Campsis*) need this form of pruning to flower well.

Climbers used as ground covers will climb up and over adjacent trees and shrubs. They need to be kept separate in the planting design.

Location

The effects of sun and shade on the growth and habit of climbers mean that it is crucial to make a correct assessment of the sun and shade over the whole of the entire growth area. As most climbers 'run for the sun', they will not simply obey the designer's wishes. Therefore, the overall planting scheme needs to reflect the likely growth of the climbers. Shade-tolerant climbers such as ivy (*Hedera* spp.), climbing hydrangea (*Hydrangea anomala* subsp. *petiolaris*), *Schizophragma hydrangeoides*, *Pileostegia viburnoides* and *Parthenocissus henryana* are very useful as they will keep to shady areas.

Aspect is important. Walls and high, solid fences give the climbers no choice but to grow in the sun or shade that they are given. Trellises and open structures allow the plant to choose its favoured aspect: sunny, shady or growing over the top.

The overall orientation is important if there is only one aspect, but most climbers are planted where orientation will change around a corner, or at upper levels of a wall or a building.

Walls usually create shelter and localised heat island effects, reducing the effects of frost and cold damage. It can be tempting to use less hardy plants (*Solanum jasminoides* 'Album' has become popular recently), but a cold winter *will* kill them off. It may be worth taking a risk with semi hardy species where they comprise only a few of the total climbers planted, but not where they are to form the structure of the planting.

Water use and subsidence

Climbers are often planted near buildings. Their potentially large leaf area is likely to lead to considerable water uptake. On shrinkable clays this could contribute to soil drying and consequent subsidence. Climbers should be chosen carefully on these soils and, on new buildings, checked with the engineer.

The effect of trees on foundations is well documented, but the effect of shrubs and climbers much less so. The main reference is the current *National House Builders Council Specification*, chapter 4.2. This is supplemented by *Tree Root Damage to Buildings* (Biddle, 1998) which illustrates many case studies alongside the principal effects of tree roots on buildings. Tree root interactions with buildings are discussed in Chapter 9.

At present, common sense must be used, and with it the information that a mature wisteria can have the leaf area of a medium-sized tree. As with trees, the real risks of subsidence exist only on shrinkable clays, and direct damage to structures is very rare.

Damage to hosts

This area is full of myths and old wives' tales – the truth is that any potential damage will either be physical or due to smothering. Any plant, except perhaps the largest trees, can be smothered by a climber shading it from the light. Match host and climber carefully. Young plants can be strangled by stem twiners such as honeysuckle (*Lonicera* spp.) and *Wisteria* spp. However, mature hosts rarely suffer physical damage. The adventitious roots of ivy, climbing hydrangea or trumpet vine will not harm a healthy tree or a sound brick wall, but the roots can penetrate the lime mortar of old walls and may cause problems. Ivy in particular protects the surface of walls from rain and can be benefi-

cial. The weight of the plant may cause a problem to unhealthy trees or unsound structures.

There does not seem to be any reliable information on the weight of climbing plants and the load they exert on structures. Damage to buildings is covered in *Bird, Bee and Plant Damage to Buildings* (BRE, 1986). Its tone is somewhat alarmist, but it is really only old and dilapidated structures that are at risk. Regular pruning to keep climbers out of eaves, roofs and gutters is necessary. Damage to drains is possible, but there has to be damaged pipework and a moist environment in the pipe for roots to enter. It is worth remembering that most surface water pipes and soakaways are dry most of the time and unlikely to attract plant roots.

In heavy soils, elevated soil oxygen levels around fractured drainage pipes and their sand or shingle surrounds may result in the opportunistic rooting of climbers into these.

Building maintenance departments are often hostile to climbing plants because of the additional costs of removing growth from windows etc. These problems are largely generated by self-clinging climbing plants: for example *Parthenocissus*. While extremely valuable plants in most regards, these do not recognise boundaries between walls and window frames. These problems can be avoided by using species that can only climb where a specific support system is provided.

Ecology

Climbers not only diversify the visual qualities of a landscape, but they also provide a variety of wildlife habitats. The dense branch structure and foliage of many climbers offer good habitats for insects and birds. Any climber of suitable growth form and size will be satisfactory for nesting birds, but native climbers are most likely to be best for insects and thus for a range of wildlife that depends on them. Ivy in particular has many niches for insects, together with nectar-rich flowers in autumn and berries in winter.

It is difficult to include climbers in native scrub and woodland plantings, as these rarely provide suitable hosts until several years after establishment. However, a few can be used in young plantings if they are given an unobtrusive support and they will provide a source from which seeds can spread in the future.

17.4 Detailing for successful establishment

Architectural supports

The design of the fixing must suit the climber. Those developing a few strong stems that can support the rest of the plant, such as wisteria and vines, need only a few supports. Tendril and leaf petiole climbers need many thin supports. Those with sucker pads just need a flat surface. If there are too few supports for tendril climbers the plant builds up a dense mass of stems by clinging to itself and this can be very difficult to manage and keep it looking good. Stem twiners behave similarly.

The material used for the support is important: timber is usually satisfactory, but metal can cause problems, as it heats up quickly in sunshine and may burn plants in direct contact. Stainless steel rods in particular are often too smooth for most plants to fasten on to, and aluminium can also cause problems in full sun. Wires cause few difficulties, so it may be possible to cover a metal structure with a light wire fixing to support the plants. Metals can be long-lasting, but even pressure treated timber has a lifespan of about 50 years. The design of climbing plant supports should be imaginative and mix metal, timber and wires to suit the chosen climbers, and respond to the design character of the landscape scheme.

Wall fixings

Wall fixings are essential for all climbers that are not self-clinging or where the surface is hostile to them. They are usually linked by wires spaced out to suit the growth of the climber. They need to be close enough together and in the right places vertically and horizontally for the climber to reach from one to the other unless the plant will be regularly tied in during the early years. Wires at

300 mm centres are generally adequate. There are many strong fixings, such as various grades of Rawlbolts™, that will support bulky climbers in the long term. Elements that are usually free standing, such as trellis and wire mesh, can also be fixed to walls. Obviously, a gap is needed between this and the wall for the support system to get a good grip.

It is even easier to fix supporting wires or trellis to timber fences and structures using galvanised nails or galvanised or brass screws. Trellis and wire mesh provide useful supports for most climbers, but can look too domestic in scale for many landscape projects. Stem twiners cannot be disentangled from trellis, however, unless they are cut out piece by piece.

Posts and pergolas are usually too big to allow all but the most vigorous stem climbers to grip them, and consequently a mesh, wires or trellis are needed on the posts. Regular individual fixing of stems, as they grow, is probably outside the maintenance scope of most landscape schemes.

Planting pits

Match your climber to its host, provide a good planting pit and you have the ideal match for early establishment and long-term maintenance. The soil near a climbing plant's host is usually dry and already exploited by the host plant. This is equally true of structures with projecting foundations or overhanging roofs. Most surface water is carried away from paved areas and the subsoil is usually well compacted under the paving (Fig. 17.2). In all these conditions, an adequate planting pit of good soil, with connections to an aerated subsoil, must be provided. A water supply is essential during establishment. In general a 600 × 600 × 1000 mm deep prepared pit is suitable, provided the surrounding subsoil is a good rooting medium.

The base of walls are often backfilled with building debris or heavily compacted at depth, and hence deeper planting pits are desirable. Data on the root volumes of small trees at maturity (see Chapter 11) suggest that at maturity, vigorous

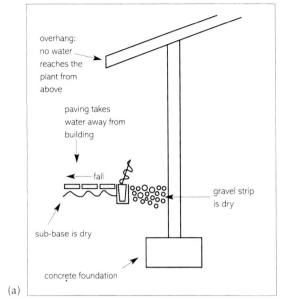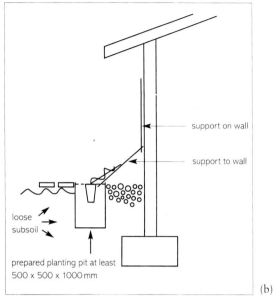

(a)

(b)

Fig. 17.2 Ensuring an adequate planting pit: (a) the climber stands almost no chance as the planting pit is too small and the overhang deprives the plant of water; (b) with a larger planting pit and shorter overhang, the plant stands a good chance of establishing successfully.

climbers need 20–30 m³ of soil for their root system.

17.5 The plants

The aim of these lists is to show the range and diversity of climbers, highlighting the important differences in the groups to help in selection for landscape planting. Each major genus is well known, but guidance is given about the variety of form, character, requirements and maintenance within each, to help with selection when confronted with lists in books and catalogues. The main characteristics for landscape selection are also given, together with a guide to plant choice.

Roses

A dauntingly large group, all scramblers with thorns, superficially similar in appearance but varied in habit. Relatively few of them are true climbers. Most demand full sun to flower well and resist diseases.

Species and cultivars

Most native species are really large, scrambling shrubs. The native *R. canina*, *R. rubiginosa* and *R. arvensis* are commonly grown. There are many other native selections, which are not readily available. *R. arvensis* 'Splendens' is a vigorous climber (or massive ground cover) that tolerates shade. Some exotic species are very vigorous. *R. filipes* 'Kiftsgate' has reached over 20 m in a copper beech in its namesake garden. There are other roses with large clusters of small white flowers that are less vigorous. *R. mulliganii* covers the pergola in the centre of the white garden at Sissinghurst. There are many other, similar 'musk rose' species and cultivars. *R. laevigata* 'Cooperi' is evergreen with single white flowers, but is not fully hardy in cold areas. *R.* 'Mermaid' has single yellow flowers and is hardier, evergreen and surprisingly shade tolerant.

Fig. 17.3 Roses require fairly intensive training and maintenance when grown as climbers, as this picture of Kew Gardens demonstrates! (Photo: James Hitchmough)

Climbing roses

Large-flowered climbers need to be selected for their vigour, colour and length of flowering period. They all need full sun and some fresh air or they tend to become infected with the defoliating disease 'black spot'. If they get too dry at the roots in late summer they tend to get mildew. The Henry Doubleday Research Association at Ryton Organic Gardens, Coventry provides a list of the most disease resistant plants.

Rambling roses

The cluster-flowered rambler roses are often ineffective climbers and require sophisticated annual pruning to remove flowered stems (Fig. 17.3). However, another group listed as ramblers are easy, vigorous, disease resistant plants. This group includes 'Alberic Barbier', 'Albertine' and 'Francois Juranville'.

Clematis

This forms a large group of similar-looking climbers that are very varied in flowering time and requirements. The spring flowering *Clematis*

montana cultivars are strong growing and need thinning out after flowering, unless they have a big space to fill. There are many new cultivars that are worth consideration. The native *C. vitalba* is a very large growing species that can be used to drape chalk cliffs. Other, spring flowering clematis are much less vigorous and both *C. alpina* and *C. macropetala* have small drooping flowers in blue, white or pink. *C. armandii* is evergreen and has a rather unevenly branching, unpredictable habit. The large-flowered climbers are of such mixed parentage that the different flowering times and pruning requirements mean that they need expert attention.

The late summer flowerers are much easier, smaller-flowered plants. *C. viticella* cultivars have a mass of elegant flowers in a wide range of colours and fairly strong growth. There are also several yellow flowered species and cultivars with pendent flowers in late summer and autumn, of which C. 'Bill Mackenzie' is one of the brightest.

As leaf tendril climbers they need a lattice with a mesh of no more than 200 mm to cling to. With careful choice for vigour, they can be matched to other plants and even other climbers such as roses. Some scrambling varieties such as *C. x jouiniana* make good vigorous ground cover.

Ivy

These are dense evergreen climbers with a huge variety of leaf shapes and variegation. The normal flexible shoots with adventitious roots to grip their host represent only the juvenile phase. When they reach sunlight, a 'shrubby' mature state develops that then flowers and sets seed. All seedlings return to the juvenile state. Each state comes true if propagated by cuttings, and so-called tree ivies are cuttings of mature phase shoots. Ivies will not normally damage sound structures.

Hedera helix is native. It will climb and smother new plantings, so should be used only in appropriate situations. *H. hibernica* is also native but does not have a wide distribution. It is an anomaly in that it does not climb in its juvenile form, and so makes a good ground cover.

The large-leafed ivies are from more southern

areas and have much bolder leaves. The common species are *H. colchica* and *H. algeriensis*. Both have brightly-coloured variegated forms that brighten up shady sites.

Honeysuckle

These are strong stem twiners that can be either deciduous or evergreen. The native *Lonicera periclymenum* is the common cream-flowered, scented honeysuckle in hedgerows. It has many cultivars.

Other deciduous and scented honeysuckles are well worthwhile. The true *L. x americana* is an outstanding plant if supplied true to its name. It is fairly short growing and almost evergreen. These honeysuckles are scented only in the evening, to attract night-flying moths for pollination.

Some are deciduous and not scented, but this is compensated for by spectacular red or yellow flowers, and *L.* 'Gold Flame' is a truly shade-tolerant plant. The main evergreen species is the vigorous *L. japonica*, with small, cream flowers that give off scent all day. 'Hall's Prolific' is the best cream selection, but *L. j.* 'Repens' has purple-flushed flowers and young shoots. It also makes a good, wide-spreading ground cover. *L. henryi* has larger leaves but smaller flowers.

Virginia creeper

These self-clinging climbers provide spectacular red autumn colour. The true Virginia creeper is *Parthenocissus quinquefolia*, and is rather vigorous and coarse. *P. tricuspidata* 'Veitchii' is a selection of a Chinese species with a neater leaf but is also vigorous. *P. henryana* has an attractive dark green leaf with a reddish tinge and a paler midrib, and performs well in shade.

Wisteria

Wisteria sinensis is the common species, but many cultivars, in all colours from white through blue to dark purple, are now available. The wisteria with very long pale blue racemes is *W. floribunda* 'Multijuga'. These are very long-lived plants that

Fig. 17.4 Wisteria climbs by twining stems and without careful training can produce a rather untidy 'bird's nest' of shoots. (Photo: James Hitchmough)

can grow to very large sizes. Regular pruning can keep them smaller and floriferous (Fig. 17.4).

Other climbers

There are many other climbers which are not commonly available in nurseries. However, as any scheme may only need a few plants, it is worthwhile insisting they are supplied true to name. The common climbing hydrangea *Hydrangea anomala* subsp. *petiolaris* is self-clinging like ivy. It can be slow to start after planting, but responds well to irrigation and fertiliser during the establishment period. Similar but perhaps rather better during flowering are *Schizophragma*. The recently introduced *H. seemanii* is a useful hardy evergreen climbing hydrangea. The closely related

Pileostegia viburnoides has handsome large ever-green leaves.

Trachelospermums are excellent, self-clinging evergreens with jasmine-like flowers and scent. *T. jasminoides* is rather slow-growing, but *T. j. var. japonicum* is vigorous, *T. j.* 'Variegatum' lightens up a shady area and *T. j.* 'Wilsonii' goes an attractive deep purple-red in cold weather.

Jasmines are good scented climbers. They are vigorous twiners. The common *J. officinale* has some good cultivars and some recent introductions with maroon-flushed flowers. True pink flowers are available in *J. beesianum* and *J. x stephanense*.

Good evergreen stem-twining climbers are few and far between. The closely-related *Stauntonia hexaphylla* and *Holboellia latifolia* are striking dense-foliaged evergreens. The latter is not hardy in the coldest locations in Britain, but is a massive large-leafed climber for screening and covering eyesores. Superficially similar in appearance to these species is *Akebia quinata*, a very tough reliable species that is evergreen in all but the most severe winters.

Vines are strong-growing deciduous climbers. They need to be regularly pruned to fruit well. The *Vitis vinifera* 'Brant' has small black fruits even if not pruned, and spectacular autumn colour in a range of reds. *V. v.* 'Purpurea' has purple or purple-flushed foliage all through summer. V.v. 'Incana' is grey leaved, unusual in climbers.

V. coignetiae has huge leaves and massive growth and a mass of reds and oranges in autumn. These are stem tendril climbers, but can be tied onto a few supports to establish a main woody framework.

The trumpet vines, *Campsis* spp., are like true vines in habit but have large orange-red flowers. The best is *C.* 'Mme. Galen'.

The true monster of deciduous climbers is the potentially huge Russian vine *Fallopia aubertii*, with large plumes of white flowers in late summer. It is a quick-growing plant for screening and looks very handsome if it has enough space to develop. It does however quickly lose its basal foliage and is essentially a plant of relatively low quality when viewed at close quarters.

17.6 Supply

Once climbers have been carefully selected it is important that they are provided true to name. As they are usually required in small numbers there is no excuse for substitution. Many of the most familiar species are available from wholesale nurseries. *The RHS Plant Finder* provides sources of supply for less common species and cultivars. Two or three litre plants are most common and small plants usually establish best. Large specimen plants are available from specialist suppliers, but should be used with care as climbers cling or twine as they grow and they need careful training onto their new supports.

Success with climbing plants is all about selecting the right plant for the right situation and giving it an appropriate means of support. Given this, climbing plants are an extremely beautiful and useful group for urban landscapes on buildings and in many locations on walls, fences and other structures.

References

Biddle, P.G. (1998) *Tree Root Damage to Buildings* (2 vols). Willowmead Publishing, Wantage.

BRE (1986) *Bird, Bee and Plant Damage to Buildings*, BRE Digest 418. Watford.

Royal Horticultural Society (published annually), *The RHS Plant Finder 2003–2004: 70 000 Plants and Where to Buy Them*. Dorling Kindersley, London.

Further reading

Davis, B. (1990) *Climbers and Wall Plants*. Viking, Harmondsworth.

Grey-Wilson, C. & Matthews, V. (1983) *Gardening on Walls*. Collins, London.

The Henry Doubleday Research Association, Ryton Organic Gardens, Ryton, Corentry. Telephone 01203 303507.

18 Roof Gardens

Steve Scrivens

There is a great deal of mysticism about growing plants on top of buildings. Plants have been growing in precarious locations ever since they first evolved. In what other landscape situation are plants provided with good quality improved topsoil, regular irrigation, high root temperatures and a high level of maintenance? Plants and gardens certainly make life more pleasant for people, and in high-density cities the only areas which are left for plants are roofs.

Because of their cost, though, it is often difficult to make a case for having roof gardens in terms of their environmental benefits alone. There are the additional expenses of strengthening the structure, the need for additional services, plus (if the site is within a major city) the extra cost of importing materials, and the cost of the ongoing maintenance of the landscape over the life of the building. By absorbing water, roof gardens can damp down peaks in run-off during heavy rain, but this buffering is limited, as the drainage systems still have to cope with peak flows.

Taking this idea to its logical conclusion, in some cases the intensive nature of the resource inputs required for roof gardens could be seen as exceeding the environmental benefits derived.

Roof gardens are more common in some countries than others because of differences in planning laws and perception of benefits. In any major city the value of the land upon which a building stands can represent a significant part of the total cost of the project. Consequently most buildings are built as cheaply as possible, which in turn means that little money is spent on landscape, unless the planning laws demand it. In Switzerland and Germany,

for example, to build on greenfield sites there has to be a gesture towards restoring the status quo.

Under German law, although development above ground is strictly controlled, there is much more flexibility when developing below ground. As a result it is often possible to develop right up to the site boundary. This can be very useful in an urban context. It also means that more extensive activities such as car parks can be hidden from view.

In most countries only clients who wish to offer something special will provide roof gardens (Plate 20). A roof garden with paving and large trees will cost double or even treble the price of a conventional garden at ground level. Few clients elect to spend money in this way unless there is a legal requirement or financial benefit. Clients who have commissioned a building for their own use are another matter and, in the main, these are the only people who fund such features.

Traditionally a roof garden was considered to be any collection of plants raised up on a structure (Fig. 18.1). Today the term 'green roof' has been adopted to refer to those systems that produce a sward of dwarf, drought tolerant to xerophytic plants, supported on a relatively shallow substrate (Fig. 18.2). In climates with low summer rainfall, for much of the year the plants are in a dormant state. If this approach is considered acceptable then it follows a long tradition of putting turf on roofs, as practised in the Middle East, Scandinavia and North America. Although many green roofs were initially required by law there is now a general acceptance on the part of businesses and developers that greening the envi-

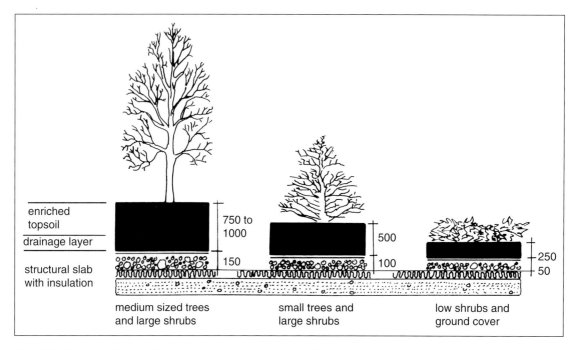

Fig. 18.1   Some typical sections through conventional roof gardens.

Fig. 18.2   The application of a green roof to an existing factory in Germany which could not support the loading of a conventional roof garden. (Photo: James Hitchmough)

ronment is a socially desirable objective. However even a minimal depth green roof is still expensive.

18.1   Loading

There are only two conventional methods of constructing roof gardens. The first is to have a free-draining roof, where surplus water is removed. The second is to retain some water on the roof. This has an additional weight penalty of up to $100 \, kg/m^2$, although with thicker profiles this becomes proportionately less significant. All modern proprietary systems seek to reduce the weight of the drainage layer, but unfortunately this is a small part of the total weight of the profile. Further effort goes into reducing the weight of the substrate but the benefit of this, from a horticultural perspective, is very questionable.

Most commercial buildings are designed to receive a people (live) load of $5 \, kN/m^2$, plus a dead load of 1 or $2 \, kN/m^2$ for furniture etc. If people have access to a garden then it must be assumed that they will congregate at the same density that they would on a crowded office floor. In other words the weight of the garden is in addition to the $5 \, kN/m^2$ set aside for the live load. If it is possible to guarantee that people will not congregate on a garden then the live load component can be removed from the calculation. Some typical roof garden loadings are shown in Table 18.1.

Table 18.1 Some typical roof garden loadings.

Overall depth (excluding insulation)	Green roof 100 mm	Traditional roof thin 300 mm	Traditional roof medium 500 mm	Traditional roof thick 1000 mm
Live load – people	0.0	0.0	5.0	5.0
Screed & insulation	0.2 (to 1.0)	0.2 (to 1.0)	1.0	1.5
Mastic asphalt	0.0	0.0	1.0	1.0
Thin layer tanking	0.1	0.1	0.0	0.0
Drainage layer	0.1	0.5	1.0	1.5
Soil	1.5	4.0	6.5	13.0
Mulch	0.1	0.1	0.2	0.3
Plants	0.2	0.5	1.5	2.5
TOTAL	**2.2 kN**	**5.4 kN**	**16.2 kN**	**24.8 kN**

Most floor slabs are designed to take a uniform load. However, point loads can sometimes be placed over columns and beams. The structural engineer will usually suggest that he should comment on proposals. This is a very laborious method; it is better to have a drawing marked up with the capabilities of the slab and to design within these constraints. Even if a slab is designed to take a uniform load it is often possible to adopt a 'swings and roundabouts' approach. For example if paving is of minimal depth then the adjacent soil may be deeper. Similarly large blocks of expanded polystyrene can be used to allow a flexible reduction in weight (Fig. 18.3).

If there is a major change in level or if there is a need for a slope then slabs of extruded polystyrene can be used as a lightweight void filler (Fig. 18.4). The slabs should sit directly on the membrane so that they are stable. Drainage can be provided by chamfering the lower corners of the blocks. The blocks seldom need pinning together as the weight of the soil holds them in place but if it makes installation easier and safer then this would be advisable. Once they have been placed it is usually advisable to cover the formation with a geotextile to keep the voids open.

18.2 Drainage

It is rare to find drainage problems with roof gardens; architects and engineers are aware of the problems that have been associated with flat roofs in the past. Most 'flat' roofs are now designed with falls, and drainage outlets are detailed for maximum efficiency. With a roof garden it is necessary to ensure that rainwater is able to flow through the drainage layer and that it is not possible for the drainage points to become blocked. Experience would indicate that a fall of 1:30 is more than adequate to carry water to the nearest drainage point. The gulleys should be located at no more than 30 m intervals so that the maximum distance for lateral movement does not exceed 15 m although 30 m can be made to work. In reality gulleys are often positioned in a way that suits the services in the ceiling void below rather than the garden. Any area of roof should always have at least two drainage points.

If the area is predominately hard then the paving can be placed on spacers directly on the membrane or insulation layer. If the landscape is to contain hard and soft elements then the drainage layer must be contiguous across the area. Traditionally clean gravel was used. The author's studies of established roof gardens have found that drainage materials do not offer any real resistance to the lateral movement of water.

There are several proprietary products on the market which are formed from plastic and which perform a very similar function to aggregates in that they create open voids. In fact in many ways they are more efficient, as the void to solid ratio is higher (as is their cost).

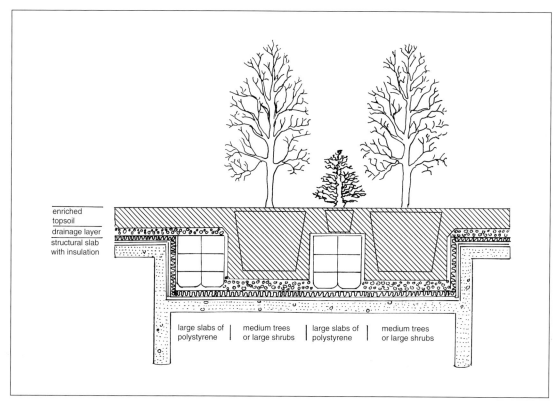

enriched
topsoil
drainage layer
structural slab
with insulation

large slabs of | medium trees | large slabs of | medium trees
polystyrene | or large shrubs | polystyrene | or large shrubs

Fig. 18.3   Blocks of expanded polystyrene can be buried within a deep planter to reduce the overall weight of an area while still allowing enough topsoil in a limited area for the growth of small trees and large shrubs.

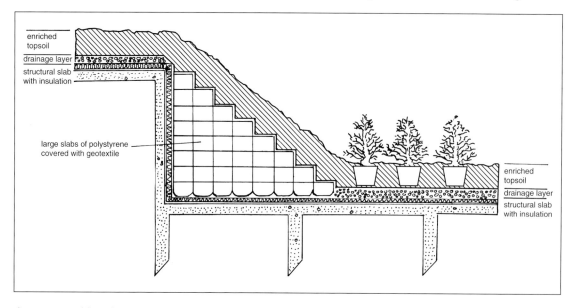

enriched
topsoil
drainage layer
structural slab
with insulation

large slabs of polystyrene
covered with geotextile

enriched
topsoil
drainage layer
structural slab
with insulation

Fig. 18.4   Sudden changes in level can be converted into slopes by the use of slabs of expanded polystyrene.

Fig. 18.5 The Scottish Widows building in Edinburgh: here the landscape sits on a considerable depth of 'Lytag' overlying a 'Leca' drainage area. (Photo: Steve Scrivens)

Traditional granular base

The traditional approach is to have a free-draining roof, which is laid to a gentle fall to encourage run-off through a granular base material. The drainage layer is then formed in 'Leca', 'Lytag' or gravel. Lightweight aggregates are usually favoured, but pea gravel appears to be slightly more water retentive than 'Leca'.

'Leca' (lightweight expanded clay aggregate) is strong, inert and admirably suited for use as a granular drainage material. Non-calcareous pea gravel may be preferred for thin substrate profiles, with 'Leca' for the deeper ones. The drainage layer only needs to be deep enough to remove excess soil moisture. Studies of established roof gardens have shown that a drainage layer of 50 mm thick is often adequate (Fig. 18.5). To be completely certain a layer of 100 mm is more appropriate;

more than 150 mm is seldom of benefit. The only need for caution is the standard requirement that the drainage system should be able to handle the worst storm in 100 years. Aggregates must create some hydraulic resistance and impede the flow of water across a roof. As a result lengths of flexible perforated land drain can be used to link drainage points. These routes are also useful if cables or flexible pipes need to be threaded across a roof at a later date.

Plastic 'egg crates' and plastic formers

A number of proprietary systems employ plastic 'egg crates' that can be laid on the membrane or insulation layer to form drainage voids. The deeper sections come in sheets measuring 2 m × 1 m. The thinner sections come in rolls, sometimes with geotextile fabric bonded to the upper face. Some proprietary systems use a mat of three-dimensional plastic cubes in a sheet form. In some cases plastic cellular grass reinforcing systems have been inverted, although the long-term effect on the wellbeing of a membrane must be questionable if they are used sharp side down.

Expanded polystyrene slabs

Sheets of open porous expanded polystyrene slabs or profiled expanded polystyrene slabs have a low weight but in the main have relatively small interstices.

'Enkamat'

This is a light open filamentous material reminiscent to a pan scourer. Some of the heavier grades are marketed with a geotextile fabric lightly bonded onto their upper surface. This product was devised to act as a vertical drain against a retaining wall or basement, with thinner sections preventing soil erosion along water courses etc. This material has been used to provide a drainage layer under a thin profile roof garden.

Inclined base

If a roof is inclined there is no need for any identifiable drainage layer other than a thick hydroscopic geotextile. The optimum slope is uncertain, but seems to be between 1:3 and 1:5. This approach has a considerable weight advantage. One problem with steep roofs is that the substrate can work its way down the roof. A heavy plastic mesh can be fixed at the top of the roof, and run underneath the geotextile to avoid this problem.

Flooded drainage layer

If a roof is level then it may be appropriate to use a flooded drainage layer. In Europe such a system has been marketed under the trade name of 'Optima' for more than 40 years. With this technique a layer of low density aggregate is placed over the roof to a depth of between 75 and 150 mm. It is then covered by a hydroscopic geotextile soil separator and the substrate. The 'Leca layer' is then flooded with water so that at its highest level there is an air gap, between the surface of the water and the geotextile, of 10 mm and more normally, a gap of 20 mm. The surface of the drainage level must be level, otherwise there will be areas of drought and others of waterlogging. The system works well and has much to commend it although the number of species that are truly successful is limited. However it is ideally suited to more robust, drought tolerant shrubs such as *Cotoneaster*, Pines and Junipers. This is because the substrate dries out from the top down and after a few weeks the moist substrate is restricted to a thin zone towards the bottom of the profile.

Drainage points

Many different ways have been devised to handle drainage points. These range from large manhole covers 600 mm square through to tiny covers 150 mm in diameter. Sometimes drainage points are totally hidden below the substrate. This might have certain aesthetic advantages but can be hazardous: drainage points should be capable of being inspected from above and accessed from below. Often gulleys and their associated pipework require cleaning after the construction work is complete. Rodding points and silt traps should be placed below every garden outlet. Being able to view the rate at which water leaves a roof is vital when calibrating the irrigation system. All drainage points should be surrounded by pre-formed manhole rings and covered with a lid. Pre-cast concrete manhole sections and nowadays 500 mm diameter plastic manhole rings are widely used. Lids may need to be lined with extruded polystyrene to guard against frost action. Where possible all hose points should be placed adjacent to drainage points in case there is a leak.

18.3 Thermal insulation

Many people assume that roof gardens contribute to the thermal insulation of a building. It is not a cost-effective solution in itself, since a garden costs considerably more than any insulation material.

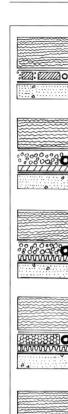

Derry and Toms (1930s)
Membrane covered with well spaced bricks laid flat with clinker infill covered with hessian and top soil

1940s to 1960s
Membrane protected by a sand and cement screed with a gravel drainage layer covered with a fibre-glass quilt, a layer of peat, and topsoil

1960s to date (traditional)
Membrane covered with an extruded polystyrene insulation layer and a 'leca' drainage layer covered with a geotextile and modified topsoil

1980s proprietary system
Membrane protected with an extruded polystyrene insulation layer covered with sheets of open expanded polystyrene covered with geotextile and enriched topsoil or compost

1990s proprietary system
Membrane protected with an extruded polystyrene insulation layer covered with vacuum formed plastic 'egg crate' covered with geotextile and enriched topsoil or compost

Fig. 18.6 Various coverings for the membrane or insulation layer have been developed over the course of the twentieth century but the mastic asphalt layer on the Derry and Toms' building is still in very good condition after 70 years.

The roof garden does buffer the roof membrane against any extremes of climate and so must extend its life. A good example of this effect is Derry and Toms' roof garden (Fig. 18.6), where the mastic asphalt layer is in almost perfect condition after 70 years. The buffering effect of a garden can also reduce the need for certain structural elements, which in turn can produce a saving. For example, it has been claimed that the roof garden at the Willis Faber and Dumas building in Ipswich, England was cost neutral because its

presence enabled a single movement joint to be omitted.

As a general rule, plants only start into growth where the temperature of their root system rises over 10°C. Above this threshold growth rates accelerate as root zone temperatures rise. Preliminary readings would seem to indicate that it is common for the soil of a roof garden, built on a heated structure, to be at least 3°C warmer than a conventional landscape. The elevated temperature of the soil brings the plants into growth earlier in spring and sustains their growth in the autumn. In the case of unheated structures, such as multi storey car parks, the converse is true. In colder climates insulation is needed to reduce the speed at which, and the degree to which, the substrate cools. Fortunately the effect of frost on both the root system of plants and growing mediums would appear to be minimal.

18.4   Hard landscape elements

Low density porous concrete

If there is a need for an area of hard landscape to be placed over a drained layer then a bed of low fines 'Lytag' concrete (1 : 1 : 7) can be placed on top of a proprietary drainage layer (Fig. 18.7).

Pools

If there is a need to separate a water feature from planting then a wall can be formed in-situ which is connected directly to the roof slab (Fig. 18.8). All water features generate a positive water pressure permanently acting on the membrane and this will find the smallest flaw. As a result a supplementary membrane, to provide 'belt and braces' protection, is usually to be recommended. If an informal design is required then there is no need for apprehension as the perimeter wall can be hidden under soil and/or cobbles.

Planters

A soft informal edge to a planter can be formed by trapping a geotextile vertically between topsoil

Fig. 18.7 Jacobs Island, near Tower Bridge in London: stable paving can be formed in situ on a low fines 'Lytag' concrete bed. This lightweight bed allows water to flow freely and even retains some moisture. (Photo: Steve Scrivens)

and cobbles. This simple approach is very successful (Figs. 18.9; 18.10). Paving can be placed on top of slabs of extruded polystyrene and the adjacent voids filled with topsoil. Hollow preformed grc and stainless steel hollow box forms have been used to produce light weight kerbs. They use the weight of the substrate to hold them in place (Fig. 18.11). These offer a low weight solution to retaining soil.

Planters can be formed from materials such as brick and timber. The advantage of timber structures is that they can be placed on top of a flexible insulation layer. They can also be relocated easily if access to the membrane becomes necessary.

Having said this, extruded expanded polystyrene slabs are surprisingly strong, and it is possible to construct planters in-situ. Engineering bricks with a cement-sand mortar are probably the best materials to use. If soft facing bricks are to be used then tanking will be necessary to prevent water penetration. If a strong waterproof render is required then grc (glan reinforced cement) can be very useful as it has structural properties of its own. As a rule hard landscape elements are heavy and expensive to construct. If it is possible to design out the need for them then it is advantageous.

Hard paving can be laid on pads directly on a roof. Research has shown that concrete and brick paving can be successfully laid on a sand bed overlying extruded polystyrene boards. This layer will even support the weight of cars.

Timber

Bulks of timber can be used to construct planters. Thinner sections can be used to construct boardwalks and bridges. However, there is sometimes a concern about a potential fire risk. As a general rule timber that measures more than 100 mm by 100 mm is deemed not to prove a threat. Thinner sections can be a hazard. Intumescent fire protection coating can be applied but does not last well outside.

Artificial rocks

Roof gardens must be the classic location for the use of artificial boulders. They weigh a fraction of real boulders and if correctly handled can look more realistic than nature.

18.5   Proprietary systems

Many proprietary roof garden systems are available in Europe, most of them originating in Germany. These systems seek to minimise the weight and depth of the drainage layer by using open sheets of expanded polystyrene or convoluted moulded plastic forms. Some of the drainage systems are designed to retain a small amount of water, e.g. some convoluted plastic sheets can

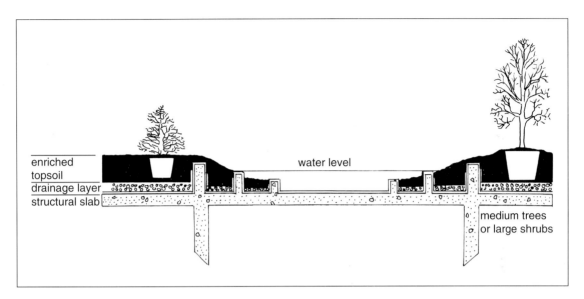

Fig. 18.8 Section through a 'natural' water course constructed on a roof. The taller upstand walls retain the water. The shorter upstand walls retain the soil that supports the aquatic plants. This detail was used at Jacobs Island, London.

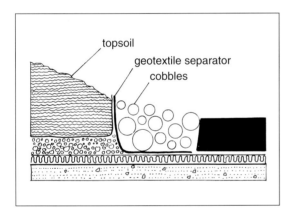

Fig. 18.9 A barrier formed by a black geotextile fabric trapped between cobbles and topsoil offers a very simple solution to forming a planter. This option was used at Jacobs Island, London.

contain up to one litre of water per square metre. This is the equivalent of two or three days' evapo-transpiration loss. The value of such small quantities of water is not clear but the manufacturers list this as a bonus for their systems. The scientific logic behind the design of some proprietary roof garden systems is not always apparent.

Almost all companies that provide proprietary waterproofing systems insist that their root barrier is used between the membrane and the garden. As a rule the root barriers tend to consist of a layer of thick roofing felt lightly bonded to the membrane itself or a sheet of very thick polythene. The point where root activity is at its maximum is around the outside of a planter and particularly in the corners. However no special techniques are available for protecting these weaknesses. The thick polythene systems usually rely on overlapping adjacent sheets by a metre or so to prevent roots getting under them. The problem of corners and up-stands is conveniently ignored.

18.6   The growing environment

When a plant is grown on a roof it requires no more or less from its environment than any other plant.

The aerial environment

Light has a major impact on plant growth and flowering. The potential arc of visible sky area will

Fig. 18.10 Jacobs Island, near Tower Bridge, shows what can be done with only 200 mm of water and 450 mm of topsoil. (Photo: Steve Scrivens)

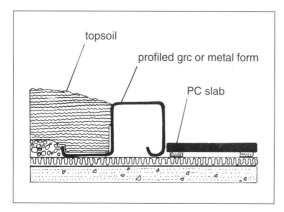

Fig. 18.11 An 'S' shaped metal or grc profile can be used to create a lightweight planter surround. The weight of the soil pressing down on the horizontal element holds the unit in place.

often be reduced by adjacent structures. The more southerly the orientation of a garden the higher will be the level of illumination. In most locations half the light which is received outside is indirect light scattered by clouds etc. As a general rule any plant used within 10 m of the base of an east- or north-facing wall should possess some shade tolerance. Many species benefit from the shelter at the base of buildings e.g. in shallow courtyards, although flower production may be reduced and foliage colour altered. However, if the adjacent building is more than three stories high and obstructs the sun for most of the day, there is a case for using hard landscape at the base of the building, as even the most shade tolerant plants may have difficulty growing satisfactorily.

The subterranean environment

Key aspects of this are described below; of these, lack of water is the primary limitation in most roof gardens.

Mechanical support

The extent of a root system is related to the volume of soil available for occupation, the irrigation regime and the ultimate size of the plant in question. Large volumes of soil are able to support large foliage canopies and vice-versa. If low groundcover is acceptable then the depth and volume of the substrate becomes much less important. Very shallow substrates are incapable of supporting tall plants against wind throw. A tree grown in 100 mm (4 inches) of soil would inevitably blow over. Heavy and regular pruning of more vigorous plants can however help overcome this danger.

If trees need guying, then it should only be for a few months while the roots grow out. In many cases it will not be necessary as most specimen plants are moved with large root balls. If semi-mature trees are well tended for three months their own root system should be more than sufficient to hold them upright. The traditional approach to guying was to provide bolt fixings to the roof and/or parapet. With careful detailing this approach can be made to work. Timber dead men can be used to anchor trees but are of questionable value in a thin profile. One approach which does work is to place sheets of aluminium between a half and one metre square in contact with the insulation layer or membrane protection layer underneath the garden. Galvanised steel hawsers can be threaded through holes drilled through the centre of these plates. The weight of the soil then offers anchorage.

When trees and shrubs are to be used whose nursery root balls are deeper than the general profile of the garden, it may be necessary to increase the soil depth in the immediate area.

With exposed sites there may be some apprehension about the stability of the substrate, especially where very sandy or peaty, and subject to wind erosion on drying. It is possible to stabilise a substrate by placing a layer of fine woven polypropylene mesh on the surface, although it is necessary to anchor it at regular intervals. However, the movement of substrates by both wind and rain is usually less than might be expected. The rapid development of ground cover gives a useful defence against erosion.

Nutrients

Almost all natural topsoils contain clay particles, which absorb nutrients onto their surface. The organic components of a substrate are also very good at absorbing nutrients, but clay particles have the advantage that they will absorb potassium ions that the organic component will not. A good substrate must have the capacity to retain nutrients and to release them slowly as required. The ability of a substrate to donate certain nutrients can be quantified in terms of its cation exchange capacity (CEC). Clays generally have high CECs but some materials such as peat and vermiculite can have even higher values. Where substrates have low CEC it is possible to use slow release and controlled release fertilisers to provide nutrients to plants over a long period.

Water

With a conventional soil the irregularly-shaped inorganic particles do not fit closely together and so give rise to voids in which water is held against drainage. The organic materials used in substrates have a natural sponginess that ensures the presence of pores which contain air and/or water. A film of water is attached to the constituents of the substrate by molecular attraction and as this is lost it is replaced by air. As a saturated substrate drains, the film of water around each particle is reduced in thickness and the attraction between the remaining water and the substrate is increased. Ultimately an equilibrium is reached where the water ceases to move, and the substrate is then said to be at 'field capacity', i.e. retaining its maximum amount of water. Even at field capacity a good substrate should still contain at least 15 per cent of its volume as air. A plant which is growing in a substrate at field capacity can absorb water with little effort but as the water content falls water uptake becomes more difficult. Eventually a point is reached where the attraction of the substrate becomes so great that uptake ceases, with the result that the foliage wilts. The point at which this occurs is called the 'permanent wilting point'.

It follows that between field capacity and permanent wilting point there is water that the plant can abstract. The actual amount of water available depends upon the composition of the substrate and is very variable. Sand contains a smaller volume of water than clay; it is more readily available but quickly exhausted. A similar situation exists with organic materials, which usually have a high moisture retention capability. The fastest growth is achieved with an open substrate provided that the water content is frequently restored.

To maintain optimum growth rates all roots require a continuous supply of oxygen for respiration. Much of the gaseous exchange with the soil occurs by simple diffusion. As the substrate drains, fresh air is drawn into the medium and quickly saturated with water vapour.

18.7   Soil and substrate

The depth of substrate that can be placed on a roof owes more to the load bearing capabilities of the structure than any horticultural considerations. As a rule the rooting medium on a green roof will be less than 150 mm thick. In a conventional garden the overall profile can be as little as 300 mm deep, although 450 mm is to be preferred and up to 1000 mm of topsoil can be used. In reality the maximum depth of the substrate is determined by the size of the rootballs of the plants which are to be used; if they are (for example) 300 mm deep, then with a minimum of 50 mm of soil beneath them and with an allowance for levelling, a 400 mm profile becomes the minimum. It is possible to mound the soil around each specimen plant, but the overall effect can look incongruous, though after a year of plant growth the underlying profile should be lost from view.

The traditional substrate for roof gardens has always been improved topsoil. Materials used to 'improve' the topsoil include expanded polystyrene, 'Leca', grit, perlite, and bark, but most commonly peat. All tend to produce a more open texture with improved drainage properties. Incorporating organic material encourages water retention and facilitates root growth because it allows roots to penetrate freely through the material. Newer materials such as coir are available and there are many different types of peat, but for high quality projects there is still no alternative to coarse sphagnum peat. The younger, coarser grades are more appropriate as they last much longer than the more normal grades. The peat should not be screened as this destroys its structure. However, organic materials such as peat and bark degrade. Peat oxidises at a rate of 15 to 20 per cent per annum. Coarse bark is less susceptible to degradation but will still 'vanish' at a rate of 10 per cent per annum.

In some cases standard nursery potting composts based on a mixture of peat and sand, and peat have been used. Unfortunately much of the peat oxidises out from these mixes within ten years and leaves the plants to grow in sand.

A wide range of soil types have been used for roof gardens. Silty clays have often been used without any major problems other than they are a little 'heavy' and easily compacted when wet. In many cases considerable effort has gone into 'improving' topsoil to resemble John Innes' potting compost. Unfortunately some of these mixes compact very badly following settlement, often due to mixing, spreading or trafficking when wet.

Much of what passes for topsoil in landscape practice today has been reclaimed from construction waste or even manufactured from subsoil and animal waste. Sourcing a good quality topsoil can be a long, expensive process but cannot be skimped. Even real topsoil is often screened to remove stones and grass, but this destroys the natural structure of the soil and should be avoided. Only natural sandy loam topsoil should be used.

In some cases there is no choice but to ameliorate a soil before it is brought to site. An effective formula is described below, but needs to be adjusted to suit the materials that are available. These percentages are by volume. Caution needs to be exercised with peat as the industry assumes that the peat is fluffed up and full of air. This is irrelevant when the peat is squashed by the loam fraction:

- high quality sandy loam topsoil – 60 to 70 per cent
- coarse sphagnum peat – 20 per cent
- composted horticultural bark – 5 to 20 per cent
- nutrients.

Bulk substrate materials – organic

Peat

There are many sources of peat in Northern Europe and North America but unfortunately there is no standardised international method of classification available, although for horticultural purposes the following are accepted.

Sphagnum

Sphagnum moss peats come from peat bogs and should consist of at least 75 per cent of partially decomposed sphagnum moss. The leaves of the moss usually consist of a single layer of cells which give them a high rate of water absorption and retention. The general characteristics of sphagnum peat are:

- spongy fibrous texture,
- a high porosity with high water retention,
- a low inorganic content and usually
- a low pH.

Commercially developed peat deposits occur naturally in Germany, Finland, Canada and Ireland and have similar properties to the hypnaceous moss peats of the USA.

Sedge

These peats are formed mainly from sedges and reeds during the silting up of shallow lakes. As a result they will typically hold more nutrients than sphagnum peats, have a higher CEC per unit weight, and be more humidified and decomposed. They have a lower porosity than sphagnum moss peats, a less durable structure and are particularly difficult to re-wet although these problems can be overcome by careful management.

Shredded bark

Bark has the advantage that its rate of decomposition is about one third that of peat. However, in certain cases it can suffer from nitrogen deficiency and generate toxic compounds, although these problems usually moderate after the first six months. To avoid problems of toxicity from compounds arising from natural resins and turpenes, only those barks that are specifically marketed for substrates should be used. Most of the bark used in Britain comes from larch and pine, while in North America Douglas, red and white fir are common sources. The best barks have a loose open structure that provides good drainage, although in extreme cases this can reduce the volume of water available to the plants. For this reason bark should not be used as the main bulk constituent of a substrate.

When well-decomposed, barks have a high CEC which can exceed that of peat. Before bark can be used as a growth medium it requires composting with additions of nitrogenous fertiliser and super phosphate for about three months. Most hardwood barks are acid, with pH values of 3.5 to 6.5. This can rise quite rapidly due to the high level of calcium which they contain naturally, although this is not always the case with softwoods.

Paper can be composted in the same way as bark and used to open up a substrate. Its properties are very variable and it should not form more than 10 per cent of the total volume of a substrate.

Soil separators

It is usual to separate the growing medium from the drainage layer by the use of a geotextile membrane. At the Scottish Widows building a separation layer of hessian sacking was used between the topsoil and a thick 'Lytag' layer which was placed so as to add a third dimension to the garden. This decomposed gently so that the stability of the substrate was maintained. Ten years after it was installed no mixing had occurred. It seems that the role of a geotextile is to keep the drainage layer clean when the soil is being placed rather than during its operational life.

Before the development of geotextile fabrics, filter layers were formed from a glassfibre mat up to 50 mm thick. This was compressed by the weight of the growing medium to a layer only 5 mm thick. Such mats are easily torn and must have caused problems during construction. It was also common practice to cover the fibreglass with a 50 mm thick layer of peat. Many properties have been attributed to this layer, including improved filtering and the storage of moisture. There does appear to be increased root activity in this zone; however, when this layer is compressed by the overlaying substrate and oxidised for a few years it soon becomes reduced to a few millimetres in thickness. One reason for this layer may have been a desire to protect the glassfibre mat during construction. With the introduction of polypropylene and polyethylene geotextiles this problem was eliminated.

The latest geotextiles are ideal filter layers because they combine considerable strength with efficient filtering. However, most of them are designed for civil engineering work and tend to be hydrophobic. This has the effect of holding water in the substrate as well as obstructing the upward movement of water with subterranean irrigation systems. A fully synthetic hydroscopic geotextile such as Trevira Spunband by Hoechst AG or Polyfelt by Polyfelt Geosynthetics (UK) Limited is to be recommended.

18.8   Plant selection

No group of plants can be said to be unsuitable for use in a roof garden. Large forest trees may be impracticable because of problems with anchorage, but other than that almost any plant that is used in general landscape is capable of prospering. However, before selecting plants it is important to consider how they will tolerate the environment that exists on the roof. These factors include:

- *exposure*

  The danger of exposure is often exaggerated and plants on roof gardens rarely show evidence of wind pruning. However, it is prudent to avoid tall herbaceous plants subject to stem breakage and those which produce fragile flowers if the garden is exposed.

- *drought tolerance*

  The need to tolerate drought needs to be balanced with the presence or absence of an irrigation system, and the volume of substrate. If a typical range of decorative plants are required, the need for an irrigation system cannot be overemphasized. It is possible to produce a fairly basic drought-resistant landscape that will survive without irrigation, but this may be somewhat unsightly during periods of moisture stress and at odds with urban landscape design. Most plants, and particularly those trees and shrubs which are commonly used in urban landscapes, cannot survive prolonged periods of drought. Among the plants that are better able to tolerate drought, the following are robust and reliable: *Juniperus* spp., *Cotoneaster* spp., *Pinus mugo* and *Hedera* spp.

  If there is no irrigation system then the plants must possess durable perennating organs or the ability to withstand total desiccation, e.g. *Sedum* and some grasses. Current research at the University of Sheffield (Nolan, 2001) is adapting the rather spartan planting of continental European green roofs to the lower evaporation and higher rainfall climates of northern Britain. One of the most commonly used elements in any landscape is turf-grass. Turf-grass has a high maintenance requirement and the fine leaved grasses are subject to many problems including fungal attack, drought damage, and intolerance to low light levels. Even a relatively brief period of drought will defoliate and in some cases kill the finer grasses in a lawn.

- *stability*

  When selecting plants it is important to try and select plants whose root systems would naturally suit the rooting environment. For example, Birch (*Betula pendula*) and Scrub Pine (*Pinus nigra*) naturally have shallow root systems.

The selection of plants for roof gardens is surrounded by myths, and some plants are thought unsuitable because they are believed to have 'tap roots'. Some plants do have tap roots when they are small, but it is doubtful whether they have any effect after the first year. The modern nursery practice of undercutting young trees encourages the formation of a fibrous root system, and recent studies (for example, see summary in Harris *et al.*, 1999) show conclusively that even in large trees, most root development is horizontal, and relatively close to the soil surface.

Depth of rooting is determined by soil penetrative resistance and soil oxygen thresholds. On clay-based soils there is rarely sufficient oxygen to support roots below 900 mm, so most roots are restricted to these depths. Roots are most numerous in the top 450 mm of profiles. Root systems are discussed in greater detail in Chapter 9.

* *planting density*

  During the 1980s research work was carried out at the University of Bath on the optimum planting density for a number of ground cover plants. One unexpected result of these studies was that during periods of severe drought, the plants which were closest together died long before the plants that were well spread out. This was due to competition between the plants for water. Although the foliage might have looked uniform, the surface area of the more closely planted shrubs was three times that of the least. Extremely high planting densities are liable to lead to greater stress or even death in severe drought conditions. Plant spacings should be increased where such conditions are likely to prevail (see Chapter 14).

18.9 Water

Water is necessary not just to keep a plant alive, but to allow active growth to take place. A shortage of water reduces the efficiency of the photosynthetic machinery significantly, leading to reduced carbohydrate production and reduced growth.

In addition to this latter form of stunting, if water is not readily available during growth periods, cells do not expand to their full size. If a plant is to achieve its full growth potential its roots system needs to be surrounded by soil which is at field capacity or with a maximum soil moisture deficit of 25 mm. In other words it is only necessary to apply a maximum of 25 mm (one inch) of water for the soil to be fully saturated.

When water stress is eliminated, many trees and shrubs will grow over one metre per year. This means ground cover will be achieved in the second year and maturity in the third year. Where the client requires vigorously-growing, luxuriant planting, a comprehensive irrigation system is necessary. If the client will tolerate woody plants, or herbaceous plants that will be stressed and potentially unattractive for part of the summer months, then irrigation may not be essential. If an area of landscape is to dry out several times a year, then only plants that can survive acute desiccation will be possible.

Having an irrigation system does not mean that it is necessary to maintain all plants at field capacity. In many cases the more drought tolerant components can be exposed to moderate moisture stress without showing any obviously adverse symptoms. Plants grown at field capacity may require excessive levels of maintenance to manage their growth. However managing the irrigation system in this way does require informed judgement, which may or may not be available.

18.10 Water availability

The amount of available water contained in a substrate varies with its composition. It varies from 50 mm in 300 mm for a sandy soil to in excess of 100 mm in 300 mm for a clay soil or one which has a high organic matter content. Organic ameliorated loams suitable for roof garden plantings fall into the 'high availability' range, with a figure of 65 mm per 300 mm depth. As the rate of water loss from a landscape is often in excess of 25 mm per week this means that irrigation is required every two weeks. Frequent, shallow irrigation encourages surface rooting.

It is possible to do theoretical calculations on the rate of water loss, but the best way to judge the irrigation requirement of a garden is to watch the drains. If water is just draining away for one or two days a week in dry weather then the soil is probably close to its optimum. As it is only possible to 'flood' a soil to make water pass down through its profile it is best to apply the water in relatively large volumes at well spaced intervals, e.g. 25 mm per week. It is necessary to add 25–50 mm in a single application. This will be a considerable volume of water on a large scheme and so it maybe advisable to subdivide the irrigation system into zones which are triggered on different days.

Water is lost from an area of landscape by one of three processes:

- drainage to waste,
- evaporation from the substrate,
- transpiration by plants.

Water can enter soil from above or below. Entry from below is often referred to (incorrectly) as a capillary process; it occurs when surface tension lifts water around and through the various substrate components. Entry from above is governed by the rate of infiltration. Should water be applied faster than this rate, then run-off will occur. When water is applied to the surface of a substrate it must bring each successive layer to saturation before further downward movement can take place, i.e. gravity tries to draw the water downwards, while the surface tension of the constituent parts attracts it to themselves. The lower (drier) layers may still exert suction on the upper layers but further downward movement cannot occur if there is no free water available.

It is impossible to moisten a soil 'lightly'. The typical water spread associated with cultivated soils is shown in Fig. 18.12. The onion shaped spread indicated in the diagram is characteristic of all substrates. In most loam soils the maximum useable width is 1.2 m, whilst in heavy soils the water spreads in a circle 2.0 m in diameter but with

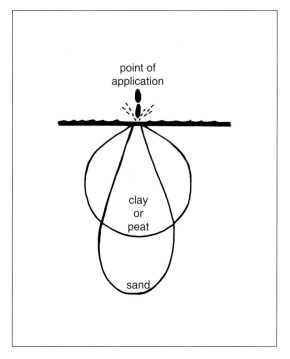

Fig. 18.12 The pattern of water spread through different soils.

a reduced depth of penetration. In a sandy soil, the maximum lateral spread of water is reduced to 0.90 to 1.20 m while the penetration depth is considerably increased. In a planter where the substrate depth is not great the water spread will be as indicated in Fig. 18.13. The lowest portion of the water penetration spreads to form a moist layer on the base of the planter. From this layer water is lifted by surface tension to a height of only 200 mm.

Water loss from total vegetation cover is very close to that of an open water surface. The basic principle is modified slightly with the seasons. The theoretical rate of water loss is approximately 80 per cent of an open water surface in the months of June, July and August, 60 per cent in spring and autumn and 40 per cent in winter. The evaporation loss from wet soil is slightly higher than that of an open water surface. This is due to the irregularity of the surface, which increases the evapora-

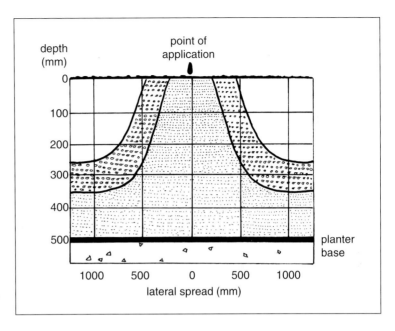

Fig. 18.13 The pattern of water spread in a planter.

tive area. It is also due to the soil warming more rapidly than a body of water. The water loss from the surface of the soil extends to a depth of approximately 300 mm. Below this the only way that water can escape is if it is removed by plants. This is important because in most roof gardens the depth of the substrate is seldom much more than 300 mm.

In the UK the rate of evapo-transpiration is commonly far in excess of precipitation for several months each year. As a result it is necessary to make an allowance for evaporative losses when designing a roof garden, and to have some awareness of what levels of precipitation are normal in the area. Tables and maps of moisture deficits are available to assist farmers, for example Smith (1984), but these have to be treated with caution as they relate to the open country and not the dry turbulent air of cities.

The layering effect of multiple canopies further complicates matters. In fact treble the theoretical rate for evapo-transpiration can be appropriate, particularly where trees grow out of a shrub bed. In other words on an exposed roof there can be a double canopy situation where full ground cover is achieved by shrubs but another dominant canopy exists in the form of trees. The figures also need to be increased when the canopy extends beyond the edge of a planter (e.g. with climbers a large foliar canopy can be drawing water from a very small planter). Preliminary models that assist making decisions on irrigation frequency in relation to soil volume have been developed (for example, Hitchmough, 1992).

18.11 Flooded drainage layer irrigation

This system (Fig. 18.14) reduces the irrigation requirements by retaining rainwater over the body of the roof. A layer of water up to 100 mm deep can be retained, although when the aggregates are discounted the actual water layer is seldom more than 40 mm thick. This would not last for more than two weeks, except for the fact that the bulk of the profile will have dried out to provide a barrier to further water loss. In other words the system automatically puts the plants under increasing stress and cuts down the rate of evaporation from the surface. The extra weight of the water has to be carried by the structure but it can provide the plants' water requirements for at least

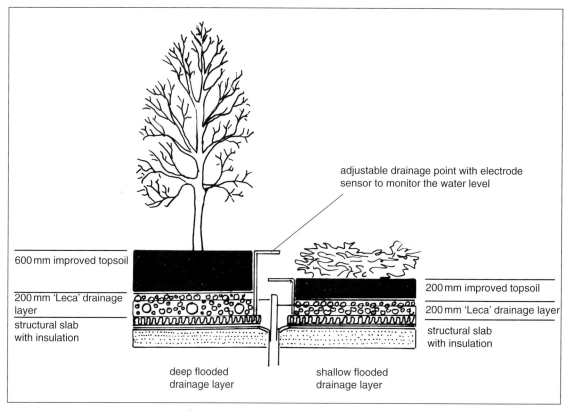

Fig. 18.14 Typical sections through a flooded drainage layer roof garden.

six weeks in a dry summer without the need for irrigation.

The principle behind a subterranean irrigation system is that the standing water in the drainage layer passes round the surface of the 'Leca' granules and into the soil separator. From here surface tension lifts it up through the soil, helped by the saturated vapour that permeates the voids between the 'Leca' granules. As the distance between the substrate and the standing water increases, so the resistance within the system increases until a point is reached where the surface tension exerted by the substrate is insufficient to raise the water any further.

The capillary lift is dependent upon a number of factors, and in particular the composition of the substrate, but the most powerful regulating factors are the characteristics of the drainage layer and the size of the aggregate. The ideal separation distance between the water and the soil separating membrane is 20 mm. However, this distance can be increased to 75 mm and still leave an adequate layer of moist earth to sustain plant growth in a dry summer. This would therefore be a good starting point for designing a system, although careful adjustment will always be necessary on site because of the specific characteristics of the materials employed.

Traditionally the water level in the drainage layer was regulated by a ball cock fitted with a large flat float to make its operation more precise than is normally the case. Such mechanical equipment has been rendered obsolete by electronic water level controls. An electrode sensor consists of either two or three adjustable stainless steel rods connected to an electronic circuit that activates a solenoid valve. A three-probe sensor gives both an upper and a lower level control and is to be preferred. The longest probe acts as a return for the current. When the water level falls below the bottom of the middle probe, the circuit is switched on, the solenoid valve opens and the water flows. When the water level reaches the shortest probe the circuitry switches off and the solenoid valve closes.

The great appeal of such a system is that all the components, with the exception of the stainless steel rods, can be placed in a weatherproof housing some way from the probes or within the building. It also means that the inlet pipe can be at a considerable height above the water in the drainage layer, avoiding any danger of back siphoning. The other advantage of a solenoid valve is that it will operate at almost any water pressure.

With a flooded drainage layer there must be an adequate overflow system to cope with the natural precipitation. This can only be achieved by having a drainage point with an adjustable weir. The weir needs to be relatively watertight and therefore usually relies upon a neoprene 'O' ring seal around a short length of pipe which slides up and down inside the gulley. Such an adjustable riser needs to be lifted upwards in summer and lowered in winter.

18.12 Water delivery methods

Water can be delivered to planted areas in three basic ways:

- At ground level (drip emitters)
- Above ground (sprinkler systems)
- Below ground (flooded drainage layer).

The choice of which system to use will depend upon the nature of the planting, the availability of water and the topography of the area. Drip irrigation systems are useful but can suffer from abuse or neglect. Sprinkler systems have the advantage that the application of water can be monitored visually. If a lawn is required then there is no real alternative to sprinklers, but they need to work forever. Underground capillary systems, such as

are used under golf tees, do work but are expensive, fragile and not relevant to this discussion. The specific details of the different systems are described below.

At ground level

There are two main types:

- Drip emitters – these are small plastic units that fit onto a small plastic pipe and 'weep' water gently into the soil. The more modern types are hidden within the pipe itself.
- Perforated tubes – these are thin walled plastic tubes that have a row of perforations along their length from which water can 'weep'. They have some of the properties of drip emitters but can suffer from blockages and have limited pressure-compensating properties.

Drip emitters

The major advantage of drip emitters is that they are economical with water. Outlets can be placed next to the individual plants and 100 per cent of the water can be absorbed. Also the delivery of water is much slower than with sprinklers, so that drip emitters can be used on sloping sites without the risk of erosion. The disadvantage of drip emitters is that they are not suitable for lawns as they produce stripes. In their earliest forms drip systems were no more than perforated pipes. These were later enhanced by the use of pressure-compensating nozzles that allowed a constant flow of water irrespective of pressure. This was useful because it meant that irrigation systems could be run across surfaces at different levels.

The problem with drip irrigation systems is that they are designed for commercial use, where they are not expected to last for more than a year or two. Most of the components are built cheaply in low-grade materials. Unfortunately in the landscape world there is little interest in ongoing maintenance, and so most drip systems are rendered ineffective within a few years. On a well-managed site the whole system will need to be replaced every few years.

Perforated tube

With emitters the water is discharged at given points, but in certain cases it may be preferable to produce bands of irrigated substrate. A perforated tube system permits a greater area to be wetted than with emitters and so is useful with ground cover. There are many types of perforated tube systems available but most are made of high quality black ultra-violet resistant polyethylene between 0.25 mm and 0.50 mm thick. The simplest consist of a folded strip of polyethylene, stitched along its length. More precise systems use an accurately perforated tube but the most advanced systems consist of two fused tubes: the larger carries the main flow which is bled into the smaller tube and discharged from there. This more complex structure reduces the effect of pressure loss along the length of tubing, which can be significant at the normal low operating pressures of 0.3 to 1.0 kg/cm^2.

A wide range of perforation frequencies are available to give different discharge rates, but for most roof planting situations the perforations should be 0.5 mm in diameter at 100 mm intervals. Due to the small apertures the water supply should be passed through a filter with a mesh size which is no greater than 100 microns. Despite their flexible construction, perforated tubes can be hidden below ground at depths of between 50 mm and 100 mm.

Above ground

Sprinklers

Their major advantage is that, for lawns and areas of low planting (i.e. less than 600 mm to 700 mm), a very even distribution of water is possible with relatively few outlets. Disadvantages include:

- sprinklers are not economical with water. As little as 60 to 70 per cent of the water sprayed may eventually be absorbed and the rest can be lost due to evaporation
- constant use of sprinklers can compact the soil
- they will cause erosion problems on sloping sites

- they can be obstructed by bushes and solid planting areas (trees are not a problem as the canopy tends to be above the sprinkler arc)
- sprinklers may be a nuisance to people trying to use the garden while they are in operation.

A *sprinkler* is any unit that emits a definite jet or number of jets and rotates to achieve full coverage. The selection of a sprinkler head will depend upon the size and shape of the area to be watered and should take into account any possible obstruction, the amount of water available and its pressure, the soil type, and any specific plant requirements.

A *spray head* is a fixed position unit that emits a stream of water through a fixed arc. The application rate of a spray head is usually very high, i.e. 25 to 50 mm/h. However, it covers a relatively small area, ie from 3 to 7 m radius, and operates well at low pressures (10 to 20 m head). Models are available which can water in full circles as well as 90, 120, 180, and 270 degree, circular and square patterns. This range of capabilities permits the selection of a system to suit a given area.

The 'throw' of some spray heads can be varied by an adjustment screw, to compensate for pressure variations throughout the circuit. However, if such adjustable units are to be employed the system should be designed assuming a throw of only 60 per cent of the potential maximum. The surface type of spray head can be permanently mounted flush with the ground, and used for small areas of lawn, flower borders and planters. The fixed elevation shrub spray head is used in the main for flower and shrub borders and open ground plantings. Both these types are available with a low-angle watering pattern that can be very useful on windy sites, or for situations where it is beneficial to water under the canopy.

On no account should sprinkler and spray heads be mixed on the same circuit because their widely varying application rates will lead to some areas being over-watered while others will be under-watered. Even with the same type of sprinklers or spray heads on a single circuit, it is important to remember that part circle models will discharge less than full circle heads in a given time period.

Pop-up heads

Pop-up spray heads are used predominantly in areas of turf and are installed flush with the ground. When the water is turned on, the heads rise above the ground to prevent the grass from interfering with their operation. When the water is turned off, the pressure within the circuit falls and the heads retract. These pop-up spray heads are ideal for lawn areas but care needs to be taken with their installation otherwise they can be damaged during mowing operations. Ideally the mounting should be set a few millimetres into the ground.

The installation of surface or pop-up spray heads is relatively simple. A connection is made to the supply pipe by the use of either a T-junction or a pipe saddle; to this is connected a short length of flexible pipe. The top flange of the head assembly must be flush with the ground. This operation is greatly assisted by the use of a length of flexible pipe immediately below the nozzle.

Impact heads

An impact sprinkler is a unit producing a jet of water that is broken up mechanically to achieve a greater coverage over a wide area. These have a relatively low rate of application of 5 to 12 mm/h. They operate at a pressure of 20 to 55 m head and usually have a throw of 12 to 25 m. Such sprinklers are available in full or part circle models. The part circle models are adjustable to give a cover of any segment up to 360 degrees.

Sprinklers of this type are available in a pop-up form and so are ideal for irrigating large areas. Unfortunately the size of the head itself means that the pop-up assembly is large and not as discreet as the spray type. Because of their size impact head sprinklers are sometimes mounted on a permanent risor. Some are produced with a lance that can be connected to a quick coupling ball valve for individual point operation.

On established turf, where settlement of the soil medium is complete, pop-up sprinklers may be installed with the top of the housing flush with the ground surface. In this case a direct connection between the supply pipe and sprinklers can be made with a riser of the correct length. Where further settlement is likely, flexible pipework should be used: the heads may need to be raised or lowered at some future date to compensate for changes in surface levels. To allow the assembly housing to drain, and so prevent corrosion, a small amount of pea gravel should be placed under each unit.

Where sprinklers are installed on a a sloping site a stopmatic valve can be fitted underneath the sprinklers to prevent head drainage, ie to prevent water from draining out of the lower sprinkler so creating a puddle or wet area around the head. Stopmatic valves will hold back from 15 to 25 psi of water pressure and eliminate this problem.

Small spray emitters

A range of nozzles are available that produce fan shapes or circular coverage. The nozzles are usually fixed directly onto the pipe but for aesthetic reasons, or to achieve extra throw, the nozzles can be elevated from the supply line on a 5 mm polyethylene riser. These emitters will deliver at a rate proportional to the water pressure, and so each line needs to be horizontal. The advantage of these emitters is that a low-level spray can be directed under the foliage to cover an area on each side of the supply line. They provide an economical and convenient compromise between a drip system and overhead sprinklers by producing a reasonably large wetted area from a spray.

18.13 Irrigation control

As the water passes through the air so it evaporates, with the result that much of it never actually arrives at its target. The vegetation that it strikes traps some of it and in turn this evaporates very rapidly during the daytime. When well sprinkled a large bush will hold many litres of water on its foliage. The cooler the air, and the cooler the surface upon which the water lands, the lower the rate of loss. The most efficient time at which to apply water is the early morning when wind speeds are low and the foliage has time to dry before the full force of the sun acts upon it. Most landscape plants are very durable and so leaf scorch is not often a problem.

An advantage to applying water at night is that because the evaporation rate is lower, there is less of a tendency for salts to be deposited on the foliage.

All irrigation systems require a control input to activate them. This can be supplied in a number of ways.

Manual

The operation requires human input to initiate it, from personal observation or readings taken from instruments such as tensiometers. Regular inspection is required to determine the moisture level in a substrate, and this does represent a considerable ongoing maintenance input.

Time clock

If the environment is reasonably uniform the human element can be standardised into a timed operation, although adequate drainage is important. The best way to calibrate a system is to catch the water in a number of buckets and measure how long it takes to apply the desired volume of water. Monitoring the drains shows the moment at which the ground becomes saturated. This information can then be used to set the time clock.

Automatic

With existing technology this can be an effective solution to the problem of irrigation control but needs good technical support, which is unusual with most landscape projects. There is still much resistance to fully automatic irrigation controls although their value is proven.

The easiest way of monitoring an irrigation system is to inspect the drains. If they dribble for one or two days a week then the moisture content of the soil is probably correct. The problem of determining the moisture level in a substrate can be overcome by regular inspection, and for the first few months after installation digging into the substrate can also be a useful guide.

18.14   Problems with roof gardens

Membranes

Membrane penetrations

One problem with all membranes is to find a way of penetrating them without the risk of a leak. Penetrating through the top of an upstand can help to avoid a problem. At no time should bolts pass straight through a membrane; a two-step approach should always be adopted. A heavy steel plate should be bolted to the structure. The membrane should then be fixed to the plate with a sealing ring and an adhesive layer so that there is no possibility of a leak. The object to be anchored can then be bolted to studs that are fully welded to the steel plate so that water cannot track along the threads.

Membrane testing

All membranes should be tested before they are covered. Electronic testing is now replacing flood testing. This involves passing a tiny electric current over the upper surface of the membrane to see if it can escape to earth through the underlying structure. This approach is so sensitive that tiny penetrations can be identified. If a roof is to be flood tested, then a 72 h test is to be recommended: finding a leak after the garden has been finished is very difficult.

Root barriers

The membrane under a roof garden has traditionally been protected by a sand cement screed. These have sometimes caused problems with lime leaching out and being precipitated in the drainage gullys. Precast concrete paving slabs were also widely used. GRC tiles have been used to provide a light-weight solution. More recently extruded polystyrene sheets with a grc coating on one side have been tried. In the last thirty years upside-

Fig. 18.15 Tennis courts on a casino roof, Atlantic City, New Jersey, USA. (Photo: Steve Scrivens)

down roof insulation has become popular. It takes a great deal of force to drive a garden fork through a sheet of extruded expanded polystyrene; this fact is usually taken as a good reason to omit the traditional protection layer.

Companies providing proprietary waterproofing systems insist that their root barrier should be used between the membrane and the garden. These systems rarely deal satisfactorily with the corners of planters, where root penetration is most likely to occur.

Safety

Handrails

As a rule handrails are placed around the outside of a roof (Fig. 18.15). Fixing handrails to the structural edge of a building is relatively straightforward, but unfortunately it makes them very obvious. The visual impact of the handrails can be minimised by using stainless steel hawsers. Another successful alternative is to place the handrails away from the edge. This may present some interesting detailing problems with the waterproofing, but it allows the planting to run continuously to the edge of the building. The only disadvantage is that maintenance personnel must wear safety harnesses if they are to work outside the barriers.

Objects falling from a roof

Children who drop objects from roof gardens can be a problem. Some roof gardens have had to be closed because of such behaviour. If children are to remain unsupervised on an elevated roof garden there may well be a good case for erecting a high close-mesh fence around the outside. If ball games are contemplated then a totally enclosing cage is essential (Fig. 18.15). There can also be problems with debris, such as cans, rolling off the edge of a roof, so there is a need for some form of upstand wherever paving abuts a roof edge.

Vertigo

Vertigo is a problem that affects many people. A broad perimeter planting or heavy balustrade will help to reassure those who suffer from vertigo.

18.15 Summary

Many plant users find roof gardens intimidating because they are seemingly divorced from ground level soil profiles. Designers and managers need to have a greater technical understanding of plant growth and associated support systems such as drainage and irrigation, and in particular an understanding of water movement in soil media, but with this level of knowledge and attention to detail successful roof gardens are perfectly feasible.

References

Harris, R.W., Clark, J.M., & Matheny, N.P. (1999) *Arboriculture: Integrated management of landscape trees, shrubs and vines*, 3rd edn. Prentice-Hall, Englewood Cliffs, New Jersey.

Hitchmough, J.D. (1992) Calculating the earth. Technical Section No. 4, *Landscape Design*, 213, 42–4.

Nolan, A. (2001) Plant choices for extensive green roofs in the UK. Unpublished MA Dissertation, Department of Landscape, University of Sheffield.

Smith, L.P. (1984) *The Agricultural Climate of England and Wales*, MAFF, HMSO, London.

Website

www.landscapetechnology.co.uk

V Establishment and Management of Herbaceous Plants

19 Wildflowers in Rural Landscapes

Neil Bayfield

Wildflowers are freely-flowering herbaceous species *(forbs)* which are typically selected to add colour or texture to sites of high landscape value at visibly prominent locations, such as road intersections, bridges and recreation sites. There is a fine line between wildflowers and weeds, which may also be colourful, but have undesirable properties: for example ragwort (*Senecio jacobaea*) is poisonous to stock, thistles or willowherbs (*Epilobium/Chamaenerion* spp.) are invasive.

Wildflower swards are not only visually attractive but they help newly-constructed sites to blend with the surrounding landscape and provide islands and corridors of nature conservation value. This chapter looks at seeding and planting using native species, as recommended by most nature conservation agencies and local authorities for rural locations.

In creating wildflower swards, careful attention must be paid to:

- site characteristics (Fig. 19.1)
- selection of appropriate mixtures and methods of establishment
- ground preparation and
- subsequent management.

Establishing wildflowers from seed may take two or more years, and there will be a need for ongoing maintenance; these factors should be considered when preparing specifications.

19.1 Where to sow wildflowers

The public image of wildflower swards is probably of meadows full of flowers with luxuriant growth and rich soils. In fact highly fertile soils are generally unsuitable for wildflowers because they result in a dense growth of grasses which compete with other species. Unlike grasses, most sown wildflowers (other than annuals) take more than a season to reach flowering, and some have slow or delayed germination, so are slow to establish. Consequently, suitable soils should generally be of low or moderate fertility, and sown companion grasses should be short growing and not aggressive, so that a fairly open turf is produced, with space for young wildflower plants to colonise.

In arable countryside, subsoil may be preferable to topsoil because it is less fertile, and should contain fewer weed seeds. However, situations where topsoil is likely to be suitable include:

- sites where there was previously an existing wildflower community (such as semi-natural parkland on chalk or limestone soils);
- infertile upland or heathland soils;
- sites of high nature conservation status.

Any application of fertiliser should take account of soil fertility status; often it may not be needed at all.

Wildflower mixtures are relatively expensive compared with amenity grass seeding, and will need careful management, particularly in the early stages. They should therefore be restricted to locations where the likelihood of success is high, where they blend in with the landscape and where they enhance the environment by making it more attractive to users or by providing habitats for wildlife (Table 19.1). Wildflower mixtures are particularly appropriate where the countryside

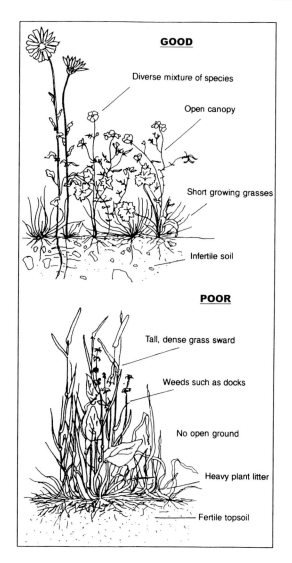

GOOD

Diverse mixture of species

Open canopy

Short growing grasses

Infertile soil

POOR

Tall, dense grass sward

Weeds such as docks

No open ground

Heavy plant litter

Fertile topsoil

Fig. 19.1 Characteristics of good and poor wild-flower swards.

Fig. 19.2 Surviving fragments of regional wild-flower meadows are often found on roadsides – as with this community of *Geranium pratense*, *Filipendula ulmaria* and *Cirsium heterophyllum*. Such fragments provide a guide to local meadow character and a potentially valuable source of local seed. (Photo: James Hitchmough)

still retains a colourful and varied vegetation, but they may sometimes look out of place in areas where the scenery consists of monocultures of crops or intensive grassland.

Places to consider include conspicuous banks, cuttings, and other earthworks (Fig.19.2). It is important to try to maintain the landscape character by using appropriate mixtures: for example, in a moorland setting highly coloured mixtures of lowland species could be out of place.

Wildflowers are generally not recommended on road verge fronts within 2.5 m of a major road (where salt spray and cutting could prevent establishment) and on areas that have to be mown frequently for safety or security, where taller species would rarely reach flowering stage. In such locations it may be feasible to sow short, cutting-resistant leguminous species such as clovers and birds foot trefoil.

19.2   Site investigation

The landscape, topography and any nature conservation interests are likely to influence a decision

Table 19.1 Advantages and disadvantages of wildflower swards compared to grass seeding.

Advantages	Disadvantages
• Wildflowers can usually be grown on subsoil: topsoil can be used for landscape work elsewhere. • Mixtures can be selected to suit the locality and the surrounding ground. • Along a road, only part of the route need be sown to create a strong visual effect. • Sown earthworks usually blend better with surrounding landscapes than uniform areas of grass. • Sowings demonstrate the willingness of the developers of a scheme to minimise environmental impacts. • Although more expensive than uniform grass, cost of wildflowers is minimal in terms of overall contract costs, particularly when planned from an early stage. • Increased biological diversity.	• Wildflower seed is relatively expensive. • Establishment is slower than with ordinary grass seed. • Cover and flowering in the first year may be poor. • Some wildflower swards need mowing annually or more often. • Selection of mixes is more complicated than for standard grass seed mixes for amenity use. • Flowers may be in bloom for only a small part of the year. • Need to match seed mix and short and long term maintenance to soil and environmental conditions.

to sow wildflowers, but additional site investigation will be needed before a detailed specification can be drawn up. Information on soil type and fertility, drainage and soil seed bank composition, data on previous vegetation or crop composition and past management are useful (Fig. 19.3). Soil fertility is probably the single most important factor influencing wildflower establishment. Ideally a soil should have just sufficient nutrients for the sown species to establish, without favouring nutrient-demanding grasses or weeds.

There is no simple way to gauge high or low fertility in relation to wildflowers. Help can often be obtained from information on previous land use, including any recent applications of nitrogenous fertiliser (N), and from soil nutrient analysis. Where a site has been recently managed for arable crops or leys receiving more than 200 kg/ha N, the topsoil is likely to be too fertile and should be stripped off and used for some other purpose such as tree or shrub planting. However, where soils are sandy or have only low clay content, then nutrient retention will be low, and despite previous fertiliser dressings it may still be suitable for wildflowers.

A standard agricultural soils analysis can be helpful. For example, ADAS has developed an index for extractable potassium (K) phosphorus (P) and magnesium (Mg) which ranges from low (0) to high (9), and this can be used as a guide to suitability for wildflowers.

Soils with an index of 0–3 (that is, 0–45, 0–400 and 0–100 ppm of P, K and Mg respectively) are likely to be suitable if N values are also low. As a rough guide, recently cultivated or fertilised ground is likely to be moderate to high in N, whereas ground that has been fallow for a few years will generally be low.

Total N values of less than 0.1 per cent of soil mass are considered low. However this figure can be deceptive for much of this N may be unavailable to plants. A value of 10 ppm or less of nitrate N indicates fairly low available nitrogen, but this value should also be viewed with caution since it can vary at different times of year and may rapidly decline due to leaching in wet weather. For these reasons, standard soil analyses do not include N values. It is possible that in future some simple bioassay tests might be available for assessing soil suitability but these are not yet sufficiently reliable or well tested for routine use.

Observation has shown that flower mixtures establish more easily and successfully on some soil types than on others. This provides another means

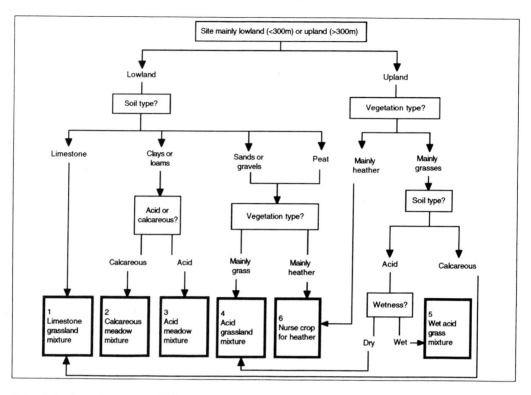

Fig. 19.3   Selection of grass or wildflower mixtures in relation to landscape type.

of identifying suitable ground, especially at sites with varying substrate types.

Most suitable:
  Chalk and limestone
  Calcareous clays
  Calcareous sands and marsh
  Acid clays
  Alluvium
  Poor sandy soils
  Upland peaty soils
  Lowland peaty soils

Least suitable:
  Coarse gravels
  Fen peats.

Gradient is relatively unimportant: where other factors are equal, growth is similar on flat or sloping ground. However very steep slopes are difficult to mow, and maintenance costs can be kept

down by sowing wildflowers on these sites. Rainfall erosion may also increase the difficulty of establishing wildflowers on steeply sloping sites. Drainage will be an important consideration in selecting appropriate mixtures.

A buried seed bank test can reveal if topsoils have large viable seed populations. Soils with a high weed seed count of more than 20 seedlings per sample may be subject to weed infestations (depending on species composition) and may need to be discarded. Rushes and docks can be particularly troublesome.

To determine the size of the seed bank, collect a sample from the top 5 cm of soil. Spread a dried sub-sample of 100 ml thinly over capillary matting in a shallow seed tray, and keep it moist in a warm (6–25°C) greenhouse. The sample should be stirred weekly, to ensure that as many seeds as possible are exposed to light. Germinating seedlings are counted and categorised as grasses, forbs, rushes or ericoids, then removed from the tray. Using this technique, seedlings can still appear after more than a year, but the largest numbers are usually recorded in the first few months. A six-week period provides a minimal estimate, but still gives a reasonable comparison of the relative numbers of seeds at different types of site.

19.3 Choosing the right mixture of grass and flowers

In rural landscapes wildflowers should generally be sown in combination with grasses, which germinate quickly and establish a fibrous root system that helps stabilise the soil. Grasses are winter green and protect the soil surface at all times of the year. In contrast many wildflowers are slow to germinate, may die back in winter and benefit from the shelter and soil stability provided by grasses, as long as growth is not too vigorous.

Mixtures usually comprise about 80 per cent by weight of grasses and 20 per cent wildflowers. This will produce a sward with a natural appearance and some colourful flowers which generally blends with the surrounding countryside. The ratio can, however, be varied to produce a more economical mixture or to give a more colourful sward with less grass. In urban landscapes the imperative for greater colour may favour wildflower only sowings as discussed in Chapter 20.

There are about 500 species of wildflowers offered for sale in the UK, but many are available in only small quantities. Some are very expensive, and many have proved difficult to establish. The Department of Transport *Wildflower Handbook* (1993) gives data for 64 species that are particularly suitable for sowing, based on good performance in trial sowings, field experiments and on seed availability. These data sheets can be used to tailor mixtures to suit specific site requirements, but a small number of basic mixtures will suit most situations. Site information such as altitude, soil type, acidity, vegetation and wetness can be used to help select one of six basic mixtures, or a general purpose mixture can be chosen that will suit most soils. An example of a suitable seed mix for calcareous meadow is given in Table 19.2.

Table 19.2 Example of a seed mixture for upland limestone grassland (National Vegetation Classification CG9).

% by weight grasses		% by weight forbs	
Agrostis capillaris	10	Achillea millefolium	2.0
Dactylis glomerata	10	Anthyllis vulneraria	1.0
Festuca rubra	20	Galium verum	1.0
Festuca ovina	40	Leontodon hispidus	3.0
		Lotus corniculatus	3.0
		Plantago lanceolata	3.0
		Sanguisorba minor	2.0
		Scabiosa columbaria	3.0
		Succisa pratensis	2.0

Chambers (1994) gives information on growing and maintaining a wider selection of native species. Advice on selecting seed mixtures can also be obtained from reputable suppliers and several firms offer a range of mixtures for different types of habitat, often with guidance for selection and cultivation. Some websites giving lists of suppliers and technical advice can be found at the end of this chapter.

Only a few wildflowers such as ox-eye daisy (*Leucanthemum vulgare*) will flower in the first season. A way of achieving quick colour is to add seeds of annuals such as poppies (*Papaver rhoeas*), cornflower (*Centaurea cyanus*) and scentless mayweed (*Matricaria perforata*), but it is worth noting that though most annuals do not persist after the first season, they can look out of place in some situations, particularly in heathland and upland locations.

Although native species are usually specified, not all may be available as of British origin, and when available these are often more expensive than foreign seed. Seed should be ordered from reputable suppliers who should provide a detailed list of the proportions and sources of species included in mixtures. Substitute species should not be accepted unless these are clearly suitable for the purpose required. It is not unknown for different species to appear from those listed. A sample of the seed supplied should be retained for subsequent checking, in case of disputes

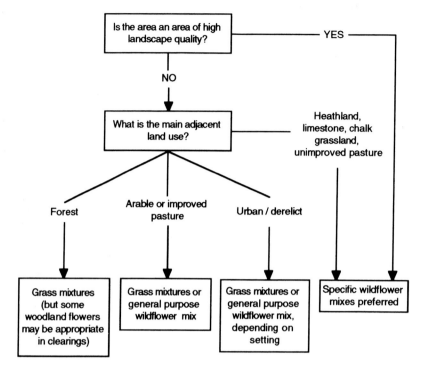

Fig. 19.4 A simple key to selecting seed mixtures.

over quality or content. Wildflower seeds are not subject to the usual minimum germination regulations. Although most have more than 70 per cent germination, a few are lower than 50 per cent, and some have delayed germination or dormancy.

The composition of a seed mixture is usually a compromise between what is desired and what is possible in terms of cost, germination and availability. General guidance on suitably colourful or characteristic species can be gained by examining lists of species for broad vegetation categories or for appropriate National Vegetation Classification vegetation types. Some of these species will be ruled out because they are weeds, because they are unavailable commercially or are too expensive. Further species may be unsuitable because they have low or erratic germination. This leaves a much shorter list.

The proportions of those finally selected will be determined by their seed weight: large-seeded species such as *Festuca rubra* and *Plantago lance-*

olata are normally sown at higher proportions by weight than small seeded species such as *Agrostis capillaris* or *Campanula rotundifolia*. The difference in the weight sown will usually only give a partial correction for variation in seed size, and small seeded species may still have much higher seed rates (seeds per square metre) than large seeded species.

Finally, some consideration may need to be given to cost and germination factors. For example the grass *Deschampsia flexuosa* has medium sized seeds, which suggests relatively high sowing weights, but the crop varies from year to year and so can be expensive, so proportions could be reduced relative to more reasonably-priced species. On the other hand, germination rates for the *Deschampsia* tend to be erratic, so higher sowing rates could still be justified. It is easy to appreciate that there can be considerable variation in seed mixtures for the same vegetation type, depending on circumstances and the judgement of the seedsman (Fig. 19.4).

19.4 Origins and provenance

The origin of wildflowers can be of great importance in some situations (such as at sites of nature conservation importance) and for some clients. There are two main issues. Much wildflower seed of UK native species is still imported from Eastern Europe and elsewhere. This may not always be very suited to growth in the UK. Also it may sometimes not turn out to be the same species or subspecies as those growing native in this country. Such material can be regarded as potentially diluting the native plant gene pool by directly replacing indigenous stands of plants or indirectly through crossing with closely related forms. In recent years there has been increasing emphasis on selecting and propagating only UK sourced material for projects with a nature conservation or biodiversity focus (Flora Locale 2000). A Code of Practice issued by Flora Locale and Plantlife (2000) suggests that to clarify plant origins, 'native plants' should be taken to be of species native to Britain and of origin within the UK. Such plants should not have been selectively bred or genetically modified. The term 'native origin' should only be given to native material from a known location and for not more than six generations from collection. 'Native provenance' should only be applied to material from a known locality but where the plants might have been planted or introduced from elsewhere. 'Local provenance' should be used for material of native origin or provenance that is close to where it is to be planted. The Code of Practice gives advice on documenting and archiving information about collected and propagated material.

There are now several firms that specialise in supplying British seed and plants and some can supply details of source localities. In most cases the cost of such material is significantly higher than material of uncertain origin, and the quantities available may be small and variable from year to year.

19.5 Site preparation, sowing and hydroseeding methods

The seedbed should have fine tilth, good drainage and aeration, satisfactory nutrient status (neither completely infertile nor excessively fertile) and be free of weeds (particularly perennial weeds such as docks or thistles). Preparatory work to achieve these conditions may include rejection of a fertile topsoil or deep ploughing to invert it, ripping to decompact and drain subsoil, and the use of herbicides to kill weeds.

On slopes, it is generally easiest to undertake ripping operations up and down the slope, whereas finishing operations should be across the slope to minimise the likelihood of surface erosion. Finishing can involve using tractors, small horticultural rotovators or even hand work, depending on the scale and location of the site and the equipment available.

Some soils may require supplementary treatment to improve seedbed conditions. Excessively well-drained soils such as chalk, rubble, gravels and sands may benefit from a mulch of bark, peat or paper pulp or a dressing of alginates to improve moisture retention. Very acid soils (less than 4.5 pH) benefit from a light dressing (100–200 g/m^2) of ground limestone to help release plant nutrients. Such soils usually require moderate dressings of fertiliser to help establishment of both grasses and wildflowers.

Very infertile soils such as gravels should also be given light to moderate dressings of fertiliser (e.g. 25–70 kg/ha of 5:10:10 NPK).

On steep slopes (greater than 10°) use of plastic or jute geotextile netting or a tackifier can help prevent erosion during establishment, but can add considerably to the cost of the project.

Sowing can be done by hand, by back-mounted spreader, or machine-mounted spreader. On large areas with machine access seed may also be drilled. Because of the great variation in size of flower and grass seeds, thorough mixing is desirable throughout the sowing operation. If flower seeds are sown separately from grass, a bulking agent such as silver sand, sawdust or fine barley meal can be added. The light colour of the mixture helps show where the seed has been sown. After sowing (and spreading of any fertiliser required), it is beneficial to rake the seeds in and roll the surface.

An alternative approach is to apply seeds and any surface amending agents such as fertiliser, mulch and tackifier by hydroseeding. Hydroseed-

Table 19.3 Typical hydroseed slurry mixture (specifications must be varied to suit soil and site conditions).

Seed	5–20 g/m²
Mulch	100–200 g/m²
Fertiliser	10–30 g/m² (15:15:15 NPK, slow release)
Tackifiers	70–75 g/m²
Water	1.5–2 litres/m²

ing is quicker than conventional seeding and requires less ground preparation. It is also well suited for steep or rocky slopes where access is difficult. Hydroseeding is most cost-effective on large sites. Materials costs are higher than with conventional seeding since seed rates should be about doubled, and mulch and other additives are usually included at extra cost. Application costs are, however, relatively low. Table 19.3 shows a typical hydroseeding slurry mixture.

The choice of hydroseeding or conventional seeding may be specified, or left to the contractor. It can be difficult to check on the composition of a hydroseed mixture, so it is worthwhile using a reputable contractor and retaining a small sample for possible analysis in case of dispute. A seed tray of sterile compost can be placed on the surface before hydroseeding, and germinated in controlled conditions later to test the mixture; or a seed laboratory can be asked to check composition from seed characteristics.

Sowing date

It is generally agreed that the best results are obtained from late summer sowings (August–September), with spring (April–May) next best. Spring sowings have the benefit of a full season's growth, autumn sowings from generally damp weather and young plants get well-established over winter for vigorous growth next spring. Some flower seeds require winter vernalisation (chilling) and will not germinate until the spring. In midsummer there is often a shortage of moisture and establishment may be poor. To save possible waste of seed, materials and labour, the time of sowing should be specified to suit the mix and site condition.

19.6 Plugs, pot plants and direct transplants

Seeding is usually the most economical method of creating wildflower swards. However, in some situations there may be advantages in using grown material in the form of plugs, pot grown plants or direct transplants. Examples include:

- where it is desirable to produce a rapid display;
- where suitable seed material is unobtainable;
- for planting into established habitats such as existing grass swards or hedgerows;
- where the aim is to create small patches of pattern or colour.

The two most widely used types of material are pot-grown plants, which may flower in a single season and have a substantial soil and root mass, and much smaller plugs (usually supplied in trays) which have minimal soil mass and may take more than a season to flower. Costs vary considerably depending on source and species, but pot plants may cost about 70p–£1 and plugs 15–30p. Clearly large scale plantings will be very costly and careful site selection and location for maximum effect are needed. Plant in groups to create patches of colour.

It is essential to select appropriate species carefully; the site may need to be managed by cutting or selective weeding to ensure that young plants are not swamped by vigorous growth of grasses. It may not be practical to provide water except at the time of planting, so the rate of successful establishment will be higher if planting is done in autumn or early spring, when the ground is more likely to be moist. Success in planting both plugs and pot-grown plants can be very variable; the main problems seem to be neglect and drought. To achieve satisfactory results it is even more necessary to monitor growth and manage the site regularly than with seeded swards (Fig. 19.5).

Transplanting material direct from intact ground may be an appropriate and cost-effective method in a few situations (Bayfield and Aitken, 1992), such as path restoration schemes and some types of heathlands and wetlands. Suitable species are those that have a tussock or creeping growth

Fig. 19.5 Cowslips established initially by planting plugs, which have then spread outwards by self seeding. Many other species do not appear to respond so co-operatively. (Photo: James Hitchmough)

form. Plants should be extracted carefully from intact ground so as to cause minimal damage. They are then torn apart to provide numerous bare rooted fingerling transplants, which are immediately transplanted to the host site and planted at 10–50 cm, depending on species and location (Fig. 19.6). Companion seeding with grasses is usual to provide rapid overall cover. Species with a single rooting point such as heathers are generally not suitable to make fingerlings but can be planted as turves (minimum 15 cm square soil block).

These plant materials have the advantage of being local and therefore should be well adapted to the site. Careful selection of species, planting to create maximum effect and attention to subsequent management are still essential to ensure success.

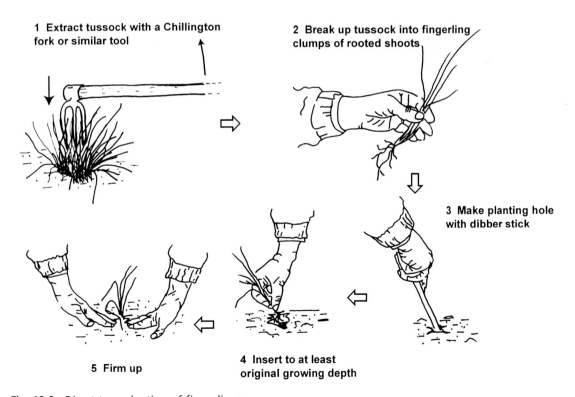

1 Extract tussock with a Chillington fork or similar tool

2 Break up tussock into fingerling clumps of rooted shoots

3 Make planting hole with dibber stick

4 Insert to at least original growing depth

5 Firm up

Fig. 19.6 Direct transplanting of fingerlings.

19.7   The management of wildflower areas

Areas sown or planted with wildflowers need special management. During the first twelve months this is particularly crucial, but long-term management is also important, and should be included in specifications. In the first year the main aims should be to:

- establish rapid plant cover to stabilise the soil surface and prevent erosion;
- control weeds; and
- create a sufficiently open sward to permit the survival and spread of wildflowers.

Ideally the timing and detail of management activities should be decided by staff who know local conditions well, responding to the state of growth and development of the swards.

Sites sown in autumn should not need any management until spring, when vegetation taller than 100 mm should be cut back to 75 mm and cut material removed so that young plants are not smothered. This should be repeated when the new growth exceeds 200 mm. On fertile sites this may be three or four times in the first year, but on thin or infertile soils no cutting may be needed (Table 19.4). Where colourful annuals have been included, a single cut in early April and again in September/October will usually be appropriate. Sites sown in spring should be cut after about six weeks, then at intervals when the growth exceeds 200 mm.

In subsequent years, management will involve preventing a build-up of plant litter and reducing dominance by grasses. On low fertility sites where vegetation is not thick enough to hide the surface, cutting with a flail mower or forage harvester once a year may be all that is needed. Ideally the cut material should be removed, but where this is not feasible it is better to cut and leave the material than not to cut.

On fertile sites it is advisable to cut twice a year: in late July or early August after flowering, and again in October. However these regimes are only guidelines: in hot dry years when growth is slow, it may be necessary to cut only once, but in wet years three cuts may be required.

19.8   Quality control and monitoring

Records of vegetation height, cover, species composition and overall appearance should be used to assess what management regime is required and note the overall wildflower status of the sward. Sites should be inspected after about two months to check on germination and see if there is likely to be a weed problem, though recording the species present will not be possible for at least six months. It is worth comparing these with the list sown. Missing or unexplained species could be checked against relevant samples of seed, and

Table 19.4   Management requirements and actions indicated by monitoring.

Indicator	Action
Cover	
• Very dense ground cover or only dense	• Cutting or raking mat of litter
• Very low cover (<20%)	• Consider reseeding or light fertiliser dressing
Height	
• Excessively tall (usually in conjunction with high density and lack of bare ground)	• Cutting.
Species composition	
• Very low frequency of wildflowers (<1/m²)	• Cut. Consider spot planting of potted seedlings
• Frequent weeds	• Spot weeding or cutting
• Wrong species appear	• Complain and change supplier

where a species has failed it should be left out of mixtures for similar sites in the future.

References

Bayfield, N.G. & Aitken, R. (1992) *Managing the Impacts of Recreation on Vegetation and Soils.* Institute of Terrestrial Ecology, Banchory, Scotland.

Chambers, K. (1994) Th*e Wildflower Compendium.* NPK Landscapes, Manchester.

Department of Transport (1993) *The Wildflower Handbook.* The Stationery Office, London.

Flora Locale (2000) *Planting with Wildlife in Mind: Guidance on the Supply and Use of Native Flora for Projects in the Town or Countryside. A Cross-cutting Action Plan for UK Biodiversity.* Flora Locale, Newbury.

Flora Locale & Plantlife (2000*) Code of Practice for Collectors, Growers and Suppliers of Wild Flora.* Flora Locale, Newbury.

Further reading

Bradshaw, A.D., Goode, D.A., & Thorp, E. (eds) (1986) *Ecology and Design in Landscape.* Blackwell, Oxford.

British Gas (1988) *Heathland Restoration: a Handbook of Techniques.* British Gas, Southampton.

Lickorish, S., Luscombe G., & Scott, R. (1997) *Wildflowers Work.* Landlife, Liverpool.

Wells, T.C.E., Bell, S., & Frost, A. (1981) *Creating Attractive Grasslands Using Native Plant Species.* Nature Conservancy Council, Shrewsbury.

Wells, T.C.E., Cox, R., & Frost, A. (1989), *The Establishment and Management of Wildflower Meadows.* Nature Conservancy Council, Peterborough.

Useful websites

www.naturebureau.co.uk
www.landlife.org.uk
www.powen.freeserve.co.uk/Links/
supplieraddresses.htm
www.hartlana.co.uk/natural/wfsm.htm

20 Wildflower Landscapes in the Urban Environment

Richard Scott

Over the past 26 years, Landlife, an urban wildlife charity based in Merseyside, has pioneered new approaches and developed the philosophy of creative conservation. Creative conservation is creative in a literal sense, creating new ecological landscapes, but also creative in the sense of celebration and inspiration. It can be defined as making places for wildlife to flourish and for people to enjoy (Landlife and the Urban Wildlife Partnership, 1995).

Working from practical research programmes, Landlife has demonstrated that sustainable new wildflower landscapes can be created on urban sites of previously little ecological value; by getting the starting point right, natural processes of evolution can create valuable new habitats for wildlife and people. Working on suitable substrates and introducing core common species, a framework can be established for the development of long-term, floristically diverse meadows.

Landlife's work began with low-cost naturalistic landscaping techniques in the inner city, and has grown to more directed ecological landscaping (based on species selection and substrate modification) located largely in areas adjacent to high-density housing. Experimental field trials were conducted as part of a Nature Conservancy Council research contract with the Groundwork Trust, directly targeted at the problem of how to provide ecologically interesting and attractive grassland in urban areas. This resulted in the English Nature publication *Flowers in the Grass* (Ash *et al.*, 1992). Landlife applied these wildflower landscape techniques on a large scale, working with Knowsley Metropolitan Borough

Council on the award-winning Knowsley Wildflower Project, which subsequently resulted in the establishment of the Millennium National Wildflower Centre at Court Hey Park.

Landlife's work has been unique in combining sustainable wildflower seed production with community involvement and ecological landscaping; it led to the practical guide, *Wildflowers Work* (Lickorish *et al.*, 1997), which details individual specifications for particular projects.

The basic approach to creating wildflower meadows in urban areas is often similar to the approach for rural areas (discussed in Chapter 19) but there are a number of practical and philosophical differences. The first of these is that in urban areas many of the sites for wildflower sowing do not involve agricultural land. Some sites are very fertile, but others consist of 'waste' substrates, derived in some cases from centuries of urban re-development and re-use: building rubbles, old industrial spoils and compacted sub-soils are common.

The major philosophical difference between urban and rural wildflower meadow creation is that in urban areas there is often no nearby habitat-stereotype to serve as a convenient model. Even where one exists, site conditions are often so different because of urban development that to attempt to create a facsimile flies in the face of ecological reality. This should not however be seen in a negative light: it allows the creation of novel plant communities that rarely occur in rural landscapes, which add to both the ecological and cultural richness of urban places. These factors have played a significant role in encouraging the development of creative conservation, rather than the more traditional defensive, 'conservative' view of nature conservation that is the orthodoxy in Britain.

20.1   Problems of terminology

A major problem associated with sowing wildflowers relates to terminology, and in particular the word 'wild'. This leads many people to assume that maintenance can be neglected almost completely. This is a dangerous assumption: even in rural areas, almost all of the habitats that are valued for nature conservation are semi-natural, managed environments. As soon as active management of these landscapes ceases, the process of succession re-asserts itself, and change begins. In fact change is endemic in all landscapes; at best we can only direct that change. Even if we manage areas in a consistent manner change continues to happen anyway, in response to particular weather conditions.

Good management practice means responding to circumstance: in urban situations the circumstances for planting wildflowers vary enormously from traditional park settings to derelict land. Funding for environmental project work has often been a problem, and necessity has led to creative approaches to wildflower landscapes; sites involving rubble and subsoil, that are traditionally considered to be problems, can become aides to effective solutions.

Traditional wildflower meadows in the countryside are in fact a happy accident of hay production, which until the twentieth century did not involve Italian rye grass leys or large inputs of inorganic fertilisers. However, the stewards of these old landscapes were interested in the grass rather than the flowers. Flowers were the by-product of a cropping system whose ecology fitted in with the life cycle of persistent meadow species. The hay was cut and carted away and then usually grazed quite heavily, creating new spaces for wildflower seedlings to establish. In these systems competition in time and space for room to grow is intense. Wildflowers and grasses together perform a balancing act, with the stress generated by some

kind of management or site factors enabling the two competing groups of plants to co-exist.

Productivity, in terms of the amount of growth that a site will produce per unit area (often discussed in terms of grams of herbage per square metre) is one of the biggest problems in terms of establishing attractive long-life wildflower landscapes. Under highly-productive conditions, the grass will outcompete the wildflower species, taking all the available space. In the agricultural meadows of old, where hay was the priority, it is often forgotten that these areas were periodically manured to keep up hay yields. The key factor that maintained such a diversity of species in these sites was the continuous management, removing the biomass of vegetation (the hay) at its peak of growth. After a second flush of growth, grazing by cattle would leave the meadows looking heavily poached and scarified in the late autumn. The wildflower species that survived in these areas adapted to fit in with this particular management regime.

In urban areas we are sometimes faced with fertile soils, but a very different tradition of amenity land management. We cannot adopt traditional meadow options – or it is hard to do so; local authorities are generally more used to landscape management by sixteen annual cuts with a gang mower. The most important management activity is to prevent establishing seedlings being swamped by tall vigorous grasses. In rural areas agricultural contractors have access to appropriate machinery, but in urban areas there is usually no system of dealing with long grass, other than cutting with hand-held brush-cutters and sending the material to landfill, at a further cost. Clearly this is hardly a sustainable solution.

20.2   The value of infertile substrates in urban meadow-making

Sowing directly onto low fertility substrates means that there is a reduced need for cutting (the mechanical equivalent of heavy grazing by animals) from the very beginning of the project; wildflowers have more time to establish without experiencing severe competition. These kinds of materials are also generally free from the weeds that are apparent when we disturb topsoil, the 'soil weed banks' that persist in the surface layers of fertile topsoil. The bare ground that persists on very infertile soil is also very beneficial to invertebrate populations.

Frequent cutting and removal of biomass is often expected to lower soil fertility, but is somewhat of a myth: the scientific evidence suggest this takes a very long time, and in urban areas inputs from atmospheric nitrogen may actually be greater than nitrogen removal in cutting. A typical hay-crop removes about 30 kg N per ha per year; many urban areas receive the same amount of nitrogen from rainfall alone (Ash *et al.*, 1992). Long-term studies have shown it takes many years to deplete soil reserves of phosphates and nitrogen. Johnson and Poulton (1976), for example, estimated that it could take over 70 years to deplete fertiliser residues by vegetation removal.

If the cuttings are chopped very finely, they will not have a significant impact in terms of species diversity. An 18-year experiment on cutting road verges found in 1988 that when the cuttings were chopped up finely, only the levels of extractable potassium in the soil decreased, and that most other nutrients remained unaffected. They concluded that any increase in species diversity was due to physical disturbance and scarification rather than change in nutrient status. However, unmanaged grass and long grass that has been cut and left is an effective mulch and eliminates any seedlings beneath it.

The main point of this is that in productive soils the imperative for management (i.e. cutting) is much greater, and it is difficult to meet these requirements in an urban environment. The situation in which grass excludes all but the most aggressive plants is often seen on old road verges that have been sown with aggressive strains of red fescue. Low fertility soils help to solve the problem of having to respond to grass productivity.

20.3   Critical fertility levels

High levels of phosphate are generally recognised as a main factor behind the loss of botanical inter-

Table 20.1 Fertility guidelines for chemical analysis (after Ash *et al.*, 1992).

Mineralisable nitrogen µg/g (equivalent to PPM)	
<2	infertile
2–20	intermediate
>20	fertile
Extractable phosphate µg/g	
<20	infertile
20–80	intermediate
>80	fertile

est in 'improved' semi-natural grassland. Inputs of organic nitrogen (through manures, for example) were a common addition to meadows in the past. It can be difficult to categorise fertility but a simple guideline is given above in Table 20.1. Methods of analysis differ and can cause confusing results; the analyses in this table follow Allen (1974).

A high P low N substrate such as brick rubble can, over time, become a fertile soil through the action of legumes. Fertility is also affected by pH; at high and low levels, phosphate becomes unavailable to plants, which is why for example many alkaline waste materials prove so suitable for wildflower projects.

These principles are well demonstrated in the success of a meadow in Knowsley created by Landlife on a site stripped of topsoil (Plate 21). This is unique in that nearly two hectares were landscaped at virtually no cost; the sale of topsoil paid for the whole project, and the reduction of fertility has resulted in one of the most sustainable landscapes in the United Kingdom. The number of plant species has increased from an initial introduction of 16 core species to a naturalistic community of 57 species. The cost of sowing was only £0.03 per square metre (because this was offset by the sale of topsoil) and sowing took place at low rates. Management costs in the long term have been minimal, and the site has yielded more valuable seed for other project sites. The weed problem has been almost nonexistent, with just a small amount of ragwort (*Senecio jacobea*) pulled in year seven.

Such sites become very important in demonstrating how biodiversity can be established prac-

Table 20.2 Species that have proved to be suitable for sowing in simple combinations on subsoils.

Sandy subsoils		Clay subsoils	
Lady's bedstraw	(*Galium verum*)	Cowslip	(*Primula veris*)
Bladder campion	(*Silene vulgaris*)	Lesser knapweed	(*Centaurea nigra*)
Centaury	(*Centauria erythraea*)	Field scabious	(*Knautia arvensis*)
Wild carrot	(*Daucus carota*)	Betony	(*Stachys officinalis*)
Ox-eye daisy	(*Leucanthemum vulgare*)	Devils bit scabious	(*Succisa pratensis*)
Musk mallow	(*Malva moschata*)	Meadow buttercup	(*Ranunculus acris*)
Vipers bugloss	(*Echium vulgare*)	Ragged Robin	(*Lychnis flos-cuculi*)
Kidney Vetch	(*Anthylllis vulnaria*)	Self heal	(*Prunella vulgaris*)
Yellow rattle	(*Rhinanthus minor*)		
Evening primrose	(*Oenothera biennis*)		

Note: There are always exceptions. Devils bit scabious has for example performed outstandingly well on sandy subsoils.

tically. Where there is a failure to capitalise on the site conditions, importing materials and laying them out may lead to a cost of up to £1.40 per square metre (for stripping topsoil, adding material, ground preparation, seed and sowing). By targeting low fertility soils, and deliberately avoiding species or approaches that are poorly fitted to the site, costs are kept down from the very beginning and the chances of success increased.

20.4   Dealing with urban contexts

Working in public open space is likely to involve a very diverse group of people, and great sensitivity to their views and needs is often required. A considerable amount of information needs to be assessed before any project works begin. This involves a process of negotiation with (for example) local authorities, community groups, parish councils and key individuals. Ideally groups should visit successful wildflower sites and talk to individuals who have been involved in successful projects about what works best and why. Good examples are never used well enough, and sadly people often experience failure first.

Failures in the urban sphere become highly significant, because they are likely to be seen by a large number of people. If the project is a community initiative and things go wrong, the individuals or groups involved are unlikely to try anything again for a long time, perhaps never. Many landscape initiatives now dictate commu-

nity involvement as part of the grant requirement. Success becomes an imperative in such projects and so the planning stage is a critical part of the process, where sufficient time must be spent on accentuating the positive and using the process of change as part of the community development. Landlife's project work has also heightened local interest with community events, wildflower buttonhole days in busy local centres, and by producing attractive postcards of the fields in flower.

It is important that a logical process is followed: for this reason Landlife produced a set of guidelines with the Urban Wildlife Partnership, highlighting the essential elements of good practice (available from Landlife on request). Basically they state the importance of surveying the existing area. Many urban areas (if managed correctly) can actually already have an interesting flora, simply by relaxing the mowing regime at the correct time of year.

Creative conservation projects should be planned with long-term management in mind. The project needs to be of sustainable size: if schemes are too small they rapidly suffer from management problems because they invariably require special attention which is likely to be at odds with the surrounding landscape.

- Undertake a survey of the area for existing wildlife value.
- Don't sow if you can't cut resulting meadows.

If you can't cut but still need to sow, choose species that will persist without management.

- Secure the right permissions.
- Choose a suitable seed mix for the ecological conditions prevailing.
- Use good ground preparation and sow the expensive seed with care.
- Ensure the right cutting management every year, or design for neglect.
- Enable people to enjoy the project; don't be too precious.

20.5   Ground preparation for sowing

The key to good ground preparation is minimising disturbance of the weed seed bank in the soil and taking enough time to create a sterile seedbed. Good results have also been achieved by using a surface mulch layer of approximately 25 mm of sand to suppress weed seed germination. Seed is then sown directly into this ideal seedbed (Dunnett and Hitchmough, 2001). This can be a practical solution for even quite large areas, as sand is a cheap medium, and this will save a lot of time in the longer term in the management effort needed to suppress vigorous weedy species. A specification for the preparation and sowing of highly fertile soils is given in Table 20.3.

Low fertility sites obviously give a lot more options, with calcareous or sandy soils the most desirable. Heavy soils are more problematic, as working such soils is dependent upon dry weather. Specifications for meadow establishment on infertile substrates are similar, but generally less intensive, than those shown in Table 20.3. It is notable that on many richer sites ox-eye daisy (*Leucanthemum vulgare*) will dominate for a few years and then disappear; on less rich sites this species persists (Plate 22). The continued presence of ox-eye daisy is a useful indicator of how receptive a sward is likely to be to self-colonising new species.

By sowing a simple combination of species on a selected infertile substrate we are applying the ecological theories of Grime (2001). These recognise that a peak of species diversity occurs when plants are stressed by environmental circumstances. For example, materials like cockleshells, crushed con-

crete, motorway scrapings, and waste clothing have all been successfully used in creating diverse and attractive landscapes. Below in Table 20.4 is a sample specification for a crushed concrete meadow; alternatives such as limestone gravel or shales or 'crusher run' from builders' yards can similarly be used (Fig. 20.1).

20.6   Choice of species and mixes

Landlife advocates the use of a simple matrix of species which can be established with confidence, allowing nature to shape the final result in relation to the level of management available

Table 20.3   Specification for sowing on topsoil.

Planting

- Flail grass to produce the closest-cropped turf possible.
- Spray area with Roundup herbicide, and wait until grass has died back.
  If time permits wait a couple of weeks to allow secondary germination, and spray again. This is a sterile seed bed technique. Wait at least three days after the second treatment before cultivation.
- Chain harrow the area several times to produce a scratch cultivation. Avoid excessive disturbance of soil, which will encourage weeds.
- Broadcast seed at a rate of 1 g/m^2 or less as pure wildflower seed, or with grass at 1–2 g/m^2.
- Chain harrow area again, or roll using Cambridge Roller to maximise seed-soil contact.
- Seed should be bulked up with a neutral carrier such as barley meal to act as a seed carrier at a ratio of approx. 10:1.

Management

- In the first year keep well cut to a height of approx. 50 mm, to prevent tall weeds shading wildflowers.
- In second and subsequent years allow to flower and cut in late July after seed has dropped.
  Flail several times to reduce to fine cuttings, or take hay crop.
- Chain harrow periodically in August/September in future years to create new spaces for new wildflower seedlings.
- On infertile soils the sterile seed bed technique is obviously less Important.

Fig. 20.1 A bank of wildflowers growing on lime-stone shale, without topsoil. (Photo: Landlife)

(DoE, 1994). Mathematical theory evolving from the chaos theory of Poincaré illustrates that complex and unpredictable results can evolve from simple starting points. Adams (1996) states the need for using the applied skills of habitat creation and restoration, but also simply letting nature take its course and seeing what kind of landscapes may evolve. Wildness, he points out, cannot normally be planned with any degree of precision.

Often in specifications ecologists target particular seed mixtures according to National Vegetation Classification (Rodwell *et al.*, 1992). This is a useful reference point in composing seed mixtures, but if followed slavishly its complexity at the outset demands a greater effort to obtain the seed mix and get it to establish satisfactorily. There is of course a place for this kind of habitat creation, but it demands time, patience and considerable cost. Standard wildflower seed mixtures only approximate to the species that could occur on a given site, and many species listed in the National Vegetation Classification are not available commercially.

There is a good case for sowing mixtures of pure wildflower seed, because many of the problems relating to management result from grass competition. Industry standards have dictated a mixture of 20 per cent wildflowers to 80 per cent grass, but

Table 20.4 Crushed concrete or crushed tower block meadow.

Crushed concrete specification
- Scrape off the upper portion (10 cm) of topsoil with a JCB to remove the seed bank of unwanted species (Fig. 20.2).
- Apply a fine grade of crushed concrete evenly, to make up the soil to the original level. Approximately 2 tonnes of waste will be required for each 10 m².
- Rotovate or power harrow the crushed concrete into the remaining soil as evenly as possible.
- Sow a calcareous wildflower at the rate of 0.5–1 g/m² as pure wildflower seed or 5 g/m² as wildflower grass mix. Broadcast by hand or precision sow. (Seed is best bulked up with a carrier to ensure even spread.)
- Harrow or rake to tickle in soil.
- Roll to maximise seed-soil contact if possible.

Management
- Few species will flower in first season, and cover in first year may be thin. If sown with grass, cut when the grass height exceeds 50 mm to prevent the young wildflowers being overshadowed.
- Employ a two-cut mowing regime: once in April, and a second cut in September. Cut as close as possible, leave cuttings finely chopped. This can be achieved by several passes with a tractor mounted flail. On sites where the fertility is very low one cut in September should be sufficient.

Fig. 20.2 Topsoil removal in progess. (Photo: James Hitchmough)

certainly in urban areas a dense flowering effect can be achieved using a pure wildflower mix, or with very small quantities of grass seed. Most seed houses will make seed mixtures to the customer's specification. Grass species will often arrive very quickly without being sown. Aggressive grasses such as Yorkshire fog (*Holcus lanatus*) can quickly dominate a meadow, sometimes threatening to eliminate newly-established wildflowers. In these circumstances the adverse effects of dominating grasses can be reduced by the application of a selective grass herbicide.

20.7   Landscape effects

Perhaps one of the delights of wildflower landscapes is in composing simple yet spectacular colour combinations. Certainly when we come across vibrant wildflower displays in the countryside it is often due to a single or perhaps two or three species of wildflowers, and there is no reason why we cannot design these effects, as we would in a conventional landscape planting. Suggestions for simple combinations that work well are listed in Table 20.5. Ecological processes will mould and add to the resulting meadow, especially where low fertility substrates are used. For example, on wildflower projects sown on crushed concrete and subsoil, bee orchids (*Ophrys apifera*) have been known to colonise within three years.

On fertile soils, cornfield annuals are an excellent solution, giving a first year show of colour which is important in demonstrating benefits to community groups. Sown annual meadows are discussed in detail in Chapter 22. However it is worth stating that annuals grow best on the more difficult rich soils, rather than the infertile soils which makes perennial wildflower landscaping much easier. Annuals also require annual cultivation, which can be a considerable commitment if not understood initially.

Nevertheless annuals can be sown successfully with perennial species to give a good effect in the first year, and when working with schools and community groups this is very important (Fig. 20.3). A sowing mix which works well in this

Table 20.5 Visually effective, simple wildflower combinations (sown as pure wildflower mixes at $1\,g/m^2$).

Infertile to moderately infertile soils
Longevity is partly dependent on soil conditions and management, and on poor open soils will be much better.

Ox-eye daisy	(*Leucanthemum vulgare*)
Kidney vetch	(*Anthyllis vulnaria*)
Wild carrot	(*Daucus carota*)
Vipers bugloss	(*Echium vulgare*)
St.John's wort	(*Hypericum perforatum*)
Cowslip	(*Primula veris*)
Self heal	(*Prunella vulgaris*)
Birdsfoot trefoil	(*Lotus corniculatus*)
Musk mallow	(*Malva moschata*)
Yarrow	(*Achillea millefolium*)
Self heal	(*Prunella vulgaris*)
Field scabious	(*Knautia arvensis*)
Greater knapweed	(*Centaurea scabiosa*)
Musk mallow	(*Malva moschata*)

Moderately fertile soils

Teasel	(*Dipsacus fullonum*)
Cow parsley	(*Anthriscus sylvestris*)
Red campion	(*Silene dioica*)
Lesser knapweed	(*Centaurea nigra*)
Meadow buttercup	(*Ranunculus acris*)
Cow parsley	(*Anthriscus sylvestris*)

situation (though attention to weed control and management are important) is shown in Table 20.6.

20.8   The use of nursery grown plants

This is expensive, as a large number of plants will be required to have a significant impact in terms of making an area look attractive. As a comparison, establishing wildflowers from seed costs approximately in the region of £0.18 per square metre when sowing pure wildflower seed at $1\,g/m^2$, and typically results in hundreds of plants within this area. Purchasing nursery grown stock costs approximately £7.00/m². For urban projects, when funding is often a problem, these costs are not always feasible. Undoubtedly the best use of plants is to involve the community and children in particular in planting days.

Fig. 20.3 It is important to sow annuals for immediate effect when working with schools and community groups. (Photo: Landlife)

Table 20.6 Recommended wildflower seed mix for schools (% by weight).

20% Red campion	(*Silene dioica*)
20% Meadow buttercup	(*Ranunculus acris*)
20% Cowslip	(*Primula veris*)
10% Ox-eye Daisy	(*Leucanthemum vulgare*)
5% Cow parsley	(*Anthriscus sylvestris*)
10% Field scabious	(*Knautia arvensis*)

- Sow at 1 g/m^2 as pure wildflower seed with 2 g/m^2 of standard cornfield annual mix as below.

72% Corn cockle	(*Agrostemma githalgo*)
22% Cornflower	(*Centaurea cyanus*)
5% Corn marigold	(*Chrysanthemum segetum*)
1% Corn Poppy	(*Papaver rhoeas*)

- Best sow in spring to get an even distribution of cornfield species (autumn sowings tend to be dominated by corn cockle). Sowing in late May produced a meadow in which the annuals were in full flower for the return of schools after the summer holiday.
- Cut back as soon as annuals are past their best and remove cuttings. Cut at least once again to help light reach perennial meadow plants.
- Second season; cut up to three times a year. Once late March\early April, once in late July\early August, and the end of September.
- Weed control: because the soils are more fertile spot treatment of unwanted weeds is important. Allow at least two visits per year.

The best wildflowers for planting are therefore those that are most difficult to establish from seed and fairly tolerant once established. Prime candidates therefore are cowslip (*Primula veris*), meadow cranesbill (*Geranium pratense*), betony (*Stachys officinalis*), meadowsweet (*Filipendula vulgaris*) and purple loosestrife (*Lythrum salicaria*), the last two working extremely well together in damp locations. Plugs are of course an option and cheaper, but supply tends to be variable, and because of their small size and vulnerability to drought, planting times must therefore be confined to wetter periods of the year. They are an extra weapon in the armoury, but should be used to heighten interest rather than be the main thrust of a project.

20.9   Conclusion

Rather than seeking high complexity at the outset, creative conservation looks at making the right start, working with the existing ground conditions to introduce or manage simple but ecologically valuable landscapes that can evolve through natural processes over time. In places of low ecological potential, where natural seed banks are poor or non-existent and where natural colonisation of desired species is likely to be very slow, creative conservation can give a helping hand.

Plant selection in many urban spaces can be more diverse and responsive than in the countryside. There is a real opportunity to work with urban park managers to enable them to become more intuitive to the practical ecology of their situation. Sometimes this may involve selecting plants of non-native form and origin, which is what has always happened with the use of trees and shrubs in urban parks. Landlife has for example completed successful projects in Kirkby (a new town), using a combination of native wildflowers with naturalised plants like the lupin (*Lupinus polyphyllus*) which was in the past a local landmark, before the areas where they grew were built on. The use of species like this, which can survive neglect, is an important dynamic in urban areas.

In these situations we need to act flexibly and pragmatically, treating each site on its merits in the context of the diversity of a changing urban world. Given the recent warnings of the Hadley Centre's climate model (predicting a general North–South shift in natural habitats at a rate of 50–80 km a decade), adopting a flexible creative conservation strategy may be the only sensible approach. Biodiversity Action Plans based on the premise that environments are more or less static may well be out of date already, and unsustainable as a means of conserving local biodiversity in a dramatically changing climate.

References

Adams, W.M. (1996) *Future Nature*: a vision for conservation. Kogau Page, London.

Allen, S.E. (ed.) (1974) *Chemical Analysis of Ecological Materials*. Blackwell, Oxford.

Ash, H.J., Bennett, R., & Scott, R. (1992) *Flowers in the Grass; creating and managing grasslands with wildflowers*. English Nature, Peterborough.

DoE (1994) Partnerships in Practice.

Dunnett, N. & Hitchmough, J. (2001) First in last out. *The Garden*, March 2001, 182–3.

Grime, P. (2001) *Plant Strategies, Vegetation Processes and Ecosystem Properties*. John Wiley, Chichester.

Johnson, A.E. & Poulton, P.R. (1976) 'Yields on the exhaustion land and changes in the NPK content of the soils due to cropping and manuring 1852–1975'. *Rothamstead Experimental Station Report 1976. Part 2*, pp 53–86. Rothamstead Experimental Station, Harpenden.

Landlife and the Urban Wildlife Partnership (1995) *Guidelines for Creative Conservation*. The Wildlife Trusts, Newark. [Available from Landlife.]

Lickorish, S., Luscombe G., & Scott, R. (1997) *Wildflowers Work*. Landlife, Liverpool.

Rodwell, J.S., Piggott, C.D., Ratcliffe, D.A., Malloch, A.J.C., Birks, H.J.B., Proctor, M.C.F., Shimwell, D.W., Huntley, J.P., Radford, E., Wigginton, M.J., & Wilkins, P. (1992) *British Plant Communities. Vol. 3. Grasslands and Montane Communities*. Cambridge University Press, Cambridge.

21 Aquatic Planting

Kevin Patrick

Aquatic plants form an ecological rather than a taxonomic group, and cannot be defined with any degree of precision. These plants occupy a continuum from open water to dry land, and some species can exist across the entire hydrosere. This chapter deals with those plants that grow in water, up to and including the water's edge: submerged, floating, emergent and marginal aquatics. It considers the establishment of aquatic vegetation in British rivers and streams, ponds and lakes, including urban watercourses and ornamental ponds.

Aquatic habitats, and especially rivers, are a subject that has been neglected until recently. It was not until 1988 that the former Nature Conservancy Council began to systematically designate our most ecologically important rivers as Sites of Special Scientific Interest (SSSI).

This is unfortunate because recent studies have shown that wetland habitats, and especially watercourses, are one of the last widespread bastions of biodiversity in the British countryside. They are under-represented in designations such as SSSI, National Nature Reserves, Areas of Outstanding Natural Beauty and Environmentally Sensitive Areas etc.

Aquatic and wetland communities have been in serious decline in the UK for decades and many are still under threat. Agricultural drainage, incremental urbanisation of the flood plain, pollution and eutrophication (nutrient enrichment), water abstraction and unsympathetic flood defence schemes are among the main threats to our river and wetland ecosystems.

The neglect of aquatic and wetland habitats has been reflected in the training of landscape architects; most of them graduate with a knowledge of trees and shrubs, but few will have been taught about aquatic plants or wetland landscapes. This is a pity because aquatic plants are immensely rewarding: the right plants in the right place can grow very quickly, creating dramatic and dynamic landscape features as well as superb natural habitats (Plate 23). Compared with aquatic plants, trees and shrubs can seem rather dull.

21.1 Objectives for aquatic planting

It is important to think about the objectives of any planting scheme at the outset, and aquatic planting is no exception.

Habitat creation

Aquatic plants fulfil many vital functions in wetland ecosystems; Fig. 21.1 classifies them into their main groups. Submerged species provide shelter and food for aquatic invertebrates, small fish and some bird species. These plants are essential as the egg laying sites for coarse fish such as pike and bream and in waterbodies where the underwater landscape is uniform (e.g. new lakes, dredged channels etc.), these submerged plant communities often provide the only source of habitat complexity and diversity. The oxygenating function of submerged plants is well known.

Floating plants can provide much-needed shade in the summer and a valuable 'island' habitat for many invertebrates. The red-eyed damselfly, for example, is closely associated with water lilies.

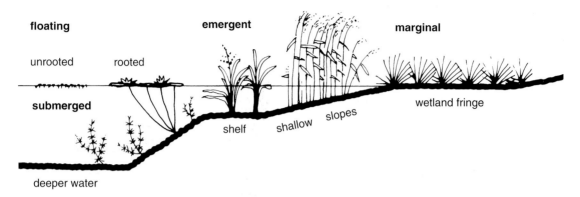

Fig. 21.1   A basic classification of aquatic plant types and bank profile features.

Emergent plants have a crucial role for many invertebrates, forming the essential link between water and air for the aquatic larval stages of dragonflies and others.

Water bodies with a species-rich and complex plant community are likely to support animal communities that are correspondingly species-rich and numerous.

If habitat creation is the main objective for a planting scheme, special attention should be paid to selecting species appropriate to both the location and the particular environmental parameters of the site. The source of the plant material is also of major importance if ecological and genetic authenticity is to be achieved. If the site is adjacent to an existing, quality aquatic habitat, then natural colonisation may be a sensible alternative to planting, providing that a longer time scale is acceptable.

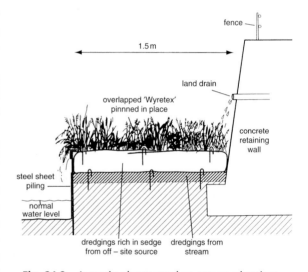

Fig. 21.2   Aquatic plants used as screen planting.

aquatic plants in otherwise hostile situations (see Fig. 21.2).

Bank protection

Bank protection is a specialised use of aquatic vegetation for bioengineering purposes and may involve the use of additional structures or geotextiles. Coppin and Richards (1990) give commonly available aquatic species recognised as having inherent bank and channel reinforcing abilities (Table 21.1).

Screening bankside structures

Steel sheet piling, concrete walls, weirs, revetments and pipes are all too often the human contribution to wetland landscapes. Nothing looks quite as desolate as high vertical walls rising straight out of a river or lake, unrelieved by vegetation at the water's edge. It does not have to be like this, and some designers and ecologists have been experimenting with artificial edge creation by constructing shelves, pockets and troughs of substrate for

Table 21.1 Aquatic plants with bank and channel reinforcing abilities.

Greater pond sedge	Carex riparia
Lesser pond sedge	Carex acutiformis
Reed sweet-grass	Glyceria maxima
Reed canary-grass	Phalaris arundinacea

Table 21.2 Aquatic plants most tolerant of turbidity.

Rigid hornwort	Ceratophyllum demersum
Yellow water-lily	Nuphar lutea
Amphibious bistort	Persicaria amphibia
Arrowhead	Sagittaria sagittifolia
Common club-rush	Schoenoplectus lacustris

Buffering

Buffering is another specialised objective that may become more important now that the European Union Nitrate Directive has been adopted. Pollution and nutrient enrichment of freshwater has become a serious problem both for wildlife and for drinking water supplies. The use of wetland buffer zones has been shown to be one way of alleviating this problem (Young, 1995).

Aesthetics

Aquatic vegetation can create a supremely lush and luxuriant effect and there is no need to utilise exotic species or cultivars of native species. Indeed these potentially endanger our native flora through competitive exclusion, and possible genetic introgression. These threats are discussed in greater detail in Chapter 2. Most native wetland species are robust, beautiful and self perpetuating. Crowfoot (*Ranunculus aquatilis*), water-lilies (*Nymphaea alba*), yellow iris (*Iris pseudacorus*), purple loosestrife (*Lythrum salicaria*), flowering rush (*Butomus umbellatus*), bulrush (*Typha* spp.) and marsh marigold (*Caltha palustris*) create the rich scene depicted in 'Ophelia' by Sir John Everett Millais (Plate 24).

21.2   Species selection

To make use of the ecological data available for aquatic plants, it is necessary to assess the following environmental parameters of the planting site.

Shade

Shade has a profound impact on aquatic vegetation. Very few submerged, floating and emergent species will thrive in shade, although several marginal species are well suited to almost woodland conditions. One of the best ways to enable diversification of aquatic vegetation is to reduce the shade caused by adjacent trees, either by coppicing, pollarding or crown lifting. Shade can also occur where turbid water drastically reduces the light available for bottom-rooted and emergent plants. Among truly aquatic plants, Haslam (1978) cites unbranched bur-reed (*Sparganium emersum*), as most tolerant of overhead shading, with branched bur-reed (*S. erectum*), and starwort species (*Callitriche* spp.), as confirmed shade tolerators. Aquatic plants most tolerant of turbidity are shown in Table 21.2.

Water flow

Several aspects of hydrology need to be taken into account when defining water flow: velocity, turbulence, discharge and location within the channel are all important. None of these factors alone are adequate to describe a flow regime in relation to aquatic plants; they are also difficult to measure. For this reason Haslam (1978) suggests four visual categories of flow conditions affecting river plants:

- negligible flow; for example, canals, fen and dykes
- slow flow; trailing plants hardly move
- moderate flow; trailing plants clearly move and the water surface is slightly disturbed
- fast flow; trailing plants move vigorously and the water surface is markedly disturbed.

To this list of categories can be added:

- nil flow conditions as found in ponds and lakes

Table 21.3 Aquatic plants tolerant of spate conditions.

Canadian waterweed	*Elodea canadensis*
Spiked water-milfoil	*Myriophyllum spicatum*
Amphibious bistort	*Persicaria amphibia*
Curled pondweed	*Potamogeton crispus*
Perfoliate pondweed	*Potamogeton perfoliatus*
River water-crowfoot	*Ranunculus fluitans*
Branched bur-reed	*Sparganium erectum*

- high liability to 'spate' (a sudden water surge after heavy rain). This is often a characteristic of upland streams and urbanised catchments.

Flow regimes are a key limiting factor in urban watercourses subject to spate events. Intervals of dry weather resulting in very low flows are periodically interrupted by rainstorms: the rain is immediately conveyed via all the hard surfaces and drains to create a raging torrent. This combination of dry periods and spate floods creates a hostile environment for aquatic plants.

Haslam (1978) suggests a limited range of species that can tolerate spate conditions (see Table 21.3). They are able to do this because they are rapidly able to replace damaged parts, or can quickly re-grow from detached rhizome fragments.

Fast-flowing water exerts considerable wear and tear on plant roots and leaves. This environment is associated with a limited range of specialised plants such as mosses and common water-crowfoot (*Ranunculus aquatilis*). Still and slowly-moving water has the greatest potential for plant diversity. Indeed, this is the only habitat for unrooted species such as rigid hornwort (*Ceratophyllum demersum*), and frogbit (*Hydrocharis morsus-ranae*).

Depth

While most aquatic plants can grow across a range of water depths once they are established, it is advisable to be specific about water depth at the time of planting. For example, common reed (*Phragmites australis*) can be found growing in water over a metre deep, but will only establish itself if planted at, or just above, water level, so that undamaged shoots or rhizomes are in contact with the air (Ebstam, 1992). It is not advisable to plant into water more than one metre deep, as deep water is too cold for most plants to establish. Once established in the shallows, some species (e.g. water lilies) will need to spread into deeper water to develop their full potential.

Trying to predict water depths over different parts of a landscape design drawing is very difficult, so planting plans which show intricate patterns and exact locations for aquatic plants are usually inappropriate. It is better to give a general indication of planting arrangement, together with notes on where to plant in relation to water level, and supervise the planting on site.

On sites where water level cannot be predicted or is likely to vary markedly over time (perhaps due to prolonged flooding or drought) it may be worth planting across a range of water depths.

Designers often have more control over water depth than other environmental factors, so the design of the bank profile is a powerful tool for determining the extent and type of aquatic plant communities.

Only unrooted floating plants and the very largest aquatic plants, such as river water crowfoot (*Ranunculus fluitans*), and yellow water-lily (*Nuphar lutea*), can grow in water that is more than 1.5 metres deep. To ensure areas of open water it is therefore advisable to design profiles which extend to a greater depth. Turbidity and water flow often combine with depth to control the distribution of aquatic plants and so precise depth limits for individual species are not reliable. However, for practical purposes a depth of 1.5 metres is suggested for controlling the spread of common reed (*Phragmities australis*) (Ward, 1992), and this is probably deep enough to control other invasive emergents such as bulrush (*Typha latifolia*), in most circumstances. While there are no hard rules for bank profile design, a wide range of depths with shallow slopes (and/or shelves) will usually enable the establishment of a more diverse aquatic community. Steep slopes into deep water, without shelves, make for poor marginal communities as well as posing a potential drowning risk to young children.

Substrate

Aquatic substrates are determined by the interaction of water flow and surface geology. Rivers and streams are essentially mechanisms for transporting sediments from the land to the sea. As a result they may contain a range of particle sizes from boulders to stones, gravel, sand and silt/mud, with the underlying geology exposed in areas of scouring. Most aquatic plants will grow in medium to fine substrates with moderate to rich nutrient levels.

At a recent project in the south of England, marginal aquatics were planted into an excavated gravel substrate without topsoil on a 1:4 river bank exposed to wave action. In order to assess establishment of marginal aquatic vegetation in this hostile environment, a trial planting was implemented in the summer of 2000. By the autumn it was clear that some species were establishing better than others. Table 21.4 provides interim results of this trial.

Lakes and ponds typically tend to involve a narrower range of substrates, as they are essentially sediment sinks and quickly accumulate a layer of mud rich in organic matter. Choice of species is less critical in such habitats.

Water chemistry and quality

The pH of water is another factor influencing natural plant distribution and, like substrate, is closely related to geology. Plants like rigid hornwort (*Ceratophyllum demersum*) and watercress (*Rorippa nasturtium-aquaticum*) are associated with base rich waters (water having a pH of more than seven), often originating from chalk aquifers; plants such as bulbous rush (*Juncus bulbosus*) are typical of the base poor waters and acidic geology of the north and west.

Only a few species favour or avoid waters with a high pH (Andrews and Kinsman, 1990) and little research has been done on the precise pH requirements of aquatic plants. It is more usual to take a

Table 21.4 Plant establishment on gravel substrate after one season.

Species	Number planted	Plant establishment after first season
Lesser pond sedge *Carex acutiformis*	80	81%
Yellow iris *Iris pseudacorus*	576	79%
Water-plantain *Alisma plantago-aquatica*	80	76%
Soft rush *Juncus effusus*	328	73%
Hard rush *Juncus inflexus*	80	72%
Greater pond sedge *Carex riparia*	576	64%
Water mint *Mentha aquatica*	80	56%
Water forget-me-not *Myosotis scorpioides*	80	42%
Gypsywort *Lycopus europaeus*	80	11%
Total	1960	68% (mean)

practical and holistic approach by referring to the geology of the waterbody, e.g. chalk, sandstone, clay streams.

Water pollution takes many forms but enrichment from sewage or agricultural fertilisers, and hydrocarbons from urban or road run-off, are perhaps the most widespread causes of chronically-poor water quality. Such pollution may not be as dramatic as headline-catching events such as chemical spills, but the impact on aquatic ecology is just as profound.

Site indicators of chronic pollution include 'sewage fungus' – a straggling grey-white mass covering everything under the water. This can smother submerged aquatic plants and is sometimes the only plant in watercourses downstream of foul water connections or inadequate sewage treatment plants.

In slow-moving or still waters, algal blooms can be caused by enrichment from agricultural fertilisers. Floating and submerged plants may be impossible to establish in these conditions. Urban watercourses can appear to have good quality water. After rain flushes surface debris of adjacent hard surfaces they can however become sludge-rich, oily torrents.

Disturbance

The soft tissues and lax forms of many aquatic plants are particularly unsuited to withstanding disturbance and damage from trampling, grazing and spate flows, especially during the establishment phase. An assessment of the potential for disturbance from these and other causes should be done before finalising any planting proposal.

Plant selection

As with any type of landscape plants, the first step towards competent planting design with aquatics is to identify appropriate species. May, June and July are the best months for looking at aquatic plants. A good beginners' guide is *Aquatic Plants* by Spencer-Jones and Wade (1986). For a comprehensive identification guide, there is *British Water Plants* (Haslam *et al.*, 1982).

A good source of information on the ecological preferences of aquatic plants can be found in *The New Rivers and Wildlife Handbook* (RSPB, 1994). For a more limited range of aquatics, *Comparative Plant Ecology* (Grime *et al.*, 1988) is a good guide. A systematic review of British aquatic plant communities can be found in *British Plant Communities Volume 4* often called the National Vegetation Classification (Rodwell *et. al.*, 1995).

From the point of view of the plant specifier, the problem with such reference books is that they make no concession to the commercial reality of what is readily available for planting 'off the shelf'. For this reason the ecological information presented later in this chapter is restricted to those common native species that are generally available from commercial nurseries.

In both urban and rural contexts, the use of native aquatic plant species is strongly desirable

Fig. 21.3 Aesthetically pleasing effects can be created with native species: this is amphibious bistort (*Persicaria amphibia*) forming a floating mat with delicate pink flowers. (Photo: Kevin Patrick)

(Fig. 21.3). There have been many ecological problems caused by introductions of non-native wetland plants in recent years. In the 1960s, species such as New Zealand pigmyweed *Crassula helmsii*, Nuttall's waterweed *Elodea nuttallii*, least duckweed *Lemna minuta* and parrot's-feather *Myriophyllum aquaticum* were very rare or unrecorded in the UK; today these species are widespread and some are becoming pest species. It is not easy to tell which species will, and which will not, escape from the garden pond and colonise the wider environment. Under no circumstances should non-natives be planted in rivers and streams.

Just as importantly, it is unnecessary to use non-native aquatic plant species in even the most urban context. Dramatic effects can be achieved by the simplest of detailing; the strong arrow-like foliage of bulrush or yellow iris emerging from a reflecting pool or a sheet of duckweed in a courtyard can create a memorable image. For courtyard pools and garden ponds, the species listed in Table 21.5 are suggested as a basic urban palette.

Information on a wide range of common, native aquatic and wet marginal plants that are commercially available and recommended for planting

Table 21.5 Native plants for urban pools.

Species		Function
Yellow iris	*Iris pseudacorus*	Form and flower
Common duckweed	*Lemna minor*	Water covering
Purple loosestrife	*Lythrum salicaria*	Late summer colour
Common Water-starwort	*Callitriche stagnalis*	Oxygenator
Flowering rush	*Butomus umbellatus*	Form and flower
Marsh marigold	*Caltha palustris*	Spring colour
Water plantain	*Alisma plantago-aquatica*	Form
Spiked water-milfoil	*Myriophyllum spicatum*	Oxygenator
Water mint	*Mentha aquatica*	Scent
Hard/soft rush	*Juncus inflexus/effusus*	Form
Pendulous sedge	*Carex pendula*	Form, shade tolerant, evergreen

is given in Table 21.6. Nomenclature follows Stace (1991).

21.3   Sources of aquatic plants

Once a list of aquatic species has been chosen to achieve the objectives of the scheme and match the environmental parameters of the site, it is necessary to consider the plant source. There are four main options.

Nursery grown

Specialist aquatic nurseries are able to provide moderate quantities of native aquatics at short notice during the growing season. These plants are offered rooted in pots or, for submerged and floating aquatics, they are sold in tied bunches. Aquatics can also be specified bare-root. Bare-root plants are normally delivered to site immediately after packaging by the nursery. Wet plants are typically packed into plastic bags, sometimes with damp newspaper, moss or gel, and placed in cardboard boxes or, for large quantities, wooden crates or pallets.

Specifying from a nursery catalogue is convenient but it does have disadvantages. The range of available species is inevitably restricted. This can preclude a high degree of ecological sophistication for habitat creation schemes. Native or other specific provenances cannot always be guaranteed; indeed few of the specialist nurseries even claim to propagate from native provenance stock. The use of non-local populations or cultivars of native species may lead to adverse changes in the genetic structure of local populations of aquatic plants (see Chapter 2). Plant specifiers have a responsibility to seek, and create the demand for, stock of at least native provenance; they should avoid planting garden cultivars and non-natives species. Any planting in or near to a riverine SSSI should utilise not just native but local provenance stock, to ensure the genetic authenticity of local plant populations.

Commercially-produced aquatics can harbour undesirable weed species, notoriously New Zealand pigmyweed (*Crassula helmsii*), an extremely invasive alien plant which can form extensive blankets in lakes and ponds. Nursery grown plants are also expensive for large-scale schemes.

A recent innovation is the production of ready-grown aquatic and marginal plants in a reinforced substrate, known as rolls, pallets, mattresses or carpets. This is a specialist bio-engineering technique and liaison with the supplier is essential. Experience in the Environment Agency has shown some of these products to be very successful for the establishment of marginal vegetation in situations where substrate would not normally occur.

Table 21.6 Ecological and other characteristics of important British aquatic and wetland species (Adapted from RSPB, 1994; nomenclature follows Stace).

Key: ■ preferred conditions, most frequently found or high tolerance; ▲ very commonly found or fair/good tolerance; ❑ occasionally found or moderate tolerance; blank – rarely found, absent or intolerant; ○ information not available or not applicable; U = upland only; L = lowland only; T = transitional; Thr = throughout.

	Altitude	Substrate						Flow			
		Clay	Silt	Peat	Sand	Gravel/pebble	Cobble/boulder	Nil/slow	Moderate	Fast/rapid	More than 1 m
Free-floating unrooted											
Rigid hornwort, *Ceratophyllum demersum*	L	▲	■		❑	❑		■			■
Frogbit, *Hydrocharis morsus-ranae*	L	▲	▲					■			■
Submerged narrow leaved											
Mare's tail, *Hippuris vulgaris*	L	▲	❑		❑	■		❑	■		❑
Bulbous rush, *Juncus bulbosus*	UT				▲	■		❑	▲	■	
Common water crowfoot, *Ranunculus aquatilis*	Thr					■	❑	▲	▲	❑	
Arrowhead, *Sagittaria sagittifolia*	L	■	■					■	❑		
Spiked water milfoil; *Myriophyllum spicatum*	Thr	▲	■			▲		■	▲	▲	▲
Submerged broad leaved											
Common water starwort, *Callitriche stagnalis*	Thr	▲	▲			▲	❑	▲	■		
Curled pondweed, *Potamogeton crispus*	T-L	▲	❑		❑	▲		▲	▲	❑	
Rooted floating-leaved											
White water lily, *Nymphaea alba*	Thr	■	❑		▲			■			▲
Broad-leaved pondweed, *Potamogeton natans*	Thr	▲	▲	❑	❑	❑	▲	▲	❑	❑	■
Emergent narrow-leaved											
Water plantain, *Alisma plantago-aquatica*	L	■	❑					■	❑		
Flowering rush, *Butomus umbellatus*	L	■	❑		▲			■	▲		
Common spike-rush, *Eleocharis palustris*	Thr	▲	▲	▲		❑	❑	▲	▲	❑	
Water horsetail, *Equisetum fluviatile*	Thr	▲	▲	▲				■			
Common reed, *Phragmites australis*	L	▲	▲	▲				■			❑
Emergent broad-leaved											
Watercress, *Rorippa nasturtium aquaticum*	L	▲	▲					■	❑		
Water dock, *Rumex hydrolapathum*	L	■	▲					■			
Encroaching plants											
Lesser pond sedge, *Carex acutiformis*	L	■	▲		❑			■	▲		
Greater pond sedge, *Carex riparia*	L	▲	▲	▲				■			
Bogbean, *Menyanthes trifoliata*	Thr	▲	▲	▲				■			
Amphibious bistort, *Persicaria amphibia*	L	▲	▲		▲			▲	❑		
Pink water-speedwell, *Veronica catenata*	T-L	▲	▲					■	▲		
Narrow-leaved marginals											
Slender tufted-sedge, *Carex acuta*	L	▲	❑		❑			■	❑		○
Common sedge, *Carex nigra*	U-T		❑	▲		▲		▲	▲	▲	○
Pendulous sedge, *Carex pendula*	L	■					■		❑		○
Yellow flag iris, *Iris pseudacorus*	T-L	▲	▲		❑			■	▲	❑	○
Jointed rush, *Juncus articulatus*	U-T	▲	❑	❑	▲			▲	▲		○
Soft rush, *Juncus effusus*	U-T	■		❑				▲	▲	❑	○
Hard rush, *Juncus inflexus*	U-L	■			❑			■	▲		○
Branched bur-reed, *Sparganium erectum*	T-L	▲	■					■	❑		○
Lesser bulrush, *Typha angustifolia*	L	▲	■	❑				■			○

Depth			River width				Chemistry			Water quality							Where to plant					Plant size		
0.5–1 m	0.1–0.5 m	dry–0.1	More than 20 m	10–20 m	5–10 m	Less than 5 m	Base poor	Neutral	Base rich	Clean	Moderate	Polluted	**Shade tolerance**	**Disturbance tolerance**	**Stabilising ability**	**Scour resistance**	Open water	Just submerged	At water level	Just above	30 cm above	Taller than 1 m	0.5–1 m	Shorter than 0.5 m
❑			▲	▲	▲			❑	▮	▲	▮	❑	▮	▮	○	○	○	○	○	○	○	○	○	○
❑			▲	▲	▲				▮	❑	▮			❑	○	○	○	○	○	○	○	○	○	○
▮	▮		❑	▮	▮	❑		❑	▮	▮	❑			❑	○	○	○	○	○	○	○	○	○	○
▲	▮			▮	▮	❑	▮	❑		▮			▮	▮	○	○	○	○	○	○	○	○	○	○
❑	▮	❑		▲	▲	▲	▲	▲		▮	▲			▮	○	○	○	○	○	○	○	○	○	○
❑	▮		▲	▲	▲	▲		▲	▮	▲	▲	▲		▮	○	○	○	○	○	○	○	○	○	○
▲			▲	▲	▲				▮	▲	▲		❑	❑	○	○	○	○	○	○	○	○	○	○
▮	▮		❑	▲	▲	▲	❑	▮	❑	▮	▲		▮	❑	○	○	○	○	○	○	○	○	○	○
▲	▮		▲	▲	▲	▲		▮	▲	▲	▲	▲	❑	▮	○	○	○	○	○	○	○	○	○	○
▲	❑		▲	▲	▲	❑	▲	▲	❑	▮			❑		○	○	○	○	○	○	○	○	○	○
❑		▲	▲	▲	❑	▲	▲	▲		▲	▲			▮	○	○	○	○	○	○	○	○	○	○
	▲	▮			▲	▲		❑	▮	▲	▲			▮		❑			▮	▮			▲	▲
❑	▮	❑	❑	▮	▮				▮	▲	▲			❑	○	○	○	○	○	○	○	○	○	○
	▲	▮	▲	▲	▲	▲	❑	▮	❑				❑		▮	▮		▲	▲		▲			▮
	▮	❑	▲	▲	▲	▲	❑	▲	▲		▮	❑	❑		○	○	○	○	○	○	○	○	○	○
▲	▲	▮	❑	❑	▲	▲		▲					❑		❑				▮			▮		
	▲	▮		❑	❑	▮		❑	▮	▲	▲		❑			❑		▮	▮				▲	▮
	❑	▮	▲	▲	▲				▮	▲	❑				○	○	○	○	○	○	○	○	○	○
	▲	▮	no preference					▲	▲	▲	▲	▲		▮	▮	▮			▮	▲		❑	▲	▮
	▲	▮	no preference					▲	▲	▲	▲	▲	❑	▮	○	○	○	○	○	○	○	○	○	○
❑	▮	▲	❑	❑	❑	▲	▲	▲	▲	▮				❑	○	○	○	○	○	○	○	○	○	○
		▮	no preference					▲	▲	▲	▲	▲	❑		❑					▮			▲	▲
	❑	▲		▲	▲	▲		▲	▲	▮	▲			❑	○	○	○	○	○	○	○	○	○	○
○	○	○	○	○	○	○		▮	▲	○	○	○		○	▮	▮			▮				▮	
○	○	○	○	○	○	○	❑	▮	❑	○	○	○	❑	○	▮	▮			▲	▲				▲
○	○	○	○	○	○	○	▲	▲		○	○	○	▮	○					▮				▮	
○	○	○	○	○	○	○		▲	▲	○	○	○	❑	○	▮	▮		▮	▮			▮	❑	
○	○	○	○	○	○	○	▮	❑		○	○	○	❑	○	▮	▮					▮			
○	○	○	○	○	○	○	▮	▲		○	○	○	❑	○	▮	▮					▲			▲
○	○	○	○	○	○	○		▲	▮	○	○	○		○	▮	▮					▮		▲	▲
○	○	○	○	○	○	○		▲	▲	○	○	○	▮	○	▮	▮		▲	▲	▲		▮	▲	
○	○	○	○	○	○	○		▲	▲	○	○	○		○	▮	❑			❑	▮		▮		

Table 21.6 *Continued*

Key: ■ preferred conditions, most frequently found or high tolerance; ▲ very commonly found or fair/good tolerance; ❏ occasionally found or moderate tolerance; blank – rarely found, absent or intolerant; ○ information not available or not applicable; U = upland only; L = lowland only; T = transitional; Thr = throughout.	Altitude	Substrate						Flow			
		Clay	Silt	Peat	Sand	Gravel/pebble	Cobble/boulder	Nil/slow	Moderate	Fast/rapid	More than 1 m
Broad-leaved marginals											
Water mint, *Mentha aquatica*	T-L	▲	❏		▲	▲		▲	▲	❏	○
Water figwort, *Scrophularia auriculata*	T-L	▲	❏		▲			■	▲		○
Marsh marigold, *Caltha palustris*	U-T	▲		▲				▲	▲		○
Meadowsweet, *Filipendula ulmaria*	Thr	▲		▲	❏			▲	▲	❏	○
Purple loosestrife, *Lythrum salicaria*	L	▲	▲	❏	▲			■	❏		○
Gypsywort, *Lycopus europaeus*	L	▲	❏		▲			■	▲		○
Marsh woundwort, *Stachys palustris*	T-L	▲	❏		▲			▲	▲		○
Butterbur, *Petasites hybridus*	T-L	❏			▲	▲		❏	■	❏	○
Hemp agrimony, *Eupatorium cannabinum*	T-L	▲	❏		▲		❏	■	❏		○
Large bittercress, *Cardamine amara*	T-L	▲		▲				▲	❏		○
Common marsh bedstraw, *Galium palustre*	T-L	▲	▲	▲	❏			■	❏		○
Water avens, *Geum rivale*	Thr	▲	■	■				▲			○
Water forget-me-not, *Myosotis scorpioides*	T-L	▲	▲	▲	▲	❏	❏	▲	▲	❏	○
Water chickweed, *Myosotis aquaticum*	L	▲	▲		▲			■	❏		○
Lesser spearwort, *Ranunculus flammula*	Thr	❏		▲		▲		■	❏	▲	○
Greater spearwort, *Ranunculus lingua*	T-L	❏	❏	■				■	❏		○
Celery leaved-buttercup, *Ranunculus sceleratus*	L	▲	■					■	❏		○
Ivy-leaved crowfoot, *Ranunculus hederaceus*	U	❏	▲	▲				■			○
Brooklime, *Veronica beccabunga*	Thr	■	❏	❏	▲	❏	❏	■	▲		○

Natural colonisation

Natural colonisation is a sensible alternative to planting if the site is adjacent to an existing and comparable habitat that already contains a good range of aquatic species. Ecological authenticity is thereby guaranteed at no cost. However, this is a risky option if any problem or alien species occur near the site (or, for riparian sites, anywhere upstream) as these species will often colonise the site to the exclusion of more desirable species.

Naturally colonising vegetation will not resemble established communities for at least several years: the new community will probably be dominated by competitive and ruderal species such as bulrush (*Typha latifolia*), celery-leaved buttercup (*Ranunculus sceleratus*) and fool's watercress (*Apium nodiflorum*), although exact species composition will depend on location and habitat. Natural colonisation can be augmented by any of the other source options to enhance habitat diversity.

Collect and import

The main advantage of the collect and import option is that it provides ecological authenticity, providing that the donor site is a natural habitat without alien species.

Propagules of naturally occurring plants can be collected from other sites and imported to a com-

Depth			River width				Chemistry			Water quality							Where to plant					Plant size		
0.5–1 m	0.1–0.5 m	dry–0.1	More than 20 m	10–20 m	5–10 m	Less than 5 m	Base poor	Neutral	Base rich	Clean	Moderate	Polluted	**Shade tolerance**	**Disturbance tolerance**	**Stabilising ability**	**Scour resistance**	Open water	Just submerged	At water level	Just above	30 cm above	Taller than 1 m	0.5–1 m	Shorter than 0.5 m
○	○	○	○	○	○	○		▲	▲	○	○	○	▮	○	▮	▮				▮			▲	▲
○	○	○	○	○	○	○		▲	▲	○	○	○	▮	○		❑				▲	▲		▮	
○	○	○	○	○	○	○		▮	❑	○	○	○	▮	○					▮		▮		▲	▮
○	○	○	○	○	○	○		▲	▲	○	○	○	▮	○	▮	▮				▮			▮	
○	○	○	○	○	○	○		❑	▮	○	○	○	❑	○	❑			❑	▮	❑			▲	▲
○	○	○	○	○	○	○		▲	▲	○	○	○	❑	○	❑	❑				▲	▮		▲	▲
○	○	○	○	○	○	○		▲	▲	○	○	○	❑	○	▮						▮		▲	▲
○	○	○	○	○	○	○		▮	❑	○	○	○	▮	○	▮	▮			❑	▮		▲	▲	
○	○	○	○	○	○	○		▲	▲	○	○	○	▮	○	▮	▮				▮	▮	▲	▲	
○	○	○	○	○	○	○		▮	❑	○	○	○	▮	○	❑	❑				▮	▮			▮
○	○	○	○	○	○	○		▲	▲	○	○	○	❑	○		❑					▮			▮
○	○	○	○	○	○	○		❑	▮	○	○	○	▮	○	▮	❑		▮	❑				❑	▮
○	○	○	○	○	○	○	❑	▮	▲	○	○	○	❑	○	▮	▮				▮			❑	▮
○	○	○	○	○	○	○		❑	▮	○	○	○	▮	○					▮				▲	▲
○	○	○	○	○	○	○	❑	▮	❑	○	○	○	❑	○	❑	▮								▮
○	○	○	○	○	○	○		▲	❑	○	○	○		○	❑	❑				▮				▲
○	○	○	○	○	○	○		❑	▮	○	○	○	❑	○	❑	❑			▮				❑	▮
○	○	○	○	○	○	○	▮			○	○	○	❑	○					▲	▲				▮
○	○	○	○	○	○	○		▮		○	○	○	❑	○	❑	❑				▮	❑			▮

patible receptive environment, providing that the permission of the donor site landowner is obtained and the species involved are abundant. In the event that the donor site is an SSSI, or a rare species is involved, the consent of English Nature or the relevant national agency is mandatory. A recent planting trial of common water-crowfoot (*Ranunculus aquatilis*) on the River Kennet SSSI was carried out by planting surplus plant material cut from the same river. This was preferred to importing commercially-grown stock because it ensured genetic authenticity.

Plants can be imported in three ways: as root rich dredgings, as individually collected plants and as seed.

Root rich dredgings

The Environment Agency and other water managers regularly dredge silt from selected waterbodies for operational reasons. Such dredgings often contain a wealth of aquatic rhizomes.

This can be an effective way of providing large-scale aquatic planting. However, the technique should be used with restraint and due regard for the donor site. It is not good practice to damage one habitat solely for the purpose of re-creating it elsewhere.

Unfortunately the logistics of dredged spoil transfer are complex and this can restrict the technique to transfers within a site, or between adjacent sites where road transport is feasible from riverbank to riverbank.

The de-watering period for dredged spoil varies from two to seven days. If the spoil is too wet, expensive watertight containers are needed; if it is too dry, plant establishment is impaired. The timing of operations at site is therefore critical.

Individually collected plants

This technique usually requires skilled supervision if it is to be successful but it can be very useful for small-scale projects, perhaps involving local interest groups. Most landscape contractors are also willing to carry out this work, if they are given enough information at the tender stage.

The period between collection and planting should be kept to a minimum. Same day transplanting between compatible sites can achieve near 100 per cent success rates for many wetland species.

Seed

Little is known about the seeding of aquatic plants, and without close control of water levels, propagation from seed is unlikely to be successful. However it is probably worth trying locally collected seed for annuals and biennials, and for rushes (*Juncus* spp.), yellow iris (*Iris pseudacorus*), and water-plantain (*Alisma plantago-aquatica*).

Contract growing

For really large habitat creation schemes, e.g. reedbeds, it is advisable to think ahead and propagate plants from native provenance stock. If more than a thousand of any one species is required, contract growing should be investigated (one or two hundred is the threshold for uncommon species), especially if container grown plants are specified. The nursery that wins a tender for supply will normally expect some form of written commitment from the purchaser.

Virtually all aquatic plants can be contract grown if a supplier is given nine months notice, and for planting in late summer, many species can be provided at only three months notice. However, aquatic plants are dormant over the winter season, so if large quantities are required for planting before May contract growers should be appointed by the previous August at the latest.

21.4 Planting

The ideal time for aquatic planting is May. Most species can be planted throughout the summer and pot-grown plants are available and can be planted all year round, although planting in mid-winter is not recommended. Submerged and floating species are not generally available until May, and for bare-rooted plants it is advisable to discuss seasonal availability with the nurseries. Bulrush (*Typha* spp.), for example, is best planted in winter if bare-root stock is used.

There are three vital components to a successful aquatic planting operation.

- Achieve good contact with the substrate.
  This is not relevant to unrooted floating plants but it is important for all the others, especially those planted in flowing water which must achieve a good root hold before the next flood. Planting bunches of submerged plants into shallow water can be done by notch planting and firming down. For water over 50 cm deep, the plants must be well-weighted (binding to stones or perforated bricks is one technique) and dropped onto the substrate.

  For water-lilies and some rooted emergents, deep water planting (not deeper than 1 m) can be done by enclosing the root ball in a coarse hessian sack containing stones, tying the top and dropping into place. Pot grown plants tend to be buoyant and are best planted at, or just above, water level. Emergent species with colonising roots can then spread into deeper water. Planting into soft substrates is normally straightforward but when gravel river beds are encountered it may be necessary to use steel spikes to create notches.

- Use fresh plant material.
  Aquatic plants can deteriorate quickly once out of their normal environment; floating and sub-

merged plants are especially vulnerable to mis-handling. It is important to specify a maximum duration between dispatch from supplier to planting. Same day planting is ideal, but within 48 hours is acceptable if the plants are kept damp and cool.

- Place each species in the correct situation for its ecological preferences, especially in relation to bank profile and water depth.

Site supervision and knowledge of the plant species is essential. Contractors are sometimes unfamiliar with aquatic planting and it is unlikely that drawings will be sufficiently detailed or accurate to help. Planting by contractors without adequate site supervision may result in aquatic species being planted in soil that is either too wet or too dry to support their successful growth.

On riparian planting sites, especially in urbanised catchments, it may be advisable to do the planting in two phases: plant 50 per cent of the plants and treat the rest as a provisional item. This cautious approach has two advantages. First, even a moderate flood soon after planting can be devastating if the plants have not had time to root into the substrate properly, so planting in consecutive years simply spreads the risk. Second, it gives the designer a chance to observe which plants do best, and in which locations. This allows the opportunity for design modifications or manipulation of environmental variables (e.g. crown lifting to reduce tree shade). In addition, if the first phase has been successful, the second batch of plants may not be needed at all.

Planting density and size

As previously noted, aquatic plants have the potential to grow and spread at a speed which is spectacular compared with most terrestrial plants. This has two important consequences for the plant specifier.

First, fewer plants per square metre can be specified than for terrestrial planting. It is helpful to think of aquatic planting in terms of inoculating the site with highly dynamic life forms, instead

Table 21.7 Planting rates according to plant type.

Plant type	Planting rate
Unrooted floating	1 or 2 per 10 m²
Submerged floating	1 per 10 m²
Emergent	1 or 2 per m² (more for reed beds)
Marginal	2 or 3 per m² or 2–3 per linear metre at water's edge

of ground cover or carpet bedding. Table 21.7 provides an approximate guide to planting rates according to plant type.

Second, there is little point in specifying large container sizes. Specialised situations such as courtyard pools in commercial settings may require the instant effect of mature plants in large tubs, but in the majority of aquatic planting schemes the 9 cm pot can be thought of as the upper end of the size range. Where a quick cover is required with 'sheet forming' species such as common reed (*Phragmites australis*), or brooklime (*Veronica beccabunga*), the logical approach is to use the smallest available size planted at a density of three or four plants per m².

However, in the previously reported planting trial on excavated gravel substrate (see Table 21.4) the 9 cm potted plants established best (81 per cent establishment in the first year) while 5 cm modular plants (61 per cent establishment) fared worse than bare rooted plants (75 per cent establishment). Smaller plants are likely to be less suitable for sites subject to severe wave action, and other forms of physical disturbance.

21.5   Problems

Aggressive species that competitively exclude other species

Site managers should be able to identify all of the species listed in Table 21.8 so that they can be controlled if found on site. *The Wildlife and Countryside Act 1981* makes it an offence to plant or cause Japanese knotweed and giant hogweed to grow in the wild.

Table 21.8   Invasive alien species.

Japanese knotweed	*Fallopia japonica*
Giant hogweed	*Heracleum mantegazzianum*
Indian balsam	*Impatiens glandulifera*
N.Z. pigmyweed	*Crassula helmsii*
Water fern	*Azolla* spp.

Table 21.9   Invasive native species.

Duckweed	*Lemna* spp.
Canadian waterweed	*Elodea canadensis*
Yellow water-lily	*Nuphar lutea*
Fools water-cress	*Apium nodiflorum*
Reed sweet-grass	*Glyceria maxima*
Hemlock water-dropwort	*Oenanthe crocata*
Bulrush	*Typha latifolia*

The Environment Agency can offer guidance on the control of these plants, and has produced a booklet (NRA, 1994) which deals with the first three species on the above list.

Native species can also be problematic, depending upon location and site conditions. Species listed in Table 21.9 have a reputation for colonising sites unaided and rapidly establishing mono-specific stands. These species are not recommended for planting other than in situations where nothing else will survive, such as heavily polluted or problematic urban sites.

Common reed (*Phragmites australis*) also has a tendency to spread beyond its bounds and unless an extensive reedbed is wanted, this species should be used with caution. On small sites it can be planted in situations where its spread is limited by deep water on the water side, and by some form of restraint (physical or management) on the landward side.

Captive wildfowl

With the possible exception of Canada geese, free flying waterbirds are to be welcomed but the introduction of clipped-wing ducks to lakes and ponds should be avoided. They can graze out most aquatic plant species.

Fish

Unless angling is to be an objective, coarse fish should not be introduced to ponds and lakes because they tend to suppress populations of invertebrates and amphibians through predation. On fine sediment substrates, bottom-feeding fish can increase turbidity, which suppresses submerged aquatic plant growth.

Algal blooms

Mechanical removal of algae is onerous and rarely successful. Algal blooms can be combatted by introducing bales of barley straw to the water at a rate of $20-50 \, g/m^3$ for still waters, more for flowing water. Although it is still not fully understood, this is a proven and well-documented technique (Ridge *et al.*, 1995).

21.6   Management

The management of aquatic vegetation is a subject in itself, and this chapter does not attempt to cover it in detail. However, the guiding principle that must always be observed is that the success of any planting scheme is largely dependent upon achieving a close match between anticipated and actual aftercare. It is therefore essential at the design stage to liaise with the persons who will be responsible for the site.

Design for minimum management and do not rely on traditional weeding techniques during the defects liability period or in the long term. Establishing aquatic communities is more akin to wildflower seeding than to tree or shrub planting; it is not possible to avoid the earlier stages of ecological succession. The site will probably be colonised to some degree by ruderal species and although these may be perceived as 'weeds', it may not be appropriate or economically viable to try and remove them. In some cases they will disappear after a couple of years as the longer term species develop. The competitive alien species listed in Table 21.8 should be tackled as a priority. In some cases it may also be desirable to reduce the dominance of monoculture-forming native species.

Fig. 21.4 A typical riverside management approach: cut and stack all emergent vegetation on alternate banks in late summer. (Photo: Kevin Patrick)

In the longer term, no site manager will want the onerous task of selectively controlling certain plants, in what may be an intimate mix of species, under the difficult conditions of aquatic habitats. Instead, management will take the form of broad brush, often brutal, operations such as dredging or weed cutting (Fig 21.4). It is important to minimise the ecological impact of such operations by working on areas in rotation or on alternate banks.

The long-term management of aquatic vegetation usually generates large quantities of material for disposal, either as dredged silt or cut vegetation. This raises questions about machine access and whether the material can be spread on adja-

cent land or must be taken to a pre-determined dump site. It is important to consider these points at the design stage and incorporate them in a management plan.

Most newly-planted aquatic sites will have achieved some level of stability and pattern by the third growing season, although for ponds and lakes this is only the start of the long process of ecological succession which leads inexorably towards dry land. For unmanaged rivers and streams, this process usually culminates in bank sides dominated by trees such as willow or alder, sometimes to the detriment of aquatic plants that need light. Clear management objectives are necessary to decide whether maintenance works should actively check the natural colonisation and growth of woody plants.

References

Andrews, J. & Kinsman, D. (1990) *Gravel Pit Restoration for Wildlife*, RSPB, Bedfordshire.

Coppin, N.J. & Richards, I.G. (1990) *Use of Vegetation in Civil Engineering.* CIRIA, Butterworths, Kent.

Ebstam, B. (1992) Establishment of reedbeds. In: *Reedbeds for Wildlife*, D. Ward (ed.). RSPB / University of Bristol, Bedfordshire.

Grime, J.P., Hodgson, J.G., & Hunt, R. (1998) *Comparative Plant Ecology.* Unwin Hyman Ltd, London.

Haslam, S.M. (1978) *River Plants.* Cambridge University Press, Cambridge.

Haslam, S.M, Sinker, C.A., & Wolseley, P.A. (1982) *British Water Plants.* Field Studies Council, Shrewsbury.

NRA (1994) *Guidance for the control of invasive plants near watercourses.* National Rivers Authority, Bristol.

Ridge, I., Pillinger, J., & Walters, J. (1995) Alleviating the problems of excessive algal growth. In: *The Ecological Basis for River Management*, Harper, D.M. & Ferguson A.J.D. (eds.). Wiley, Chichester.

Rodwell, J.S., Pigott, C.D., Ratcliffe, D.A., Malloch, A.J.C., Birks, H.J.B., Proctor, M.C.F., Shimwell, D.W., Huntley, J.P., Radford, E., Wiggington, M.J., & Wilkins, P. (1995) *British Plant Communities Volume 4: Aquatic and Swamp Communities.* Cambridge University Press, Cambridge.

RSPB, NRA and RSNC (1994) *The New Rivers and Wildlife Handbook.* RSPB, Bedfordshire.

Spencer-Jones, D. & Wade, M. (1986) *Aquatic Plants.* ICI Professional Products, Farnham, Surrey.

Stace, C. (1991) *New Flora of the British Isles.* Cambridge University Press, Cambridge.

Ward, D. (1992) Management of reedbeds for wildlife. In: *Reedbeds for Wildlife*, D. Ward (ed.). RSPB / University of Bristol, Bedfordshire.

Young, S. (1995) Fertilisers in freshwater. *Enact*, (English Nature), **3**, (1), 16–17.

Further reading

EA (1998) *Flood Defence Conservation Requirements for Watercourse Maintenance Works.* Environment Agency, Bristol.

22 Direct-sown Annual Meadows

Nigel Dunnett

In a horticultural sense, the concept of an annual plant has become rather blurred, linked more to use than to a strict botanical definition. Indeed, many of the plants used in annual bedding schemes (see Chapter 23) are actually frost-sensitive perennials that are discarded after one growing season. Technically, however, an annual is a plant that completes its life cycle (from germination, flowering and seed production to death) in the space of a single year. These plants have evolved an annual life cycle as an adaptation to the environmental conditions in which they originate. This chapter suggests an approach to the use of annuals that mimics these environmental conditions to produce a relatively low-input method for introducing dramatic colour to small and large-scale sites (Fig. 22.1).

The advantages of using annuals as landscape plants are that:

- there is little delay between establishment and final growth form,
- flowering is rapid,
- the intensity of colour is unrivalled, and
- direct-sown annuals are very cheap, compared to other planting methods.

Of course, the downside is that the vegetation is transient and to some extent has to be renewed each year, so that there are periods when bare or cultivated ground is apparent, but even this enables experimentation and refinement of plant mixtures from year to year.

This chapter looks at the use of direct-sown mixtures of annual species to produce meadow-like displays, and is based upon the author's ex-perience of creating such meadows in parks in Sheffield. The use of the term 'meadow' in this context refers to the visual nature of the display: naturalistic and spontaneous intricate associations of flowering plants; compared to the image of a traditional native wildflower meadow, there may be no grass, or certainly a much reduced grass component.

22.1 Characteristics of annuals

The key characteristics of annuals are that they complete their life cycle in a short space of time, and that they reproduce by seed (often producing copious amounts). This 'ruderal' strategy has evolved to enable these plants to survive frequent disturbance events (such as floods, unstable ground conditions or droughts) in their native habitats. The rapid growth rate allows the plants to make the most of favourable growing conditions, while quick flowering and the production of large numbers of seed allows the plants to survive the next environmental disturbance through dispersing their seed in space or time (as buried dormant seed).

Longer-lived plants are unable to survive in these habitats because disturbance prevents them from gaining a hold. However, if that disturbance ceases (for example if annual cultivation of an arable field stops) then grasses and perennial flowering plants will rapidly become dominant.

It follows that to recreate the natural conditions that promote dominance of a piece of land by annuals, some form of regular disturbance to the system is essential. However, things are not quite

Fig. 22.1 Native-exotic annual meadow in a housing estate in Sheffield: annual meadows are low cost, high impact plantings for community spaces. (Photo: Nigel Dunnett)

Fig. 22.2 Spontaneous wild poppies on shingle at Dungeness, Kent – the natural model for direct-sown annual meadows. (Photo: Nigel Dunnett)

so simple. In order to achieve high growth rates and rapid flowering, annuals require fertile soil. This contradicts the usual wisdom that meadow-like vegetation establishes and persists better on lower-fertility substrates. It is no coincidence that the most familiar annuals (apart from those cultivated deliberately) are weeds of gardens or arable fields, or are actually the crops themselves. Weed control is another major consideration: creating conditions to foster desirable annuals also fosters undesirable annual weeds (such as groundsel, *Senecio vulgaris*) or disturbance-adapted perennials such as creeping thistle (*Cirsium arvense*) or couch grass (*Elymus repens*).

22.2   Sources of inspiration

Until 50 or 100 years ago, meadow-like displays of mixed annuals had been a part of the British summer landscape for centuries as cornfield weeds. Species such as corn flower (*Centaurea cyanus*), corn marigold (*Chrysanthemum segetum*), corn cockle (*Agrostemma githago*) and corn poppy (*Papavar rhoeas*) were common. The widespread use of herbicides has rendered all but the poppy more or less extinct from most of the British Isles. With reduced herbicide use at field

margins, field poppies are again becoming prominent at the edges of arable fields. The vibrant shimmering sheets of red amongst ripening corn ears gives a hint of what can be achieved with controlled sowings (Fig. 22.2).

Similar and even more intensively colourful displays can be found in other parts of the world. Mediterranean-type climates with mild winters and hot dry summers foster spring carpets of annuals such as are seen in southern Europe, South Africa and the Southwest USA. Impressive flowering sheets are not limited to natural examples: flowering crops, whether it be oil seed rape, sunflowers, flax or linseed, show just how easy it is to achieve impressive displays through simple techniques.

There is a drawback to these examples: in most cases the length of actual flowering display is short, from a matter of weeks to a couple of months. Designed landscapes must usually aim for better value from the space that the plantings occupy. For this reason it is best to use a range of species to extend the length of flowering display (as well as adding variations in texture and form) rather than relying on one or a few different plants to carry the effect.

Traditionally in direct sowings of annuals, these

different species would be sown in interlocking single species drifts or blocks to produce an annual bed or border. Not only is this time-consuming to produce, but it can result in a gappy or open structure to a planting if some species fail to establish, or when one of more of the plants have finished their display. It also lacks a naturalistic, spontaneous effect. For these reasons this chapter concentrates primarily on vegetation created through direct sowing of intimate mixtures of annuals.

22.3 Plant selection and mixture composition

Native species, non-natives and site context

The most commonly available mixtures of annuals for direct sowing are the so-called 'cornfield annual' mixtures of British native species. Other mixtures are available from a variety of sources that may be composed partly or entirely of exotic species. It is important to consider the context of a site when deciding whether or not to use a mixture containing non-native species. There is a real possibility that if non-native species are introduced in rural locations (such as roadsides or sites adjacent to arable fields), they may spread into adjacent disturbed sites or habitats, in much the same way that certain annual crops, such as oil-seed rape, persist in a location for several years after the original crop has been taken. Therefore, non-native mixtures should only be used in urban areas, or within the boundaries of what are clearly amenity or garden sites in rural areas. Such mixtures should never be used in the open countryside or adjacent to sites of nature conservation interest.

Outside of these areas, however, there need be no such scruples about the use of non-native annuals. For the majority of the species in native-only annual mixtures, the whole concept of nativeness is questionable: most species are either extinct or have an extremely localised distribution. For example, in the wild the corn marigold is largely restricted to coastal locations in Western Scotland. It certainly does not make sense in most general landscape situations to promote the use of local provenance seed sources for native annuals: they are either absent, or so mobile as to render the idea of locally adapted populations rather meaningless.

Monocultures

Monocultural sowings can produce extremely dramatic effects, perhaps best exemplified by the field-scale displays of flowering agricultural crops, such as sunflowers, maize, oil-seed rape and flax. These effects can be reproduced in designed settings, but in most instances the period of flowering display will be unacceptably short compared with the time from sowing to flowering, and post-flowering decline. Some species do however have attractive foliage and seed heads. Monocultural blocks are useful when used in conjunction with others to produce pattern-based designs, such as strips or geometric shapes.

Mixtures

In addition to the mixtures of 'native' annuals, several seed companies also supply non-native mixtures. In some cases these are rather random assortments of species to produce a 'riot of colour'. Other mixtures may be based on colour themes, or targeted at the overall length of display. Some seed companies will formulate a mixture to a client's specification. It is also possible to put together one's own mix from the component species if a pre-formulated mix is unsuitable. This can be a costly operation if done on a small scale. It is often more cost-efficient to 'top-up' or add additional species to a basic pre-formulated mixture (such as a native cornfield mix) if a wider diversity of species is required. Species that have proved valuable in mixes are shown in Table 22.1.

Precise mixture lists are outside the scope of this chapter, which deals rather with how a mixture may be composed. A satisfactory mixture for general landscape purposes will begin flowering within 6–8 weeks of a spring sowing, and should continue in flower into the autumn. It should also remain in an attractive condition throughout that

Table 22.1   Recommended annuals for use in direct sown mixes.

Name	Long Season	Rapid Flowerer	Late Flowerer	Emergent	Seed Plant	Star Performer	Suitable for monoculture	Dependable re-seeding
Agrostemma githago					•			•
Ammi majus	•							
Artemisia annua	•			•			•	
Atriplex hortensis 'Rubra'	•			•	•		•	•
Borago officinalis						•		
Calendula officinalis	•						•	•
Centaurea cyanus	•			•				
Chrysanthemum carinatum			•					
Chrysanthemum coronarium	•		•					
Chrysanthemum segetum	•						•	•
Coreopsis tinctoria			•	•			•	
Cosmos bipinnatus			•				•	
Crambe cordifolia		•			•			•
Delphinium ajacis			•					
Eschscholtzia californica	•							•
Gaillardia pulchella						•		
Gypsophila muralis		•						
Helianthus annua				•		•	•	
Helichrysum bracteatum	•							
Iberis umbellata						•		•
Limnanthes douglasii		•						•
Linaria maroccana		•						
Linum grandiflorum var rubrum	•							
Nicandra physaloides	•			•	•		•	
Nigella damascena					•	•	•	•
Papaver rhoeas						•		•
Papaver somniferum					•	•	•	•
Phacelia tanacetifolia		•						•
Raphanus raphanistrum		•				•		•
Reseda odorata						•		
Rudbeckia hirta			•					
Viscaria oculenta		•						

time. To achieve this, a well-balanced mixture may contain the following categories of plants.

Long-season species

These species will form the backbone of the mixture, providing a display over several months. Examples include *Centaurea cyanus*, *Ammi majus* and *Chrysanthemum segetum*.

Rapid-flowering species

These shorten the period between sowing and the beginning of an effective display. In most instances these species will be coming towards the end of their flowering period when the main flowering of the mixture begins. A number of such species (e.g. *Linaria* spp., *Gypsophila* spp. and *Viscaria* spp.) produce very slender plants with fine leaves that create little shade and allow later flowering species to grow up through them. Such species can be a relatively high component of the mixture. Others, such as *Phacelia tanacetifolia*, make much more bulky plants and are unattractive out of flower. Such species should be used at low density.

Late-flowering species

This is an extremely useful group that extends the life of a sown meadow into the autumn; as well as injecting additional colour, it also adds a degree of freshness to the vegetation at this time. Examples include the North American annuals *Coreopsis tinctoria* and *Cosmos bipinnatus*.

Emergents

Such species rise out the general mass of the vegetation and provide visual and structural diversity. To achieve this effect they should not be used in great quantity; if spread thinly throughout a mixture, they provide a visual rhythm to large areas. An example is *Atriplex hortensis*.

Species with attractive seed heads

These help to extend the season of display and provide structural interest. Many of the ornamental annual grasses fall into this category, as do species such as *Papaver somniferum*.

Star performers

These species have outstanding flowering or foliage attributes but may not have a particularly long season of display. Nevertheless, the inclusion of a number of such species in a mixture will ensure a succession of flowering effects over the season.

22.4 Site preparation and establishment of direct-sown annual mixes

The conditions required for an effective annual display are different to those specified for longer-term wildflower meadows, and are perhaps more akin to traditional horticultural practice. Low fertility substrates, and sites suffering compaction or impeded drainage, will tend to produce open, short and sparse vegetation that will generally be unsatisfactory.

It will be necessary to remove any existing perennial vegetation cover before site cultivation. In general this can be achieved through the application of a translocated herbicide prior to cultivation, allowing a suitable period of time to elapse as recommended by the manufacturer.

Once the perennial weeds have been dealt with, it will be necessary to plough or cultivate the site. The top 150 mm should be reduced to a tilth suitable for further grading. There is no need to strip or remove topsoil prior to sowing. On soils where fertility is known to be low, an application of a general purpose fertiliser three to five days prior to sowing may be beneficial, but in most cases this will not be necessary. On very dry or exposed sites, the incorporation of moisture retaining granules has also been recommended as a means of maintaining summer displays (Norfolk City Council, pers. comm.).

Prior to sowing, the site should be raked or harrowed to a depth of around 25 mm to produce an even, lightly firmed seed bed with good crumb structure. Seed can be sown broadcast directly onto this surface, or in evenly spaced drills at, for example, 300 mm apart. Drill sowing has the advantage that some weed management is possible in the early stages, but is more time consuming to undertake the sowing, unless using specialist equipment.

Broadcast sown seed can be mechanically distributed from hand-held, pedestrian-operated, or tractor-mounted spreaders. The temptation to sow too thickly should be avoided. Over large areas, seed can be sown at $1-3\,g\,m^2$; over smaller areas, or around the edges of larger areas, seed may be sown at $3-5\,m^2$ to increase flowering drama close to viewers. Following sowing, the mixed seed should be lightly raked or harrowed into the soil surface. On dry soils it may be necessary to roll the site to firm the ground.

Germination of weeds from the soil 'seed bank'

Unfortunately, the conditions that suit the germination and establishment of the sown annuals are also ideal for the establishment of weed seedlings, particularly those already present in the soil seed bank. On some sites this can be a real problem, swamping and out-competing the desired species. Several options are available to deal with this situation.

- A period can be left between the initial cultivation and the subsequent sowing, sufficient to allow germination from the seed bank. This weed cover can then be physically removed by hoeing or cultivation, or removed chemically through herbicide application. The downside to this approach is that only a proportion of seeds in the soil will germinate at any one time; any subsequent disturbance or cultivation will bring a fresh supply to the surface. A long-term programme of site treatment in this manner, over at least one complete growing season, may be necessary to have any impact on the soil seed bank.
- A second, and much more effective technique is to spread a weed free material over the top of the cultivated soil surface and to then sow onto that. Trials conducted at the University of Sheffield show that relatively thin layers, for example 10mm, can be sufficient to produce

annual vegetation dominated by desired species on very weedy sites (Dunnett and Hitchmough, 2001).

When to sow

Annuals can be direct-sown in spring or in autumn. An autumn sowing (September) will produce seedlings that will over-winter and flower early in the summer (May and June). While this may be welcome, there will be relatively little display at the end of the summer and into autumn, unless late season performers such as *Rudbeckia hirta* are included. A spring sowing will ensure flowers through summer and the autumn. Sowing at various times through the spring in Sheffield has indicated that there is little advantage to early sowing. The optimal time appears to be mid-late April, but sowing can continue up until the end of May. The later sowings tend to catch up rapidly because of warmer temperatures, and these later sowings will flower further into the autumn. As an indication, an annual mixture sown in the third week of April in Sheffield will start flowering at the end of May, be producing an effective display by the third week of June, and will then flower for at least four more months.

Subsequent maintenance and weed control

Maintenance requirements are minimal over the entire first growing period. The mixed annuals can be cut back at the end of the flowering period in late autumn, or the vegetation can be left standing over the winter. The dried skeletons of the annuals and their seed heads can be attractive and provide good feeding grounds for seed-eating birds such as goldfinches. There is no doubt that some people will find such vegetation untidy. Research at the University of Sheffield indicates that this is linked to familiarity: people who know what the mixed annual sowings look like in the summer and autumn tend to accept their winter appearance (Mynott, 2001). Certainly in Sheffield parks, where direct-sown annual plantings have been established alongside standard seasonal bedding in similar sized and shaped beds, the public reaction to the sown meadow has been animated and excited compared to the standard bedding (Plate 25).

In most instances it will be necessary to re-sow the meadow each year. Many of the component species will re-seed in subsequent years, and it is usually possible to sow at a reduced rate in later years, but is not a long-term strategy to rely on spontaneous re-sowing alone. The conditions that suit the desired annuals also suit undesirable weeds, and while the colourful annuals may mask the presence of the weeds in the early years, after a number of years the weeds will gradually build up. In addition, relying totally on re-seeding will also mean that the area will be come dominated by a small number of species that re-seed successfully.

In Sheffield, the annual meadow sites are cultivated afresh each spring. Weed control using a translocated herbicide is carried out at least every second year prior to cultivation. Unfortunately, perennial weeds that regenerate readily from broken fragments of roots or rhizomes can be strongly promoted by this annual disturbance regime. Such species include the field thistle, (*Cirsium arvense*), nettle (*Urtica dioica*), and couch grass (*Elymus repens*).

Many of these species can be controlled by a spring application of translocated herbicide prior to site cultivation. However, *Cirsium arvense* emerges relatively late in the year, and may not be controlled by such an application. This species has proved to be the most problematic in the Sheffield sowings: there is little option but to hand-pull it in early summer, when it is conspicuous above the annual seedlings, or to spot treat with herbicide when it is growing strongly. Other problem weeds will be specific to site, but in the first two years in Sheffield, creeping bent grass *(Agrostis stolonifera)* and heath speedwell *(Veronica officinalis)* both produced large spreading stands beneath the annual cover. Again, spring herbicide treatment prior to re-cultivation has been sufficient to control these species.

More problematic are annual and biennial species that grow and set copious seed within the sowings. In particular, rapid germinating species with fast growth rates can out-compete the sown annuals. Groundsel (*Senecio vulgaris*) is one such species that dominated areas in the Sheffield sowings in the first two years. An effective treatment for such species is to over-cut or strim the affected areas at flowering height, six to eight weeks after sowing (i.e. mid-June following a mid-late April sowing). This has the effect of preventing seed-set in the spontaneous weed species, while allowing the sown annuals to grow through. In Sheffield this has been sufficient to prevent the problem recurring. The best approach to dealing with such spontaneous annual contaminants is to use mulches to reduce weed germination rates.

22.5 Biennials and quick-to-flower perennials

Biennials and short-lived perennials are adapted to periodic environmental disturbance in the same way as annuals (albeit on a longer timescale) and can be managed from direct sowings in a similar way. Inclusion of some annuals (at about 10 per cent of the total weight) will ensure first year colour. Such a mix was sown in a Sheffield park in spring 1998 (Plate 26). Included in the mix were:

Digitalis purpurea 'Sutton's Apricot'
Hesperis matronalis
Leucanthemum vulgare
Salvia sclarea var. *turkestanica*

Flowering commenced in May 1999 with the first three species, while the *Salvia* bloomed in July and August and its dried skeletons remained as a conspicuous feature through the winter. The vegetation achieved a complete cover in the second year, leaving little opportunity for re-seeding of the biennials. However, the last three species are short-lived perennials and a repeat performance occurred in 2000, this time without the foxgloves. In spring 2001 the entire area was given an application of a translocated herbicide, cultivated and subsequently sown at a low rate with an annual seed mixture. In summer 2001, a survey of the area found abundant seedlings of the four original components, in approximately their original pro-

Table 22.2   Biennials and rapid-flowering perennials for direct sowing.

Species	Season	Type
Achillea 'Summer Pastels'	Summer	Short-lived perennial
Buphthalmum salicifolium	Summer	Perennial
Coreopsis lanceolata	Summer	Short-lived perennial
Digitalis purpurea & cvs	Spring/early summer	Biennial
Hesperis matronalis	Spring/early summer	Short-lived perennial
Hypericum perforatum	Summer	Short-lived perennial
Leucanthemum vulgare & cvs	Spring/early summer	Short-lived perennial
Linaria purpurea	Summer	Short-lived perennial
Lunaria annua	Spring	Biennial
Rudbeckia fulgida	Late summer/autumn	Perennial
Rudbeckia triloba	Late summer	Short-lived perennial
Salvia sclarea var. turkestanica	Summer	Short-lived perennial
Salvia nemorosa	Summer	Perennial
Verbascum thapsus, V.bombyciferum, V.olympicum	Summer	Biennial

portions, amongst the annuals. This suggests that biennial clearance and disturbance, combined with sowing an annual mix, will result in one year's biennial display interspersed with a year's annual flowering.

The results of other (as yet unpublished) work show that the use of annuals as a 'nurse crop' can be beneficial in reducing competition from grasses and unsown weeds in a longer-term perennial sowing. The major disadvantage of sowing perennial vegetation in public spaces is that it is visually unsatisfactory for at least its first year. The inclusion of annuals in a mixture overcomes this problem. It is essential that the annuals used are slender and do not produce foliage at ground level (although they may make a sparse canopy higher up). *Linaria maroccana, Linum grandiflora* var. *rubrum, Centaurea cyanus* and *Coreopsis tinctoria* were used effectively.

In trials the amount of grass invasion was effectively and significantly reduced to zero under the annuals. In the same sowings minus the annuals, a ten per cent cover of grass weeds was recorded. The numbers of sown perennials that established were not reduced significantly by the inclusion of annuals, but the mean height and spread of those perennial species was significantly reduced. It remains to be seen whether this has a serious effect

on performance in subsequent years, or whether the benefit of first year colour and the elimination of grass competition outweighs the possible disadvantage of smaller perennial species after the first year.

Biennials and rapid-flowering perennials are best used where relatively short-term displays are required; combinations of annuals, biennials and rapid-flowering perennials are useful for providing low-cost and low maintenance displays for up to three years. Table 22.2 lists some dependable species. While very many perennials will flower in their second year from seed, Table 22.1 includes species that will dependably make large, floriferous plants by their second year.

22.6   Summary

Where dependable, relatively low-cost and exciting naturalistic colour effects are required, meadow-like vegetation that flowers rapidly from direct-sown seed offers a variety of opportunities. There is an annual maintenance requirement to ensure year-on-year continuity, but this is much less than what is required to sustain standard bedding schemes. In more formal areas, small areas or garden-scale sites, this is a feasible means to introduce more relaxed types of planting.

On larger sites, annual meadows provide what is perhaps the most reliable and dependable means of producing colouful displays on more fertile sites in high profile locations. However, the ongoing commitment to weed control and re-cultivation must be recognised. Without this, the use of direct-sown annuals is probably best viewed as a short-term measure, perhaps for use on vacant sites or temporary sites, or as a precursor to more permanent vegetation types.

List of suppliers

Pictorial Meadows Ltd,
The Innovation Centre,
217 Portobello,
Sheffield,
S1 4DP
Tel. 0114 222 4432,
Fax 0114 222 4430

Moles Seeds
Turkey Cock Lane
Stanway
Colchester
Essex
CO3 5PD
Tel. 01206 213213
Fax 01206 212876

Suttons Seeds
Woodview Road
Paignton
Devon
TQ4 7NG
Tel 01803 696321
Fax 01803 696345

Mr Fothergill's Seeds Ltd
Gazeley Road
Kentford
Newmarket
Suffolk
CB8 7QB
Tel 01638 751161
Fax 01638 751624

References

Dunnett, N. & Hitchmough, J.D. (2001) First In, Last Out. *The Garden*, March 2001.
Mynott, L. (2001) User Perception of Naturalistic Meadow Vegetation in Parks. MA research dissertation, Department of Landscape, University of Sheffield.
Rice, G. (2001) *Discovering Annuals*. Frances Lincoln, London.

Further reading

Dunnett, N. (1999) Annuals on the Loose. *The Garden*, March 1999.
Lloyd, C. & Rice, G. (1996) *Garden Flowers from Seed*, Timber Press, London.
Phillips, R. & Rix, M. (2002) *Annuals and Biennials*. Pan, London.

23 Bedding Plants

Richard Bisgrove

'Bedding' is a system employing plants for temporary seasonal effect, usually in a more-or-less formal display. Conventionally summer bedding is planted in late May or early June (in the Northern hemisphere) to flower from June to September/October. It is then removed in October to be replaced by spring bedding of bulbs and biennials. These flower in April/May and are in turn removed to make way for the next cycle of summer bedding. There are, however, many variations on this simple theme.

Bedding is a much-maligned aspect of plant use. In the modern era, when anything and everything Victorian has been viewed with deep disdain, it has been seen (mistakenly) as synonymous with Victorian gardening. For several decades in the twentieth century, its use continued in the world of public parks in a debased form guaranteed to turn away those who might well have been attracted to the spectacle of real Victorian bedding. Bedding has also marked an important social divide between horticulturists, who are interested in plants, and landscape architects, who have had to decry decorative planting or any hint of humour in order to establish the dignity of their young profession.

As the Victorian period has receded into historical distance it has become increasingly respectable. Many facets of Victorian gardening have been rediscovered as entirely fitting for the twenty-first century. With the rediscovery of our public parks, and reinvestment in them (most notably through Heritage Lottery Funding), a now-mature landscape profession can realise the enormous opportunities for the use of bedding to enrich and enliven the public and private landscape.

23.1 Historical development

The origins of bedding lie much farther back than the nineteenth century, in the simple rectangular beds of the mediaeval garden. Throughout the fifteenth, sixteenth and seventeenth centuries these beds increased in size and complexity, incorporating ideas from the Renaissance gardens of Italy, France and the Netherlands and expanding into complicated 'knot gardens' of low, interwoven hedges. These developed into larger and grander parterres with elaborate scrollwork of box or other low evergreens against a background of sand, gravel or coloured minerals. Within this permanent framework, flowering plants – especially rare and novel plants – were displayed as individual specimens rather like ornaments in a china cabinet, or as ribbons of mixed colours. As each plant ceased to flower it was removed and replaced by later flowering plants from the greenhouses or reserve ground to maintain a continuous succession of interest (Green, 1956).

In the eighteenth century formal terraces and elaborate parterres were swept away. With the development of the English landscape garden, a naturalistic setting of grass and trees crept up to the walls of the house. The loss of flowers that was supposed to have resulted from the rise of landscape gardening is, though, greatly exaggerated. Enthusiasm for plant collecting increased rapidly throughout the eighteenth century, with town gardens and the walled garden complexes of rural estates becoming repositories for the swelling collections of new exotics from the colonies (Lemmon and Musgrave, 1968). *Pelargonium zonale* was introduced to Britain in 1710 and crossed with *P. inquinans* by 1714. 'Geranium africanum', the zonal pelargonium, was a popular flower by 1750 when Lancelot Brown was launching into practice as a landscape gardener.

The nineteenth century saw a return of formal gardening around the house (Fig. 23.1), and with it a revival of interest in the 'ancient or geometric' garden. Humphry Repton proposed a changing array of flowers for the Prince Regent's garden around the Brighton Pavilion and by 1826 J.C. Loudon was writing about the 'changeable flower garden' as an established feature (Elliot, 1986).

The early nineteenth-century parterre bore a superficial resemblance to its seventeenth-century precursor but its function as a display cabinet for rarities vanished. The decorative role became paramount and the practices of geometric gardening rapidly diversified. Initially the repertoire of plants familiar to George London and Henry Wise in the late seventeenth century were supplemented by many hardy annuals introduced from western North America by David Douglas and other collectors (Fletcher, 1969). By the 1840s, gardeners realised the potential of tender perennials – and most notably the zonal pelargonium or 'geranium' – for providing a long season of intense colour.

That recognition coincided with political changes in Central and South America and the introduction of a whole new range of half-hardy annuals and tender perennials: salvias, petunias, begonias etc. The flood of new introductions also coincided with the rapid expansion of industry, of wealth, new houses and new gardens, and the industrial technology to build and heat glasshouses in which the new flowers could be produced by the tens of thousands to supply the new gardens (Bisgrove, 1992).

The evergreen hedges diminished, and the new flower parterre became a geometrical pattern of annuals only, with the beds bare in the winter months. The brief season of the flower parterre was not important when families moved from their summer seats to winter 'in town', but by the 1860s the bareness of the winter garden near the house was noted (Fleming, 1870). At Cliveden and Dropmore in Buckinghamshire, the concept of spring bedding was developed, using biennials and short-lived perennials (forget-me-not, wallflower, arabis, aubrieta) interplanted with tulips, hyacinths and other bulbs.

The exotic and vividly colourful effects possible with bedding appealed to the professional gardener and to the very rich, whether *ancien* or *nouveau*, because of the opportunities it provided for spectacular display of skill and conspicuous display of wealth. The flower parterre took pride of place on terraces around the house alongside

Fig. 23.1 Prince Puckler Muskau's 'flower garden near the house' (1826), reproduced from M.L. Gothein (1928), *History of Garden Art*, Dent.

the many other garden features: herbaceous borders, shrub walks, rose gardens, arboreta and rock gardens etc.

The end of the nineteenth century saw an inevitable decline in the most elaborate forms of bedding. As gardening filtered down the social scale the bedding plant, formerly a sign of wealth and conspicuous consumption, appeared in the smaller gardens of the middle and even the labouring classes (Loudon, 1838).

The new generation of wealthy garden owners yearned for a simpler and more natural effect. A reaction to the 'vulgar excesses' of bedding was spearheaded by William Robinson in fierce tirades against 'pastry-cook gardening' and the 'painted gravel gardens' of W.A. Nesfield (Robinson, 1883, 1892). While Robinson attacked the old style, Gertrude Jekyll provided a more sophisticated yet more restrained example of garden making for the new generation. Her defence and extensive use of 'bedding' plants (Jekyll, 1914) went largely unnoticed by succeeding generations of gardeners, determined to see only evil in the bedding system.

Although bedding continued to be a component of most large gardens well into the twentieth century, the cumulative and combined effects of World War I, the 1929 Wall Street Crash and the soaring cost of labour spelled an end to lavish display in private gardens. Annuals were largely replaced by herbaceous perennials and by the new repeat-flowering Polyantha roses.

The growth of bedding in the second half of the nineteenth century had also coincided with the expansion of public parks. Here the enthusiasm of horticultural staff was unrestrained by the aristocratic 'good taste' of an employer and, especially in many industrial towns, bedding became the main feature of the public parks and a major focus of civic pride. More and more flower beds were planted, until the only function of a park was to be walked through and gasped at. Municipal bedding survived the vicissitudes of wars and depressions of the early twentieth century, but gradually lost its vitality. With a few notable exceptions local authority bedding schemes became increasingly hackneyed: concentric circles of red geraniums, white alyssum and blue lobelia.

Rising standards of living led to a decline in support for public parks: spiralling under-funding and declining standards left them vulnerable to competitive tendering in the 1980s, and death by a thousand budget cuts. In a new era of modern architecture, New Towns, motorways and other public landscapes, the new profession of landscape architecture cut its teeth on a new diet of simplicity and dignified professional restraint in which the bedding plant had no place.

All of these factors should have led to the extinction of the practice of bedding: but a further combination of factors has led, instead, to its spectacular revival. New mobility (including the mobility to visit garden centres), new interest from a greatly expanded property-owning class, and the new technology of plug plant production have created both the demand and the capacity to supply bedding plants of increased quality and acceptable price. Annuals provide instant colour for quick-fix gardens in a population moving frequently from one house to another.

Foreign holidays to France, Spain, Italy and other countries which retained the tradition of exciting, even garish, bedding showed the exciting potential of an erstwhile hackneyed tradition. The invention of the patio and outdoor living stimulated a demand for summer-long colour that only the annual or tender perennial could satisfy. The bedding plant, though not often the extensive bedding scheme, swept back into favour in private gardens.

In the public domain the Garden Festivals of the 1980s and 1990s, like the patios of the mobile executive, needed instant and summer-long colour. Landscape architects started using flowers, and often in exciting and creative ways, just at the time when globalisation of the market provided a wider range of plants bred specifically for use as bedding (Figs 23.2 and 23.3).

Finally, the historical revival and restoration of gardens led to the re-discovery of the annual (Fig. 23.4). This came first with the need to reinforce the colour schemes of Gertrude Jekyll-inspired borders and with the gradual realisation that

Fig. 23.2   Liverpool Garden Festival: sunburst bedding scheme. (Photo: Richard Bisgrove)

Fig. 23.3   Stoke Garden Festival: a 'waterfall' of violas. (Photo: Richard Bisgrove)

Fig. 23.4 Hardy annuals sown as a mixture. (Photo: Nada Jennett)

Miss Jekyll herself used many annuals and tender perennials in what others had assumed to be her 'herbaceous' borders. As the Victorian era finally faded sufficiently into the past to be taken seriously, The National Trust began to embark bravely on full-blooded Victorian revivals – at Biddulph Grange, Lyme Park and most recently at Waddesdon Manor, where the 'carpet bed', formerly the low-point of Victorian excess, is being re-discovered.

As the twenty-first century opens, the enormously exciting programme of restoration of public parks (supported by the Heritage Lottery Fund) signals the return of the bedding plant to acceptance by polite society. All these factors, public and private, have combined to demonstrate to the landscape world at large what Gertrude Jekyll and Edwin Lutyens demonstrated to their own smaller world a century ago: the advantage of artists and gardeners, landscape architects and historians working together.

The prospect (real or imagined) of global warming, plus a spate of colourful garden books by Rosemary Verey, Penelope Hobhouse, Christopher Lloyd, Andrew Lawson and many

others, has made it not only acceptable but a social imperative to embrace once more the scarlet salvia, the dahlia and the canna. These are now seen by some (Waite, 1994; Lloyd, 2000) as antidotes to the labour-saving, ground-covered shrub gardens of the post-war era and the blocks of berberis, cotoneaster and viburnum that had been the mainstay of the landscape architect's vocabulary.

In summary, bedding is a versatile system of planting offering the potential for a whole range of effects. While the emphasis has been on the exciting, exotic, colourful and spectacular – sometimes bordering on the crude – soft harmonies and delicate textures are equally part of the bedding plant spectrum.

23.2 Bedding systems

Conventionally two systems of bedding have been widely practised.

Summer bedding came first, using (mainly half-hardy) annuals and tender perennials to create a display from June to September. In warmer regions (and that could soon include southern Britain) two batches of bedding may be necessary, with a second display of rather later-flowering plants for the cooler autumn months replacing the scorched remains of high summer bedding.

Spring bedding soon followed, employing biennials, short-lived perennials and bulbs which overwinter in the beds to flower in April and May. Some so-called 'spring' bedding plants such as polyanthus actually flower intermittently during mild winter spells before the main flush of flower in April / May (Fig. 23.5). The breeding of pansies, in particular, has been directed with some success at producing strains that flower more-or-less freely throughout the winter months.

In addition to these two mainstays of the bedding repertoire various other systems have been employed to a more limited extent.

Winter bedding utilises some winter-flowering plants, especially heathers, but primarily foliage plants such as ivies, euonymus, dwarf conifers and variegated box to create interest in the winter months. The plants used in winter bedding are, in general, much slower growing than the annuals

Fig. 23.5 Spring bedding: tulips and forget-me-nots in teardrop beds at Stoke. (Photo: Richard Bisgrove)

and tender perennials used in spring and summer and are therefore more expensive. Furthermore, because there is effectively no growth during the winter months the plants need to be of sufficient size and sufficiently closely spaced to achieve a well-furnished appearance at once. There is no opportunity for plants to grow and weave together during their season of display.

Because winter bedding prevents spring bedding from being planted in the autumn (unless bulbs alone are used), the plants for spring display need to be grown on to larger sizes and planted just before their flowering season, rather than planted in October and left to develop in the beds. For all these reasons, winter bedding has been used far less than spring and summer bedding – except in window boxes and other containers, where it can be used very effectively for a cheering winter display.

Plunge bedding is essentially large-scale outdoor flower arranging. Specimen plants in full growth and full flower are plunged in the ground (either removed from the containers in which they have been grown, or with containers left in place) to create literally instant, mature effects. These are usually for a very short duration such as Ascot week or for a special occasion such as a wedding.

Container-grown annuals, flowering herbaceous perennials, shrubs and/or bulbs (including summer bulbs such as lilies) may all be employed to create the required effect. The technique ranges from conventional plunge bedding (in which a formal bed of flowers and perhaps foliage plants is created for a short period) to exhibition planting where a much wider range of plants, including trees and shrubs, and perhaps other 'props' such as furniture and water features, are moved in to create a temporary garden.

Where there is any regular demand for plunge bedding it is useful to maintain a core collection of large plants in containers, perhaps flowering shrubs such as rhododendrons or hydrangeas, to provide stability for the scheme and to reduce the need for large numbers of smaller plants. The danger with this is that it can lead to overly-repetitive schemes and to dull predictability. Also it is notoriously difficult to maintain infrequently-used plants in vigorous condition; they always tend to become neglected, pot-bound and moribund until it is too late to rejuvenate them.

In many instances plunge bedding is more-or-less opportunistic: a balance between the effect required for a particular occasion and place, and the availability of appropriate plants. This is even more the case when seasonal flowering plants are used. The need to time flowering for a particular date may require several batches of plants to ensure that one batch will be in peak condition, unless the brief is sufficiently flexible to permit shopping around in the period leading up to the display for whatever plants are available and suitable.

Plunge bedding is obviously very expensive, and appropriate only in very special circumstances but given modern materials-handling technology there is no reason why modern schemes should not equal in inventiveness the efforts of nineteenth century gardeners who had only manpower at their disposal.

23.3   Bedding styles

The stereotype of a bedding scheme is a formal, geometric pattern of flowering plants: in its most clichéd expression an edging of low plants, a central panel of something of medium height and 'dot' plants of much taller species (or the same species grown as standards) to break the flatness of the bed.

A wider range of plants can be employed to create more complex patterns, whether purely abstract or representational. Colour, form and foliage texture can all be exploited to achieve the desired mood or character, whether exhilarating or restrained.

At its most extreme this patterning becomes carpet bedding, in which very low foliage plants of various colours are used, with regular trimming, to delineate civic or family crests, commemorative messages and other devices. Occasionally carpet bedding has erupted into the third dimension either with the soil mounded into jelly-mould shapes or with wire frames packed with compost and fed by trickle irrigation (Plate 27). Perhaps the most tongue-in-cheek interpretation of the carpet bed is the simulation of an unrolling carpet but animals, people, even the Great Wall of China have been constructed by such means. Although many professional horticulturists and landscape

Fig. 23.6   The City of Bath is one of a small number of local authorities which continue to produce bedding on a lavish scale. (Photo: James Hitchmough)

architects would dismiss such products as evidence of debased taste they are undoubtedly eye-catching and, where a sense of humour is appropriate, infinitely more effective than a bed of berberis full of trapped litter.

From three-dimensional bedding the opportunities extend into hanging baskets, globes, columns and other devices for raising plants – especially trailing plants, and most recently surfinia petunias – into the air (Fig. 23.6). However, once plants are separated from the earth and exposed to drying conditions on all sides, the need for an effective and reliable watering system becomes absolutely vital. One day of desiccation can destroy airborne plants for the rest of the season.

If the tight, geometrically precise patterns and mottoes of carpet bedding represent one extreme of the bedding system, then the millefleur style represents the other (Fig. 23.7). The millefleur bed is the modern equivalent of the mediaeval flowery mead without the grass. A portfolio of plants, often embracing annuals and herbaceous perennials (including clump-forming grasses) is assembled to give the desired range of heights, colours and textures. These plants are then distributed more-

Fig. 23.7 Millefleur bedding at Le Havre. (Photo: Richard Bisgrove)

or-less at random throughout the bed to produce a tapestry of plants widely varying in height, form and (usually) colour. The main criterion for inclusion in the portfolio is that plants should have a long season of interest or, at least, that they should not occupy much space with uninteresting or unsightly foliage before or after their flowering season. The overall effect is rather similar to the grass and gravel gardens of Piet Oudolf or Beth Chatto. The beds are of a more ephemeral nature, requiring more resources but with none of the problems of balancing a composition of competing plants in the second and subsequent years, as in the case of perennial planting.

One final variant on the theme of bedding systems is the foliage or 'subtropical' bed, using plants with bold foliage to create an exotic character. The plunging outdoors for the summer months of bananas, sugar cane, palms and other plants of exotic appearance became popular in the 1860s. Before he began to decry bedding schemes, William Robinson advocated setting these exotic specimens in beds of lower foliage plants (Robinson, 1870). From the bold jungle gardens of bananas, cannas, daturas and papyrus to the geometrical precision of the carpet bed, the late Victorians practised every intermediate style of

bedding display (Cole 1877). William Robinson also went on to explore how the 'subtropical' garden could be simulated using hardy perennial foliage plants, but that is beyond the scope of this chapter.

A new impetus for subtropical gardens came in the mid-twentieth century, with the bold swathes of brightly coloured foliage plants used by the South American Roberto Burle-Marx (Eliovson, 1991). The sweeping abstract curves of Burle-Marx' gardens had instant impact on landscape professionals and his outstanding achievements as artist / gardener / botanist helped to encourage in his landscape architectural acolytes a new respect for plants in landscape design. The obviously tender contents of his planting schemes had less immediate impact on the exterior landscape of temperate regions. The steady spread of Burle-Marx' ideas, the re-discovery of the splendours of Victorian subtropical bedding, first-hand acquaintance with the exciting vegetation in exotic holiday destinations and the prospects of global warming have all combined to raise awareness of the exciting potential of foliage bedding. As an example, this process has raised the canna to near-cult status in the new millennium (Hayward, 2002), and made the banana an essential item on the patio.

23.4 The place for bedding

There are annuals that will grow in almost any soil type, aspect or climate. In the designed landscape annuals can be used as temporary fillers or for their inherent qualities as usually vigorous, colourful symbols of vitality. When used in bedding schemes, though, there are certain constraints and implications that need to be considered.

Bedding is essentially a formal and transparently artificial system of plant use. The geometry should therefore be decisive and the setting appropriate. To sprinkle a few amoeboid beds across a large expanse of parkland grass will complicate mowing with no gain in visual impact.

Scale is all-important. A tub of petunias in a vast plaza of a modern office complex or a string of hanging baskets on Westminster Abbey can only look ridiculous. The mass of the bedding scheme and its siting need to be in proportion to the scale and character of the space around it and to the building or buildings to which the space relates.

This is becoming especially important as the commercial sponsorship of landscape schemes increases. Bedding is a very identifiable form of planting and so it is a popular vehicle for sponsorship, most notably on roundabouts. Both the sponsor and the recipient of the sponsored roundabout need to be sure that the scale, quality and appropriateness of the planting convey the intended message of quality. A thin row of marigolds in a sea of rough grass on a busy intersection is not likely to send a helpful message about the dynamism or product quality of the company named on the sponsorship sign. Planting must be in scale with the space.

Conversely, as bedding is an expensive commodity, the scale of the space in which bedding is to be used should where possible be reduced so that bedding is able to create the required impact. Sinking or raising part of a plaza or enclosing part of a large expanse of paving or grass with trees or hedges will create a space within a space of human scale in which bedding can achieve real impact. Sprinkling the same amount of bedding over the whole of a large plaza or lawn will only emphasise the vastness and desolation of the expanse.

Unity is also important. The beds in any one field of vision need to unite into a single composition. Where grass is the dominant element in the design, beds may be used along paths, for example, to frame panels of lawn but the widths of beds and the spaces between them need to be carefully considered in relation to path widths and the scale of the lawn. Where the bedding itself is the dominant element, with the beds combining into a flower parterre, the shape of the grass or paths between the beds is very important – both for design and ease of maintenance. The beds should unite into a single design. Humphry Repton's 'rule of thirds' remains as appropriate as ever: There should be a major (two-thirds) and minor (one-third) element in any landscape picture rather than equal amounts of lawn and flower bed, for example, vying for attention.

Bedding relies on uniformity of effect. Shade, root competition from large trees, water or nutrient gradients on steep slopes and any other environmental factors causing uneven growth will spoil the effect. The site should therefore be open, but sheltered, level or terraced into a series of levels and of uniform fertility.

Bedding usually relies on rapid growth of initially small plants. Although the optimum conditions for growth of individual species vary widely, the horticultural ideal of a well-cultivated, moderately fertile, moist but well-drained and more-or-less neutral soil will provide the best growing conditions for the widest range of plants of use in bedding. After establishment most bedding plants will grow satisfactorily in most summers on well-prepared soil without further irrigation. On light or shallow soils and in dry summers irrigation may be desirable, and sometimes essential, for success. For subtropical bedding the richer and moister the soil and the more sheltered the location, the better.

Bedding is environmentally resilient in the sense that bedding plants can be cultivated almost anywhere with suitable soil cultivations (as shown by their success in the Garden Festivals on reclaimed sites) but the plants themselves are soft and easily damaged, whether by accidental trampling of bed corners or deliberate vandalism. As any imperfections will destroy the sense of high culture which the bedding scheme is there to express, bedding should only be contemplated where it can be protected from abuse, or where resources are available to repair the damage promptly and, if necessary, repeatedly.

Bedding is conspicuous, conspicuously located and often very bright. It is therefore more than usually important that plant associations are successful in terms of heights, colour harmonies / contrasts, environmental tolerances etc. Whenever possible it is wise to experiment on a small scale with planting schemes a year before the full scheme is to be put into effect. Care must then be taken to ensure availability of the same cultivars in that second year. In a sector in which novelty seems all-important, the commercial lifespan of some cultivars is very short.

23.5 Cultivation

The main requirement of bedding plants is for a fertile soil. Beds should be cultivated (by digging, rotary cultivation etc.) to a minimum depth of 200 mm and preferably to 400 mm every third year. Organic matter such as manure, composted green waste etc., should be incorporated (preferably annually) and a top-dressing of balanced (10:10:10) fertiliser spread before planting of summer bedding.

There is usually a narrow window of time between removal of one bedding scheme and planting of the next, so soil should be trodden (unless excessively wet) and raked level after any cultivations and prior to planting. Care should be taken to avoid damage to surrounding grass areas and periodic checks are needed to ensure that bed shapes are true: uneven trimming of grass edges can soon destroy the crispness of finish of a symmetrical pattern.

Plant raising is now almost invariably left to commercial nurserymen. If plants are to be raised in-house, seed will need to be ordered in late autumn and seed for summer bedding material sown in a heated greenhouse or frame. January / February sowings are necessary for many fine-seeded species (antirrhinum, begonia, lobelia, petunia); March /April is preferable for larger-seeded subjects (dahlia, tagetes, zinnia). Traditionally seeds were sown in boxes and pricked out to a wider spacing before gradually hardening off in readiness for planting. Modern techniques employ various methods of seed pelleting, mechanical space sowing, and cellular trays to produce plug plants suitable either for potting on or for direct planting into the final situation. In particular situations a combination of buying-in material that is readily available from commercial suppliers, contract-raising less common species or cultivars, and in-house production may be needed to achieve the range and quality of material needed within a given budget.

23.6 Types of plants

Many hundreds of species and many thousands of cultivars of plants lend themselves to use as bedding plants when there is adequate time to experiment but a few are so reliable in flower and therefore so extensively developed by the breeder that they play a particularly important part in bedding. The following descriptive lists contain some of the most useful plants. Varieties / cultivars are not given as they tend to change rapidly. Seed catalogues provide up-to-date, colourfully illustrated and free guides to current availability.

Low annuals: suitable for edging and for carpeting of smaller beds

Ageratum houstonianum

Low mounds of powder-puff flowers in 'blue' (more accurately lavender / lilac) and now in white or pink. New cultivars can be excessively dumpy.

Begonia semperflorens

The fibrous-rooted begonias have fleshy green or bronze leaves and non-stop succession of white, pink or red flowers. They are tolerant of full sun or partial shade. Very compact, so not good blenders with other plants but suitable for precise patterns.

Brachycombe iberidifolia

Very fine-textured carpets of mid-green foliage topped by long succession of lavender-blue daisies. Drought tolerant but much more productive in more fertile conditions.

Cineraria maritima

This is grown for its densely felted and dissected grey foliage. The bright yellow flowers are removed if they occur. A woody perennial in nature it is capable of growing beyond the low edging category but if grown as an annual it can be kept low by pinching if required.

Felicia amelloides

Forms a neat mound of dark green leaves with bright blue daisies held well above the foliage on slender stems. This is a very drought tolerant plant and one that will overwinter in a very sheltered situation to become a short-lived perennial; it flowers more freely in good growing conditions.

Impatiens

Busy lizzie is currently a major focus for the plant breeders' efforts. Fleshy stems are topped by flat flowers often forming a near-solid sheet of white, pink, red, orange or mauve/purple. Popularity and ease of cultivation brings its own problems of abuse (in purple and orange circles on roundabouts for example) but this is not the plant's fault.

Lobelia erinus

Blue lobelia has been one of the mainstays of the bedding plant tradition, forming carpets (sometimes very low carpets) of tiny but rich-green leaves topped by delicately formed flowers in deep or pale blue or white. Reddish maroon is a more recent addition. Compact cultivars are becoming ever-more compact and need close spacing. Spreading cultivars are easier to use and trailing types are popular in containers.

Lobularia maritima

Universally known by its redundant name of *Alyssum maritimum*, Sweet Alyssum is a very low carpeting plant with sweetly scented white flowers. There is a dark purple form. It can be grown as a hardy annual but is more conveniently handled for bedding as a half-hardy annual.

Pyrethrum tanacetifolia

This is similar to *Cineraria maritima* but its grey leaves are much more finely dissected and lace-like in effect.

Tagetes patula, T. signata

For reasons known only to seedsmen, *Tagetes signata* is to be found under 'T' in catalogues while *T. patula* is found under 'M' for (French) marigold. The former is a very neat edging plant with domes of fine-textured foliage and myriads of small flowers in yellow or orange. The latter, one of the most popular, easiest and robust of bedding plants, is somewhat larger and coarser. Flowers vary from dark red through bright orange and tangerine to yellow or combinations of these colours, and now to white, though the white form fades to an unpleasant brown as the flowers die.

Verbena x hybrida

This more-or-less trailing plant produces a colourful carpet of domed flower heads in white, pink, lavender, cherry red or bright scarlet. In addition to the clear colours of older cultivars several muted colours have been produced in recent years including buff yellow and the self explanatory 'Peaches and Cream'. In dry summers verbena is prone to mildew which will eventually disfigure the plant.

Intermediate annuals: suitable for the groundwork of most beds

Antirrhinum majus

The snapdragon is available in a very wide range of colours and colour combinations and in heights ranging from 15 cm to 100 cm or more, but the most useful for bedding are those of intermediate height. The distinctive 'snapdragon' or 'bunny rabbit' flowers are ranged in stiffly upright spikes which, *en masse*, give a very attractive vertical rhythm to the bed. Rust resistant strains only should be grown and even these will succumb to rust in hot, dry summers.

Begonia x tuberhybrida

The 'non-stop' begonias are the most suitable tuberous begonias for bedding because of their freedom of flowering and weather-resistance of the flowers. A good colour range (white, yellow, orange, red) and freedom of flowering over handsome foliage make them very suitable for bedding.

Clarkia rubicunda (Godetia)

Although once very popular as a bedding plant, godetia has languished in obscurity for many years. The neat domes of foliage are smothered by large white, pink or red flowers unfurling from long pointed buds. Godetia is easy to grow but needs generous cultivation if it is to continue flowering until the end of summer.

Dahlia hybrids

Seed-raised dahlias are now available in a wide range of heights and as double flowers in addition to the older single 'Coltness Gem' types. Some of the newer strains have attractively bronzed foliage. The flower colour range is very wide but seed-raised dahlias are usually available only in mixed colours and can be rather variable in height. Where a more uniform effect is desired tubers or rooted cuttings of named cultivars can be used.

Echium vulgare

Viper's bugloss is normally grown as a hardy annual but can be raised as a half-hardy annual if care is taken not to allow plants to become root-bound and not to disturb the roots unduly when planting out. Flowers of the species change colour on opening from pink to lavender but in modern cultivars the pink is suppressed and the lavender intensified to a good blue, a rare colour among bedding plants. The flower spike continues to unfurl over a very long period so the plants remain colourful, though increasingly tall, over a long period.

Heliotropium peruvianum

Heliotrope is one of several tender perennials (a large, woody shrub in the subtropics) which was enormously popular in the nineteenth century but fell from favour in the twentieth because of difficulties in propagation. It was then rescued by transformation at the hands of plant breeders into half-hardy annual mode. It is still not the easiest plant to raise as it is slow to reach flowering size, and the colour range from seed is very limited – just purple. However, the durability of the flat purple heads of flowers above very dark green leaves and the sweet 'cherry pie' scent place heliotrope among the aristocrats of bedding plants. A number of named, vegetatively propagated cultivars from nineteenth-century collections are gradually coming to light again for the more adventurous.

Pelargonium x hortorum

The zonal pelargonium or 'geranium' has remained at the top of the bedding plant stakes for more than a century. It was transformed in the latter part of the twentieth century from a wide range of cultivars managed as tender perennials to a more limited but expanding range of half-hardy annual strains. Once established from seed the plants can, of course, be treated as tender perennials thereafter if required. Stout stems, often with attractively bronze-zoned leaves, carry an indefinite succession of large, rounded flower-heads in red, orange, pink or white until frost ends the display.

Petunia x hybrida

The petunia is one of the mainstays of the bedding plant repertoire, with more-or-less trailing domes of sticky, grey-green foliage and a long succession of funnel-shaped flowers in various shades of red, purple, pink, white or pale yellow. The purple strains especially are often scented. Plant breeders are not noted for their restraint in the manipulation of plant characteristics but even the more bizarre and bright colours among modern petunias are fairly gentle in overall effect. They should therefore be kept well away from that other mainstay of bedding, the French and African marigolds, whose solid domes of brassy colours will kill the softer petunia colours.

Salvia spp.

Salvia is one of the very few genera which embraces all three primary colours among its diverse range of species. For bedding there are two main options, each very different from the other. *Salvia splendens* is the scarlet salvia, tortured by the plant breeders into ever more dumpy format but admirable for its intense scarlet spikes of flowers (the colour is from the bracts, so much more durable than flowers) over dark green foliage. There are now 'interesting' variations on the scarlet salvia with bracts of salmon pink or purple; these can be attractive or nauseating depending on their setting. Entirely different in effect from the scarlet salvia is *S. farinacea*, a taller, more upright and slender plant with finely dissected grey-green leaves and narrow spikes of small, deep purple-blue flower heads emerging from a dense grey/white farina.

Tagetes erecta

The African marigold is similar to the smaller French marigold (see *T. patula* above) but taller and larger in all its parts. The more extreme products of the plant breeders' efforts can only be described as gross but the looser plants and those with less solidly globular flower heads are useful

in creating bold effects in the larger bedding schemes.

Tall annuals suitable for large bedding schemes

Amaranthus caudatus

'Love-lies-bleeding' is an upright leafy plant with long, pendulous tassels of tiny beetroot red flowers. There is also a pale green form. Both are more attractive when used as specimens than when crowded together in groups, as this latter obscures the trailing habit which is the main attraction of the plant.

Argyranthemum frutescens

A bushy and eventually large tender perennial with finely dissected grey-green foliage (very finely dissected in some cultivars) and a continuous succession of daisy flowers, (single, anemone-centred or double) in white, pale yellow or pink. Like many tender perennials this may be trained as a standard as well as being allowed to grow naturally as a rounded bush.

Bassia (Kochia) scoparia

The very fine-textured pale green foliage of Kochia gradually builds up during the summer to a neat, elongated dome like a soldier's busby or bearskin hat, an ideal contrast or anchor to many bright flowers. In autumn the foliage turns from pale green to the fiery beetroot red which gives the plant its common name of 'burning bush'. In world regions with a hot, dry climate Kochia can become a serious weed, so is not cultivated, but there is currently no risk of this in Britain.

Cleome pungens

A very striking half-hardy annual with compound leaves and rounded domes of spider flowers in pink, rose or white. The inflorescence continues to elongate over the whole summer. This is a plant of exotic appearance that has more the substance of a shrub than of a temporary annual.

Cosmos bipinnatus

An easily grown hardy or half-hardy annual making a tall mound of finely dissected, dark green foliage topped by large, broad-petalled composite flowers of white, pink or red. Dwarf strains (a relative term as these are still 50 cm or so in height) are more compact and more concentrated in flower effect than the elegant but metre-plus tall older hybrids, so are usually more useful for bedding.

Fuchsia hybrids

One of the few tender perennials still to be grown as such, rather than as a half-hardy annual, the fuchsia embraces many hundreds of cultivars. Nearly all have pendulous flowers, some neat and simple in outline, others huge, ruffled affairs, but all of soft colouring; pink, purple, red or white in various combinations. In most cultivars the flowers are loosely arranged at the tips of extending shoots so the whole effect of the plant is subtle, never a solid mass of colour. Fuchsias are easily raised from cuttings and plants may be kept from year to year especially if large standards, pyramids or other trained forms are required.

Lavatera trimestris

A vigorous and easily grown annual, somewhat similar to hibiscus in appearance, with pink or white funnel-shaped flowers unfurling from long pointed buds. Tall, intermediate and now dwarf strains are available, with the flowering effect more concentrated in the smaller types.

Nicotiana affinis

The flowering tobacco plant, *Nicotiana affinis*, bears loose branching spikes of white flowers which, in the species, open only at dusk or in dull, cloudy conditions to release their exquisite scent. Modern strains open their flowers during the day

and the colour range has been extended to pink, lilac or red, and to green but the scent of these modern types has all but vanished and in some the graceful habit of the parent has been transformed into a flat-topped, dumpy tuft.

Nicotiana sylvestris

This is a much less well-known plant but a strikingly statuesque one. Large rosettes of softly hairy pale green leaves give rise to tall stems, each topped by a fountain of long-tubed, scented white flowers. The inflorescence continues to expand throughout the summer until the flowers are at, then above, eye level.

Zinnia elegans

'Elegans' is not an epithet which most people would apply to the modern zinnia but the tight, intricately spiralled domes of brilliantly coloured flowers are ideal for the livelier bedding schemes. Heights and flower sizes vary from the diminutive to the gigantic. Modern strains are fairly tolerant of the indeterminate British summer but the zinnia excels in sunshine.

'Subtropical' plants

Abutilon x hybridum

A large shrub in the subtropics, abutilon adapts well to the role of tender perennial in British bedding schemes and can be propagated by cuttings each year. With exotic hibiscus-like flowers in red, yellow, orange or pink and the variegated foliage of some cultivars, abutilon will grow to a metre or two in height in one season.

Brugmansia (Datura) suaveolens

Angel's trumpet is the common name for this rather coarse but exotic potato relative. The huge, fragrant trumpet flowers, white, yellow or pink, hang from thick branches. Brugmansia needs a rich soil and reliable water supply to flourish but it is then a spectacular sight. It is highly poisonous (though not in the least tempting to eat) so should be kept away from the easy reach of children.

Canna indica

Many hundreds of cultivars of this exotic, banana-like plant with vivid spikes of red, orange or yellow flowers were grown in nineteenth-century gardens. Many of these have been rediscovered and many more have been bred in the late twentieth century as the canna has surged back into popularity. Rhizomes need to be lifted and stored overwinter in a frost-free place, either in unwatered pots of soil or in well-ventilated bags, and started into growth in a heated greenhouse in early spring.

Eucalyptus gunnii

The blue gum is one of the greyest of the eucalypts and, in its young state, one of the most attractive. A very tall tree at maturity, it grows sufficiently quickly to reach 2–3 metres in height in one year from an early sowing, and makes an elegant specimen.

Grevillea robusta and Jacaranda mimosaefolia

Although quite different at maturity, both of these trees can be grown from seed to make, in their first year, elegant, upright columns of dark green, dissected foliage – doubly dissected in the case of Jacaranda. If it can be kept overwinter in a well-lit glasshouse the Jacaranda may produce its attractive lavender-blue flowers in the second year but it then becomes too unwieldy to use as a bedding plant.

Musa basjoo

With the even larger *M. ensete* and other bananas, the huge, paddle-shaped leaves are more effective than any other plant at creating an exotic character in a bedding scheme. The leaves are susceptible to wind damage so need a sheltered position. William Robinson recommended plunging large, container-grown bananas on the fringes of a lawn, replacing the turf around the plants to give the impression that the plants were permanent inhabitants of the garden.

Ricinus communis 'Gibsonii'

The true castor oil is a bold plant with large, palmate leaves of bright green or reddish-bronze depending on variety. If sown early in the year and given good growing conditions it will reach at least 2 m in height and nearly that in width. The seeds are extremely poisonous.

Solenostemon scutellarioides

Better known under its old name of *Coleus blumei*, the flame nettle resembles a nettle in habit and leaf except that the leaves are soft to the touch and brightly coloured in various combinations of red, green, yellow, brown and near-black. Some are self-coloured; others have one colour margined by another while others have multicoloured zones or venation. They may be raised from seed or are very easily propagated from cuttings. Pinching plants regularly to remove flower spikes will prolong their useful life.

Zea mays

Maize striped in green and white or green, red and white was a frequent component of Gertrude Jekyll's borders when a vertical accent was required. The pin-striped effect of the variegation creates a fresh, crisp effect among lower plants. Good strains of seed are now difficult to find but worth searching for.

Biennials and short-lived perennials for spring bedding

Arabis albida and Aubrieta deltoidea

Arabis (white and pink) and *Aubretia* (pink, lilac, red or purple) are both low, compact, carpeting plants with neat grey foliage almost smothered by flowers in late spring. Where an even effect is required *Aubrieta* in particular is best propagated by cuttings; seed-raised plants are variable in compactness and vigour.

Bellis perennis

These giant offspring of the common daisy have rich green leaves and large mop-head flowers of white, blush, pink or red on 15 cm stems. They are effective on their own or form a good carpet beneath tulips of similar colouring.

Cheiranthus cheiri

The wallflower is the one spring bedding plant that is tall enough to stand alone without tulips or other bulbs to give added height, so it is especially useful where budgets are limited. The colour range extends from white, cream and yellow through tawny orange and deep red to purple. Whites, creams and purples are much less vigorous than the yellows, oranges and reds. The latter range, especially, are delightfully scented.

Myosotis sylvatica

The forget-me-not forms rounded clumps of soft green foliage topped by slowly unfurling spikes of clear blue flowers. There are white and pink forms but neither can compare in clarity with the blues. Plant breeders seem to be focusing on deep gentian-blue colouring and excessive dumpiness. Older strains with their somewhat looser habit and paler blue flowers are more effective at forming a good carpet and are much more visible in the poor light conditions of spring. Forget-me-nots are ideal companions for tulips of harmonious colouring.

Primula x polyanthus

Polyanthus, or bunch-flowered primrose, have been bred in a bewildering array of colours including subtle brown, grey/purple and almost black in addition to the older reds, yellows and blues. Some, especially the yellows, are sweetly scented.

Although good perennials, they need to be treated as biennials if they are to produce a flower / leaf ratio suitable for bedding. The plants form compact crowns of crinkled foliage from which upright flower stems emerge, so close spacing is necessary to give good coverage of the bed. Rich soil is needed for free flowering.

Viola x wittrockiana

Pansies have been enjoyed for many decades for their large, rounded, velvety flowers and their bright colours; many flowers having whiskery markings giving the appearance of a face. The colour range is enormous and there are many good mixtures as well as single-coloured varieties, literally from white to black. This versatile plant can be sown in early spring for use as a summer bedding plant (though it is only really successful in cool situations), or in summer to flower in spring. Plants from a summer sowing often produce a scattering of flowers in mild winter spells before the main spring flowering season, and this useful characteristic has been seized upon and developed by plant breeders to produce strains which flower continuously, though not always prolifically, through the winter months.

23.7　Economics

Bedding is by its nature a labour-intensive and expensive form of planting. Trying to achieve the exciting results of which it is capable on a low budget is like shopping around for a cheap Ferrari substitute. However, the two main methods of achieving good value at reasonable cost lie in plant selection and materials handling.

Cultivars of easily grown and popular species that are widely available will be less expensive than novelties or more difficult plants (for example requiring a long growing period under heated glass). Small, compact plants (fibrous-rooted begonias, lobelia, lobularia) are needed in much larger quantities than are larger and more spreading plants (petunia, lavatera, cosmos). The cost per square metre for plants and for planting will be greater for a scheme using mainly small plants. Small increases in spacing can achieve substantial savings in the number of plants required (plus cost of planting) but will increase the time taken for the scheme to achieve maturity. Many modern cultivars are too compact and may never knit together unless closely spaced. Given that plants may vary in cost from 20 p to £20-plus (for a re-usable palm tree or other specimen), and that spacings vary from 100 mm to a metre, there are clearly many permutations of factors by which the budget can be managed.

One bedding scheme, for example, employed a chain of *Ricinus communis* and the tall *Nicotiana sylvestris* along the spine of long, matching narrow beds (Plate 28). On either side of this spine, blocks of green *Amaranthus caudatus* provided intermediate height while the rest of the beds were filled with white petunias. Planting densities for the three larger plants were only one, two and three plants per square metre respectively, with a filling of inexpensive petunias at six or seven per square metre. The planting quickly developed into an undulating mass of pale green and white, a restrained and refreshing scheme for a hot summer.

Handling is the other main cost involved in bedding. Careful organisation and attention to detail can make large differences in cost, from the earliest stages of sowing and pricking out to the final planting. Soil preparation and timing of planting to achieve high rates of planting, delivery of plants to the site, proximity of plants to beds, avoidance of complex sorting of plants on site, ease of handling and disposal of containers etc. will all contribute to saving of time and therefore money.

At Waddesdon Manor, one of the most elaborately splendid houses of the nineteenth century, the flower parterre has recently been restored. Lord Rothschild has decided to bring the tradition of carpet bedding into the twenty-first century by commissioning a different artist each year to prepare a design for the beds. Each design is scanned into a computer and translated into a planting plan. This enables plants to be assembled in the nursery in coded trays to be transported to the garden. The large carpet beds are now planted in two days instead of three weeks.

23.8 Summary

Bedding is one of the most exciting and versatile forms of planting design. Although much maligned in the past it offers fun for the designer, a welcome creative challenge for the maintainer and fun, freshness and vitality for the consumer, with a 'wow factor' greater than in any other aspect of planting design.

References

Bisgrove, R. (1992) *The English Garden*, 116–19. Penguin Books, Harmondsworth, Middx.

Cole, N. (1877) *The Royal Parks and Gardens of London.* Journal of Horticulture Press.

Eliovson, S. (1991) *The Gardens of Roberto Burle-Marx.* Thames and Hudson.

Elliott, B. (1986) *The Victorian Garden.* pp 51–2, Batsford.

Fleming, A. (1870) *Spring and Winter Flower Gardening*, Journal of Horticulture Press.

Fletcher, H. (1969) *The Story of the Royal Horticultural Society*, OUP, Oxford. [This deals very well with the role of the RHS in the introduction of garden plants.]

Green, D. (1956) *Gardener to Queen Anne.* OUP, Oxford. [This provides a list of plants used by Henry Wise c.1700 to furnish the parterre in each month of the year.]

Hayward, K. (2002) *Hart Canna Handbook*, Farnborough. (Nursery Handbook)

Jekyll, G. (1914) *Colour Schemes for the Flower Garden.* Country Life.

Lemmon, K. & Musgrave, T. (1968) *The golden age of plant hunters.* Dent, London.

Lloyd, C. (2000) Dynamite plot. *The Garden* May 2000, 268–73.

Loudon, J.C. (1838) *The Suburban Gardener and Villa Companion.* Longmans.

Robinson, W. (1870) *The Subtropical Garden.* John Murray.

Robinson, W. (1883) *The English Flower Garden.* John Murray.

Robinson, W. (1892) *Garden Design and Architects' Gardens.* John Murray.

Waite, R. (1994) Sub-tropical splendour. *The Garden* August 1994, 358–61.

Further reading

Various seed catalogues of major commercial seed producers, for example, Thompson and Morgan and Moles Seeds, and Ball and Colegrave Ltd.

Evison, J.R.B. (1958) *Gardening for Display.* Collingridge. Though dated in some respects, this remains an excellent source, including 18 pages of recipes of successful bedding schemes. Evison was Superintendent of Parks and Gardens at Brighton, one of the few local authorities to maintain an active tradition of bedding into the late twentieth century.

Phillips, R. & Rix, M. (2002) *Annuals and Biennials.* Pan, London. The best photographic study of annuals.

Rice, G. (1986) *A Handbook of Annuals and Bedding Plants,* Croom Helm.

Rice, G. (2001) *Discovering Annuals.* Frances Lincoln, London.

24 Bulbous Plants for Use in Designed Landscapes

Fergus Garrett and Rory Dusoir

The term 'bulb' as defined by botanists has a strictly limited compass. It is a modified bud consisting of separate scales attached to a fleshy basal core. Slice an onion lengthwise in half for a clear illustration of this structure. Daffodils, snowdrops, lilies and tulips are amongst the plants that possess a bulb in this true sense. But this definition excludes genera such as *Crocus*, *Gladiolus*, *Cyclamen* and *Dierama* that produce corms or tubers. The latter are modified stems or stem-bases and have a solid, not a scaly consistency. For the purposes of plant users, bulbs, corms and tubers need not be rigorously differentiated (and generally aren't) as they behave in the same way. They all act as storage organs and allow plants to retreat underground for long periods of dormancy. While they are in this dormant state they can be stored dry for several months, which allows mature plants to be moved before flowering. Therefore almost instant and often spectacular effects can be achieved in plantings at comparatively small expense.

24.1 Ecological characteristics

Bulbous plants occur in habitats where climatic conditions are regularly hostile to vegetative growth for significant periods of time, normally (but not always) on a predictable annual basis. Although the same conditions may not prevail in cultivation, they are still the most important factor in determining the conditions a particular bulb species needs to grow, persist and flower satisfactorily.

Winter and spring-growing bulbs

Very cold winters, very dry summers

The steppes and mountain ranges of Central Asia, with their parched summers and freezing winters, possess an incredibly rich bulbous flora. In this climatic type plants must complete their vegetative growth cycle by late spring, the only time of year when both warmth and moisture coincide. Flowering normally takes place early on in the cycle to allow time for pollination and the formation of seed, although the final stage of ripening may not require moisture and can take place when the plant is vegetatively dormant. However, some winter-green bulbs (e.g. *Allium*, and some aroid species) flower at the end of their vegetative growth cycle.

As with all bulbs, photosynthates created in the leaves are stored in the bulb to fuel the following year's flowering and growth. Therefore the current season's performance of a bulbous plant in flower is largely dependent on the growing conditions of the previous year, a fact which is important to bear in mind in cultivation. This can be used to advantage when bulbs are bedded out: although the growing conditions may not be ideal, the plant still performs reasonably well for the first year utilising the photosynthates stored in its bulb, and can then be discarded. Bulbs that have been grown in more favourable positions may find it possible to put back enough carbohydrates into a storage organ to enable them to be used again.

Spring growth gives way to summer dormancy, which is known as aestivation. The majority of bulbs in cultivation as ornamentals are spring flowering and summer dormant. In their natural habitat their aestivation is generally essential because there is little or no summer rainfall. In cultivation, plants from these habitats become dormant with or without summer drought.

Mild winters, dry summers

The type of climate where a wet relatively mild winter and spring is followed by a dry summer is known as 'Mediterranean'. Apart from the Mediterranean region itself such conditions occur in four areas of the world: California, Central Chile, the south-western tip of South Africa and Western and Southern Australia. All of these (apart from Australia) have a very diverse bulbous flora.

The Mediterranean region itself supports many winter-growing bulbs, quite a few of which are hardy in Britain. Although the Mediterranean coastline rarely suffers severe frost, in the high mountains of the hinterland frost and snow cover are commonplace. Many aroids (including *Arum creticum*, *Crocus*, cyclamen such as *C. hederifolium* and *C.coum*), and most of the alliums in cultivation produce winter foliage which is perfectly frost hardy. Periods of frosty weather will slow down growth but will not in any way damage this foliage. Growth resumes in mild weather.

Perhaps the most variable factor amongst Mediterranean regions is the winter temperature. 'Mediterranean' type climates in the southern hemisphere occur approximately five degrees of latitude closer to the equator than their counterparts to the north, and their winters are correspondingly milder. The vast majority of winter-spring growing bulbs from southern latitudes will not tolerate British winters.

Bulbs from these areas tend to be winter green, starting their growth with the autumn rains. This makes them vulnerable to frost when grown in Britain, although hardier forms of some plants occur at higher altitudes. South African species such as *Zantedeschia aethiopica*, *Amaryllis belladonna* and *Nerine bowdenii* tolerate British winters by suspending growth until the spring. The growth of *Zantedeschia aethiopica* is delayed further if it is planted deep or grown underwater,

Fig. 24.1 Bluebells (*Hyacinthoides non-scripta*) in a woodland setting. (Photo: Fergus Garrett / Rory Dusoir)

in which case it will flower in June, turning a naturally winter-spring growing plant into a summer-flower. There are few bulb species whose growth cycles are so malleable. The form known as 'Crowborough' is hardy down to −15°C under these circumstances. *Amaryllis belladonna* and *Nerine bowdenii* require a well-drained, sun-soaked position, and given this, can be equally hardy. It is important to bear it in mind that hardiness does not merely depend on the lowest winter temperature in a given area. Good drainage, shelter from cold winds, and summer ripening all play an important part in maintaining the health and survival of Mediterranean bulbs grown in our climate.

Cold wet winters, moist wet summers

Bulbs also occur in temperate/maritime climates with wet summers. The native daffodil (*Narcissus pseudonarcissus*), bluebells (*Hyacinthoides non-scripta*) and snowdrops (*Galanthus nivalis*) are familiar examples (Figs 24.1, 24.2). In these climates the most important factor in determining dormancy is often competition with other plants rather than summer drought. Once the woodland canopy above them has leafed out fully (around mid-May), very little light will reach bulbous

Fig. 24.2 *Narcissus* species in short turf. (Photo: Fergus Garrett / Rory Dusoir)

plants. Therefore, they must complete their vegetative growth for the year before June, and will be dormant for the rest of the year. Some European *Narcissus* species grow primarily in grassland where the competition from grasses and other strong-growing meadow plants is at its height during the summer months; rather than directly competing with the growth of neighbouring grasses, the daffodils go into summer dormancy. They have evolved to grow and flower in spring to avoid competition. The energy stored in the bulb from the previous year allows it to grow vigorously early in the spring when most herbaceous and deciduous plants are barely breaking dormancy. Similar adaptations to summer competition occur throughout central and northern Europe and eastern and central USA. Species from these areas are eminently suited to cultivation in the British Isles, as their hardiness is not an issue, nor does summer rainfall cause problems.

Some aestivating bulbs flower in autumn rather than in winter or spring. Their flowering is naturally triggered by autumn rains. In cultivation also, the flowering of species such as one of the true autumn-flowering crocuses, *Crocus speciosus*, can be advanced by irrigation in September or October. Some species such as *Cyclamen hederifolium* proceed to grow leaves during and after flowering, which then grow through winter.

Others, such as *Crocus speciosus*, resume dormancy after flowering, until vegetative growth restarts in late winter.

Summer growing bulbs

Cool dry winters, warm wet summers

These climatic conditions give rise to bulbs that grow and flower during the summer months. Eastern South Africa and mountainous regions of central and eastern Asia (including the Himalayas) are two areas where these climatic conditions co-occur with a wide range of summer flowering bulbs. Snow cover in eastern Asia keeps the bulbs dry over winter, whereas in eastern South Africa there is simply a lack of winter precipitation. The combination of winter drought and summer moisture is difficult to provide in our climate and in general bulbs from these habitats are less robust in cultivation, and less well suited to cultivation in the public landscape than some of the previously mentioned ecological groups.

Some species of Asian *Lilium* are an example of a group that is often unpredictable in cultivation, requiring good drainage in winter, but plenty of summer moisture. Some Asian lilies are intolerant of alkaline soils (e.g. *L. auratum*), but most will tolerate some lime as long as their soil has a high humus content. *L. regale*, *L. tigrinum* and the european *L. pyrenaicum* are amongst the most robust and persistent of the montane lily species.

There are a number of summer growing and flowering bulbs from the southern hemisphere (Southern Africa and South America) which can be successfully cultivated in the British Isles, with the proviso that they are often borderline in terms of winter hardiness. Unlike *Lilium* species (the bulbs of which are sensitive to drying out) many of these southern hemisphere species can be lifted in the autumn and stored dry over winter (e.g. *Acidanthera, Ferraria, Gladiolus, Polianthes,* and *Tigridia*). In Southern Britain they are often better left to clump up *in situ* with a heavy mulch to improve their prospects of winter survival. *Crinum × powellii, Gladiolus papilio, Dierama pulcherrimum, Galtonia candicans, Schizostylis coccinea,* many *Crocosmia* and *Eucomis* species are essentially hardy in all but the most extreme winters. The evergreen *Dierama pulcherrimum* can be successfully cultivated in the cracks between stone paving, where it will self-sow abundantly. The paving slabs prevent the soil from drying out in the summer, as well as providing relatively dry zones of soil during the winter months. Most of these species are best thought of in a design sense as permanent planting, rather than ephemerals as their foliage is generally present from spring to autumn.

Warm, dry winters, hot wet summers

Some herbaceous plants from tropical regions form bulb-like organs in response to alternating periods of wet and dry weather. Vigorous, luxuriant leaf growth and continuous flowering occur in the rainy season, giving way to dormancy below ground when the rains either cease or fail. Cannas and dahlias are examples of this group of species and occasionally survive a mild winter without protection in SW England. Generally though tropical bulb species cannot be considered hardy in temperate climates. Nevertheless, Cannas, dahlias, and tuberous rooted begonias grow well in the British Isles given winter protection, and are frequently used in summer bedding schemes in this country and in continental Europe.

Bulbous plants from tropical climates are exceptional in that they do not require an annual period of dormancy. Given the right conditions (i.e. continuous warmth and moisture), they can often be kept growing and flowering indifferently at all times of year. In practice plants are left where they flowered until the first autumn frosts have killed the top growth, then bulbs are lifted and stored in a cool, but frost-free building. Alternatively, they may be protected in situ, but this may not be sufficient if the winter is cold.

24.2 Cultivation and use in the designed landscape

A very diverse range of bulbous plants is available commercially from wholesale nurseries. Many of these are relatively inexpensive to purchase, and easy to handle and plant. Traditionally bulbs have featured strongly in bedding schemes and in mixed borders in public parks and gardens. They have also been used to enrich deciduous woodland plantings and add colour to meadows and grassland, although this has been largely restricted to institutional and large private gardens. Bulbs are very popular with the public and can provide almost instant results in a wide range of colours and forms. Often wrongly associated just with spring, bulb displays can in fact be all year round from the summer, into autumn, and well into winter.

Although knowledge of a plant in its native habitat (see Chapter 2) can provide pointers to successful cultivation, it is not always necessary to imitate these conditions slavishly. Wild tulips tend to grow on stony, arid hillsides, but their garden descendants are often perfectly happy in heavy clay soil. Plants whose aestivation occurs naturally as a response to summer drought will retreat into dormancy indifferently in the absence of drought. Indeed the distinction between drought-driven aestivation and competition-driven aestivation is not at all clear cut in the wild. *Cyclamen hederifolium* for example grows naturally both in deciduous woodland and in sun-baked maquis. It is equally flexible in cultivation, thriving in deciduous shade or in full sun providing that it receives sufficient light during its winter and spring growing period.

Many aestivating bulbs will show a similar adaptability. They are well adapted to grow underneath deciduous shrubs (provided they are exposed to adequate light during their main growth period before the shrub is in leaf) and can also be combined with robust, later growing herbaceous perennials such as *Anemone* × *hybrida* or *Astilbe chinensis* var. *tacquetii* 'Superba'. These plants will completely cover the ground once the bulb's leaves have disappeared, but will themselves go dormant in winter, once again providing bulbs with spring growing space. By combining plants in this way, plant users are imitating the natural behaviour of plants such as daffodils and bluebells, and the same ecological principles can be extended to plants whose aestivation is naturally triggered by drought rather than by competition. When associating plants in such a way timing is all important; you

Table 24.1 Bulbs tolerant of wet, poorly drained soils.

Camassia
Canna
Crinum
Fritillaria meleagris
Leucojum
Watsonia (many)
Zantedeschia aethiopica

Table 24.2 Bulbous plants tolerant of planting locations that are partially shaded from late spring to autumn.

Anemone apennina, A. blanda, A. nemorosa
Arisaema spp. and cvs
Arum italicum and cvs
Begonia spp., and cvs
Cardiocrinum giganteum
Chionodoxa spp.
Colchicum spp. and cvs
Corydalis spp.
Cyclamen spp. and cvs
Dicentra spp. and cvs
Eranthis hyemalis
Erythronium spp. and cvs
Galanthus spp. and cvs
Hyacinthoides hispanica, H. non-scripta
Leucojum aestivum, L. vernum
Lilium spp. and cvs (some)
Ranunculus ficaria and cvs
Scilla bifolia, S. bithynica, S. sibirica
Trillium spp. and cvs
Zantedeschia aethiopica and cvs

must find two plants whose respective growing periods do not overlap too much.

Soil conditions

As a general principle, most bulbs require adequately drained soil in order to thrive. Exceptions to this are shown in Table 24.1. Most bulbous plants also require reasonably fertile soils to perform satisfactorily.

Sun or shade?

The vast majority of bulbs require full sun during their growing season, but are relatively indifferent to shade once they are dormant. Exceptions to this are species that perform best when the bulbs are grown in soil that is hot and dry during the summer months, (for example in Britain, some *Allium*, *Nerine*, and *Tulipa*). Many species associated naturally with deciduous woodland, (for example bluebells, *Hyacinthoides non-scripta*) are in actual fact highly intolerant of shade when it coincides with their growth period, and if planted in the shade of evergreen trees or overhead structures, perform very poorly.

There are few bulbs that are hardy in temperate regions that will thrive and continue to flower well in year-round shade. Some species that will tolerate shade between spring and autumn are shown in Table 24.2.

Time of ordering and planting

The majority of bulbs will not emerge above soil level until late winter or spring. This does not nec-

essarily mean that the bulbs are dormant during this time. Root growth of many spring bulbs commences in the autumn, well before the leaves start to move. The roots of *Narcissus* and *Allium* species (both of which are winter green) are generally in growth by August, and sometimes earlier. For this reason, it is important to order spring flowering bulbs in late summer to allow planting early in the autumn before root growth commences. In many cases the quality of bulbs purchased late in the season is substantially lower than material sent out in September-October. However, many bulbs are exceptionally forgiving in this respect and if kept cool and dry can be held back into the New Year. Even when planted as late as January stalwarts such as tulips will perform almost as normal in the following spring.

Planting conditions and depth of planting

Although it is difficult to generalise too much on the planting requirements of specific bulbs, it is true to say that a well prepared friable soil, with good drainage will give you the best results.

Table 24.3 Bulbous plants requiring full sun during their growing season for satisfactory performance in Britain.

Acidanthera spp.
Allium spp. and cvs (most)
Alstroemeria spp. and cvs
Amaryllis belladona
Asphodeline spp.
Brodiaea laxa
Camassia spp. and cvs
Canna spp. and cvs
Crinum x powelli
Crocosmia spp. and cvs*
Crocus spp. and cvs
Dactylorhiza spp.
Dahlia spp. and cvs
Dierama spp.
Eremurus spp. and cvs
Eucomis spp. and cvs
Fritillaria spp. and cvs
Galtonia spp. and cvs
Gladiolus spp. and cvs
Hedychium spp. and cvs*
Hyacinthus cvs
Ipheon spp. and cvs
Lilium spp. and cvs (some)
Muscari spp. and cvs
Narcissus spp. and cvs
Nectaroscordum siculum and ssp. *bulgaricum*
Nerine bowdenii
Ornithogalum (many)
Scilla spp. and cvs (some)
Sparaxis spp. and cvs
Sternbergia lutea
Tigridia cvs
Tropaeolum spp. and cvs
Tulbaghia violacea and cvs*
Tulipa spp. and cvs
Watsonia spp. and cvs
Zantedeschia aethiopica and cvs*
Zephyranthes candida
Zigadenus spp.

* Tolerate shade in warmer sunny climates.

Compacted, waterlogged, structureless soil should provide much poorer growing conditions. The latter conditions are very common in public landscapes where surface compaction results from pedestrians or site construction machinery. Spring flowering bulbs such as narcissus are often remarkably tolerant of these compacted soils, probably because during their winter growing period, the soils are so wet that they offer little resistance to root growth. The bulbs are dormant by the time the soil dries out and becomes highly resistant to root penetration. On such sites bulbs that tolerate wet conditions (see Table 24.1) are most likely to be most successful.

Bulbs such as lilies require a moist soil during their growing season but must never be waterlogged for long periods. Where it is necessary to cultivate specific species, sharp, washed horticultural grit (3–5 mm) can be incorporated into heavy soils to improve drainage. Soils that are too freely drained need plenty of fibrous organic matter to increase moisture-holding capacity.

Woodland species generally perform best in humus-rich soil. This can be provided both by conserving autumnal leaf litter and mulching with organic matter in the form of leafmould or composted bark. Well-rotted farmyard manure can be used for lilies, trilliums, arisaemas and other bulbs that require highly fertile soils.

Where bulbs are planted in beds and borders, once the soil has been cultivated a general fertiliser (with an NPK ratio approximating to 10:10:10) may improve establishment and flowering. Spacing of the bulbs will depend very much on the effect wanted. The planting depth should be at least as deep as the length of the bulbs in question (measure the main body only and don't include the neck). There are exceptions to this general rule of planting depth. Dry sandy soils may force you to plant deeper as the bulb is more prone to drying out. Whatever the soil conditions, Nerines need shallow planting for reliable flowering. Tuberous begonias also prefer a shallow depth whereas bluebells (*Hyacinthoides* spp.) prefer to be much deeper. Most bulb catalogues provide guidance on depth of planting. Within limits however depth isn't absolutely critical: many bulbs have contractile roots and are able to re-position themselves in the soil to some degree.

Care should be taken that the bulb is placed the right way up, with the growing tip pointing upwards. Tulips and daffodils often manage to re-orientate themselves even when planted upside down. Less robust species are likely to be more sensitive to this. Where possible bulbs should be

Fig. 24.3 *Crocus vernus* cultivars planted in mown grass at Kew. (Photo: James Hitchmough)

Table 24.4 Small bulbs that require short turf during their growth period.

Anemone nemorosa, A. apennina, and *A. blanda*
Chionodoxa spp.
Colchicum spp. and cvs.
Crocus spring types: *C. chrysanthus, C. biflorus,* and *C. tommasianus*
Crocus autumn types: *C. speciosus*
Erythronium dens-canis, E. revolutum
Fritillaria meleagris
Galanthus nivalis
Leucojum vernum
Muscari spp.
Narcissus (smaller species including *N.pseudonarcissus, N. bulbocodium, N. minor*)
Ornithogalum spp.
Ranunculus ficaria
Scilla spp.
Tulipa sprengeri, T. sylvestris

planted to rest firmly on the soil at the base of the planting hole, avoiding any unnecessary air-pockets prior to backfilling with soil.

24.3 Planting bulbs in grass

Many bulbs are natives of grassland habitats and cope with the competitiveness of that environment. The majority of bulbs grown in our temperate climate are autumn and spring flowering, making them ideal to use in meadow communities as they fit in with the natural growth cycles of managed temperate grasslands. The use of *Crocus* and *Narcissus* in the grasslands of urban parks is relatively common (Fig. 24.3), and is attractive to managers because the grass can be returned to mown grass after the leaves of the bulbs die down, generally in June-July. Bulbs can also be used very effectively in meadow-type grasslands that contain native wildflowers that are cut in August and September. Bulbs in grass are one of the most cost-effective means of providing dramatic seasonal colour events in public parks.

The nature of the turf to be planted determines which bulbs are suitable. Coarse, strong growing grasses will overwhelm smaller growing bulbs unless they grow and flower early in the year. In spring, the grass is low enough to allow the smaller spring bulbs to show themselves without having to fight through a tall sward. Bulbs that need short turf in early spring to flourish are shown in Table 24.4.

As the season progresses larger growing bulbs need to be used in order to compete with the taller grass. Late flowering spring bulbs such as Green-winged orchids (*Orchis morio*) and Common spotted orchids (*Dactylorhiza fuchsii*) are easily swamped if the grass is too vigorous and a thoughtful cutting regime may need to be undertaken to favour these (Plate 29). An early spring cut, carefully timed so as not to defoliate the orchid foliage rosettes, may be sufficient but this would inevitably exclude earlier flowering bulbs such as crocuses and daffodils. These orchids maintain a symbiotic relationship with soil fungi that enables them to multiply; if the appropriate fungus is not present then populations may remain static or diminish irrespective of cutting regime.

Many bulbs are visually unsuitable for use in borders primarily because their long strap shaped leaves look unsightly for a long time after the flowers have finished. Bulbs with these characteristics include the large flowered hybrid daffodils such as 'King Alfred' and 'Emperor'. Growing them in grass has the advantage that in May/June the dying foliage of the daffodils is progressively masked by rapid growth of the sward.

Table 24.5 Bulbs that will grow satisfactorily in rank, tall grass during their growth period.

Camassia spp.
Gladiolus communis subsp. *byzantinus* (Fig. 24.4)
Iris latifolia
Leucojum aestivum
Lilium martagon, L. pyrenaicum
Narcissus (tall to medium cultivars)
Nectaroscordum siculum

Fig. 24.4 *Gladiolus communis* ssp. *byzantinus* in long meadow grass. (Photo: Fergus Garrett / Rory Dusoir).

Hybrid tulips can also be used in grass for similar reasons, and can look quite stunning, however most cultivars decline and need to be supplemented by additional bulbs on a two-to-three-year cycle.

The majority of bulbs suitable for planting in grass are summer dormant, and the grass can be mown immediately after the leaves of the latest-flowering bulbs die down. If self seeding is to be encouraged then you have to wait until the seeds have ripened and this may be as late as the second week in August in the case of the Common Spotted Orchid (*Dactylorhiza fuchsii*). Self seeding is important for some smaller bulbs to maintain their populations, but is unimportant with long lived bulbs such as large flowered Daffodil cultivars.

In many public spaces it is not always possible to delay grass cutting this long. As a general principle many bulbs will continue to perform satisfactorily provided at least five or six weeks elapses between flowering and cutting.

The gap between raking up of grass cut in late summer and the grass greening up with the autumn rains, provides the perfect window for autumn-flowering bulbs which are activated into growth by the increase in soil moisture content. These include *Crocus* such as *C. nudiflorus*, *C. speciosus*, *Colchicum autumnale* and *C. speciosum*, all of which flourish in turf.

Very often a second cut is recommended either before the autumn flowering bulbs emerge or after they have finished flowering. If grass growth is too rapid after the first cut (in August) then a second cut before the autumn bulbs emerge is preferable, so that the long grass does not mask the flowering of the bulbs. If you miss this then the cut can be undertaken after flowering as long as care is taken to assess whether emerging buds will be cut off, as flowering of these autumn bulbs is spread out over a couple of weeks, especially if different strains are present. As well as showing off the autumn flowering bulbs in short turf the other advantage of the second cut is that as winter commences the grass remains short and it remains that way, to the advantage of the display in the following spring.

The timing of any sort of cutting regime in a meadow is always a demanding decision: it requires the balancing of practical issues such as machinery availability and public reaction with an understanding of the impact of cutting on the persistence of different species. Waiting for bulb leaves to die down can take a long time, up to six weeks after flowering in the case of the larger leaved daffodil hybrids. Snowdrops and crocuses generally require a much shorter time of approximately four weeks.

This post flowering photosynthesis is essential for next year's flowering and for the bulbs to persist. Seed ripening takes even longer and can be further delayed by wet weather. The cutting regime is an important tool in guiding the development of a meadow, as the timing of the cut always favours certain species over others.

Establishing bulbs in grass

The easiest, cheapest, and the most reliable way to establish bulbs in turf is to plant dry bulbs purchased from the supplier directly in the autumn when the ground is soft enough to cultivate. Planting can be done efficiently by lifting sections of turf with a turf cutting machine, and placing the bulbs in position under the turf, which is then laid back on top of them. A large number of bulbs can be planted very quickly, but it is rather a cumbersome method and the subsequent display can look static with concentrated clumps that do not flow from one group to another.

A preferred method of planting is to use a long-handled bulb planter which when punched into the soil pulls out a 125 mm plug of turf and soil. One bulb is placed in the bottom of each hole (sometimes more for species with small bulbs) and the plug replaced. Such bulb planters enable you to cover a large area very effectively in a short space of time. Also your plantings can be more random taking on a more natural rhythm. In the wild bulbs usually spray outwards from the core of their colonies and this effect should be imitated whenever possible. Block planting of bulbs in grass often looks very uncomfortable; ideally groups should flow in an informal manner. In public landscapes, community groups can readily undertake bulb planting.

Another important point to make about bulb planting styles is that although with certain bulbs such as crocuses planting in mixtures may be acceptable, with others such as daffodils their different flowering times in a mixture often spoils the effect, deadheads being next to fresh flowers in the same group. It is sometimes better to keep varieties separate so that as one finishes your eye can move from that to another group that is just coming into flower.

24.4   Bulbs in woodland

Although the majority of bulbs, corms, and tubers are not adapted to cope with constant deep shade, many will thrive in semi-shaded conditions of woodland. 'Winter growing' bulbs make up a good deal of the northern temperate species, and it is these that make their new roots in the autumn and winter and leaf and flower in the spring. This fits in ideally with a deciduous woodland habitat where the leaf cover on the trees begins to thin and then fall in the autumn and winter allowing moisture and light to reach the woodland floor. The leaves are 'off' the trees until the following spring, which enables the bulb to grow, flower and begin seed set before the canopy starts to close in. With this the bulb starts its dormant season.

As the tree and shrub cover comes into active growth, the water requirement increases dramatically and the soil remains relatively dry for the rest of the summer. The bulbous storage organ is ideally adapted to cope with these conditions, remaining dormant until activated by water, temperature and light the following autumn.

Another adaptation of many woodland bulbs is that unlike many bulbs of open sunny habits they do not need warmth in order to form their flower bud for the following year. Most of the species listed in Tables 24.2 and 24.4 perform very well in deciduous woodland.

24.5   Bulbs in mixed borders

Bulbs planted in between or underneath herbaceous perennials or under the canopy of deciduous shrubs can greatly enhance the appearance of plantings. This is particularly so during winter and spring, a time when many of the more structural components are often relatively unattractive.

Winter and spring flowering species

Galanthus species and their cultivars flower at this time of year utilising the spaces vacated by dormant herbaceous perennials. They can even be placed at the back of a wide plantings because in winter the vegetation is dormant and the view to the bulbs unobstructed. There are many species and cultivars of snowdrops including rare single and double forms. *Galanthus nivalis* is the commonest and most inexpensive snowdrop available and is without doubt the most versatile and useful member of the genus. Tough and reliable, it is not

Fig. 24.5 *Galanthus* species can be used to occupy vacant winter spaces under the canopy of deciduous shrubs. (Photo: Fergus Garrett / Rory Dusoir)

Fig. 24.6 *Ranunculus ficaria* 'Brazen Hussy' can occupy the same space as *Crocosmia* 'Lucifer'; the celandine grows, flowers and recedes before the crocosmia emerges fully. (Photo: Fergus Garrett / Rory Dusoir)

however the showiest snowdrop, but planted 'en masse' it is still very effective. The larger flowered hybrids such as G. 'S. Arnott', G. 'Atkinsii', and G. 'Colesborne' are more dramatic but are not economical for use on a large scale. All snowdrops are winter growers so need to be planted in the autumn. It is also recognised that they are well adapted to be planted 'in the green' i.e. in full leaf in the spring. They can be inter-planted or under-planted, amongst summer flowering herbaceous material where they can grow, flower, and die down before the latter take over the space in late spring. They can also occupy vacant winter spaces under the canopy of deciduous shrubs that are later obscured as the shrub comes into leaf (Fig. 24.5).

Ranunculus ficaria, the lesser celandine, may perhaps be too aggressive for very detailed planting, but is highly ornamental in naturalistic woodland edge type plantings. The less vigorous, dark leafed cultivar 'Brazen Hussy' can be grown 'on top' of a late spring/ early summer active perennial like *Crocosmia* 'Lucifer'. The *Crocosmia* allows the early starting *Ranunculus* to colonise the same space: grow, flower and recede before the former emerges and completely envelopes the space (Fig. 24.6). The celandine remains dormant with bulbils just below the surface of the soil around the stems of the crocosmia. Both plants co-exist in harmony without getting in each other's way. *Anemone blanda*, *A. nemorosa*, and *A. ranunculoides*, *Crocus biflorus*, *C. chrysanthus* and *C. vernus* hybrids as well as many other winter-growing bulbs can be treated in a similar manner. *Crocus tommasinianus* is particularly useful because it seeds itself freely through plantings, its leaves never so voluminous as to be a nuisance. It works well underneath and flowers with the pink blossom of the dwarf shrub, *Prunus tenella* 'Fire Hills'.

Spring flowering species

Daffodil species and cultivars need careful positioning because the leaves of the large flowered hybrids are too obtrusive in a border. They are better used in meadow planting. If planted amongst vigorous perennials such as hemerocallis which have the same engulfing effect as the grass the coarse leaves of the daffodils can be hidden. The smaller jonquils and cyclamineus types are much more suitable for mixed planting, their dying leaves insufficiently coarse to detract from the other plants. *Narcissus* 'Tete-a-tete' planted between phloxes and similar herbaceous perennials provides a good example of how a bulb can work in with a herbaceous perennial to extend the season. *Narcissus* 'Hawera' is a jonquil that can be used in the same way.

Tulips have an important role to play in plantings not only as bedding subjects but also as permanent planting. Some cultivars are highly permanent, for example, clumps of *Tulipa* 'Red Matador' have grown undisturbed for over 25 years in the Long Border at Christopher Lloyd's garden Great Dixter, in East Sussex. In the same garden *Tulipa* 'Dillenberg' has been very successful amongst *Phlox paniculata* hybrids, and so has the lily flowered tulip 'White Triumphator' in between clumps of *Inula magnifica*. Even when they do not prove so permanent they can be simply 'topped up ' from year to year by planting new bulbs.

Temporary plantings of tulips running through permanent planting can be very effective. The permanence of different tulip cultivars and species is difficult to predetermine. Not only does it depend on the specific growing conditions of that site but also on the adaptability of the variety itself. Species tulips such as *Tulipa orphanidea*, *T. eichleri*, *T. batalinii*, and *T. sylvestris* appear to persist most satisfactorily in warm, well-drained sunny sites, though this may be a generalisation. In complete contrast, *Tulipa sprengeri* is a vigorously self seeding species that will naturalise in mixed plantings as well as under deciduous trees and shrubs in most garden soils. This is an expensive species to purchase (for reasons that are never clear) but is an ideal scarlet permanent species for use in public plantings.

Crown Imperials, *Fritillaria imperialis* are striking bulbs for fertile, well-drained soils. They are one of the tallest spring bulbs and make an imposing feature in mixed planting. They need annual fertilising to prevent them diminishing and to maintain good flowering. *Leucojum aestivum* requires a cool moist position to flower freely in April; primroses and forget-me-nots making good partners for it. It is very robust and can be planted under deciduous shrubs such as *Cornus alba*. *Nectaroscordum* (closely related to the genus *Allium*) are ideal for inter-planting amongst herbaceous perennials such as Astilbes. *Nectaroscordum siculum*, and its subspecies *bulgaricum* are persistent perennials, seeding themselves around freely. They are happiest in a sunny position although they do tolerate semi-shade. Their pendant bell like flowers in subtle shades of cream, purple, and green, are intriguingly beautiful and are followed by pretty seedheads. They are striking emerging from low, 'dry looking' meadow planting.

Camassia thrive in most soils and make excellent mixed border components, but care should be taken in placing them as their long leaves are awkward and can look unsightly for a long time. By planting amongst a winter dormant, trailing ground covering geranium such as G. 'Ann Folkard' the leaves are soon obscured by the geranium after the *Camassia* has finished flowering. *Camassia cusickii*, *C. leichtlinii* and *C. l.* 'Alba' are commonly used in mixed plantings and are relatively trouble free.

Late spring to early summer

Hardy gladioli such as *Gladiolus communis* subsp. *byzantinus*, work well in amongst permanent plantings. By commencing growth relatively early whilst the surrounding herbaceous vegetation is still dormant, they have a head start over their competition. After flowering they, like many of the others from a similar Mediterranean climate, aestivate and melt back into their storage organs only to start growth again in the autumn. The space subsequently vacated by them is taken over by the surrounding vegetation.

Alliums are both splendid and versatile in mixed planting (Fig. 24.7). There are over 700 members of the genus, many from temperate regions of the world. Many species from the Mediterranean and central Asian region are robust and persistent in cultivation in Britain, given reasonably well-drained soil, for example, such as *Allium christophii*, *A. giganteum*, *A. moly*, *A.* × *hollandicum*, and *A. karataviense*. These make their leaf growth through the winter and spring and flower in late spring or early summer. For designers, the tall species are most valuable, as the ball like flower heads on stems up to one metre tall offer strong rhythmical possibilities as emergents

Fig. 24.7 *Allium christophii* planted to occupy the spaces between tussocks of *Molinia caerulea* before this emerges in late spring. (Photo: James Hitchmough)

from lower mixed planting. These visual qualities have been used many times in the work of Wolfgang Oehme and James van Sweden. They are however irresistible to some passers-by and this can be problematic in some urban public spaces. *Eremurus* have similar architecture to the larger *Allium*, with which they can be combined to produce dramatic effects. They are sensitive to excessively wet soils and given their height in flower are sometimes *unstable* in windy, exposed sites. This can be reduced to some degree by minimal addition of fertiliser. There are many good garden hybrids available on the market. They come in a variety of sizes and colours, and look especially at home in contemporary low naturalistic planting coming out of gravel mulches. The leaves are very untidy, especially in the really tall species such as *E. robustus*, but can be obscured by adjacent low planting. For general use *E. stenophyllus* and its hybrids are most useful in public and commercial planting.

Summer to autumn flowering bulbs

Crocosmia commence active growth in spring and are important border components for their foliage as well as their flowers. There are many hybrids available now including really striking plants such as the blazing red-flowered *Crocosmia* 'Lucifer' and the large flowered deep yellow 'Star of the East'. From the perspective of planting design they are best seen as permanent herbaceous planting, as they are in leaf from spring to autumn. They thrive in rich soil, in a sunny position and benefit from summer moisture. If kept overly dry they succumb to red spider mite.

Autumn flowering bulbs

Autumn flowering bulbs provide valuable colour and much needed freshness so late on in the season. Colchicums are one of the main highlights with *Colchicum autumnale*, *C. speciosum* and their white forms probably the most valuable. Their dark green leaves are luxuriant and attractive in the spring, eventually browning off in late July when they can be cut down and cleared away. It then takes several weeks for the flowers to emerge so a low growing, permanent carpet of *Vinca minor* or *Origanum vulgare* 'Aureum' can be used as a ground cover sheet from which the *Colchicum* emerge. Once the colchicum flowers are finished the carpet is still there covering the ground until the first frosts, when it is cleared away making way for the colchicum leaves to follow. In seasonal colour plantings a bedding plant such as *Helichrysum petiolare*, or *Petunia* 'Purple Wave' can be planted amongst the bulbs to achieve similar effects.

Colchicum are very handy in borders in vacant spaces in between shrubs and low growing perennials such as *Alchemilla mollis*. In the case of the latter the *Alchemilla* can be cut down after flowering in order to produce a fresh set of leaves to go with the colchicum.

Amaryllis belladonna from South Africa is another valuable autumn bulb that flowers before the leaves; heads of striking deep pink trumpet flowers are borne on 450 mm stems. It needs a sheltered sunny position, preferably at the base of a south-facing wall. *Nerine bowdenii* has brighter pink flowers than the *Amaryllis* and is smaller in stature although just as striking. Again it is from South Africa and loves being in a sunny open position. Its flowers in September look particularly good with dome like asters such as *Aster* 'Violet Queen' or *Nepeta nervosa*. Both of these bulbs are really only reliably hardy in the warmer regions of the British Isles.

As with the preceding species, *Sternbergia* can be more difficult to use, as they require full sun and a sheltered warm situation yet have insufficient structure to stand alone. They can work well when planted in gravel-surfaced strips or cut-outs within paving.

There are quite a number of autumn-flowering crocuses that have potential for landscape use, with *Crocus nudiflorus* and *C. speciosus* being particularly robust. They characteristically flower without their leaves with shades of violet blue flowers, *C. nudiflorus* being slightly richer in colour than the paler *C. speciosus*. They are best naturalised in grass, as in mixed plantings their leaves can look unsightly from spring to summer. *C. kotschyanus* (bluish lavender) and *C. ochroleucus* (creamy white) are also commonly available.

Crinums need a sunny position with plenty of moisture during their summer growing season. The most common and hardy species, *Crinum × powellii* has pink flowers late in summer and makes a large clump up to 1.25 m tall, with almost evergreen leaves. This and its white form *Crinum × powellii* 'Album' make impressive features in planting although their leaves can be very untidy later in the summer. Both forms are also suitable to be treated as marginals in water. *Eucomis*, and *Schizostylis*, also from South Africa, can be treated as permanent herbaceous features in mixed planting. *Eucomis* need a sheltered site in order to flower reliably; they have tall spikes bearing many star-shaped flowers from September into October. *Schizostylis* are hardier and thrive in moist, fertile soil; the red-flowered form *Schizostylis coccinea* 'Major' is the most dramatic form although there are pretty pink and white forms on the market.

Hardy cyclamen, and especially *C. hederifolium* are autumn stalwarts. Intense pink in colour with a dark rim round the lip of the flower, this species will thrive under evergreen trees providing the shade is not too dense. Their silver, green and grey marbled leaves are a strong winter feature. *Arum*

italicum 'Pictum' is another bulb with a strong winter presence. The autumn display consists of clubs of bright scarlet berries on 150 mm stems, which are soon devoured by birds. These are followed by highly decorative heart-shaped marbled leaves. This arum will tolerate dense shade and is effective in combination with snowdrops.

24.6   Bulbs in 'bedding out' schemes

Bedding out is a term used for temporary plantings aimed at providing colourful displays in spring and in summer, either integrated into a mixed border scheme or in isolated beds of their own. Bulbous plants are an important component of these schemes. Bedding out is discussed in greater detail in Chapter 23.

Spring bedding

The exciting, rich colours that are common in bulbs make them ideal for use in spring bedding schemes (see Table 24.6). Massed together on their own, or accompanied by a colourful carpeter, they provide stunning seasonal displays. Tulips, muscari, hyacinths, daffodils, and scillas are commonly used in the spring with forget-me-nots, bellis, wallflowers, arabis, primulas, and pansies (Fig. 24.8). Either flowering before, after or with

Fig. 24.8 A vibrant spring bedding scheme: scarlet and orange tulips underplanted with forget-me-nots. (Photo: Fergus Garrett / Rory Dusoir)

Table 24. 6 Bulbous plants for spring bedding.

Allium
Anemone
Chionodoxa
Crocus
Hermodactylus
Hyacinthus
Muscaria
Narcissus
Ornithogalum
Ranunculus asiaticus
Scilla
Tulipa

Table 24.7 Bulbous plants for summer bedding.

Acidanthera
Allium (late species such as *A. giganteum*)
Alocasia
Begonia
Brodiaea
Canna
Colocasia
Dahlia
Eucomis
Galtonia
Gladiolus
Hedychium
Iris
Lilium
Nerine
Tigridia
Watsonia
Zantedeschia

these plants enables endless creative possibilities. Although often seen as the height of municipal conservatism, in the hands of a designer who understands the material, this type of bedding can produce stunning, complex effects, as has been demonstrated in the planting undertaken by Schoenaich-Rees Associates at the Tate Gallery in London.

Once flowering is finished the bulbs are lifted and stored dry before planting again the next autumn. However, the relatively low cost of purchasing bulbs through wholesaler firms means that very often discarding the old bulbs and buying new ones works out more economically than the labour-intensive process of saving the old bulbs. Fresh purchases also have the added advantage of being relatively disease-free, and uniform in size, meaning a more even display.

Summer bedding

Bulbs play a lesser role in summer bedding although tuberous-rooted begonias, cannas, gladioli, *Zantedeschia*, and dahlias are important exceptions (see Table 24.7). These can be integrated into colourful schemes along with annuals and half-hardy perennials or used individually as dot plants. *Eucomis*, *Tigridia*, *Acidenthera*, *Colocasia*, and *Alocasia* are less common but exciting in more exotic schemes. Summer flowering bulbs can also be used to emerge from low, ground cover-like plantings of trailers such as *Bidens ferrulifolia*, *Helichrysum petiolare*, *Diascia*, *Nastur-*

tium, and *Petunia*. The aim in all cases is to achieve a long-lasting display that will effectively take you to the end of summer, after which the plants are discarded or stored for next year.

Cannas and dahlias can be stored relatively dry in a frost-free space only to be re-activated the following spring by potting into fresh soil, watering, and moving under glass to give them a kick-start before planting out in May. Tuberous rooted begonias can be treated and stored the same way. None of these plants should be allowed to dry out completely during winter storage so slightly moist peat moss or similar is the preferable medium. Susceptibility to fungal rot makes it worthwhile to roll bulbs, corms and tubers, in a suitable fungicide powder to cut down on winter losses. Dahlias can also be over-wintered as tubers, however it is more practical to purchase new plants derived from cuttings taken earlier in the year (Plate 30).

Tigridia and *Acidanthera* can be treated in the same sort of way to a spring flowering bulb, though both are not reliably hardy in the British Isles so an early spring planting is preferred. *Colocasia* and *Alocasia* provide dramatic tropical effects by virtue of their very large leaves, and if possible need to be stored in a heated greenhouse and kept active throughout the winter. If allowed to go dormant and over-watered, these can easily suffer from rot. If watering is tightly controlled they can be kept winter dormant and then re-activated in a similar manner to Cannas and Dahlias.

Nerine bowdenii also makes an impressive bedding ingredient flowering from late summer into autumn. The sugar pink flowers look particularly good with deep purple forms of *Heliotropium peruvianum*. It is hardy enough to safely overwinter in much of the British Isles. The dying leaves should be removed prior to flowering, allowing the display during flowering to be untarnished by the yellowing leaves. Nerines can be moved in full flower from containers or the open ground into bedding schemes if they are watered in well prior to and after the move.

24.7 Purchasing bulbs

Bulbs are usually available for purchase in a dry state when they are dormant. Spring flowering bulbs are for sale late summer into autumn, and summer flowering bulbs are available in the spring. Buying fresh when the bulbs first offered for sale is always advisable as poor storage conditions may lead to rapid deterioration, especially in sensitive bulbs such as fritillaries and snowdrops. A dry atmosphere with cool temperatures is ideal for bulb storage. Bulbs should be firm, and healthy looking. Bulbs that are soft and shrivelled should be rejected. A soft basal plate (especially in narcissus) spells danger and should be avoided. A healthy bulb should be blemish free and free of any damage. Bulbs sometimes come in a number of size grades, from 'top size'. Large bulbs may have greater flowering impact in the first year, and the extra expense may be justified in some cases, but often smaller-sized bulbs will in the long term, perform perfectly adequately.

The bulb trade has come under much criticism due to the collection of many bulbs from the wild. Though many steps have been taken to bring an end to this problem there is still evidence that sub-

stantial wild collecting is still occurring. Many endangered bulbs are protected by the Convention of International Trade in Endangered Species (CITES) and many of the firms who supply bulbs fully endorse the campaign to conserve populations in the wild. It is essential that everyone involved, from the supplier to the purchaser, play their part in putting a stop to the illegal trade in wild bulbs.

Wholesale suppliers

Bloms Bulbs, Primrose Nurseries, Melbourne, Beds MK44 1ZZ
Tel 01234 709099 Fax 01234 709799

Parkers Bulbs Co, 452 Chester Road, Manchester M16 9HL
Tel 0161 8723517 Fax 0161 8770602

Peter Nyssen Ltd, 124 Flixton Road, Urmston, Manchester, M41 5BG
Tel 0161 7474000 Fax 0161 7486319

Specialist retail nurseries

Avon Bulbs, Burnt House Farm, Mid Lambrook, South Petherton, Somerset Ta13 5HE
Tel 01460 242177
Broadleigh Gardens, Barr House, Bishops Hull, Taunton, Somerset TA14 1AE
Tel 01823 286231

Further reading

Lloyd, C. (1976) 'Meadow Gardening'. *The Garden*, **101**, pp 323–9.
Lloyd, C. (1976) 'Meadow Gardening Part II'. *The Garden*, **101**, pp 350–55.
Mathew, B. (1997) *Growing Bulbs: The Complete Practical Guide.* Batsford, London.
Mathew, B. & Swindells, P. (1994) *The Gardener's Guide to Bulbs.* Mitchell Beazley, London.

25 Herbaceous Perennials

James Hitchmough

'Herbaceous perennials' are plants that renew their above-ground parts on an annual basis and do not produce 'woody' tissues. Most are winter deciduous but there are also evergreen species. This chapter also covers bulb-like species with specialised storage organs, such as corms which are in leaf from spring to summer or later (for example, *Crocosmia* and *Dierama*) and herbaceous perennials native to the British Isles that are often seen as plants for sown meadows only. Many but not all of the recommendations in this chapter are also applicable to sub-shrubs such as *Lavandula*. Species that are subject to severe damage in a typical winter are not considered.

25.1 Herbaceous perennials and their native habitats

The term 'herbaceous perennial' encompasses a great diversity of plants originating from nearly every temperate ecosystem. Important wild habitats from which cultivated herbaceous perennials have been introduced are listed in Table 25.1.

Understanding a species' original habitat can provide a useful indication of the environmental conditions it needs to grow satisfactorily in cultivation. Information on habitats is distributed patchily throughout the horticultural literature: Phillips and Rix (1994) is readily available, but the richest sources are generally the far less accessible floras of a particular country. In addition to the type of habitat it is also important to take into account the latitude and altitude in question. Species from a given habitat in a region with a milder winter climate than Britain may prove susceptible to winter cold. However, for the vast majority of cultivated herbaceous perennials, winter hardiness is not a significant problem in Britain.

Practitioners need to recognise that habitat information will also need interpretation: for example, many species can be stretched to grow in different conditions, when competition with other species is managed as in traditional border type plantings. Species typically found in woodland may occur in full sun in more northerly situations or at higher altitudes in the mountains. This transition is apparent in a number of native and exotic species cultivated in the British Isles: in Surrey, shade may be essential while, in Scotland, the same species will perform satisfactorily in full sun.

In addition to classification by type of habitat, it is also useful in practice to categorise species on the basis of life form or growth traits.

Foliage retention

Herbaceous species can be split into three categories on the basis of winter leaf retention:

- winter deciduous;
- overwintering foliage, often as a basal rosette;
- winter evergreen.

This characteristic is of some significance not only visually, but also in terms of management. As the major cost of using herbaceous perennials in landscape plantings is generally weed control, species that have evergreen foliage may sometimes be more resistant to weed colonisation during the autumn to spring period. Conversely, non-selective herbicides may have to be sprayed over wholly

Table 25.1 'Wild' habitats and associated herbaceous perennials.

Habitat type	Typical species / comments:
Woodland	
Dense woodland	slow growing highly shade tolerant species, such as many ferns, *Helleborus orientalis*, *Luzula sylvatica*, or essentially vernal spp. such as *Primula vulgaris*. Species present vary according to moisture and light levels.
Open woodland	Wider range of less specialised species, e.g. *Geranium macrorrhizum*, *Tellima grandiflora*, *Geranium maculatum*. Many of these species grow in woodland in southern parts of their range and in full sun in more northern regions.
Woodland edge/very open woodland	Wide range of less specialised species, many of these species grow in woodland in southern parts of their range and in full sun in grassy places in more northern regions or at altitude, e.g. *Geranium sanguineum*.
Heath and scrub	These habitats are typically on relatively infertile soils, species often slow growing with limited shade tolerance, for example *Euphorbia polychroma*.
Grassland	
Dry	Species are often small slow growing, shade intolerant, for example *Pulsatilla vulgaris*, *Iris pumila*, *Inula ensifolia*, *Festuca*, *Stipa*, *Salvia nemorosa*, *Eryngium*.
Moist	Species typically larger more vigorous, *Geranium sylvaticum*, *G. pratense*, *Sanguisorba*. Large number of members of daisy family; *Aster*, *Echinacea*, *Liatris*, *Silphium*, *Solidago* associated with North American prairies. *Kniphofia* and *Agapanthus* in S. Africa.
Wet	Many candelabra type asiatic *Primula*, *Caltha*, *Trollius*, some *Aconitum*.
Fen, bog and riparian	Largely shade intolerant, species associated with more fertile sites are large and vigorous, e.g. *Iris pseudoacorus*, *Phragmites*, *Iris sibirica*, *Rudbeckia laciniata*, *Lythrum*, *Lysimachia*, *Filipendula* and *Astilbe* spp.

deciduous species to prevent build up of winter green weeds. In this sense, species that maintain some overwintering foliage as a basal rosette are the least satisfactory.

Some species retain basal foliage only in their first winter and then become totally deciduous. The leaf retention characteristics of some herbaceous species are shown in Table 25.2. Evergreenness is frequently an adaptation to habitats experiencing shortages of water, nutrients and light – such plants are often naturally relatively slow growing.

Growth form and means of reproduction

These characteristics often reflect the ecological requirements of a species habitat, and in cultivation they are an important consideration for designers. Typical growth forms and means of reproduction in herbaceous perennials are shown in Table 25.3. Knowledge of these characteristics can help designers to create plantings that are easier and cheaper to maintain. For example, tall species that spread vigorously by underground stems such as *Macleaya microcarpa* will, eventually, eliminate all clump-forming neighbours, but these will survive if an equally tall but clump-forming *Miscanthus* or *Veronicastrum* is used instead. Self-seeding can either be valuable or a problem trait, depending upon the situation. Species that spread aggressively by self-seeding generally need a vegetation-free soil surface to do this successfully.

Tolerance of sun and shade

In most cases this can be deduced from knowledge of a species' habitat, although some species possess tolerances beyond what might be expected. Tolerance of these factors is important, not only for siting species in relation to the shade cast by buildings and trees, but also for determining the persistence of species within herbaceous plantings, where taller species spread and outgrow lower-

Table 25.2 Leaf retention in some herbaceous perennials.

Winter deciduous*	Overwintering basal foliage	Winter evergreen
Astrantia	*Aster* (some)	*Bergenia*
Eupatorium maculatum	*Buphthalmum salicifolium*	*Epimedium*
Euphorbia griffithii	*Deschampsia cespitosa*	*Eryngium* (S. American spp.)
Geranium (many)	*Geranium macrorrhizum*	*Euphorbia amygdaloides*
Helianthus	*Hesperis matronalis*	*Geranium x oxonianum*
Hemerocallis	*Iris x germanica*	*Helleborus*
Hosta	*Leucanthemum*	*Heuchera*
Iris sibirica	*Lobelia cardinalis*	*Kniphofia* (many)
Liatris	*Lychnis chalcedonica*	*Libertia*
Phlox	*Miscanthus* (some cvs)	*Papaver orientalis*
Sanguisorba	*Oenothera tetragona*	*Primula heledoxa*
Thalictrum	*Origanum*	*Stipa*
Trollius	*Rudbeckia fulgida*	*Waldsteinia*

* some winter deciduous spp. produce above ground buds in late winter.

Table 25.3 Growth form and means of reproduction in a range of herbaceous perennials.

abundant self-sowing, short-lived, clump	These are referred to as ruderal spp., for example, *Aquilegia* spp., *Digitalis* (perennial spp.), *Lychnis coronaria*, *Lupinus* spp.
abundant self-sowing, long-lived clump	These species are relatively unusual, as this is essentially an ecological contradiction. Includes *Helleborus argutifolius*, *Helleborus orientalis*, *Primula veris*, *Alchemilla mollis*, *Brunnera macrophylla* and *Geranium pratense*
occasional to very rare self-sowing, long-lived clump	A very common growth form. Clumps expand slowly by new vegetative shoots forming as a concentric ring around last year's shoots, e.g., *Geranium psilostemon*, *Trollius*, *Hemerocallis*, many *Salvia*, *Iris sibirica*, many *Aster*, *Campanula lactiflora*, *Heuchera*, *Miscanthus*, *Stipa gigantea*, *Euphorbia polychroma* and *E. palustris*, *Aconitum*, *Hosta*
occasional to very rare self-sowing, short-lived clump	Without intensive maintenance these spp. are typically rather transient, for example *Achillea* cultivars, *Sidalcea*, many *Delphinium*, *Verbascum* cultivars
occasional to very rare self-sowing, sheet former spreading by surface or underground running shoots	The best know of these species have self layering shoots that potentially expand continuously, for example, *Geranium procurrens*, *Polygonum (Persicaria) campanulatum*, *Mimulus* spp., *Caltha polypetala* (hort.) *Waldsteinia ternata*, *Filipendula*, many *Bergenia*. A second group spread outwards rapidly from a central rootstock but die back annually to that point, posing fewer management spread headaches, e.g. *Geranium wallichianum* and *Anthemis tinctoria* cvs. The latter species tends to be short lived.

growing species. In meadow-like sowing and planting (see below) shade intolerant species with predominantly basal foliage (for example, many *Hemerocallis*) are eventually eliminated by the shade cast by surrounding meadow grasses. Typical tolerance for a range of species in the British climate is shown in Table 25.4. Species that are shade intolerant in Britain often grow satisfactorily in light shade in sunnier climates.

Tolerance of soil moisture

Once again this can generally be assumed from the habitat-climatic distribution. Valuable information

Table 25.4   Tolerance of some herbaceous perennials for sun and shade.

Shade tolerant	Tolerate sun and some shade	Shade intolerant
Anemone x hybrida	*Achemilla*	*Achillea*
Aster (woodland spp.)	*Aconitum*	*Aster* (prairie spp.)
Cimicifuga	*Ajuga*	*Eryngium*
Digitalis (many)	*Astilbe*	*Euphorbia* (most)
Geranium nodosum	*Campanula*	*Hemerocallis*
Helleborus	*Filipendula*	*Iris germanica* cvs.
Hosta	*Geranium* (many)	*Iris sibirica*
Polygonatum	*Ligularia*	*Kniphofia*
Primula japonica	*Meconopsis*	*Miscanthus*
Smilacina	*Persicaria* (many)	*Salvia* (most)
Tellima	*Rodgersia*	*Scabiosa*
Tiarella	*Thalictrum*	*Stipa*
Veratrum	*Trollius*	*Verbascum*

Table 25.5   Tolerance of some herbaceous perennials to soil moisture.

Tolerate very wet	Average soil moisture	Tolerate very dry
Caltha	*Aster* (many)	*Dictamnus*
Descampsia cespitosa	*Campanula*	*Eryngium*
Eupatoriun maculatum	*Delphinium* (large cvs)	*Euphorbia* (many)
Euphorbia palustris	*Dierama*	*Inula ensifolia*
Filipendula	*Echinacea*	*Iris x germanica*
Iris sibirica	*Geranium* (most)	*Kniphofia* (some)
Ligularia	*Hemerocallis*	*Melica*
Lysimachia	*Hosta*	*Origanum*
Lythrum	*Miscanthus*	*Papaver orientale*
Molinia caerulea	*Monarda*	*Phlomis*
Polygonum (Persicaria)	*Phlox paniculata*	*Salvia* (many)
Primula florindae	*Rudbeckia*	*Sedum* (most)
Thalictrum	*Solidago* (most)	*Stipa*
Trollius	*Veronica* (many)	*Verbascum*

on this can be obtained from *The Dry Garden* (Chatto, 1985), *The Damp Garden* (Chatto, 1982), and Hansen and Stahl (1993). Species can be stretched outside their preferred moisture range in cultivation, but become increasingly less robust.

Longevity

In general, short-lived species often have high self-seeding potential and can be recognised by this characteristic. Longevity is also a function of the suitability of the planting site, in terms of the appropriateness of sun and shade, soil moisture, winter cold and the intensity of slug and snail grazing. Species that are often functionally short-lived in Britain due to a combination of these factors include *Diascia, Asclepias tuberosa, Coreopsis lanceolate, Lychnis coronaria, Linaria purpurea, Digitalis x mertonensis, Meconopsis*, small growing *Kniphofia, Primula, Tanacetum coccineum, Sidalcea*, and *Verbascum* hybrids.

Table 25.6 A suggested categorisation in terms of Grime's strategies for a number of familiar cultivated herbaceous plants (after Grime *et al.*, 1988).

Stress tolerators	*Helleborus orientalis*[AB], *Iris x germanica*[A], *Polygonatum multiflorum*[BA], *Primula helodoxa*[C], *Scabiosa columbaria*[A].
Stress-tolerant competitors	*Acanthus mollis*[AB], *Bergenia* spp.[AB], *Geranium* spp. (many)[A], *Hosta* spp., *Romneya coulteri*[A].
Competitors	*Anemone x hybrida, Filipendula ulmaria, Monarda didyma, Petasites* spp., *Polygonum campanulatum*.
Ruderals	*Aquilegia vulgaris, Campanula alliariifolia, Meconopsis cambrica, Polemonium caeruleum, Silene dioica*.
Stress-tolerant ruderals	*Digitalis purpurea*[B], *Echinacea purpurea*[A], *Eryngium giganteum*[A], *Linaria purpurea*[A], *Lychnis coronaria*[A].
Competitive ruderals	*Anchusa azurea, Foeniculum vulgare, Impatiens glandulifera, Oenothera biennis, Salvia sclarea*.

Key: Nature of stress tolerance
A = Drought; B = Light; C = Waterlogging

Ecological strategy

This categorisation overlaps most of the previous categories and is potentially very valuable to professional users of herbaceous perennials. Plant strategy theory has been developed at the University of Sheffield by Professor Phil Grime and his colleagues over the past 25 years (Grime *et al.*, 1988). This work is based on ecological tests that allow a species to be pigeon-holed as possessing either a competitor, stress tolerator or ruderal strategy. There are also intermediate categories as shown in Table 25.6.

Competitors

These are typically large and long lived, grow vigorously when water, nutrients and light are abundant and eliminate adjacent non-competitor neighbours, leading to monocultural swards. Nettles are a classic weedy competitor.

Stress tolerators

These hail from either heavily shaded, drought-prone and infertile habitats or very wet anaerobic habitats, and survive these conditions by growing very slowly. Ragged robin (*Lychnis flos-cuculi*) and origanum (*Origanum vulgare*) are two native stress tolerators of wet anaerobic and dry habitats respectively. When grown on fertile moist soils in the company of competitor species, stress tolerators are soon eliminated.

Ruderals

These are short-lived species whose persistence depends on high levels of self sowing. They are eliminated when planted with competitors on fertile soils, but may persist with stress tolerators where soils are not too infertile.

These categorisations can also be applied to exotic, cultivated species to provide an indication of the likely long-term outcomes of plantings that contain species with different ecological strategies. As a general principle, mixing competitors and stress tolerators together on fertile sites is to be avoided. Although laboratory-confirmed data on the ecological strategy of cultivated species is not yet available, with detailed knowledge of herbaceous plant growth and morphology it is possible to develop a preliminary categorisation.

25.2 Plant selection and procurement

Selection of species and cultivars

In British wholesale nurseries, approximately 1 500 species and cultivars of herbaceous perennials are typically available. When specialist (mostly retail) nurseries are added to this, this number rises well above 5 000. Some of the species grown by specialist nurseries are less robust than those in the mainstream wholesale list, but there are many exceptions. New species or cultivars with outstanding appearance or reliability gradually move from specialists to wholesale nurseries (for example, *Geranium* 'Patricia'), but many do not. This represents a lost opportunity for designers who are not aware of this diversity. You are unlikely to see *Ferula communis* in a wholesale list, but it is a tall emergent species with fantastic design lines that can be obtained in small numbers from retail specialists identified through The *RHS Plant Finder*.

In selecting herbaceous perennials it is important not only to consider flower colour and form but also the ecological factors mentioned above, plus the maintenance characteristics that will ultimately determine the persistence and long-term success of plantings. The work of Professor Richard Hansen at Weihenstephan, Munich, in dividing the cultivated herbaceous flora into categories based on ecological and horticultural characteristics (Hansen and Stahl, 1993), helps in the selection of plants that are compatible with the site and with one another. However, this system was conceived in Southern Germany and is not always fully applicable to conditions in the UK.

Cultivar selections are often very useful as they provide much greater control over appearance and growth habits. *Campanula lactiflora* 'Pritchards Variety' is 1–1.2 m tall, with deep violet flowers as opposed to the milky blue, 1.5 m typical of seedlings. *Molinia caerulea* cultivars vary in overall size and vigour, autumn colour, the splay angle of the leaves and the density of the inflorescence. Some cultivars are more robust than the species, others less so. In genera that attract 'fancier' nurserymen, for example, *Iris, Hemero-*

callis, and *Hosta*, a significant percentage of cultivars are of dubious value to landscape users.

The nursery product

Herbaceous perennials are typically available to landscape users in a number of forms, the full range of which are shown in the HTA *National Plant Specification* (HTA, 1997). The best product depends on the nature of the site, design requirements and needs of the clients.

Seed

With the exception of native species used in wildflower meadows (see Chapter 22) or in woodland understorey, non-native herbaceous perennials have rarely been sown *in situ* in landscape plantings. This can be a viable means of establishing naturalistic herbaceous vegetation, and this is discussed later in the chapter. Seed from widely cultivated non-native species is often comparable in price to that of native species grown for wildflower meadows. With North American species of *Aster, Echinacea*, and *Solidago*, for example, the cost of seed to establish a naturalistic prairie-like community of 100+ plants per square metre is around £0.50–80, depending on the species chosen. The disadvantages of establishment by sowing are:

- the initial impact is low,
- the user has reduced control over composition, and
- management in the first year is more critical.

Small container grown plants

These range from plugs of various dimensions to 9 cm containers (P9s). As with all transplanted nursery stock, small dynamic plants are relatively cheap to purchase and plant, and have the potential to establish quickly. Planting can take place throughout the year, given some irrigation capacity during the summer. Small plants are also probably less attractive to thieves. Their disadvantages are due to their restricted number of growth points and rhizome reserves: they are more vulnerable to

Fig. 25.1   A traditional high quality herbaceous double border at Arley Hall. (Photo: James Hitchmough)

poor planting, unfavourable site conditions, traffic and slug grazing.

Medium to large container grown plants

These tend to be more robust than small material, although where sites are very unfavourable this may only constitute a short-term advantage. Cost is the major disadvantage. This often results in relatively low planting densities, delaying or preventing the development of a sward of foliage that will reduce the likelihood of weed colonisation.

Field grown bare-root plants

This production technique has fallen out of favour, largely because bare-root material is essentially restricted to planting only in the autumn to spring period. From the perspective of plant users, though, this is an excellent form in which to buy herbaceous perennials, other than grasses and evergreen species that are sensitive to being transplanted. Field-grown plants are generally substantially larger than container stock at the same price; they will not suffer from moisture stress and transplant problems associated with

being planted in a potentially hydrophobic pot of peat compost.

In many species planting in autumn rather than spring appears to produce better growth in the growing season that follows. Bare-root herbaceous perennials are generally less sensitive to root desiccation than bare-root trees and shrubs, but care in handling prior to planting is still required to reduce the possibility of desiccation.

25.3   Planting design

This section has been placed to precede 'site preparation and establishment' because the approach to the latter is very much determined by the type of planting design proposed. For most of the twentieth century, the main form of herbaceous planting design has been the border (Fig. 25.1). Alan Bloom's island bed concept broke away from the traditional linear shape, but did not change the form of planting from the tradition of drift-like but rarely repeating groups of species (often composed of three to seven plants) relatively widely-spaced with large areas of cultivated soil. A contemporary version of this can be seen in the main herbaceous borders at Wisley.

Fig. 25.2 Herbaceous block planting in a Heritage Lottery retro-fitted park in Sunderland. (Photo: James Hitchmough)

Some alternative forms of planting design are discussed below; many of them can be integrated with adjacent tree and shrub planting, provided care is taken in the location of species that are intolerant of shade or competition with tree and shrub roots.

Reduced maintenance herbaceous border

This is based on rigorous plant selection using only long-lived, robust species that do not require division or staking, will survive heavy annual mulching, are not subject to serious slug damage and will grow satisfactorily without additional nutrients and water. Blocks are planted at much higher densities (300 mm centres) so that areas of bare soil between and within clumps is minimised (Fig. 25.2). The aim is to produce a fused sheet of foliage, as the need for maintenance access has been minimised by plant selection.

Height is provided by species that do not require staking: for example, *Miscanthus* cvs., *Vernonia* spp., or *Silphium perfoliatum*. Blocks are repeated throughout the planting to provide rhythmical patterns of colour and texture. This approach is well suited to fertile urban soils. Some species will gradually be eliminated by others; this needs to be accepted and allowed to occur.

Clonal herb tapestry plantings

The design of this type of planting is similar to the above but the plants are selected from species that colonise by underground stems to form dense clonal patches which intermingle with other species of similar habit forming a tapestry of stems and foliage. Plantings can consist of a complex tapestry of species forming a sheet 0.6–1.2 m tall, with occasional emergents (woody or herbaceous), or as large alternating monocultural blocks.

Once established, species with these characteristics (*Euphorbia griffithii*, *E. sikkimensis*, *Filipendula rubra*, *F. ulmaria*, *Helianthus x laetiflorus* cvs., *Macleaya microcarpa*, *Senecio tanguticus*) tend to eliminate smaller growing species, so broadly compatible vigour is important in each planting layer. Most of the species with this habit are plants of wet fertile sites and are well suited to fertile urban soils. Mulching is necessary while the species establish. Given their colonising habit spacing requirements are not particularly critical and 450 mm is likely to be satisfactory for most species.

Ground cover sheets

These are generally composed on monocultural blocks rather than tapestry-like arrangements. A wide variety of species can be suitable for this purpose, but a key requirement is that the foliage is dense enough and tall enough (300 mm or above) to exclude weeds and there is some foliage retention in winter to reduce weed colonisation during this time. Dead foliage that remains attached and is slow to decay is very effective in this role (e.g. *Iris sibirica* cultivars). Species are available for full sun or in the shade of buildings or trees (see Table 25.4). Many geraniums are excellent as ground cover, particularly *G. x oxonianum*, and *G. macrorrhizum* cvs.; *Astrantia major*, *Alchemilla mollis*, *Hosta* cvs., *Aruncus dioicus* and *Brunnera macrophylla* are all suitable species. Planting densities need to be high enough to allow foliage canopies to fuse after one year's growth. Typically this means 300–400 mm centres. All of the species listed are essentially immortal, regenerating *in situ* by self-sowing or rhizomes.

Steppe-like planting

This is often referred to as 'German-style' herbaceous planting, which is misleading as it is only one part of a range of styles used in that country. The essence of this form of planting is that it involves small groups or even individuals repeated across the planting area to create naturalistic rhythmical patterns (Figs 25.3, 25.4, Plate 31). The design form is a randomised matrix. There is

Fig. 25.3 Steppe-inspired decorative planting in the West Park, Munich. The archetypal 'German style'. (Photo: James Hitchmough)

Fig. 25.4 Piet Oudolf's herbaceous planting in the 'Dream Park' in the town of Enkoping, near Stockholm. (Photo: James Hitchmough)

also contrast of rounded lower level canopies with taller emergent grasses and herbaceous perennials. Plants are widely spaced and the intervening spaces used to provide habits for spring bulbs.

This style mimics the relatively open, dry herbaceous vegetation naturally found in Central and Eastern Europe; however its openness creates substantial maintenance problems when implemented on moist fertile sites in Britain. Sensible sites for this type of planting are infertile well-drained gravel subsoils, chalky soils, amended crushed building rubble or sandy dry soil. Weed colonisation can be slowed (but not eliminated) by the use of sand, chippings or gravel as a mulch. Plantings on infertile soils are slow to develop but plants are typically longer-lived than on fertile soils.

Woodland edge planting

This is very much a continental style used in conjunction with edge shrubs and trees to create a semi-shaded environment that gives way to full sun. Typically it employs a backbone of large-leafed emergent species that wilt in full sun when soils dry out (for example *Ligularia*, *Telekia speciosa*) surrounded by lower ground cover layers of *Geranium*, *Alchemilla* and similar species (Plate 32). Shade cast by the trees and by the perennials themselves restricts invasion by common urban sun-loving weeds. Good examples of this and steppe-like planting have been undertaken by Noel Kingsbury at Cowley Manor, Gloucestershire (Kingsbury, 1996).

Dr Nigel Dunnett at the University of Sheffield is working upon an alternative system in which the woody plants are coppiced on a three to four year cycle to create alternating periods of shade and sun (see Chapter 13). The herbaceous perennials used (both native and exotic species) are sufficiently shade-tolerant to survive the shady periods, and then re-expand when the shrubs and trees are coppiced. This form of planting design is particularly valuable for producing herbaceous vegetation with some structural properties, in which shrubs with brilliant autumn colour are combined with late-flowering herbaceous species. Spring display is also substantial.

Fig. 25.5 Native-exotic meadow created by sowing a native wildflower meadow then establishing non-native herbaceous plants in it by planting. The meadow is managed by cutting for hay in August. RHS Harlow Carr, Harrogate. (Photo: James Hitchmough)

Purpose-sown native meadow with planted exotics

This is based on the idea of sowing native wild-flower species into the spaces between planted exotic herbaceous perennials that would normally be invaded by urban weeds in a low-maintenance regime. This approach allows the creation of meadows in naturalistically inspired urban parks that have either longer displays or more dramatic colour effects than purely native meadows (Fig. 25.5). Experiments on the creation of these systems have been taking place since 1994 (Hitchmough, 2000).

Meadows are cut as hay in August to check dominants and maintain native plant diversity. Relatively few exotic species can thrive under this regime, although those that can (for example, *Geranium sylvaticum* cultivars, *G. x magnificum*, *G. psilostemon*, *Papaver orientalis*, *Euphorbia palustris*, *Sanguisorba obtusa* and *Lychnis chalcedonica*) are capable of producing a striking display at very low maintenance levels. If the meadow is not cut until late autumn, more species will thrive but the meadow may become rather rank where soils are very fertile.

A key issue in the success of the planted material is the degree of establishment before competition from sown species is introduced. Generally the species that are well fitted to this cultivation regime seem to establish irrespective of this, although when little is done to alleviate competition they do so very slowly. Planting the exotic material in year one into a clean soil surface and then sowing the meadow species the following year is possibly the most effective way to establish these systems, but is more labour intensive. Sowing a wildflower-only mix at 0.5–1 g/m^2 rather than a grass dominated meadow mix at 4 g/m^2 is likely to improve establishment of the planted stock.

Exotic sown vegetation

Much of the understanding on how to do this is still in the research stage: it will be a few years before proven specifications for creating these types of vegetation in urban parks etc. are available. However work to date suggests that such vegetation can be achieved at only a fraction of the establishment cost of conventional herbaceous planting.

European meadow vegetation

Research into this vegetation has utilised a mixture of highly colourful native and non-native species to create a vegetation that flowers from spring to late summer. Based on three-year-old trials in Sheffield, successful native species include *Centaurea scabiosa*, *Daucus carota*, *Galium verum*, *Hieracium aurantiacum*, *Malva moschata*, and *Primula veris*. To these are added exotic species including *Buphthalmum salicifolium*, *Dianthus cartusianorum*, *Lychnis coronaria* (likely to disappear in the longer term) and *Papaver orientale*. Major factors in determining success have been the intensity of competition with weedy grasses from the soil seed bank such as Yorkshire fog (*Holcus lanatus*) and grazing by slugs and snails.

In northern Britain, *Salvia pratensis* and *Salvia nemorosa*, two extremely colourful species, are severely damaged by molluscs and are likely to dis-

Table 25.7   Species that established successfully from sowing and persisted for more than four years in prairie experiments in Sheffield.

Species	Notes
Aster azureus	
Aster laevis	low % emergence but reliable long term spp.
Baptisia australis	prone to slug damage post-emergence, fine in second year. Expensive seed, establish through planting?
Coreopsis lanceolata	often dominates in year 1 then dies out in year 2, avoid
Coreopsis tripteris	
Echinacea pallida	less affected by slugs than *E. purpurea*, but slower
Echinacea purpurea	
Eupatorium maculatum	
Helianthus mollis	very attractive to slugs as a seedling, untouched thereafter
Monarda fistulosa	
Ratibida pinnata	very attractive to slugs as a seedling and in spring as adults
Rudbeckia subtomentosa	slow to establish but unaffected by slug grazing
Schizachyrium scoparium	successful in southern England, but summers too cool in Sheffield
Silphium integrifolium	
Silphium laciniatum	
Silphium perfoliatum	
Silphium terebinthinaceum	
Solidago rigida	
Solidago speciosa	
Sorghastrum nutans	
Veronicastrum virginicum	completely slug proof but seed very small and establishment poor on sand mulches

appear in the longer term. A recent collaboration between Sheffield University and Writtle College in Chelmsford Essex is running the same species in an experiment in this warmer drier climate. Already it appears that *S. pratensis* is much better fitted to this climate and much more likely to succeed.

In all cases management consists of a hay cut in September. On really fertile soils an early spring or winter cut may also be required.

North American prairie vegetation

In 1997 research into making predominantly late summer and autumn flowering prairie-like communities of *Aster*, *Echinacea*, *Helianthus*, *Ratibida*, *Solidago* and *Rudbeckia* from seeding in-situ commenced and is now well advanced. A goal of this work was to produce dramatic large sheets of this colourful vegetation in urban parks, with management largely consisting of cutting at critical time periods. Only non-invasive species have been used. This work has mainly been carried out in Sheffield and at RHS Wisley in Surrey. In common with all 'ecologically' based vegetation, different results are likely to be found where there are differences in terms of site environment and climate. The species that have proved most reliable in Sheffield are listed in Table 25.7.

Success is largely a question of establishing sufficient prairie plants in the first year to compete effectively and dominate the vegetation in the second year. Spreading a layer of sharp sand 30–50 mm deep then sowing into this in winter has proved a valuable means of reducing weed seed germination from the underlying topsoil (Figs 25.6, 25.7). This system works less well however in drier climates where the underlying soils are sandy or chalky. The other factor that leads to low numbers of prairie plants is predation by slugs and snails during the spring germination period. Where slug populations are high, control

Fig. 25.6 Sowing the seed to create the prairie at the Eden Project. The site is divided into laneways to facilitate calibration of sowing, then the seed is raked into the surface. (Photo: James Hitchmough)

Fig. 25.7 North American prairie established by a combination of planting and oversowing at the Eden Project. (Photo: James Hitchmough)

measures are necessary during the period of germination and initial establishment.

Given control of weeds and slug predation in the first year, a dramatic 1.2 m tall plant community develops in the second year and flowers from July to October. Where weed control is poor in the first year, the prairie plants never achieve dominance and gradually weedy native species dominate the vegetation. The University of Sheffield project is still investigating alternative management techniques: burning over in spring with a propane gas burner, spraying with a non-selective contact herbicide and finally strimming down the dead vegetation, and removing it from the site. Given an adequate density of prairie plants in year one, all of these three techniques are satisfactory, although burning is increasingly looking to be the most effective form of weed control and promoting prairie plant regeneration within the community from self sown seed.

Species that are highly palatable to slugs (for example, *Ratibida pinnata* and *Echinacea purpurea*) tend to disappear on slug rich sites, but their demise merely creates opportunities for adjacent prairie plants. As a result the community is constantly changing, but always attractive.

25.4 Site preparation and establishment

It should now be clear that there is no one ideal type of soil for herbaceous perennials; soil parameters need to be re-assessed to meet the requirements of a chosen planting style. Whenever possible, it is most sensible to work with the site rather than against it. On ex-industrial land with raw soils of infertile crushed masonry and on subsoil surrounding new buildings, a steppe or dry meadow planting is more sensible than importing a highly-fertile topsoil to establish a traditional herbaceous planting.

Areas that are naturally wet may be used for tall species such as *Ligularia* and *Filipendula*, with woodland edge species around existing trees. These ecological approaches are increasingly accepted for landscapes to be planted with native species but are just as relevant to non-native herbaceous species.

On small-scale sites in prestige locations, it is most likely that planting areas will be topsoiled in the post-construction phase. Again the choice of soil should relate to the type of vegetation to be established. The traditional industry standard that the more nutrient-rich a topsoil is, the better it is needs to be reinterpreted. If an open, dry-looking planting composed of stress tolerator species is required, then it is important to specify a relatively infertile sandy loam (or even a gravel subsoil). Viable fragments of stoloniferous weeds are unacceptable, but they are often present in purchased topsoil. With regard to soil pH, most herbaceous perennials are tolerant of a wide range of values. In ecologically inspired plantings with less human intervention to control competition between species, pH range may be more critical to species persistence.

Irrespective of soil type, pH and nutrient status, the most important consideration is that soils are sufficiently root-permeable to a depth of at least 200–300 mm for herbaceous plants to establish within them. Soils must be adequately fractured through cultivation prior to planting, under conditions that are as dry as possible. Depending on the nature of the soil, this may require the incorporation of significant quantities of organic or mineral (coarse sand) additives.

Species differ in the degree of soil compaction they will tolerate. Wild forms of *Aster novi-belgii* and its hybrids are frequent colonisers of massively compacted subsoil clays on derelict land, while these conditions would be impossible for 'garden' perennials such as *Delphinium* cultivars. The more hostile the soil conditions, the slower, smaller and more stressed-looking the plants will be. Location and function of plantings will determine what is acceptable. As a general principle, wild-occurring forms of herbaceous perennials are likely to perform better than garden selections. Hansen and Stahl (1993) give further guidance on these distinctions under the heading of perennials for 'Open Ground' as opposed to 'Border Perennials'. Habitat type is also a useful indicator of likely tolerance of soils that are mechanically hostile; species that have evolved in woodland or woodland edges (often in highly organic soils with low penetrative resistance) are sometimes poorly adapted to raw landscape soils.

Research suggests that species which would struggle as planted container stock in very poorly structured, machine destroyed soils will often establish satisfactorily when sown on the same site (Hitchmough *et al.*, 2003). This is one of the advantages of sowing on large sites that are not in prestige locations and where short-term appearance is not so critical. Establishing species by sowing is often more successful on infertile subsoil materials because of the reduced competition with weedy species.

Pre-planting weed control

Whenever possible it is best to assess and control perennial weeds in an area to be planted, well in advance of planting. The main maintenance cost of herbaceous perennials is trying to restrict the colonisation of weedy native species that will ultimately dominate and eliminate the planted species. These weeds come from two sources: perennial weeds (present as rhizomes, for example) in the soil, and weed seeds either present in the soil or transported from outside the site.

Weed seed banks can be managed by mulching, but the rhizomatous species present on site must be eliminated before planting. It is paradoxical that the sites most in need of intensive weed management are often those that are intended to be more ecologically-managed 'hands off' areas of herbaceous planting. A key ecological principle is 'first in dominates', meaning that it is essential to start without established competitive dominants such as couch grass, docks and nettles.

While not effective on all possible weed species, the herbicide glyphosate (especially in the 'Biactive' formulations) is the most efficient means of eliminating these types of weeds. Generally two applications at least four to six weeks apart are required, and even then there will often be some regrowth that needs spot treatment post planting.

Given the contractual timescales of many projects (plus the fact that, depending on time of year, the foliage of the target weeds may or not be present) these recommendations may seem impractical, but on weedy sites you neglect this advice at your peril. Sites that are topsoiled in winter immediately before planting are potentially extremely problematic: unless perennial weeds are absent from the donor site, you may not appreciate just how many weed rhizomes are present until late spring.

Planting and immediate post-planting maintenance

With container-grown stock, planting can take place throughout the year. However from spring to autumn it is important that stock grown in peat or bark composts is soaked prior to planting. This ensures that the root balls do not shrink away from the surrounding soil, leading to plant dehydration and failure. It is worth specifying that some of the compost is knocked off the root ball to make sure that roots are in intimate contact with the surrounding soil. In general, herbaceous perennials should be planted with the buds at or just below (10 mm) the surface of the planted area; a few species do better if the rhizomes are partly exposed (for example, bearded iris). Post-planting watering is very valuable in summer, but it is rarely required in winter.

Plant spacing has been touched on earlier in this specification: with all plants it is a relative factor that depends very heavily on the purpose of the planting, and expectations of its appearance. Spacing within a group is essentially up to the designer (250–450 mm is the likely range for most species). More care needs to be taken with spacing between groups, and most critically between individuals and small groups in the matrix planting often used in steppe-like planting. Here it is important that species are spaced to ensure that they will not be eliminated in the first growing season by the lateral growth of a taller emergent. These interactions are most critical with relatively low-growing species that form tight clumps and (unlike species with laterally spreading canopies) do not have the capacity to move out of shaded zones created by taller species.

Mulching is important to reduce germination from the soil seed bank, and, to some degree, weed seeds transported from outside the planting. The choice of materials depends on the style of the planting. Steppe-like planting looks better with pea gravels, grit sands and coarse sand (Fig. 25.8). A depth of 50 mm is normally adequate. Mulching around plants in growth is straightforward; however some species (for example those with evergreen basal foliage in winter) tend to die if

Fig. 25.8 Dry planting at the Beth Chatto Gardens, Elmstead Market, Essex, showing the extensive use of gravel mulches. (Photo: James Hitchmough)

50 mm of mulch is placed onto their foliage at this time of year, so care must be exercised. Mulching is discussed in detail in Chapter 8.

Many herbaceous perennials grow relatively slowly in the first year after transplanting, and then take off much more dramatically in the second year. It is often important to make sure that clients and maintenance staff understand this, to avoid unnecessary panic. Applying large amounts of fertiliser to push plants along tends to work best with competitor and ruderal species, which are biologically able to make rapid use of these nutrients. Stress tolerators are naturally slower and unable to respond in the same way. Such additions of nutrients inevitably disadvantage the stress tolerators in the first and certainly the second year, when they have to compete with the excessively vigorous growth of either planted or weedy competitors and ruderals.

25.5 Longer-term management

Staking and tying

In landscape plantings the most sensible way to deal with this is simply to avoid any plants that may require it. Species that tend to flop include the following: some tall *Aster novi-belgii* (but not 'Climax'), *Rudbeckia* 'Herbstsonne', *Delphinium* cultivars, *Galega* spp. These are mainly tall-growing species but some low species flop outwards in a rather untidy manner: for example *Geranium* 'Johnsons Blue', *Centaurea montana*, and *Sedum* 'Autumn Joy'. High fertility and moisture encourage flopping. Strimming off plantings of species prone to flopping in mid summer results in shorter plants that are less prone to flop.

Division

Species that require division on a regular basis are of dubious value in landscape planting. On less fertile soils the need for frequent division is significantly reduced by slower growth rates. *Achillea* cultivars are a good example of this. Advice on division in gardening texts is often based on the assumption that you want to produce plants that would win first place in the flower show, rather than perform adequately in landscape planting.

Cutting back post-flowering

There are two categories in relation to this:

Plants which need cutting back because they are scruffy post-flowering

These species are mainly early spring to early summer-flowering species, and include the following: *Aconitum napellus* (and other early flowering spp.), *Doronicum*, *Lupinus* cvs., *Papaver orientale*, *Aquilegia*, *Polemonium* (especially under dry conditions), *Thalictrum aquilegifolium*. Some of these species essentially enter dormancy after flowering. They are most readily used in planting designs and locations where this decline is not evident or problematic; for example many of the sun-requiring species can be grown in meadow-like planting or sowings which are cut as hay in August. Shade-tolerant species can be cultivated in coppice or woodland edge plantings.

Plants which can be cut back to encourage a second flowering, or to tidy up their leaf canopy

Cutting back these species is more discretionary, but in prestige locations it is desirable to obtain an extension of the flowering season. Species that respond in this way include; *Salvia x sylvestris* and *S. nemorosa* cultivars, *Delphinium* (small flowered belladonna group), *Geranium* 'Kashmir Purple', *G.* 'Johnsons Blue' and some *Nepeta* spp. The traditional practice of cutting down the dead stems of herbaceous species in late autumn is not recommended. Apart from the attractive colours and texture of some dead stems, leaf litter and other debris is better retained among the stems and can significantly reduce winter weed invasion. Stems can be cut down in late winter or spring to allow mulching if this is to be practised. However, slug damage may increase.

Pests and diseases

In a landscape situation, species with significant pest or disease problems are generally not worth considering. Some pests and diseases are highly specific to a species or genus; for example phlox eelworm is a problem primarily in *Phlox maculata* and *P. paniculata*. Other pests and diseases are more catholic and sporadic: for example mildews may affect some species, (e.g. *Pulmonaria*) and need not preclude use.

The real *bête noire* of herbaceous planting are slugs and snails. Information on the palatability of herbaceous perennials is inherently unreliable, as location, the mollusc species present, and the feeding alternatives have a major impact. Some perennials are heavily grazing in spring (for example, *Hemerocallis*) but are able (under border conditions) to recover; other species simply disappear. There is a tendency for species of dry habitats to be attractive (and sensitive) to slug grazing in Britain, but there are many exceptions. Many herbaceous *Salvia* are also quite sensitive, especially as seedlings or small vegetative plants. In general, seedlings are much more attractive to slugs than established plants of the same species. Some species that never appear to suffer significant damage are listed in Table 25.8. Collection, analysis and publication of information on slug damage from gardens etc. would be extremely valuable.

Table 25.8   Herbaceous plants that appear immune to slug grazing as established plants.

Aconitum	Geranium (most)	Rodgersia
Astilbe	Helleborus	Silphium (most)
Astrantia major	Iris sibirica	Thalictrum (most)
Baptisia	Lychnis chalcedonica	Trollius europaeus (highly attractive as seedlings)
Bergenia	Papaver orientale	Tussock forming grasses (most)
Euphorbia (most)	Polygonum bistorta 'Superba'	Veronicastrum

Weed control

This is the major maintenance issue in herbaceous plantings. The most common invading weeds vary depending on the site, planting design and maintenance regime, but stoloniferous grasses such as Couch (*Elymus repens*) and Creeping Bent (*Agrostis stolonifera*) are particularly common. Whether weeds such as these are a significant problem depends on the role, location and form of the planting. In plantings of tall canopied species (as described in Section 25.3 on 'planting design') coexistence with these species may be possible as the tall summer leafage may restrict the extent of these and other shade-intolerant weeds.

In lower more open plantings, these weeds create a visual sense of dereliction, and gradually lead to the elimination of planted species – either directly (through competition) or by changing the structure of the vegetation. The latter leads to an increase in snails and slugs that feed on palatable species, which previously were relatively ungrazed. Physical removal of some weeds is feasible given sufficient maintenance capacity, but for species such as couch grass this often isn't possible once significant establishment has occurred.

Herbicides are the most effective means of addressing such problems, given a management regime that is sufficiently competent to apply these compounds selectively. There are grass-specific herbicides that are tolerated by non-grasses, and can be sprayed over the top of plants infested with grasses. 'Off label' permission is available for overspraying herbaceous perennials with some of these grass herbicides.

In addition to grass-specific herbicides, glyphosate (Roundup Biactive) and glufosinate ammonium (Challenge) can be used selectively as carefully directed applications onto the weeds only. Glyphosate has the advantage of extremely low mammalian toxicity, and is effective on broad leaves and grasses. Its extensive translocation means that it needs only to be applied to a small percentage of the foliage to kill weeds. However this does increase the chance of accidentally killing desirable plants.

Many but not all of the weeds that invade herbaceous plantings are winter green, in contrast to most cultivated herbaceous perennials. This greatly reduces the risk of accidental damage, although care must be taken adjacent to species with some form of overwintering foliage. Application via a small wick wiper minimises risk further. Weeds treated with glyphosate during the winter months die very slowly, but the treatment is generally quite effective. Application during summer requires great care, but is perfectly feasible with wick and similar applicators. For example bindweed (*Convolvulus arvensis*) can be treated by inserting canes in plantings to encourage the foliage to climb to where it can be treated without risk to surrounding herbaceous species.

Glufosinate ammonium is much less easily translocated than glyphosate, and poses less risk to cultivated species; it will adequately control clump-forming grasses and other weeds with limited rhizome development. In plantings composed of entirely winter-dormant species, overspraying plantings in December (prior to bud emergence) may be possible with both these herbicides, but there is currently no specific label recommendation to support this. It is clearly a high-risk strategy, the success of which would depend on correctly assessing whether any green shoots could be sprayed with the herbicide. Research is needed to confirm safety and efficacy.

Fig. 25.9 Burning over herbaceous plantings in spring with a propane-powered burner is an effective means of controlling some winter-colonising weeds; it is tolerated by many winter-dormant herbaceous plants. (Photo: James Hitchmough)

Another approach that may provide effective control of non-stoloniferous species (when more research has been carried out) is the use of a propane-fuelled heat gun. These are readily hired at low cost and, in addition to severely damaging some winter green grasses and killing annual winter-germinating weeds, will also kill some of the weed seeds on the soil surface, potentially reducing weediness later in the year.

This technique should be carried out in late winter, before the emergence of new shoots of planted species (Fig. 25.9). Clearly it cannot be used on species that have winter foliage without the risk of damage. Even where this treatment does not kill weed species, in some cases it can cause sufficient check to swing the balance back in favour of winter-deciduous planted species. The author is currently actively researching into these techniques of weed management in sown communities of herbaceous perennials.

Mulching on an annual or biennial basis will greatly reduce weed seed germination in plantings, but will not control existing rhizomatous weeds. Observation in gardens such as RHS Harlow Carr in Harrogate demonstrates that many herbaceous species are very tolerant of being covered with

50–75 mm of organic mulch in the winter months. Species with overwintering leaf rosettes may be adversely affected, and some species suffer a greater incidence of slug damage under this regime. There is a clear need to survey collections using mulching to gain a better understanding of which species are the really sensitive ones. Mulching is potentially expensive, but it can provide value for money when the cost of trying to retrieve weed-ridden plantings is taken into account.

Fertiliser application

Occasional light applications of granular balanced fertilisers (such as 'Growmore') will maintain adequate vigour in plantings where a reasonably high canopy density is important. As a general principle, fertiliser should not be added without a clear understanding of the purpose of doing so. Fertilisers favour the invasion and development of competitor species, and should be seen as contributing to maintenance load.

25.6 Summary

Herbaceous perennials encompass a great diversity of species and planting styles. The challenge with these types of plants and planting is to gain the benefits of brilliant colour and dramatic seasonal change, yet at the same time be able to manage the vegetation within the skills base and budget available. Employing an ecological perspective to the design and management of herbaceous plantings is one way to achieve this, working with the site conditions as much as possible, irrespective of whether the plants in question are native or exotic.

References

Chatto, B. (1985) *The Dry Garden*, Dent, London.
Chatto, B. (1982) *The Damp Garden*, Dent, London.
Grime, J.P., Hodgson, I.G., & Hunt, R. (1988) *Comparative Plant Ecology: a functional guide to common British species*. Unwin Hyman, London.

Hansen, R. & Stahl, F. (1993) *Perennials and their Garden Habitats.* Cambridge University Press, Cambridge.

Hitchmough, J.D. (2000) Establishment of cultivated herbaceous perennials in purpose sown native wildflower meadows in south west Scotland. *Landscape and Urban Planning.* 714, 1–15.

Hitchmough, J.D., Kendle, A.D., & Paraskevopoulou, A. (2003) Seedling emergence, survival and initial growth in low productivity urban 'waste' soils; a comparison of North American prairie forbs with meadow forbs and grasses native to Britain. *Journal of Horticultural Science and Biotechnology.* 78, 1, 89–99.

HTA (1997) *National Plant Specification*, HTA, Reading.

Kingsbury, N. (1996) *The New Perennial Garden.* Frances Lincoln, London.

Phillips, R. & Rix, M. (1994) *Perennials, Volumes 1 and 2,* Macmillan, London.

26 Amenity and Sports Turf Seed

John Hacker

This chapter is a guide for those concerned with the establishment of both sports and amenity turf. In recent years, great strides have been made by seed houses in their quest to improve the grass species traditionally used for amenity and sports turf. However, attempts to introduce new genera have been slow, with only a few coming to the forefront in the past ten years.

The use of specific types of grass for the production of good playing surfaces is fairly well understood, but far less is documented for amenity areas. By dividing such sites into simple categories such as areas of heavy or normal wear, and by recognising certain common site characteristics such as sun, shade, drainage and topsoil, it is possible to use sports pitch research to select appropriate grass types for amenity use.

26.1 Grass from turf or seed

Grassed areas in Britain have traditionally been established from seed or turf, although sea-washed turf often regenerates itself (at least partly) by vegetative means. In contrast, the process of planting stolons or rhizomes (often known as 'sprigs') is used extensively in warmer areas of the world, where the more aggressively creeping warm season grasses are grown. Indeed, the hybrid bermuda grasses are sterile, leaving vegetative propagation the only means of establishing a new area.

Whether a grass sward is to be established by seed or by turf from a nursery, the species and cultivars available are the same. The exception to this would be meadow turf, which is composed of the natural species growing within the area where the turf was lifted. This may include grasses sown for agricultural biomass production and other species that are considered weed grasses within the amenity market including *Poa annua*, Yorkshire Fog (*Holcus lanatus*) and Creeping Softgrass (*Holcus mollis*).

From a professional point of view, the benefits of using turf can be great. Buying the time taken for grass seedlings to establish gives an immediate maturity to a site and provides instant stability to the soil surface. This can be extremely important on sandy soils and steep slopes.

Using turf may also have important commercial implications, particularly for sports facilities where the course or pitch can be played sooner, facilitating an earlier financial return on the venue. In the property market, houses with established lawns are also likely to sell quicker than those with bare soil and an unfinished appearance.

Laying turf does not answer all the problems and can itself be the cause of some difficulties. These include reduced water permeability and the importation of pests, diseases and undesirable weeds. The leading turf companies, however, go to great lengths to provide a high quality product. Many of the drawbacks can be overcome by having the turf grown to order on specific root-zones, having the turf washed to remove native soil or by undertaking the correct maintenance practices in the first few years of establishment.

Buying time, however, costs money and the price of purchasing and laying turf is considerably greater than that of sowing seed. Sowing also allows the use of the newest or highest ranked cultivars that may not have been available when the

Table 26.1 The major turfgrass species in the UK.

Species	Common name	Area of use
Agrostis capillaris (syn. *A. tenuis*) *Agrostis castellana* *Agrostis stolonifera*	Browntop bent Highland bent Creeping bent	Fine turf areas such as golf greens and as the basal components of a mixed sward
Festuca rubra subsp. *rubra* *Festuca rubra* subsp. *commutata* *Festuca rubra* subsp. *litoralis* and others	Strong creeping red fescue Chewings fescue Slender creeping red fescue	Fine turf grass areas usually with bentgrass and as the basal component of a mixed sward
Poa pratensis	Smooth stalked meadowgrass	Basal component of a mixed sward in the UK
Poa annua *Lolium perenne* *Phleum pratense* *Cynosurus cristatus*	Annual meadowgrass Perennial ryegrass Timothy Crested dogstail	Considered a weed species Major wear-tolerant species in sports pitches Possible component on a heavy, wet soil Once used as a component of hardwearing swards

turf for sale was sown. It normally takes between 12 and 15 months to produce a turf ready for sale, depending on growth rates during the production cycle.

With turf production, the cultivar and species content of the product offered for sale cannot always be guaranteed to be the same as that sown. This is because some of the cultural practices involved in the production of turf can change the composition of the sward over time. Indeed, such changes are likely to accrue after a short while in any sown sward, as the species composition will vary depending upon such factors as the temperature at the time of sowing, soil fertility, local environmental parameters and general maintenance procedures.

In general, it is safe to say that a good selection of purpose grown turf is available from a number of high quality producers. However, before purchasing any turf it is necessary to go to the trouble of making sure of the following:

- The species and/or cultivar sown were those you require.
- Those cultivars/species are still present in the turf to be delivered to site.
- The soil on the turf is compatible with the soil/rootzone on site.

- The turf is free of weeds, pests and diseases.
- The turf contains minimal organic matter (thatch).

For those buying seed, current seed laws give good protection. However, always buy certified, or better still higher voluntary standard (HVS) seed of the most recent year's production from a reputable company. As with any product, things can go wrong and it is always well worth giving the seed a visual check to determine the various species within the bag before sowing.

26.2   Grass species and cultivars

The species of grass used within the amenity and sports turf markets are those able to cope with relatively low heights of cut, often comparable to grazing by sheep or rabbits. Selection and breeding within these species has, of course, improved their performance and given rise to many named cultivars (see Table 26.1 for the main grass species used). Timothy (*Phleum pratense*) and crested dogstail (*Cynosurus cristatus*) are now no longer commonly found in high quality seed mixtures. They may however be used in specific situations where their characteristics are desirable: in wild flora companion mixtures, and mixtures for shade or damp situations. The main grass species used are examined below.

Agrostis species

The three common bentgrass species (browntop, highland and creeping) are extensively used on fine turf areas including golf and bowling greens. Bentgrass leaves, which are slightly grey/green in colour, have a rolled vernation with a narrow flat and pointed leafblade. Members of the genus can be cut regularly between 4–5 mm and on occasions as low as 3 mm. This provides an excellent surface for putting or bowling. As its name implies, creeping bent (*Agrostis stolonifera*) has a more aggressive creeping habit than the other two species and can rapidly develop a thatch problem if not properly managed. Bred in the USA, many creeping bent cultivars exhibit a more dormant growth habit in the winter unlike the invasive weed species *Poa annua*. Incorrect maintenance practices can therefore lead to a rapid ingress of *Poa annua* during the late autumn and winter period.

More recently developed creeping bentgrass cultivars have had some success within the British Isles, and in particular Ireland, although single species swards can be more prone to disease. Highland bent (*Agrostis castellana*), which was originally classified as a cultivar of browntop bent (*Agrostis capillaris* syn. *A. tenuis*), is usually cheaper than both browntop and creeping bent and is extensively used as a basal component of tees, fairways and general amenity mixtures. It can also be used in winter sports pitches where at least 12 months establishment is possible before play is permitted. It is also used in traditional golf green mixtures where its provenance may be of benefit in terms of winter hardiness.

Bentgrasses are subject to a range of diseases including leafspot, fusarium patch and take-all patch disease, which is associated with increases in soil pH brought about either by the application of alkaline water or by inappropriate maintenance practices. It is of particular concern on newly constructed sand based greens. Well-managed bentgrass is commonly perceived by the professional golfer to give the best putting surface.

Festuca species

The fine leaved fescues or red fescues are commonly used in conjunction with bentgrass or, like bentgrass, as a basal component of a mixed sward. The needle-like leaves are light green in colour. They are naturally adapted to dry infertile soils and provide an attractive sward at different cutting heights. Like bentgrasses they will take mowing to 4–5 mm but can die out if regularly scalped or subjected to heavy wear. Nutrition is also important to a mixed fescue and bent sward, with single high nitrogen applications favouring the bentgrass and multiple or low nitrogen applications favouring the fescues.

Chewings fescue (*Festuca rubra* subsp. *commutata*), a tufted non-creeping species, was a traditional partner for Highland bent in golf and bowling greens. Nowadays, slender creeping red fescue (*Festuca rubra* subsp. *litoralis*) is more commonly part of the fine turf mixture, usually making up half the fescue component of the mix. In addition, the fescues, like bentgrass can be used as part of a pitch mixture provided the sward is allowed sufficient time to establish before use.

Strong creeping red fescue (*Festucs rubra* subsp. *rubra*) was traditionally used in sports pitch mixtures but research has found it to be less wear-tolerant than the other two species. It is also less tolerant than bents of close mowing. It is however a useful basal component of mixed swards cut at intermediate heights and not receiving heavy wear, such as golf course fairways or amenity areas. Once again, recent breeding programmes have improved the quality of strong creeping red fescue in comparison to chewings fescue and slender creeping red fescue.

Poa pratensis and *Poa annua*

Smooth stalked meadowgrass (*Poa pratensis*) is widely used in temperate regions of the USA. Known in America as Kentucky bluegrass, its blue/green colour is typical of many but not all cultivars. The leaf, which has a folded venation, is broad and of medium texture with a boat shaped tip. Its strong rhizomatous growth produces excellent turf for lifting with a high recuperative potential.

Unfortunately, it does not integrate well with other fine-leaved temperate species due to its strong growth, where its coarser darker leaves stand out to the trained eye. This species does better when cut between 25 and 50 mm and grown in hotter summer conditions more typical of continental weather patterns. Its use has not really taken off in the UK as much as was thought probable 15 or 20 years ago. Having said this, recent warmer summer periods and a better understanding of its cultural needs in the early months of establishment has led to resurgence of its use within certain turf markets.

Poa pratensis is often used as a component of swards for high wear areas such as golf tees where its recuperative ability is valuable. It is likely therefore to prove valuable in high wear amenity areas, provided the grass is not cut too low and given sufficient time to establish. It does not do well when sown in a mix with perennial ryegrass, which out-competes it in the establishment phase.

Annual meadowgrass *(Poa annua)* is considered an invasive weed species in the UK and elsewhere in the world. It exists to some extent in the vast majority of grass areas including golf greens. It is present in a number of forms ranging from the ephemeral subspecies *Poa annua erecta* to the biennial/perennial form *Poa annua reptans*. Its prolific seeding ability even when cut to 4 mm has ensured its success as a temperate species worldwide, although it does die back in hotter climates during the summer period.

Poa annua grows well under many conditions but survives on compacted soil where other species cannot cope. Factors associated with its success include wet poorly drained compact soils, high nitrogen and phosphorus levels and a lack of competition from other species. Over recent years, when golf as a sport has boomed, *Poa annua* has become a major component in many greens and high wear areas, especially those built on heavier soil likely to compact and subject to high levels of nutrition and water.

Poa annua is subject to attack by several diseases including the most common disease of fine turf, fusarium patch (*Microdochium nivale*, also known as snowmould). Recently, anthracnose (*Colletotrichum graminicola*), a disease associated with high levels of use and compacted soil, has become a significant problem on many golf greens containing *Poa annua*. This species is generally not sown in the UK, although consideration has been given to its improvement by breeding and selection. Unfortunately, the seedheads, which reduce the quality of putting surfaces in early summer, are an integral part of the species. Other *Poa* species closely related to *Poa annua* such as *Poa supina* are now available on the market and are being promoted for use as part of swards in football stadia where environmental factors such as low light intensity have a significant effect on sward growth. One cultivar of *Poa trivialis* (rough stalked meadowgrass), a close relative of *Poa pratensis*, is also available and under evaluation for use in similar situations.

Lolium perenne

Perennial ryegrass (*Lolium perenne*) is the major wear tolerant species used in the temperate world. Breeding over many years has produced a plant that is rapid to establish, very wear tolerant and desirable in texture and colour. Plant breeders continue to improve the species year after year. Perennial ryegrass has a folded venation with a shiny back to the leaf. Most, but not all, cultivars have a distinct red base to the leaf sheaf. The plant is tufted, although a few cultivars such as 'Barclay' tend to have a slight creeping habit. Under correct conditions the species can provide a top quality playing surface within 12 weeks of sowing. Perennial ryegrass today is a relatively low growing, medium textured grass compared with the old forage grasses used in the amenity world 20–30 years ago. Indeed, some of the newer cultivars are so fine they are difficult to distinguish from fine leaved fescues. In general, perennial ryegrass is an excellent species for all medium to heavy wear areas where rapid establishment is required. A perennial ryegrass, fescue and bent mixture, given time to establish, can provide an excellent general-purpose grass sward with a dense understorey.

Fig. 26.1 The colour of turf grass varies considerably between species and even between cultivars, as can be seen here from this cultivar trial. Designers could exploit these variations to produce subtle ground patterning. (Photo: James Hitchmough)

In some cases, perennial ryegrass can become a weed of finer grass swards due to its ability to lie flat when mown, thereby surviving low heights of cut. In warmer climates, it is commonly used (along with other temperate species) to oversow warm season grasses which have become dormant and discoloured in the winter period.

Phleum pratense

Timothy (*Phleum pratense*) has not lived up to the great hopes that the industry had for it 10 or 15 years ago. A medium to coarse textured species, it has a grey/green colour with a notable twist to the leaf blade. When established, the base of the stem can swell, producing a slight bulbous effect. Timothy does well on wet heavier soils where it may act as a replacement for perennial ryegrass. Wet heavy football pitches are however, becoming less and less common as they are unable to provide the desired playing surface quality. However, in certain circumstances Timothy may have a role to play in a mixed amenity sward, particularly one that is being maintained at a higher height of cut

or where grasses are part of a wild flower species mixture.

26.3 Turfgrass cultivars

The various seed houses specialising in grass have seen the sports turf and amenity markets as an important business area. Selecting grasses for sports and amenity can be done at the same time as selecting grasses for the much larger agricultural market when undertaking trials on new cultivars (Fig. 26.1).

Cultivars within the UK have for over 30 years been tested and assessed by the Sports Turf Research Institute (STRI) in Bingley, West Yorkshire. They have conducted merit tests on cultivars for a range of uses at their research centre in Yorkshire. The trials can be viewed by appointment and the results are published each year in the STRI booklet *Turfgrass Seed*.

Not surprisingly, plant breeders have concentrated their breeding/selection efforts on those growth criteria deemed important by the industry. The STRI has ranked selection criteria into those of primary and secondary importance. This is illustrated in *Turfgrass Seed 2001* by its evaluation of *Lolium perenne* for either 'winter pitches' or 'landscaping'. In the case of winter pitches, wear tolerance under high or low nitrogen regimes is the main selection criteria. Other criteria including shoot density, fineness of leaf, cleanness of cut, slow growth, freedom from red thread, and winter greenness are listed but not highlighted.

When looking at the same species for landscaping use, the primary criteria change as might be expected to include tolerance of close mowing, shoot density, fineness of leaf and slow regrowth. The practical impact of this is that cultivar 'Allegro', which is ranked Number 2 for winter pitches, plummets to Number 65 for amenity use. The lesson to be learned from this is that the days when a species alone can be specified in a contract are long since gone. Thanks to the improvements made in the commercial world of the plant breeders, a specification these days should include a range of cultivars which have the properties desired for the specific site.

The STRI evaluates over 200 cultivars annually and careful consideration should be given to the current cultivar rating. However, as the STRI points out, cultivars at the top of each list may not be the best cultivar for every use. Users should identify which characteristics are most important for their intended use and select cultivars accordingly.

In general, it can be said that the improvement in grass cultivars over the past 30 years has been enormous thanks to the seed houses providing the user with an excellent choice. The plant breeders of today are, however, no more complacent than those who started the work years ago. Without doubt the grasses available to the industry will continue to improve in the future.

New species introduction

Seed houses are always looking for new products to sell and this has led to several attempts at finding new genera suitable for amenity or sports turf usage. While some species such as crested hairgrass (*Koeleria macrantha*) would appear to be

Table 26.2   New species under evaluation.

Botanical name	Common name
Koeleria macrantha	Crested hairgrass
Festuca arundinacea	Tall fescue
Festuca longifolia	Hard fescue
Festuca tenuifolia	Fine-leaved sheep's fescue
Festuca ovina	Sheep's fescue

completely new to the sports turf and amenity world, others such as sheep's fescue (*Festuca ovina*) are not. In some cases the species may have been upgraded from a component of the golf course rough to a more intensively managed area following a period of selection by seed houses. However a number of new genera are being used within certain mixtures, while others are still being evaluated to a greater or lesser extent (see Table 26.2).

The criteria for turfgrass breeding and selection are many, but the two main lines of investigation continue to be wear-tolerance for winter sports grasses and low maintenance for amenity grasses. The new species introductions reflect this with tall fescue, (*Festuca arundinacea*) and crested hairgrass, (*Koeleria macrantha*) being promoted as possible replacements or additives for perennial ryegrass swards. As yet neither has the rapid establishment or high wear qualities of perennial ryegrass, but they have made great strides as far as the amenity market is concerned.

Crested hairgrass is a low growing species that performs best under low nitrogen regimes and does well on drier soils. Similarly, tall fescue, requires less nitrogen and water than perennial ryegrass. Many of the newer cultivars have finer leaves than the species itself and maintain a good colour during winter with better disease resistance. Hard fescue (*F. longifolia*) and fine-leaved sheep's fescue (*F. tenuifolia*) have good shade adaptation and cope well with drought conditions. The nutrient requirements are less than for the red fescues and they generally have good disease resistance.

As performance data build up on their use in the UK, it is likely that the newer species will become more widely used, particularly on low input amenity sites. Currently, they are often used as a small component of mixtures for such sites; this may indicate that they still have something to prove. Alternatively, it is a sign of the conservative nature of the landscape architect/horticulturist in the UK.

26.4   Grasses for difficult sites

While most specifiers would like to work with ideal situations this is not always possible. There are a number of difficult sites ranging from the extreme of heavy metal contamination to the more common problems of shade and wetness. In these cases, survival is often more important than performance, and species naturally adapted to these environments are often used for at least part of the mixture.

Severely contaminated areas

Areas contaminated with heavy metals such as lead, zinc and copper or toxic substances such as salt pose special problems for plant growth. Usually, these areas, often associated with industrial sites or spoil sites, are contaminated with not just one but a range of toxic metals and substances. This means that giving greenness and surface stability is the main aim of any seeding operation. It may also be necessary to correct inherent problems such as extremes of acidity before sowing is undertaken. In view of this, every site must be thoroughly assessed before specific seeding advice can be given. Grasses selected for their ability to survive in such areas include the following:

- slender creeping red fescue 'Merlin' (*Festuca rubra* subsp. *litoralis*)
- browntop bentgrass 'Parys Mountain' (*Agrostis capillaris*).

These cultivars are often mixed with other grasses and legumes, depending on site conditions. These act as nurse species to prevent surface erosion during establishment or to enhance nitrogen levels in the long term.

Shady, moist and dry areas

The maritime climate of the UK gives unique growing conditions. The Gulf Stream and prevailing south-westerly winds along the spine of northern hills and mountains give, in simplistic terms, a warm, wet west/south west and a drier, colder east/south east. It must not be forgotten, however, that within this overall picture there are numerous microclimates caused by local topography, latitude, geology and soils. It is not uncommon for a golf course of 50 to 60 hectares to have two or three quite different soil textures, microclimates and water regimes.

Many of the grass species commonly used can tolerate a range of variations in growth parameters but at the extremes it is best to use species which have evolved to cope with the problems encountered, at least as a constituent of any species mixture:

- shady moist areas: rough stalk meadowgrass (*Poa trivialis*); wood meadowgrass (*Poa nemoralis*); tufted hair-grass (*Deschampsia cespitosa*)
- open moist areas: Timothy (*Phleum pratense*)
- dry soils and low fertility areas: crested hair-grass (*Koeleria macrantha*); tall fescue (*Festuca arundinacea*); flattened meadowgrass (*Poa compressa*); sheep's fescue (*Festuca ovina*); fine-leaved sheep's fescue (*Festuca tenuifolia*); hard fescue (*Festuca longifolia*)
- shady dry areas with low fertility: red fescue (*Festuca rubra* subsp. *rubra*), (*Festuca rubra* subsp. *commutata*), (*Festuca rubra* subsp. *litoralis*); fine-leaved sheep's fescue (*Festuca tenuifolia*); hard fescue (*Festuca longifolia*).

Saline conditions

Saline conditions exist naturally along the coasts of the UK. There are, however, other areas such as roadside verges that can be subject to high salt levels for obvious reasons. Fortunately many salt-tolerant species also have other desirable factors such as the ability to survive under dry, infertile conditions. Examples of species include:

- salt march grass (*Puccinellia* spp.)
- red fescues (*Festuca rubra* and especially *Festuca rubra* subsp. *litoralis*)
- bentgrass (*Agrostis* spp.).

In nature these factors often come together, as is the case for many ecological niches.

26.5   Seed mixtures and blends

Mono-specific stands of grasses in nature are very unusual and most natural swards will be composed of a variety of grasses and other native flora. Temperate species will mix well together to form a multi-species sward where conditions allow. On the other hand tropical species, with strong creeping growth habits, do not integrate well; they give a patchy overall appearance if mixed with other species. The benefits of a multi-species sward are considerable and include the following.

Greater disease resistance for the sward

While some diseases have a broad spectrum of hosts, many turf diseases have preferential hosts. Anthracnose disease (*Colletotrichum graminicola*) and fusarium patch disease (*Microdochium nivale*) for example, tend to attack *Poa annua* although fusarium has a fairly wide host range. Take-All patch disease (*Gaeumannomyces gramminis*) is almost exclusively found on bentgrasses in the UK while Red Thread disease (*Laetisaria fuciformis*) is more likely to be associated with red fescues and ryegrass.

It is easy to conclude from this that a mixed sward is more resilient to fungal attack than a single species sward. If one grass is suffering from attack, then a second or third species can fill in the gap left by the retreating plant. An example of this is where Take-all patch disease attacks a mixed sward. In this case the symptom is that of an enlarging ring. On the other hand where it attacks a pure bentgrass sward a dead circle is left, as there is nothing available to fill in after the disease attack.

Greater adaptability to the environment

Using a number of species will allow the species most suited to the location to excel while other species may decline. Each species has its own preferred range of growth parameters under which it survives best. Major factors in need of consideration include shade, sun, soil fertility, pH, salinity, moisture levels, level of wear and closeness of cut. Usually these factors do not occur in isolation and any one ecological niche will be affected by many of these factors at one time. To give an example, in situations where fertility is low or there is a likelihood of drought or shade, fescues are likely to predominate while ryegrass will struggle. Perennial ryegrass will, on the other hand, do well in more fertile soils in full sunlight and be able to cope with heavier wear conditions.

Single species swards

In some instances single species swards are used. Such swards are more consistent in colour, texture and maintenance requirements than species mixtures. This is clearly beneficial provided the species used is well adapted to the environment in which it is being grown. In North America extensive areas of the north east and mid-west have used smooth stalked meadowgrass (*Poa pratensis*) or Kentucky bluegrass as it is known there.

A number of cultivars are often blended together to give a degree of resilience (albeit less than a multi-species mixture) to the sward as a whole. For instance, one cultivar may have better colour, finer leaf texture or better disease resistance. *Poa pratensis* has a very high wear tolerance once established and has a dark blue/green leaf colour. It does not however seem to be suited to the maritime climate of the UK, where it is more susceptible to leafspot diseases. In recent years plant breeding has improved disease resistance, but *Poa pratensis* still does not do well in the UK, probably because of the cooler summers and our tradition of mixing different species together. *Poa pratensis* is notably slower in establishment than *Lolium perenne*, which is commonly used in our high wear sport areas. This means that *Lolium perenne* inevitably out-competes *Poa pratensis* in both seed germination and seedling establishment.

During the golfing boom of the early 1990s, the American tendency to use creeping bentgrass as a single species sward was introduced on some high budget courses in southern England and Ireland. In this instance a single cultivar of creeping bent was used on the greens while other cultivars of creeping bent or other grass species were used on the tees and fairway areas. Initially, the Penn series of cultivars was used which include 'Penneagle' and 'Penncross'. In recent years Providence creeping bentgrass has been more widely used, being rated more highly for shoot density than the Penn varieties. Newer varieties of creeping bentgrass include 'Bueno' and 'Barifera' although none of the current creeping bentgrasses rate as highly for shoot density as the best browntop bentgrasses. Other new cultivars are also being developed and used across other parts of the world.

Given the tendency for bentgrass to suffer from Take-all patch disease, the risk of having a pure bentgrass sward could be considered high and maintenance practices must be adjusted to take this into account. In addition, strong creeping grasses form thatch quite readily and thatch control must therefore be a major part of annual maintenance regimes.

Seed mixtures

While most seed houses offer a range of mixtures for various purposes they are able to produce customised mixtures provided the volume is sufficient. When using pre-determined mixtures it is worth checking that the cultivars used have the performance criteria required for the specific site concerned. Clearly the cost of a mixture is part of the sales formula and the addition of low-rated cultivars can significantly reduce costs. It may be that this is acceptable for the site concerned and will save the client money. On the other hand, seeding is only a small proportion of the costs of a new golf green or football pitch where the attributes of the best cultivars can be most valuable.

Fine turf seed mixtures

For areas mown to 5 mm or less bentgrass and fescue are the main temperate grass species used. Areas commonly mown to these heights include golf and bowling greens along with the highest quality amenity lawns. The mixtures usually contain between 70 and 80 per cent fescues, with the difference being made up of browntop bent. The fescue component usually includes both chewings fescue and slender creeping red fescue with the remaining bentgrass being made up of one or two cultivars. These mixtures are generally sown at a rate of 35 g/m².

Alternatively, pure bent swards using cultivars such as 'Providence' or 'Bueno' may be suitable for parts of the country exhibiting a more continental weather pattern. As yet, pure fescue swards have not shown that they are able to take the high level of wear usual on heavily-used golf courses. They may however be suitable for lawns and general amenity areas if not cut too low. Sowing rates for pure bent blends are much reduced (10 to 15 g/m²) due to the high seed numbers (10 000 to 15 000 seeds per gram).

Intermediate wear areas

For areas such as golf tees, cricket squares and lawns the seed mixtures can be divided into those with and without perennial ryegrass. On parkland golf courses where high levels of wear are expected, the newer fine-leaved perennial ryegrass cultivars can be a valuable addition to the mixture. However, the shiny texture of the leaf does make it stand out, while its growth rate can increase frequency of cut during warm, wet periods.

In view of this, perennial ryegrass is not acceptable on many golf courses including links, heathland and upland courses where the natural species are likely to be the finer leaf fescues and bents or other native species.

For cricket wickets, lawns of intermediate quality and many other intermediate wear areas, perennial ryegrass is widely used as part of a mixture which includes the creeping and non-creeping fescues and other fine-leaved hard wearing grasses.

Generally speaking, the higher quality of the area concerned the better the quality of cultivars used.

Sowing rates for these mixtures are generally $35\,g/m^2$ but may be adjusted to take account of the species present and the time available for establishment. For instance, golf rough areas can be sown at $20\,g/m^2$ or even slightly less in order to enable local flora to establish between the grasses.

Heavy wear areas

For heavy wear areas such as sports pitches and recreational playing areas perennial ryegrass is the outstanding species in the UK. Providing there is at least 12 months establishment time, the finer-leaved fescues and bents and to some extent smooth stalked meadowgrass will be included to give a dense base to the sward. Where less time is available for establishment, it is unlikely that species other than perennial ryegrass will survive, although they may be included within the mixture on the basis that their lifespan within the sward will be relatively short.

In order to provide as much variation as possible with a monospecific sward, it is normal to have two or three cultivars with slightly different attributes to provide as dense and hard wearing a sward as possible. Where ryegrass is a significant proportion of the mixture, then a higher sowing rate of $40\,g/m^2$ may be appropriate.

Special or difficult areas

There are many special or difficult sites requiring individual seed mixtures. In these cases species with the desired attributes – drought hardiness, salt tolerance and heavy metal tolerance for example – are used. These may be used on their own or mixed with the more commonly used species mentioned earlier. Many difficult areas have problems that can be partially corrected prior to sowing by the application of lime, fertiliser or other product. In order to sustain swards in low fertility non-sports areas, legumes are often used.

For areas in which a broader flora is desired, special grass mixtures of native species can be purchased along with a wide range of non-grass native wild flora.

26.6   Seed treatments

Treatments for seeds have in the past concentrated on protection against fungi and birds. However, over the last few years, combination seed treatments have been developed and commonly used within the amenity grass sector. In addition, further research into the use of mycorrhizal fungi has been undertaken. These fungi can be beneficial in extending the surface area of the root for nutrient uptake.

Seed coatings

Two seed coatings, Fortiva and Headstart have been available for a number of years in order to enhance initial germination and establishment of seed. These materials concentrate on giving resistance against attack by soil pathogens, increasing stimulation for germination and promoting initial establishment – in some cases using trace elements. Using these treatments increases the cost of seed but may well be beneficial at marginal seeding times such as early spring and late autumn.

Mycorrhizal inoculants

Mycorrhizal inoculants are also supplied by at least two companies within the industry, in order to improve root growth and aid stress recovery in sports turf situations. Recent trials have shown that their application does enhance rooting, both in terms of root depth and density. However, the application of such material incurs a cost which is probably only justifiable in projects with high capital costs and high wear characteristics such as golf courses and stadia football pitches.

The use of germination enhancers and mycorrhizal fungi will depend upon the location being seeded. In most instances, untreated seed should provide an acceptable grass sward. However, in marginal cases where growth may be inhibited by factors such as low light, poor fertility or high wear then these products may well have a place in providing the best quality grass possible.

26.7 Summary

Currently, there are a wide variety of turfgrass species and improved cultivars available for amenity and sports turf purposes. In addition, new species are constantly being evaluated by grass breeders, to meet existing markets and realise potential markets. There is no doubt that in twenty years' time the species available will not only be better, but will probably be joined by grasses new to the amenity world.

However, no matter how good grasses become in terms of our selection criteria, using high-quality grasses alone will not bring success on intensively-used areas. The basic fundamentals of plant growth still apply and good drainage with correct maintenance practices are still essential for all but a few long-suffering species. Thoughtful use of existing species and cultivars will provide the best chance of success, provided all other issues relating to plant growth have been addressed.

Further reading

See the references and bibliography at the end of Chapter 27.

Seed agents and suppliers

Advanta Seeds (UK) Ltd.,
Sleaford, Lincs.
NG34 7HA
Tel: 01529 304511
Fax: 01529 413137

Barenbrug (UK) Ltd.,
Rougham Industrial Estate,
Rougham,
Bury St Edmunds,
Suffolk IP30 9ND
Tel: 01359 272000
Fax: 01359 272001

British Seed Houses Ltd.,
Bewsey Industrial Estate,
Pitt Street, Warrington,
Cheshire WA5 5LE
Tel: 01925 654411
Fax: 01925 416676

Cebeco Seed Innovations Ltd.,
North Cliff House,
North Carlton,
Lincoln LN1 2RP
Tel: 01522 730836
Fax: 01522 731069

DLF – Trifolium UK and Ireland Ltd.,
and Pope & Chapman
c/o Woodside,
Dunmow Road,
Bishops Stortford,
Herts. CM23 5RG
Tel: 01279 653251
Fax: 01279 505849

Johnson's Sport & Amenity,
and Perryfield Holdings Ltd.,
c/o Thorn Farm, Inkberrow,
Worcestershire WR7 4LJ
Tel: 01386 793135
Fax: 01386 792715

Nickerson (UK) Ltd.,
Rothwell,
Market Rasen,
Lincs. LN7 6DT
Tel: 01472 371220
Fax: 01472 371195

Oliver Bros (Seeds) Ltd.,
North Cliff Farm,
North Carlton,

Lincs. LN1 2RP
Tel: 01522 730836
Fax: 01522 731069

Rigby Taylor Ltd.,
Rigby Taylor House,
Garside Street, Bolton,
Lancs. BL1 4AE
Tel: 01204 394888
Fax: 01204 385276

Seeds 2000 Ltd.,
Middleton House,
Purton, Berkeley,
Gloucestershire GL13 9HY
Tel: 01453 511930
Fax: 01453 511800

Semundo Ltd.,
49 North Road,
Gt. Abingdon,
Cambridge CB1 6AS
Tel: 01223 890777
Fax: 01223 890666

27 The Management of Amenity Grasslands

Andy Boorman

All amenity grasslands require some type of maintenance. Grasslands usually represent a stage in succession from abandoned cultivated soil to forest. Without mowing or grazing the progress of this succession will be apparent in years rather than decades. Intensity of maintenance is closely but not exclusively related to height and frequency of cut. Table 27.1 illustrates the diversity of amenity grassland types and shows the interaction between categories of use and maintenance. This chapter is primarily concerned with grasslands other than wildflower meadows, which are dealt with in detail in Chapters 19, 20 and 22.

27.1 Sward types and their uses

Amenity grasslands are important components of managed landscapes. They encompass such diverse sward types as golf greens, playing fields, lawns and roadside embankments. They can be separated into three categories: grass primarily intended to be walked on, to be played on, or to be looked upon. However, there is an overlap: for example winter pitches may function as lawns in summer.

It is difficult to estimate the total area of amenity grassland, but it is thought that in the United Kingdom it could be equivalent to a good-sized county. There are over 25 000 sites containing more than 75 000 pitches in England alone. In addition, there are over 30 000 additional facilities for tennis, bowls, cricket and athletics. These figures do not include the far greater areas of parks, gardens and verges. Whether they walk, play or look upon these swards, users take them for granted until something goes wrong.

The managing agencies responsible are varied and include local and central government, private contractors, highways and airport authorities, trusts, conservation bodies and individuals. Turf management expertise is not always present at decision-making levels. There is however no excuse for failure to meet objectives and standards, as the body of knowledge for turf culture is extensive: for example, Adams and Gibbs (1994) and Aldous (1999).

In the maritime climate of Britain grass swards are usually robust and deterioration (whether in visual qualities or in playability) is often complex, involving a number of interacting factors. Bad or inappropriate practices are still common, but poor construction, pressure of use, bad weather, an over-concentration on cost and even bad luck can be contributors. This chapter concentrates on the important criteria for managing living turf surfaces, and is written primarily for non-specialists. It is designed to complement the existing turf literature.

27.2 Strategic approaches to grassland management

When developing maintenance and management programmes for grassland areas, a wide range of factors such as the environment, the concerns of staff and user groups, turf surface performance specifications and cost must all be considered. Management objectives need to be realistic and achievable.

Table 27.1 The relationship between sward types and uses.

Classifications	Walk upon	Play upon	Look upon
High maintenance – low height and frequent cut	Fine turf High quality lawns	Golf and bowling greens Golf tees Grass tennis courts Cricket squares Croquet lawns	Ornamental (velvet) lawns Grass parterres Tapis vert
Medium maintenance – medium height and/or less frequent cut	Medium turf Urban verges Urban parks, picnic areas, lawns in country parks and estates	Pitches Golf fairways Sports stadia Outfields Horse race tracks	Cemeteries airports
Low maintenance – tall grass or infrequent cut	Coarse/rough grass or turf Conservation swards General grasslands in country parks and estates	Golf rough and semi rough	Embankments Ornamental and conservation-species-rich grasslands Country verges

Environmental objectives

An obvious example might be minimising or eliminating pesticide use. As with many management objectives, what is desirable is not always very easy to achieve in practice. For example pesticides are often more effective and less costly than alternatives. Other environmentally desirable objectives are more readily achievable; for example contemporary use of fertilisers involves grass being grown 'lean' to help avoid run-off and ground water pollution. Sensitivity to the use of water for irrigation could mean that golf course fairways are not routinely irrigated.

Increasing grassland biodiversity is an example of an environmental objective that may not be simple to achieve. This is especially so where soil fertility is high, and vigorous grasses tend to dominate at the expense of broad-leaved wildflowers. Consultation with stakeholders will often help to identify the most appropriate environmental objectives for an area.

There is now a considerable body of literature about environmental issues and turf management,

for example Balogh and Walker (1992) and Taylor *et al.* (2001).

Stakeholders

These may be staff involved in the management of a resource, users or the general public. With staff, in-house discussions leading to a review of workforce training may show rapid improvements in grassland management. With the general public, consultation can be invaluable in gaining support for management initiatives: one example might involve leaving the grass in part of an urban park uncut, or with mown paths only (Fig.27.1) to increase biodiversity and reduce costs.

Stakeholders may also help to prioritise objectives. For example members of a golf course may actually wish for slower easier greens, because they want a more relaxing game. This will in turn reduce demands on the green's staff. Consulting users of a park may help to clarify their relative needs and concerns: aesthetics, tranquillity, dog walking, children's needs, safety and so on. For

Fig. 27.1 Mowing can be used to sculpt interesting pathways and spaces out of rough grass subject to only one cut per annum. (Photo: James Hitchmough)

Table 27.2 Playing quality measurements for flat bowling greens (Bell and Holmes, 1988).

Parameter	Method	Preferred	Minimum
Green speed (s)	Time taken to travel 27.4 m (30 yds)	12	10
Evenness (mm)	Standard deviation of spot heights using a profile gauge	≤1.5	≤2.0

more information about consulting stakeholders see Davis and Girdler (1999).

Performance specifications

These have been developed for many types of amenity grasslands, particularly for sports turf in relation to playing quality. A range of examples are shown in Tables 27.2–27.7. These specifications can be effective tools providing they involve achievable standards and targets. Table 27.2 shows some of the criteria used since 1988 by The English Bowls Association to assess flat bowling greens used for competition (Evans, 1992). These, along with other statements, such as sward composition, can be used as an objective for the management of greens.

The specifications for tournament golf surfaces are generally well accepted and can be used as a practicable goal for management, as shown in Table 27.3.

Not all turf quality standards are adhered to or accepted. The golf green speed ranges in Table 27.4 have been accepted in industry for years. However, standards for hardness and golf club simulations have yet to be universally adopted, although they do provide objective standards.

In consultation with players and industry, the Sports Turf Research Institute (STRI) in England has proposed a number of objective criteria for the performance of pitches (Table 27.5). They are unlikely to be used widely due to the difficulty of producing the measurements without specialised equipment and expertise. The football pitch stan-

Table 27.3 Surface specification for a golf tournament.

Area	Turf height (mm)	Surface	Additional comment
Tees	8–10	Firm and level	Use appropriate tees
Fairways	14–16	Good grass cover, firm tight and consistent	Width varies from 25–35 m. Check yardage markers
Semi-rough	35–40	Good grass cover, firm tight and consistent	2.5 m in width from fairway to rough
Rough	70–80	Ball played as it lies	Maintain to penalise golfer half a stroke
Greens collar	8–10	Firm, smooth and consistent	Trim around pop-ups
Greens	3–4.5	Fast, firm, smooth and consistent	Speed at 3.2 m on a stimpmeter. Check pin positions
Bunkers	Trim edges	Raked and topped up if needed	

Table 27.4 Golf greens speed ranges in Britain (Baker *et al.*, 1996)

Parameter	Details	Preferred range	Acceptable range
Green speed (m)	Stimpmeter	1.6–2.8	1.5–3.0
Hardness (gravities)	Clegg Impact	70–100	95–120
Stopping distance (m)	5 iron simulation	0.5–5.0	−0.5–8.0
Stopping distance (m)	9 iron simulation	0.0–2.0	−1.0–3.5
Evenness (mm)	Profile gauge	≤1.0	≤1.25

Table 27.5 Objective criteria for pitch sports (Canaway *et al.*, 1990).

Parameter	Soccer		Rugby		Hockey	
	preferred	acceptable	preferred	acceptable	preferred	acceptable
Ball rebound (%)	20–50	15–55	20–50	15–55	–	–
Ball roll (m)	3–12	2–14	–	–	≥5.5	≥5.5
Traction (Nm)	≥25	≥20	≥35	≥25	≥35	≥25
Hardness (gravities)	55–140	35–200	50–100	30–180	90–140	65–200
Evenness (mm)	≤8	≤10	≤8	≤10	≤4	≤5/6

dards in Table 27.6 are more realistic and can be used to develop others for similar sward types.

Programmes of work can be developed from these specifications. For example the greens root-zone standards in Table 27.7 could be used to develop top dressing programmes.

There is plenty of information in the turf literature that can be used to develop performance specifications. The set of specifications published by the Institute of Groundsmen (IOG, 2001) maybe useful. However, it is far better to adapt the published advice to take account of local circumstances rather than follow it slavishly.

Management costs

Budgets for turf management are inevitably restricted, particularly in the public landscape, where there is often little or no income from managed grasslands. There is the inevitable temptation to cut cost by adopting non-standard practices. This can prove to be short sighted: for

Table 27.6 Surface standards for an association football pitch used for 30 hrs per month.

Criteria	Standards
Length of grass	20–40 mm
Evenness	10 mm in firm and 50 mm in soft conditions when measured with a 3 m straight edge
Markings	As per FA rules and visible from 30 m
Presentation	Visible stripes and shoots no more than 25 mm from the vertical
Thatch	12–18 mm
Sward composition	95% perennial ryegrass
Ground cover	80% prior to playing season
Annual meadowgrass	No more than 4% in a 750 mm quadrat
Fine leaved weeds	Less than 3% in a 750 mm quadrat
Broad leaved weeds	None within a 750 mm quadrat
Diseases	None
Pests	None
Worms	Less than 20 casts per sq metre
pH	6.0–7.5
Nutrient status	Phosphorus 15–30, potassium 100–250, magnesium 50–125 and iron 20–60 ppm
Infiltration	Minimum 35 mm/hr, ideally to 250 mm/hr

Table 27.7 Root zone standards for greens and sand pitches (adapted from Aldous, 1999).

Parameter	Desirable	comment
pH	5.5–7.0	Ideally pH 6.0 or slightly less
Drainage	100–150 mm/hr for fine turf	Up to 250 mm/hr in wet areas
Moisture retention	12–18% of water by weight	Concentrate on fine turf areas
Nutrient levels	Low levels of P	Act on test results
Aeration/porosity	Total pore space between 35 and 50%	25% capillary and 25% macropores
Bulk density/compaction	1.5–1.7 g/m^2	Firm, but not compacted

example cutting down on top dressing on sports pitches can seriously affect their carrying capacity (Stewart, 1994). For facilities with a commercial role, targeting additional income can mean extra cost. The turf management demands made by 45 000 rounds of golf a year are very much lower compared to 65 000 (Perris and Evans, 1996).

Differential mowing is often proposed as a means of cutting mowing cost in grasslands in public open space. Areas under consideration are divided into three zones. Those nearest to paths, beds and borders are cut weekly and those furthest from the public can be left as rough grass. The remainder is divided into two: one half is cut every three weeks. Long grass can be seen as scruffy, particularly if there is little discernible improvement

in biodiversity, but it is an important habitat for many invertebrates and small mammals. Areas of slightly longer grass can act as a disincentive for dog walkers to pick up their pets' excreta. This can be both a health hazard and a source of friction between park users.

Differential mowing typically works best where nutrient levels are already relatively low, or have been reduced by stripping off the top 50 mm of topsoil. Re-sowing such areas with lower maintenance species and cultivars such as fescues and dwarf perennial ryegrass will achieve most of the objectives of differential mowing with fewer complaints about untidiness. Alternatively, where it is desirable for rough grass to be tidy with no more than one cut per annum, and to produce a worth-

Table 27.8 Relationships between type of mower and frequencies of cut, relative costs and finish. Adapted from Cobham (1990).

Mower type	Cutting rates h/ha	Cuts per year	Relative costs gang mower = 100%	Quality of finish
3.5 m 5 unit gang mower	0.7	24	100	Med – good
1.7 m triple cylinder mower	3.7	12	158	Med – good
500 mm cylinder mower	12.6	24	954	Med – good
500 mm cylinder mower (cuttings boxed off)	14.5	24	1098	Med – good
500 mm rotary mower	17.9	6	569	Med – good
450 mm hover mower on banks	5.3	4	1007	Rough – med
2.1 m tractor rear-mounted flail	7.5	2	57	Rough

while flowering display, tufted hair grass (*Deschampsia cespitosa*) can be sown. This very useful grass requires damp soils, but will tolerate shade, is almost evergreen and can be purchased as non-dormant seed. Reducing grassland management costs by differential mowing and other approaches are considered in greater detail in Parker and Bryan (1989). The influence of machinery selection on costs is illustrated in Table 27.8.

Whatever objectives and priorities are developed they must be interpreted as flexible management plans. These will need to allow for the inevitable contingencies that will arise due to weather, use and changes in demand.

27.3 Turf culture: principles and operations

Levels of maintenance can be intensive or extensive, depending on the management objectives, frequency and pressure of use and sward type. Maintenance should always be based on the application of sound principles.

Control of grass growth

Some form of growth control is essential for all swards. It is necessary to maintain top growth within specified limits, to produce a particular playing surface, sustain ornamental or recreational turf and control undesirable vegetation. Mowing is by far the most common practice, but in some situations grazing or burning can be used. These can be beneficial in areas where species diversity is being encouraged. However, swards that contain noxious weeds such as common ragwort (*Senecio jacobaea*) that are toxic to stock present problems. Sward burning is only viable if vegetation can dry sufficiently to be lit, and if the fire can be adequately controlled without posing an undue risk. Burning is little used these days, however it can be a very successful means of managing swards for nature conservation, as discussed by Green (1985).

Growth retarding chemicals such as mefluidide suppress grass growth, but also reduce its capacity to tolerate wear, and can have an adverse effect on other flora. Therefore their use has been confined largely to 'look upon' areas such as airports.

Effects of mowing

Unlike most plants, turf grasses are adapted to tolerate recurrent foliage removal, which is replaced from growing-points at ground level. Frequent mowing encourages the production of leaves and tillers and suppresses flowering. Constant close cutting produces a dwarfed plant with smaller leaves and shallow roots. After mowing, growth temporarily stops and diseases may enter through the wounds, but healthy plants recover quickly.

Height and frequency of cut

Frequent cutting below 10 mm favours species such as bents (*Agrostis* spp.) and annual meadow-grass (*Poa annua*). Cutting at 25 mm will encourage perennial ryegrass (*Lolium perenne*) and weeds such as clover. Frequent mowing typically reduces plant diversity within the sward. There is often a conflict between the height required for use and the optimum for the grass. Most turf grasses will survive, but not thrive, at cuts below their optimal range and will require additional maintenance.

It is best not to cut off more than a third of the growth present during any one mowing. A golf green cut at 3 mm can grow 1 mm a day, and so will need to be mown daily. A football field cut at 25 mm is likely to take at least a week to grow the required 8 mm. Do not be too prescriptive about frequency of cut, using the 30 per cent rule, prescribed height and growing conditions. Where possible it is desirable not to reduce the height too quickly in early spring. This can interfere with the flush of root growth that occurs at this time. Performance as opposed to task-based specifications are a more sensible means of controlling grass cutting.

Arisings

In general, clippings should not be collected unless they interfere with a sport or damage the surface. Clippings are routinely boxed on greens, wickets, tennis courts and high quality pitches and lawns. Arisings should be removed from wild flower areas and ornamental rough grass. This can help reduce soil fertility, which in time should discourage competitive grass growth.

There are a number of benefits, other than cost reduction, of not collecting clippings in regularly-mown grass. They re-cycle nutrients and can help reduce water stress in dry weather. However, they can lead to problems in fine turf, including worm castes and weeds. Non-collection does not cause thatch (a layer of organic debris on the soil surface) in itself, but can contribute to its build up in a susceptible sward.

Mowing machines

Purchase of a mower is an important decision that should not be based purely on cost. Sward type, finish, area to be cut, workload, speed of operation, safety and operator comfort should all be considered. A full technical discussion of mowers is beyond the scope of this work, but consultation with experienced machine operators is to be recommended. The majority of turf management books have an extensive discussion of mowing and mowers.

Cylinder mowers give the best finish, but rotary mowers are more flexible. They can cut long and wet grass and are less susceptible to damage from rubbish and other debris. They are now the most common types for general amenity turf. Cylinder machines that have 100/180 cuts per metre can also cut lower than 10 mm. They are used exclusively on fine turf, producing the requisite high quality finish. Cylinder mowers with 50/100 cuts per metre can be used on medium turf. These are available in units as gang mowers or singly; they have a good finish and produce a striped surface.

Flails, strimmers or reciprocating knife machines are used for long grass. Flail mowers can leave a poor finish, but cope well with debris and rubbish. A second cut with a heavy-duty rotary could be considered. Strimmers produce a good finish if operated correctly, but are only for relatively small areas, for example cutting around trees. Their nylon cords can damage the bark of woody plants (so-called 'strimmer blight').

Mowers must be properly set up and used correctly. Skinning or scalping occurs when the mower is set too low, the ground is uneven or the mower is turned sharply with the cutters engaged. Chewing or uneven cutting can occur if blades are blunt or poorly-set. A comparison of work rate and other characteristics of a range of mowing machines are shown in Table 27.8. In addition to choosing the most appropriate type of machine, it is also important not to compromise on power. Under-powered machines may be cheaper initially, but will have a shorter life, higher maintenance costs and be more uncomfortable to operate.

Mowing patterns

The roller or cylinder of a mower orientates shoots according to the direction of its travel and so can be used to stripe or pattern the surface as part of the presentation. The direction of mowing should be varied as much as possible. A grain or nap may occur if shoots lay in one direction, and this will interfere with ball roll on greens. In addition, a constant mowing pattern can result in compaction, uneven wear and washboarding. If the direction of mowing can not be changed, disengage some reels to alter the pattern and pressure on the ground.

Nutrition of turf grasses

In normal circumstances, this is only an important consideration for fine swards and sports turf, although there are many situations in public and commercial landscapes where relatively small areas of heavily trafficked grass areas can be improved by fertiliser application. It is difficult to be overly prescriptive when designing a fertiliser programme. The role of the nutrient, turf use, the effects of weather, the behaviour of the nutrients in the rootzone and the interaction between fertilisers and other practices are all important variables. A flexible programme based on sound principles is more effective than working to a schedule.

Nitrogen is associated with leaf and top growth. If present in excess, the grass will be deep green in colour, have lush foliage, shallow roots and be prone to disease and stress (frost, heat or drought). Deficiency shows as pale leaves, and poor production of tillers, leaves and roots. Nitrogen is highly mobile in soils and is readily leached.

Potassium's role in turf culture involves stress tolerance, disease resistance, hard wear and recovery from damage. It also seems to regulate uptake of other nutrients and so can reduce the problem of shallow rooting seen with nitrogen. Potassium is moderately mobile in soils, but highly mobile in sands from which it is leached readily.

Phosphorus is important for growth in all parts of the plant. Grasses under normal circumstances are highly efficient at adsorbing phosphorus and its removal by mowing is minimal. High levels of phosphorus are associated with weeds such as clovers and annual meadowgrass. For these reasons, use small amounts in turf fertiliser programmes. Because of overuse in the past, many soils under turf contain adequate phosphorus. It is immobile in soils, but moderately mobile in sands.

Magnesium and iron are commonly added to compound turf fertilisers. Magnesium is locked into the soil by potassium, so its use is mainly to counter this. Iron has the reputation for 'hardening' the plant, encouraging disease resistance, masking the effects of fairy rings and is used to 'green up' grass. Both of these nutrients are more important on sands than on clay-based soil.

The main aim of a turf fertiliser programme is to replace nutrients lost in clippings and by leaching. Some additional fertiliser will be needed to counter wear and maintain sward density. Grasses are comparatively efficient at extracting nutrients from well-drained and aerated soils. Current practice involves less nitrogen than was traditionally thought wise. The grass is said to be 'grown hungry' or kept 'hard'. The most obvious benefit is to produce a relatively deeper root system. It also reduces thatch and helps avoid polluted drainage waters.

Consequently, do not routinely use fertilisers that contain more than 12 per cent nitrogen, and no more than 6 per cent in autumn. It is also advisable to link the amount of potassium with nitrogen. A usual ratio is $3N:2K_2O$, but even $50:50$ is used. It is most important not to use nitrogen late in the growing season because of the risk of damage from frost and diseases. Soil testing is important, particularly with turf growing on sand based constructions, where annual tests are advised.

Light, frequent applications of fertiliser are preferred. Alternatively use controlled release fertilisers, which discharge small amounts of minerals at a constant rate. However, even small prills risk being split by mowers and so their use on low cut turf is still uncommon. There is a wide range of fertilisers, including straights, compounds, organic or inorganic. The safest approach is to use compound proprietary materials, whether organic or inorganic. The fertiliser must not be allowed to lie on the grass, as it can cause scorch. It should be washed or worked in thoroughly.

Recently the use of materials that are aimed at the soil microflora rather than the grasses has become popular. These may also encourage symbiotic mycorrhiza to colonise turf grass roots. Often called turf conditioners, many are based on seaweed, but other organic sources are used. Some contain spores and live organisms as well as vitamins, growth promoters, small amounts of nutrients and trace elements. There has been little scientific work to objectively quantify their benefits, but anecdotal evidence seems to indicate no major problems with their use. Carrow (1993) offers useful advice to practitioners when evaluating these materials.

Turf grasses will tolerate soil acidity between pH 5.0 and 8.0, but have narrower optima. Fine swards should be grown slightly acidic, but no lower than 5.0, whereas 6.5 to 7.0 is more suitable for hard wearing swards. Acid soils (below pH 5.5) lack worms and microflora, which can lead to thatch build up and increase the risk of disease. Soils above pH 7.5 can be nutrient deficient. Many turf fertilisers are acidic and can be used to lower the pH. Raising the pH can encourage the fungal disease Take-all patch (*Gasumannomyces graminis*) on susceptible grasses.

Irrigation

Water is a scarce resource and should not be used for general irrigation of amenity grasslands even during drought. However, its use is essential for highly quality fine and sports turf. It is also essential in many cases when turf is used on shallow soil profiles on roof gardens. In summary the reasons for using water on turf are:

- allowing the grass to grow during dry weather
- helping the establishment of a new sward
- preparing sports surfaces (tennis, cricket, football)
- washing in top dressings, fertilisers and pesticides and in the application of liquid formulations.

It allows the manager more control and is an essential requirement where sand has been used in sports turf construction.

A soil at field capacity contains enough moisture to supply turf for seven to fourteen days during the growing season – depending on soil texture, root depth and conditions for growth. The rate of water loss depends on factors that include rate of photosynthesis, sunshine, temperature and wind speed. The losses can be estimated by using a pan evaporimeter, soil tensiometers or from evapotranspiration figures provided by advisory services. These can help calculate irrigation needs.

However, experience of how turf behaves when it dries is also used. Fewer clippings are boxed off and the surface becomes firm, giving extra bounce to a ball. On a golf green, holes become more difficult to change. Then the grass may start to lose colour and footprints are more obvious. If no water is applied the grass goes brown and finally it will become dormant. Foot-printing and hole changing are often used to anticipate the need for water on fine turf.

If possible do not water turf little and often, as this leads to shallow rooting and encourages annual meadowgrass. It is better to allow the rootzone to dry to 40–60 per cent of field capacity, then water to saturate the root zone. However, underuse of the irrigation system will stress the grass and thin out the sward. Sand constructions should have a perched water table to give extra water storage, but the total water stored is still relatively low.

A high quality water source is important and it must not be contaminated with pollutants, salts and plant or human diseases. If the water is hard then it may be necessary to use acid fertilisers to prevent the soil pH from rising. Buying water can be very expensive. One option is to collect winter rain and store it in tanks, lakes and ponds. The expense of the outlay is usually offset in the long term and there are opportunities to develop valuable wildlife habitats.

The design of an irrigation system is very specialised and beyond the scope of this discussion. Pop-ups are ideal for turf and are common on golf courses. However, travellers and flip/flops are widespread on bowling greens, lawns etc. What is important is to have even, consistent cover over the whole of the surface, without too much overlap. Choate (1994) gives a very full treatment of turf irrigation.

Other operations

Top dressing, aeration, thatch control and pesticide use are important secondary operations. It is best to assume that problems will occur and take routine preventative measures, except when using pesticides.

Top dressing

This is the single most important secondary operation on quality turf surfaces and is used to:

- maintain surface levels and quality
- prepare sports surfaces
- improve the structure and texture of topsoil
- carry fertilisers and pesticides
- encourage rhizome, stolon and tiller production
- culturally control thatch and weeds
- help renovate sports and lawn areas and knit in newly laid turf.

A variety of materials are used including clay for cricket wickets and sand to improve texture and structure. The latter must be of a specified grade and washed to remove fines and impurities. A general-purpose top dressing should be sterilised and similar in nature to the underlying soil. Never alter top dressing materials frequently.

Top dressings must be worked well into the soil surface and never smother the grass. Apply evenly, taking care to fill hollows. If a very level surface is required, then the area can be strung-out using levelled pegs.

Only apply top dressing to grass that is actively growing, with the exception of soccer goalmouths during the playing season. Never apply during dry weather (unless irrigation is to be used), if frost is likely, or during wet weather. For most surfaces spring and early autumn are suitable, fitting in with the needs of staff, users and grass. However

golf greens should be top dressed fortnightly or monthly during the growing season. Top dress following scarification and aeration after disposing of the arisings.

Thatch control

Thatch is a layer of decomposing grass tissue on the soil's surface. It occurs naturally and small amounts are desirable in protecting the surface from damage. However, it deadens ball bounce and so is scarified from cricket and tennis surfaces during preparation for play. Scarification is also used at the end of the playing season on bowling greens and in autumn or spring on fine lawns. It can also help control moss and reduce weeds, particularly annual meadowgrass. Grass is mown a few days before scarification, making sure it is neither too short nor long. Depending on the amount of thatch, two passes may be needed in different directions.

On golf greens too much thatch leads to a poor spongy surface. Species such as creeping bent (*Agrostis stolonifera*) and bermuda grass (*Cynodon dactylon*) produce a lot of stolons, which can form a dense mat. In both these cases prevention by frequent, light scarification is used. The best system replaces the front roller of a mower with thatch control reels.

A rapid build up of thatch is symptomatic of more fundamental problems, which must be tackled. Rapidly growing grass may produce too much material for the soil's ability to break it down. Using too much nitrogen fertiliser, watering little and often, over-use of pesticides, acidic soils and compaction are usually the most important causes of thatch problems.

Aeration

Turf grasses are very sensitive to the poorly aerated conditions found in compacted soil. Pressure of play or pedestrian traffic during wet weather is likely to compact soil; this is found on desire lines across amenity turf, golf greens, goal-mouths and cricket wickets.

There are several methods of relieving compaction, but the best use a hollow tine or a deep spike (vertidrain). The former removes some of the compacted soil, which is replaced with a new sandy rootzone applied by topdressing. Vertidrains act by cracking and lifting the soil, opening fissures at depth. Rootzone replacement is most applicable on fine turf areas, whereas deep spiking is used on pitches, fairways and similar.

The vibrating mini-mole plough is an excellent tool. It cracks the soil, but leaves the surface relatively undisturbed and is suitable for fine and coarser turf. However, due to its complex vibrating action, larger machines are slow and hard on the tractor, implement and driver.

Soil compaction should be treated in spring or autumn, when the soil is warm enough for roots to exploit the freshly aerated soil. However, the soil should be neither too wet nor dry. Prevention is better than cure, so aerate before serious problems occur. Annual treatments are recommended for intensively used areas.

Using small solid tines (spikes) or triangular rotating blades (groovers) in winter does not control compaction; in fact these can add to the problem. However, they allow water to move more quickly off the surface. They should not be used in the absence of other aeration treatments because of the risk of a serious breakdown of soil structure. On a small scale the careful use of a garden fork, with a slight heaving action, is better at relieving compaction than any machine.

Pesticide use

The control of weeds, pests and diseases has traditionally involved the intensive use of pesticides. It is now recognised that to rely on these is unwise. The public is increasingly questioning pesticide use on environmental grounds. Routine pesticide use can select for resistant strains of pest or disease, and cause an increase in the populations of resistant weed species. They can be direct contributors to other problems, notably thatch build up.

There are some problems that can not be effectively controlled chemically, for example annual meadowgrass and worms. There are approved products for both, but due to restrictions or simply lack of efficacy they will need additional control methods. For example, ethofumesate can be used to control annual meadowgrass, but it should not be used on sandy rootzones, swards containing *Agrostis* spp. and the grass should not be cut until 14 days after application (Whitehead, 2001). These are all factors that can reduce its effectiveness for fine close-cut bent/fescue swards, such as greens. In these situations this weed is such a problem that many greenkeepers accept its presence. They have to adjust sward management by increasing water and fertiliser use and spray iron sulphate to mask its pale colour.

Current thinking looks to a more integrative approach. This does not correspond exactly to integrated pest management, but rather involves sound turf culture, cultural control and minimal use of pesticides. In many cases an intractable turf grass problem is the result of poor grass growth. The list of factors that are associated with moss infestation illustrate this. It includes poor drainage, excessive shade, poor aeration, acidic soil, shallow top soil, lack of nutrients, scalping, thatch, compaction and general neglect. Control strategies should start by identifying and eliminating factors that contribute to the problem.

Cultural control is unlikely to solve a problem completely, but can reduce it to acceptable levels. Scarification and top dressing can help control weeds, particularly annual meadowgrass. In combination with these practices low phosphate fertilisers can improve the effectiveness of control, as perennial turf grass is more efficient than *Poa annua* at absorbing this mineral. Oversowing may also be needed, as will hand pulling. Grass can often be a problem in amenity meadows, particularly those grown for summer flower. Two or three deep cuts, almost to the point of scalping, before re-growth in spring seems to help in reducing the taller grasses.

Weeds can interfere with a playing surface, giving uneven ball bounce and roll. In sports such as cricket, where predicting the flight of a ball is important, uneven bounce can be dangerous for players. Weeds often wear poorly and can affect the visual appearance of swards. Selective herbicides such as dicamba and MCPA can be used,

Table 27.9 Mowing heights in mm for common amenity turf surfaces.

Area	Summer	Winter
Golf green	3–6	8–9
Green surrounds and tees	6–13	13–18
Fairways	13–18	18–25
Flat bowling green	3–6	8–9
Crown bowling green	5	8
Tennis courts	5–6	8–13
Hockey pitch	13–25	13–25
Football pitch	25–38	25–38
Rugby pitch	25–50	50–75
Cricket tables	5–6	8–13
Cricket outfields	6–18	10–25
Racecourses	75–100	75–100
High quality lawns	8–10	10–13
General amenity grassland	25–50	25–50
Wildflower swards	Not applicable	75–100

Table 27.10 Typical annual fertiliser needs for common amenity turf surfaces.

Area	N g/m^2	P$_2$O$_5$ g/m^2	K$_2$O g/m^2
Greens, high quality lawns	8–20	2	6–15
Golf tees	8–20	2	6–15
Golf fairways	8–12	0	0
Cricket tables, tennis courts	8–12	2	4–10
Outfields and stadia (clippings returned)	4	0	0
Outfields and stadia (clippings removed)	8–12	4–6	4–6
Hockey pitches (clippings returned)	4–5	0	0
Hockey pitches (clippings removed)	8–20	2	6–15
Pitches and lawns (clippings removed)	8–10	2–5	2–5
High quality pitches (clippings removed)	16–20	8–10	8–10
Racecourses	8–10	2–5	2–5

particularly if complete control is required (Whitehead, 2001). Constant changes in regulation and the availability of herbicides and pesticides for turf grass make it essential to consult the most current pesticide guide.

Inevitably pests and diseases are most problematic in fine and sports turf swards, and can result in serious damage or loss of function. Identifying the source of the problem is important: in addition to pests and diseases, machinery oils, fertiliser, pesticides, urine, lightning and walking on frosted turf can all cause scorches and patches. Chemicals should be used cautiously on an 'as need' basis.

Reassuringly, turf has a remarkable ability to recover from pest and disease. The disease 'Take-all' on fine turf is an exception and will eliminate all grasses other than fescues. There is no effective chemical control, but the problem does decline by itself over time.

27.4 Example of work programmes for turf management

These are provided for guidance and should not be used as a blueprint. Turf management requires flexibility and the ability to balance the needs of

Table 27.11 Summary of irrigation use for various turf surfaces.

Area	Spring	Summer	Autumn	Winter
Golf green	Check system. Start watering programme.	Water deeply, but infrequently. Water early morning.	Check drainage system and rod.	Drain irrigation system.
Fairways	Consider minimal water use. Perhaps only water main landing areas.			
Bowling green	As for golf greens.			
Tennis courts	As for golf greens. Do not play on wet courts.			
Winter pitches		Irrigate areas that are under repair.		Water may be needed to produce a slick pitch.
Cricket tables	Start watering programme as weather dries.	As and when needed to keep the grass alive and for wicket preparation.	Water after renovation if weather is dry.	
High quality lawns		As and when needed to keep grass alive.		
Cricket outfields	Only water areas under repair or newly-laid.			
Lawns	As above.			
Racecourses	Courses in dry areas will need extensive irrigation for the safety of horses and riders. Otherwise treat as amenity grass.			

Table 27.12 Summary of secondary operations.

Area	Spring	Summer	Autumn	Winter
Golf green	Begin thatch control. Switching. Weed control.	Use thatch control reels. Top dress little and often.	High risk of diseases such as *Fusarium* patch. Spike lightly if needed.	
Fairways	Vertidrain if not done in autumn. Scarify if needed.		Vertidrain or similar. Litter and leaf collection.	
Bowling green	Switch. Scarify and top dress. Weed control.	Light scarification and top dressing.	Major renovation: scarification, aeration, over-seed and top dress.	Keep off and spike if needed.
Tennis courts	Scarify and top dress. Weed control.	Prepare for play.	Renovation as for bowls.	As bowls.
Winter games pitches	At the end of the season, a major renovation programme is required to include: scarify, aerate, top dress and oversow.		Prepare for season.	Top dress goalmouths. Divot repair.
Cricket tables	Rolling starts the process of wicket preparation.	Prepare and repair as and when needed. Scarify.	As for bowls.	As bowls.
Cricket outfields	Scarify and control weeds only if needed.		Vertidrain.	
High quality lawns	Scarify and top dress. Control weeds.	Edging.	Aerate and top dress.	As bowls.

Table 27.13 Typical annual programme for an 18 Hole Golf Club.

Area	Spring	Summer	Autumn	Winter
Fairways	Fertilise with 8–12 g/m^2 of N. Mow at 14–18 mm, 1–3 times a week. Divot every 6 weeks.	Divot regularly. Mow as spring. Selective weed control if needed.	Raise height of cut to 25 mm. Scarify and aerate as needed. Remove leaves and debris. Divot as needed. Renovate worn areas.	Mow, aerate and remove debris as needed.
Tees	Aerate and scarify as needed. Fertilise and top dress. Mow at least weekly. Move members' tee markers. Renovate winter tees.	Mow twice weekly. Mow banks weekly. Move tee markers weekly. Fertilise and irrigate as needed. Repair divots daily. Weed control if needed.	Bring winter tees into play. Mow, scarify and aerate as needed. Overseed with rye/fescue mix or smooth stalked meadowgrass at 35 g/m^2. Top dress with sand/soil mix at 1.75 kg/m^2 and work well into the surface. Raise cut to winter height. Remove leaves and debris.	Keep clear of leaves and debris. Spike as needed. Mow at 13 mm minimum.
Greens	Switch. Lower height and increase frequency to summer levels. Mow apron, approach and banks as for autumn. Fertilise in split dressings. Hollow tine or vertidrain in April or May. Scarify lightly every 2–4 weeks or fit thatch control reels to mowers. Top dress regularly. Irrigate as needed. Move hole 2/3 times a week. Trim round sprinkler heads every 2 weeks.	As spring, except lower cut to 4–5 mm. Top dress at 0.5 kg/m^2 every 5–6 weeks using sand or soil mix. Weed control if needed. Mow aprons and approaches to 7–8 mm and banks and surrounds to 25–37 mm.	Move to winter greens. In September scarify and hollow tine or vertidrain leaving for 2 weeks before top dressing up to 3 g/m^2. After early September use a 4:0:8 fertiliser at 6/8 g/m^2. Worm control as needed. Raise height of cut and reduce frequency to winter levels. Banks and surrounds cut up to 37 mm and approach and apron at 9–10 mm.	As autumn for the main greens. Cut winter greens at 7–8 mm, and change hole weekly. After winter lightly roll to firm and brush/switch daily. Cut apron and approach at 10–12 mm and banks and surrounds at 50 mm.
Bunkers	Rake Monday, Wednesday and Friday. Control weeds as needed. Edge weekly. Cut greens bunker banks at 25–50 mm and fairway banks to 50–100 mm.	As spring.	Top up with fresh sand if not done in spring to 250–500 mm. This represents 25–30% of the volume. Keep clear of debris.	Keep clear of debris.
Rough	Cut semi-rough at 35–50 mm weekly to fortnightly. Cut deep rough at 75–100 mm as dictated by flora.	As spring.	Cut all rough down to 25 mm or less.	

Table 27.14 Typical annual programme for a mixed-use park.

Area	Spring	Summer	Autumn	Winter
Lawns and cricket outfield	Fertilise with 8–12 g/m² of N if clippings are collected. Mow at 25 mm weekly. Edge around beds and strim around trees.	As spring. Raise cut during dry weather. Selective weed control if needed.	Scarify and aerate if needed. Remove leaves and debris. Renovate worn areas.	Mow, aerate and remove debris as needed.
Pitches	After the season mow, vertidrain and scarify as needed. Fertilise if clippings are collected. Top dress with sand or sand/soil mix at 1.75 kg/m² and work well into the surface. Mow at 15/25 mm. Renovate goalmouths and other worn areas.	Raise cut if possible. Fertilise and irrigate renovated areas as needed. Weed control if needed. At end of summer mark out pitches and put up goals.	Cut at 15–18 mm for hockey preferably 25 mm for general-purpose pitches. Remove leaves and debris. Replace divots regularly.	As autumn. Sand and spike goalmouths as needed. Stripe pitch prior to matches. Paint lines as needed.
Bowling greens	Remove dew using a long cane-switching. Bring cut down and increase frequency to 3–6 times a week. Fertilise in split dressings. Groom lightly every 2/4 weeks or fit thatch control reels to mowers. Top dress regularly. Irrigate as needed.	As spring, except lower cut to 4–5 mm. Top dress at 0.5 kg/m² every 5–6 weeks using sand or sand/soil mix. Weed control if needed.	Raise cut to winter height. At the end of the season scarify and hollow tine leaving for 2 weeks before top dressing. Do not carry on with summer fertiliser after early September. Use a 4:0:8 fertiliser at 6/8 g/m². Oversow worn ends. Worm control as needed.	As autumn. Top up and repair ditches. After winter lightly roll to firm and brush/switch daily.
Cricket square	Switch. Start rolling programme. Top dress and fertilise in split dressings. Start first wicket preparation 10 days before first game by cutting at 8 mm, scarifying and rolling. Mark wicket and cut to 3 mm and roll day before game.	Wicket preparations as spring. Renovate ends and raise cut before wicket use. Irrigate as needed and as part of wicket preparation.	Renovate bowler's ends and creases. Aerate, scarify and clay top dress whole square. Oversow with bent, fescue and ryegrass mix at 35 g/m². Fence off. Keep clear of debris.	Keep clear of debris. Plan wicket rotation for the next season. Roll late winter with light roller to firm surface.
Rough grass		Strim around trees, particularly if newly-planted.	Cut down to 50 mm or less. Dispose of arisings.	Possible 2 or 3 further cuts.

the users and the grasses. The first tables provide an overview and the last two are examples for particular uses. The books about specific sward types found in the list of references are useful sources for producing work programmes. Mowing heights for the more common amenity sward types are shown in Table 27.9.

Ranges are given to allow for factors such as sward composition, climate and intensity of use.

In winter grass is cut as and when needed. Cutting height is raised during periods of drought.

Fertiliser regimes for various sward types are shown in Table 27.10. Clippings contain approximately 3 per cent nitrogen, 0.7 per cent phosphorus and 2 per cent potassium.

Actual application rates for potassium and phosphorus should be calculated on the basis of a soil test. If sandy rootzones are used in turfgrass construction, also test for micronutrients. It is impossible to quantify annual use of an irrigation system as the amount of water required and frequency of watering will vary according to season, climate, sward type, species composition and construction method. However, a summary is found in Table 27.11.

A similar approach is adopted for secondary operations, such as scarification and aeration (Table 27.12).

For additional information required when dealing with a golf tournament, see Table 27.3.

27.5 Conclusion

Many aspects of turf management are beyond the scope of this text, but there is a considerable volume of literature that can be consulted and the list of references can be used for further reading. In addition, there are specialist turf management journals and periodicals and now dedicated Internet sites that can be readily accessed. Managers responsible for extensive specialist turf surfaces and sports facilities are advised to join the Institute of Groundsmen (IOG), British and International Greenkeeping Association (BIGGA) and Institute of Landscape and Amenity Management (ILAM) as appropriate. The Sports Turf Research Institute (STRI) has a consultancy service, which can be accessed for a charge and there are many excellent private consultants.

Finally, turf management at all levels is a multi-skilled activity. Using poorly trained and paid operatives rarely proves to be successful in the long term. Paying attention to staff development through training and qualifications leads to a better-motivated and more effective workforce.

References

Adams, W.A. & Gibbs, R.J. (1994) *Natural Turf for Sport and Amenity: Science and Practice*, CABI Publishing, Wallingford.

Aldous, D. (1999) *International Turf Management*, Inkata, Melbourne, Australia.

Baker, S.W. (1996) Survey of golf greens in Great Britain IV: playing quality, *Journal of the Sports Turf Research Institute*, 72, 120–32.

Balogh, J.C. & Walker, W.J. (1992) *Golf Course Management and Construction: Environmental Issues*, Lewis, Chelsea MI.

Bell, M.J. & Holmes, G. (1988) Playing quality standards for level bowling greens, *Journal of the Sports Turf Research Institute*, 64, 48–62.

Canaway, P.M., Bell, M.J., Holmes, G., & Baker, S.W. (1990) 'Specifications for the playing quality of natural turf for association football'. In: *Natural and Artificial Playing Fields: Characteristics and Safety Features*, ASTMSTP 1073 (Schmidt R.G. Ed.), American Society for Testing and Materials, Philadelphia, USA.

Carrow, R.N. (1993) 'Evaluating soil and turf conditioners', *Golf Course Management*, Oct 1993, pp 56, 58, 60, 64 and 70.

Choate, R.B. (1994) *Turf Irrigation Manual*, Weathermatic, Dallas.

Cobham, R. (Ed.) (1990) *Amenity Landscape Management: A Resources Handbook*, SPON, London.

Davis, M. & Girdler, D. (1999) *Skills for Best Value: Consultation and User Satisfaction*, ILAM, Reading.

Evans, R.D.C. (Ed.) (1992) *Bowling Greens*, STRI, Bingley.

Green, B. (1985) *Countryside conservation: the protection and management of amenity ecosystems*. 2nd Edn, SPON, London.

Institute of Groundsmen (2001) *Guidelines for Performance Quality Standards: Part 1 Sports Surfaces*, IOG, Milton Keynes.

Parker, J. & Bryan, P. (1989) *Landscape Management and Maintenance, a guide to its costing and organisation.* Gower Technical, Aldershot.

Perris, J. & Evans, R.D.C. (1996) *The Care of the Golf Course.* STRI, Bingley.

Stewart, V.I. (1994) *Sports Turf: Science, Construction and Maintenance.* SPON, London.

Taylor, R., Peake, M., & Penrose L. (2001) *The Wildside of Golf.* BIGGA, York.

Whitehead, R. (2001) *The UK Pesticide Guide 2001.* CABI Publishing, Wallingford. Please note that the *most current version* of this text must be consulted.

Further reading

Balwin, N. (1990) *Turfgrass Pests and Diseases.* STRI, Bingley.

Emmons, R.D. (2000) *Turfgrass Science and Management.* Delmer, Albany NY.

Evans, R.D.C. (ed.) (1991) *Cricket Grounds.* STRI, Bingley.

Evans, R.D.C. (ed.) (1994) *Winter Games Pitches: The Construction and Maintenance of Natural Turf Pitches for Team Sports.* STRI, Bingley.

Institute of Groundsmen (2001) Guidelines for Performance Quality Standards: Part 2 Amenity Turf, Landscape Features and Play Areas, IOG, Milton Keynes.

Lickorish, S., Lucombe, G., & Scott, R. (1997) *Wildflowers Work.* 2nd edn, Landlife, Liverpool.

Perris, J. (ed.) (2000) *Grass Tennis Courts.* STRI and The All England Tennis Club, Bingley.

Puhalla, J., Krans, J., & Goatley, M. (1999) *Sports Fields: A Manual for Design, Construction and Maintenance.* AnnArbor Press, Michigan, USA.

Radko, A.M. (1980) 'The USGA Stimpmeter for measuring the speed of putting Greens'. In: *Proceedings of 3rd International Turfgrass Research Conference.* Beard, J.B. (ed.) *American Society of Agronomy,* pp. 473–6.

Sport England (2000) *Guidance Note: Natural Turf for Sport.* Sport England, London.

Turgeon, A.J. (1999) *Turfgrass Management.* 5th edn, Prentice Hall, New Jersey.

York, C.A. (1998) *Turfgrass Diseases and Associated Disorders.* STRI, Bingley.

Index

Note: page numbers in *italics* refer to figures and tables. Plate numbers refer to illustrations in Plates section.

Plant Index

Note: this list includes names of plants suitable for planting schemes, weeds and plant pathogens. Plant names are given as both Latin and common form, where both are used in the text. Grasses are all listed under 'grass'.

Page numbers in *italics* refer to figures and tables. Plate numbers refer to illustrations in the plate section.